# Franklin D. Roosevelt and Foreign Affairs

VOLUME I: JANUARY 1933–FEBRUARY 1934

Roosevelt greets former Premier of France Edouard Herriot.
On the right is naval aide Captain Walter Vernou. April 24, 1933.

# Franklin D. Roosevelt and Foreign Affairs

VOLUME I: JANUARY 1933–FEBRUARY 1934

Edited by Edgar B. Nixon

*Franklin D. Roosevelt Library*

HYDE PARK, NEW YORK

The Belknap Press of Harvard University Press

Cambridge, Massachusetts    1969

*3 2 7. 7 3*
*R 6 1 ł*
*7 3 4 8 9*

*February, 1971*

# Foreword

The Franklin D. Roosevelt Library was built by President Roosevelt on the grounds of his estate in Hyde Park in 1939 to house his Presidential papers, his family correspondence, his books and collections, and gifts made to him and Mrs. Roosevelt while they were in the White House. In 1940 he presented this, the first of the Presidential Libraries, to the federal government. It is estimated that there are now more than twenty million documents housed in this modest fieldstone building of Dutch colonial design. The Library is administered by the National Archives and Records Service of the General Services Administration.

The wealth of material included in this gift to the nation and the promptness with which the Roosevelt Presidential papers were opened for research use are in part responsible for the continuing and increasing interest taken by scholars and students in the Roosevelt era. Since the papers were opened, within five years of his death, hundreds of studies have been published on Roosevelt and his period and a steadily increasing number of scholars have traveled to the Library in Hyde Park.

As part of its task of making the Roosevelt papers available for research the Library has instituted a documentary publication program. Since the tremendous volume of modern Presidential files makes it impractical to publish everything that comes in and goes out of the executive office it is necessary to select from them the significant and the representative papers. The Library's program is aimed at the publication of selected documents in the major fields of Roosevelt's public actions. Already published are two volumes, *Franklin D. Roosevelt and Conservation, 1911–1945,* containing well over a thousand of the most significant documents in the Roosevelt papers relating to his lifelong interest in conservation.

The present volumes containing the principal documents in the Roosevelt papers pertaining to foreign relations during his first administration will, we believe, make important materials readily available to students of diplomatic history and world politics. These volumes, to be followed by others for his later administrations, contain not only the official reports to the President but also the many unofficial and private communications with which Roosevelt kept himself informed of world conditions and of opinion in this country. His own writings and statements include letters to the Secretary of State, our ambassadors, representatives of foreign powers, and private persons, messages to Congress, conferences with the press, and speeches and addresses.

These volumes together with *The Public Papers and Addresses of Franklin D. Roosevelt* and the *Foreign Relations* series of the Department of State present the student with a full account of the conduct of foreign relations during the years 1933–1937. In them it is possible to see how much emphasis was placed by the President on foreign affairs during an administration in which it appeared that chief attention was of necessity centered on domestic problems.

The long and painstaking task of selecting, compiling, and editing these documents has been performed by Edgar B. Nixon with the assistance of the members of the staff of the Library mentioned in his preface. The project was begun under Herman Kahn, former Director of the Library. William J. Stewart joined the editor in the final phases of the work and contributed immeasurably in reviewing notes, proofreading, and preparation of the index. Mrs. Carolyn K. Stone and Miss Lisa P. Mills have given helpful assistance in proofreading and with the index.

We wish also to express our appreciation to Lawson B. Knott, Jr., Administrator of General Services, and Robert H. Bahmer, former Archivist of the United States, for their interest and encouragement.

Elizabeth B. Drewry
Director, Franklin D. Roosevelt Library

James B. Rhoads
Archivist of the United States
National Archives and Records Service
General Services Administration

# Editor's Preface

*Franklin D. Roosevelt and Foreign Affairs,* an annotated collection of documents, will ultimately cover all of Roosevelt's terms as President. The first three volumes, being published simultaneously in 1969, cover the first term, 1933 to 1937. The documents are drawn from the Roosevelt papers in the Franklin D. Roosevelt Library, Hyde Park, New York. The President's direct handling of diplomatic relations is shown in the letters, memoranda, and notes that passed daily between the White House and the State Department and other departments, the correspondence with ambassadors and other American representatives abroad, correspondence with heads of foreign states and their representatives, and exchanges with the Senate Foreign Relations Committee and other Congressional committees.

"Foreign affairs" has been broadly defined to include not only foreign relations as such but also the domestic background of these matters. Thus the papers included in Volumes I through III show the efforts of organizations and individuals to influence the administration's actions and policies on issues such as adherence to the World Court, the St. Lawrence Waterway Treaty, diplomatic recognition of Russia, naval parity, neutrality legislation, and tariff matters. Efforts of the President to gain support for his policies through speeches, press conferences, and letters to influential organizations are documented. Papers showing divisions in the Congress on various issues and on the inception and progress of relevant legislation have also been included.

The work is designed to provide students, scholars, journalists, and others with accurate texts of documents in President Roosevelt's papers concerning foreign affairs, together with such editorial comment as is necessary for an understanding of the matters treated. The approximately 1,400 documents selected for the first three volumes were drawn from over twice that number of items identified among President Roosevelt's papers for his first term as having some connection with foreign affairs. These items are about equally divided between communications sent by the President and those received by him. Included are letters, telegrams, memoranda, notes, press conference transcripts, press releases, speeches and extemporaneous remarks, and messages to Congress.

All significant Roosevelt items have been included except those readily available in Samuel I. Rosenman's *The Public Papers and Addresses of Franklin D. Roosevelt,* the State Department's *Foreign Relations* series, and Elliott Roosevelt's *F.D.R.: His Personal Letters.* References to these publications are given in the editorial notes, as necessary. A few especially important documents have been reprinted in the interest of continuity. Other Roosevelt papers not included consist of brief notes of acknowledgment, routine notes and messages required by protocol, and correspondence dealing only indirectly with foreign affairs.

A number of letters to Roosevelt from ambassadors or other representatives abroad have not been included either because they are of lesser importance or are repetitious of other communications. Those selected, however, are the more significant and are representative of the others. All important materials not included are cited in the notes.

The arrangement is chronological throughout. Division by subject was impracticable because many of President Roosevelt's letters, press conferences, and speeches dealt with a variety of topics. An arrangement of documents by date, however, has the virtue of simplicity and of showing roughly the order in which the various items reached the President's desk. It also shows the heterogeneity and widely varying importance of the matters considered by him.

It should be emphasized that the papers of a President touch only in part on the issues with which his administration has to deal. They have to do only with matters that, for one reason or another, are brought to his attention. Moreover, many important matters are handled in conversation at White House conferences or over the telephone and thus remain undocumented.

These volumes are the product of the joint efforts of a number of members of the staff of the Franklin D. Roosevelt Library and the editor wishes to make grateful acknowledgment of their many contributions.

The project was begun under the general supervision of Herman Kahn, former Director of the Library, who planned the work. The late George W. Roach assisted in the search for material and in research on the documents, and, with Mrs. Aimée C. Buchanan, collated the copy. Joseph W. Marshall, librarian, was most generous of his time in searching for obscure printed materials, as was Jerome V. Deyo in locating manuscripts. Mrs. Carolyn K. Stone and Miss Lisa P. Mills read galley proof with great care and helped prepare the index. Special acknowledgment goes to William J. Stewart who was indefatigable in his assistance and whose special skills as a researcher, bibliographer, and indexer were indispensable to the completion of the volumes.

To Dr. Elizabeth B. Drewry, Director of the Library, must go the credit for bringing the project to completion. Dr. Drewry secured the publisher, assumed all the multitudinous duties of arranging administrative and legal details with the Press and with the National Archives and Records Service, handled the day-to-day exchanges on matters of editing, format, and scheduling, and found time to review galleys and page proof and to plan the form of the index. All of us are deeply grateful to her for her never-failing encouragement and advice.

Edgar B. Nixon
Franklin D. Roosevelt Library
Hyde Park, New York
July 1968

# Editorial Method

Annotation of the text is confined to identification of persons and explanation of events mentioned; there is no attempt to provide a narrative of the events of the period. It is assumed that users of the volumes will be familiar with the general history of the years covered. However, every effort has been made to explain in the notes obscure or incomplete references. Significant items not printed are cited to source and briefly described. Cross references to related documents "above" and "below" are provided, and running heads give dates of documents on the page for easy location of cross references. Enclosures are printed directly below a document, and when not reprinted their presence or absence in the Roosevelt papers is noted.

Texts are reproduced verbatim except that obvious typist's errors were corrected. Where letters are handwritten all eccentricities of spelling and punctuation are retained. Crossed-out words are printed with a line through them and words substituted for the crossed-out words are in italics. All parenthetical words in the press conference transcripts are by the reporter unless otherwise noted. Uniform style is used in rendering headings, salutations, closes, and signatures. Annotations on the document are reproduced, with a descriptive symbol (explained in the list following) and indication, when possible, of authorship. Marguerite LeHand, private secretary to President Roosevelt, is the LeHand who appears frequently on such notations. When it is apparent that a letter or other document was drafted for the President's signature, either the name of the drafter or that of the department in which it originated is indicated. Explanatory words inserted in the text by the editor appear in italics in brackets.

The different kinds of texts of President Roosevelt's speeches and messages to Congress are indicated in the notes. They may be drafts, the final copy or reading copy, the press release of the final copy, the stenographic transcript, or in the case of speeches a recording of the radio broadcast. The broadcast recording is used as the text when available and differences between this and other texts are noted.

The citation in brackets at the end of each document gives the particular section of the White House files in which the document is located, the subfile, and a descriptive symbol. These designations are explained in the list of abbreviations below. (The Roosevelt Library has in large part retained the White House filing system.) The documents printed are from the Roosevelt papers in the Library (the White House papers) or, in the case of one or two items, Group 14, Roosevelt family papers, or from other collections acquired by the Library. Of the latter, several items are from the papers of R. Walton Moore, Assistant Secretary of State and Counselor to the State Department, 1933–1937. Other collections in the Library from which a few items have been selected for publication are the papers of Louis McHenry Howe, President Roosevelt's personal secretary until his death in 1936, and the papers of Rear Admiral Wilson Brown, Naval Aide to President Roosevelt.

The index to the first three volumes is at the end of Volume III.

## Abbreviations

File division

OF: Official File
PPF: President's Personal File
PSF: President's Secretary's File
RL Recordings: Roosevelt Library Recordings

Descriptive symbol

A: autograph, not signed
AS: autograph, signed
CT: carbon typescript, not signed
CTS: carbon typescript, signed
M: mimeographed
T: typescript, ribbon copy, not signed
TS: typescript, ribbon copy, signed

# Contents

FOREWORD                                    v

EDITOR'S PREFACE                          vii

EDITORIAL METHOD                          xi

ABBREVIATIONS                            xii

DOCUMENTS

1933  January                              1

      February                             8

      March                               19

      April                               31

      May                                 91

      June                               194

      July                               266

      August                             342

      September                          383

      October                            417

      November                           451

      December                           509

1934  January                            567

      February                           623

INDEX FOR VOLUMES I–III (see Volume III)

## Roosevelt to Henry L. Stimson, Secretary of State

New York City, January 4, 1933

My dear Mr. Secretary: I am inclosing a copy of a note which I am sending to the President in tonight's mail. It would be delightful if you could run up to Hyde Park to lunch with me next Saturday or Monday, if the President approves.[1]

With my sincere regards, Faithfully yours,

[PPF 20:CT]

[1] Stimson accepted in a note of January 5 (OF 20).


## [*Enclosure*] Roosevelt to President Hoover

New York City, January 4, 1933

My dear Mr. President: I should much like to have the privilege of discussing with the Secretary of State certain matters relating to the State Department. It would be of great assistance to me to obtain first hand information on these matters from him. I hope that you will have no objection to his coming to see me some day at his convenience, especially if this could be arranged before I go down to Warm Springs two weeks from now.[1]

Very sincerely yours,

[PPF 20:CT]

[1] Printed also in Elliott Roosevelt, with Joseph P. Lash, eds., *F.D.R.: His Personal Letters, 1928–1945,* 2 vols. (New York: Duell, Sloan and Pearce, 1950), I, 320–321; hereafter cited as *Personal Letters*. The events leading up to this letter may be followed in Raymond Moley, *After Seven Years* (New York: Harper, 1939), pp. 68–94. The post-election Hoover-Roosevelt correspondence, in which Hoover attempted to persuade Roosevelt to take part in certain decisions of policy with respect to war debts, disarmament, and world economic recovery, is printed in Samuel I. Rosenman, ed., *The Public Papers and Addresses of Franklin D. Roosevelt, 1928–1936,* 5 vols. (New York: Random House, 1938), I, 873–884; hereafter cited as *Public Papers*. It is also published in William Starr Myers and Walter H. Newton, *The Hoover Administration* (New York: Scribner's, 1936), pp. 280–281, 282,

290–291, 294–297. On Nov. 12, 1932, Hoover informed Roosevelt that the British had asked for a suspension of their December 15 debt installment; in view of the importance of the issue, he asked for a conference. Roosevelt agreed in a note of November 14 (*Public Papers,* I, 873–876, 876–877), and the two met in Washington on November 22. This meeting is described by Roosevelt in a note to the correspondence just cited, and by Moley, *After Seven Years,* pp. 72–76. Both issued press statements on Nov. 23, 1932 (Myers and Newton, *Hoover Administration,* pp. 283–288). In his, Roosevelt restated his policy on the debt issue and again declared that responsibility for resolving the immediate questions raised by the British, French, and other notes rested with those "now vested with executive and legislative authority." In a second exchange, Hoover asked Roosevelt to join with him in selecting a delegate to the coming Monetary and Economic Conference. Roosevelt declined and suggested that the questions of delegates and agenda be postponed until after the inauguration (*Public Papers,* I, 877–884). The meeting here requested by Roosevelt took place January 9. See press release of Jan. 17, 1933, below.

## Norman H. Davis, Chairman, American Delegation, London Naval Conference, to Roosevelt

New York, January 10, 1933

Dear Franklin: I am enclosing a copy of a cable which I have just received from Arthur Sweetser at Geneva.[1] As you probably know Sweetser is an American who has been on the Secretariat of the League since its formation and is now acting as the head of the information section. He has also been acting as a liaison to keep us informed as to developments in the Far Eastern situation. His cable is so condensed that it requires considerable reading to get its full meaning. My interpretation of it, however, is as follows:

Hope for a solution of the Far Eastern controversy through conciliation is now practically abandoned and it is feared that the area of trouble will be extended. The meeting of the Committee of 19 (appointed by the Assembly) to be held on the 16th will probably terminate the conciliatory phase of the negotiations and prepare for the full Assembly a report under paragraph 4 Article 15 of the Covenant. There is considerable division of opinion regarding the nature of the report. Some favor a statement of the facts based on the first 8 chapters of the Lytton Commission Report recommending a settlement along lines of the 9th chapter of the Report and probably fixing responsibility as a result of the failure at conciliation; while others would give a wider scope to the responsibility including specific violations of Articles 10 and 12 of the Covenant. The outcome will affect developments both generally and locally for years. One of the fundamental elements is that despite a flood of news from here on other questions, practically nothing has appeared for months—indeed since before elections—on the Far Eastern situation and almost nothing with regard to the views of the incoming Administration. While he hesitates to urge a statement he believes that in view of the vital import of the decisions and the deeply genuine desire on the part of the nations to synchronize their actions with ours and the very natural uncertainty as to the forthcoming changes, it is clearly in our interest to make a statement if only to show a continuation of policy and of anxious watchfulness. He would appreciate any possible personal guidance by cable.

I presume, of course, that you discussed that entire question with Stimson[2] and after you have had an opportunity to consider the above I should be glad to confer with you if you so desire. My own opinion is that the most practical procedure would be for us to talk the situation over now very frankly with England and France with a view to maintaining a similar policy for coping with the situation which is of such vital importance to the three countries.

Very sincerely yours,

Norman H. Davis

P.S. After dictating the above Dr. Sze, the Chinese Minister, came to see me and gave to me the paraphrase of a very confidential cable he has received from Dr. Yen, the Chinese representative at Geneva. I am enclosing this for your very confidential information.[3]

[Group 12:TS]

[1] The cable, dated Jan. 10, 1933, contained a pessimistic forecast of the fate of the Lytton report, then being considered by the League's Committee of Nineteen. The report (findings of the Commission of Inquiry, headed by the Earl of Lytton, on the Japanese encroachments in Manchuria) had been made public on Oct. 2, 1932. Sweetser had been on the press section of the American delegation at the Versailles Peace Conference and had been with the League of Nation's information section since 1919. He was known but slightly to Roosevelt in 1933. In the years following, however, he sent him long and informative reports from Geneva and by 1937 the President spoke of him as "an old friend of mine" (Roosevelt to Cordell Hull, Feb. 11, 1937, PPF 506). On Dec. 31, 1933, Sweetser was appointed director of the League Secretariat (New York *Times,* Jan. 1, 1934, p. 18).

[2] In Hyde Park on Jan. 9, 1933.

[3] The cable, W. W. Yen to Alfred Sze, is not present.

## Press Statement by Roosevelt

[New York, January 17, 1933]

Any statement relating to any particular foreign situation must of course come from the ~~State Department~~ *Secretary of State* of the United States.

I am however wholly willing to make it clear that ~~one of the keystone cornerstones of~~ American foreign policy must ~~be the stressing of~~ *uphold* the ~~sacredness~~ *sanctity* of international treaties. That is the a cornerstone on which all relations between nations must rest. F[1]

[PPF 1-F:A:FDR]

[1] Roosevelt drafted this statement in pencil, on January 17 and handed it to the reporters who had called at his New York house that day; it appeared the next day (see New York *Times,* Jan. 18, 1933, p. 1). Deleted words are indicated and inserted words are in italic.

Stimson and Roosevelt had talked for six hours in Hyde Park on Jan. 9, 1933; see Henry L. Stimson and McGeorge Bundy, *On Active Service in Peace and War* (New York: Harper, 1947), pp. 292–293, and Moley, *After Seven Years,* p. 94. Stimson says that he warned the president-elect that the League was approaching "a final judgment" on the Sino-Japanese dispute and that the Administration might have to make a further statement. He also says that Roosevelt gave "general approval" of his Manchurian policy and promised that he would do nothing to weaken his stand.

On January 16 Stimson notified the European chancelleries that United States policy on Manchuria would not be changed. When the statement here printed appeared the next day it was taken for an endorsement of the Stimson policy, as it was intended to be (New York *Times,* Jan. 17, 1933, p. 1). Apparently Roosevelt had consulted none of his advisers on this news release; Raymond Moley and Rexford G. Tugwell regarded the endorsement as calamitous (Moley, *After Seven Years,* pp. 94–95). The "final judgment" of the League that Stimson spoke of took the form of a report of the League Assembly; this report is printed in Stimson's *The Far Eastern Crisis: Recollections and Observations* (New York: Harper, 1936), pp. 273–285. For the situation at the outset of 1933 as seen in the diplomatic correspondence, see *Foreign Relations of the United States, Diplomatic Papers, 1933,* III, *The Far East* (Washington, 1949), hereafter cited as *Foreign Relations.*

## Henry L. Stimson, Secretary of State, to Roosevelt, Warm Springs

Washington, January 25, 1933

*Personal and Confidential*

Dear Governor Roosevelt: I have just received from the British Ambassador a reply to the invitation which I transmitted for you to the British Government last Friday. I enclose herewith a copy of this reply.[1]

Very sincerely yours,

Henry L. Stimson

[PPF 20:TS]

[1] Present. Roosevelt's invitation to the British government to discuss war debts in Washington in March, dated Jan. 20, 1933, with Stimson's memorandum on the subject of the same date and the British reply are printed in *Foreign Relations, 1933*, I, 828–829, 832–833. Stimson telephoned the reply to Roosevelt in Warm Springs (*ibid.*, pp. 833–834).

# Henry L. Stimson, Secretary of State, to Roosevelt, Warm Springs

Washington, January 25, 1933

My dear Mr. Roosevelt: In the course of our telephone conversations, you suggested that it would be interesting to have a report from our representative in France regarding the impression left on the French Government and the French people by the discussions that have been taking place between this Government and the British Government.[1] I requested Ambassador Edge to cable a report, and I am enclosing a paraphrase of his reply.[2]

Sincerely yours,

H. L. Stimson

[PPF 20:TS]

[1] Memoranda of the Roosevelt-Stimson telephone conversations of Jan. 23, 24, and 25 are printed in *Foreign Relations, 1933*, I, 829–830, 831–832, 833–834. France had defaulted on the Dec. 15, 1932, installment of her war debt to the United States, one of seven nations to do so; it was therefore necessary to formulate a policy on the issue. On Jan. 19, 1933, Stimson, Roosevelt, Moley, and Tugwell conferred at the Mayflower Hotel in Washington on war debts and on the next day Roosevelt conferred with President Hoover and Treasury Secretary Ogden Mills at the White House (Moley, *After Seven Years*, pp. 97–101). On Jan. 22, 1933, Stimson reminded Roosevelt that he (Stimson) had suggested at the Mayflower Hotel meeting that it might become necessary to make representations to the French government about the debt. He thought that if this were not done the French might feel that the default was not taken seriously, and enclosed a draft note that he thought represented the American position (*Foreign Relations, 1933*, I, 867–868).

[2] In this dispatch of Jan. 24, 1933, and in another of the next day also sent to Roosevelt (PPF 20), Ambassador Walter E. Edge reported that the French press was assuming

that the discussions could in no way affect the French position. Moreover, there was confidence that the British would defend French interests. A Warm Springs dispatch of Jan. 24, 1933 (New York *Times,* Jan. 25, 1933, p. 1) was widely quoted to the effect that Roosevelt's advisers left no doubt that defaulting nations such as France would also be eligible to lay their case before the United States. The two dispatches were telephoned to Roosevelt on January 25; on January 27 Roosevelt telegraphed to Stimson that he thought "a more informal oral suggestion would be more effective in permitting France to arrive at the reconsideration of their failure to pay"; Stimson replied January 30 that he would act accordingly (*Foreign Relations, 1933,* I, 833–834, 871).

## William C. Bullitt to Roosevelt, Warm Springs

Paris [January 26, 1933][1]

[*Telegram*] Today held two intimate conversations with Boncour.[2] Your good will toward France has moved him and he hopes by following plan we decided on that it will be possible to obtain payment due last December. Shortly after inauguration he expects to ask Herriot to go to America ostensibly on lecture trip but in reality to have confidential talk with you.[3] This would begin February twenty first. In case the Boncour ministry should fall a new government would adhere to this project. He gave definite promise that no loan would be given to Japan. I am leaving for Germany tomorrow.[4]

Bill

[PPF 1124:T]

[1] Date derived from the New York *Times,* Jan. 28, 1933, p. 6.

[2] Joseph Paul-Boncour, French Minister of Foreign Affairs. Bullitt was in Europe as an unofficial observer for Roosevelt and was there particularly to take note of the rumored French-British-German rapprochement and European attitudes toward the debt installments due Dec. 15, 1932. Bullitt reported to Roosevelt on his conversations with European statesmen on Dec. 27, 1932; his second trip to Europe, Jan. 13 to Feb. 15, 1933, was followed by denials by him and Roosevelt that his missions had any official status. See Louis B. Wehle, *Hidden Threads of History: Wilson Through Roosevelt* (New York: Macmillan, 1953), pp. 110–115, 118–119; New York *Times,* Feb. 6, p. 6, Feb. 11, p. 9, Feb. 16, 1933, p. 3; and Moley, *After Seven Years,* pp. 135–137. Bullitt took part in the preliminary talks with the French and British in Washington in the spring. On April 20 he was appointed special assistant to the Secretary of State.

[3] Edouard Herriot had resigned as Premier in December 1932, following a vote of no confidence on the issue of the payment of the Dec. 15, 1932, debt installment, which he favored. Concerning the lecture trip, see Davis to Hull, April 13, 1933, in *Foreign Relations, 1933,* I, 494–496.

[4] From London, Bullitt had reported that Neville Chamberlain and J. Ramsay MacDonald had told him that it would be possible for England to return to the gold standard, that MacDonald would come to the United States after the inauguration, and that the Japanese would not be permitted to float a proposed half-billion dollar

loan in London. From Berlin he reported that he believed full reliance could be placed on German support for return of England to the gold standard (Bullitt to Roosevelt, Jan. 23, 24, 30 (?), 1933, PPF 1124).

## Harvey H. Bundy, Assistant Secretary of State, to Roosevelt, Warm Springs

Washington, January 27, 1933

*Personal and Confidential*

My dear Governor Roosevelt: Secretary Stimson has asked me to send you the enclosed memorandum, with regard to which he spoke to you on the telephone this afternoon.[1]

Very sincerely yours,

Harvey H. Bundy

[PPF 20:TS]

---

[1] In this long memorandum of Jan. 27, 1933 (published in William Starr Myers, *The Foreign Policies of Herbert Hoover, 1929–1933,* New York: Scribner's, 1940, pp. 242–249), Hoover reviewed United States policy on the war debts. We would recognize no connection between the reparations due the debtor nations and the payments they owed us; debt settlement should be based on ability to pay; any adjustment of debts owing to inability to pay must be compensated for by "tangible benefits." Hoover saw the American position challenged in Chamberlain's speech of Jan. 24, 1933 (printed in New York *Times,* Jan. 25, 1933, p. 2), and the British note of Jan. 25, 1933 (*Foreign Relations, 1933,* I, 832–833). These statements appeared to assert that the United States–British settlement must be final and must be a nominal one based on reparations payments.

Hoover believed that the American position should be informally reaffirmed to the British by Roosevelt's future Secretary of the Treasury and Secretary of State. On January 27 British Ambassador Ronald Lindsay cabled his office that Under Secretary of State William Phillips had asked him to go to Warm Springs the next day to confer with Roosevelt on war debts (E. L. Woodward and Rohan Butler, eds., *Documents on British Foreign Policy, 1919–1939,* 2d series, V, 1933, London, 1956, p. 747; hereafter cited as *British Documents, 1919–1939*). Presumably Roosevelt had Hoover's memorandum in time for his conference with Lindsay on Sunday, January 29. In Warm Springs, Lindsay said that the idea of the meeting had originated with Roosevelt who had suggested it to Stimson on January 27 (New York *Times,* Jan. 29, 1933, p. 1).

## Press Statement by Roosevelt and Ronald Lindsay, British Ambassador

[Warm Springs, January 29, 1933]

The British Ambassador & Mr. Roosevelt have had a wholly informal and unofficial but very satisfactory conversation covering ~~principally~~ *tentatively*[1] the arrangements for the coming meetings in Washington. It is hoped that these meetings will be able to start early in March.[2]

[PPF 1-F:A:FDR]

[1] In reproducing drafts, deleted words are indicated and inserted words are in italic.

[2] Lindsay and Roosevelt prepared this statement for the press following their four-hour conversation in Warm Springs on Sunday, January 29; it appeared in the New York *Times* (p. 1) the next day. On his way back to Washington on Sunday Lindsay had misgivings about the wording and telegraphed Roosevelt from Greenville, S. C.: "Seems to me word 'satisfactory' in press statement may create exaggerated impression. To avoid this would you agree to our indicating in talk to press that conversation was exchange of views with object of facilitating agreement but that we did not expect or attempt to reach actual agreements in the conversation" (PPF 1-F).

Lindsay's summary of the talk is published in *British Documents, 1919–1939,* V, 748–751, as is his memorandum of Roosevelt's proposal for a debt settlement: a lump sum payment of from twelve to fifteen hundred million dollars in full discharge (*ibid.,* pp. 751–752). Lindsay said that both he and Roosevelt were aware that this was equally unacceptable to the Congress and the British government.

## Prime Minister J. Ramsay MacDonald to Roosevelt, Albany

[London] 10th February, 1933

*Personal & Private*

Dear Mr. Roosevelt: I am making bold to write you this letter explaining some of our difficulties here, so that you may understand them at first hand. It is in no sense official.

I am most anxious that we should find a way to solve the really great difficulties which have to be surmounted in dealing with the Debt. (You know how I put Anglo-American good relations in the forefront of the things absolutely essential to the regeneration of the world). We have a double problem with the United States on the one hand and Europe and the world generally, on the other. How are we to bring both together in one solution, or any solutions? Were we dealing with you alone, the problem would be comparatively simple and would proceed somewhat on the lines which a friend of yours explained to us a fortnight ago.[1] We should consider together something which would substantially scale down our indebtedness and leave it in a position which both of us could accept. When we turn to the other side of our problem, the matter is not so easy. At Lausanne we had to meet the European situation, the characteristic features of which may be summarised thus:

(1) The German payments had become impossible, especially after the Moratorium, and we were faced a year ago with repudiation. Had that begun, nobody could foresee the terrible disasters both in finance and in politics which would have followed. Repudiation is a malady which spreads like foot and mouth disease. Not only would Government financial obligations be smashed, but commercial debts would be involved, and a series of bankruptcies would have followed of the gravest character.

(2) Our debtors, especially France and Italy, would have ceased payment to us. The Moratorium had already cost us a good many millions of pounds which we were perfectly willing to forego had a final settlement been reached, but no such settlement appeared to be possible and a complete breakdown was facing us.

(3) The virtual bankruptcy of certain mid-European States would have become operative. Whole masses of the people of Europe would have been reduced to starvation; international trade on this side would have been brought to a standstill, and we should have had to face a condition of things in finance, trade and political unsettlement, which have not been experienced for many generations. Communism would undoubtedly have planted its flags over the greater part of Europe.

When I went to Lausanne, the outlook was of the most gloomy kind. The difficulties, however, were overcome for the time being, but, in the process of settlement, we had to face hard realities. I have always regretted that at Lausanne we were deprived of the benefits of American participation or even American advice. You will remember that Mr. Hoover's attitude was "let Europe settle its own difficulties and then approach us"; and the approach, we were warned, would not have to be of a representative European body, but of individual nations. We were put in a very hard corner. During the whole of the hectic weeks of the Conference I did my best, with the loyal backing of my colleagues, to keep in mind at every stage the American position.

The result is that whether America formally recognises it or not, no settlement with any European nation can meet the present situation

9

unless it is, in fact, one which will keep the Lausanne Agreement going and enable it to be ratified. In other words, the American settlement must be a European one as well, so that when it is made you and we together will have enabled Europe and America to begin anew a restoration of commercial transactions and trade. This will have to be based upon confidence between the nations, and the establishment of currencies which will have something like a stable international value, to be used for the ordinary operations of international commerce. All this, however, will be fully explained to you when you see our Ambassador.

What prompted me to have this direct personal communication with you was another set of problems, namely, how are we to conduct our negotiations? My last visit to America was preceded by a very full exchange of views between Washington and London. The naval positions of both countries were discussed through your Embassy here, with myself; and all the points that were to be raised in the course of the discussions were thoroughly explored and differences brought down to very definite proportions. When that was done, I went to America and finished the business. We have found that, on this occasion, that could not be done, so that if any Minister were to go to Washington now, he would have to deal with a great budget of questions upon which no exchange of opinions has taken place. After seeing you and discovering what you wished to have discussed and how the discussion should take place, he would require [sic] to send very lengthy and elaborate reports to the Cabinet here and begin with the Cabinet an exchange of views under rather unsatisfactory conditions. Things would go, at any rate at first, very slowly. The press in both countries would as likely as not, be pernicious, and as our House of Commons is sitting, questions would be put daily on how matters were proceeding. That is a situation which I do not like.

Moreover, we should desire to exchange views with you—and I believe you reciprocate that desire—on some important subjects which are really international and which, if other European nations felt were being agreed to without their presence, might make it impossible for either you or us to reach the wider agreement upon them which is absolutely necessary if they are to become part and parcel of a world settlement. You will find again and again that it is not always the substance of proposals which creates trouble, but the way they are brought out. We ought, therefore, before any Minister goes to Washington, to agree upon what we are to discuss and how we are to discuss it. I think you will agree with these proposals:

(i) you and I in our hearts wish to secure for the next half century or so the closest friendship between our two countries and the firmest confidence in each other;

(ii) not only a settlement of Debts, but a co-operation in world policy on such matters as peace, disarmament, a restoration of trade, is to be our aim; and

(iii) we must secure between ourselves an exchange of views which will, by the sheer consequence of mutual understanding, give us a very great measure of co-operation in all the international conferences now sitting in which we are mutually interested, not only as separate states but as states responsible for the peace and happiness of the world.

I am afraid that as the outlook now is, we cannot get into real touch until after the beginning of March, though our Ambassador will see you before then and give you much information. But I would suggest that you discuss at once with our Ambassador your views upon the subjects about which you would like to confer with us. We shall then give you our opinions and by rapid exchanges of reactions, settle the purpose of a conference between you and a British Minister, which might be held quite soon so as to help you with your public opinion.

There will be no attempt at this stage of our relations to settle Debts but to examine various possible schemes so that we might officially understand each other's position and the conditions in which each of us find ourselves making an agreement difficult. When that is done, the personal negotiation stage would have been reached.

The objection to this way of handling is only too apparent. It will mean time, however rapidly we may get through it. But as an offset to that, it will mean—I hope—success, for the inevitable consequence of failure to agree is really too terrible for me to contemplate.

Before leaving the thoughts which I am now trying to express, I must point out again, and emphasize, that in everything we do we must not isolate ourselves from the rest of the interested nations, otherwise we on this side will only have gone out of the frying pan to find ourselves in the fire. This is a very difficult problem. I suppose you find that public opinion in your country presses you to carry out your decision that you can only deal with nations separately. I think you will find that to be very awkward in actual working, and the only way that I can see through it is that in any conversations we may have you and we will have to strive to come to understandings which can be applied to your debtors and ours for we are both a debtor and a creditor state.

Then the question arises, what Minister or Ministers should go to

11

Washington, when the stage has been set. Of course, I should like to go myself. A sea voyage and friendly contacts with you afterwards would be to me, however difficult the work, a pleasant interlude, but my hands here are so full almost beyond imagination that to leave the country for any length of time and for such a far away destination, is not very possible. Moreover, if you and I met we would have to pull off some big agreement. Failure in that respect would do both of us very serious damage and would badly affect our Governments. Therefore, good preparation would have to be made for the visit, and we should have to find ourselves in a position when a satisfactory agreement would be very possible. Before I went to see your predecessor we spent some months in preliminary negotiations through the American Embassy here.

I believe, however, that if a British Minister went to Washington as soon as possible the effect would be excellent, but even a Cabinet Minister must bring away something.

I have been turning this over again and again in my mind since I saw your friend here a few weeks ago. I think you are a little bit too optimistic as to the time-table, and if you are to meet your Congress shortly you will not be able to go very far as regards settlements. You might be able to go a good long way so far as understandings are concerned, but I come more and more definitely to the conclusion that, if we agree that War Debts must be set in a large programme of agreements, you will have to face the possibility of postponing payments in June. That will, no doubt, be a hard thing for you to do, and you can depend upon my helping you in every way I can to avoid it, but the more I think it over the more the doubt in my mind of the possibility of this deepens. It would not require to be a very long moratorium, as far as I can see at the moment, and it could be arranged between us not for itself and in relation merely to the specific problem of War Debts, but in order to allow time for a full consideration of the wider set of problems which we would be reviewing. When all these preliminaries were done, I should then be very delighted to run over to Washington for a comparatively brief time and help to dot the 'i's and stroke the 't's and finish the sentences, and with you do something that would draw our two countries closer together and launch them on a great policy of world recovery, inspired by ideals far firmer than mere cash relationships or political documents that are only patched up affairs. In my mind there is a common ideal and a common outlook which I should so like to be made effective during your term of office and my own.

I repeat that this is purely a personal communication which I have been emboldened to make because I am so convinced that we look upon all these problems from the same standpoint and that we have enough influence to bring our two countries to see them as we do. You will therefore please not use this letter in the official communications which must pass between our respective Governments. Our Ambassador will meet you and tell you everything official about us, and he will have his instructions as to what to say to you about our thoughts and intentions.

I hope most sincerely that you have entered upon a term of office which will give you much satisfaction and bring you great success, and in sending my kindest regards to you I make bold to join Mrs. Roosevelt's name with your own. I have had a good many letters during the last month or two from mutual friends on your side, and the warmth of their references to you warms my own heart as regards the prospects of our relations.[2]

Believe me to be, Yours always sincerely,

J. Ramsay MacDonald

P.S. I am still pondering over the problem of time because I am not quite happy about it. If you could get on rapidly with Lindsay the visit I am willing to make might be materially hastened. JRM [3]

[PSF:Great Britain:TS]

[1] William C. Bullitt.

[2] MacDonald's argument that the Lausanne agreement be sustained and ratified and that a final settlement of the British debt be made echoed Neville Chamberlain's speech at Leeds on Jan. 24, 1933 (New York *Times,* Jan. 25, 1933, p. 2).

[3] Lindsay saw Roosevelt at his New York house on the evening of Feb. 20, 1933; his report of his conversation to Sir John Simon, British Secretary for Foreign Affairs, is printed in *British Documents, 1919–1939,* V, 769–771. The president-elect had admitted that wiping out the debts would be the best solution but neither public opinion nor the Congress would countenance this or even far less drastic solutions. He thought the wisest course would be to push the debt question into the background for the time being and to concentrate on the economic questions to come up at the London Conference.

## Roosevelt to Prime Minister J. Ramsay MacDonald, London

[New York, February 20, 1933][1]

*Personal and Confidential*

Dear Mr. MacDonald: I was delighted to receive your letter of February 10th,[2] and I hope that you will continue to write to me unofficially until I have the pleasure of talking with you face to face.

I regret that you feel our meeting must be long delayed. I had hoped to see you soon. And your letter strengthens my belief that if you should visit America we would not find it difficult to establish a personal relationship of absolute confidence. You express my own thoughts when you write: "You and I in our hearts wish to secure for the next half century or so the closest friendship between our two countries and the firmest confidence in each other."

I thank you also for stating so frankly your view of the line by which we should approach our task. I shall attempt to be equally frank, since it is only by mutual frankness that we shall be able to achieve the collaboration we both desire.

I was glad to note at the outset of your letter the statement: "Were we dealing with you alone, the problem would be comparatively simple and would proceed somewhat on the lines which a friend of yours explained to us a fortnight ago." From the remainder of your letter, I gather that your difficulty in accepting that line of approach arises from an apprehension that we desire to "isolate ourselves from the rest of the interested nations." I can assure you that we desire no such thing. On the contrary, I have already established contact with the French and shall do so shortly with the other interested nations.

Your difficulty in regard to the Lausanne agreement I think I understand. But I feel that I must add a comment to your statement: "no settlement with any European nation can meet the present situation unless it is, in fact, one which will keep the Lausanne Agreement going and enable it to be ratified." Is it not true that in view of recent developments in Europe it may be most difficult, even impossible, to obtain ratification of the Lausanne Agreement but that, ratified or not, it will "keep going"? The possibility of payments by Germany over and above those envisaged by the Lausanne Agreement seems to me somewhat remote.

We cannot, of course, take any official responsibility for the maintenance of the Lausanne agreement, and obviously we cannot comment in any way on settlements which you may or may not make with your own debtors. But we may say that we hope to reach agreement with each of our debtors by way of the line of approach which you discussed with our mutual friend some weeks ago. I am under the impression that such settlements could in no way diminish the chance that the Lausanne Agreement may "keep going." In any case, please do not forget that so far as we are concerned the Congress of the United States has the final word in this matter, and that I am certain Congress will not under any conditions go beyond the line indicated. Congress may well not go that far. Congress will certainly not go further.

That brings me to the question you raise toward the end of your letter: the question of a possible moratorium on June 15th. It is entirely beyond my constitutional powers to promise any such moratorium. I am bound by the resolution of Congress. Furthermore, in the interest of establishing a real collaboration between us, I must tell you frankly that if we were still in disagreement over questions of importance I should not recommend such a moratorium to Congress. If on the contrary we had reached agreement and all that was needed was in your own words, "to dot the 'i's and stroke the 't's and finish the sentences," and if you were about to come over for that purpose, I should in courtesy to you recommend a slight delay.

The entire matter presents itself to me at the moment in the following light: There are a number of problems which must be solved if the economic life of the world is to be revived. It is undesirable to establish an order of priority in regard to these problems because the solution of each and every one of them is essential for a restoration of prosperity. We should seek together the best solution for each problem individually and not bargain one solution against another; but we should reach our final solutions of all at the same time. We should, therefore, discuss simultaneously methods to revive international commerce, tariffs, monetary questions, the gold standard, silver, debts, etc. For example, concurrently we should attempt to devise ways and means to enable countries, which today have depreciated currencies, to return to the gold standard at the same time that we adopt our other remedies for curing the present economic illness of the world.

In these problems today it seems to me that speed is of the essence. Let us above all avoid a long drawn out conference like the disarmament conference. But let us also avoid an abortive conference. I heartily second your proposal that we should enter upon a rapid exchange of views through the embassies in Washington and London. And I thank you for your thoughtfulness in suggesting that a British Minister might perhaps come over. But I must tell you frankly that such a visit, however agreeable to me personally, would not "help me with my public opinion," and that since Sir Ronald will have the matter at his finger tips it seems to me that the introduction of another personality might tend to delay rather than expedite agreement.

Of course I do not refer to a visit of yourself. I remain most anxious to talk with you at the earliest possible moment. A thought in this connection occurs to me. Sir Ronald communicated to me your suggestion that the Economic Conference should perhaps be held in Washington rather than in London. The French, I find, would also approve of Washington. If you and I should decide that was desirable, would you consider coming over to open the Conference? Then without prejudice to either of us, we could establish the personal relationship which I believe may be of the utmost importance for the future relations of our countries. And we could give orders to our subordinates to reach solutions in these economic questions which are, after all, but obstacles on the road to the great collaboration we both desire.

In my opinion it is essential that we should from now on approach our mutual problems not as traders intent on driving hard bargains but as intimate friends attempting to help each other to find solutions for questions which involve the welfare not only of our own countries but of all mankind.

Every good wish to you and the hope that we may meet soon.

Yours always sincerely,

[*Notation:*A:LeHand] Not sent
[PSF:Great Britain:T]

---

[1] A supplied and approximate date. This letter was not sent.
[2] Above.

## Press Statement by Roosevelt

[New York, February 21, 1933]

After conferring with Secretary Stimson in Washington on Monday, the French Ambassador came to see Mr. Roosevelt in New York today. We discussed unofficially all questions relating to collaboration between France and the United States. These included, of course, the World

Economic Conference and intergovernmental debts. These conversations will continue and the new Secretary of State, after his selection is announced, will doubtless see M. Claudel.[1] I had a delightful meeting with Mr. Herridge, the Canadian Minister.[2] This was the first time I had the privilege of meeting him and we discussed many matters of mutual interest to Canada and the United States.[3]

[PPF 1-F:T:Draft]

[1] Paul Claudel's summary of his talk with Roosevelt was sent to Sir John Simon by A. De Fleuriau, French ambassador in London, and is printed in *British Documents, 1919–1939,* V, 772–773.

[2] William D. Herridge was minister to the United States from 1931 to 1935.

[3] This statement appeared (somewhat revised) in the New York *Times* of Feb. 22, 1933, p. 3. Details of the conversations were not reported but the *Times* said that it was understood that Claudel had brought a proposal for payment of the Dec. 15, 1932, debt installment, and that Herridge had discussed the St. Lawrence Seaway Treaty and the possibility of a reciprocal tariff agreement. The *Times* noted also that Roosevelt "read from a sheet on which he had written in his own hand what he wished to say." The handwritten statement is present (PPF 1-F) but contains only a part of what is printed here.

# Draft of Press Statement by Roosevelt

[New York, February 21, 1933]

Mr. Roosevelt announced tonight that ~~selection~~ he has invited Senator Cordell Hull[1] of Tennessee to be Secretary of State, and Mr. William H. Woodin[2] of Pennsylvania and New York to be Secretary of the Treasury, & they have accepted.

Senator Hull will resign ~~from the~~ as a member of the Senate in time to assume his duties after the 4th of March.

Mr. Woodin was ~~literally~~ drafted by Mr. Roosevelt as there were many difficulties in severing ties with the industrial companies with which he is connected.[3]

[PPF 1-F:A:FDR]

[1] Hull was first offered the secretaryship on January 20. He asked for time to consider and accepted after talking with Roosevelt on February 16, when he boarded the president-elect's train at Richmond and accompanied him to Washington. Formal announcement was made February 21 (Hull, *The Memoirs of Cordell Hull,* 2 vols., New York: Macmillan, 1948, I, 156–158; hereafter cited as Hull, *Memoirs*).

[2] William H. Woodin, a financier and industrialist, had known Roosevelt as governor.

[3] Only the first sentence of this draft was issued to the press; cf. New York *Times,* Feb. 22, 1933, p. 3.

## Draft by Sumner Welles of a Statement on Pan-American Policy

[Washington, February 21, 1933][1]

The creation and maintenance of the most cordial and intimate friendship between the United States and the other republics of the American Continent must be regarded as a keystone of our foreign policy. The erroneous interpretations given to the Monroe Doctrine over a period of many decades have constituted a constant cause for apprehension and for misrepresentation of the true purposes of the Government of the United States. The Monroe Doctrine declares that the United States will not permit any non-American nation to encroach upon the political independence of any American republic; and that the United States will not consent to the acquisition in any manner of the control of additional territory in this Hemisphere by any non-American Power. These principles have until now been proclaimed solely on the authority of the United States and they will not be abandoned. But they are essentially principles of continental self-defense. And they are as vitally important to every other republic of this Hemisphere as they are to the United States itself. I would welcome their adoption by every American republic as a portion of its national policy. In that manner alone, in my opinion, can there be permanently abolished the impression which has persisted that these simple principles of self-defense can involve a threat to the sovereignty or to the national well-being of any republic of the Western Hemisphere. In the same spirit of mutual understanding and of cooperation for the promotion of the welfare of the American peoples, I favor the principle of consultation between the governments of the American republics whenever there arises in this Continent any question which threatens the peace and well-being of the American world. I believe that in such emergency there should be summoned immediately an inter-American conference, in which the American republics can determine, as individual powers bound together by a common interest, what policy best behooves them in a crisis which may be of potential danger to each one of them in varying degree. The United States should take the ground that pan-American responsibilities must be accepted by all the American republics on equal terms. I would stress, in particular, the continental responsibility for the maintenance of peace in this Hemisphere, and the necessity for the perfection of the mechanism required for the carrying out of that obligation.

The lives of our citizens abroad must, of course, be protected, wherever they may be, when they are in imminent danger and the local authorities are patently unable to afford them security, but such protection by this Government should never again result in armed intervention by the United States in a sister republic. I believe that the dispatch of the armed forces of the United States to any foreign soil whatsoever, save for the purpose of dealing with a temporary emergency such as that just described, should never be undertaken by the American Executive except with the consent of the American Congress.

There is no more effective means of enhancing friendship between nations than in promoting commerce between them. We cannot expect to preserve the sincere friendship of our neighbors on this Continent if we close our markets to them. We cannot enjoy the markets of the American Continent, which have as vast a potentiality for development as any in the world, unless we permit the citizens of our sister nations to trade with us. The interest of the peoples of this Continent demands that the American governments individually take without delay such action as may be necessary to abolish those barriers and restrictions which now hamper the healthy flow of commerce between their respective nations.

[*Notation*:A:LeHand] Inaug speech
[PSF:Cuba:T]

---

[1] This document is undated and has been given this date for convenience. It was sent to Roosevelt sometime in the period "between his nomination and his inauguration" (Charles C. Griffin, "Welles to Roosevelt: A Memorandum on Inter-American Relations, 1933," in *The Hispanic American Historical Review*, XXXIV, May 1954, pp. 190–192). It was placed with the inaugural speech material but was not used for the speech; compare, however, with Roosevelt's Pan-American speech of April 12, 1933, in *Public Papers*, II, 129–132.

## From the Inaugural Address of March 4, 1933

[*Excerpt*] Our international trade relations, though vastly important, are in point of time and necessity secondary to the establishment of a sound national economy. I favor as a practical policy the putting of first things first. I shall spare no effort to restore world trade by international economic readjustment, but the emergency at home cannot wait on that accomplishment.

The basic thought that guides these specific means of national recovery is not narrowly nationalistic. It is the insistence, as a first consideration,

19

upon the interdependence of the various elements in and parts of the United States—a recognition of the old and permanently important manifestation of the American spirit of the pioneer. It is the way to recovery. It is the immediate way. It is the strongest assurance that the recovery will endure.

In the field of world policy I would dedicate this Nation to the policy of the good neighbor—the neighbor who resolutely respects himself and, because he does so, respects the rights of others—the neighbor who respects his obligations and respects the sanctity of his agreements in and with a world of neighbors.[1]

[Speech File:T]

[1] This is but a small part of the inaugural address; see *Public Papers*, II, 11-16. The original autograph draft, composed by President Roosevelt in Hyde Park on Feb. 27, 1933, and two succeeding drafts, are in the Roosevelt papers.

A statement by the President on the origin of the term "Good Neighbor" was dictated by him in 1942 in response to a request from Vice-President Henry A. Wallace for use in a speech. The statement follows (Tully to Roosevelt, May 13, 1942, PSF: Wallace):

May 17, 1942

The origin of the Good Neighbor Policy dates back to a day in the President's life when, as Assistant Secretary of the Navy at the beginning of the first Wilson Administration, the United States realized that Mexico had become critical. President Wilson decided that the insult to the American Flag at Tampico was more than this country could tolerate, in view of the unfriendly and undemocratic Administration then in power in Mexico. The Fleet was ordered to take Vera Cruz, which United States Forces occupied for several months. History may show that this whole episode was realistically necessary but the fact remains that many were killed on both sides and the bad feeling throughout Latin America created by this action lasted for a generation. The President has always believed that the germ of the Good Neighbor Policy originated in his mind at that time.

In 1915 the atrocious conditions in the Republic of Haiti, ending with the brutal murder and cutting up of the President of Haiti, was causing unrest in other parts of the Caribbean, including Cuba, Santa Domingo and Jamaica. The United States, under a policy which had lasted for many years, restored order both in Haiti and in Santa Domingo by sending Marines there and by occupying both Republics for a long period.

In all of these operations, President Roosevelt was impressed with the great emphasis placed on trade and finance in lieu of an approach from the standpoint of the right of self-determination and the use of a quarantine system for the restoration of order rather than the use of force in occupations. After he left Washington at that time, the President saw a rebirth of dollar diplomacy and the occupation of Nicaragua.

Soon after he became Governor of New York the terrible depression, starting in this country, spread all over the world, including Central and South America, and during the next four years most of our discussions with Latin America were still largely based on dollar diplomacy. This was accentuated by the fact that during the period from 1925 to 1930, New York banks, aided by the trips of Professor [Edwin W.] Kaemmerer to various Republics, forced on most of these Republics unnecessary loans at exorbitant interest rates and huge commission fees.

The President, therefore, began to visualize a wholly new attitude toward other American Republics based on an honest and sincere desire, first, to remove from their minds all fear of American aggression—territorial or financial—and, second, to take them into a kind of hemispheric partnership in which no Republic would obtain undue advantage.

After the President's election in the Autumn of 1932, he discussed this subject with Senator Hull, Senator [Joseph T.] Robinson and with a number of others.

In February, 1933, he began to formulate his Inaugural Address. In a discussion of the Address with Professor Moley he drew the analogy between the relations of the American Republics and the relations between a citizen in a small community with his own neighbors and said "What we need in the small community is the man who is a good neighbor to the people he associates with every day". This use of the words "Good Neighbor" was seized on by Professor Moley as just the right term, and the President put it into his first draft of the First Inaugural.

## Roosevelt to Cordell Hull, Secretary of State

[Washington] March 9, 1933

Memorandum for the Secretary of State: Will you be thinking about the following tentative suggestions:

Ambassador to Belgium—Dave H. Morris of New York[1]
Ambassador to Spain—Claude Bowers of Indiana[2]
Minister to Holland—William Gorham Rice of Albany[3]
Ambassador to Japan—Ambassador Grew to remain[4]
Minister to China—Minister Johnson to remain[5]

[OF 20:CT]

[1] Morris, a New York lawyer and a friend of Roosevelt, was appointed ambassador to Belgium on May 18, 1933.
[2] Bowers, a journalist and historian, was appointed ambassador to Spain on April 6, 1933.
[3] See Roosevelt to Rice, April 20, 1933, below.
[4] Joseph C. Grew had been ambassador to Japan since 1932.
[5] Nelson T. Johnson had been minister to China since 1929.

## Frederic A. Delano to Roosevelt

Washington, March 14, 1933

My dear F.D.R.: The writer of the enclosed letter and telegram was associated with your Uncle Warren in All Souls' Church in New York City. He has always been a hard working, loyal citizen, and has been

21

connected with many good causes. While I am passing Mr. Strong's letter along to you, it does not mean that I am urging his point of view.

Your affectionate Uncle,

Frederic

P.S. Another letter on the same text from Sam Eliot[1]—my view of the League of Nations is that it can do a vast amount of good as a method of interchanging ideas, for the present (at least) without physical force but with the force of public opinion—we should join as an Associate Party. F.A.D.

[OF 184-A:TS]

[1] In his letter of March 13, Samuel A. Eliot, minister of Arlington Street Unitarian Church in Boston, urged that Roosevelt's anti-League statement of Feb. 2, 1932, be omitted from his forthcoming book, *Looking Forward,* the subject of the enclosures in this letter.

## [*Enclosure 1*] Charles H. Strong to Frederic A. Delano

New York City, March 11, 1933

My dear Mr. Delano: I am greatly disturbed over the announcement that the President's publishers, on Thursday next, are to place on sale a book by the President, entitled, "Looking Forward." It will contain the statement on the enclosed slip.

Irrespective of my own views concerning the advisability of this country's becoming a member of the League of Nations, I greatly fear that this publication at this time will seriously interfere with the plans of the President and the State Department with respect to disarmament, and many other international problems. It undoubtedly will be a crushing blow to the friends of the League, both in this country and abroad. The President might wish to ascertain the views of Secretary Hull as to this. I have no means of knowing what he would think of it.

It is, of course, too late to delete this paragraph, even if the President were so disposed, but possibly the publication could be delayed.

With reference to the statement that "the country is overwhelmingly against it"—meaning the League—I am wondering if the President knows that in Massachusetts, on Election Day last November, on a referendum in eleven cities, as to whether the voters favored the admission of the United States into the League, every city voted heavily in favor of the proposition. The total vote cast was 40,510, and the vote stood 25,631 in favor and 14,897 against. The cities were representative of many interests.

The League of Nations Association has organized groups in every state in the Union, and in some cases branches in several cities.

Many of us in New York are very anxious about this. We may be mistaken about the probable effect of this statement, but we fear we are not.

You are at liberty, of course, to show this letter to the President, and I would be glad to come to Washington to discuss the matter with anyone, if that seems advisable.

Sincerely yours,

Charles H. Strong

[OF 184-A:TS]


## [*Enclosure 2*] Extract from "Looking Forward" by Franklin Roosevelt, to be published March 16, 1933

In common with millions of my fellow countrymen, I worked and spoke, in 1920, in behalf of American participation in a League of Nations, conceived in the highest spirit of world friendship for the great object of preventing a return of world war. For that course I have no apology to make.

If, today, I believed that the same or even similar factors entered into the argument, I would still favor America's entry into the League; and I would go so far as to seek to win over the overwhelming opposition which exists in this country today. But the League of Nations today is not the League of Nations conceived by Woodrow Wilson. It might have been had the United States joined. Too often through these years its major function has been not the broad overwhelming purpose of world peace but rather a mere meeting place for the political discussion of strictly European political national difficulties. In these the United States should have no part.

American participation in the League would not serve the highest purpose of the prevention of war and a settlement of international difficulties in accordance with fundamental American ideals; the League has not developed through these years along the course contemplated by its founder, nor have the principal members shown a disposition to divert the huge loans spent on armaments into the channels of legitimate trade, balanced budgets and payment of obligations.[1]

[OF 184-A:T]

[1] This extract from Roosevelt's speech before the New York State Grange in Albany on Feb. 2, 1932, appears in this form in *Looking Forward* (New York: John Day, 1933), pp. 254–255. As the speech was given, however, and as printed in the official New York state compilation, *Public Papers of Franklin D. Roosevelt, Forty-Eighth Governor of the State of New York. Second Term* (Albany, 1939), pp. 550–552, the last paragraph is as follows: "The fact remains that we did not join the League. The League has not developed through these years along the course contemplated by its founder, nor have the principal members shown a disposition to divert the huge sums spent on armament into the channels of legitimate trade, balanced budgets and payment of obligations. American participation in the League would not serve the highest purpose of the prevention of war and a settlement of international difficulties in accordance with fundamental American ideals. Because of these facts, therefore, I do not favor American participation." A part of the speech appears in Rosenman, ed., *Public Papers,* I, 155–157, but this does not include any part of the text just quoted nor several following paragraphs in the original speech on foreign debts.

## Roosevelt to Lillian D. Wald, New York

[Washington] March 16, 1933

*Personal*

Dear Miss Wald: I am delighted to see the enclosed.[1] I do so wish that the P.M. and I could have a quiet weekend together. I am confident that we would not only agree as to principles, but that we could work out some practical methods of solution. I still hope that he can come here a little later on—even though complete agreements are not pre-ordained!

I do hope you are better.

Very sincerely yours,

[PPF 114:CT]

[1] Not present; an accompanying note indicates that the enclosure, a letter from Ramsay MacDonald to Miss Wald, was returned to her. Miss Wald, a pioneer social worker (founder of Henry Street Settlement House in New York), was active in international peace movements and was chairman of the American Union Against Militarism. She and MacDonald were old friends.

## Press Conference, Executive Offices of the White House, March 17, 1933, 4:05 P.M.

[*Excerpt*] Q: Mr. President, there has been considerable curiosity and speculation over the visit here yesterday of the German and French and British Ambassadors.

The President: All I can tell you is to tell you the truth, of what Steve[1] told you—that the thing was a coincidence entirely. The British Ambassador asked to see me to tell me merely that the Prime Minister was going to have a plan that he hoped we would give favorable consideration to. The plan has not come and I have not seen the plan yet. It was coming in at the State Department about two hours ago but had not been written out yet.

Then I happened to mention to Robbins[2] yesterday morning that I would be very glad to see the German and French Ambassadors before they left and he arranged to have them come in right away. As a matter of fact, I had not thought that I would see them for two or three days so it really was a coincidence. It made a good story.

Q: Do you expect to see Phil La Follette?

The President: Has he come back?

Q: You did not know it?

The President: I did not know it.

Q: Did you discuss the disarmament situation?

The President: Oh, yes.

Q: What did you say about it?

The President: Steve, really—(Laughter)

Q: There is a British Treasury official of high consequence arriving today on the same boat with La Follette. Does that have anything to do with conversation about debts?

The President: Who is it?

Q: Alverson, or something like that.

Q: Sir Percy Thompson.

The President: Who is he?

Q: An Under Secretary—he is Comptroller of the British Treasury.

The President: I am learning a lot from the Press.

Q: And there are a couple of Frenchmen and one German who are said to be financial advisors of the League of Nations, and they are said to be in Washington.

The President: Is that so? (Laughter)

Q: Mr. President, can you tell us or give us an idea of what the attitude of the new Administration is on disarmament?

The President: I do not believe that I had better talk on disarmament today because—and this is off the record—we do feel that is one of the principal keys to the world situation and things are changing so fast that the only thing I can do or say in answer to that question—off the record—is that we are going to use every possible means to make some kind of a very, very definite and practical success of this disarmament conference, and use every means we can to prevent it from either blowing up or arriving at some patch-work thing.

Q: Couldn't you make that "background," Mr. President?

The President: Yes, use it for background, that is all right. I cannot go into details, however, because things are changing so fast every twenty-four hours.

Q: Do you expect to pass judgment in any form whatsoever on the MacDonald proposals?[3]

The President: I have not read them yet; we have not got them yet. At one o'clock the Secretary of State told us that they were coming in but had not been written out.

Q: Is Mr. Davis likely to go back to use his good offices?

The President: Off the record, before he goes we will have something on that, but I cannot say anything on it because I am not certain as to what form it will take. It may be in the form of a statement from the State Department.[4]

[President's Press Conferences:T]

[1] Stephen T. Early, Assistant Secretary to the President, was in charge of press relations.

[2] Warren D. Robbins, a cousin of the President, was at this time chief of the Division of Protocol of the State Department, and was appointed minister to Canada on May 11, 1933.

[3] The reference is to the disarmament protocol proposed by MacDonald to the Geneva Conference on March 16; it is printed in *Foreign Relations, 1933*, I, 43–54, and discussed in the correspondence following therein.

[4] Davis had been working with Hull on preparations for the Disarmament Conference and a week before Roosevelt had asked that he come to the White House for a conference (Roosevelt to Marvin H. McIntyre, March 9, 1933, OF 29). Davis saw the President for forty-five minutes on March 16, and Davis and Hull talked with him for an hour on the next day (PPF 1-0).

## Roosevelt to Senator Key Pittman of Nevada

[Washington] March 20, 1933

Memorandum for Senator Pittman: How do you think I should answer Governor Olson? The last thing Senator Walsh said to me was that he hoped his going into the Cabinet would not interfere with the quick ratification.[1]

[*Notation*:A:LeHand] What is the status of this?
[OF 66:T]

[1] Senator Thomas J. Walsh of Montana had died March 2, 1933, while on his way to Washington to take office as Attorney General. Roosevelt refers to a telegram from Governor Floyd Olson of Minnesota, March 17, 1933 (OF 66), urging him to ask Congress to ratify the Great Lakes–St. Lawrence Deep Waterway Treaty between the United States and Canada that had been signed in Washington on July 18, 1932. See Roosevelt to Olson, March 27, 1933, below.

## Roosevelt to Cordell Hull, Secretary of State

[Washington] March 20, 1933

Memorandum for the Secretary of State: Mr. Howe has shown me your note of March 14th in regard to representatives sent to attend meetings of international conferences, congresses, etc.[1]

It seems to me that we have an opportunity here to get in new blood and I hope you will work up lists that will be more representative of this country than some of the lists I have seen in the past. It is an excellent opportunity. This should apply even to meetings of secondary importance.

[*Notation*:A:LeHand] FDR
[OF 20:CT]

[1] Hull to Louis M. Howe, March 14, 1933 (OF 20). He explained that persons appointed to represent the government were in some cases "officials of the Government and in other cases . . . individuals outside of the Government service selected because of their particular knowledge of the subjects to be discussed." He added that proposed appointments were first submitted to the President for approval except those of delegates to scientific, humanitarian, and educational meetings who had nothing to do with matters of policy.

## Roosevelt to Senator Arthur Capper of Kansas

[Washington] March 22, 1933

Dear Senator: Yes, I am much interested in steps to give the President authority to place an embargo on arms. Will you have a talk with Senator Pittman about it?[1]

Very sincerely yours,

[OF 178:CT]

[1] This letter was in reply to Senator Capper's letter of March 17, 1933 (OF 178), in which he referred to newspaper reports that the Administration was considering taking some action "in the way of an embargo against shipment of arms to nations which have violated the Peace Pact." He enclosed a copy of a resolution that he had had before the Senate for nearly two years and that he had reintroduced on March 13: Senate Joint Resolution 23, "Providing that it shall be unlawful . . . to export to any country violating the terms of the pact of Paris arms, munitions, implements of war, or other articles for use in war, or make any such trade or financial arrangements with the violating country or its nationals as in the judgment of the President may be used to strengthen or maintain the violation."

The resolution was referred to the Senate Committee on Foreign Affairs which took no action (*Congressional Record,* vol. 77, p. 414). Roosevelt had declared himself in favor of an arms embargo, under certain conditions, as early as Jan. 11, 1933. This was after President Hoover had sent to the Senate his message of Jan. 10, 1933, asking for ratification of the 1925 Geneva convention for the control of arms and munitions traffic, or, alternately, the right to place an embargo on arms and munitions destined for warring nations (New York *Times,* Jan. 12, 1933, p. 1). The *Literary Digest* of Jan. 28, 1933, quoted Roosevelt as having said: "I have long been in favor of the use of embargoes on arms to belligerent nations, especially to nations guilty of making an attack on other nations—that is, against aggressor nations."

## Roosevelt to Howard S. Cullman, New York

[Washington] March 27, 1933

Dear Howard: You are right about reciprocal tariff readjustments. The Secretary of State is, of course, keenly interested and we hope it gets somewhere this summer. It is certainly vital.[1]

Always sincerely,

[OF 61:CT]

[1] Cullman, commissioner of the Port of New York Authority, and a friend of Roosevelt, had written March 20, 1933 (OF 61), to ask that tariff readjustments be made with the country's import and export business in mind. He noted that the combined value

of New York City's import and export trade had dropped since 1928 from almost $4 billion to a little over $1 billion, and that stevedores were out of work, warehouses empty, and the shipping trade demoralized.

## Roosevelt to Governor Floyd B. Olson, St. Paul, Minnesota

[Washington] March 27, 1933

My dear Governor Olson: Thank you very much for your telegram of the seventeenth.[1] I am taking up the matter of the St. Lawrence Treaty with Senator Pittman's Committee in the Senate. The Treaty was reported favorably on February 21st and was referred back on March 10th.

Very sincerely yours,

[OF 66:CT]

[1] See Roosevelt to Pittman, March 20, 1933, above.

## Press Conference, Executive Offices of the White House, March 31, 1933, 4:12 P.M.

[*Excerpt*] Q: May we switch over to the foreign field for a moment? We understand that France has been sending some hints on the World Economic Conference to Washington. Can you tell us your attitude on that?

The President: I have not heard anything about French hints. I can only talk about it entirely off the record at this time. It has been suggested that Prime Minister MacDonald be named chairman and that the conference be held in London.

Q: He has been named chairman?

The President: He has been named chairman and of course it simply is one of those things we cannot discuss at all.

Q: There is another report that you intend to appoint both Republicans and Democrats to the delegation. Have you been considering that?

The President: I had not thought of what the politics were. We have got a fairly good group that is working on it at the present time, and I don't know their politics. I don't know what the formal and official delegation will be—it might be three or it might be twenty-three. I don't think there will be much politics in it . . .

Q: Do you feel like giving us any background about your visit with the Japanese, Mr. Matsuoka?

The President: No background, because I had a very pleasant conversation about when he was a student at the University of Oregon and how his classmate later became my classmate. It was a very friendly talk—just a friendly talk.[1]

[President's Press Conferences:T]

[1] Roosevelt saw Yosuke Matsuoka for fifteen minutes on March 31, 1933 (PPF 1-0). He later wrote to Colonel Edward M. House that he had kept the conversation formal; that Matsuoka had talked too freely to newspapermen and his suggestion about where the United States fleet should be kept had brought the White House thousands of protests (Roosevelt to House, April 5, 1933, *Personal Letters, 1928–1945*, I, 342–343).

# Roosevelt to Jeanne Rosat-Sandoz, Le Locle, Switzerland

[Washington] March 31, 1933

My dear Madame Sandoz: I am delighted to have your letter and it brings back many memories of those two very happy years that you were with us at Hyde Park.[1] I have often thought that it was you, more than anyone else, who laid the foundation for my education. The lessons in French which I began at that time have stood me in good stead during all these years and here in Washington it is a great pleasure to be able to converse with the members of the Diplomatic Corps in a common tongue.

I wish much that it were possible for me to go to Switzerland. When I have finished my task in Washington I shall be able to travel again and in that event I trust that I shall have the pleasure of seeing you once more.

Very sincerely yours,

[PPF 199:CT]

[1] Mme. Sandoz, who wrote to Roosevelt Jan. 30, 1933 (PPF 199) congratulating him on his inauguration, was his governess from 1891 to 1893. See Frank Freidel, *Franklin D. Roosevelt: The Apprenticeship* (Boston: Little, Brown, 1952), I, 30–31. Mme. Sandoz and Roosevelt continued to exchange letters until her death in 1937.

## William Phillips, Under Secretary of State, to
## Louis M. Howe, Personal Secretary to the President

Washington, March 31, 1933

Dear Colonel Howe: In accordance with my instructions, the Department sent you over this morning, for the President's information, copies of telegrams regarding the proposed boycott of Jews in Germany.[1]

You will note that these telegrams were coded in confidential code. At one time the Department followed the practice of transmitting such telegrams in paraphrase. However, considering the delay occasioned by the time necessary to make paraphrases and the desirability that the President should be in a position to peruse the actual texts of important telegrams, the Department will continue, if you approve, to send copies of telegrams in the original text.

I should like to emphasize, however, that the protection of the code makes it essential that the telegrams be carefully guarded and that no portion of them be made public at any time without prior paraphrasing.

In addition, may I suggest that when the copies of these telegrams have served their purpose they be returned to this Department?[2]

Sincerely yours,

William Phillips

[OF 20:TS]

[1] Not present; presumably returned to Phillips. For these exchanges, between George A. Gordon (chargé in Berlin) and Hull, and Phillips and Gordon, see *Foreign Relations, 1933*, II, 334–335, 335–337, 337, 342–346. The boycott was begun as scheduled on April 1 but President Paul von Hindenburg's intervention prevented excesses (Gordon to Hull, April 2, 1933, *ibid.*, pp. 347–350).

[2] Answered April 7, 1933, below.

## Roosevelt to Cordell Hull, Secretary of State

[Washington, April 1, 1933][1]

Memorandum for Secretary of State

Do *please* keep me in daily touch with what Davis is doing—I hear several despatches have come from him showing that Davis is talking debts and economics. That is *not* his job! Will you and Phillips run over and see me this morning?[2]

FDR

[OF 29:A]

---

[1] Date derived from an accompanying typed copy.

[2] Norman Davis, appointed a member of the organizing committee of the Economic Conference by President Hoover, was named a delegate to the Disarmament Conference by Roosevelt on March 14, 1933. On arriving in London, he at once told MacDonald that the thing to do was "to put debts completely in the background for the time being and to concentrate on ways and means for recovering from the depression" (Davis to Hull, March 30, 1933, *Foreign Relations, 1933,* I, 474–476). In a telegram to Roosevelt of March 31 (*ibid.,* pp. 477–479), he said he believed that failure of the Disarmament Conference would endanger the chances of success of the Economic Conference and that the questions of disarmament and economics were inseparable. Hull agreed with Davis in this view (*Memoirs,* I, 254–255); for the dispute between Moley and Davis on the issue see Moley's *After Seven Years,* chaps. 3 and 7.

## William Phillips, Under Secretary of State, to Roosevelt

Washington, April 3, 1933

Dear Mr. President: You asked me recently a question in regard to the Japanese mandates in the Pacific.[1]

I am sending you herewith a memorandum dated February 2nd, prepared by Doctor Hornbeck, of the Division of Far Eastern Affairs, together with a covering memorandum, dated April 3rd, also prepared by him. These two memoranda give, I think, an excellent summary of the whole question up to date.[2]

Faithfully yours,

William Phillips

[PSF:Japan:TS]

---

[1] Possibly during a two-hour White House conference on March 30 (PPF 1-0).

[2] The former, entitled "Manchuria Situation," is about 4,000 words long; the covering memorandum (printed below) is an adequate summary.

## [*Enclosure 1*] Stanley K. Hornbeck, Chief, Division of Far Eastern Affairs, to William Phillips

April 3, 1933

Mr. Phillips: On the subject Manchuria situation: Question of the Japanese mandates in the Pacific; relation of the United States thereto, herewith, as requested by you, a copy of the memorandum of February 2, 1933.[1]

Since the date on which this memorandum was submitted, Japan has withdrawn from the League of Nations. Also there have come from various Japanese official sources statements (but, so far as we know, no official pronouncement) to the effect that, regardless of considerations which may be advanced in opposition thereto, Japan regards the Mandated Islands as Japan's territory and intends to keep them. It would seem that the League will have to come to some decision with regard to the technical problems involved.

The United States, as one of the Allied and Associated Powers, acquired an interest in law in these Islands; and, as a "Pacific Power" and as a party to various treaties relating to the Far East, has a practical interest in the fate of and the use made of them. However, there is no need of and probably no useful purpose to be served by action on our part in anticipation of and before action by Japan or the League or both. This Division is therefore still of the opinion expressed in the last paragraph of the summarizing page immediately hereunder, it being our belief that there would be nothing to be gained—and there might be something to be lost—by a manifestation by the American Government at this time of interest or concern with regard to the matter.

(Note: In so far as our "conclusions" are given consideration, it is suggested that when or before any action by the American Government with regard to this matter may be in contemplation the whole subject should be examined by the Legal Adviser.)[2]

S. K. Hornbeck

[PSF:Japan:TS]

---

[1] The résumé only has been printed below.

[2] On Feb. 20, 1933, the Japanese Cabinet had voted to withdraw from the League; formal notice was sent to Geneva on March 27. On March 10, Hornbeck notified Warren D. Robbins, protocol officer, that the Japanese ambassador in Washington had requested an appointment with Roosevelt for Vice-Admiral Osami Nagano, Japan's delegate to the Disarmament Conference (OF 197). Nagano was in Washington only two days;

Roosevelt saw him on March 15, together with Ambassador Katsuji Debuchi, for fifteen minutes (PPF 1-0). Hornbeck, in urging that the request for appointment be granted, said it was "understood" that politics would not be discussed.

## [*Enclosure 2*] Résumé of Memorandum

February 2, 1933

The memorandum hereunder deals with the question of the relation of the United States to the status and possible problem of the Japanese Mandates in the Pacific.

It has been prepared on the basis of a study and memoranda by Mr. Field of WE,[1] together with some other materials.

The statement of facts and analysis which it contains lead to the conclusions that

(a) it cannot be assumed that a Mandatory upon leaving the League would automatically lose its rights in relation to a Mandate;

(b) it is questionable whether the Council of the League has the right to divest a Mandatory of its Mandate without the consent of the Mandatory;

(c) the rights of the United States in relation to Japan's Mandate would not be affected (either increased or diminished) by the fact of Japan's ceasing to be a member of the League; but that

(d) it might be possible for the United States to cooperate with the League in any change which, in the event of Japan's resignation from the League, the League might contemplate making in regard to the Japanese Mandate.

It is the view of FE[2] that up to such time as the League may have had to consider this question and shall have taken an initiative with regard to it, the American Government should give no sign of interest or concern with regard to it.

[PSF:Japan:T]

---

[1] Noel H. Field, of the Division of Western European Affairs.
[2] Division of Far Eastern Affairs.

## State Department Memorandum on United States Monetary and Economic Policy

Office of the Economic Adviser, April 3, 1933

Second draft of American policy on monetary and economic topics to be discussed in bilateral conversations and eventually at the Economic Conference.

(1) Central Bank Bullion Reserves

a. The United States Government believes that it would be desirable to establish a uniform legal gold reserve ratio for all the major countries. At the present time, various countries have various reserve requirements. It is the belief of this Government that uniformity will contribute greatly toward world stability in monetary affairs.

b. The United States Government believes that it is desirable to establish a uniform ratio lower than the average of the present legal ratios on the ground that a lowering of the legal gold reserves will tend to expand credit throughout the world. The United States Government has in mind a uniform ratio in the neighborhood of 30 per cent.

c. In the interests of general uniformity, the United States Government is prepared to suspend gold redemption of the currency. This Government is of the opinion that gold redemption of the currency acts as a healthy brake on over-expansion and that in a normal world it would be desirable to retain such redemption. This Government feels, however, that it is more important today to reestablish the free flow of trade by removal of restrictions and uniformity of practice than to adhere to the principle of a redeemable currency.

d. The United States Government believes that one of the most important things to be accomplished is to prevent a rushing about in the world of a large quantity of homeless money such as we have witnessed in the past. To this end the United States Government suggests the establishment of uniform buying and selling points for gold with a spread of possibly 5 per cent in place of the arbitrary import and export points which are today determined by cost of shipping.

(2) Silver

The United States Government believes that it is in the interests of all concerned to bring silver into line with the general commodity price level, and so far as possible, to stabilize it in terms of the general commodity price level. The United States Government is opposed to any form of fixed-ratio bimetallism and is further opposed to any proposal for artificial raising of the price of silver, just as it is opposed to any valorization scheme in any commodity.

The United States Government is convinced that silver at its present level is substantially below the general commodity price level (see separate memorandum showing that if silver had not been subject to special depressing influences—demonetization of subsidiary coinages and action of Indian Government—it would probably be selling today in the neighborhood of 50 cents per ounce, as against an actual present price of about 27 cents per ounce). The United States Government believes that it is desirable to offset the special depressing influences upon silver and that it is desirable so far as possible to restore the confidence of the Far East in its exchange medium, silver, by dignifying silver by means of including it to some extent in the gold family.

To this end the United States Government believes (a) that a remonetization of the debased subsidiary coinages would be desirable and (b) that it would be desirable to include a limited amount of silver in the bullion reserves of the various central banks. Specifically, the United States Government suggests that if, for example, a uniform gold reserve of 30 per cent is agreed upon in accordance with section (1) hereof, that then an additional 5 per cent or 7 per cent gold reserve be superimposed upon the 30 per cent reserve, such additional 5 per cent or 7 per cent reserve to be in gold or optionally in silver, if obtainable below a price corresponding to the commodity price level. For example, if it is determined that the price for silver which corresponds to today's price level lies somewhere in the neighborhood of 50 cents, then the central banks could optionally maintain the additional 5 per cent or 7 per cent reserve in silver to the extent that they could purchase silver below 50 cents an ounce.

The effect of this suggestion would be to create an enormous buying power for silver below 50 cents an ounce, and an equally large potential selling power above that price. It would be desirable in the view of the United States Government as a condition precedent to the adoption of such a plan, to obtain an agreement from the large silver producers who are very few in number, to a sensible limitation of production, and likewise to obtain from the Indian Treasury an assurance that the Indian Treasury would not dump unreasonable quantities of silver upon the world market.

(3) Exchange Restrictions

It is the view of the United States Government that it is in the interests of all concerned to remove all artificial exchange restrictions as soon as possible. It is further the view of this Government that such removal can only be accomplished after the debt structure of many of the debtor countries has been reorganized. In some cases, such as Chile, it will be impossible to remove exchange restrictions until the funded as well as the floating debt has been scaled down and refunded. In other cases, such as Germany, the short term debt, so-called, now bound under standstill agreements or exchange restrictions, will have to be so reduced by funding operations that the residue will no longer constitute a menace to the exchange of those countries. The United States Government, in so far as it can properly exert an influence upon American banks and other American citizens who are private creditors of such countries, is prepared to advocate such refunding and funding operations. The American Government is also prepared to submit a definite plan which it has worked out for handling the specific German problem.

(4) Correlated Central Bank Money Policy

The United States Government is in favor of close cooperation between the various central banks in their money policy. It is the belief of this Government that it would be to the advantage of all if the central banks of the major countries should uniformly agree either (a) to engage in open market operations such as are now carried on by the Bank of England and the Federal Reserve System, or (b) to limit their activity to note issuing function, as is now the case of the Bank of France. It is the present belief of the United States Government that it would probably be better for all central banks to engage in open market operations, and that in these operations the central banks take close and frequent counsel with each other. (This section is obviously susceptible of much greater development.)

(5) Gold Standard

The United States Government believes that the maintenance of an international gold standard in some form is an essential to world recovery. In this connection it is fully prepared to discuss with an open mind whatever sacrifice may be necessary on the part of such countries as the United States which have not devalued their currency in order to bring about world uniformity and equilibrium.

(6) Synchronized Expenditure Program

The United States Government believes that the general price level cannot be raised except by means and measures which will ultimately restore the willingness of individuals to engage in the normal risks of trade and that this willingness alone can keep the industrial machinery operating at a point where the natural sources of employment provide employment for all requiring work. The United States Government believes that a continued process of paying people to do nothing without a program for the rehabilitation of industry and commerce must lead to progressively greater unemployment; and if carried to its ultimate extreme, must lead to strangulation of industry by inordinate taxation, the strangulation of imports to protect threatened budgets, the ultimate unbalancing of budgets, with the final result of uncontrolled inflation and complete chaos.

The United States Government recognizes that in order to bring about the desired improvement in prices, action must be taken in many directions. Certainly one of the most important directions must be the effort to clear the channels of international trade, thereby making possible the assertion of normal demand for commodities. This effort to clear the channels of international trade is certain to be a protracted and difficult one, and full reliance cannot be placed upon it as a sole measure to produce the desired price movement.

The United States Government therefore suggests that consideration be given to the development of a plan of simultaneous action by various nations covering a period of say two to four years, under which plan each national government would undertake to engage in a program of rehabilitation proportionate to and of a character consistent with the individual requirements of each nation. It should be left within the discretion of each national government to determine the precise objects of expenditure as well as the methods, but the various national programs should be coordinated in general purpose, namely, the stimulation of the natural sources of employment either by direct Government expenditure or in the form of subsidies to private interests. In either case it should be borne in mind that a stimulation of those industries which are already over-producing is to be avoided.

The advantages of international action over uncorrelated similar action by individual nations would be:

(a) That inasmuch as the effect desired is largely to be attained through a restoration of confidence in private economic life, it is reasonable to suppose that this confidence will be stimulated to a greater extent by impressive international action than it would be by scattered individual efforts.

(b) It is further reasonable to suppose that coordinated action by several nations will bring about similar action by other nations which would otherwise not undertake the steps contemplated, and that the aggregate effect in restoring consumer demand will therefore be increased by a coordinated program.

38

(c) Whereas in the case of individual action, the individual nation is exposed to an immediate effect if it engages in a program of expenditure uncorrelated to similar programs of other nations, a synchronized international action will to a large extent remove the unfavorable effect upon the exchanges.

In the development of such an expenditure program, the United States Government believes that the basic thought should be to do whatever is necessary in the different countries to set going the machinery of trade and through the reestablishment of trade to restimulate the natural sources of employment. In the interim, it will be a part of the program for each government to take such action as is necessary to provide subsistence relief.

[*Notation*:A] Warburg's initials on this—last page—[1]

JPW:LEW
EA:HF[2]

[OF 17:T]

[1] This notation appears at the top of the first page of the original.

[2] James P. Warburg, financial adviser to the American delegation to the London Economic Conference; Herbert Feis, economic adviser to the State Department.

# Roosevelt to Representative Theodore Christianson of Minnesota

[Washington] April 4, 1933

*Private*

My dear Governor: I have not had a chance before this to thank you for your note of March 15th. I wish very much you would let me have any information in your possession regarding arms factories in Japan owned by American manufacturers.[1]

Very sincerely yours,

[PPF 238:CT]

[1] Christianson had written (PPF 238) that he had learned that American manufacturers of munitions had factories in Japan. An embargo on the sale of arms to belligerents would therefore be ineffective unless shipment of raw materials was also barred. Replying to Roosevelt's letter on April 12 (PPF 238), Christianson said he had been unable to find out who had told him about the American-owned factories.

## Roosevelt to Representative John E. Miller of Arkansas

[Washington] April 4, 1933

Dear Mr. Miller: Thank you for your letter of March 27th.[1] The chief problem involved in your suggestion is that it would probably greatly increase the cost of manufacture of nearly all of our steel products—at least, so I am informed.

Very sincerely yours,

[OF 342:CT]

[1] Miller called attention (OF 342) to the unemployment in the manganese industry and urged application of the recently enacted "Buy American" statute to all purchases of steel by the federal government (*Statutes at Large of the United States of America*, Washington, 1933, XLVII, 604–605; hereafter cited as 47 *Stat.*).

## Roosevelt to George McAneny, President, National Civil Service Reform League, New York

[Washington] April 4, 1933

Dear Mr. McAneny: Thank you for your letter of March 29th with its memorandum.[1] Some day I hope to have a chance to talk over the Foreign Service with you. May I suggest that as one who helped in getting the "career service" established, I am anxious that it be maintained—nevertheless, the situation is not so delightfully simple, so far as merit and good government are concerned, as the memorandum suggests!

Very sincerely yours,

[OF 67:CT]

[1] McAneny enclosed a list of Foreign Service career officers and on behalf of the National Civil Service Reform League urged that they be retained (OF 67). Roosevelt had been a member of the League and its predecessors since 1908 (Group 14).

## Press Conference, Executive Offices of the White House, April 5, 1933, 10:40 A.M.

[*Excerpt*] Q: Reports from London say that Mr. MacDonald has booked passage for arrival here on the 15th.

The President: Steve Early has a statement on that for you. It will be ready for you as soon as you get out of here.[1] I can only tell you, off the record, we have not heard a thing.

Q: One report said that he was waiting for some invitation.

The President: We haven't a thing. Steve will give you the story on it.

Q: Mr. President, in connection with Ramsay MacDonald's visit, the London papers this morning say that Norman Davis has submitted an informal debt funding agreement proposal which will—

The President: Off the record, that is crazy. He is not over there on debts at all. That is off the record.[2]

Q: Does Steve's statement cover the possibility of our extending an invitation to MacDonald to come over?

The President: I think it covers the whole thing.

Q: Does it include a conference?

The President: You will have to wait and see . . .

Q: This London report also says something about extending invitations to other governments to send over experts to cover preliminary meetings before the Economic Conference. Is that covered in the statement?

The President: No, that is not covered in the statement. That is a newspaper story which is based on just about 20 per cent of fact. The facts are, of course, that we are at the present time carrying on economic conversations right here and that is all there is to it. We are continuing those economic conversations with respect to various governments. There are no formal conferences. When we get to some particular point, we ask the Ambassador from Germany to drop around or the French financial adviser to drop around to the State Department. It is being handled in a very informal and thoroughly practical way.

Q: Is that why you talked to the French Ambassador?

The President: He merely came in to say "good-bye."

Q: Can you say anything on the nature of the trade agreement legislation which the State Department apparently has under consideration?

The President: I was talking with the Secretary of State about that last night and I think you can use this as background, that we have not got to anything further than a preliminary discussion of what may be necessary to ask Congress for before they adjourn. We have not got anything down on paper at all. But, as I said in the message to Congress three days ago, I am going to ask them for something that will enable us to at least try to break down some of the tariff barriers.

Q: Will that follow the Argos (?)[3] plan?

The President: What was that?

Q: The Argos (?) plan proposition of the Donnelly tariff of 1897.

The President: I don't know. I never heard of it. I am too young. (Laughter)

Q: Mr. President, in that connection do you intend to ask Congress also for any authority in connection with the negotiation of war debts?

The President: I have not discussed that at all.

[President's Press Conferences:T]

[1] Printed below.

[2] See Davis' dispatches to Hull dated April 2, April 3 (two), and April 4, 1933, in *Foreign Relations, 1933,* I, 479–485, on a proposal to move the Economic Conference to Washington, thus making the United States more amenable on debts; bringing China and Japan in on the discussions; and on the relation of MacDonald's visit to the debt question.

[3] The question marks, here and below, are in the original.

# Statement by Roosevelt on Prime Minister MacDonald's Visit

[Washington] April 5, 1933

In the course of informal exchanges of views between the British and ourselves regarding the general economic situation and the problem of disarmament the President has felt that a visit to Washington by the Prime Minister would be helpful.

The President ever since his first conversation with the British Ambassador at Warm Springs has emphasized his hope that the Prime Minister could come over.[1]

[White House Press Releases:M]

[1] This statement, which was rewritten by Roosevelt, originally read as follows: "In the course of informal exchanges of views between the British and ourselves regarding the general economic situation, it developed that a visit to Washington by the Prime Minister would facilitate the preparations of the forthcoming world economic conference. This idea appealed to both Governments and the President has expressed to the Prime Minister the pleasure with which he is looking forward to the meeting" (PPF 1-F). Roosevelt's letter of invitation to MacDonald of April 6, 1933, is printed in *Public Papers,* II, 116.

## Roosevelt to Senator Clarence C. Dill of Washington

[Washington] April 7, 1933

*Private and Confidential*

Dear Clarence: Since your note of March 24th came I have been working hard on the silver situation.[1] I wish much that you could have a talk with Moley and Warburg and they can tell you verbally about the progress we are making. I think they are on the right track.

Always sincerely,

[PPF 243:CT]

[1] Dill urged (PPF 243) legislation to support the price of silver to give the American representatives in the economic conference a weapon "to use with England and France in insisting that they shall not hereafter dump silver below a certain minimum price."

## Press Conference, Executive Offices of the White House, April 7, 1933, 4 P.M.

[*Excerpt*] Q: Can you tell us what your plans are for these conversations you are going to have with Ramsay MacDonald and the other European statesmen?

The President: Not yet.

Q: After you have had a series of conferences with the different Ambassadors—

The President: As a matter of fact, so far as I am concerned, they will be very informal, so much so that it will be very difficult to write about them.

Q: Oh! (Laughter) We will have to write a lot then. (Laughter)

Q: Are you going to sit around a table and discuss it with all of them?

The President: No.

Q: Just individually?

The President: Yes.

Q: Does that include Canadian negotiations?

The President: I would not put it that way. Don't say those "negotiations." Now, this stuff is off the record. I think I had best give you some idea of the way it is being handled. As we are going along, the State Department is discussing various phases, let us say with England, then they will discuss it among themselves and then possibly some others will discuss it with France. Thus, there won't be any gathering or anything that you can call "those negotiations." There won't be any general conference. It will be selective in its treatment—I think that is the correct word.

Q: Has any consideration been given to financing public works by a popular construction bond issue?

The President: No, we have not got to that yet.

Q: You have got your bill ready for reciprocal tariff, have you not?

The President: No.

Q: There is a story in that connection this afternoon in the *Times* that a 10 per cent cut is on your program.[1]

The President: I heard of it.

Q: There is some discussion that you have some sort of proposition by which Cuba can send in 10% of the amount of sugar at a reduced rate and the other 90% will be at the present rate. Wouldn't that be a good way to solve that problem?

The President: I suppose there have been an average of fifteen plans sent in a day. That would come under the category of one of the different plans. We have not got down to a discussion of the different plans.

Q: Is Russia to be received in the economic discussions?

The President: (The President gave a negative response by shaking his head.)

[President's Press Conferences:T]

[1] A Washington dispatch, "Roosevelt Drafts Tariff Proposals," was published in the New York *Times* of April 7 but contained no mention of a "ten per cent cut."

## Norman H. Davis, Chairman, American Delegation, Disarmament Conference, to Roosevelt

[London] April 7, 1933

*Confidential*

Dear Mr. President: I think that I have covered very fully in my dispatches to the Secretary of State the substance of my conversations with Mr. MacDonald and some of his colleagues relative to his proposed visit to the United States.[1] Since it has now been decided that the Prime Minister is to go it is perhaps well for me to give you certain "high spots" which may be of some assistance in the conversations which you are to have.

In our first talk after my arrival in London I discovered that the Cabinet had been quite opposed to his making the visit and that while the opposition was diminishing it still existed. The chief opposition was from the Tories, who being in the majority were afraid that the visit, if a success, would increase MacDonald's prestige, and if a failure would weaken that of the Government. Chamberlain was the principal obstruction because he wanted to go himself and also because he was determined to try to force a debt settlement prior to the Conference or at least to get an assurance that we would not ask for any payments during the Conference negotiations and would carry on debt negotiations concurrently with those of the Conference.

They contended that it would be most dangerous for MacDonald to go to Washington to negotiate an agreement without some previous assurance that there was a basis for agreement. I told them that if he should go solely for the avowed purpose of a general exchange of views with you, and not to negotiate specific agreements himself, it would seem that their preoccupation should disappear. This seemed to satisfy them somewhat but they then raised the question that it would be risky for MacDonald to go unless there were at least some assurance as to a postponement of the June 15th payment, intimating that it would make their position more embarrassing if they were afterwards called upon to pay. In other words they seemed to think that if they should decide to default they could do so with better grace if he had stayed at home. I explained to them that I was satisfied you would not give any such assurance and that I would not be willing to even put such a suggestion up to you, which I thought was unreasonable, with which MacDonald agreed. As they pressed for this it became more necessary for me to fall over backwards because, as I told them, in view of the position they had taken, anything that was said that could be construed as holding out any hope whatever that the Prime Minister's visit might result in a postponement of the June 15th payment, might lead to a misunderstanding and that in my judgment they should merely decide whether or not an exchange of views between you and the Prime Minister on other matters, which were of more vital importance to the two countries, would not justify the trip.

I succeeded in convincing MacDonald, and I think all of them, except perhaps Chamberlain, that recovery from the depression must be put in the foreground and debts more or less in the background. While I personally think that it would be advisable for you to get authority, if possible, to prevent any serious situation arising with regard to the June

15th payments, because it would put us in a better trading position later on if we do not get in a jam at that time, I have not told them so and I have not said or done anything which could be construed as any commitment whatever.

In one of my talks with MacDonald, at which Simon was present, he was laying much stress upon the importance of getting beyond the June 15th payment without raising serious political difficulties. He said, in fact, that the problem was most serious because, in the present state of mind in both countries, it was as much of a political difficulty for them to get the approval of Parliament to pay as it was for you to get the approval of Congress to postpone payment, but that it was of the utmost importance to find some way to get beyond this without a real crisis. He then inquired what I thought could be done about it. I told him that it seemed to me that it ought to ease the situation in both countries if we would concentrate our efforts in pulling out of this depression; that if this were done it might possibly somewhat change the attitude of Congress and also the attitude of Parliament; that so far as the British debt was concerned I personally had always felt that after we had made a better settlement with the French than we did with the British it would have been fair and logical to put the British debt on the same basis and that it might have been done had it not been for the Balfour note which had been a deterring factor.[2] He then told me that when he was at Rapidan in 1929 Hoover told him he thought the British loan ought to be put upon the same basis as the French and indicated that it would be done but that nothing was ever done about it. Simon then spoke up and said that it would not solve the problem even if that were now done because it would not relieve the situation on June 15th with regard to the French. He thus indicated it might put them in an embarrassing position as regards the French if we were to do this. I then said that while I had thought at one time that a readjustment of the British debt on that basis might be one thing which Congress would be inclined to do I had no idea what its attitude would be, especially now, and furthermore that what I had said was a purely personal and unofficial view and not intended in any way as even a tentative proposal. I also said that in fact I had no idea how you would feel about even considering such an approach to the problem and could not speak for you. I mention this to you because subsequently, in the last talk which I had with MacDonald, at his request, and at which Baldwin, Chamberlain, Runciman and Simon[3] were present, he raised this question in such a way as to try to infer that I had advanced it as a proposal. I then made it very clear that I had done nothing of the kind. Nevertheless, my reaction was that such an arrangement would appeal to all of them except Simon and to a lesser extent MacDonald who would be rather embarrassed because of the United Front Agreement.

I may say, however, that I am more than ever convinced that it would be good strategy, if you think it advisable to ask for authority from Congress, for us, of our own volition, to announce that as a matter of fair play, we were going to stop this discrimination and put the British debt on the same basis as the French, making the adjustment retroactive. I am satisfied this would have such a good effect in England that it would greatly weaken the sentiment in favor of defaulting and would disrupt the united front. It would, in fact, put the British Government on the defensive. While it would not take care of the French and other payments maturing on June 15th, in case you should not get authority to deal with those as you see fit, it would relieve the tension with regard to the British payment, which is much more than all the others put together. If the British debt were readjusted as indicated it would give them a credit of something like $900,000,000. My idea would be to apply most of this to reducing the capital indebtedness and merely to set enough aside to cover say the next two installments.

Another thing which you may bear in mind is the possibility that MacDonald may not last much longer unless he can do something in the near future to strengthen his hand. I am sorry because I am extremely fond of him. He has much imagination and ability and back of his ministerial exterior he has a subtle capacity for trading.

I am inclined to think that it was not necessary for him to act in such a hurry in submitting the British Proposal recently in Geneva[4] and that his visit to Rome was mainly with a view of strengthening his hand. If something comes of the proposal and of the proposed Four Power Pact it will help him. If not, it will do the opposite. I am satisfied it would have been better for them to have waited for us and to have put in a joint proposal which would have had a much greater chance of success.

There are many excellent features in their disarmament proposal, most of which in fact are not new. They have not laid enough stress on the strengthening of the defensive position of nations and the weakening of their powers of offense and I think it a mistake to propose a five year instead of a ten year treaty. As soon as I have had some further talks with the French and get a better line on the German situation I may make some suggestions for your consideration. I am inclined to think that the time may come within the next few weeks when you could give

47

the necessary push to get through a real disarmament agreement which, of course, would do more to insure the success of the Economic Conference and restore confidence and good will than almost anything else.

I hope also within a few days to give you my considered views about the so-called Four Power Pact. Just now it looks as if it would not be born—certainly not without considerable change.

To return to the debt question, England and France can think of nothing but debts. Many of their papers have in every way tried to give the impression that I have been discussing debt settlements although I have scrupulously refrained from doing so and have insisted that any negotiations about debts must be carried on in Washington. This has been done, I am sure, to keep the debt question before the public and to embarrass us. Nearly every move they make has some relation to debts. The British and French Treasuries are acting very closely together, in fact much more so than the political sides of the two Governments. I have a very strong suspicion, based upon considerable circumstantial evidence, that the British Treasury has encouraged the French in their continued failure to make the December 15th payment.

Strange as it may seem, one of the chief causes of the failure to make the payment now is due to the fact that Herriot, who is the leader of the majority political party, has stated that he would not assume the leadership of the Government again as long as it is in default on these payments. Many of his political enemies, and in fact some within his own party now, who wish to hold office and who by conviction are not opposed to paying, are refraining from giving their approval just in order to keep Herriot out of power.

It may interest you to know that you have caught the imagination of Europe to a remarkable extent. It makes me proud as an American to have a President with so much prestige and to feel that this may enable you to exercise an effective influence in coping with the critical world situation. The excessive amount of publicity which I am at present getting—much to my dislike— is largely due to the fact that I am looked upon as your direct representative.

I am sorry to burden you with such a long letter but hope it may be of some use.

With warmest personal regards and best wishes to Mrs. Roosevelt and yourself, in which Mrs. Davis joins me, I am,

Faithfully yours,

Norman H. Davis

[PSF:Great Britain:TS]

[1] See Davis to Hull, March 30, 1933, and the dispatches following, in *Foreign Relations, 1933*, I, 474–476.

[2] The Balfour note of Aug. 1, 1922, to representatives of the Allied powers, in which Great Britain offered to give up all claims to German reparations and to debts owed her by the Allies, provided this formed part of a general debt settlement (*Foreign Relations, 1922*, I, 406–409).

[3] Stanley Baldwin, Neville Chamberlain, Walter Runciman, John Simon.

[4] The MacDonald proposal of March 16, 1933 (*Foreign Relations, 1933*, I, 43–54).

## Louis M. Howe, Personal Secretary to the President, to William Phillips, Under Secretary of State

[Washington] April 7th, 1933

My dear Mr. Secretary: I have issued strict instructions to Mr. Forster[1] and everyone else who in any possible way may be in a position to receive messages from your department—that in no case should an envelope addressed to me and marked confidential or personal, be taken from your messenger, but that they should be taken into my room and handed either to myself or to Miss Durand[2] for whose responsibility I vouch.

I will, of course, then be responsible, and I will see that the messages go directly to the President and the President will see that they are returned directly to me. Through this arrangement I hope we will prevent any unfortunate leaks.

I would like to request that if this arrangement is satisfactory to you that such unparaphrased cables be sent over addressed to me marked personal or confidential, for if I am going to be held responsible I have to be sure that they do not fall into other hands en route, and if they are addressed to the President, they are very apt to be handed to one of several people to be delivered to the President at their leisure.

Of course, if the President is at the White House, send the messages to him there and not to the Executive Offices, addressing them directly to him, and this will insure against their going into other hands.

Very truly yours,

[OF 20:CT]

[1] Rudolph Forster entered the White House Executive Office as a stenographer in 1897. From 1903 until his death in 1943 he was director of the Executive Office staff, and as such was responsible for the orderly routing of documents and letters.

[2] Margaret Durand, Howe's secretary.

## William Phillips, Under Secretary of State, to Roosevelt

Washington, April 8, 1933

My dear Mr. President: If you are ready to make the changes in the Diplomatic Service which I had the pleasure of discussing with you some days ago, I should be very grateful if you would so indicate on the accompanying memorandum.[1] Perhaps you could do this by writing the word "approved" after each country or indicate such other wishes as you desire.

May I also send you the accompanying personal telegram, which I have received from Hugh Gibson in Brussels?[2] In the circumstances, I wonder whether you would care to consider him for Turkey instead of Brazil.

Inasmuch as Mr. Curley is slated for Poland[3] I suggest that we send Caffery, whom we discussed for that post, to Brazil in the event that Gibson goes to Turkey. Caffery[4] is one of the best men in the Service in the ministerial rank and might appropriately be promoted to Brazil. Such a promotion will be well received throughout the entire Service.

I told Francis White[5] that you were glad to offer him Czechoslovakia, which we regarded as one of the most important legations in Europe. He is still considering it, but is somewhat fearful for his children on account of climatic conditions and the apparent impossibility of living in the Legation, which is in an almost impossible condition. If White persists in this viewpoint, would you care to offer him Hungary?

We did not settle the other day on a place for John V. A. MacMurray,[6] although I understood you to say that you would like to restore him to the service. He might be willing to take Riga, which is important in view of its Russian affiliations.

There is only one other person, I believe, about whom you asked me to speak to you and that is John Nicholas Brown.[7] According to my recollection, we did not discuss him at our meeting the other day and I do not, therefore, know whether you desire to find a place for him.

Please do not hesitate to let me know if there is anything further I can do to help you in this connection.

Faithfully yours,

William Phillips

[OF 20:TS]

[1] The memorandum is present; it is a list of countries and suggested appointments. There is but one notation. Under Brazil the President wrote: "Weddell—of Va   Pollard's man?"

[2] April 5, 1933, requesting transfer to Istanbul in the event he was moved from Brussels; however, his appointment to Brazil became effective May 11, 1933 (OF 20).

[3] Mayor James M. Curley of Boston had hoped to be named ambassador to Italy but Under Secretary of State Phillips, another Bostonian, opposed this and with Moley's and James A. Farley's aid so arranged matters that Poland was offered to Curley and Italy went to Breckinridge Long (Moley, *After Seven Years,* pp. 132–133). Roosevelt's letter of April 11, 1933, to Curley, offering him the Polish post is printed in Curley's *I'd Do It Again* (Englewood Cliffs: Prentice Hall, 1957), p. 251. Asked about the Curley appointment at his April 14 press conference, Roosevelt said that Curley felt it his duty to remain as mayor of Boston during the emergency: "There was much regret. We will have to withdraw his name."

[4] Jefferson Caffery was appointed Assistant Secretary of State on July 11, 1933.

[5] Appointed minister to Czechoslovakia, June 13, 1933.

[6] MacMurray had resigned from the State Department in 1929; he was named minister to Estonia, Latvia, and Lithuania in 1933.

[7] Brown, a Providence real estate man, received no appointment.


# Roosevelt to Governor I. C. Blackwood, Columbia, South Carolina

[Washington] April 12, 1933

*Personal & Confidential*

My dear Governor Blackwood: I am glad that you wrote me an expression of your deep concern over the alleged outrages against Jews living in Germany.[1]

For your own personal information I want you to know that this matter has been very seriously considered for some time and I think that very appropriate action has been taken.

Confidentially, I instructed the State Department recently to carefully observe the situation in Germany and to take every step that one Government can take in a situation where another Government is dealing with a domestic problem of its own.

Very sincerely yours,

[PPF 256:CT]

[1] Blackwood wrote (March 31, 1933, PPF 256) that he was writing at the instance of Jewish friends in South Carolina but was not attempting to suggest what Roosevelt should do.

## Press Conference, Executive Offices of the White House, April 12, 1933, 10:30 A.M.

[*Excerpt*] Q: Is Ramsay MacDonald going to stay at the White House?[1]

The President: You can say and use this as background, that I hate to fish or cut bait on where the distinguished visitors are going to live. Of course, with a great many of them coming in, it is obviously impossible to have them all at the White House. There may be three or four of them here at the same time and the White House is not sufficiently elastic. In view of that, I adopted what might be called a rule of thumb and that is that the Prime Ministers would stay at the White House but that Members of Cabinets, very much to my regret, would have to stay at their own embassies.

Q: Are you likely to see Herriot and MacDonald together, or will there be separate conversations?

The President: Do you know the date that Herriot leaves?

Q: He leaves next Monday and ought to be here by Friday. Mr. MacDonald will still be here at that time?

The President: Very likely, if he gets here before MacDonald leaves, we will all sit around the table.

Q: How is your French? They don't talk much English.

The President: Between us, we can make a go. It always reminds me of the time back in 1913, which the older people will remember, when Doctor Miller of Brazil, their foreign minister,[2] came up here to return Secretary Root's[3] call. I took Secretary Root and others down with me and Doctor Miller got on board at Hampton Roads and he spoke German, French, Italian, Spanish and Portuguese, and not a word of English. None of the others spoke a word of anything except English and I had to do the translating. I lost ten pounds in one evening.

[President's Press Conferences:T]

[1] MacDonald arrived in New York on April 21 and went at once to Washington where he was the guest of the Roosevelts at the White House.
[2] Lauro S. Müller.
[3] Elihu Root, Secretary of State, 1905–1909.

## Cordell Hull, Secretary of State, to Roosevelt

Washington, April 12, 1933

My dear Mr. President: On numerous occasions during the past few years the Rumanian Government has urged that the United States recognize Rumanian sovereignty over Bessarabia. This territory, which was formerly a part of the Russian Empire, proclaimed its independence on December 2, 1917, and on November 26, 1918, its Supreme Council decided to unite with Rumania.

The union of Bessarabia with Rumania was recognized by the Principal Allied Powers in a treaty signed at Paris on October 28, 1920. This treaty has been ratified by all of the signatory Powers except Japan and it appears that no Power, except the United States and Soviet Russia, now questions Rumanian sovereignty over the territory. In reply to requests from certain of the Allied Powers as to the American attitude toward the question of Bessarabia, Mr. Colby[1] stated in 1920 that the United States was of the opinion that all decisions of vital importance to Russia, and especially those concerning its sovereignty over the territory of the former Russian Empire, should be held in abeyance. Consequently this Government declined to be drawn into any discussion as to the Rumanian claim to Bessarabia. This attitude has been maintained up to the present time despite the fact that Rumania has continued to exercise sovereignty over the territory uninterruptedly and despite the fact that we have recognized the detachment from Russia of other territories such as the Baltic States.

The manner in which the American Government has manifested its unwillingness to recognize the de facto situation has been by the establishment of a separate immigration quota for the Bessarabian territory. However, this Government has acquiesced in the situation to a certain extent by including Bessarabia in the jurisdiction of our consular representatives at Bucharest, by granting visas to natives of Bessarabia bearing Rumanian passports, and by other acts.

After a careful examination of the facts I have come to the conclusion that there is no longer any reason why we should continue to adhere to the doctrine enunciated by Mr. Colby in 1920. On the contrary, I feel that we should now recognize the de facto situation. This can be accomplished in the following way by a simple administrative act. A proclamation must in any case be issued in the near future to effect certain administrative changes in the immigration quotas for the year beginning July 1, 1933. It would be my idea to omit any reference to

Bessarabia in this proclamation. The elimination of the Bessarabian quota and the inclusion of the territory within the Rumanian quota area would have the effect of according American recognition to Rumanian sovereignty over Bessarabia and would set at rest the contention of Rumania that the existence of the Bessarabian quota constitutes a "public discrimination" against that country.

If you approve of this proposal I shall make the necessary arrangements to have it put into effect.

Faithfully yours,

Cordell Hull

[*Notation*:AS] Approved—It is sensible—Franklin D. Roosevelt April 15—1933

[OF 428:TS]

---

[1] Bainbridge Colby, Secretary of State under Wilson.

## Roosevelt to Arthur Murray, London

[Washington] April 14, 1933

My dear Arthur: I have been so rushed since your letter came that I have not had an opportunity to do more than act on your suggestion.[1] However, as you know by this time, the delicate suggestions did not bear fruit, though I am very certain that you were right—and I am very grateful to you for writing me as you did.

I am, of course, delighted that the P.M. is coming—I am very certain that the very fact of the trip will greatly help with public opinion—both here and in England. Both of us believe in realistic action on broader lines than the isolationists concede. Things seem to be complicated a bit by the development in Germany but I still believe that in every country the people themselves are more peaceably and liberally inclined than their governments.

As you will have read, events are moving swiftly here and there is a splendid uplift of morale. It is putting many of our 12,000,000 of our unemployed to work but the big question is whether it will put enough of them to work.

Do write me whenever you have any news.

Always sincerely,

P.S. I shall be delighted to have that book about our common ancestor. As T.R. used to remark—"He was probably very common." I take that back—no outlaw could be so described. F.D.R.

[PPF 435:CT]

[1] Feb. 13, 1933 (PSF:M), suggesting that Walter Runciman, president of the British Board of Trade and a close friend of Murray, be invited to come to the United States as one of MacDonald's advisers. Murray, Viscount Elibank, a Scottish Liberal M.P., had known the Roosevelts since 1917, when he was assistant military attaché at the British Embassy in Washington, and they had continued their acquaintance since then. See Elibank, "Franklin Roosevelt: Friend of Britain," in *The Contemporary Review* (June 1955), pp. 362–368.

# Press Conference, Executive Offices of the White House, April 14, 1933, 4 P.M.

[*Excerpt*] Q: Mr. President, can you tell us anything of the conversation with Colonel Cooper?[1]

The President: I can tell you entirely off the record. He talked about the possibility of selling things to Russia. But that has to be off the record.

Q: What is the possibility?

The President: We talked about the need in Russia for all kinds of machinery and materials of various kinds.

Q: Colonel Cooper—that was Colonel Hugh Cooper?

The President: Yes.

Q: That is all off the record?

The President: Yes, that has to be off the record.

Q: On that same subject, did he urge recognition?

The President: No, we did not talk about that. We only talked about the need of Russia for these various materials.

Q: Can you sell them without recognition?

The President: We have been selling some without recognition.

[President's Press Conferences:T]

[1] On the day before (PPF 1-0). Hugh L. Cooper was a distinguished hydraulic engineer who had been in charge of the construction of the Dnieper Dam in Russia and Dam Number Two at Muscle Shoals. Senator George W. Norris had recommended that Roosevelt consult him on the question of Soviet recognition (Norris to McIntyre, March 31; McIntyre to Cooper, April 6, 1933, OF 220-A).

## Pierrepont Moffat, Chief, Division of Western European Affairs, to William Phillips, Under Secretary of State

[Washington] April 19, 1933

Mr. Phillips: At your suggestion I went up this morning to call on Mr. Stimson and discussed with him in considerable detail telegrams Nos. 163 and 164 from Norman Davis.[1]

Mr. Stimson was immensely interested and considered that the Davis suggestions were a logical development of this Government's policy of the past few years.

(1) He has from the beginning considered the General Disarmament Conference as in essence a European peace conference. Before it started he warned the European leaders that they should, as a preliminary step, settle the outstanding European questions. As this was not done, he has been foreseeing a breakdown in the conference in some form or other. It has taken a crisis to convince Europe of the necessity of putting its own house in order. Germany, by threatening to bolt the conference and to repudiate the Treaty of Versailles, has precipitated an issue which sooner or later would have had to be faced.

(2) It is obvious that the United States could not enter into the discussion of how Europe should set its house in order. Political and territorial changes or the evolution of a strong peace machinery involve political considerations from which we must disassociate ourselves. The best we can do is to give Europe a sympathetic and helpful understanding.

(3) On the other hand, if Europe will make this effort, if Europe will set its house in order and build up a machinery of security, we must not be the country to block it. The broadest conception of our policy is that at small risk we should encourage peace in Europe and view it as a big national insurance.

(4) Two of our wars have been fought on the issue of the *maintenance of our neutral rights.*[2] If (under given circumstances) we can avoid similar dangers in the future, we stand to be the gainer. This point of view is susceptible of further development.

Mr. Stimson, therefore, thoroughly agrees with the purpose of the Davis suggestion. He queries, however, whether there are not sufficient elements in it which would arouse political opposition to endanger the success of the treaty. In other words, is it necessary to tie up in contractual form the Davis suggestions?

Mr. Stimson therefore wonders whether we could not obtain the desired results by making our contribution in the form of a declaration of the President. This would to a large degree meet the preoccupation of Europe and yet would not be used as a political football in the Senate with possible adverse repercussions on any treaty which might be signed. It would also make certain beyond peradventure of doubt that we retained the final right of independent decision. He had tried to persuade President Hoover to issue such a declaration but the latter had been unwilling.

As far as a consultative pact is concerned, he suggested that we look up two telegrams sent from Senator Swanson in Geneva last March to Senator Robinson suggesting that Congress take the initiative and authorize the President to consult with other nations under certain circumstances.[3]

P.M.

[PSF:Disarmament Conference:TS]

[1] Both dated April 16, 1933 (*Foreign Relations, 1933,* I, 89–92, 93–97), in which Davis proposed a "consultative pact" to provide for consultation by the United States with other states in the event of aggression by one European state against another.

[2] Underscored in the original, apparently by Roosevelt.

[3] Claude A. Swanson, a senator from Virginia, was appointed Secretary of the Navy on March 4, 1933. He had been a delegate to the Geneva Disarmament Conference. Moffat says Hull was unwilling to go beyond the vague provisions for consultation as set forth in the Democratic party platform (Nancy Harvison Hooker, ed., *The Moffat Papers: Selections from the Diplomatic Journals of Jay Pierrepont Moffat, 1919–1943,* Cambridge, Mass.: Harvard, 1956, p. 93).

## [*Enclosure*]

Questions from Mr. Davis's telegrams to which he requests answers:

1. Assuming a general disarmament treaty which represents a substantial achievement, are we prepared in connection therewith to agree to consult in case of a threat to the peace?

2. Assuming that in connection with such a disarmament treaty the Continental European powers agree among themselves upon special measures for maintaining or guaranteeing peace in Continental Europe and for determining and taking collective action against a continental state responsible for a breach of peace (or of the Briand-Kellogg Pact) are we prepared to agree to refrain from any action, and to withhold protection from our citizens if engaged in action, which would tend to defeat the collective action which the European states may have decided

upon; such action on our part to be predicated upon our independent decision that the state in question has in fact been responsible for the breach of the peace?

3. Is it our policy to press for a regional treatment of disarmament along the lines suggested by Mr. Davis, with provisions for active disarmament limited in large measure to Europe and leaving the United States and Japan unbound?

4. Should Mr. Davis attempt to bring about an adjournment of the Disarmament Conference after it meets on April 25 for a period of three or four weeks, in an endeavor to work out a political appeasement in Europe, leaving the technical commissions to continue their work and thus avoid an adjournment of the conference?

5. If the President agrees with Mr. Davis's recommendations, should our policy be announced at the appropriate time by the President in Washington or should it be held back and used as a bargaining point during the actual negotiations at Geneva?

[PSF:Disarmament Conference:T]

## Roosevelt to Cordell Hull, Secretary of State

Washington, April 20, 1933

Memorandum for the Secretary of State: What would you think of our asking Newton Baker to go as Ambassador to Germany?

FDR

[*Notation:*AS] Fine—but on account of War, might be best unofficially first to sound out German Government.[1] Hull

[OF 198-B:TS]

[1] Baker had been Wilson's Secretary of War.

## Roosevelt to William Gorham Rice, New York State Civil Service Commission, Albany

[Washington] April 20, 1933

Dear Colonel Rice: I would have written you before this in regard to Holland but for the fact that I have been trying to smooth out a somewhat difficult situation, which I want you to know of with perfect frankness. I do not need to tell you that I have wanted you to go as Minister to the Hague, but it has developed that there is another friend of mine who is most anxious to go and who, I must tell you quite candidly, has at least an equal claim.

May I, therefore, ask you to serve as Minister to the Netherlands with the understanding that you would come home after a year? I need not tell you that I should be very happy to have you and Mrs. Rice represent the United States at the Hague, and I know from many sources how very acceptable your appointment would be to our Dutch friends.[1]

With my warm regards to you both, Very sincerely yours,

[PPF 288:CT]

---

[1] Rice, an old friend of Roosevelt, replied April 23 (PPF 288), that he could not accept the appointment under the conditions stated. (He was seventy-seven years old at this time.) Grenville T. Emmet, Roosevelt's former law partner, was appointed minister to The Netherlands on Jan. 15, 1934. See Roosevelt to Rice, June 16, 1933, below.

## Press Conference, Executive Offices of the White House, April 21, 1933, 4:08 P.M.

[*Excerpt*] The President: I have been talking to Steve about the handling of the news during the course of the next four or five days. This is just between ourselves and in the family. I think probably the easiest way to do it and the best thing all around is to handle the foreign end of it—any foreign news—with either statements by Mr. MacDonald, or Mr. Herriot, or Mr. Bennett[1] or by formal statements from Secretary Hull or me. In other words, that we should not have a round-table discussion about foreign matters when the heads of foreign governments are here. I think it is better all around to keep it more or less formal. Of course, that does not mean that we cannot speak about domestic questions in the same family way we have been doing it before. I think that is the best thing.

Q: Will you get right down to business tonight with Mr. MacDonald?
The President: It depends on what you call business.
Q: Just what is your program?
The President: Just going to have a nice, family party this evening.
Q: Who is going to be there?
The President: Two Roosevelts and two MacDonalds[2] and that's all.

Q: Could you tell us what you intend to take up with Mr. MacDonald?

The President: Well, ships and kings and sealing wax and things like that.

Q: You can't get down on page one with that. (Laughter) . . .

Q: To go back to MacDonald's visit again, is there any likelihood of a formal statement being issued tonight, that you know of?

The President: Not by me.

Q: Is there any possibility that you might give Mr. Early something for us after your first talk with the Prime Minister?

The President: It will be along the lines that we are sitting around the fire and chatting; that is about all.

Q: Do you not believe that our action regarding gold makes the monetary situation the most important topic that you will have in your conversation?[3]

The President: No; there are a great many important topics. I don't know of any particular one. We are going to settle as many as we can simultaneously.

Q: Have you any more ten-yard plays in mind right away?[4]

The President: There is one up in Congress at the present moment.

Q: What is that?

The President: The Thomas Amendment, which I regard as very, very essential.[5]

Q: It is being discussed in the newspapers as a move to act as a lever—

The President: I can tell you, off the record, on that—I will have to tell you off the record because I simply had no thought of it at all. As a matter of fact, and again off the record, the problem we faced last week—this is what I think I told you Wednesday morning—the problem last week was one of going ahead and protecting the value of the dollar. Mind you, this is off the record. Protecting the value of the dollar was one of the proposals, and it meant experimenting with it to the tune of 100 or maybe 200 million dollars, a pretty costly experiment. It might have worked and, if it did not work, we might be right in the middle of these conversations. It seemed a great deal better not to risk losing that money but, rather, to take the bull by the horns. It had nothing to do, of course, with the fact that we had delegates coming from different nations all over the world.

[President's Press Conferences:T]

[1] Richard B. Bennett, Prime Minister of Canada.

[2] MacDonald was accompanied by his daughter Ishbel.

[3] The embargoing (with certain exceptions) of the export of gold coin, gold bullion, or gold certificates, announced by Roosevelt at his April 19 press conference and proclaimed officially the next day (*Public Papers*, II, 137–141, 141–143).

[4] At the April 19 press conference Roosevelt compared his problem in the monetary crisis with that of a football quarterback: each play determined the nature of the next one.

[5] This was an amendment to the Agricultural Adjustment Act of 1933 (H.R. 3835). Introduced by Senator J. W. Elmer Thomas (Okla.) on April 20, 1933, it authorized credit expansion through the Federal Reserve System by issuance of United States notes, reduction of the gold content of the dollar up to 50 per cent, and acceptance of silver in payment of foreign debts (*Cong. Rec.*, vol. 77, pp. 2004–2005). The amendment became law May 12, 1933 (48 *Stat.* 31).

# Press Conference Held by Prime Minister MacDonald in the President's Office, April 21, 1933, 6:35 P.M.

The Prime Minister: How do you do? I think some of us have met before, have we not?

Mr. Durno:[1] Yes. There is quite a large crowd, Mr. Prime Minister; they will all be in in just a second.

The Prime Minister: Yes. Well, I am very glad indeed to see you again. Will we come to an agreement with each other? Please do not quote me verbatim because I make it a rule that when that takes place I must always see the copy before it is printed and that is much too great a bother to you and, besides, I am not going to say anything that is worth quoting.[2] (Laughter)

Well, you understand that I have only just set foot again in America this forenoon and it would quite obviously be most improper for me to make any statements whilst I am still full of innocence. I must know a little more before I venture to make statements. And I am sure that you understand quite seriously that the importance of my meeting your President now is so very great—not merely for your country and for mine, but for the whole world—that any one occupying my position must be very, very careful that a loose word or an ill-considered sentence is not going to make misunderstanding and difficulty for the final success of our meeting. My experience with the American journalists has always been that they are faithful copywriters when you are perfectly honest and straight with them. Sometimes, in other quarters, I have heard how difficult the American journalist is. I always say I have never experienced that. Someone else might have but that has never been my experience

61

and I am sure that an old experience of mine is going to be repeated on this occasion. Well, now, what can I say to you?

Q: Mr. Prime Minister, is Great Britain prepared to cooperate with the United States in restoring—

The Prime Minister: If you wouldn't mind—just one minute. What can I say to you? Whatever I say to you must be prefixed by an expression of most sincere pleasure in meeting you all again.

You know the purpose of the conversations—the great purpose of the conversations. It is in a sentence to try, with the President and myself— with others—with other nations—to try and find some sort of solution for the most extraordinary and very, very tragic breakdown of our economic mechanism. The farmers and some of the very best types of human beings—and certainly some of the hardest working and most honest of men and women. Our skilled mechanics—I know them so well—I can sit by their firesides and talk to them as man to man. Their skill is great; their thrift is magnificent; they are self-respecting and their uprightness is beyond reproach. They have been saving; they have been men and families of most exemplary character, yet they with their families are today in a state of dire distress. There must be something wrong when that is true.

It is not a national problem. Of course, nations can do a good deal to alleviate it within their own boundaries, but what we have all got to get into our heads—you of America, we of Great Britain, is this: That no nation can solve it of itself. We have got to lay our heads together as friendly cooperators, and that is why I have come here and why your President has invited me to come here and why I have come here on this occasion.

We want to discuss together the calling of this international conference which is going to be held and more clearly define national problems and the situation which I have just described. We want to consider how those problems can be solved. Why is it that the international faith of the world is shrinking and shrinking and shrinking? There are a great many of us, those in particular described by Abraham Lincoln as people for whom God must have had a special affection because he has made so many of them, who really work for a living, some by muscle, some by brains, some by imagination—the man or woman who writes a great poem that inspires us to good life and great deeds is as much a producer in the world as the man who by the exercise of his muscles takes coal from the bowels of the earth and sends it up so that it may be available for our grates. Why is it that the exchange of goods, the volume of international commerce upon which we have to live, is getting smaller—smaller—the stream is getting shallower and shallower? God didn't mean that! It certainly must be a mistake on the part of man.

We are going to talk about that during this weekend. As I said, I don't know that at the moment I can say very much more than that. I dare say there will be other subjects—I don't like—you certainly are not to quote this now, but somehow I feel very fond of your President. I have got a sort of feeling that there is a good colleague with great spiritual power. And what can we do in public life without sincerity and spiritual power? A lot of people think that politics is a somewhat degrading occupation. Rubbish!—rubbish! It is the most elevating of occupations. I call it service. It is the most elevating service that any man or woman can be called upon to perform. It all depends on the spirit in which you do it. Some of us come from very humble origin—haven't forgotten and never will forget—and using their influence and authority in order to place people where they can put their energy to useful purpose. What better service can we give to the community? And I believe that is the spirit of President Roosevelt, who is now my host. I say, "Don't quote that," for I am just talking to friends, talking to men and women with whom I should like to come into a personal understanding so that if you damn me, your conscience will trouble you in doing it. I know—I know perfectly well. I whirled a pen myself and probably, when these hectic days have gone over, I may have to return to it and I shall do it with a great deal of pleasure if I do. So I know the insides of newspaper offices. I know that newspapers will oppose and object to things, but I should like, especially on this matter, which is not a parliamentary matter, which is not a sectional matter, which is not an American matter, which is not a British matter, that the critical press should be seized with the determination to help. Because if we could only get that—but don't make any mistake about it, it is going to be very difficult, but we will. When we went through a crisis in Great Britain a little over a year ago—getting on to two years ago, what did we do? We said that all those things that are petty and small-minded and partisan must go. We have fought, but now for the time being a truce to this pettifogging partisanism and I am glad to say that every newspaper of any reputation in the country responded—I say every newspaper of any reputation.

My friends, it calls for a union of nationalities. Not that we get in alliance with each other—not that we get tied up one to another—not at all. But it is a union of nationalities, appreciating the nature and importance of the problems and laying their heads together in order to find common ways to get commonly held solutions. My friends, we hope so to do it.

I am not going to say any more because I am going to speak tomorrow at the Press Club and by then I shall, perhaps, have been able to find my bearings a little more. This is only just a "How do you do?" This is an introductory—a re-introductory to many of us—shaking of the hand. If you would like to put questions I hope you will be discreet. If you are not discreet, I can assure you that I shall show you a very good example. (Laughter)

Mr. Boettiger:[3] May we put one very discreet question? Will you discuss war debts with the President?

The Prime Minister: The question of debts is one of those things—one of those features in the landscape that we have got to survey.

Q: Have you any suggestion to make to the President in your discussion of the debts when you survey that far?

The Prime Minister: That I don't know.

Q: Do you think it would be indiscreet to ask if Great Britain is prepared to cooperate with the United States in the restoration of the monetary standard based on a reduced rule?

The Prime Minister: You have not put one question; you have put a dozen. The United Kingdom has been hoping for a long time for the opportunity of considering with other nations how best to establish stability in monetary systems.

Q: Will you discuss the stabilization of Sterling—(inaudible)

The Prime Minister: We have been trying for a long time to give more stabilization and certainty to money.

Q: Can you tell us your idea of some things that might be done to meet present problems?

The Prime Minister: Not at this stage. You see, we have come to just exchange views—especially myself. I am your guest. You see, I am your guest and I must behave as a guest. But I can assure you all that there is going to be no holding back. No holding back. We are going to pull what is in our heads, whatever it may be and whatever value it may have.

Now, during the time I am here—it is only just this week end—as you can imagine, there is a tremendous amount of work that has to be done in London and it is not convenient to be away long, so I am really only going to spend, much to my regret, what we call at home a "long week end." A long week end is from Friday to Tuesday and I am afraid that is about all I can spend here—as I say, very much to my regret. But during that time my friend, Mr. Wright[4]—I think probably some of you know him, he has been in Washington before—he will be the liaison officer between and I am sure he will help you with information in every possible way. I think he would like to say something to you before we part this afternoon.

Q: Might I ask this question? I think it is timely. In your opinion, is there any intrinsic validity in the criticisms—we have cables reporting the editorials in London papers as criticizing the monetary policies of the United States—the motive because of the effect on the proposed conversations.

The Prime Minister: Well, I have seen nothing—I have seen nothing. What you might call the crisis—the change, took place while I was on the *Berengaria* and I cannot say.[5] I have read no newspaper. It is literally true that I have read no newspaper. I will try to do it tonight before I go to bed or after I get to bed.

I am quite willing to say this: All this talk about conveying enmity—it is not in my heart—it is not in the hearts of my colleagues nor the British Government. If little bits have cropped up, well, we are all human—but even that is not in my heart and I am sure it is not in the hearts of my colleagues. Realize that we are going through a very difficult crisis and do not let us begin to say—do not let our people say the U.S. have been working under some curious policy and do not let you say that we have been working under some curious policy. I can assure you—I certainly can speak for ourselves. It is not true—it is not true. It does not exist.

Now I think I will leave you in charge of Mr. Wright. I had a rather tiring day.

(Discussion about pictures)

Well, so far as I am concerned, I have no objection to a photograph being taken in this room of my friends and myself. (Pictures)

I was just going to say that so far as I am concerned I am standing at this particular spot on the instructions of the President who wished me to interview sitting in his chair and standing at this desk.[6] So you see, we are getting on. (Applause)

I am very glad to be photographed here with you and I talked very sincerely.

Thank you. Thank you so much for coming here.

[President's Press Conferences:T]

[1] George Durno, International News Service representative.

[2] MacDonald arrived in Washington on April 21, 1933, and on the next day held the first of five talks with Roosevelt. Five joint statements were issued from April 21

to 26; all are printed in *Public Papers*, II, 145–149, and in *Foreign Relations, 1933*, I, 490–493, 837. The President went into the conferences with a complicated debt settlement plan worked out principally by James P. Warburg. The plan involved cancellation of interest charges on the debts owed; redetermination of the principal then owed; and reaffirmation by the debtor of his obligation (Moley, *After Seven Years*, pp. 202–203). The conversations with Édouard Herriot began while MacDonald was still in Washington; they were concluded with the issuance of two noncommital joint statements on April 28, 1933, printed in *Public Papers*, II, 151–152.

[3] John Boettiger, at this time on the staff of the Chicago *Tribune*. He married Anna Roosevelt in 1935.

[4] Michael Wright, liaison between the Prime Minister and the British press.

[5] The gold embargo was proclaimed April 20.

[6] Roosevelt was not present.

## Cordell Hull, Secretary of State, to Roosevelt

Washington, April 21, 1933

My dear Mr. President: You asked me this afternoon[1] for further information in connection with our commercial treaty with Great Britain. I enclose a brief explanation of why the United States has up to the present consented to the Imperial preferences.

Faithfully yours,

Cordell Hull

[PSF:Great Britain:TS]

[1] At the meeting of the Cabinet (PPF 1-0).

## [*Enclosure*] Herbert Feis, Economic Adviser to the State Department, to Cordell Hull

April 21, 1933

Convention of Commerce and Navigation with Great Britain—1815: The essential provisions of the Treaty of 1815 are: "There shall be between the territories of the United States of America, and all the territories of His Britannick Majesty in Europe, a reciprocal liberty of commerce," and

". . . No higher or other duties shall be imposed on the importation into the territories of His Britannick Majesty in Europe of any articles the growth, produce or manufacture of the United States, than are or shall be payable on the like articles being the growth, produce or manufacture of any other foreign country."

In 1815 and for many years thereafter, the present Dominions of the British Commonwealth cannot have been regarded as being within the meaning of the phrase "any other foreign country" as used in defining the obligation of His Brittanic Majesty in the treaty. If at present it be arguable that the self-governing Dominions are in fact foreign countries in regard of Great Britain, it would still remain true that the Treaty of 1815 must be construed as a conditional most-favored-nation treaty in the sense that the parties are not required to extend free to each other any favor which they extend to a third country in return for some reciprocal concession or compensation. The Imperial preferences granted by the United Kingdom to the Dominions are part of a system of mutual concessions between the United Kingdom and the Dominions. The Supreme Court of the United States has construed the treaty as "conditional."

[PSF:Great Britain:T]

## Prime Minister Benito Mussolini of Italy to Roosevelt

[Rome, April 24, 1933]

My dear Mr President,

in response to your request to have an exchange of views concerning the world economic and political problems in wich the United States and Italy are mutually interested, I have asked the Minister of Finance Hon: Guido Jung to come to Washington as my representative.[1]

Mr Jung is bringing you my kindest personal regards and greetings. He will tell with how great an interest I am following the work of the United States Government for the solution of the world present difficulties wich only can be solved by the mutual cooperation and goodwill of the nations.

It is with great pleasure that I entrust Mr Jung with the reproduction of the manuscripts of Virgil and Horace which are kept at the "Laurenziano" Library in Florence; my representative will have the honor of conveying them to you as a mark of my most cordial feelings.

I choose these two authors not only because their poetical works represent the greatest legacy of Rom in the field of letters but also because they stand as exemples of that greatness of spirit and human understanding wich I believe are the two central qualities of the American Character.

With best wishes and sentiments of exsteem, believe me

Very sincerly yours

Mussolini

Roma 24 Aprile 1933—XI

[PSF:Italy:AS]

[1] Roosevelt's "request" was in the form of an aide-mémoire from Stimson to the Italian ambassador, Jan. 24, 1933 (*Foreign Relations, 1933,* I, 888–889). Roosevelt had not had previous correspondence with Mussolini, and there is little to indicate that the Duce had engaged his especial interest earlier. In 1925 Roosevelt and Howe made a study of the Italian war debt issue with regard to Democratic party policy (Freidel, *Franklin D. Roosevelt,* II, 223–225), and in the same year a family friend, Baron Bernardo Quaranta di San Severino, sent to Mrs. James Roosevelt a copy of his book, *Mussolini, as Revealed in His Political Speeches (November 1914—August 1923)* (London: Dent, 1923), autographed by Mussolini and San Severino. Mrs. Roosevelt gave the book (a collection of speeches) to her son as a Christmas present in 1925. Roosevelt had some subsequent correspondence with San Severino, a minor diplomat serving in Turkey, and in this he called Roosevelt's attention to Mustafa Kemal's activities (Roosevelt to San Severino, July 20, 1929; San Severino to Roosevelt, Aug. 23, 1932, Group 12). Another who brought Mussolini and Kemal to Roosevelt's attention was Charles H. Sherrill, a former West Sixty–Fifth Street neighbor of the Roosevelts, ambassador to Turkey in 1932–1933. In 1936 Sherrill sent Roosevelt a copy of his book, *Trois Hommes (Kamal-Roosevelt-Mussolini)* (Paris: Librarie Plon, 1936).

# William Phillips, Under Secretary of State, to Roosevelt

[Washington] April 24, 1933

Memorandum on the MacDonald Plan. From all indications that have reached us, the French are opposed to the MacDonald plan on several counts.

(a) It permits German rearmament to the extent of doubling the number of men allowed her and permitting her to supply herself without quantitative restriction with certain types of weapons.

(b) It leaves Germany free from armaments provisions of the Treaty of Versailles at the conclusion of the term of the MacDonald Treaty and thus faces France with the prospect of seeing Germany able to rearm, starting from a more favorable basis than would be possible today.

(c) The security clauses of the MacDonald plan are vague and would not give France a precise picture of the commitments accepted by the other signatory powers.

(d) It gives Russia more men than Poland and Rumania combined, a provision unacceptable to France's allies.

Unless Germany obtains enough disarmament from France she threatens to bolt the conference and declare that the Treaty of Versailles is null and void. However, in view of the definite warnings that Japan has given the conference that she desires an increase in armaments, it is clear that a universal treaty reducing armaments becomes a virtual impossibility.[1]

[PSF:Disarmament Conference:T]

[1] Roosevelt, MacDonald, and Sir Robert Vansittart, Permanent Under Secretary of State for Foreign Affairs, had discussed the MacDonald plan on Sunday, April 23, 1933. The text of the plan, and Vansittart's summary of the talk (held aboard the *Sequoia* on the Potomac), are in *Foreign Relations, 1933*, I, 43–54, 102–104. Roosevelt agreed with the greater part of the plan but the provision for a conference of the signators in event of a breach of the peace troubled him. He suggested, according to Vansittart, that he could accomplish by a declaration or a unilaterally signed note what he would have difficulty doing by a multilateral treaty, which would have to be approved by the Senate. The idea of a declaration eventually took the form of the message to heads of state of May 16, 1933, below. See Hull to Davis, April 25, 1933, *Foreign Relations, 1933*, I, 107–108, sending Roosevelt's statement of the United States position on the MacDonald plan, and the correspondence following.

# G. F. Warren, Cornell University, to Roosevelt

Ithaca, New York, April 24, 1933

Dear President Roosevelt: The newspaper comments make me quite uneasy. They sound as if there were an inference that the right to lower the gold content of the dollar is not to be exercised but merely used as a club over foreigners.[1]

The primary reason for reducing the weight of gold in the dollar is to improve the internal conditions in America, so that we will not have to complete the bankrupting process which deflation means. The mere issuance of paper money or expansion of credit, so long as each dollar is kept at par, will have very little influence on prices. The world determines the value of 23.22 grains of gold in terms of commodities. We determine the grains of gold in the dollar, and only by this means can we set our price level out of line with the world value of gold.

This principle is unknown to a considerable number of economists who have been steadily wrong in all their forecasts. In fact, a large group of economists petitioned Hoover a year and a half ago to do just what he did, thinking that they could raise prices by credit expansion. They are just as wrong now as they have been for fifteen years.

There is one and only one way to raise our commodity price level; that is, by reducing the amount of gold in the dollar. A rise in prices this week of basic commodities was directly in proportion to the decline in the value of the dollar in foreign exchange. Cotton did not rise in Liverpool.

If we allow or force the dollar to sink in foreign exchange and then bring it back to par, we will again be deflating. There can be no permanent gain by leaving the gold standard unless the dollar is revalued. To restore the price level, it must be reduced to between 12 and 16 grains. There is only one safe course, reduce the gold value of the dollar.[2]

Very truly yours,

G. F. Warren

[OF 229:TS]

[1] Under the pending Thomas amendment to the Agricultural Adjustment Act, Roosevelt was empowered to reduce the gold content of the dollar as a means of raising prices. An article in the New York *Times* of April 22, 1933, p. 2, said that the impression was strong in Administration circles "that the President would be very slow in adopting a program for increasing issues of currency." Warren had presumably seen this and similar reports. Warren, professor of agricultural economics and farm management at Cornell, had known Roosevelt since his governorship and had been a teacher of Henry Morgenthau, Jr., when he was a student at Cornell. Warren was at this time, with Irving Fisher of Yale, economic adviser to the Committee for the Nation.

[2] According to an attached note, copies of this letter were sent to the Secretary of the Treasury, the Budget Director, and Raymond Moley.

# Press Conference held by Prime Minister MacDonald in the President's Office, April 26, 1933, 10:10 A.M.

The Prime Minister: Good morning. Well, I brought good weather and I have left good weather. I think that ought to be reckoned in in whatever settlement is going to be made between us. How much value do you place upon a good day? You had better credit me with that. Are you all in?

Mr. Wright: Not quite in.

The Prime Minister: Time is flying so fast—all in yet?

Mr. Boettiger: All in.

The Prime Minister: Well, I am very sorry to leave you again. It seems only an hour or two since I said "How do you do" to you just after I arrived in Washington. I think you have been so admirably served by our press men behind us that it was unnecessary for you to see me myself, and I should like to thank you for the fine help you have been to us. I would like to thank our press experts for—and I think you perhaps will join me in this—for the way they have placed themselves so unreservedly at our disposal. The success of our conversations has depended very largely upon that admirable body of experts who, with great patience and great knowledge and unlimited good will for each other—both sides—have worked away to advise possible ways of coming to agreements when the time arrives.

You will remember I told you that I was not calling to come to agreements—to draft papers and sign them so that the last word had been said. I have kept my promise, my friends, we have not done that—we have never tried to do it. This has been preliminary conversation—just like when you are going out on some big expedition you send scouts ahead to see what is the best trail for you to take and to see how far the ground will enable you to carry out your purposes.[1] Well, that is what we have been doing the last two or three days and I think—though I have had many experiences that between the cup and the lip there are many slips—I think that I can say to you, without any reservation at all, either in my heart or on my lips, that these two or three days of friendly, pleasant conversations have been fruitful in a way that I hardly imagined would be possible when I came. But still—and I repeat it—no agreements, no settlements. I leave your President as free as he was when I found him and he lets me go home to see my own colleagues in the British Empire as free as I was the day I left them—that is the day before I sailed for New York.[2]

But, nevertheless, it has been real good business we have done—real good business. I am very glad that I have had the pleasure also of meeting Mr. Bennett down here. It was absolutely impossible for me to get to Canada at this time. You saw this morning that yesterday was our budget day, and the Prime Minister's supreme duty is to be at home whilst the budget is being discussed and settled in the House of Commons, so I am hurrying back. I must hurry back in order to be there with as little delay as possible. So I couldn't go to Canada and I hope the Canadian journalists who are present will convey to their readers my profound regret that fate has been against me on this occasion but that I still remember my pledge to go to Canada on a holiday. In the meantime, I am very glad indeed that I am having the opportunity of talking with Mr. Bennett.

Now, I would like to put it to you this way: I came here as—apparently as a Minister of Great Britain and as the destined—perhaps for my sins, because it is going to be no easy job—Chairman of the International Economic Conference. The burdens and the worries of both offices were lying in a most terrible way on my back when I saw you last. I am going away as a friend, for I am taking away with me a memory of a most genial man, who is your President, and a really friendly crowd representing, I hope—I flatter myself by hoping—representing the spirit of the American people.

I have learned more clearly than I knew before of the difficulties of the American Government—the American nation—and I hope that in return for that you folks and your Government appreciates perhaps a little bit more vividly the great troubles and the great difficulties that I have to face as Prime Minister and my colleagues have to face as responsible cabinet ministers.

We are going away leaving behind us and taking away with us a closer understanding than before. We understood each other at a little distance off. We now understand each other, as it were, elbow to elbow. You know the human difference in that and, believe me, my friends, the very highest diplomacy and the most accurate and searching diplomacy always take into account the value of personal and human understandings between both sides. I think we have got that as the result of the conversations.

It therefore has come to this: That we have got above and beyond mere market haggling and foggling. We are not going to cooperate in finding solutions of the great troubles of the world if we maintain ourselves in the position of mere bargainers. "I will give you six pence in silver if I am perfectly certain that you are going to give me six coppers." Bah! That is not the way of going to work together. That is not a way we are going to live together. That is not the way we are going to aspire and achieve together. We have got above that. We have got to an understanding now. There is to be a real human understanding and the bargains we want and the exchanges we want are the bargains and exchanges which will make us both—both separately and cooperatively—more efficient in removing the burdens that are oppressing the world at the present moment.

We are also—and this is the last I want to say—we are also going away not only convinced of the fact that we hope to come to an agreement—we are going away with a greater thought than that—we are going away with a determination we are going to come to an agreement because it is our moral duty to come to an agreement; that if we don't come to agreements—I am only telling you what I have been trying to do. I said "we"; there are others here and "we" includes, in one's throat even though not in one's language. But can you imagine what is going to happen if America and Great Britain cannot devise a means of marching side by side? No alliances! Don't you have any fear of that. No entanglements! We are not going to be brought into the maelstrom of Europe. You are going to remain where you are, but no man lives to himself alone. The man who is strongest and most independent is the one who has stretched out his hand to somebody else and grasped it. That is the idea that is in my mind and I think—I think we have got. I think we have got it.

And you have been awfully good in helping us to get it, and with all the gratitudes that I take away with me—I believe in about an hour and a half—I am sorry but it is true—but amongst all the things I am going to take away with me—not in my luggage but in my heart—one of the strongest of them will be my gratitude to the American Press, whom you represent here today.

Well, I hope we will meet again. I cannot bear to think that this contact is not going to be a continuing one. I hope that your President will be spared many years of life to give us opportunities for these meetings and I can assure—I can assure him through you that every opportunity that comes to me to go out in your woods, to go down your river, I will fly to take them.

So, my friends, goodbye for the time being.[3]

[President's Press Conferences:T]

[1] See the Roosevelt-MacDonald statement of April 26, 1933, in *Public Papers,* II, 147–149.

[2] The preceding paragraph was quoted (in large part) in a memorandum prepared by Early dated April 28, 1933, and headed, "For the information of Senator Robinson" (OF 212). Early also quoted from the joint statement issued by Roosevelt and MacDonald on April 25, 1933: "It is wholly misleading to intimate that any plan or any settlement is under way. It is the simple truth that thus far only preliminary explorations of many different routes have been commenced." (See *Public Papers,* II, 147.)

Early concluded: "You can assure your friends in Congress that there has been no agreement nor agreement to make an agreement in relation to debts, cancellation of debts or moratoriums between the President and the Prime Minister of Great Britain, and that the same is accordingly true as to conversation between the President and the representative of France. The rumor that the President was about to send up a request for a moratorium on debt interest payments until after the Economic Conference is, of course, started by the active propaganda now being started under the general direction of Mr. Mellon."

Andrew W. Mellon, as ambassador to Great Britain (1932–1933), had had numerous discussions with MacDonald about the war debts but on returning to the United States in January 1933, denied that he had been given any special instructions by President Hoover (New York *Times,* Jan. 13, 1933, p. 1).

[3] Printed also in the New York *Times,* April 27, 1933, p. 2.


## Press Conference, Executive Offices of the White House, April 26, 1933, 4:07 P.M.

(M. Herriot was present as were the French correspondents who had accompanied him and the English correspondents who had accompanied Prime Minister MacDonald.)

The President: I am very glad to see all of you, especially those who are here from France and from Great Britain. Just for your benefit, I perhaps might mention that nothing that is said in these conferences is for quotation.

I think that the only news is that Mr. Herriot and I have had a very satisfactory conversation this morning and that the talk is going to continue and that we are getting on very well. The only addition I can make to that is that my French is improving. (Laughter)

Q: Mr. President, what of these reports that you are considering the possible abandonment of some of the rights of neutrality in order to satisfy the demand for security?

The President: Of course, off the record, I am not responsible for any reports unless they come out in the form of official communications.

Q: Tell us what you have been talking about with Mr. Herriot.

The President: Well, I think that it is fair to assume that so far, the principal substance of the conversation has been disarmament. As you know, the disarmament conference resumed in Geneva yesterday, but I think probably that most of the news of the conference will emanate from Geneva and not from Washington. I think you can assume that both the French and the British and ourselves have been in fairly close touch with Geneva during the past twenty-four hours.

Q: The afternoon papers are carrying a story about Norman Davis coming out for the consolidated ticket in all particulars at Geneva; is that true?

The President: I don't know; we have not heard from Davis at all.

Q: Do you care to state your ideas on that?

The President: No. You see, as a matter of politeness, the International Conference is being held in Geneva and anything pertaining to the Conference should come from there. So far, in Washington, we have only had consultations with the British and French. It is merely a matter of politeness that the news should come from Geneva and not from here.

Q: Has the debt question been discussed so far?

The President: No.

Q: Daladier, the French Premier, is quoted as saying today that if the United States grants a postponement of the June 15th payment, France will be glad to pay the December 15th installment.

The President: That, literally, is true. We have not discussed it in any way . . .

Q: Are you and Mr. Herriot going to have an announcement after today's meeting?

The President: We have not got to that yet. What do you think, Mr. Ambassador or Mr. Under Secretary?[1] I don't know that we really need an announcement. I think you know as much now as I would be able to give out in an announcement today. We are still in a preliminary stage. The French experts and the American experts are hard at work with each other and we have not seen them since yesterday.

Q: They are working on the economic problems?

The President: Yes, on the economic problems—monetary and tariff.

Q: May we expect a statement on the subject of international exchange within the next week?

The President: I don't think—this is off the record, just for your information—I don't think that there will be any formal statement on international exchange because we still have to have conversations with a good many other nations. The Italians are coming next week. The Germans are coming next week. Also we have people coming from the Argentine; the Japanese are on their way or, rather, the Chinese are on their way because I don't think the Japs have started yet.

Q: Has the date for the economic conference been fixed as yet?

The President: Bill,[2] are we at liberty to say anything on that? No, that is supposed to come out of London. There again, I think we know about it pretty well—the French Government, the British Government and most of the other governments know about it but, as a matter of courtesy, it should come from the Chairman of the Organizing Committee, Sir John Simon, so we cannot make an announcement at this end.

Q: Have you reached any decision as to the personnel of our delegation?

The President: No, I have not taken it up at all . . .

Q: Can you tell us anything about the conversations with respect to the Canadian Minister? Can you tell us whether they will involve trade agreements and the St. Lawrence River?

The President: I cannot tell you. You are about twenty-four hours ahead of time. Prime Minister Bennett and I are having our first talk tomorrow morning at ten o'clock . . .

Q: May I ask whether stabilization of currency is prior to stabilization of markets in your plan?

The President: Gosh, that sounds like the Baltimore *Sun.* (Laughter) Is it Fred who asked the question?

Q: (Fred Essary) No, sir; Mr. President, I am keeping very quiet.

The President: Stabilization of currency to go ahead of what?

Q: Stabilization of markets.

The President: I don't know. I should say, off the record, the best answer is that they should be considered a pair of dice(?)[3] which we hope will grow at the same rate during the coming year. (Laughter)

Q: Would you ask Mr. Herriot for us, in your improved French, if he is going to have a press conference today.

(The President asked Mr. Herriot in French and Mr. Herriot indicated that he would not have a press conference.)

Q: Have you used the long-distance phone here this afternoon?

The President: No.

Q: How do you figure your legislative program for this session of Congress? Is the railroad bill the last thing you had in mind?

The President: I should say, for your information and off the record, that that is about the last message—the last new thing that will go up except, of course, the possibility of resolutions later on in relation to tariff and also, possibly, in relation to debts, but that is purely speculative at this time because we haven't got to it. But, as far as the actual legislative program is concerned—as far as I can tell now, there is only one more major thing going up and that is railroads.

Q: Can you indicate what the tenor of the resolution on debts will be?

The President: Resolution on debts? That is speculative yet. We haven't come to that.

Q: What kind of a resolution should we speculate on?

The President: Don't. (Laughter)

Mr. Durno: Thank you, Mr. President.

(The Press Conference adjourned at 4:22 P.M. Immediately thereafter the President shook hands with the French and British correspondents. Having spoken to the British correspondents the day before, the President addressed himself to the French correspondents as follows.)

The President: I want to tell you all one story about the conference which I had with the French press in July, 1918. M. Clemenceau felt that it was time in 1918, in the summer, to tell the world all about how we were stopping the German submarines. So, at the Meurice Hotel in Paris, I had a conference with the French press at eleven o'clock in the morning.

I proceeded to tell them what the three governments, the French Government, the British Government and the American Government, were doing about submarines. When I got through, I said, "Now, gentlemen, if you want to ask me any questions, I will answer the questions as long as it is not a secret matter." Thereupon one of the editors said to me, "Is it the custom in the United States for the members of the Cabinet to answer questions from the press?" And I said, "Yes, it is the custom in the United States for the members of the Cabinet to answer questions from the press." Whereupon everybody exclaimed and they wanted to know all about it, and I explained our custom here where every member of the American Cabinet receives the press twice a day and they thought that that was perfectly wonderful.

The next morning I had an appointment with Clemenceau and when I came into the room he came forward and he said, "You have caused my Government to fall here, right in the middle of the War and before we have the War won. You will make my Government fall." I said, "What have I done?" He said, "You told all the French press how they were received by the American Cabinet and now they have come to me and demanded that all my French Cabinet should receive the French press twice a day and," he said, "before we do that we will resign."

It is awfully nice to see you.

[President's Press Conferences:T]

[1] Phillips and André de Laboulaye were present.
[2] William Phillips, Under Secretary of State.
[3] Question mark in the original; possibly this should read "mice."

## Press Conference, Executive Offices of the White House, April 28, 1933, 12:40 P.M.

[*Excerpt*] Q: Tell us about the resolutions you might ask for to deal with debts?

The President: I haven't any more idea than you have; absolutely haven't any more idea than you have.

Q: Down in Warm Springs, I think you mentioned the possibility of asking for a commission to advise with you—a Congressional commission. Have you still got that in mind?

The President: No, I can only talk about that entirely off the record and in the family. It seemed possible, at that time, to have some kind of a more or less formal commission, but that would entail probably a debate and so forth and so on. It is probably better, from the standpoint of the present situation, to handle it in just an informal way, keeping in touch with the Foreign Relations Committees in the two Houses and with the leaders in the different groups. That would make it much simpler. We will arrive at the same result without any formalities.

Q: Is the conversation with the Canadian Prime Minister still in process?

The President: Yes, he is coming in at half past two this afternoon, right after the Cabinet meeting. We are getting on extremely well.[1]

Q: Can you tell us anything about the tariff? The French tell us that they want a safeguarding clause, enabling them to increase the tax in the event the dollar should take a sudden drop.

The President: I cannot tell you anything at this end because it is a thing that should break from London tomorrow.

Q: Will you conclude your talks with Bennett today?

The President: Yes.

Q: Will there be an announcement of any kind?

The President: I think so, yes.

Q: May I ask one more question: Is it fair to assume that the trade treaties with Canada will depend on the treaty powers you get from the Senate?

The President: Not necessarily.

Q: Should this break from London—the tariff treaties?

The President: The tariff treaties? Yes, because it will come up on a motion by Mr. Davis.

Q: Is Mr. Davis in London now?

The President: Yes; he left Geneva this morning to get to London either tonight or tomorrow morning.

Q: May I ask if the conclusions arrived at in the conference last summer proved any element of embarrassment in your conversation with the Prime Minister?

The President: Off the record, I can only tell you that so far we have not mentioned the Ottawa Conference . . .[2]

Q: Is there anything new about the Ambassador to Germany?

The President: No.

Q: Will the agreement made with Canada have to wait until after the World Economic Conference?

The President: That is too difficult a question to answer. I don't know.

Q: Can you give us any idea?

The President: In other words, entirely off the record, the way I would put it would be this: There are quite a number of matters in which Canada and the United States can act by a bilateral agreement that would not affect the rest of the world and, of course, we could go ahead on that right away.

Q: Will any attempt be made to stabilize the currency of Great Britain and the United States in advance of the Economic Conference?

The President: That I cannot answer; it is too complicated.

Q: It is not so complicated.

The President: We are not ready for it.

Q: Has the French Government made any overtures for the payment on December 15?

The President: We have not discussed it.

Q: Speaking of those matters as to which we could conclude treaties with Canada before the Economic Conference, those would also have to await receipt of authority from Congress, would they not? In other words, there is nothing you can do with respect to Canada at the present time?

The President: On tariff matters, that is perfectly true, but there are a lot of other things.

Q: There are a lot of other things?

The President: We have quite a lot of things that are subjects of negotiation at the present time. Some of them have proceeded to the actual treaty stage, others are before the International Joint Commission. For instance, I am taking up again with the State Department and the Foreign Relations Committee the treaty in relation to Sockeyed Salmon. (Laughter)

Q: But tariff matters would have to wait?

The President: Yes.

Q: Is there any chance of an agreement on wheat control?

The President: That is a thing still under discussion with Mr. Bennett. We are talking about that this afternoon.

Q: Was the matter of the Consultative Pacts deliberately left out of the statement this morning?[3]

The President: What was that?

Q: The pact—discussing it with France—the statement does not mention it.

The President: I think the language covers the whole thing pretty well. I haven't got a copy of it here. (Mr. Early handed the President a copy of the statement.) There is something in the statement in regard to—(reading statement)—

Mr. Early: It mentions the word peace.

The President: Well, you get to the top of the second paragraph and it reads "at no moment has understanding been more necessary between France and the United States for maintenance of peace." You see, there are various elements here—the maintenance of peace, progressive and simultaneous disarmament, the restoration of stable monetary conditions in an atmosphere of general security. There you have four things. Draw your own conclusions.

Q: Mr. President, what kind of a consulting pact would you get? Would it be more of a modified—

The President: That is it; you have to draw your own conclusions from the four things mentioned there.

Q: Well, some of your Senators say there won't be any such a consultative pact—only in name only.

The President: Wait and see.

Q: Where will that develop, at Geneva?

The President: I don't know.

Q: How long are we going to have to wait?

The President: I don't know that either. I am not an awful good guesser this morning . . .

Q: Have you any statement on the departure of M. Herriot?

The President: You mean from me?

Q: From both of you.

The President: Yes, there is a very fine statement that is coming out in about half an hour, as soon as it gets mimeographed.[4] All I can say is to repeat how very, very happy I was in having the chance, not only of meeting him but of becoming real friends with him. I feel that the conversations have very greatly advanced the understanding between the two countries. (Mr. Early spoke to the President.) Steve says his statement is all ready.

Then, the only other thing I have is that in ten minutes I have to attend a luncheon to the Philippines [*sic*] who are visiting here, Señor Quezon and two or three others—I believe there are six of them—and the Secretary of War and the new Governor General.[5]

Q: I understand that Señor Quezon is returning somewhat disappointed because he found, on the Hill at least, quite a bit of antagonism toward any change in the Independence Bill. Does that represent the Administration attitude? He did intend to stay quite a while but now he is returning.

The President: It would have to be off the record, merely with the idea of giving you a slant on my own feeling on it. We have got to remember that this is a special session of the Congress and, as such, we want to take up only the things that are special from the domestic point of view—in other words, emergencies.

It is only a very short time since the Philippine Bill went through and we all feel that nothing should be done during this special session of Congress to raise the question in any way.

Q: But that does not preclude action later on?

The President: No human being can tell what future Congresses will do but, so far as the present Congress is concerned, our general position is "no changes."

Q: That is off the record?

The President: Yes.

[President's Press Conferences:T]

[1] Bennett also talked with Roosevelt on April 24 and 28 (PPF 1-0); a joint statement was issued on April 29 (*Public Papers,* II, 150). They agreed that the commodity price level should be increased, that an international monetary standard should be restored, and that U.S.–Canadian trade should be increased. For Bennett's ideas on Canadian relations with the United States, see Pierre Boal to Phillips, April 14, 1933, in *Foreign Relations, 1933,* II, 44–49.

[2] The Imperial Economic Conference held in Ottawa the previous summer. Bennett (a strict believer in the gold standard) had been a member of the Monetary Committee. The Monetary Committee failed to recommend that the Empire return to the gold standard but it agreed that the level of commodity prices should be raised.

[3] The second joint statement of April 28 (*Public Papers,* II, 151–152).

[4] Presumably Herriot's farewell statement to the American public; see New York *Times,* April 29, 1933, pp. 1, 2.

[5] George Dern and Frank Murphy.

## Michael J. McDermott, Chief, Division of Current Information, State Department, to Stephen T. Early, Assistant Secretary to the President

[Washington] April 28, 1933

Dear Steve: Enclosed is a copy of my notes on Mr. Moley's conference in your office yesterday, which I hastily pounded out last night. I have given a copy to the Secretary of State and Mr. Phillips so that they may know fully what was said and not cross wires when they see the Press.

I keep them fully informed by similar reports with what the President says at his press conferences on foreign affairs. I make no notes on anything that does not relate to foreign affairs.

I believe that Mr. Moley's talk did a great deal of good in putting the correspondents straight and we will have no bad reactions from it. The correspondents certainly owe you much for arranging it. Thanks for letting me sit in.

Sincerely,

M. J. McDermott

[OF 17:TS]

## *Enclosure*] Confidential Memorandum of Mr. Raymond Moley's Talk for Background Purposes with Correspondents at the White House, April 27, 1933

Mr. Stephen T. Early first spoke to the correspondents (all Americans) in confidence. He reminded the correspondents that they had been informed of an understanding with Prime Minister MacDonald that all information given the press would be in the form of communiqués, without oral supplement. The British played ball very well. It had come to Mr. Early's attention that rumor had it that Mr. Michael Wright, liaison between the Prime Minister and the British press, had been present at the conversations, but this was not true. Neither Mr. Wright nor Mr. Early sat in during any of the conversations. Now Mr. Early was informed that M. Herriot was seeing the French press and discussing matters with them. Certainly the American press should be put in the same position as the French press, and Mr. Early had therefore arranged

82

that Mr. Moley should talk with the correspondents for background purposes with the understanding that nothing said would be attributed to the White House. This talk would be in the nature of an experiment.

Mr. Moley spoke as follows, for background: Going back to the meeting in January when the subject of having these informal meetings prior to the Economic Conference with individual nations came up and had been agreed to by President elect Roosevelt after conferences with Secretary of State Stimson, the question of form and method came up and the second White House Conference was held.[1] At that conference, just how the meetings should be held and when was discussed. There was some confusion about how the discussions were to be held and what ought to be the form of the American memorandum to the British, they having signified a desire very early in November to talk about debts. After the numerous exchanges between the President Elect and the President, this meeting finally took place to discuss what the Secretary of State, Mr. Stimson, and the President Elect had tentatively agreed upon, namely, that somebody come over from England to talk about debts and subjects related to the Economic Conference. It was agreed that we should suggest that the English send representatives to discuss economic questions and a representative to discuss debts. There was no hard and fast rule but the general policy was that the two things were to be "considered concurrently but separately." That phraseology Mr. Stimson and I agreed upon after the White House Conference was over. When the group came over the intent of that policy was carried out insofar as the conferences of the experts and also conferences in which the experts and the principals were together did not mention debts. Debts were reserved for a private and confidential discussion between the President and the Prime Minister alone. This was the strict rule I impressed on everybody connected with our staff, that there was to be no discussion of debts either in groups or privately.

Following the debts through, the President and the Prime Minister discussed debts and the result of their discussion is in the statement given out, and I want to assure you that that statement is the complete truth.[2] The complete truth is: they did talk about it; they did discuss various possibilities, they did it only tentatively and they left the subject without ending in disagreement but with an illumination as to possibilities. There was no disagreement, and neither was there an agreement of any kind. I think I can make it more clear: They went into this conference without the equipment, and deliberately so, to reach even tentative agreements, because if you go into that kind of thing you have to get exact figures, dates, etc. In order that the conversation could be held on a lofty high plane those things were left out.

Correspondent: Was silver touched on as one of the possibilities?

Mr. Moley: That is one of a number of things that have been in conference. That has been talked over. It is contingent on the payment of the June 15th payment. I say it is contingent—it is one of the methods of paying that installment. As Senator Pittman has explained publicly many times, the British, in his opinion, are owed sums by the Indian Government, which Government is willing to pay it in silver. It would be much easier for the British. The French would probably have to buy it. Some arrangement could be worked out but I don't think they (the President and the Prime Minister) talked about that. That is the general thought. It is within the realm of possibility and before Congress.

Correspondent: Would you go on with the discussion of the French debt?

Mr. Moley: Inasmuch as there has been this misapprehension, I will lay the cards on the table. Our position with reference to the payment of the French default is simply that it would manifestly be a difficult thing to explain to the English, inasmuch as the English paid up, however reluctantly, without promises on December 15th, to make promises in order to secure the payment of $19,000,000 and that $19,000,000 is due. The position of the United States is that we would be awfully glad to get it, and after we get it that means we will just try to forget that it is a little late and therefore the French and the British will be looked upon on the same basis, but without a promise, which the British did not get. They didn't get any promises however reluctantly they paid. Here is a detail which is no diplomatic secret given me by an American, not by a French representative, away back in December after the Herriot Government went out of power. He got the information confidentially that the Herriot Government, if we would give some new fact, just a new fact whatever it might be, would find it acceptable and provide the excuse for paying the $19,000,000. That new fact never took form because there isn't anything to say about the new facts. The facts are all on the table, have been discussed and made plain. If France had been given a new fact, England would have been put on a disparity. I said, not to a representative of the French Government but to the American, that it might be very well to read carefully all the statements made by the President elect, including his November 22nd statement which was a friendly gesture to the debtor countries and he might be willing to talk to them and tell them they might get a new fact out of that, but so far as making any previous promises was concerned they could not be made. I can say this in great frankness. Apparently the French opinion has hardened a bit over that and now we get the discovery of what the fact should be, and that fact is that we ought not to press the payment of the June 15th installment—not an absolute promise we will let them off—but a statement we will not be hard about it. They haven't any such assurance. They have not been treated any differently from England.

Correspondent: How could we be less hard?

Mr. Moley: We could refrain from dunning them, sending them notes, bringing it to their attention, talking about it.

Correspondent: Have the British been given any assurance of a consultative pact in connection with disarmament?

Mr. Moley: On that subject I wouldn't be able to express any opinion at all.

Correspondent: If we could go into a consultative pact with France, what would that mean to us?

Mr. Moley: I know nothing about disarmament proceedings. I personally haven't made any attempt to keep myself informed about disarmament.

Correspondent: Is it the attitude of the administration that the June 15th payments shall be made?

Mr. Moley: We are exactly in the position of anybody who has a debt coming due the 15th of June and who has heard rumblings of difficulty about payment and some intimations that it will not be paid. We can't take any other position than remain silent in regard to that. I won't say it is a mere hope but it is something that is not on our mind.

Correspondent: There was a broad intimation in the British note that accompanied the last payment to the effect that it was the last payment under the existing system.

Mr. Moley: Yes?

Correspondent: Supposing France and England should not pay on the 15th of June, might it not interfere with our entering into agreements at the World Economic Conference?

Mr. Moley: I don't think so, personally. I am glad you brought that question up. It is a point on which I think Mr. Hull's policy has been already justified. The policy has been explained by him over and over again. Certainly we would attend the Conference. I said this very hopefully and directly to the British Ambassador because we see these various questions as questions which must be adjusted to the mutual advantage of both parties when you come to trade agreements. You will agree on that. When you come to monetary agreements, or to tariffs, or to anything else, then that subject has to be agreed upon, and when you come to the debts that subject must be agreed upon without reference to the other subjects. There has been a disposition in the past to a quid pro quo diplomacy. Mr. Hull has given the expression that there is no quid pro quo diplomacy in existence so far as we are concerned. I think that is the only sound policy because you can't trade one thing against another. You can't reduce them to the same terms. That is my personal opinion. Hour after hour in the discussions I have stated it: that each question can be adjusted with reference to the advantage of all parties concerned and without reference to another question. I think that is fundamental.

Correspondent: Is it possible that debts will be discussed at the Economic Conference?

Mr. Moley: No. I think it is perfectly correct to say that the established policy of the American Government, published in Mr. Roosevelt's statement of November 24th, is that a debt is a debt.

Correspondent: Is it possible that American representatives in London will be authorized to deal with various representatives of other governments separately on the subject of debts?

Mr. Moley: That could be possible, but it isn't an immediate probability.

Correspondent: The American attitude has been that when the experts were together debts were not discussed?

Mr. Moley: I may say this in confidence. At this meeting when the suggestion was made by the French, in the first experts' meeting, we made it clear we were not authorized to discuss debts. This policy has succeeded because we have gone down the line and taken every question and we have really found signs of mutually advantageous adjustments without reference to other questions. The moment you get other questions in and try to trade one against the other you get into trouble. You can't reduce them to a common denominator. In dealings of Governments there are often claims against which counter claims can be set off, because they can be reduced to money; but you can't reduce a trade agreement because you don't know what you are going to get out of it. The tremendous, hopeful thing is that you get along much faster, and we have, on that basis, and the meetings have been perfectly pleasant. The foreboding that they would not discuss economic questions until debt settlements were reached has not been borne out. It is a fine thing. It comes down to an expression of the terms under which in each of these various matters an approach to a final agreement can be reached. I can't go into that much further. Take the question of silver for example, or any other question on the agenda for the Economic Conference—the preliminary exploration of the Committee. Take the question of silver and it comes to a question of reviewing what the problem is; what it means to the various countries of the world, and I don't believe there is a man who came here who has not been impressed by the masterly way in which Senator Pittman has explained silver. He demonstrated that it does mean something, as a commodity, to the trade of the world, and we discussed various conditions regarding improvement in the price of silver and ended in a clear understanding of the possibilities of making some effort to improve it. That is what we did with all these questions.

Correspondent: Will M. Herriot enter the Economic Conference without debts being settled?

Mr. Moley: There has been no intimation so far as we are concerned of any refusal. The World Economic Conference is one of thirty, forty, or fifty nations, all interested, and for a government to refuse to take part would be—my guess is that they would. All these nations are not merely concerned in restoration of the economic world stability and prosperity but they realize that it is essential, and the idea that any nation would refuse to participate would mean cutting off noses to spite faces.

Correspondent: Did the President discuss debts with Herriot this afternoon?

Mr. Moley: I do not know; I haven't seen the President since the meeting.

Mr. Early: Those discussions have commenced.

Correspondent: Would you indorse the statement made by Mr. Wright of the British Delegation last night that these conferences had been so satisfactory that they give good hope of a successful understanding at the Economic Conference if the conference with all the countries went as well as the British?

Mr. Moley: Yes, and after the meeting with the French there is still ample room for such a feeling.

Correspondent: Going back to silver, is there any talk of establishing an international bimetallic standard?

Mr. Moley: Nothing has been talked about. But if you follow the policies of Senator Pittman you will find he has never believed in the necessity of a bimetallic standard but by treating silver not as a commodity but as a means of world trade. Most earnest and impressive on other nations is Pittman's statement that more than half the people of the world use silver and if we are to get together we have to consider that. Not to do so would be to leave half the cast out of the play. You can't just talk about gold. You have to talk about silver in the terms which he uses and when you do that you establish a ratio, it is true, but a ratio not called a bimetallic standard. We have to get trade moving and know it will by raising prices on commodities. We know that it should improve and it is natural that it should.

Correspondent: Was there any discussion of some countries using some silver instead of small paper?

Mr. Moley: Now we are getting into details. I do not think we should go into that. Naturally the whole subject was gone into thoroughly in many ways.

Correspondent: Any further revision of debts depends on the payment of the June 15th installment?

Mr. Moley: That is a question not determined yet. It has not yet been worked out. I do not think that is a bargaining point at all.

Correspondent: If debts are not to be disposed of before the World Economic Conference and should France default wouldn't it be difficult to come to understandings on tariff matters, stabilization of money, etc., inasmuch as the debtor countries will say that they couldn't balance their budgets?

Mr. Moley: That point of view is answered by the statement that the balancing of all the budgets in the world is more than the wildest optimist could expect to come from the Economic Conference. It is one of the minor questions in the conference.

Correspondent: Do you expect debts to be settled in some form or other before the conclusion of the Economic Conference?

Mr. Moley: I wouldn't answer that question. The question of whether the Economic Conference can be concluded before debt settlement is reached is one nobody can predict, but a very fine World Economic Conference could be concluded without a settlement of the debts.

Correspondent: Will negotiations as to debts continue between the ambassadors and President Roosevelt?

Mr. Moley: The formula of November holds good. Through the channels of diplomatic intercourse debt questions can always be raised.

Correspondent: Were debts discussed when the British Ambassador was discussing the topics included in the agenda of the Economic Conference?

Mr. Moley: The British Ambassador never raised the question in those conferences.

Correspondent: Do I understand the situation that we expect France to make the December 15 payment past due as well as the June 15 payment?

Mr. Moley: Were I to answer that question I would be doing what we should not do. As I see it, the question isn't raised and it is better not to speak about it. That is the proper position for us to take.

Correspondent: Can you tell us about the Canadian conversations?[3]

Mr. Moley: The Canadian conversations followed the same general line as the others with the additional questions related to the fact that we live close to each other.

Correspondent: There is nothing between us that we are likely to stumble upon?

Mr. Moley: Of course trade between the United States and Canada is governed by tariffs. I cannot stress too much the fine impression the Prime Minister has made on everybody.

Correspondent: The President said yesterday that he might send a resolution on tariffs and another on debts to the Capitol and today Senator Pittman in the Senate said that there would be no resolution from the administration on debts. He said he thought the President had in mind this amendment to the inflation bill offered today, which authorizes the President to receive a certain amount of the debt payments in silver.[4] Can you say that the Administration has no thought of asking any further resolution on the debt question?

Mr. Early: Please let the President clear that up tomorrow at his Press Conference. I think he wants to.

M. J. McDermott

[OF 17:CT]

---

[1] See White House press release of Jan. 20, 1933, and memorandum by Stimson, same date, in *Foreign Relations, 1933*, I, 827–828, 828, and in *Public Papers*, II, 147–149.

[2] Printed *Foreign Relations, 1933*, I, 492.

[3] Between Roosevelt and Prime Minister Bennett on April 27 at the White House. Others present were Hull, the Canadian minister to the United States, W. D. Herridge, and Raymond Moley.

[4] The "inflation bill" was the Thomas amendment to the Agricultural Adjustment Act (Title III) which authorized the President to reduce the gold content of the dollar (48 *Stat.* 51). The amendment here referred to was that offered by Senator Carl Hayden to authorize the acceptance of silver in debt payments up to a total of $200 million. This was approved as sec. 45 of the Act.

## Bishop G. Ashton Oldham, Diocese of Albany, to Roosevelt

Albany, New York, April 28, 1933

My dear President Roosevelt: I had the great pleasure of renewing my acquaintance with Prime Minister Ramsay MacDonald the other day, meeting him in the afternoon quite informally and hearing him again at the Pilgrim's dinner that night, which was a really great occasion.[1] His admiration for you, as you must have heard, is unbounded, though he told me somewhat humorously that he had told you there was one great difference between his position and yours, namely, that you had not the power of ecclesiastical appointments! To this I replied that his own appointments had been admirable, and from what I know of you and your appointments I would not mind at all if you also had this power, though I fancy you would be the last to want it.

Seriously, I cannot refrain from just a line to tell you how I am enheartened by everything you have done, and so are all my friends, including many rock-ribbed members of the G.O.P. I believe I know something of the tremendous issues at stake and the great battle you are waging, and trust and pray that you may continue to have both the wisdom and courage to carry on. You know something perhaps of my long interest in international affairs, and I am increasingly convinced that here is the real crux of the whole problem. By other means, such as you have initiated, we may be able to stave off actual distress for ourselves, but unless the leading nations of the world can be brought to some kind of real cooperation, then the building of the new structure of our civilization will be postponed indefinitely. It almost looks as if a miracle will be required to bring such cooperation about, but I have the greatest hopes in your method of personal conferences; and if all your visitors go away with the friendly and hopeful feeling that Ramsay MacDonald expressed, I really believe the miracle can happen . . .[2]

With warm personal regards and every good wish to you all, I am,
Faithfully yours,

G. Ashton Oldham

P.S. If ever you get time from your pressing duties, please do not forget your promise to send me that autographed photo.[3]

[PPF 418:TS]

[1] Bishop Oldham was born in England and presumably had known MacDonald there. From 1929 to 1949 he was bishop of the Albany Diocese of the Protestant Episcopal church. During the governorship period the Roosevelts frequently attended services in Albany at the Cathedral of All Saints, where Oldham was in charge. He wrote frequently to Roosevelt, giving his views as a churchman on international matters. Oldham was a vice-president of the National Council for Prevention of War and president of the Albany branch of the Foreign Policy Association during the 1930's. He was also a member of the Pilgrims of America, at whose dinner on April 26 Ramsay MacDonald was the honored guest.

[2] In two paragraphs here omitted, Oldham urged a substantial decrease in military appropriations and the elimination of the Citizens Military Training Corps and the Reserve Officers Training Corps.

[3] Answered May 12, 1933, below.


# William Phillips, Under Secretary of State, to Marvin H. McIntyre, Assistant Secretary to the President

Washington, April 28, 1933

Dear Mr. McIntyre: The President asked me yesterday to let him have the definition of "an aggressor nation" which was made by Litvinoff at the meeting of the General Disarmament Conference on February 6, 1933. I enclose herewith the definition in question, which I shall be grateful if you would hand to the President.[1]

Sincerely yours,

William Phillips

[PSF:State:TS]

[1] Maxim Litvinov had defined an agressor nation as one who committed any one of these acts: declaration of war; invasion without declaration of war; bombardment by land, sea, or air; crossing of frontiers without permission or infringement of such permission when granted; and naval blockade (New York *Times,* Feb. 7, 1933, p. 10).


# Roosevelt to William Green, President, American Federation of Labor, Washington

[Washington] May 3, 1933

My dear President Green: I am very glad to have a representative of Labor go to the Economic Conference, to be held in London on June twelfth, as a member of the Advisory Staff of the United States Government.

Will you be good enough to let me have a suggestion for appointment?[1]

Very sincerely yours,

[OF 17:CT]

[1] Roosevelt was replying to Green's letter of May 1, 1933 (OF 17), urging appointment of a representative of labor to the United States delegation to the Economic Conference. Green pointed out that Coolidge had appointed a representative of the American Federation of Labor to act in an advisory capacity at the 1927 Economic Conference in Geneva. Green replied May 5, 1933 (OF 17), and recommended James Wilson of Cincinnati, president of the Pattern Makers League of North America and fourth vice-president of the American Federation of Labor—a Democrat, he noted. With this letter is a note, Roosevelt to Hull and Moley, May 9, 1933: "This is O.K. Will you see that he is duly placed on the advisory Staff? F.D.R."

## Roosevelt to Roger L. Scaife, London

[Washington] May 3, 1933

Dear Roger: It was good to get your note from London. I understand the feeling in England, especially among the old line Tories. Nevertheless, I think our conversations here did do good.

I am delighted to hear about Elizabeth.[1]

Always sincerely,

[PPF 373:CT]

[1] Scaife, at this time with Houghton Mifflin, wrote frequently to Roosevelt on literary matters. In his note of April 13, 1933 (PPF 373), he discussed the political situation in England where he had been on business. He said he had heard nothing but praise of Roosevelt and expressions of strong belief in his abilities. At the same time, he had found some people doubtful of the wisdom of the coming MacDonald visit. Elizabeth was his daughter, who was shortly to be married to the son of the former senator from Indiana, Albert J. Beveridge.

## Press Conference, Executive Offices of the White House, May 3, 1933, 10:45 A.M.

[Excerpt] Q: News from abroad indicates that you will agree to this pact and that you are also backing this French proposal for disarmament.[1] Can you tell us anything about it?

The President: I cannot, because everything on that has to come out via Norman Davis.

Q: Norman Davis has indicated that we should get it via you.

The President: Yes, but it would be discourteous to the Conference to have anything come out of here.

Q: The French are accusing us this morning of bad faith because of our refusal to meet gold bond interest payments in gold.[2] Have you any comment on that?

The President: Entirely off the record. The general thought is this: A government gets out an issue of bonds in its own country and they are payable within that country. The overwhelming majority of that issue is taken by its own citizens, payable here. Now, if citizens of other countries, to a very, very small number, purchase those bonds, they know in the first instance that the bonds are payable in the country of origin. Is there any moral reason why they should be favored over the 98 or 99% of the holders of those bonds who are our own citizens? Should not foreign purchasers take exactly the same risks in buying those bonds that Americans do? That is the simplest explanation of it. The idea is to treat everybody the same way. That is off the record.

Q: Mr. President, I take it from that that there will be no exports of gold allowed for service on those bonds.

The President: Yes.

Q: That is off the record, or can we use that?

The President: Yes, you can use that. Of course, that does not apply to earmarked gold and the necessary amount for trade balances.

[President's Press Conferences:T]

[1] Presumably referring to the MacDonald disarmament plan through restriction of types of weapons and armaments, and the French counterproposal that the Germans be denied the right to build sample types of prohibited weapons. See Hull to Davis, April 27, 1933, in *Foreign Relations, 1933,* I, 111–112.

[2] On May 1, 1933, the Treasury Department had barred the export of gold to meet the interest payments on securities held abroad. The move was a discretionary action under the executive order of April 20, 1933, barring export of gold.

# Press Conference, Executive Offices of the White House, May 5, 1933, 4:05 P.M.

(There were present: The Secretary of State, Mr. Jung of Italy, and the Italian Ambassador.)

[*Excerpt*] Q: Can you tell us whether you expect the St. Lawrence Waterway Treaty to go through this session or not?

The President: I don't know. I am in the same position I was two weeks ago. I have not talked to Senator Pittman about it . . .

Q: May I read you a very brief dispatch. It says that Premier MacDonald told British leaders tonight that he and President Roosevelt are in agreement that if the World Economic Conference is to be a success, then the debt question must be settled one way or the other before the conference ends. "We both pledged ourselves to leave no stone unturned and to use every means in our power to find a way to settle these debts."[1]

The President: Thank you for telling me about it.

Q: In regard to the first part: Are you in such an agreement?

The President: No . . .

Q: Has Mr. Cox[2] agreed to be a member of the Economic Conference delegation?

The President: That is what they call a "leading question." It assumes that he has been asked.

Q: Has he been asked?

The President: No comment.

Q: Mr. President, with the return of the gentlemen from England and France to their countries, the papers are full of reports of what happened—reports that are somewhat mysterious to us over here. Could you clarify your position on the debts particularly, at this time?

The President: No.

Q: Or with respect to the consultative pact?

The President: No.

Q: Can you tell us what you have taken up with Doctor Jung this afternoon?

The President: Everything.[3] (Laughter)

Q: Won't you deny these reports that we are going to have a moratorium in June?

The President: (Laughter) You are being laughed out of court.

Q: Your joint statement with Premier MacDonald said that a joint debt agreement had been reached. Does that still stand?

The President: Whatever was said here and in what they call the official communiqué still stands.[4]

Q: That statement also said that negotiations would be carried on in Washington and London in the meantime. Are they going on now?

The President: No.

Q: When are they going to be started?

The President: I don't know.

[President's Press Conferences:T]

[1] In a radio address of May 5, 1933 (printed New York *Times,* May 6, 1933, p. 2), MacDonald said, "As we both pledged ourselves to leave no stone unturned to make that conference a success, this agreement means that we are to use every means in our power to find a way to settle those debts." Atherton reported to Hull on May 6 that this statement was generally understood in England to mean that some sort of an agreement had been reached to get relief on the debts from Congress; if this proved impossible, Britain could not be condemned if she did not meet the next installment. In two cables of May 8 and 9, Davis informed Hull that in Britain the tariff truce proposed by Roosevelt was becoming "definitely tied up with some assurance or action on the debts." For himself, he believed that unless the President had some liberty of action to use the debts in economic negotiations, the United States could not use its best weapon (*Foreign Relations, 1933,* I, 493–494, 594, 597–600).

[2] James M. Cox, former governor of Ohio.

[3] See statement issued by the White House on May 6, 1933, in *Public Papers,* II, 158–159. Jung sailed for Italy on May 7.

[4] The Roosevelt-MacDonald Statement of April 25, 1933, said that no plan was under way and that only "preliminary explorations" had begun (*ibid.,* p. 147).

# Roosevelt to Cordell Hull, Secretary of State

Washington, May 6, 1933

*Very Confidential*

Memorandum for the Secretary of State: I talked this afternoon with Dr. Schacht for one half hour and made it perfectly clear that the United States will insist that Germany remain in status quo in armament and that we would support every possible effort to have the offensive armament of every other nation brought down to the German level. We discussed only land armament and not naval. I intimated as strongly as possible that we regard Germany as the only possible obstacle to a Disarmament Treaty and that I hoped Dr. Schacht would give this point of view to Hitler as quickly as possible.

You might consider whether it is worthwhile bringing this to the attention of Davis.[1]

F.D.R.

[OF 198:CT]

[1] Hjalmar Schacht, president of the Reichsbank, had taken part in the Dawes Committee discussions in 1924 and in the Reparations Commission discussions in 1929. Roosevelt's talk with him on May 6 followed a White House luncheon in his honor. See *Moffat Papers,* pp. 95–96; William E. Dodd, Jr., and Martha Dodd, eds., *Ambassador*

---

*Dodd's Diary, 1933–1938* (New York: Harcourt, Brace, 1941), pp. 4–5; and Hull, *Memoirs,* I, 237–238. Schacht's reports to the German Foreign Ministry on this and succeeding conversations with Roosevelt and Hull are in *Documents on German Foreign Policy, 1918–1945,* Series C, I, 390–394, 403–404, 423–424. Roosevelt talked with Schacht again on May 8, 10, and 12 (PPF 1-0), and a joint statement was issued on May 12 (*Public Papers,* II, 174–175). On May 11, Hull, Ambassador Hans Luther, Senator Pittman, chairman of the Foreign Relations Committee, Herbert Feis, economic adviser to the State Department, and Rexford G. Tugwell, Assistant Secretary of Agriculture, conferred with Schacht on Germany's economic and financial situation. Schacht intimated that the German government would soon be forced to declare a moratorium on payments on her external debt of five billion dollars (memorandum by Feis, May 11, 1933, *Foreign Relations, 1933,* I, 532–533). Germany declared the moratorium on June 8, 1933, excluding only funds involved in the Dawes and Young Plan loans.

# Joint Statement by Roosevelt and Tomas A. Le Breton of Argentina

[Washington] May 6, 1933

The conversations in which we have been engaged had as purpose the fullest possible exchange of views and ideas between our two countries upon the tasks that confront all countries at the coming Economic Conference. They were inspired by the wish to examine all possible phases of economic and monetary policy which by international action might restore employment, improve prices and the turnover of trade, and aid in the solution of financial and monetary difficulties. The exchange of views was to prepare the way for action between all countries, and not to lead at the moment to definite agreements.

The conversations have been characterized by the spirit of warm friendship that has long existed between these two countries, and by the quick and friendly understanding of each other's minds and spirit which has grown up between the two countries whose history has made us neighbors in mind and feeling.

We have joined in the realization that the gradual and simultaneous economic disarmament of the world is imperative, and the restoration of stable monetary conditions. We have surveyed with a close similarity of views and judgments the ways and means of bringing about an increased movement of trade between the two countries and throughout the world. We have entered into related questions of trade policy in which the two governments have an important and immediate concern.

These conversations, we believe, will greatly help to forward the common purposes that we have, and to prepare the way for undertakings at the Economic Conference and the development of the mutual interests of the two countries. In warm friendship we will continue to carry forward this work.[1]

White House
[Press Releases:M]

[1] Le Breton, Argentinian ambassador to France, had been designated, with Felipe A. Espil, Argentinian ambassador in Washington, to represent their country in the pre-Conference talks. This statement is typical of those issued by the White House on the conversations held by Roosevelt with the representatives of other countries in preparation for the World Economic Conference. (A number are printed in *Public Papers*, II, 145–149, 149–150, 150–152, 158–159, 174–175, 206–207, 211–213, 218.) Roosevelt referred to the meetings in his "Fireside Chat" of May 7, 1933 (*ibid.*, pp. 160–168), listing "four great objectives": a general reduction of armaments, a lowering of trade barriers, stabilization of currencies, and the re-establishment of friendly relations between nations.

# D. Y. Thomas, University of Arkansas, to Esther E. Lape, New York

Fayetteville, Arkansas, May 7, 1933

Dear Miss Lape: While in Washington, April 26–29, I had a conversation with Senator Robinson about the World Court. Of course you had learned from the press some time ago why it had not been brought up. Senator Robinson said that President Roosevelt requested him not to bring it up this session of Congress because it would interfere with the passage of more urgent matters. The Senator said that he had a majority on the committee ready to report it out, but deferred to the President's wish.[1]

My own opinion is that the attitude of the Hearst newspapers has had something to do with it. They will fight it to the bitter end. You probably recall what Mr. Roosevelt said about the League of Nations when a candidate for the Democratic nomination and that this was acceptable to Hearst.[2] Perhaps the President thinks it bad politics to incur the hostility of Hearst in the first few months of his administration. If he should put forward the World Court just now, Hearst probably would fight him on his domestic policy. My hope is that, when the major part of his domestic policy is out of the way, he will take up the World Court and defy Hearst. I should not be surprised if the Hearst papers open up on him before the end of the economic conference.

I do not think that you need to worry about Senator Robinson much more. Whenever the word comes from the White House, he will act.

Very truly yours,

D. Y. Thomas

[OF 202-A:TS]

¹ Cf. New York *Times,* April 5, 1933, p. 5. Thomas was a professor of history and political science; his letter was sent by Miss Lape to either the President or to Mrs. Roosevelt. She was an old friend of the Roosevelts and had been identified with the American Foundation ever since its organization by Edward Bok in 1923. She had edited *Ways to Peace* (New York: Scribners, 1924), a selection of the peace plans submitted for the Bok peace prize of 1923. Roosevelt had submitted one, which is printed in Eleanor Roosevelt's *This I Remember* (New York: Harpers, 1949), pp. 353–366. A draft of the original is in the Roosevelt papers, PSF: Roosevelt.

² Roosevelt's speech before the New York State Grange of Feb. 2, 1933; see Delano to Roosevelt, March 14, 1933, above.

## Prime Minister J. Ramsay MacDonald to Roosevelt

Whitehall, 8 May 1933.

*Personal & Unofficial.*

My Dear President, The weather on my way home was as fair and kind as my stay at the White House, and I reached Southampton much benefitted by my six days at sea. Whatever may be the results of our conversations as regards national understandings, they have given me memories of great friendship and an interesting companionship which I shall always be swift to try and renew. During the next week or two, as we anticipated, the great advantages to both our countries which our meeting could bring, if they are given a chance to mature, will have to undergo criticisms and attacks both in Washington & London, designed to render them of no avail. According to our press, you seem to be going to have a specially troublesome time. You know how well I understand your difficulties and how much I sympathise with you in meeting them. I have tried to keep you and your task in mind in everything I have said since my return, and I hope that I have not embarrassed you by anything I have done.

To an inner Committee of the Cabinet & to the Cabinet itself in more general and less specific terms, I have reported what things we reviewed. I can assure you that my colleagues are as anxious as ever to find ways of reconciling your difficulties with our own so that both your Government & ours may deal with our problems & the International Economic Conference work determined to find solutions & secure agreements.

Our good-will, however, cannot blind us to the realities of the exceedingly treacherous country we have to cross before we reach easier times. I shall refer to two points specifically:

1. *The Tariff Truce:* You know how much I favour the idea and how much I wish to cooperate in making it possible. You will remember when our experts first brought up the subject, I had to warn you of the position in which I found myself owing to negotiations which we had begun, and to objectives e.g. land settlement and agricultural protection, which had been embodied in legislation giving instructions from the House of Commons to the Cabinet to proceed immediately to apply the law. What had actually been begun and announced, we could not suspend on the chance that, six or seven months from now, the International Conference would be a complete success. All that we are now doing will be reported at the Conference when the subjects arise. On an examination of our actions, we have come to the conclusion that if our work in hand were completed, we should still be in a better position than other States whose agreement is essential, to accept proposals which would make a real success of the Conference. Moreover, it must be remembered that we were forced to begin this policy when our European competitors were hard at work setting up new barriers to damage our trade, and when every attempt we had made to fix the date for the meeting of the International Conference had failed. For instance, the Argentine Agreement (regarding which Mr. Norman Davis called upon me on Friday to say he had been instructed to protest & to indicate the possibility of some hostile action in Congress) was virtually concluded before I left for Washington. I told you of the unfortunate effect on our minds of the behaviour of some European Governments when we ourselves tried to get a Tariff Truce at Geneva a few years ago, and nothing could persuade us to go through the same experiences. Before I got home, the position which I had explained to you was worsened owing to a heavy propaganda by some newspapers, and the House of Commons had become suspicious that the proposal was another attempt to take advantage of our existing weak points & that it would mean a sacrifice of our interests alone of all our competitors. You will readily understand how difficult it is, when lack of confidence is about, to meet the plausible argument that, if there is to be a truce, it should be not only a stabilisation of the *status quo* which exposes us all the time to damaging attacks, but should be upon a standard of protection and prohibition as low as our own. I made some suggestions as to how

the truce resolution should be worded, but I do not know what was the result of your conversations with the French on the subject and whether they were helpful or otherwise. No doubt Sir Leith Ross will be able to tell us.

2. *War Debts:* I am sorry to see in the press that new troubles appear to have gathered round this question, and the quiet and steady working out of the negotiations which we had planned has been interfered with by newspaper head-lines. If the quieter ways cannot be followed, failure threatens the other good work we did, the friendly cooperation between our two countries and the International Economic Conference itself. All these misfortunes I shall strive to the end to prevent. If we are thwarted— well! the world will regret it as it reaps the consequences. Since my return, I find that the position I explained to you regarding a June payment still holds good and that there is increasing nervousness lest from good-will we should ask the country to do what it believes it cannot & ought not to do. You seem to be beset by pressure to exact all payments; I am beset by deputations demanding that I should make none. At the same time, the Government is still anxious to find some means of final settlement though economic conditions continue to narrow the margin within which we can turn. This final settlement is to be difficult enough in all conscience, but if during debt negotiations and the sittings of the Economic Conference something happens which is to create confusion in Europe and an upset in commercial as well as Government debts all over the world, I cannot visualise in what state we are all to be left. To reach a final debt settlement within three or four weeks is impossible, for it entails not only an agreement between us two, but between us separately and all our debtors and creditors. The negotiations between us will have, from stage to stage, to be examined in relation to this wider complexity, because, if not, results may break down in their application to existing facts. I can see no way out of this disaster other than one we considered: viz, a suspension of the June payment on the ground that it would seriously interrupt the negotiations for a final settlement and jeopardise the Conference, and on the definite and announced understanding that you were in no way committed to anything beyond the specific act of temporary suspension. The latest news from Washington is rather ominous as to this possibility and, frankly, it depresses me. If this cannot be arranged, then I fear much that nothing can be done; if it can be arranged, an agreement though it be difficult is within the bounds of possibility.

Supposing that the shock of disagreement on the 15th June could be avoided in the way I have indicated, the question of procedure is important. It would mean an exchange of notes and I am anxious that they should be helpful to both of us. We cannot expect you to take the initiative by informing us that in view of the great work in which we are both engaged you do not expect us to make a payment on the 15th June. If we addressed you first, our note would have to be on the lines that owing to the negotiations for a settlement which are begun and the importance of the work of the International Conference we ask that we may hold up our payment for the time being without prejudice to either of us and you might respond emphasising your views on the importance of the negotiations and the Conference, and agreeing not to regard a failure in June as a default, but making it plain that such a gesture on your part must not be taken to commit you to this, that and the other thing. If your leading representatives at the Economic Conference could come to London a day or two before the opening, these arrangements could be made easily—provided of course that we know you can accept them. It would be most desirable that the terms of our letters be settled beforehand.

I return to those pleasant days we spent together discussing how we could get over our troubles, if there were no one but ourselves charged with overcoming them. There is an open green park in front of my window (I am writing at Chequers) & thrushes singing in the garden, and I wish that you and Mrs Roosevelt—and may I add the gay and the faithful How[e] trailing a doubtfully fragrant halibut in his wake? —were here now paying me your return visit. You will all come one day, I hope however, to Lossiemouth before we get to regions more sublime, but not more attractive, & through our tobacco smoke—even if yours comes from miserable Chesterfields or Lucky Strikes—survey a ramshackle world which we strove together to help.

With my kindest regards & best wishes to both of you, I am

Yours very sincerely

J. Ramsay MacDonald

[PSF:London Economic Conference:AS]


## Felix Frankfurter, Law School of Harvard University, to Roosevelt

Cambridge, Massachusetts, May 9, 1933

Dear Mr. President: 1. When Woodrow Wilson was taunted with being a professor I ventured the remark—and it was before I was tarred with

101

the professorial stick—that all the great Presidents of the United States have essentially been educators. You are again proving that. Sunday night you again took the nation to school—as I hope you will, from time to time, take it to school.[1] With admirable simplicity and lucidity you are making known to the nation what you are doing. But you are also making the people feel—and nothing is more important for a democracy—that in a true sense of the word it is their government, and that their interests and their feelings are actively engaged.

2. You might like to have your recollection refreshed with the exact words of George Washington to which I referred the other night: "Let us raise a standard to which the wise and the honest can repair. The event is the hand of God." They were used by Washington at the Philadelphia Convention when lesser and less daring men than he opposed proposals for an effective Constitution.

3. I was, and still am, excited by your suggestion of appealing, through the heads of states, to the peoples of Europe to save the Disarmament Conference. There is every reason for hoping that the peoples of Europe will respond, as our people are responding, to an appeal by you. I am confident that the governments of Europe are much more timid and lethargic about daring action than their peoples. These governments are apparently willing to take all the risks of non-action and timid action. But they are unwilling to take risks for peace and recovery, although Europe stands at the edge of an abyss. An appeal such as you outlined Sunday afternoon—and I am not concerned with the details now—would touch the imagination and hopes of men everywhere.[2]

I was particularly heartened by your remark that it would not matter if you did "fail." Such an appeal could not in any true sense of the word "fail." You may not secure the adoption of a particular proposal. In any event you would tap new forces for peace and recovery. Such courageous assertion of leadership in behalf of right and reason would set in motion the latent forces of right and reason in men. You would thus give coherence and organization to the scattered feelings and purposes of men. I profoundly hope, therefore, that you too will raise a standard "to which the wise and honest can repair."

Always faithfully yours,

Felix Frankfurter

[PPF 140:TS]

[1] Roosevelt's second "Fireside Chat" of May 7, 1933, printed in *Public Papers,* II, 160–168.

[2] Apparently Frankfurter had talked with the President on Sunday afternoon, May 7.

# William Phillips, Under Secretary of State, to Roosevelt

Washington, May 9, 1933

Dear Mr. President: It occurs to us that, before you have a talk with Mr. Soong on political matters, that you would be interested to see the accompanying confidential memorandum prepared by Doctor Hornbeck.

You will note that Hornbeck has already been approached by Mr. Sze, the Chinese Minister, on the subject of possible action by the powers in relation to the hostilities in North China. The memorandum attached gives an account of the conversation and proceeds with comments in support of the view that the American Government should not let itself be drawn into the matter in advance of an initiative by other interested powers.

Faithfully yours,

William Phillips

[PSF:China:TS]

# [*Enclosure*] Memorandum by Stanley K. Hornbeck, Chief, Division of Far Eastern Affairs

May 9, 1933

Manchuria Situation. Tientsin-Peiping Area. China's Tentative Appeal to the Powers.

I. I called on the Chinese Minister at his request last evening. The Minister stated that Mr. T. V. Soong had received a telegram from Wang Ching-wei (China's Premier) in which the Premier, after referring to the state of hostilities in China south of the Wall, instructed Soong to inquire whether the powers could not take some step, in the nature of mediation, to bring the hostilities to an end. It had been arranged between Soong and Sze that the latter should inform me of this and discuss the matter with me.

There followed a conversation lasting an hour. In the course of the conversation I gained the impression that the Chinese Government had not formulated any project for the course which it would pursue if the powers were to offer "mediation"; also, that they entertain the hope that the President of the United States might become seized of the idea of an offer on his part to assume the role of mediator or of taking the lead in organizing a movement among the major governments either toward united action calling upon Japan to halt or toward calling upon the disputants to call an armistice and proceed to negotiations.

I made it a point throughout the discussion to make it clear that in what I said I would be expressing merely personal and unofficial opinions. I reminded the Minister of the statement which I had made to him on several previous occasions to the effect that the logic of the situation calls for the taking of the initiative, if to be taken, by the League of Nations or by powers members thereof. I said that in the immediate situation the material interests most acutely menaced in China (at Tientsin) are those of Great Britain and France. I then spoke of the risks which always confront governments which contemplate taking action in the nature of intervention or toward mediation. And I reminded him of various of the special difficulties inherent in any attempt of the powers to inject their views or wishes in connection with the present Sino-Japanese dispute. I referred to statements which I had made in our last previous lengthy conversation to the effect that it is difficult for any foreign government to act as a go-between on China's behalf for the reason that China speaks not through one but through several mouths. At this point the Minister said that Mr. T. V. Soong is authorized to speak with authority for China. I then referred to the efforts which the League and the American Government severally and collectively have made since September 18, 1931, and I said that it seemed to me logical and fit that any new effort which it might be possible now to make should be discussed first at Geneva or at capitals of states members of the League and that the United States was on record to the effect that if and when the League decided upon measures which its members were prepared to take the United States would be predisposed favorably toward cooperation. I said that I see no reason calling for or which would seem to warrant a departure by the United States from that position.

There followed a discussion of various possible courses which events may take in China.

(See memorandum of comment attached.)

II. Referring to my memorandum giving account of conversation with the Chinese Minister: It is my belief and that of other officers of this Division that the American Government should avoid taking any initiative, for the present at least, along the line apparently sought by the Chinese Premier. Were we to take such an initiative, the first effect would be to re-invigorate Japanese animus against this country. If, not withstanding that, our effort proved successful, one of the ultimate results would be a lasting "soreness" on the part both of the Japanese and of the Chinese (in general) toward us. In all probability, the effort, being led by us, would fail by virtue of refusal on the part of the Japanese to desist from the military operations in which they are engaged. If, however, they yielded, there would begin the negotiations between Japan and China which the Japanese have long been demanding. Those negotiations could have but one successful issue, a capitulation on the part of China in terms of recognition of the new status quo in Manchuria and a pledge to refrain from any further efforts to upset that status quo. The consummation of such an agreement between Japan and China would mean stultification to the position taken by and the efforts of the League and the American Government in relation to the Chino-Japanese conflict during the past two years. It would mean military and diplomatic victory for Japan. It would enable the Japanese to consolidate their position on the Continent and prepare for their next move (either further coercion of China or conflict with Russia or conflict with the United States). It is not to the interest of the United States or of China or of the world that such an agreement, under such circumstances, be concluded. Better that the situation between Japan and China remain fluid, even though it mean further suffering for the time being for the Chinese and a continuation of uncertainty and apprehension by and on behalf of foreign nationals in China and foreign powers in general. In some of the major foreign countries neither the governments nor the people appear as yet to have grasped the full significance of the movements which have been and which are being made by the Japanese military machine. Events at Shanghai a year ago almost (but not quite) made the thing clear to the British. Probably impending events, if the thing be not checked now and prematurely, in North China should serve to make it clearer to them. Likewise, the French. Enlightenment with regard to this matter comes slowly. Some people learn by observation, reasoning, and the use of the imagination. Others learn only by experience. It can no longer be contended by the Japanese with any approximation to appearance of reality that the movements in which their army is engaged on Chinese soil are in "defense" of the lives and property of their nationals. They are now engaged in movements the objective of which is to compel the Chinese to sign an agreement the substance of which would be China's assent to the amputation of Manchuria and the ultimate purpose of which would be dismemberment of China. They are making "war" in fact (though not in name) an instrument of national policy. This is a clear violation of the Kellogg Pact. The conclusion of the agreement which they have in contemplation would be in violation, on the part both of Japan and of China, of provisions of the Nine-Power Treaty. The whole transaction has been and is in violation of the Covenant of the League. Such being the case, the American Government should by no means become the original sponsor of the idea that such a course be pursued. We should be one of the last, rather than the first, of the foreign powers to take up with that idea. The initiative, if from any quarter, should come from one or more of the major countries members of the League. It might best come to us from the League; next best, from the British and the French Governments. If and when it thus comes, there would be warrant for our giving it serious consideration.

It should be kept in mind that approaches have already been made to our Minister[1] and to the British Minister[2] and probably to the French Minister in Peiping, by Chinese in certain different capacities, and by officials of Japan, in this connection. The British Minister explored the problem and finally decided that there was nothing further that it seemed wise to do. The potential go-between would find himself in the impossible position of trying to bring together two parties neither of whom could be relied upon in relation to the transaction contemplated. We gave our Minister instruction that he was to take no initiative but was to keep in close contact with his colleagues and if he were approached with a definite, practicable, constructive proposal by the British and the French he should receive it in a cooperative attitude. We suggested to him various of the hazards of the situation and told him that he might discuss the whole matter with his British colleague. He informed us that the British Minister had received instructions indicating that the British Government's attitude was similar to ours. There the matter stands. Any change can best be worked out by the Ministers of the powers at Peiping who are in close contact with events and men on the spot. If and as the hostilities bring the contending armies into close proximity to Peiping and Tientsin, British, French, Italian, Belgian and to some extent German anxiety will increase. We can afford to wait and watch.

As Japanese armed forces advance into China proper, the whole problem for Japan becomes greater, more complicated and increasingly unsusceptible of an early and satisfactory solution. At the same time, the strength of Chinese nationalism should be increased and some of the problems of the Nanking Government be diminished. Occupation by Japan of the whole Peiping-Tientsin area would tend to increase the amount of apprehension with which the situation is viewed by Great Britain and by Russia. Those two countries in particular stand to lose as Japan gains. The United States has not much to lose. The principles of our Far Eastern policy and our ideals with regard to world peace may be further scratched and dented (they have been considerably so already in this connection); and our trade prospects may be somewhat further impaired; but from the point of view of material interests there is nothing there that is vital to us. In the long run, our interests would be best served by a complete exposure of Japan's program, her strength and/or weakness, and as complete as possible involvement of herself in the situation which she has created and is developing there: given time, the flood tide of her invasion will reach its height and the ebb will follow. For that reason, among others, we should avoid pressing, so far as we are concerned, for an early, premature and inconclusive "peace." Let those whose interests would be better served by such a development take the initiative toward its consummation.

It is realized that the above is not a humanitarian view. It also is realized that a continuation of military reverses to the Chinese armies, and possible loss of Peiping and Tientsin, may result in serious political repercussions adversely affecting the stability of the Nanking Government. That Government, however, is between the devil and the deep sea: the devil being the prospect of further military adversities and the deep sea being the potential conclusion of a disastrous "peace." Its security will not be ensured by the acceptance of either of these hazards.

[PSF:China:T]

[1] Nelson T. Johnson.
[2] Sir Miles Lampson.

# Press Conference, Executive Offices of the White House, May 10, 1933, 10:49 A.M.

The President: Good morning. The really important news is that we are going to have a moratorium on news over Saturday and Sunday.

Q: Speaking of moratoriums, did you see the speech that Ramsay MacDonald made yesterday in which he said that an agreement had been reached that we should enter into a consultative pact?[1]

The President: Careful; don't misquote him, get it right.

Q: Will you read it and comment on it, please.

The President: You can print his language.

Q: What was that, Mr. President?

The President: You can print his language.

Q: What he said was that agreements were entered into here—

The President: What did you say? I will have to read it to you.

Q: You will find it on the front page, in the box, in the *Times*.

The President: For your information, I will read what he said. I take it that it was properly transmitted.

One of the points we both considered and had very clearly in front of us was the menace to the tranquillity of mind of Europe which the recent events in Europe had created. We saw quite clearly the new risks with which the Disarmament Conference was being faced.

Yet I am very happy to say that the United States Government is prepared to play a further part in tranquilizing Europe by agreeing, if the Disarmament Conference comes to anything like a satisfactory issue, to take its part in consultative pacts, the effect of which will be to increase the security of Europe and the safety of threatened nations against war.

This is a very considerable advance. Secretary of State Stimson began it in that courageous statement he made before he went out of office regarding the need to redefine neutrality and the present government has expressed its intention of going further in making its obligations quite definite and authoritative. An announcement will be made in Washington in due time, when the matter is further considered and its details dealt with.

I will tell you what I am going to do. I will talk to you off the record about it. We haven't got to the point of saying anything, so it has to be entirely off the record and just informative.

Both Platforms, I think certainly the Democratic Platform, favored consultative pacts. Now, what is a consultative pact? It means, and it meant in the Platform, that if all the nations agreed to set up some kind of machinery for consultation in the event of an act of aggression, we will be very glad to have somebody there to consult with. I consider that to be a step forward. But it is not, and do not get the idea that it means that we bind ourselves in the first instance to agree with the verdict. Now, that is a very different thing. We agree to consult. Therefore it does not tie the hands of the United States in any shape, manner or form and leaves our final action entirely up to us. Now, that is the simplest way of putting it. We in no way—in no way—are limiting our own right to determine our own action after the facts are brought out.

Q: Mr. President, did MacDonald give you to understand that that would be sufficient to satisfy the political security demands of Europe?

The President: Again, I can tell you off the record that that position of ours seems satisfactory to the British and to the French.

Q: To what end do we consult?

The President: Let me again illustrate, off the record.

This disarmament proposal of MacDonald's which has been before the Disarmament Conference in Geneva quite a long time—a good many months—it is divided into two parts. Part one is called security and part two is called disarmament. Parts two, three, four and five are called disarmament and parts two to five bring up for discussion a definite plan for the taking of what might be called the first steps towards the objective. The objective, most simply stated, is to reduce and eventually to practically remove the weapons of offensive warfare, in other words, the weapons of attack. If we can limit and eventually remove the weapons of attack, you automatically build up and strengthen the weapons of defense. If you remove the weapons of offense and thereby strengthen the weapons of defense, you give security to every nation, including the small nations.

The simplest illustration is by asking what are the weapons of offense that render the weapons of defense ineffective? Well, there is gas. You can flood a fort with gas and make it untenable. Then there is heavy, mobile artillery, because you can smash a fort with heavy artillery and you can smash trenches with heavy artillery, and you can smash barbed wire entanglements with heavy artillery. Then there are bombing planes—probably planes of all kinds—because they can drop things on top of forts, on top of trenches and on top of barbed wire. Then there is what I call land battleships. Those are the perfectly enormous tanks— they are getting bigger and bigger every day—that will walk through a ditch and over various entanglements and very soon, probably, be able to walk over a fort.

If you can eliminate those eventually—I am talking about a long-distance picture—if you can eliminate the weapons of offense, you have accomplished something and you have made the nation secure against a sudden attack.

Well, that is something that has got to be done by steps. The MacDonald plan contemplates taking the first step.

That is the simplest way of describing what the MacDonald disarmament plan is and, if the first step can be taken, there is a better chance of being able to take the second step and the third step and the fourth step towards the ultimate objective.

109

So much for the disarmament clause of the MacDonald plan.

Then you come down to what is called part one, security. Part one, security, proposes to set up certain machinery to determine who is the aggressor, and what will be done to the aggressor. There is a desire to work out some means of consultation in the event of an act of aggression in order to implement the Kellogg-Briand Pact.

Now, what that machinery may be is still very much in the air—the details of it. There are objections to the MacDonald proposal because it presupposes that if a nation commits an act of aggression that then there would be called a conference and that the conference would meet and act as what might be called a jury on the act of aggression complained of. It also presupposes, and here is the weakness of it, that the aggressor nation would be very quietly sitting still during this whole period. That is a practical objection and they are trying to work out some more practical means of consulting together to put some kind of a determination on an act of aggression.

The position that I have taken—this has got to be off the record, I am sorry, because it is a thing that has got to break on the other side if it does break at all—the position I have taken is that both parties here are entirely ready to sit at whatever kind of a consultative meeting is provided for. The idea is to work out some sort of machinery and then, having sat there, there would be a report to Washington as to what the other nations think and then we will be entirely free to do whatever we want to do. In other words, we would not be bound by the American who happened to be sitting in the consultative pact. He would report home.

Q: Mr. President, it seems to me that the consultative pact is almost identical to our relations with the League of Nations.

The President: It is an entirely different thing. You cannot use comparisons in that connection.

Q: So far, they have talked very frequently about consultative pacts.

The President: Oh, yes.

Q: But we always took the stand that we would consult as things came up but do nothing obligatory—not be obliged to consult. With this new arrangement, would we be obliged to consult?

The President: We would say quite frankly that we would sit in and consult. There is nothing particularly startling about that, when you come down to it.

Q: But we have that machinery now.

The President: Sure. In other words, it sounds like a huge change in policy, but it is very little change in policy. It is an announcement that we are going to do something that we would do anyhow.

Q: Would the other countries be more bound by their delegates to the pact?

The President: As I see it, the MacDonald suggestion was that in this consultation pact, at this meeting, this conference, that the European nations and Russia and Japan should agree, the larger powers, by unanimous vote and the smaller powers by a majority vote. But you had better, some of you, read the language of it, because part of it is still very much in the air. It is simply something to try to build on.

Q: Mr. President, inasmuch as Premier MacDonald said something for publication and this that you have said is off the record, cannot you give us something on the record?

The President: This is study, off the record.

Q: But it is not news. (Laughter)

The President: I am just trying to be helpful.

Q: May we use anything as coming from our own imagination or knowledge?

The President: No, I think it is just to enable you not to get stampeded by things coming over from the other side.

Q: In that connection, there are a lot of things coming over on debts. Do you care to comment on that?

The President: I will talk off the record also on debts. Now this is entirely off the record. Do not get stampeded by anything you hear from the other side on debts. Well, I will tell you frankly what the situation is. It is not very much further than it was a long time ago. And the position is exactly the same position that I took, I think it was last November. In other words, that a debtor nation has, at any time, the right to come before a creditor nation and lay its case before the creditor nation. Now, that has not been done by any of them officially. So, you see, we are not nearly as far along as most of the stories, and especially the headline people, would have you believe.

And then, the other part of it is, if you will read the joint statement of Mr. MacDonald and myself, you will find that that part is wholly true.[2] In other words, that we were informally exploring, that is all. No proposal has been made by us and no proposal has been made by the other fellows or any of them. You know those headlines—where is the *Herald-Tribune*—I don't blame anybody for writing stories and the headline writers have a bad time of it too because they have so very little space. For example, "U.S. to discuss war debts concurrently at

London." That does not say if they want to talk to us, it says they are to talk to us. If our fellows go off to the Economic Conference, they are not going to have authority to discuss debts. That stays with Pop— right here. (Laughter)

Now, if somebody should happen to speak, let us say it is in London, to one of the American delegates—I almost said who—about that, probably the American delegate will say, "That is interesting. If you want me to transmit something to the President, I will be glad to do it," but it is going to stay right here.

Also, the word "concurrently" does not mean that they will gang us any more than I would have suggested that or permitted that two or three months ago. They talk with us individually.

Q: But, Mr. President, public opinion, particularly over here, has probably been more stampeded by these headlines than we have. Couldn't we clear it up on our own authority, otherwise they will be still stampeded.

The President: No, go to the headline man privately.

Q: Would you be willing to say what legislation you are going to ask Congress for in order to deal with the situation after recess?

The President: There again. I have forgotten which story it was this morning, but one of the stories—I guess it was the *Times*. Oh, I know, it was Arthur's story.[3]

Q: Little Arthur? (Laughter)

The President: Why, he talked to—I wish they would put the names down, it would be so much clearer. He says that an Administration leader today—oh, come on and tell me what his name is—and then a whole paragraph about the impression the Administration leader is supposed to have conveyed. Then he goes on to say that an Administration leader of almost equal rank had another idea and then he gives another paragraph.

For example, there was a story—what was it, three weeks or a month ago—that said there was a possibility that I would send a message to the Congress on debts. Now, I suppose I could have stopped it by saying there is also a possibility that I will send no message to the Congress on debts. Well, that is still the situation. I don't know. I don't know any more than you do whether I will send a message or, if I did send a message, what would be in it. Now, that is literally true, I don't know.

Q: Isn't there a possibility that somebody will offer a resolution instead of your sending a message?

The President: No.

Q: Are you giving it consideration or do you not know yet what you will do?

The President: There isn't enough material to work on as yet. That is the easiest way to put it.

Q: Abroad, do you mean?

The President: Either abroad or here. There is no material to work on.

Q: You said that our willingness to agree to the consultative pact would be dependent on something like success by the Disarmament Conference. What do you consider "something like success?"

The President: I will say, offhand, that we are one hundred per cent behind the idea of taking the first step in the removal of the weapons of offensive warfare. We are for that step. And we will consider it successful if we can get a substantial part of the proposed step. We want it to be very substantial, because, actually, we would like this first step to go a great deal further than it proposes to go.

Q: Is that off the record too?

The President: Yes, that is off the record, all of it. . . .

Q: Mr. President, there is a third subject that has been very much in the print and that is the tariff. What may happen in the way of getting authority from the Congress to deal with tariff?

The President: Well, that is still like the debts. There is the possibility of sending something up there in the way of a message. I think there is a greater possibility there, I would say almost a probability, but what it will be, I don't know.

I am a little bit cheered up this morning about tariff, because apparently Great Britain is going along with the temporary tariff truce, and, if we can get substantial unanimity on this preliminary tariff truce between now and the twelfth of June, when we make our motion, there will be more chance of getting the second truce to last through the Conference.

Q: What other countries so far would have agreed to the truce—Italy and Belgium?

The President: Italy and Germany and Belgium, I think.

Q: Japan?

The President: China—I have not heard from Japan. They may have others over there but, of course, there again, Davis may have some that have come into London, but have not come here.

Q: Mr. President, do you or do you not consider the solution of the war debt vital to the success of the Economic Conference?

The President: Have I stopped tickling the soles of my mother-in-law? (Laughter) Yes or no.

I don't know, it is too difficult a question to answer. Are my mother-in-law's feet ticklish? In other words, of course some cleaning up of the debt issue would be a fine thing, but it is not necessarily tied in with the success of the Economic Conference. The two are not necessarily wired together. They may be, what shall I say, "platonic friends". . . .

(Mr. Early spoke to the President)

The President: For the sake of our visitors from overseas, I want to repeat very simply that "off the record" means merely "in confidence." It is only for information to prevent, more than anything else, the wrong kind of stories from being written.

Q: Do I understand that everything you said on debts is off the record?

The President: Yes.

Q: Your remarks on tariff?

The President: What did I say on tariff?

Q: You said there might be a resolution.

The President: I think we can use that as background, if you want.

Q: Can we say that you approve that dispatch of what Ramsay MacDonald said—the dispatch you read there?

The President: No.

Q: Would you regard the raising of the tariff under the provisions of the Farm Bill as a violation of all these tariff treaties we are working for?

The President: I think so. I don't think we can raise any tariffs until the twelfth of June. I don't think it would be necessary . . .

Q: Do you expect to see Schacht again today?

The President: This afternoon, I think about three or three-thirty.[4]

[President's Press Conferences:T]

[1] MacDonald's speech in Commons on May 9 was reported in the New York *Times* of May 10, 1933, p. 1.

[2] The joint statement of April 25, 1933, printed in *Public Papers*, II, 147.

[3] An article by Arthur Krock in the New York *Times* of May 10, p. 1 quoted an "Administration leader" on what war debt legislation the President would seek from Congress, and other "leaders" to the effect that he expected the debtor nations to meet the June 15, 1933, deadline; that he expected a general default; that he would ask Congress for authority to reduce debts; and that he would ask authority to suspend all June payments of nations who had met the December installment.

[4] Part of this press conference transcript is printed in *Public Papers*, II, 169–174.

# Herbert Feis, Economic Adviser to the State Department, to Louis M. Howe, Personal Secretary to the President

Washington, May 10, 1933

Dear Mr. Howe: This matter was talked over with the President yesterday, and the President gave me a letter addressed to Senator Fletcher and Mr. Rayburn.[1] I submit the attached as a way of reporting to the President on the subject.

Sincerely yours,

Herbert Feis

[OF 100-B:TS]

[1] Senator Duncan U. Fletcher of Florida and Rep. Sam Rayburn of Texas were co-sponsors of the Securities Act of 1933. The letter referred to is presumably the one also sent to Senator Hiram W. Johnson, May 20, 1933, below.

# [*Enclosure*] Herbert Feis to Cordell Hull, Secretary of State

[Washington] May 10, 1933

Mr. Secretary: I spent this morning down at the Capitol trying to assure that when the Federal Securities Act went into conference that Title 2—creating a foreign securities corporation—which has been attached to the Senate Bill would be rejected.

I saw Senator Fletcher, who is Chairman of the Banking and Currency Committee of the Senate, Representative Rayburn, Chairman of the Judiciary Committee, and Senator Wagner,[1] who will be one of the Senate conferees. To all of them I showed the President's letter.[2]

May I take this occasion to emphasize again the importance for the proper operation of the State Department of dropping this feature of the Bill for the following reasons:

(1) It would create a quasi-official body that would deal with foreign governments, outside of the control of our ministers, and more or less ignorant of the state of our relations with that foreign government. The dangers of confusion would be very great. In some instances, such as, for example, Mexico, financial relations are the very core of the relations with the foreign governments, and if an outside body of an unofficial character were bringing pressure on these foreign governments or making proposals, the whole conduct of the Department's work would be complicated and confused.

115

(2) When this body put through debt settlements and recommended them to the bondholders, the bondholders would consider that the Government was recommending these settlements, and in the case of later defaults, would charge the Government with the responsibility.

In other cases where, because of poor financial conditions, this body could do nothing, the bondholders would charge the Government with neglect.

(3) There could be no assurance as to the character of the personnel selected.

(4) Private bondholders could charge that since their own efforts to secure repayment were being blocked by the semi-official body, they had a grievance against the Government.

I could add much to this critical statement, but I think this is enough to bring out the dangers inherent in the piece of legislation.[3]

[OF 100-B:CT]

---

[1] Senator Robert F. Wagner of New York.

[2] See Feis to Howe, May 10, 1933, n. 1, above.

[3] Title 2 of Senate bill 875, here discussed by Feis, had been added on motion of Senator Hiram Johnson on May 8, 1933 (*Cong. Rec.*, vol. 77, pp. 2987–2995). The State Department favored a nongovernmental organization modeled on the British Council of Foreign Bondholders (Feis to Hull, March 15, *Foreign Relations, 1933,* I, 934–936).

## Richard Washburn Child to Roosevelt

Washington, D.C., May 11, 1933

My dear Mr. President: To relieve the holders of seven billions of foreign securities, a part of which is in default, I proposed to you that there should be created by Congress a Federal Corporation to act as a source of information and as a collection agency. You, approving that plan, told me that certain groups of New York gentlemen had volunteered this function, which I said would be dangerous for you, the Secretary of State, or of the Treasury to recognize as a self-appointed monopoly, because it might be like a burglar who came back as the doctor in the ambulance.[1]

If I am not mistaken you asked me to see Senator Johnson to introduce a bill which would have, undoubtedly, an appeal to the small and suffering holders of private foreign indebtedness, who should be protected by the best efforts that the government can put forth. This amendment to the securities bill has been accepted by the Senate and informally by the House Conferees. It would relieve you and the Secretary of State of the importunings of those who would use the State Department or the Executive Office as a collection agency; it would relieve you and the Department of State of the odium of giving approval by special privilege to any group of self-appointed and volunteer representatives, whether or no they stand in the stead of the bankers who distributed bad risks and now continue to speculate in those bad risks for the racket which nets the foreign debt as a profit.

I now learn from the Congress that you have sent an informal note asking that this legislation shall be dropped. Inasmuch as you deputed me to see the Senator from California in behalf of this legislation, I am unable to credit these rumors since Senator Johnson to whom you referred me and I have not been notified directly by you.[2]

Always faithfully,

Richard Washburn Child

[OF 242:TS]

[1] Child, a lawyer and writer, was ambassador to Italy from 1921 to 1924. He had talked with Roosevelt at the White House on April 8 and 20 (PPF 1-0). The "New York gentlemen" are not further identified here. Those forming the original group of advisers were Charles P. Howland, Pierre Jay, Thomas Nelson Perkins, George Rublee, Prof. Edwin Kemmerer of Princeton, and Allen W. Dulles (Feis to Hull, March 15, 1933, *Foreign Relations, 1933*, I, 934–936). This group was later enlarged; see White House statement of Oct. 20, 1933, in *Public Papers*, II, 411–413. Directors of the organization as finally formed are listed in an editorial note to Roosevelt to Senator Frederick Steiwer, Nov. 6, 1933, below.
[2] No reply to this letter has been found.

# Press Conference, Executive Offices of the White House, May 12, 1933, 4:06 P.M.

[*Excerpt*] Q: You said that there would be a possibility that you would have some request to make of Congress for authority with respect to war debts.[1] Is it a probability now in the face of the French action?

The President: There has been no change since last Monday.

Q: As to the European conferences, can you give us your impression, off the record, as to whether we are getting anywhere at all?

The President: I don't dare talk on it extemporaneously, that is my trouble. I would say, off the record, that things are in better shape than they were when the conferences began, because then we had nothing to go on at all and today we have something pretty definite to go on. I think the Secretary of State got word from London this afternoon—you had better check with him—that there is practical agreement on the part of the eight powers represented on the organizing of the conference.[2]

Q: That has been announced?

The President: Now, there we have something tangible.

Q: Is it tangible, considering all the reservations that have been made?

The President: I think so, yes. It is pretty tangible and it is a step toward the goal. Furthermore, we are substantially agreed on the various economic principles. And I think the course of disarmament has been distinctly clarified. In other words, as a result of a month's work, the general atmosphere, I feel, is distinctly better.

Q: Would there by any objection to writing generally along those lines?

The President: Writing along those lines; that would be all right.

[President's Press Conferences:T]

---

[1] See press conference of May 10, 1933, above. On May 11 the French government decided to ask the Chamber of Deputies to authorize payment of the defaulted Dec. 15, 1932, payment if the United States would agree to a moratorium during the Economic Conference. This would have meant a postponement of the June 15, 1933, payment pending a final settlement (New York *Times,* May 12, 1933, p. 1).

[2] Roosevelt here refers to Davis' dispatch to Hull of May 12 (*Foreign Relations, 1933,* I, 601–602). Davis reported that the American tariff proposal as described in his dispatches of May 8 and 9 (*ibid.,* pp. 594–595, 596), had been approved by the eight governments represented on the organizing committee. The eight governments agreed that they would not, before June 12 or during the Conference, "adopt any new initiatives which might increase the many varieties of difficulties now arresting international commerce." The British obtained a reservation to the effect that nothing in the resolution would prevent them from imposing "reasonable" export quotas; these and other refinements were discussed in further dispatches to Hull from Davis of May 12 and 13, and from Marriner (in Paris) of May 15 (*ibid.,* pp. 602–605, 605–606, 606–607).

Hull acknowledged the dispatch from Davis mentioned above with the words: "This is a splendid job. You have my best congratulations" (*ibid.,* p. 602). The New York *Times* correspondent in London (Ferdinand Kuhn, Jr.) cabled that the declaration was accepted there as a triumph for Roosevelt's international policy (New York *Times,* May 13, 1933, p. 1).

## Roosevelt to Bishop G. Ashton Oldham, Albany Diocese, Albany

[Washington] May 12, 1933

My dear Bishop Oldham: I am really grateful for that fine letter you have sent me.[1] Thank you ever so much for it. It is splendid of you to say those nice things about what we are doing. The conferences with the Prime Minister and others were most interesting indeed and I hope and confidently believe they will prove helpful in the solution of the problems which are facing all of us.

We have had strenuous times here, but I am enjoying it all immensely and feeling very fit.

It was good to hear from you.

Very sincerely yours,

[PPF 418:CT]

[1] April 28, 1933, above.

## William Phillips, Under Secretary of State, to Roosevelt

Washington, May 12, 1933

Dear Mr. President: Richard Washburn Child has just sent me a communication, which he says that he "strongly suspects will be personally presented" to you.[1]

I know of your attitude towards this matter, but venture to send you the enclosed memorandum prepared by Doctor Feis,[2] in the event that Mr. Child should call upon you for a further discussion of the "Federal Corporation." The memorandum sets forth consecutively the reasons against the suggested Federal Securities Bill.

Faithfully yours,

William Phillips

[OF 242:TS]

[1] Presumably Child's letter of May 11, above. No other communication from Child to the President has been found and Child may have asked Phillips to transmit his letter to the White House.
[2] An elaboration of Feis's statement of May 10, 1933, above.

## Owen Johnson to Roosevelt

Stockbridge, Mass., May 12, 1933

Dear Mr. President: I am sending you herewith the results of a rather intimate contact with French political elements covering a period from November 20th to April 23rd, the date when I landed here with the Herriot party. Due to the fact that I was one of the first to present the French side here during the war I have been on friendly terms with the Foreign Office and a number of their political leaders. I tried in my articles for the French press this winter to point out the blunder of a December default and later in my contacts told them plainly of the full extent of the reaction in public opinion here and the difficulties which they themselves had imposed on you in your desire to be generous and wise in the treatment of the whole debt question. During this time I knew Mr. Herriot, Mr. Laval, Béranger, Tardieu, Paul Reynaud, Daladier, Sarraut, Monzie and other members of the governing party, and had intimate contacts with the leading journalists of the different political groups. I likewise discussed with Mr. Rist[1] on several occasions the value of a complete exposition on his part of the history of the French gold reserve in order to answer current German propaganda as to the wrecking of the pound sterling and the threat against the dollar. I heard a very frank account from Mr. Laval of his conference with Mr. Hoover in which he placed the initiative of the cancelling of German debts directly on England. Some correction of this was made by Mr. Rist.

In accordance with my thesis that France must help you to help them, I suggested to Mr. Laboullaye and later at luncheon to Mr. Leger, now head of the Foreign Office, the advisability of France's official announcement of its recognition of the full sum of four hundred and seven million dollars on the commercial debt of the war stocks. I pointed out that they had officially reported, some years ago, a resale of over three hundred millions of dollars and that, as there was no question in the mind of any responsible Frenchman as to whom this money belonged, it would be politic to receive the benefit of the gesture rather than risk an attack where they were most vulnerable. (I know personally that Ambassador Edge is contemplating such a criticism at a future date. As a matter of fact it was in the deleted portion of his farewell speech before the American Club, you may recall.) Every public man I talked to, without respect of party, agreed that there could be no question of the acknowledgment of this indebtedness of four hundred and seven millions. This fact may be of value to you in estimating the final sum; and I venture to suggest that an intimation to the French Ambassador might bring an official declaration which would present France in a more sympathetic attitude here and so give aid to you in handling American public opinion.

In all my contacts I tried to arrive at some idea of what the French really expected to pay. I should place it at a minimum of a lump sum of one billion dollars. Mr. Caillaux stated at a finance committee meeting of the Senate, considering the first Daladier budget, that certain temporary concessions had to be made to the taxpayers because they would be asked within the year for at least eight hundred million dollars. A member of the commission, himself present, told me this. The French are naturally extremely cagey on this subject, but I found on the boat when discussing it with the opposition press—Lauzanne, Pertinax, Le Chartier—that a billion dollars was really the sum in the back of their minds. This coming from the opposition was significant. Rist himself took this suggested figure extremely calmly.

In this connection, Ambassador Edge told me that he had been negotiating with Tardieu on the basis of a lump payment of one billion dollars, but that Mr. Hoover had felt that Congress would not agree. (Mr. Tardieu is extremely anti-American and is the one man who is blocking the 15th of December payment. He personally sent for Paul Reynaud, who was going to vote favorably, and asked him as a personal favor to refrain from voting.) Would it be of value to Mr. Herriot's party to get Ambassador Edge to publish this story as part of his reminiscences? I am on good terms with him and could make the suggestion. It would show that the leader of the opposition to payment was himself considering such a sum. At any rate it would force him to some explaining and might weaken his authority.

On the question of disarmament I hope I am a false prophet, but I am extremely doubtful of the French yielding an inch now that Hitler has shown his hand. Up to Hitler's arrival nine out of every ten Frenchmen in every class and party believed two things; that no real peace could be guaranteed without a genuine rapprochment with Germany and that the Polish Corridor was a great blunder. Today the French are afraid of the same peace they have been arguing for. This peace now seems to them permitting the growth and strength of their declared enemies, Germany and Italy. I lunched with Mr. Herriot and five of the present ministry on the day after the Mussolini-MacDonald interviews. They were in a panic. For forty-eight hours they felt themselves politically isolated. The full racial megalomania of the Hitler program has completely shifted French opinion. I dined with Mr. Herriot on the night we left the gold standard. He discussed the German question with his accustomed freedom and remarked that he had completely reversed his attitude; that no understanding with them was now possible and added "we shall have to fight them again." All this has a bearing on the disarmament proposals. Even if we should be willing to back up a ten years truce I do not really believe that French opinion will now favor binding France's hands for that period. I believe they are reluctantly convinced that no change in sentiment can be expected from either the German or Italian masses, that since war is inevitable in the future better to allow it to be provoked now with the object of dismembering Germany and isolating Prussia. To link disarmament and debts is dangerous. Mr. Hoover offended them deeply by this course. They naturally will not endanger their security for any compensation offered.

The danger to American interests is the political situation of Mr. Herriot. He has enemies in his own party. Daladier, Boncour and Chautemps each considers himself a leader and has no desire to see Mr. Herriot return to power. I saw this plainly during the period between December 15th and March 15th when the attitude of the Daladier-Boncour group was frankly critical of Mr. Herriot's utterances. I believe the more Mr. Herriot himself is protected from making decisions or influencing decisions the better for his political future and American interests. His friends will willingly make him the scapegoat. I return to my original suggestion that Mr. Daladier himself should be influenced to make an official declaration concerning the debt due on the war stocks. Even Mr. Tardieu would not dare to oppose this and we would start with that much in the bag. The funding of the debts by the Mellon-Béranger agreement has had a very confusing effect on public opinion. It might clarify the situation to unscramble them.

Under ordinary circumstances I should have come down to Washington feeling as I do that my experience would be of some value to you, but knowing how completely taken up every moment of your time must be, it seems better for me to embody some of my ideas in a letter. In conclusion let me say, do not underestimate the power that you have over mass opinion in France. Throughout France today is a rising demand from all quarters that the French governmental system should have the same ruthless pruning and reorganization which you have so miraculously brought to the United States. Everything you do or say is followed with the greatest interest. You will always have this trump card up your sleeve—a direct appeal if necessary to public opinion over the heads of politicians.

Hoping that my facts may be of some use at least in confirming your own information,

I am always faithfully yours,

Owen Johnson[2]

[PPF 611:TS]

---

[1] Charles Rist, economic adviser to the French government and former deputy governor of the Bank of France. He was one of the group of financial specialists who accompanied Herriot to Washington for the talks preliminary to the London Economic Conference.

[2] Johnson, playwright and novelist (probably best known today for his stories of school life such as *The Tennessee Shad* and *The Varmint*), was an active Democratic party worker in Stockbridge, and in 1936 and 1938 ran unsuccessfully for Congress from the first Massachusetts district. He wrote occasionally to Roosevelt and Democratic party leaders on party matters (PPF 611). The letter here printed was sent by Johnson to Mrs. Roosevelt, to be shown to the President if she thought it of value. Mrs. Roosevelt wrote Johnson on May 27 that she was giving his letter to the President, and Roosevelt wrote Johnson from Pulpit Harbor, Maine, June 24, 1933, saying he had been "delighted to read it—especially because it goes along with my own views to such a large extent" (PPF 611).

# Roosevelt to Benito Mussolini, Prime Minister of Italy, Rome

Washington, May 14th, 1933

My dear Mr. Prime Minister: I am asking Ambassador Long, who is a very old personal friend of mine, to give you this note when he presents his credentials. I only wish that I might have the opportunity to see you myself, to give you my greetings and to talk over many things in which you and I have a common interest.

May I tell you how much I appreciated my talks with Signor Jung? His frankness, his complete understanding of our mutual problems, and his delightful personality gave me great pleasure and great confidence. Thank you for sending him.

Those two very wonderful volumes have thrilled me, not only because of their great artistic merit, but also because Vergil and Horace were my favorites in my student days—and I shall keep them among my treasures. When I am gone they will repose in the Library of Congress.[1]

And in the meantime they will be symbols of the greatness of the spirit and understanding of the Italian people—and of you their leader whom I hope some day to meet.

I am, my dear Mr. Mussolini, Very sincerely yours,

Franklin D. Roosevelt

[PSF:Italy:T:Copy][2]

[1] See Mussolini to Roosevelt, April 24, 1933, above.
[2] This letter, including the President's signature, is a typed ribbon copy on White House stationery. It is the official copy of the autograph letter sent.


## Roosevelt to the Congress, May 16, 1933

To the Congress: For the information of the Congress I am sending herewith a message that I have addressed this morning to the sovereigns and presidents of those nations participating in the Disarmament Conference and the World Monetary and Economic Conference.[1]

I was impelled to this action because it has become increasingly evident that the assurance of world political and economic peace and stability is threatened by selfish and short sighted policies, actions and threats of actions.

The sincere wish for this assurance by an overwhelming majority of the nations faces the danger of recalcitrant obstruction by a very small minority, just as in the domestic field the good purposes of a majority in business, labor or in other cooperative efforts are often frustrated by a selfish few.

The deep-rooted desire of Americans for better living conditions and for the avoidance of war is shared by mass humanity in every country. As a means to this end I have, in the message to the various nations, stressed the practical necessity of reducing armaments. It is high time for us and for every other nation to understand the simple fact that the invasion of any nation, or the destruction of a national sovereignty, can be prevented only by the complete elimination of the weapons that make such a course possible today.

Such an elimination will make the little nation relatively more secure against the great nation.

Furthermore, permanent defenses are a non-recurring charge against governmental budgets while large armies continually rearmed with improved offensive weapons constitute a recurring charge. This, more than any other factor today is responsible for governmental deficits and threatened bankruptcy.

The way to disarm is to disarm. The way to prevent invasion is to make it impossible.

I have asked for an agreement among nations on four practical and simultaneous steps:

First, that through a series of steps the weapons of offensive warfare be eliminated;

Second, that the first definite step be taken now;

Third, that while these steps are being taken no nation shall increase existing armaments over and above the limitations of treaty obligations;

Fourth, that subject to existing treaty rights no nation during the disarmament period shall send any armed force of whatsoever nature across its own borders.

Our people realize that weapons of offense are needed only if other nations have them and they will freely give them up if all the nations of the world will do likewise.

In the domestic field the Congress has labored in sympathetic understanding with me for the improvement of social conditions, for the preservation of individual human rights, and for the furtherance of social justice.

In the message to the nations which I herewith transmit I have named the same objectives. It is in order to assure these great human values that we seek peace by ridding the world of the weapons of aggression and attack.

Franklin D. Roosevelt

The White House
May 16, 1933

[*Notation*:A] V.P. Read For Rel & Print[2]
[Speech File:TS:Microfilm]

---

[1] Printed below.

[2] A draft of this message, with a number of revisions in Roosevelt's hand, is present (Speech File). It is possible that Howe had a hand in the drafting for it is typed in his characteristic manner. In the Senate the message was referred to the Committee on Foreign Relations; in the House, to the Committee on Foreign Affairs (*Cong. Rec.*, vol. 77, pp. 3479, 3499). The text here printed is that of a microfilm of the original in the National Archives. It is also printed in *Public Papers*, II, 192–193.

## Roosevelt to the Heads of Nations Represented at the London and Geneva Conferences

[Washington, May 16, 1933]

A profound hope of the people of my country impels me, as the head of their government, to address you and, through you, the people of your nation. This hope is that peace may be assured through practical measures of disarmament and that all of us may carry to victory our common struggle against economic chaos.

To these ends the nations have called two great world conferences. The happiness, the prosperity, and the very lives of the men, women and children who inhabit the whole world are bound up in the decisions which their governments will make in the near future. The improvement of social conditions, the preservation of individual human rights, and the furtherance of social justice are dependent upon these decisions.

The World Economic Conference will meet soon and must come to its conclusions quickly. The world can not await deliberations long drawn out. The Conference must establish order in place of the present chaos by a stabilization of currencies, by freeing the flow of world trade, and by international action to raise price levels. It must, in short, supplement individual domestic programs for economic recovery, by wise and considered international action.

The Disarmament Conference has labored for more than a year and, as yet, has been unable to reach satisfactory conclusions. Confused purposes still clash dangerously. Our duty lies in the direction of bringing practical results through concerted action based upon the greatest good to the greatest number. Before the imperative call of this great duty, petty obstacles must be swept away and petty aims forgotten. A selfish victory is always destined to be an ultimate defeat. The furtherance of durable peace for our generation in every part of the world is the only goal worthy of our best efforts.

If we ask what are the reasons for armaments, which, in spite of the lessons and tragedies of the World War, are today a greater burden on the peoples of the earth than ever before, it becomes clear that they are two-fold: First, the desire, disclosed or hidden, on the part of Governments to enlarge their territories at the expense of a sister nation. I believe that only a small minority of Governments or of peoples harbor such a purpose. Second, the fear of nations that they will be invaded. I believe that the overwhelming majority of peoples feel obliged to retain excessive armaments because they fear some act of aggression against them and not because they themselves seek to be aggressors.

There is justification for this fear. Modern weapons of offense are vastly stronger than modern weapons of defense. Frontier forts, trenches, wire entanglements, coast defenses—in a word, fixed fortifications—are no longer impregnable to the attack of war planes, heavy mobile artillery, land battleships called tanks, and poison gas.

If all nations will agree wholly to eliminate from possession and use the weapons which make possible a successful attack, defenses automatically will become impregnable, and the frontiers and independence of every nation will become secure.

The ultimate objective of the Disarmament Conference must be the complete elimination of all offensive weapons. The immediate objective is a substantial reduction of some of these weapons and the elimination of many others.

This Government believes that the program for immediate reduction of aggressive weapons, now under discussion at Geneva, is but a first step toward our ultimate goal. We do not believe that the proposed immediate steps go far enough. Nevertheless, this Government welcomes the measures now proposed and will exert its influence toward the attainment of further successive steps of disarmament.

Stated in the clearest way, there are three steps to be agreed upon in the present discussions:

First, to take, at once, the first definite step toward this objective, as broadly outlined in the MacDonald Plan.

Second, to agree upon time and procedure for taking the following steps.

Third, to agree that while the first and the following steps are being taken, no nation shall increase its existing armaments over and above the limitations of treaty obligations.

But the peace of the world must be assured during the whole period of disarmament and I, therefore, propose a fourth step concurrent with and wholly dependent on the faithful fulfillment of these three proposals and subject to existing treaty rights:

That all the nations of the world should enter into a solemn and definite pact of non-aggression: That they should solemnly reaffirm the obligations they have assumed to limit and reduce their armaments, and, provided these obligations are faithfully executed by all signatory powers, individually agree that they will send no armed force of whatsoever nature across their frontiers.

Common sense points out that if any strong nation refuses to join with genuine sincerity in these concerted efforts for political and economic peace, the one at Geneva and the other at London, progress can be obstructed and ultimately blocked. In such event the civilized world, seeking both forms of peace, will know where the responsibility for failure lies. I urge that no nation assume such a responsibility, and that all the nations joined in these great conferences translate their professed policies into action. This is the way to political and economic peace.

I trust that your government will join in the fulfillment of these hopes.[1]

Franklin D. Roosevelt

[Speech File:T:Microfilm]

[1] This message was sent by cable; no copies of the cable itself are present in the Roosevelt papers. The text is that of the message as appended to Roosevelt's message to Congress of May 16, above. It has been separately printed here for convenience and the list of fifty-two heads of state has been omitted. These names may be found with the message as printed in *Public Papers*, II, 185–191. (It is also printed in *Foreign Relations, 1933*, I, 143–145.)

The two messages were intended to offset the effects of the address Hitler had announced he would make to the Reichstag on May 17. Norman Davis feared that if Hitler announced Germany's intention to rearm, the Conference was doomed. He thought the only hope was to induce Hitler to accept the British disarmament plan, and he urged Roosevelt to make a statement on American policy before Hitler's speech (Davis to Hull, May 15, 1933, two cables, *Foreign Relations, 1933*, I, 140–141, 141–142). It was decided to do this and Roosevelt, with Hull, Phillips, Howe, and Bullitt, prepared the message to the heads of state; Moley helped with the final draft (Hull, *Memoirs*, I, 226–227; Moley, *After Seven Years*, p. 214). A preliminary draft, with many changes in Roosevelt's hand, is present (Speech File). The replies are present (OF 404). A few of the more substantive are printed below, pp. 136–137, 137–139, 148–149, 149–150, 153, 155–158. Some are also printed in *Public Papers*, II, 193–201, but for the most part in excerpt only.

MacDonald regarded the message as an indication that in the future the United States would be "indifferent to nothing that concerns the peace of the world" (New York *Times*, May 17, 1933, p. 1). Both Davis and Hull were of the opinion that the message had influenced Hitler to take a more conciliatory attitude (Davis to Hull, May 21, 1933, *Foreign Relations, 1933*, I, 165; Hull, *Memoirs*, I, 227). However, cf. Moley, *After Seven Years*, p. 214.

# Press Conference, Executive Offices of the White House, May 16, 1933, 4:03 P.M.

[*Excerpt*] Q: Mr. President, isn't it a fact that the very fact you sent a message to Moscow means that you recognize the existence of the Soviet Government?[1]

The President: I think probably the easiest way to answer that is this: That that list of countries was the list of the countries participating in the World Economic Conference and the Disarmament Conference.

Q: Some of the people up on the Hill are interpreting that to mean that the United States—that the next move is to recognize Soviet Russia.

The President: No, that was just sent to the people participating, that is all. That is the beginning of it and the end of it.

Q: Mr. President, have you received any reaction from abroad on your message?

The President: No. Has anything come in over the wires of the Press Associations?

Q: Our wires just say—the sum and substance of them—that they are studying it.

Q: Our reports are that Italy has accepted it.

The President: Really? Well, that is quick action.

Q: That was the United Press report.

Q: Suppose the non-aggression pacts and trouble cropped up in China? In that case, would you be permitted to send soldiers or marines there to protect our nationals?

The President: That is too speculative. It is too much of an "if" question.

Q: How does it apply to the South and the Far East, as far as Japan and Manchuria are concerned?

The President: All I can say is that I hope this will go into effect. In other words, cross bridges such as that when we come to them.

Q: I take it that this is aimed at the European situation—

The President: The whole world; it is aimed at the whole world situation.

Q: Is it directed chiefly to Germany?

The President: No, the whole world.

Q: Can you give us the names of the delegates to the Economic Conference?

The President: The Secretary of State, Governor Cox, Senator Pittman, and that is all so far. I don't know who else will go. Nobody else has been asked as yet.

Q: Have you determined on the number?

The President: No.

Q: Mr. President, what reason have you to believe that nations which will violate the Kellogg Pact and thus violate their words, would any more observe a Pact of Non-aggression?

The President: Just the general hope that nations will, more and more, respect their treaties.

Q: Do you have any intention—

The President: That is all you can say on that.

Q: It is somewhat the same sort of type of treaty, isn't it?

The President: Well, section four is a pretty stiff thing. If people sign up on section four, it is a pretty difficult thing to get around. It has to do with sending your armed forces beyond your own frontiers.

Q: You regard that as an advance beyond the Kellogg Pact?

The President: It is an absolutely definite thing.

Q: What about the forces already on the outside, like the Japanese forces?

The President: As I said, there are—I will have to say this off the record entirely—there are three situations at the present time where there is actually armed conflict going on. All we can say is that we hope that those will be resolved into a peaceful situation. That is about all you can say.

Q: Those conflicts are in the Far East and where else?

The President: Two are in South America. One of them is the war which Paraguay has declared—I don't know whether Bolivia has declared war or not—and the other is a war going on between Colombia and Peru in which neither side has declared war.[2]

Q: In case hereafter a country, in violation of section four, did cross a border, would we consult with other signatories of the Kellogg Pact about that?

The President: On consultation? Why, under the Kellogg Pact, we have agreed to consult and, of course, in a question involving the peace of the world, there is no reason why we should not consult.

Q: There was some comment on the fact that there was no mention of the consultative pact in these messages.

The President: I should say again, off the record, on that, that the question of consultative pacts are really details in carrying out principles.

Q: Could you tell us whether the non-aggression features of your proposal are to be made part of the Kellogg Pact, or are these new treaties?

The President: Those are details I have not considered at all.

Q: How long have you been working on this?

The President: About four months.

Q: About four months?

The President: I started working on it in January.

Q: Similar statements went to Italy and Great Britain. Is this a concerted thing?

The President: No, I have not consulted with anybody at all on this except the Secretary of State.

Q: Mr. MacDonald?

The President: No. It is probably more news to them this morning than it was to the Press last night. I had no communication with them at all.

Q: In considering this matter of non-aggression pacts, have you examined at all any of the non-aggression pacts that have been put into effect between Russia and her neighbors and Russia and France? Have you examined any at all?

The President: No, this is world-wide.

Q: Yes, I know, but I was just wondering if, in considering this matter of non-aggression pacts, you had looked into the wording of those and the effect of them.

The President: No, I have not at all.

Q: Under the non-aggression pact, is the United States free to send marines into Latin American countries to protect life and property?

The President: Yes.

Q: It would be?

The President: Yes. I told you, off the record, that the places where war is actually going on have to be specially treated.

Q: In China, the marines and the others who are stationed there under treaties have nothing to do with this proposal?

The President: No, it has not. Of course, our marines and soldiers in Tientsin and Peking are there under international treaties already in existence.

Q: That does not enter into non-aggression at all?

The President: No. Of course, number four says specifically (reading) "I therefore propose a fourth set concurrent with and wholly dependent on the faithful fulfillment of these three proposals and subject to existing treaty rights."

Q: This will be the chief thing in the Disarmament Conference?

The President: I don't know.

Q: Won't you follow it up by making—

The President: This was telegraphed to Davis last night.

Q: Who will lay it before the Disarmament Conference?

The President: I don't know.

Q: Did he have instructions to that effect?

The President: I don't think any instructions have gone out. It is a statement from his own government.

Q: Do you care to say at this time whether you are willing to participate in an international commission to supervise disarmament?

The President: I have not considered that at all, Steve.[3]

Q: Mr. President, have you considered the possibility—

The President: In other words, these are principles. We have not gone any further.

Q: Have you considered the possibility of sanctions against aggression?

The President: No; that would be the same thing, it would be a method of carrying out the principle.

Q: I assume that Secretary Hull will be Chairman of the Economic delegation, won't he?

The President: Yes.

Q: Will Cox act in his stead when he comes back?

The President: I don't know; I have not considered that.

[President's Press Conferences:T]

[1] Roosevelt to Heads of Nations, May 16, 1933, above.
[2] The Chaco war and the Leticia dispute.
[3] F. M. Stephenson of the Associated Press.

## Joseph P. Tumulty to Roosevelt

Washington, D. C., 16 May 1933

My dear Mr. President: Sitting back of the lines, I stand, as Woodrow Wilson would say, "in amaze" at what you are doing to build up the hopes and faith of a sorely stricken world. Your Message today goes straight to the heart of the world and will bring notable and handsome reactions. After all, we cannot discount the moral pressure which you have brought to bear at the psychological moment. A great surgeon once said to me that high technique was necessary in the surgeon but more than that was his ability "to know when to operate." You have that ability in the highest degree. You are leading us to the heights, and God help the men who will not be willing to sacrifice and sorrow even a little bit to bring to fruition the ideals you sponsor.

Your statement today proclaims a new Monroe Doctrine to the world. No reply to this is necessary from so busy a man.[1]

Sincerely yours,

J. P. Tumulty

[PPF 153:TS]

[1] Tumulty had been secretary to President Wilson. Roosevelt thanked him in a note of May 19, 1933 (*Personal Letters, 1928–1945,* I, 346).

# Roosevelt to Jonathan Bourne, Jr., Washington

[Washington] May 17, 1933

My dear Senator: Thank you much for your note about my old and close friend Senator Wheeler.[1] My difficulty is that I can only take one Democrat for the Delegation and that should be the Chairman of the Foreign Relations Committee. I know you will understand.

Very sincerely yours,

[OF 17:CT]

[1] Bourne, a senator from Oregon from 1907 to 1913, writing May 15, 1933 (OF 17), urged appointment of Senator Burton K. Wheeler of Montana as a delegate to the London Economic Conference as the recognized leader in Congress of the silver bloc. Wheeler, on May 3, 1933, had introduced S.R. 67; this declared it the sense of the Senate that the delegates to the Conference should "work unceasingly for an international agreement to remonetize silver on a basis of a definite fixed ratio of not to exceed 16 fine ounces of silver to 1 fine ounce of gold." The resolution was agreed to unanimously without debate on May 8, 1933 (*Cong. Rec.*, vol. 77, pp. 2775, 2967). Bourne said that although the adoption of this resolution did not legally bind the President or the delegates it carried a moral obligation to an "aggressive effort to secure in the International Conference, if possible, an agreement to remonetize silver."

# Raymond B. Stevens, Adviser on Foreign Affairs to the Government of Siam, to Roosevelt

Bangkok, Siam, 17th May, 1933

Dear Mr. President: I have several times begun a letter to you giving an account of the political situation in Siam. That situation, however, was for a time so uncertain and changed so much inside that I kept postponing a final appraisement.[1]

I believe now that the situation is finally clarified and that the present elements in control are quite firmly seated. Fortunately they have judgment and experience as well as liberal ideas. The great danger after the first Coup d'Etat was that the extreme element would get control of the Government—in which case the ruin, at least temporarily, of Siam would have followed with surprising speed. As it is financially the country is in an unusually strong condition considering world conditions. This year the budget is really balanced and last year there was a surplus of two million on a budget of 71 million.

The elimination of the small group of extremists has been carried out quietly and I believe with the support of the Siamese people—I mean those who think. Of course the great bulk of the farming population in the country have no understanding of what any form of communism really means.

My regular six-months leave was due this spring. I had intended to let it accumulate and take it at the end of my contract. I find , however, that my health will not permit me so great a strain. In fact the doctor has just ordered me to take a long and immediate rest. I am therefore sailing for America within a few days. I will spend the summer in good old New England with my family and then return to Siam in the early autumn for the remainder of my term.[2] Of course I desire to see you while I am there. I think an inside account of the very unique revolution in Siam would be interesting to you and might be a temporary relief from some of the tremendous responsibilities that you now carry. Fortunately you have the temperament to face great responsibilities not only with courage but with optimism. That is a very fortunate gift for a President. I have watched the proceedings of your administration so far with very great pleasure and also great astonishment that the Congress would be willing to abdicate so much of its power. There is certainly a marked feeling of optimism throughout the world as a result of the courage and initiative of your administration.

Permit me to extend to you my congratulations and my very best wishes.

Yours sincerely,

Raymond B. Stevens

P.S. I am pleased to know that you still have time to get some pleasure out of hobbies. My boy for a time was much interested in stamps, but his interest did not continue. I am sending you a selection of Siamese stamps which I hope will add something to your collection. I got these originally for my boy.

I can tell you much about the revolution that cannot be written. S.

[PPF 605:TS]

[1] Stevens, an old friend of Roosevelt, was at this time adviser on political affairs to the Siamese government. He here refers to the events following upon the coup d'etat of June 1932, which transformed Siam from an absolute to a limited monarchy.

[2] Stevens, however, accepted appointment to the Federal Trade Commission on June 26, 1933, and served the rest of the year. In 1935 he was appointed to the Tariff Commission and was chairman from 1937 on.

# Roosevelt to Richard Washburn Child, New York

[Washington] May 18, 1933

Dear Dick: I am glad that you have inquired whether anyone has been authorized by me to deal with political groups outside of the constituted Cuban Government. Naturally, it goes without saying that neither I nor the State Department would undertake to set up any such official contacts.[1]

Sincerely yours,

[OF 159:CT]

[1] This note was apparently written after Child had talked with Roosevelt on May 18 (PPF 1-0). The only other reference to the matter found in the Roosevelt papers is in a letter from Child to Roosevelt, May 25, 1933 (OF 159), in which Child says, "Your letter to me has cleared the air as to negotiations with certain Cuban Gentlemen."

# Roosevelt to Representative Parker Corning of New York

[Washington] May 18, 1933

Dear Parker: Thank you for letting me see that letter.[1] We have sold all the government wheat but we are most anxious to discuss reciprocal agreements with Brazil. Their Delegate arrives today.[2]

Very sincerely yours,

[OF 307-A:CT]

[1] Corning, writing May 2 (OF 307-A), enclosed a letter from Frank M. Garcia of Rio de Janeiro, who, he said, was probably remembered by Roosevelt because he had worked in the Democratic campaign headquarters in 1928. Corning said that since that time he had handled "one or two matters" for him in Brazil in a most satisfactory manner. Garcia's letter was returned to Corning and nothing further is known of its content.

[2] For the talks preparatory to the London Economic Conference.

## Roosevelt to Judge Irving Lehman, New York

[Washington] May 18, 1933

*Personal*

Dear Irving: I am delighted to have your note[1] and am only sorry that I could not see you when you were in Washington. I wish you could have been present when I was talking with Dr. Schacht. At last the German Government now knows how I feel about things. It is probably better to do it this way than to send formal notes of protest because, frankly, I fear that the latter might result in reprisals in Germany.

I do hope to see you one of these days soon. Herbert has done and is doing a fine job.

Give my best regards to your wife.

Always sincerely,

[PPF 436:CT]

[1] Lehman, a judge of the New York State Court of Appeals and brother of Governor Herbert H. Lehman of New York, had written May 10, 1933 (PPF 436), to express his gratification at Roosevelt's attitude on certain matters, presumably the Nazi persecution of the Jews.

## President Paul von Hindenburg of Germany to Roosevelt

Berlin, May 18, 1933

[*Radiogram*] I acknowledge with sincere thanks receipt of your message telegraphed to me.[1] This declaration, in which you show the world the way to eliminate the international crisis, has met with hearty approval throughout Germany. The statements which the German Reich Chancellor made yesterday, with the unanimous agreement of the German

Reichstag, prove that Germany is decided to cooperate unselfishly in overcoming the political and economic difficulties of the present moment.[2]

von Hindenburg

[OF 404:T]

[1] Roosevelt to Heads of Nations, May 16, 1933, above.
[2] The text of Hitler's speech was published in the New York *Times* of May 18, 1933, p. 3.


# President Gazi Mustafa Kemal of Turkey to Roosevelt

Ankara, 1933 May 18

[*Telegram*] I have had the honor of receiving the message which Your Excellency addressed to all the heads of States, under the loftiest humanitarian inspiration and with an objective and practical understanding of the evils from which the world is suffering through the political and economic crises which prevail.[1] With very special attention, I have read and studied the analyses and suggestions which you made with a view to preventing the failure of the Disarmament Conference and insuring the success of the World Economic Conference. I render homage to the new effort which the Chief of State of the great American Republic is exerting for the purpose of bringing about the union of the peoples in support of certain formulas, which, in their totality, impose sacrifices only for the purpose of preventing catastrophe and of facilitating passage to the era of tranquillity and perhaps of prosperity which is awaited by all mankind with feverish impatience. In advising you of the viewpoint of the Government of the Turkish Republic with respect to the principles set forth by Your Excellency in the economic and political domain, I must first assure you that in the different declarations which we have made, the general guiding lines of our policies have been set forth in a manner which most approximates the suggestions which Your Excellency has offered in your message. In fact, as regards world economy, in our memorandum addressed to your Government at the time of the preparatory work in Washington, we have dealt with the monetary question by requesting the maintenance of the gold standard convertible for international exchanges and not convertible within the countries, and we have thus advocated the type of stabilization which is best adapted to the exigencies of the hour and which in no way departs from the general principle which you have set forth. The organization of world trade was also the subject of our suggestions in the said memorandum in which we advocated the measures calculated to increase international exchanges, which methods we deem of such a nature as to insure the prosperity of the peoples and not their economic decadence. We fully agree concerning the necessity of completing the efforts made in each country for the economic revival by an ensemble of logical and well-conceived international steps. We have always held, in this connection, that the coordination of national and international efforts should be effected in such manner as to afford to each nation the possibility of development adapted to its own peculiarities and that the generally accepted spirit with respect to world economic prosperity should be respect for the rights of each one in the pursuit of progress and prosperity under conditions suited to it. I believe that on this matter again our point of view is in perfect harmony with the guiding lines of your message with respect to the Disarmament Conference. Like Your Excellency, I am of the opinion that the goal to be attained is so important that individual interests must make place for the lofty ideal, the realization of which is alone capable of insuring the tranquillity and confidence which will bring about prosperity in the entire world. Your Excellency outlines with admirable clearness and frankness the reasons underlying the failure of the efforts exerted hitherto at the Geneva Conference. You are aware of the fact that as regards disarmament the Government of the Turkish Republic has gone even beyond the principles advocated in the MacDonald plan. I must add that your own suggestions, which are inspired, with true realism, by the idea of the destruction of the offensive and the strengthening of the defensive, correspond in every respect to the viewpoint which we have constantly defended at Geneva. The complete elimination of offensive arms in the broadest sense, that is, the progressive but speedy decrease, pending elimination, of the possibilities and powers of attack, for all countries, is the aim which we have had in view from the beginning. In the speech delivered by our delegate at Geneva with respect to the MacDonald plan, Your Excellency probably noted that in posing the question of the Straits we had in view only the elimination of the offensive and the consolidation of the defensive. For this reason, I consider that on this subject Your Excellency's proposals correspond fully and in every respect to our desire for peace and to the universal ideal of good understanding in the international domain. In view of these considerations, and to pass on to the study of your concrete proposals, I must say that we have considered the MacDonald plan as a commendable effort towards reduction, and that we are prepared to discuss it with a view to giving it the form which best corresponds to the principles set forth by Your Excellency, which principles in no wise depart from those which we ourselves have stated before the Geneva assembly, that the determination of the time and procedure for the new steps to be taken along these lines fit in with our viewpoint, that in the matter of rearmament, my Government, while refraining, at present, from taking any position in the great controversies on that subject, deems that any step toward assuring peace cannot but be favorably received. Moreover, we fully agree that a general pact of non-aggression and that a pledge of limitation and of reduction of armaments would be extremely helpful. In stating to you the viewpoint of the Turkish Government, I am happy to note that no difference exists between this viewpoint and the views of the great American Republic. I am therefore especially happy to express to Your Excellency my most fervent and most sincere congratulations on the new pledge which you have just given to the cause of peace, and to state that the Government of the United States, in this respect, will find a fervent advocate of the desire of its realization in my Government, the only aim of which, in the economic realm, is to insure its own liberty for the prosperity of the country by contributing to world prosperity through the welfare of each one, and, in the political realm, to live peacefully, to cancel its own means of the offensive as a corollary to such cancellation by others, while keeping intact its legitimate means of defense towards and against all.

Gazi M. Kemal

[OF 404:T]

[1] Roosevelt to Heads of Nations, May 16, 1933, above.

## Sumner Welles, Ambassador to Cuba, to Roosevelt

Habana, May 18, 1933

My dear Mr. President: I want, in the first place, to offer you my heartiest congratulations on the message addressed by you yesterday to the Chiefs of State throughout the world. It has been splendidly received here. Nothing could have been more inspiring and at the same time nothing more practical if a world catastrophe is to be avoided. The world today is looking to you for leadership and, thank God, it is getting it.

I have been here now for nine days and I have had sufficient opportunity to realize that the situation is both more precarious and more difficult than I had anticipated.[1]

I have requested the Department to send you, for your information, those of the cables which I have sent up that I felt might be of interest to you. If you have had time to glance at them, you will have seen the policy I desire to follow out. This policy, in general terms, is:

First. A continued effort to fix the attention of that portion of public opinion in Cuba which is neither solely political nor solely fanatic upon the economic benefits to be derived by the Cuban people as a whole from the negotiation of a new commercial agreement with the United States.

Second. To cooperate with the Machado Government until such time as the electoral law can be properly revised as the result of the recommendations of some impartial American expert (President Machado's[2] agreement to my suggestion that Professor Dodds, of Princeton University, be employed as quickly as possible by the Cuban Government for this purpose has been an encouraging symptom).[3]

Third. Subsequently, the formulation by the Congress of much needed reforms to the Cuban Constitution and thereupon the election under the new electoral code of a Constituent Assembly to approve the amended form of the Cuban Constitution.

Fourth. The feeling is so bitter and the state of agitation so general that I feel it may be necessary to suggest a change in the Presidency, through constitutional procedure, some time before the electoral period commences. But I am confident that in any event General Machado should be replaced, at least during the electoral period, by some individual in whom all parties have confidence.

Fifth. The holding of national elections in which the next Constitutional President of the Republic can be elected without imposition of candidates by the present Government, or the exertion of control in any form by the existing authorities.

This, very briefly, is the policy which I think should be pursued. There are many attendant and contingent questions involved, with which I shall not burden you, but which, of course, must be taken up and be decided from time to time as they come up. Principal among these is the necessity, in my belief, of the adoption of a policy of conciliation by the present Government and the refusal on the part of the President to permit acts of retaliation, other than those provided for by law, in reprisal for acts of terrorism committed by the antagonists of the Government.

This policy is not sensational. It will satisfy neither one side nor the other down here. I have a very definite conviction, however, that it is the policy which, in the long run, if we have any luck at all, will be the one to the best interest of our own Government. I can imagine nothing more prejudicial to our whole Latin American policy than the need for the United States to intervene in Cuba, either by force of arms or by open diplomatic action. It would create grave disquiet throughout the Continent at a moment when every Republic of Latin America has confidence in you and in your policy, and it would militate strongly against the building up in a relatively brief time of that sane and beneficial Latin American policy, commercial and political, which you have often discussed with me.

Your personal letter to President Machado created a precedent in this country, the President told me, and I do not think anything could have predisposed him more favorably to my mission and to the adoption of those measures which I shall from time to time suggest to him.[4] President Machado has, of course, been painted very much blacker than he is in reality. During the first four years of his Government, he gave Cuba what has probably been the best government it has had, and the practical results of those years in the form of public works, stimulation of agriculture, etc., are concrete evidence of this. Many of the leaders of the opposition to him today, General Menocal[5] included, were among those who lobbied for his re-election. The economic depression was the basis of the original opposition to him. But his tainted and probably unconstitutional re-election, and, most of all, his pathological obsession that only repressive measures, culminating in acts of hideous cruelty, could stifle that opposition, have fanned the flames of opposition into a detestation of the President's person which is unparalleled, I think, in Cuban history.

President Machado is almost childlike in his inability to understand why the American press is so violently antagonistic to him and why you yourself are not willing to take measures to stop these attacks on the President of a friendly country by the American newspapers. I have explained to him that the American press is not, and has never been, subject to interference by the Executive. I have also suggested that if he would take certain measures which I have recommended in dealing with the American press correspondents here, the Cuban Government could at least have printed in reports sent up from Habana its own view of the situation in Cuba, as well as any statements which it might care to issue regarding the occurrences which take place here. General Machado has already carried out my suggestions; I have explained them to the American press correspondents; and I am very hopeful that this experiment will provide a change for the better.

I hesitate to ask it, because I know, of course, the tremendous pressure upon you, but if you can find time to send me two lines, either approving or disapproving the policy I have formulated, I shall deeply appreciate it.

You may be sure in any event, that at all times I shall be doing the best I can.

Believe me, Faithfully yours,

Sumner Welles

[OF 470:TS]

[1] Welles was appointed Assistant Secretary of State on April 6, 1933, and ambassador to Cuba on April 24, arriving there on May 8. His cables to Hull on the revolutionary movement there are printed in *Foreign Relations, 1933,* V, 290ff.

[2] Gerardo Machado.

[3] Harold Willis Dodds, professor of politics at Princeton, became president of the University in June 1933 and thus Welles's suggestion was not adopted. Howard Lee McBain of Columbia University was eventually chosen in Dodds's place.

[4] Roosevelt had written to Machado on April 7, 1933, thanking him for his telegram of February 15 congratulating him on his escape from assassination at Miami (OF 159).

[5] Mario Garcia Menocal.

## William Phillips, Under Secretary of State, to Roosevelt

Washington, May 18, 1933

My dear Mr. President: I took up with the Secretary this morning the four names which you mentioned yesterday in connection with the American Embassy in Berlin. They were, as you recollect, Harry Emerson Fosdick, Glenn Frank, William Mather Lewis, President of Lafayette College, and Ernest Hopkins of Dartmouth. Mr. Hull did not know any of them personally, and he was, therefore, unable to express any opinion other than that he was under the impression that Glenn Frank was of Jewish extraction and, for that reason, would be unsuitable for the post.[1]

I can give you a little further information about Doctor William Mather Lewis, whom I do not know personally. He is fifty-three years old; he spent two years of study in Germany just before the World War; he is a Democrat; and he and his wife have a private fortune. He was in the Treasury Department towards the end of the War and later became President of George Washington University. I am informed that he is a good speaker and business administrator. The personal equation is highly important, and I wish I could give you more help in this direction.

Faithfully yours,

William Phillips

[OF 198-B:TS]

[1] Frank was not a Jew. William E. Dodd, professor of history at the University of Chicago, was the one appointed. Dodd had received his doctorate from the University of Leipzig in 1900 and was fluent in German. House had suggested his appointment to Roosevelt, with Nicholas Murray Butler as his second preference (Dodd, *Diary*, pp. 3, 9–10). Earlier, the Berlin post had been offered to James M. Cox, former governor of Ohio and the Democratic candidate for president in 1920. Cox had declined because he wanted to train his son to follow him in his publishing business (Roosevelt to Cox, March 9, 1933, *Personal Letters, 1928–1945*, I, 337–338; Cox to Roosevelt, March 16, 1933, PPF 53).

## Charles W. Taussig to Roosevelt

[Washington] May 18, 1933

Memorandum to the President: If Ambassador Welles' suggestion[1] to send Professor Dodds to Cuba to study the electoral laws is carried through, and I think it most advisable that it be done, I would recommend that consideration be given to an effort to establish a political truce in Cuba for the duration of the reciprocal trade negotiations.

The opposition has expressed its alarm that in the event of a successful outcome of the trade negotiations between the United States and Cuba, it would serve to entrench further President Machado. Some supporters of the Government have expressed the opinion that should the negotiations result in higher prices for sugar, it would enable the opposition to finance a revolution. In view of the extremely disturbed conditions, it might be advisable to submit to Ambassador Welles a suggestion that the President of the United States, in a public message, request a political truce during the period of the negotiations. Without a reasonable degree of political stability during that period, it will be very difficult successfully to carry on these negotiations.

There is some indication that such procedure might have salutary effects. President Machado, in his talk with Ambassador Welles last Saturday, indicated that he might be willing to resign at some period prior to the election which normally would occur in 1934. It is not beyond a possibility that our Ambassador might, during the period of the truce, induce the President of the Cuban Government to move the date of the elections forward, in which case, if President Machado carried out his suggestion of resigning, it might solve the Cuban problem.[2]

Taussig

[OF 470:T]

[1] See Welles to Roosevelt, May 18, 1933, above.
[2] Charles W. Taussig, one of the original members of Roosevelt's "Brains Trust," was technical adviser to the State Department on economic matters during the April–May conferences in Washington and was technical adviser to the United States delegation at the London Conference. He was connected with numerous sugar and molasses producers and was an authority on the history of sugar production.

## Senator Arthur H. Vandenberg and Others to Roosevelt

Washington, D.C., 18 May 1933

The President: The Great Lakes-St. Lawrence Deep Waterway Treaty can be promptly ratified in our opinion if made a part of the administration program for action at the present session.

While the Treaty is in control of the Senate and will so remain, we recognize as a practical matter that its consideration at this session will be determined by its inclusion with, or exclusion from, the administration program.

It is our conviction that conditions are more favorable to ratification now than they are likely to prove at the January session, when nearly two years will have elapsed since the treaty was signed.

As friends of the St. Lawrence project, to which you have given most effective support, we respectfully urge avoidance of any course that might defeat years of effort to open the mid-continent to the sea and to provide for development of the power resources on the St. Lawrence River in the public interest.

The construction of this great project will furnish immediate employment and it may thus properly be included as an essential and productive part of the administration's program for public works, now before Congress. The net cost to the federal government for the project, which will be largely self-liquidating, will not exceed $24,000,000 a year during the period of construction.

Uncertainty as to the administration's attitude toward action at this session is seriously prejudicial to its early and favorable consideration. If your previously expressed personal desire for ratification of the treaty prior to adjournment is officially confirmed, we are confident the treaty can be ratified without undue delay.

But we frankly recognize the critical importance, under existing legislative circumstances, of whatever you may conclude to say to the Senate respecting administration plans in this connection. Indeed, it may well prove the controlling factor. It is for this reason that we take the liberty of urging a conclusive statement at the earliest moment.

We tender our cooperation to that end. We take this position recognizing that the treaty is a nonpartisan measure endorsed by both major political parties.[1]

> A. H. Vandenberg (Michigan)
> Robert M. La Follette Jr. (Wisconsin)
> B. K. Wheeler
> Henrik Shipstead
> F. Ryan Duffy, Wis.
> G. W. Norris
> Edward P. Costigan
> Bronson Cutting

[OF 156:TS]

[1] The St. Lawrence Waterway Treaty with Canada was signed July 18, 1932. Both parties endorsed the project in their platforms and Roosevelt came out for it in his speech of July 30, 1932 (*Public Papers*, I, 659–669). During the campaign he reiterated his support in a letter to J. Adam Bede, a former representative from Minnesota. Bede read Roosevelt's letter to the National Rivers and Harbors Congress, meeting in Washington, D.C., Jan. 18, 1933. In it the president-elect said: "I cannot understand why anyone would be trying to give out the impression that I was silent on the St. Lawrence waterway. I have expressed my views on this many times. I am sure that the statement in the Democratic platform . . . must reassure the country that I believe in the construction of a deep waterway from the Great Lakes to the ocean via the St. Lawrence. There are certain details of construction and costs which may have to be worked out, but so far as the principle of the thing is concerned, the party, as well as I, is committed to the idea" (New York *Times*, Jan. 19, 1933, p. 35). No copy of this letter has been found in the Roosevelt papers. The date of the letter is not given; Bede said he received it Oct. 15, 1932.

The treaty was favorably reported by the Senate Foreign Relations Committee on Feb. 23, 1933, and placed on the executive calendar. During the rest of the session a combination of eastern seaboard and Mississippi Valley opponents succeeded in blocking ratification. In spite of Roosevelt's earlier avowals of support, there apparently was some doubt concerning his position about the time of the date of the letter here printed. Urging ratification in the Senate on May 29, Senator Vandenberg said that he thought the President wanted the treaty ratified but he regretted that he had not thus far "seen fit to step squarely forward with an affirmative recommendation." Vandenberg added, however, that he was "perfectly confident" that the Senate would have heard from the President in no uncertain terms before the session was over (*Cong. Rec.*, vol. 76, p. 4789; vol. 77, pp. 1789–1790, 4477–4509).

## Press Conference, Executive Offices of the White House, May 19, 1933, 10:34 A.M.

[*Excerpt*] Q: Do you still feel optimistic about the Geneva Arms Conference?

The President: Put it this way: I think I feel the same kind of optimism that everybody else does, but I have not any more reports or information about it than what they have. I have had replies from different heads of nations and we have these reports from a number of ambassadors and others from our embassies and legations. We have not heard anything further, but I should say that the general tenor of the reception, both on my cable and on Hitler's speech, has distinctly not only eased the situation but has improved the whole tone of the Conference itself. And if the action, or, rather put it the other way around, if the intent as expressed can be translated into similar action, we really ought to get somewhere and get something definite done.

Q: There was a cable from Paris this morning that some French senator asked for a five percent cut in the Army and that Premier Daladier got up and made a speech and said "Nothing doing."

The President: A five per cent cut?

Q: A five per cent cut in the French Army.

The President: I hadn't heard.

Q: Nothing on that, then?

The President: No.

Q: He further said that it was impossible to go on because they had already reached the limit and could not further disarm. There is a meeting at Geneva tomorrow and that brings it into a rather queer situation.

The President: I don't think so. This is a perfectly simple situation. Nobody is cutting their armies until we get an agreement from everybody to cut. Nobody could go before Congress and say, "Please make these cuts now," until we get an agreement on which to base it.

Q: But Congress will pass anything. (Laughter)

Q: Have you finished your selection of delegates as yet?

The President: I have not done anything further than those three I mentioned the other day.[1] I am going to talk about it this afternoon.

Q: Who are you going to talk with?

The President: The Secretary of State.

Q: With respect to reports about cooperating with the rest of the world, is it not a safe assumption that you do not expect any development at Geneva which will get us into foreign entanglements or alliances?

The President: I think that is a perfectly safe assumption . . .

Q: Can you confirm for us those reports in the papers this morning that we are seeking stabilization of all currencies in advance of the World Economic Conference?

Q: Off the record.

The President: That is new to me.

Q: Mr. President, is there any Ambassador to Berlin in sight?

The President: Not yet . . .

Q: Reports from Geneva indicate that the exporting countries have agreed on a ten per cent cut on wheat. Would that be carried out by the terms of the Farm Bill in this country?[2]

The President: I think it is a little bit premature to put it that way. What we are trying to do on wheat is to get all the exporting wheat countries together on some method of reducing the world wheat surplus so as to stabilize world wheat prices. Proper reduction is, of course, one of the methods of doing it and, for the first time, the United States is in a position, because of the Farm Bill, to make an effort to go along if the other nations agree to do the same thing. That is about as far as we have got . . .

Q: Can you tell us anything further about a joint statement by Pani, the Minister of Mexico?

Q: Yes.

The President: No, I don't believe I had better because they are working on it at the present time.[3]

[President's Press Conferences:T]

---

[1] Although the preceding discussion concerns the Disarmament Conference, the reference here is apparently to the London Economic Conference; see press conference of May 16, 1933, above.

[2] Representatives of Argentina, Australia, Canada, and the United States had been

meeting in Geneva in an attempt to settle on a means of controlling world production of wheat. The conference had adjourned May 17 to enable the delegates to ask advice of their governments. The United States representative was Henry Morgenthau, Sr. (New York *Times,* May 18, 1933, p. 6).

[3] See statement of May 18, 1933, by Roosevelt and Alberto J. Pani, Finance Minister of Mexico, in *Public Papers,* II, 206.


## Roosevelt to Robert Cromie, Publisher, The Vancouver *Sun,* Vancouver, B.C.

[Washington] May 19, 1933

*Private*

Dear Mr. Cromie: I like that editorial and I hope that you have liked my effort to head Europe and Japan in the other direction![1]

Do be sure to come and see me when next you come East.

Very sincerely yours,

[PPF 452:CT]


[1] Cromie, writing May 11, 1933 (PPF 452), had sent Roosevelt an editorial from his newspaper the Vancouver *Sun* of May 11, 1933. The editorial said that world leadership had now shifted from Europe to the United States; if the world accepted this leadership it would mean "a new deal for humanity."


## President Lin Sen of China to Roosevelt

Nanking, May 19, 1933

[*Telegram*] It was with a sense of satisfaction and hopefulness that I received the exceedingly important communication you addressed to me and, through me, the people of the Chinese nation.[1]

The Chinese government and people, like the American government and people, are convinced that world peace can be assured only through the united efforts of all nations to remove any possibility of aggression not only by reduction of armaments, but also by a common pledge not to invade each others' territory. They are equally certain that world prosperity can be regained only by the establishment, out of the present chaos, of an economic order based upon the greatest good to the greatest number of people. With a sincere desire for durable peace in every part of the world, the Chinese government has cooperated and will continue to cooperate with other governments in the deliberations of the Disarmament Conference. It will be with like sincerity and open-mindedness on her part that China participates in the labors of the Economic Conference about to be held in London.

China has been the victim of aggression; the victim of excessive armaments, of offensive modern weapons of war. Large numbers of armed forces have without right crossed China's frontiers and remain on her territory. Cities are being destroyed, men, women and children are being slaughtered. This foreign invasion has shaken the political and economic fabric of the Chinese nation. What is a mere fear of aggression to other countries is a terrible living reality to China. No government is therefore more anxious than the Chinese government to see all nations enter into a solemn and definite pact of non-aggression, reduce armaments to strictly defensive purposes, and subscribe to and fulfil the engagements to send no armed force of whatever nature across their frontiers.

Chinese government is prepared to associate itself with other governments in undertaking the various steps indicated in your message, which it considers as constituting one complete plan for the maintenance of the national security of all countries, and confidently hopes that the obligations envisaged in these proposals, especially the fourth proposal, will be executed to their fullest extent, so that world peace, political as well as economic, will prevail.

Lin Sen

[OF 404:T]

[1] Roosevelt to Heads of Nations, May 16, 1933, above. Lin Sen, one of Sun Yat-Sen's lieutenants in the 1911 revolution, became state councillor of the National Government in 1926 and president in 1932. Long residence in California had made him familiar with the American viewpoint on Chinese affairs.


# President Thomas G. Masaryk of Czechoslovakia to Roosevelt

Praha, May 19, 1933

[*Radiogram*] Personally I like your initiative in advocating and defending with very good arguments the necessity of universal peace and in struggling so energetically against the economic chaos. The President of the greatest republic had the right and, allow me to say so, the duty to say such decided words to us all. Our government is working in your intentions all the time. My best wishes for the success of your under-taking. I am convinced that thinking citizens of all nations having experienced the war will join you in your effort. It is really time to make a reasonable and honest policy.[1]

T. G. Masaryk

[OF 404:T]

[1] This reply to Roosevelt's message of May 16 appears to be in Masaryk's words and not a translation.

## Senator Robert M. La Follette, Jr., of Wisconsin to Roosevelt

[Washington] 19 May 1933

Dear Mr. President: I am pleased to advise you of the results of a poll of minority Senators on the St. Lawrence Treaty made by Senator Vandenberg and myself.

This poll was made upon the suggestion of Senator Pittman to Mr. Frank P. Walsh that if a majority, exclusive of the Democrats, is now favorable to the Treaty it would justify sending in a message and insure ratification.

Senators strongly for ratification are: Borah, Capper, Carey, Cutting, Fess, Frazier, Hatfield, Johnson, La Follette, Norbeck, Norris, Nye, Schall, Vandenberg and Shipstead.

The above Senators have authorized the listing of their names as committed to ratification.

In addition, the following Senators have authorized listing their names as favorably inclined toward the Treaty but not committed to ratification in advance of debate: McNary, Robinson (Ind.), and Dickinson.

Senator McNary, the minority leader, not only stated that he was favorably inclined toward the treaty, but also stated that he favored action at this session.

Senators who stated they have an open mind on the whole matter are as follows: Couzens, Davis, Hastings, Reed, Steiwer and Townsend.

There are 35 Republican and 1 Farmer-Labor Senators. Of these, 15 are definitely committed to the Treaty, 3 are favorably inclined, and 6 are open-minded.

This leaves 12 Republican Senators, all of whom come from New England or Atlantic Seaboard states with the exception of Senator Patterson of Missouri. It is my own view that on the question of ratification some of them would shrink from voting against the Treaty, in the teeth of the party's unequivocal pledge in the 1932 platform for a Treaty negotiated under a Republican administration. It is very likely the Treaty would gain a distinct advantage from the fact that some of those opposed on both the Republican and Democratic sides would absent themselves rather than vote against party pledges, whereas the advocates of the Treaty would poll their full strength.

I am strongly of the opinion, confirmed by this poll, that the St. Lawrence Treaty can and should be ratified at this session. I am convinced, also, that your expressed intention to send a strong message in its behalf is sound from every point of view. There can be no question that delay will encourage the opposition and give certain interests more time in which to foment sectional prejudice against the Treaty, endangering the whole project.[1]

Respectfully yours,

Robert M. La Follette Jr.

[OF 156:TS]

[1] See Basil Manly to Roosevelt, June 3, 1933, below.

# Roosevelt to Senator Hiram W. Johnson of California

[Washington] May 20, 1933

Dear Senator Johnson: The enclosed copy of letter to Senator Fletcher and Congressman Rayburn carries out our conversation I think.[1]

Very sincerely yours,

[OF 242:CT]

[1] The copy of the letter to Senator Fletcher is identical with the one to Rayburn. This letter is presumably the one mentioned by Feis in his letter to Howe of May 10, 1933, above, and the date, May 20, is very likely a typist's error.

## [*Enclosure*] Roosevelt to Representative Sam Rayburn of Texas

[Washington] May 20, 1933

My dear Mr. Rayburn: In regard to Title #2 of the Senate Bill creating a Foreign Securities Corporation, the State Department believes that, as drawn, it might conflict with the work or policies of the State Department, the other agencies of the government or of the Congress, in foreign countries, or involve the government in unwanted responsibilities. The State Department suggests the selection of personnel by private and semi-public bodies of good reputation. This would correspond to the arrangement followed by the British Council of Foreign Bond Holders.

I personally am not wedded to that idea and all that I want to make clear to you is that whatever method of selecting personnel is set up, the bond holders' committee should not in any shape, manner or form be given powers which would directly or by implication overlap or conflict with the Executive or Congressional authority. There must be no possibility of involving the government nor must there be anything which would lead either our own American bond holders or foreign debtors to assume that this committee speaks for the government.

I feel confident that in line with this thought you can work something out.[1]

Very sincerely yours,

[OF 242:T]

---

[1] The "something" took the form of an amendment to Title 2, the text of which was telephoned by Rayburn to Roosevelt for his approval on about May 21 or May 22 (White House memorandum, undated, filed May 23, 1933). The amendment declared that nothing in the Securities Act could be construed to mean that anyone in the proposed corporation could act for or represent the State Department or could interfere in any way with any diplomatic negotiations being carried on by the Department. It provided further that Title 2 should not go into effect until the President so proclaimed. The Securities Bill was at this time before the Senate-House conference committee. Presumably the President agreed to the revision for the conference committee report of May 22 included the proposed amendment as telephoned to the White House, and it was passed that day as sec. 210 of the Securities Act of 1933, approved May 27, 1933 (*Cong. Rec.*, vol. 77, pp. 3879–3884; 48 *Stat.* 74).

In an undated memorandum apparently written shortly after approval of the act, Child urged Roosevelt to put Title 2 into effect (OF 242). He asked that he be consulted on the appointment of the directors of the Foreign Security Holders Corporation because he could help "without prejudice or axe-grinding." Child saw the President on Sept. 13, 1933, and on September 15 he sent him his recommendations; according to his accompanying note to Howe of the same date, the President had asked him to send his recommendations "as soon as possible" (OF 242). However, the Administration decided not to make use of Title 2. On Oct. 20, 1933, the White House announced the formation of a private organization, entirely divorced from the government, to further the interests of the holders of the defaulted securities (*Public Papers*, II, 411–413). See Roosevelt to Steiwer, Nov. 6, 1933, below.

## Emperor Hirohito of Japan to Roosevelt

Tokio, May 20, 1933

[*Radiogram*] There has been duly come to my hands on the seventeenth of this month the telegraphic message which you as the head of the American government have addressed to me.[1] I thank you for this communication inspired by the desire of assuring the peace of the world and overcoming the universal depression. I have caused your message to be transmitted to my government for their earnest consideration.[2]

Hirohito

[OF 404:T]

[1] Roosevelt to Heads of Nations, May 16, 1933, above.
[2] The implications for Japan of the May 16 message were discussed on May 16 by the Japanese ambassador, Katsuji Debuchi, and Under Secretary of State Phillips. Phillips emphasized that the message was as applicable to the Far East as it was to the rest of the world (memorandum by Phillips, May 16, 1933, *Foreign Relations, 1933*, I, 146–147).

## Roosevelt to Prime Minister J. Ramsay MacDonald, London

Washington [May 22, 1933]

[*My dear Mr. Prime Minister:*][1] I have read with great care your gracious letter and also the personal message handed to me by the Ambassador.[2] You may be assured that I fully sympathize with your expression of views as to the desirability of avoiding difficulties concerning the debts at the opening of the Economic Conference. I note with appreciation what you say of your understanding of the views held by our Congress and by the American people.

As I told you when you were here, I am most anxious that the Conference begin in an atmosphere of mutual good-will.[3] To that end I am discussing the subject informally and privately with leaders of the Congress. No doubt we shall find some way of meeting the situation in ample time before the opening of the Conference. I am finding a good deal of sentiment to the effect that if your Government is unable to pay the entire amount, it might find it possible to pay a part, perhaps in silver, as has been authorized by Congress. This feeling is based on the thought that it would make it clear in both countries that there had not been a default. It avoids a debate on terminology.[4] This is a mere suggestion, however, and is not intended to be a definitive request.

Another question, however, concerns me much more. I am disturbed lest the deliberations of the Conference be unduly affected by the desire of the debtor governments to bring about a new settlement of the debt question, even though this question does not form a part of the Agenda. While we all recognize certain economic relationships between the debts and a few of the subjects at issue, the major questions to be discussed at the Economic Conference, in my opinion, can be brought to a satisfactory and mutually advantageous determination at the Conference, without reference to the debts at all, and without their settlement being made in any way contingent upon a debt settlement. Hence, I am deeply pleased to note that you do not place a new debt settlement as a necessary prerequisite to a successful conclusion of the Conference.

I hold to my policy of free debt discussion whenever the debtor governments desire them. It is obvious of course that such discussions must be held here in Washington with whatever representatives the British Government designates for that purpose.

As to procedure, I note that your letter suggests an exchange of notes, but your personal message sent subsequent to the letter, suggests that in your opinion it would be best not to wait for a formal request from you.[5] I am inclined to the point of view that we can consider that the communications and conferences which I have had amount to a representation of your views. I will have a clearer picture of the Congressional situation by the end of this week and will cable you then.[6]

I am delighted that the disarmament conference is moving forward on the lines on which you and I are in such full accord. If things again get in a jam, be sure to let me know if you advise any action by me.

Tell the Lady Ishbel that Howe ate that halibut for breakfast.[7]

My warm regards to you both.

[Very sincerely yours,]

[Franklin D. Roosevelt]

[PSF:London Economic Conference:T]

[1] This text is that of a State Department fair copy of a White House draft; the letter was cabled by the Department to London. No copy of the cable itself has been found

in the Roosevelt papers, and the date, greeting, and close are from the text as published in *British Documents, 1919–1939,* V, 810–811. In this version, the last line (about Howe) is omitted. The author of the draft has not been identified; to judge from the typing it may have been Howe. The White House draft contains a number of additions and excisions in Roosevelt's hand; the more interesting are noted below.

[2] The letter is that of May 8, 1933 (above); no personal message of this date has been found.

[3] Before revision by Roosevelt, this sentence read: "As I told you when you were here, I am so anxious that the Conference begin in an atmosphere of good-will that I am willing to attempt to bring about the deferment of the June 15th payment by your Government if practicable means can be found."

[4] The two preceding sentences were added by Roosevelt.

[5] The following concluding clause was crossed out by Roosevelt: "but to announce that because of the danger of disturbing the atmosphere in which the Economic Conference will meet, we are not pressing for the immediate payment on June 15th."

[6] This sentence, and the rest of the letter, were added by Roosevelt.

[7] Ishbel MacDonald accompanied her father to the United States and she and Howe became well acquainted.


# President Augustin P. Justo of Argentina to Roosevelt

[Buenos Aires, May 22, 1933]

[*Radiogram*] I have the honor to transmit to Your Excellency the reply to the circular message which Your Excellency addressed to me under date of the 16th instant.[1] Feeling certain of interpreting the sentiments and traditions of the Argentine people, my Government is glad to express its decided adherence to the ideas contained in the circular message which Your Excellency has been good enough to address to me. The opinions on which it is based coincide with the courses followed by this country in so far as they spring from the recognition of interdependence and recognize the necessity for cooperation in international and economic matters. They interpret our desire for constant respect for international justice and they satisfy the tendencies to peace to which we have paid tribute in our relations with all peoples, both in positive conventional law and in the principles and doctrines that we have maintained at gatherings of American or world scope. This Government accepted the invitations to participate in the two great conferences to which Your Excellency refers in the telegram which I am answering. The delegations which will participate in them will associate themselves with every effort intended to improve a situation which really presents disquieting prospects for economic restoration and the preservation of peace. I share with you the idea that definitive peace can be firmly established only on the basis of a more perfect organization of economic activity, which will allow the standard of living of the collectivities to be raised. With this in mind, the lowering of protective tariffs, which has been called customs disarmament, should be followed, I believe, as you affirm, by limitation of armaments in convergence of two forms of action which should both tend toward the same great end. Argentina, as her delegation announced at the proper time at the Disarmament Conference held at Geneva, is resolved to collaborate in the limitation of land, naval and air armaments, on the basis of the general principles which Your Excellency enumerates. This is shown by the proposal formulated by the said delegation, in the sense of agreeing upon the non-acquisition of capital ships during a given time, by countries which are not bound by the agreements on naval limitation signed at Washington in 1922 and at London in 1930. Your Excellency expresses the fervent wish that the World Economic Conference may quickly reach positive conclusions, declaring that the world can not await deliberations long drawn out. This highly proper wish is therefore linked with the well grounded hope derived from Your Excellency's own affirmation in giving assurance of your decided cooperation in reducing tariff barriers which have caused international commerce to fall off to a more and more alarming extent. The measures elaborated by the Geneva Economic Conference of 1927, which did not succeed in putting those same aspirations into practical application, with respect to the action of the States, multilateral treaties and a customs truce, thus acquire prospects brightened by the support of the great nation over which Your Excellency so worthily presides. It is to be hoped that proper solutions may be reached in regard to the stabilization of currencies, avoiding the present disarticulation that Your Excellency points out, facilitating the resumption of world interchange and stimulating national economic life, without the excesses of economic nationalism, which has been one of the causes of the present situation. I trust likewise that proper attention will be paid to the position of the agricultural countries such as ours, producers of raw materials and foodstuffs, which have been affected intensely, and that by restoring to their natural play their interchanges with other nations, which have characteristics differing with the geographical distribution of production, there may be re-established their necessary influence in the dynamics of international commerce. In investigating, in your lofty proposals, the deep-seated causation of the world economic depression, Your Excellency points out the maintenance of armaments which burdens the budgets and has repercussions in every local economic unit.

You thus come to pointing out the ambition to extend territorial dominion, which inspires some countries with respect to neighboring nations, as a factor of disturbance which must be eliminated. I believe that I can say that, in general, the states of this continent repudiate such tendencies. They have no conception or need of them in their mutual relations. With their slight density of population and fortunate divisions as to production, which harmonize with one another in different zones, they do not require subtle combinations to attain an international equilibrium which is indicated by the spontaneous work of nature. For this reason we have been and shall always be far removed from any desire for hegemony, and imperialism is a policy which would have no application among us. Out of all the complex problems that will be dealt with by the conferences mentioned by Your Excellency, the one which preoccupies us above all is that of seeing the shadows and the obstacles that disturb world exchange or menace the industrial field dissipated, without being unmindful of the profound repercussion to which inter-dependence subjects us in the general situation. The message to which I am replying culminates in the proposal for a solemn and definite pact of non-aggression, into which all nations of the world would enter. The last war demonstrated the appalling facility with which the best solutions of law and the firmest postulates of juridical conscience may fail. In my opinion, a new instrument must be drawn up, which will coordinate and perfect those already ratified, such as the Briand-Kellogg Pact, the Locarno Pacts, and the Covenant of the League of Nations, with a new conception which may strengthen their effectiveness. On this subject, my Government has definite convictions that have been accepted by various countries of America. It believes that the Briand-Kellogg Pact must be provided with a sanction amplifying its moral force by others of a political, juridical and economic character, contractual in origin, for the imposition of peace, in order to exclude any diplomatic or armed intervention. It must be assured by an organ of conciliation, submitting conflicts to an obligatory proceeding and supplemented by the principle that territorial questions must not be decided by force in the international field. I am sure that the contribution of the United States in such pact of non-aggression would consolidate the universal character of the work planned by Your Excellency. My concurrence in the proposal stated in the message takes concrete form in the draft of the anti-war treaty of non-aggression and conciliation which has been presented by the Argentine Government and which it submits to your high judgment, in the hope that you may desire to renew the study thereof. I take pleasure, in this connection, in expressing to Your Excellency the assurance of my highest consideration.

Augustin P. Justo<br>
President of the Argentine Nation

[OF 404:T]

[1] Roosevelt to Heads of Nations, May 16, 1933, above.

## Roosevelt to Charles Lyon Chandler, Vice President, Corn Exchange National Bank and Trust Company, Philadelphia

[Washington] May 22, 1933

My dear Chandler: Many thanks for letting me see those interesting excerpts. I hope our foreign friends will continue to go along.[1]

Very sincerely yours,

[PPF 659:CT]

[1] Chandler had extensive knowledge of South American financial and business affairs and wrote frequently about them to Roosevelt. In his letter of May 19, 1933 (PPF 659), he quoted from letters received from acquaintances in Buenos Aires to the effect that public opinion there was most favorable to Roosevelt's ideas of finance.

## Robert W. Bingham, Ambassador to Great Britain, to Roosevelt

[London] May 22, 1933

Dear Mr. President: I cabled you about what I felt had been the effect of your address.[1] This opinion has been strengthened and confirmed by press utterances and press contacts, and especially by personal contacts with old friends who have talked to me freely and frankly.

For your information, I am sending you a letter from a very old friend of mine who is a wise and well-informed woman. Her husband had a distinguished career and she has lived in all parts of the world. I have marked in the letter the particular passage which shows her attitude.[2] I have had this same idea expressed to me and I am convinced the chances for success, both of the Disarmament Conference and the Economic Conference, have been greatly increased. Moreover, I think the attitude of the British towards us has been changed for the better in a marked and unmistakable manner since you came into the Presidency. From my knowledge of England and the English, I had come to the conclusion that our country and countrymen were never so unpopular. I felt this strongly when I was in England last summer. I believe that attitude of mind has changed to a marked degree, thus laying a foundation for hope for such cooperation between the British and ourselves as will be helpful to both.

In addition to Lady Grogan's letter, the important passage of which I have marked in order to save you time, I am enclosing the editorial from *The Times* about which I cabled you.[3]

My wife joins me in warm regards to you and Mrs. Roosevelt.

As ever, Sincerely your friend,

Robert W. Bingham

[OF 491:TS]

[1] Roosevelt to Heads of Nations, May 16, 1933, above.
[2] The letter, of May 19, 1933, was from Ellinor F. M. Grogan, of Bingham's Melcombe, Dorchester, Dorset (not otherwise identified). The sentences underlined read: "The President's splendid message to the world is all of good augury. I feel he is to be the protector of the peace of the world."
[3] Not present.


# Lillian D. Wald to Roosevelt

New York City, May 22, 1933

Dear President Roosevelt: Of course you are deluged by messages by air, by post and by wire! But in memory of the unforgettable discussion we had at Hyde Park,[1] I cannot resist adding my congratulations to express my great happiness over your plea to the nations of the world.[2]

And soul-satisfying as that message is in every particular—its formulation, its phraseology, the unassailable common sense and philosophy of it—I have, as many of my comrades have, an additional enthusiasm because Soviet Russia was included. In all good time a further step will be taken, I feel sure. I have unswerving faith in your leadership, and I think the whole world may give thank-offering that a man of power has arisen.

You were good enough to return the original correspondence about the Prime Minister's visit.[3] Would you care to have that correspondence or copies of it for your archives? If you would like it, I shall be glad to send it to you.

With devout admiration and everlasting gratitude for what you are doing not only for our country but for the rest of the world, I am
Faithfully yours,

Lillian D. Wald[4]

[PPF 114:TS]

[1] The date of Miss Wald's visit is not known.
[2] Roosevelt to Heads of Nations, May 16, 1933, above.
[3] Roosevelt to Wald, March 16, 1933, above.
[4] Answered May 26, 1933, below.

## Ronald C. Lindsay, British Ambassador to the United States, to Louis M. Howe, Personal Secretary to the President

British Embassy, Washington, May 23rd, 1933

Dear Colonel Howe: I have received from my Government the enclosed communication to the President in reply to the message which he addressed to His Majesty The King and to other Heads of States in regard to disarmament.[1] I shall be grateful if you will bring it to the President's notice as soon as possible, as it is being released in London this afternoon.

Yours very sincerely,

R. C. Lindsay

[OF 404:TS]

[1] May 16, 1933, above.

## [*Enclosure*] Reply of the British Government to Roosevelt's Message on Disarmament

[London, May 23, 1933]

His Majesty's Government in the United Kingdom have read with much appreciation the message which the President of the United States of America addressed to the Heads of all countries participating in the Disarmament and Economic Conferences on May 16th. His Majesty's Government feel that the action which Mr. Roosevelt has taken in addressing this message to the peoples of the world is of the highest importance and is well calculated to further the aim which His Majesty's Government have striven to secure, namely, the success of the two World Conferences. They entirely share the President's view that on the successful outcome of these Conferences hang the future happiness and prosperity of the world. They are all the more encouraged by Mr. Roosevelt's message because the President places as the first step of his programme the adoption of the draft Disarmament Convention presented to the Disarmament Conference by the Prime Minister on March 16th last.[1] His Majesty's Government see in this an earnest of the intention of the United States Government to collaborate at Geneva in pressing the general adoption of this draft Convention as a whole. His Majesty's Government believe for their part that if this can be attained the result will be a restoration of confidence between the nations of the world and that thus the best preparation will be made for the vital decisions which the Monetary and Economic Conference will be called upon to take.[2]

[OF 404:T]

[1] See *Foreign Relations, 1933*, I, 43–54.
[2] Printed also in *British Documents, 1919–1939*, V, 273.

## Arthur Sweetser, Director, Information Section, League of Nations, to Roosevelt

Geneva, 23rd May, 1933

Dear Mr. President: The other night at dinner at my house Mr. Morgenthau[1] was giving a few of us a most interesting review of recent events in Washington, and especially of some of the problems with which you are faced. Just as an aside he happened to mention your interest in stamps. I told Mr. Morgenthau that there was a special set of Swiss stamps surcharged for the "Société des Nations" and stamped in the same way, and wondered whether you would be interested to have them. He was sure you would be and thought it would be a good idea for me to send them to you. I, accordingly, enclose a full set which, as you will see, are all cancelled, as the Swiss authorities will not sell them uncancelled.

We are having most exciting and most gratifying days here. Your recent communication to Heads of States was like an electric current, and should have a most salutary effect on both the Disarmament and Economic Conferences.[2] Norman Davis' speech yesterday was a most happy follow-up.[3]

We are hopeful of progress at London, though I must confess the magnitude of the Conference and its issues is almost shattering.

With the most heartfelt congratulations on the amazing results you have achieved almost overnight, I am,

Yours most respectfully,

Arthur Sweetser[4]

[PPF 506:TS]

[1] Henry Morgenthau, Sr., representative of the United States at the International Wheat Conference.

[2] May 16, 1933, above.

[3] Davis' statement to the Disarmament Conference of May 22 that the United States was willing to enter into consultative pacts with other nations is printed in his dispatch to Hull of May 19 in *Foreign Relations, 1933*, I, 154–158, with the exception of certain revisions noted in the two dispatches immediately following.

[4] Answered June 3, 1933, below.

# Press Conference, Executive Offices of the White House, May 24, 1933, 10:35 A.M.

[*Excerpt*] Q: We were under the impression that you were not in favor of imposing these import taxes under the Tariff Bill during the tariff truce. The indications are that you may have changed your mind. Is that so?

The President: No, neither is true. In other words, as the original tariff truce was drafted, it would have been a doubtful question but, as it was finally approved, I cannot remember the exact language, but it was to the effect that no tariff changes would be allowed which changed the actual status quo. Now, a very small import tax, as I understand it, to go on in conjunction with the processing tax would not change the status quo. Importers would have exactly the same rate as they had before. It does not change the status quo. Secretary Hull has gone over it quite carefully and he says that it does not, in effect, raise the import tax.

Q: Is it the intention to put it on?

The President: I don't know.

Q: It is mandatory in the act?

The President: I think it is. I think it goes hand in hand, as I remember it, with the processing tax.[1]

Q: What happened to that tariff truce, Mr. President?

The President: The tax?

Q: No, the tariff truce.

The President: It has been signed by the eight powers.

Q: It has?

The President: Oh, yes. By "signed," I mean it is the joint statement of the eight powers on the Organizing Committee, which they agreed to and sent out to all nations.

Q: But it has not been put into effect, has it?

The President: Oh, yes; it is in effect today . . .[2]

Q: Can you tell us about the tariff resolution?

The President: Nothing further; I haven't talked with Secretary Hull about it either.[3]

Q: France seems to have thrown another monkey wrench into the Disarmament Conference. They insist that instead of scrapping weapons, some should be kept for use by the League against an aggressor nation.

The President: What will they do with them?

Q: Keep a certain amount in the respective countries for use by the League against an aggressor?

The President: I could only talk about that off the record. If you are going to eliminate guns, it is better to keep them about 5,000 fathoms. That is the best and safest place for them.

Q: Down with the German fleet. (Laughter)

Q: Have you made any further progress on the selection of the American delegation to the London Conference?

The President: No, only Chairman McReynolds—I think it is perfectly all right to announce him . . .[4]

Q: Will the delegates be allowed their expenses? There is some doubt about that?

The President: I think they only get $6 a day.

Q: Isn't that one of the difficulties—trying to get more?

The President: No, they are not going to ask for more than that.

Q: That is all they are going to get?

The President: Yes; that is what Congress says.

Q: Isn't there danger of somebody offering them a good meal over there? (Laughter)

Q: They would have to go to those week-end parties they have?

Q: In regard to the tariff resolution, is it still your intention to send it up to Congress?

The President: I think it is probable. I have not got beyond the word "probable" yet.

Q: Do you know what form that will take?

The President: No; I haven't any idea . . .

Q: Anything further toward stabilization of currency?

The President: How do you mean that—on an agreement?

Q: Yes.

The President: No, nothing at all.

Q: Anything doing on stabilization of the dollar in international exchange?

The President: No.

Q: Nothing in sight?

The President: No.

Q: Does the appointment of Professor Sprague indicate that there will be stabilization?[5]

The President: I think I can tell you off the record—this is really off the record—that we are patting ourselves on the back because Sprague is a perfectly good American and he has been one of the financial advisors of the Bank of England and he knows, probably, the foreign exchange situation as well as anybody in the world. He is coming to us at a very great financial sacrifice so that we will have all the inside dope about what everybody is doing in the other countries. It really is a grand stroke for our Government to get Sprague back here, but it does not mean any policy. I do not know what is going to happen.

Q: Any possibility of him going to the Economic Conference?

The President: I don't know; I do not think that has been decided, but it is perfectly possible.

Q: It would be an advantage—

The President: Yes, but of course you must remember that on the Economic Conference I have to keep somebody back here to hold my hand . . .

Q: Mr. President, can you tell us whether you have replied to the communication La Follette and Vandenberg and others sent in regard to—[6]

The President: I have not, but I can tell you, off the record, that it presents really a question of fact as to whether they are right in saying they have the votes for it or whether the other fellows are right in saying they have not got the vote. That is really the situation. There is no question about my being for the St. Lawrence Treaty and if we have the votes for it, it means cloture in the Senate. I would like to see it go through now. On the other hand, if it means two weeks of debate with the question of whether it goes through in the end in doubt, I think it better not to take it up.

Q: Has there been any thought of holding the Senate over for a special session with a view of the St. Lawrence Treaty?

The President: No, I want to go off on that cruise.[7]

Q: Are you having trouble getting Republicans on the delegation on account of the tariff issue?

The President: No; nobody ever suggested it.

Q: I know, but you don't seem to have any yet. (Laughter)

Q: Do you figure on diplomatic relationships with the Soviet Republic? (Laughter)

The President: Well, I have nothing to be said on that.

Q: Is it necessary to have that tariff resolution passed before the delegation goes to London?

The President: No. Obviously, of course, I should like to get it passed before the present special session adjourns, if I send it up. We have not definitely decided it because I have not got down to the question of wording. It looks probable that I will send something up.

[President's Press Conferences:T]

[1] Section 15 of the Agricultural Adjustment Act approved May 12, 1933 (48 *Stat.* 40), authorized the imposition on agricultural imports of a tax equal to the amount of the processing tax.

[2] The tariff truce had been approved on May 12 by the governments represented on the Organizing Committee of the Economic Conference; on May 24 the Council of the League asked all governments invited to the Conference to observe the truce (*Foreign Relations, 1933,* I, 601–602, 614).

[3] See press conference of June 9, 1933, below.

[4] Rep. Samuel D. McReynolds of Tennessee, chairman of the House Committee on Foreign Affairs.

[5] Oliver M. W. Sprague had been professor of banking and finance at Harvard for many years and Roosevelt had studied economics under him as an undergraduate. He was economic adviser to the Bank of England from 1930 to 1933. Early in 1933 he resigned and returned to the United States. On May 24, 1933, he was appointed executive assistant to the Secretary of the Treasury, and shortly afterwards he was named financial adviser to the American delegation of the London Economic Conference. With George L. Harrison, governor of the Federal Reserve Bank of New York, he preceded the delegation to London to confer with British and French central bank executives on currency stabilization.

[6] La Follette to Roosevelt, May 19, 1933, above.

[7] Roosevelt left Washington June 16, 1933, for a cruise by sail to Campobello.

## Roosevelt to Senator Key Pittman of Nevada, Chairman, Senate Foreign Relations Committee

[Washington] May 24, 1933

My dear Senator Pittman: I earnestly recommend the immediate passage of S.J. Res. 32.

It is my understanding that this legislation has been favorably reported out by the Senate Committee on Foreign Relations but that it has not as yet been considered by the Senate. A motion to strike out the enacting clause of a similar bill was carried last Saturday by a small majority in the House. It is obvious from the published debates as they appeared in the *Congressional Record* that the opponents of this legislation entirely misunderstood the purposes of the Resolution. The International Institute of Agriculture is not an Italian organization but an international organization founded in pursuance of a Convention to which this Government is a party. The purpose of this legislation is not to provide a gratuity for any foreign government nor to provide for a junket for any American citizen. Its purpose is to authorize the appropriations necessary to enable this Government to contribute to the support of the Institute on the same basis as other member Governments and to enable this Government to share effectively in the direction of the affairs of the Institute. There is no authorization in this bill for any appropriations for purposes other than those which I have specified.

Defeat of this legislation would place this Government in an exceedingly embarrassing position. We should be faced with the alternative of (1) continuing to pay our contribution to the Institute in paper francs when the other governments' members of the Institute were paying in gold francs and taking no part in the direction of the Institute, or (2) denouncing the Convention of 1905 and withdrawing from the Institute.

Either of these courses of action would result in placing the Institute in a precarious financial situation which would result in seriously crippling the organization. Thus this Government would be obliged to expend a far greater sum in order to obtain the services now rendered by the Institute. Neither of these courses of action would be in accordance with the fair dealing and good faith which should characterize all of the foreign relations of this Government.

The International Institute of Agriculture is rendering an important service to American agriculture.

1. As a clearing house of statistical information, collecting and publishing statistics from all parts of the world, it is giving all the member governments the benefit of the information collected by the Government services of all the members of the Institute.

2. As an international organization it is in a position to persuade the various governments to build up their statistical services in the common interest.

3. As an international forum it serves as a meeting place for discussion of the broader phases of the agricultural situation of interest to farmers everywhere.

It is only just that we should pay our fair share of the expenses of this organization. With renewed American support and with American participation in the direction of its affairs, we look forward to deriving increased benefits from our membership in the Institute.

I am sending similar letters to the Vice President and Senator Robinson.[1]

Very sincerely yours,

[OF 456:CT]

[1] The International Institute of Agriculture in Rome had its inception in 1905 in a plan proposed to the king of Italy by David Lubin, a Sacramento businessman who was interested in farming. The United States had been a member since 1907. Senate Joint Resolution 32, to appropriate $48,500 annually for the expense of participation by the United States, was introduced March 23, 1933, by Johnson; the companion House Joint Resolution 149 was introduced by McReynolds on April 11. When the House resolution was debated on May 19–20, it was strongly attacked by Thomas L. Blanton and others who described it as a junket for the American representative and unnecessary in so far as our agriculture was concerned. After lengthy debate the House voted to strike out the enacting clause (*Cong. Rec.*, vol. 77, pp. 785, 1532, 3764–3769, 3810–3811, 3813–3834).

The action of the House caused concern in the State Department and a memorandum, prepared by Joseph C. Green of the Division of Western European Affairs, May 22, 1933, was sent by Hull to Louis Howe with a note (undated) asking Howe to talk to Green (OF 456). The memorandum pointed out that to permit the regular appropriation to lapse would gravely embarrass the government which would either have to repudiate its obligation or withdraw from the Institute; either course would probably cause the end of the organization. Green suggested that the State Department and the White House push the companion Senate resolution and submitted a draft of a letter to be sent by the President to Senators Pittman and Robinson and the president of the Senate. This letter, printed above, was read in the Senate May 30. Robinson then offered an amendment to the Independent Offices Appropriation Bill, H.R. 5389 (then before the Senate) to provide the funds needed. The amendment was accepted by the Senate on June 2. In the House, on June 10, a motion by Blanton to instruct the House and Senate conferees to reject the Senate amendment as an improper action on an appropriation bill was rejected and the funds were appropriated as part of H.R. 5389, approved June 16, 1933 (*Cong. Rec.*, vol. 77, pp. 4576–4578, 5689; 48 *Stat.* 303).


# Roosevelt to Katherine Aspinwall Hodge Egerton, London

[Washington] May 25, 1933

My dear Mrs. Egerton: I am delighted to have your letter and I did know of your existence and of the fact that you are living in England.[1]

I shall always remember that my father used to call your great-grandmother Aunt Hodge.

You will have an interesting time following the Economic Conference and I wish that I might get over there myself but, of course, that is impossible.

I shall soon make changes in the Department of Commerce foreign service.[2]

If you ever come over here do be sure to come and see me.[3]

Very sincerely yours,

[PPF 475:CT]

[1] Mrs. Egerton, an employee of the American Consulate General in London, had written on May 13, 1933 (PPF 475), to tell Roosevelt of her impressions of his inaugural address, which she had heard by radio, and of British attitudes toward the issues to come before the Economic Conference. She was a distant relative of the President (her great-grandmother, Margaret Aspinwall Hodge, was a sister of his grandmother, Mary Rebecca Aspinwall Roosevelt) and she addressed him as "Dear Cousin."

[2] Mrs. Egerton had referred to duplication of effort in the work of the Consular Service and the foreign service of the Commerce Department.

[3] Mrs. Egerton came to the United States later in the summer and asked for an

appointment at the White House in a letter to Roosevelt of Sept. 14, 1933 (PPF 475). An attached note indicates that Roosevelt directed that an appointment be made for her but her name does not appear in the appointments list.

## Roosevelt to Lillian D. Wald, New York

[Washington] May 26, 1933

Dear Miss Wald: Thank you ever so much for that nice letter.[1] Of course, I should be delighted to have copies of the Prime Minister's letters. He is a wonderful person in every way and we very much enjoyed having him stay with us.

I do hope by now that you are feeling better and that Mrs. Roosevelt and I shall have the pleasure of seeing you very soon.

Very sincerely yours,

[PPF 114:CT]

[1] May 22, 1933, above.

## Press Conference, Executive Offices of the White House, May 26, 1933, 4:15 P.M.

(Present: The Secretary of State and Viscount Kikujiro Ishii.)[1]

[*Excerpt*] Q: Mr. President, what effect will that have on the foreign debts? Do they have to pay in United States currency or in gold, as the contract provides?[2]

The President: I don't know; I have not thought of it.

Q: There was a discussion of that up on the Hill today in which they said that they could pay their debts in any kind of currency they choose?

The President: I should say, offhand, that I am open to suggestions of any kind as to payment. (Laughter)

Q: Have you had any such suggestions?

The President: No.

Q: In that connection, Herriot, before the Chamber of Deputies today made a speech in which he said you insisted that, as a part of any further consideration for France on debts, that she pay her $19,000,000 which was due last December 15. Has he a pretty good memory?

The President: I think so.

Q: Is there any conflict between this bill and the clause in the Thomas Amendment to the Farm Bill, that was called the Inflation Bill, under which the gold content of the dollar could be cut to 50 per cent?[3]

The President: Oh, no; there is no relationship.

Q: Does it eliminate the prospects of any act?

The President: Oh, no.

Q: Does this change affect our position at the Economic Conference?

The President: I do not think it has any effect on the discussions there at all.

Q: It was not motivated in any way by that?

The President: No, it had no relationship. I think Steve's suggestion was about right.[4] In other words, to do what we are doing is to tell people that they cannot have gold in their private possession in this country. Why go through the rigamarole of paying them the gold and then tapping them on the shoulder and taking it away from them. Why not pay them currency in the first instance. It is practical.

Q: Do you care to say anything about the World Economic Conference as to our own individual program that will be followed?

The President: No. The delegates will have what might be called "general instructions" before they go. Those general instructions, in general, will follow the line of the accord on principles that we have made in these discussions with other nations during the past six weeks. It will only be general in form. They will establish certain principles for which we will work.

Q: Has the personnel been fixed as yet?

The President: Only the four names you have so far.[5]

Q: Will that be extended?

The President: I don't know.

Q: Have you decided as yet as to whether you are going to send up a tariff resolution?

The President: I have not done a thing about it as yet. The status quo is as it was a month ago.

Q: Can you tell us whether reorganization is in the same category?

The President: Except that we have made a good deal of progress on it. We have got somewhere.

Q: Will it come out next week?

The President: Yes, I think so . . .

Q: Going back to the World Conference, do you see any conflict between some of the basic measures that have been put in effect here or are about to be put into effect and the general program of breaking down the trade barrier?

The President: No, I don't think there is any conflict at all. We are trying to frame emergency measures so as to foster international trade.

Q: But wouldn't they tend to foster an isolation policy? Wouldn't they require for their successful operation a rather closed door and a policy of isolation?

The President: Oh, no, not necessarily. Of course, our hope is that we will raise commodity prices not only here but all over the world. That is the real international objective. Of course, as to certain things in which we have a very large surplus, like wheat, for instance, there it becomes a question of getting the countries that are in the same condition, like the Argentine and Canada and Australia, that also have surpluses, to try to work out some world method for the disposal of the surplus. Obviously, we are not going to bring in Australian or Argentine wheat here any more than in the past.

Q: That would be another policy, trying to get everybody to do the same thing we are trying to do?

The President: What we are trying to do is to raise the level all over the world.

Q: Mr. Baruch has said that under the Industrial Recovery Bill,[6] which would raise wages, that higher tariffs would be necessary to protect the American market?

The President: Not necessarily; it depends entirely on the individual product and, if commodity prices are raised in proportion in other nations at the same time, the present tariff will be equally protective.

Q: Can you tell us what you are talking to Viscount Ishii about?

The President: I think about everything. We have had a most interesting and satisfactory talk . . .[7]

Q: The Disarmament Conference apparently is on the rocks again over there. Are we correct in assuming—

The President: You ought to start that "it is my assertion."

Q: Are we correct in assuming that our effort at cooperation with the rest of the world for disarmament is contingent upon such disarmament by the rest of the world. That was the original principle, was it not?

The President: In other words what you want to know is whether our effort is dependent on all nations going along on disarmament. Of course that is the whole object of the Disarmament Conference. The Disarmament Conference will either accomplish something for disarmament or it won't. If we don't accomplish anything for disarmament, I cannot see any use in staying on.

Q: Have you any new delegates to the London conference?

The President: No, no new ones yet . . .

Q: Did England and other countries take the same action we did when they went off the gold standard?

The President: You mean about payment on their bonds?

Q: Yes, payment on their bonds.

The President: As I remember it, and you will have to check on this, no British security is payable in gold. Am I right on that?

Q: Yes, in sterling.

The President: It is payable in sterling and not gold.

Q: In other words, they did not have the gold clause and we did?

The President: Yes.

Q: Can you tell us more about your pleasant talk with Ishii?

The President: No, I don't think so; I think there will be a communiqué tonight or tomorrow.

[President's Press Conferences:T]

[1] Ishii was author of the 1917 "Gentleman's Agreement" between Japan and the United States to restrict Japanese immigration. At this time he was head of the Japanese Privy Council and chief of the Japanese delegation to the London Economic Conference.

[2] The preceding discussion had been about the proposed repeal of the gold payment clause.

[3] Senator Elmer Thomas' amendment to the Agricultural Adjustment Act, approved May 12, 1933 (48 *Stat.* 51).

[4] F. M. Stephenson of the Associated Press.

[5] Cordell Hull, James M. Cox, Key Pittman, and Samuel D. McReynolds.

[6] The National Industrial Recovery Act, approved June 16, 1933 (48 *Stat.* 195).

[7] Ishii and Roosevelt had four conversations: May 24 (at lunch), on economic matters; May 25, on disarmament and the Far Eastern crisis; and May 26, on "political matters." A joint statement was issued following their talk of May 27 (New York *Times,* May 25, p. 12; May 26, p. 3; May 27, p. 3; May 28, 1933, p. 3; *Public Papers,* II, 212–213).

# Roosevelt to Cordell Hull, Secretary of State

Washington, May 27, 1933

*Confidential*

Memorandum for the Secretary of State: This is an extremely interesting confidential memorandum. Please let me have it back when you and the Chief of the Division of Western Europe have read it.

FDR

[*Notation*:AS] Read with much interest. W. P.[1]

[*Notation*:AS] Read with interest WE/P. M.[2] May 31st
[PPF 2616:TS]

[1] William Phillips, Under Secretary of State.
[2] Pierrepont Moffat, chief, Division of Western European Affairs.

## [*Enclosure 1*] S. R. Fuller, Jr., to Roosevelt

11 May 1933, Washington, D.C.

Subject: Germany:

1–Has Hitler his feet under him?

2–What do the common people think of him?

3–(a) Does he know where he is going? (b) What are his ends? (c) Where is he going?

4–Is he going to last?

5–Is he going to have war?

6–(a) Is he going to keep the Jews out for good? (b) Or is he just punishing them temporarily to make them be good?

7–What is the general impression the German situation left upon me?

My opinions are as follows:

Ans. 1–Has Hitler his feet under him? "Yes: in the sense that a successful dictator fully organized and in full power has his feet under him; his organization and himself absolutely self confident."

Ans. 2–What do the common people think of him? "So far as can be judged, he is almost a God and is assuredly a hope to the vast majority of the common people, who trust him implicitly and believe that a new day has come to them through him."

Ans. 3–(a) Does he know where he is going? "Apparently yes." (b) What are his ends? "To arouse Germany to an enthusiasm for the Fatherland, which is sacrificial in that it is militaristic and communal in its peace-time efforts. Apparently he has succeeded in this to an almost complete degree."

(c) Where is he going? "Apparently he will endeavor to keep this viewpoint ever before the German people. It is the viewpoint of the intensest Nationalism and pride of race. Even some of his enemies concede that probably he is the most powerful man with the common people ever to appear in German public life. Amongst the people generally, multitudes of indications exist which show at least the most tremendous power over the people; hence it is believed he will attain his ends, unless he dies prematurely or makes a major domestic mistake or is defeated in war."

Ans. 4–Is he going to last? "In my opinion, yes."

Ans. 5–Is he going to have war? "It seems quite probable."

Ans. 6–(a) Is he going to keep the Jews out for good? "Yes, in so far as they already are out." (b) Or is he just punishing them temporarily to make them be good. "It does not seem that he is punishing them temporarily to make them be good."

Ans. 7–What is the general impression the German situation left upon me? "Of a nation enthralled to a point of self-sacrifice by a spiritual arousing new to it, which is so intensely nationalistic that the chances of its destroying itself through war are about equal to its chances of success through communal domestic effort; and of a nation from which all personal liberty, as we know it here, has gone. To us, it seems also that Germany, a nation which loves to be led, is again a marching nation; and so a danger."

The above opinions are the conclusions from experiences as shown in the attached memorandum.

S. R. Fuller, Jr.

[PPF 2616:TS]

## [*Enclosure 2*] S. R. Fuller, Jr., to Roosevelt

Written at Washington, D.C. 11th of May, 1933, from notes made on the S.S. *Olympic* at Sea, 8th May, 1933 by Mrs. Fuller and S. R. Fuller, Jr.

Memorandum of conversation with Dr. Schacht at the Reichsbank, Berlin, during and after luncheon, 24th April, 1933. Through business Mrs. Fuller and I have known the Schachts some years.

Those present: Dr. Schacht, Geheimrath Schmidt, Mr. Schacht, Jr., Mrs. Fuller, Mr. S. R. Fuller, Jr.

Regarding the Jews: Dr. Schacht stated that the Jewish situation had been much exaggerated in the American press. No one had been killed; no persecutions had taken place in the sense that the Jews were made to suffer personal violence.

A large number of Jews entered Germany after the War. These had joined, to a great extent, the Communists' party. The Government for the past 10 years had been filled, in the bureaucratic places to a very large extent by Jews. The majority of places were held by Jews. Germany is not a Jewish nation. The appointed judges of the Courts were largely Jewish. The ministry of Education was filled with Jews. The Chief of Police of Berlin was a Jew. 2600 out of the 3200 Berlin lawyers were Jews. In the University of Berlin 3 per cent to 4 per cent of the student body were Jews, and 40 per cent of the professors were Jews. Germany felt that this was wrong; and they put them out and filled their places, or places where necessary, with Gentiles. "But," said Dr. Schacht, "there were many unnecessary places in the Government. A movement to make the Government more efficient was not alone directed against the Jews, but where Government places were unnecessary and were occupied by Gentiles, the Gentiles were removed the same as the Jews."

Regarding the dollar: "Inflation never succeeds, Mr. Fuller. Look what it did to us. I can see no reason for it with all your gold. The German situation was different; Germany was bankrupt."

Dr. Schacht expressed a hope that an Ambassador from the United States would not be long in coming. "We were nine months without one once," he said.

Dr. Schacht expressed appreciation of the President's handling of the banking situation, but he felt uneasiness regarding the inflation.

Dr. Schacht said the people of the world must realize that this is a revolution, a glorious revolution for Germany. He repeated at intervals the phrase "glorious revolution."

In speaking of the revolution, he explained that it also involves non-Jews; that it was a campaign against graft, etc. He used the phrase "this is a campaign of purification."

I told him that the Jewish situation had caused in New York a boycott against Glanzstoff and Bemberg goods, because the Bemberg and Glanzstoff Corporations are assumed by Jewish users of yarn to be controlled by Germans.

Dr. Schacht, at a later date, and again speaking of the Jew stated: "If I were a Jew I would be concerned; I am not a Jew and I am concerned."

He asked me whether or not I thought it would be a good idea that a special Ambassador go to the United States now from Germany. I answered, "Yes, if the man selected were politic and wise, because anything would be good which would make the two nations understand each other better and so contribute to the general peace and under-standing among the component nations of the world."

Dr. Schacht did not tell me that he, himself, had been appointed that special Ambassador; he told me this on the day following.

Dr. Schacht apparently believes in the doctrine of force with respect to industry. He stated that in the "glorious revolution" the control of industry as to operations, selling, and its relations with itself should be maintained by the Government alone, and that the force of Government was necessary because industry had proved itself incapable of handling itself to the advantage of the nation.

Geheimrath Schmidt, who is interested in the I. G. Farbenindustrie, contested this opinion above mentioned.

Dr. Schacht further stated that it would be politically impossible for Germany to leave the gold standard and again to inflate. She would rather lose her foreign trade.

Dr. Schacht further stated that the Hitler movement was not autocracy but the most perfect democracy. I made no answer to this—there seemed no use.

I wanted to see Hitler in order to get a mental picture of the man. I expressed the desire to Dr. Schacht to meet Hitler. Dr. Schacht the next day took me to see Hitler. The interview was merely perfunctory, lasted three or four minutes; and is mentioned in my main memorandum.

S. R. Fuller, Jr.[1]

[PPF 2616:CTS]

[1] Samuel R. Fuller was president of American Bemberg Corporation. He had served in World War I as a commander in the Naval Reserve and had known Roosevelt then. Fuller made frequent business trips to Germany and the Netherlands and sent the President voluminous reports on his observations of political and economic trends there. His business position, together with his connection with Roosevelt, gave him access to top officials all over Europe.

## Roosevelt to the State Department

Washington, May 27, 1933

Memorandum for the State Department: Will you prepare a letter to King Albert of Belgium saying that I am asking my very old friend, our new Ambassador, David Hennen Morris,[1] to present this personal note to him. Also say that I shall never forget the very delightful visit which I paid to him at La Panne[2] during the war and also the great pleasure of seeing him in Washington and New York after the war.

Will he be good enough to extend my compliments and good wishes to Her Majesty and to the Crown Prince and also to his daughter who reminded me so much of my own daughter when I saw her at La Panne?

F.D.R.

[*Notation*:T] This letter to be prepared for the President's signature.[3]
[OF 14:T]

[1] Dave Hennen Morris, a New York lawyer, was first considered for the post of ambassador to Germany (New York *Times,* March 17, 1933, p. 15). His appointment to Brussels was confirmed by the Senate May 10, 1933.

[2] Roosevelt, with Ambassador Brand Whitlock, had called on King Albert in Brussels on Feb. 3, 1919, while in Europe to attend the Versailles Peace Conference (Diary of Livingston Davis, Group 10).

[3] See letter of June 3, 1933, below.

## Cordell Hull, Secretary of State, to Roosevelt

Washington, May 27, 1933

Memorandum for the President.

Dear Mr. President: The accompanying letter from Minister Joseph Grew at Tokyo is so exceedingly interesting that I feel sure you will desire to read it.[1]

Cordell Hull

[PSF:Japan:TS]

[1] An attached note by Stanley K. Hornbeck, chief of the Division of Far Eastern Affairs, May 29, 1933, unaddressed, reads: "This, on Japan's military strength (both material and moral), is one of the most important documents that has come in for a long time. I think that the Secretary will by all means wish to read it carefully before reaching London."

## [*Enclosure*] Joseph C. Grew, Ambassador to Japan, to Cordell Hull

Tokyo, May 11, 1933

*Confidential*

My dear Mr. Secretary: For your information I am enclosing a copy of a special report from the Military Attaché of the Embassy, describing the Japanese Army's methods of increasing its strength by means of voluntary contributions from the people and indicating, in the closing paragraphs, the tremendous military power which Japan is developing.[1] This report gives an admirable picture of one phase of Japan's fighting strength, but I would like to describe to you, briefly, the whole picture as I see it; that is, the strength of the Japanese nation as a whole and particularly the strength of the combined Japanese fighting machine. Japan is so often spoken of as a small, over-crowded nation, cooped up within the confines of a few small islands, without natural resources, and largely dependent upon foreign sources for its foodstuffs, that people in other countries sometimes fail to appreciate the facts and to realize the actual and potential power of these people.

The Japanese Empire is not a small country, as compared with the countries of Europe, at least. The Empire itself, without "Manchukuo," has an area considerably greater than that of France or Germany and much more than that of either Spain or Italy. Including the area of "Manchukuo," which to all practical purposes is under Japanese control, the total area of Japan and its dependencies is greater than that of France, Germany, Spain, Switzerland, Belgium, Netherlands and Denmark combined. The population of the Japanese Empire proper is 90 millions; with that of "Manchukuo" it is around 120 millions, or nearly the same as that of the United States. And these people (or that part of them which is of the Japanese race) are intelligent, industrious, energetic, extremely nationalistic, war-loving, aggressive and, it must be admitted, somewhat unscrupulous. So Japan cannot be considered as a small or a weak country. Nor is it living on the verge of starvation, keeping the wolf from the door by super-human exertions. Japan can and does raise enough foodstuffs (even without "Manchukuo") to feed the population quite comfortably, and in years of large harvests is embarrassed by the surplus of foodstuffs. However, if the population continues to increase at its present rate, the food problem will become real and pressing within the next generation. Moreover, the nation has developed its industries in recent years until it is able to supply itself with all of the necessities of life, and can build all the ships, and make all the airplanes, tanks, guns, ammunition, chemicals, etc., needed to wage a severe war, if it is not too protracted. Furthermore, it has large reserves of war materials, such as petroleum, nitrates, etc., not produced within the country.

So much for the country and its people and industries. Turning to the armed forces of the country, it is my opinion that Japan probably has the most complete, well-balanced, coordinated and therefore powerful fighting machine in the world today. I do not refer to the army only, but to the combination of sea, land and air forces, backed up as they are by enormous reserves of trained men, by industrial units coordinated with the fighting machine and by large reserves of supplies. The different units in Japan's machine may be exceeded in size by equivalent units of other nations, but taken as a whole the machine, I believe, is equal, if not superior, to that of any other nation. Thus, France has a larger army, but a much smaller navy; Great Britain has a larger navy, but a much smaller army. The United States is weaker than Japan on land and about equal on the sea, but is probably potentially superior in the air. Of course, it would take a group of naval, military, aviation and industrial experts to calculate accurately the relative strengths of the fighting machines of the world, but I think that if such could be done, the strength of Japan's combined machine would give a shock to many people. The machine probably could not stand a protracted, severe war, as industrial supplies would become exhausted, but for a quick, hard push I do not believe that the machine has its equal in the world.

Relative to the strength which could conceivably be brought against it, I consider Japan's fighting machine immeasurably stronger than any other. Thus, France's army is not large if all the forces which could be brought against it in Europe are considered, nor is Great Britain's navy large when compared with the combined naval forces of the European Powers. But Japan has no potential enemy in Asia capable of defeating her fighting machine as a whole, not even Soviet Russia it is believed, while American and European countries are too far from Japan to offer any serious menace. Japan's relative strength, therefore, is much greater than that of any other Power.

However, although we are faced with this tremendously powerful fighting machine across the Pacific, I think that our anxiety can be lessened by the fact that this machine does not seem to be designed for aggressive action outside of the Far East. The Japanese fighting machine, unless I am very much mistaken, is designed for the purpose of keeping Western nations from interfering while Japan carries out its ambitions in Asia, whatever they may be. It is true that the Japanese fighting forces consider the United States as their potential enemy, and sometimes direct their manoeuvres against a potential American attack by sea or air, but that is because they think that the United States is standing in the path of the nation's natural expansion and is more apt to interfere with Japan's ambitions than are the European nations.

Whether directed at us or not, however, I believe that it would be well for us to keep this tremendous Japanese fighting machine in mind when discussing disarmament.

More than the size of the nation or the strength of its fighting machine, however, the thing which makes the Japanese nation actually so powerful and potentially so menacing, is the national morale and esprit de corps—a spirit which perhaps has not been equalled since the days when the Mongol hordes followed Genghis Khan in his conquest of Asia. The force of a nation bound together with great moral determination, fired with national ambition, and peopled by a race with unbounded capacity for courageous self-sacrifice is not easy to overestimate.

Respectfully yours,

Joseph C. Grew

[*Notation*:A] Noted by Mr. Philips 5/29/33
[PSF:Japan:TS]

[1] This report, not printed here, consists of excerpts from bulletins issued in April and May 1933 by the prefectural office, Chiba Prefecture.

## Cordell Hull, Secretary of State, to Roosevelt

Washington, May 27, 1933

Memorandum for the President: Mr. Taussig handed me the accompanying documents with a request that I send them over to the White House with such comment as I might feel justified in making.

The truth is that I have really not had a split second of time in which to study the proposal. I can only say, therefore, that at first glance this appears to offer a feasible plan to deal with the sugar situation in a way that would include the so-called quota plan.

As to whether the treaty arrangement in contemplation would violate the temporary tariff truce,[1] and as to whether it would conflict with the cabled request of Ambassador Welles to the effect that no concessions of any character be made to the Cuban government until a final decision has been reached by the President (of Cuba) regarding a solution of the political problems,[2] would to any extent negative the idea of taking such preliminary steps regarding authorization by Congress as are proposed in the accompanying document, are matters about which you will doubtless have your own opinion.

Cordell Hull

[OF 159-A:TS]

[1] In effect from May 12, 1933, for the life of the London Conference.
[2] See Welles to Hull, May 25, 1933, in *Foreign Relations, 1933*, V, 295–296.

## [*Enclosure*] Charles W. Taussig to Cordell Hull.

[*Undated*]

The Department's policy towards Cuba is directed to assisting the Cuban Government to terminate the existing political difficulties and to rehabilitate its national economy. In order to accomplish the latter, Ambassador Welles has explored the basis under which it might be possible for the United States to give to Cuba a more profitable participation in the American sugar market. The granting by the United States of this advantage is to be dependent, however, upon the taking by the Cuban Government of certain measures to settle the distressing political situation. In other words, the prospect of increased economic advantages is a plum which will not be granted until the Cuban Government has taken positive and satisfactory steps to conclude the present unrest.

It is apparent, therefore, that the success of the Department's policy depends upon the enactment of the legislation which will make it possible for the Executive to make certain trade concessions, in return for equivalent concessions. The passage by Congress of the Farm Bill[1] has paved the way for this law and will make it possible for the Executive to establish sugar quotas among the various producing groups, including Cuba. So far as Cuba is concerned this will be insufficient, however, unless supplemented by legislation authorizing the Executive to enter into reciprocal trade negotiations with that country.

There is attached hereto a draft of the legislation intended to cover this need. As it is imperative that the legislation receive Congressional approval this session, it is suggested that it be attached as a rider to the General Revenue Bill.

Since the success of the Department's policy towards Cuba depends, in the last analysis, upon the enactment in some form of the necessary legislation, the importance of securing the President's approval and support of this or of some other satisfactory project is at once apparent.

[OF 159-A:CT]

¹The Agricultural Adjustment Act.

## [*Enclosure*]

Subject to ratification by the Republic of Cuba, Article II of the convention between the United States and the Republic of Cuba which became effective December 27, 1903, is hereby amended by adding the following at the end of said Article II:

Provided, however, that the President may increase such reduction of twenty per centum up to but not to exceed fifty per centum upon such articles in such quantities and for such period or periods of time from time to time and under such terms and conditions as he may determine whenever he finds that Cuba has reduced or removed, or will reduce or remove, any tariff or other burden or restriction upon the importation into that country of any articles the growth, produced or manufacture of the United States and that the export trade of the United States will be benefitted thereby. This amendment of Article II shall become effective when ratified by the Republic of Cuba and upon proclamation of the President of the United States and the President of Cuba, and any such increase of the reduction of twenty per centum up to but not to exceed fifty per centum upon any article or articles, shall become effective upon the proclamation thereof by the President of the United States.

[OF 159-A:CT]

## Cordell Hull, Secretary of State, to Roosevelt

Washington, May 27, 1933

Dear Mr. President: The Governments of Colombia and Peru have accepted the recommendations of the Advisory Committee of the League of Nations for a peaceful settlement of the Leticia dispute between those two countries. One of the recommendations of the Advisory Committee was that the Council of the League should appoint a Commission to go to Leticia to take charge of the administration of the territory in the name of the Government of Colombia, while the two governments, with the good offices of the Council of the League, negotiate in such place as they desire a settlement of their difficulties.

We are advised by Minister Wilson from Geneva that the League's Advisory Committee unanimously suggests that there should be three members of the Commission to go to Leticia, one from Brazil, one from the United States, and one from Spain. It has been suggested that the American should be an army officer with administrative experience who speaks Spanish, the Brazilian member should be a naval officer, and the Spaniard a diplomat. It is my understanding that the American officer would be appointed by the Council of the League and would of course in no wise represent the Government of the United States while serving on the League's Commission at Leticia. His status would be similar to that of General McCoy when the latter served on the League's Commission in the Far East.[1]

Inasmuch as we have cooperated fully with the League in order to bring about a peaceful settlement of this conflict, thus carrying forward your policy of the "good neighbor," I earnestly recommend that we should informally advise the League that there would be no objection to an American army officer serving on the Commission in Leticia under the conditions set out above, and that we should suggest the name of the officer in question. If you approve I will take the matter up at once with the Secretary of War, in order to select an officer of the proper qualifications.[2]

Faithfully yours,

Cordell Hull

[*Notation*:AS:FDR] OK FDR
[OF 313-C:TS]

[1] Major General Frank R. McCoy was United States member of the 1932 League of Nations Manchurian Inquiry Commission (Lytton Commission).

[2] The United States had agreed on March 18, 1933, to cooperate with the League in settling the Leticia dispute. Spain, Brazil, and the United States formed a commission to supervise the removal of the troops of Colombia and Peru from the disputed areas, and the removal was accomplished in 1934 (Hull, *Memoirs,* I, 310–311). See *Foreign Relations, 1933,* IV, "The Leticia Dispute," pp. 384–548.

## Cordell Hull, Secretary of State, to Roosevelt

Washington, May 27, 1933

Memorandum for the President: I gathered the impression from Key Pittman that he had conferred with you about a compromise amendment to the arms embargo resolution pending before the Committee on Foreign Relations in the Senate, and that Pittman had decided to make the measure apply to both parties to any particular conflict.[1] I did not learn whether you had finally and definitely agreed to this proposal.

If you have not committed yourself definitely, I would suggest that since the proposal is directly in conflict with our position at Geneva as expressed by Norman Davis,[2] it would be well for the government to deal with the matter in the light of this situation.

If, in other words, certain extremists among the senators desire to take the responsibility of preventing the adoption of the policy of peace that is being pursued by every other enlightened nation, they might be given the privilege of tying up proposed peace legislation over the next few months.

Cordell Hull

[OF 404:TS]

[1] This reference is to House Joint Resolution 93 introduced by McReynolds on March 16, 1933. The resolution, drafted by the State Department, authorized the President to act in concert with other countries to bar the export of arms and munitions to such countries as he might designate. (President Hoover had recommended the same legislation to the Congress in his message of Jan. 10, 1933.) The resolution was approved by the House on April 17, though Representative Edith Nourse Rogers of Massachusetts voiced the objection of the minority when she asked the House if their constituents had sent them to Congress "to give the President the authority to make a declaration of war against any country?" In the Senate Foreign Relations Committee an amendment offered by Johnson was approved. The amendment required that the embargo be applied to all parties to a dispute; no punitive or passive action against a particular country could therefore be taken without specific action by Congress. So amended, the resolution was reported on May 30. No action, however, was taken (*Cong. Rec.,* vol. 77, pp. 581, 1683–1702, 1746–1777, 1848–1850, 4577–4578).

[2] Davis' statement on May 22 was that the United States would accept the MacDonald plan for general disarmament and was willing to consult with other states in determining aggression. The United States would also agree to do nothing to defeat collective efforts in dealing with an aggressor (*Foreign Relations, 1933,* I, 154–158).

## William Phillips, Under Secretary of State, to Roosevelt

Washington, May 27, 1933

My dear Mr. President: Referring to my letter to you of May 25th in which I enclosed telegram No. 660 of May 25th from Mr. Davis at Geneva requesting instructions on the aviation question,[1] I have just received a further telegram from Mr. Davis (No. 668 of May 27th)[2] in which he asks urgent replies to the following questions:

(1) Can we accept for the life of the Disarmament Convention the provisions relating to civil aviation, as set out in Annex II of the British draft? (A copy of the British draft convention is attached; you will find Annex II on pages 9 to 10 thereof.)[3]

*Yes*[4]

(2) Can we accept the method of limitation of airplanes by unladen weight, as set forth in articles 37 and 41 of Chapter 3 of the British draft, and in Annex I to that Chapter? (See pages 8 and 9 of attached copy of draft convention.) Mr. Davis states that this method of limitation is opposed by the War and Navy Departments, but that it can probably not be eliminated without a public debate with the French and British, who support this method.

*Yes, as to principle but send us final text before approving—*

(3) Can we accept the figure of 500 for the number of our military and naval aircraft, as set forth in the table annexed to article 41 of the British draft? (See page 9 of the attached copy of the draft convention.) *Yes FDR*

Discussion of the air chapter of the British plan started in the Geneva Commission of the Disarmament Conference this morning and will continue on Monday. Mr. Davis is therefore very anxious to receive instructions as soon as possible, and in any case not later than tomorrow evening. We have not taken up the above points with the War and Navy Departments and shall not do so unless you wish us to. For reference purposes, I am enclosing a copy of Mr. Davis's telegram.[5]

Faithfully yours,

William Phillips[6]

[OF 404:TS]

---

[1] Phillips' letter of May 25 is present (PSF:Disarmament Conference) but the telegram is not.

[2] Printed in *Foreign Relations, 1933,* I, 171.

[3] This is not found with Phillips' letter. According to *Foreign Relations, 1933,* I, 171,

Annex II is printed in League of Nations, Conference for the Reduction and Limitation of Armaments, *Conference Documents,* II, 487.

[4] This and the succeeding italicized interpolations are written in the left margin in Roosevelt's handwriting.

[5] Not present.

[6] The President's instructions were sent to Davis by Hull in a telegram of May 28, *Foreign Relations, 1933,* I, 171–172.

# Henry A. Wallace, Secretary of Agriculture, to Roosevelt

Washington, D.C., May 27, 1933

Dear Mr. President: Relative to the proposed loan to China for the purpose of buying our wheat and cotton, I wish to call attention to one aspect which it is very easy to overlook at the moment. It is an aspect which the Republicans overlooked during the period from 1921 to 1929 which had a lot to do with bringing on the depression and the Republican defeat.

In brief the point is this: It is dangerous to loan money to other nations to buy your surplus unless you are definitely prepared sooner or later to receive goods in equal value from them.

I want to register my conviction that it is exceedingly dangerous to build up prices of export products by loans of money abroad unless we are willing on the one hand to keep our producers fully informed as to the ephemeral nature of this matter, and on the other hand to keep our people, as a whole, informed of the necessity for importing large quantities of goods from abroad within the relatively near future.

For ten years, I denounced the Republicans for failing to think clearly on this matter, and I am going to do everything I can to keep myself from being a party to the same kind of mistake in this administration. I think it is all right to loan considerable quantities of money abroad during the next year or two provided we make a real effort to educate the people in the United States to exactly what such loans mean.

I think there are real possibilities of developing continuing trade with the Orient provided we can educate our people in the United States to buy large quantities of Chinese handmade stuff, such as cloisonné vases, silken tapestries, embroidered goods, jades, etc., etc. It will be a tremendous public relations job to get the people of the United States willing to accept the necessary quantities of such things from abroad.[1]

Respectfully yours,

H. A. Wallace

I hope that our loaning of money abroad can be made a part of our national planning program. It is possible for a loan like the Chinese loan to interfere with other parts of our program.

[OF 150-D:TS]

[1] Discussions concerning a $50,000,000 loan to China by the Reconstruction Finance Corporation were begun by Finance Minister T. V. Soong during his visit to Washington in May 1933. The loan was granted on June 4 and ratified by the Nanking government on June 16, with about four-fifths of the amount earmarked for cotton and the remainder for wheat (New York *Times,* June 5, p. 1; June 17, 1933, p. 4).

## Roosevelt to Cordell Hull, Secretary of State

[Washington] May 30, 1933

Dear Mr. Secretary: I have the pleasure of appointing you Chairman of the Delegation which is to represent this Government at the monetary and Economic Conference, which is scheduled to open in London on June 12th.[1] The general subject matter for the Conference discussions is contained in the report of the Preparatory Commission of Experts, of which a copy is attached.[2] While this report may be taken as a useful presentation of the matters which require consideration, the opinions expressed therein are in no way to be considered as binding upon the American Government.

The American Delegation is instructed to set forth the American policy as outlined in the attached memorandum of instruction. In consultation with your colleagues you are authorized to use your best judgment in deciding upon minor variations in form or substance that may arise in the course of discussion. If, however, decision must be reached on matters not covered in the attached memorandum,[3] or if major changes of substance in matters covered by the memorandum seem to you necessary, you are instructed to refer decision to Washington.

It will, of course, be necessary for the Delegation to use its best judgment as to the most effective means and procedure for bringing about a speedy and successful outcome of the Conference. I wish to urge upon you that delay in conferences of this nature usually makes it more difficult to secure results and that agreement on main principles should be reached as expeditiously as possible.

There is one other thing which I wish to point out; namely, that neither you nor any other member of the Delegation is to carry on, formally or informally, any discussion of either war debts or disarmament. These two problems will be handled by me in Washington, and any questions in regard thereto should be referred to Washington.

I need not emphasize the importance to the welfare of the American people of the mission you are about to undertake. You may be assured that in your effort you may rely upon the full cooperation of myself and the whole American Government.[4]

Sincerely yours,

Franklin D. Roosevelt

[PSF:London Economic Conference:TS]

[1] Other members of the delegation were James M. Cox, former governor of Ohio, Senator Key Pittman of Nevada, chairman of the Senate Foreign Relations Committee, Rep. Samuel D. McReynolds of Tennessee, Senator James Couzens of Michigan, and Ralph W. Morrison of Texas. Morrison, a utilities and ranching magnate, was a friend of John N. Garner and Farley; Moley says his views on financial matters were unknown to the President (*After Seven Years*, p. 218). William C. Bullitt was chief executive officer; Herbert Feis, economic adviser to the State Department, was chief technical adviser; James P. Warburg was financial adviser. Roosevelt held a last conference with the delegates on May 29. Moley says the discussion was "desultory," the delegates were of different minds, and the instructions were not clear (*ibid.,* pp. 218–219). Perhaps the most optimistic member of the delegation was Hull, who had every expectation that the conference would deal with tariff reform (see his *Memoirs,* I, 249–251; and Moley, *After Seven Years,* pp. 196–198).

[2] *Draft Annotated Agenda* (League of Nations: Geneva, Jan. 20, 1933).

[3] Two pages of general instructions on organization of the American delegation and a ten-page memorandum on policy for the guidance of the American delegation, labeled, in Hull's handwriting, "Copy of Hull."

[4] Printed also, with the enclosures just cited, in *Foreign Relations, 1933,* I, 620–627.

## Augusto Rosso, Italian Ambassador, to Roosevelt

Washington, May 30, 1933

Mr. President: Availing myself of your kind authorization, I take the liberty of writing informally to you on the subject I had the privilege of discussing lately at the White House.[1]

When I had the honour to report to you the answer given to our ouverture in Tokyo, you told me of your intention to communicate to the Department of State, for their files, a confidential record of what had taken place.

I have now been informed that in the course of a recent conversation with the Under Secretary of State, the Japanese Ambassador at Rome had made a direct reference to our move in Tokyo, showing a particular interest to ascertain the motives of the Italian initiative.

The Japanese Ambassador was duly informed of the objective reasons which had prompted Signor Mussolini to enquire, privately and confidentially, about the chances of success that the Japanese Government could see in an offer of mediation from the Great Powers.[2] The Ambassador was told at the same time, as it had already been said at Tokyo according to your suggestion, that such a step had been made on the personal initiative of Signor Mussolini, without the knowledge of anybody and under no inspiration whatsoever from outside.

Signor Mussolini has now pointed out to me that the presence of a record on the subject at the Department of State would materially contradict the declaration made by us, both to the Minister of Foreign Affairs in Tokyo and to the Japanese Ambassador in Rome, and that the knowledge of such a document or the future revelation of its contents would challenge the sincerity and loyalty of our dealings with the Japanese.

Signor Mussolini would therefore much prefer that the matter continue to remain strictly secret, unless it were deemed advisable to let the Japanese understand that we had kept the American Government informed of our move.

As you see, Mr. President, it is a genuine "cas de conscience" that Signor Mussolini has asked to submit to your consideration, and I would appreciate your kindness in enabling me to tell him what is your view on the subject.

I wish to add that I have received also another cable from Signor Mussolini concerning the present situation in China, and with instructions to discuss it with the Department of State. Of course, I would be only too glad to have the privilege of bringing this communication to your knowledge at your best convenience, if so desired.[3]

I have the honour to be, Mr. President, Very respectfully,

A. Rosso

[OF 197:TS]

[1] On May 19 and 22, 1933 (PPF 1-0).

[2] The Japanese delegation to the League of Nations walked out of the Assembly on Feb. 24, 1933, when the report of the Committee of Nineteen, appointed to study the Lytton Report on the Sino-Japanese crisis, upheld its findings against Japan. On March 27, Japan gave notice of her intention to withdraw from the League. During April and May 1933, Mussolini was actively promoting his Four Power Pact (*Foreign Relations, 1933*, I, 396ff), and Rosso's reference to an "offer of mediation" in the Sino-Japanese difficulties is apparently related to this.

[3] Answered June 8, 1933, below.

## Press Conference, Executive Offices of the White House, May 31, 1933, 10:37 A.M.

[*Excerpt*] The President: But there is another—and I am talking between us—there is another angle that does disturb me. There are a lot of people in other parts of the world who take what they read as true. They haven't got on to the fact that we are a nation of spoofers in our press.

I will give you a couple of examples that I, frankly, feel rather badly about. It is not a question of mentioning the name of any one newspaper or two newspapers—that is beside the point. What I am thinking about is this country and also about things we are trying to do in the world, that we are trying to do for the peace and the peoples of the world that have been seriously hurt by things that have appeared that were not true in our American papers. I will give you two examples: The day before I sent the Round Robin letter to all the crowned heads,[1] et cetera, of course we had been working on it for a couple of days and I suppose I must have talked to fifteen or twenty people about it. I was not the least bit concerned over the fact that there was what might be called a leak to this extent; the leak was to the extent that a message was going out. That was on Monday afternoon. It was telephoned by some people who were not Press—a very lovely lady in town telephoned on to New York to her friends and said, "For God's sake, buy all the stock you can at the opening tomorrow morning because the President is going to send an important message on disarmament tomorrow morning." That is all there was in the way of a leak, the fact that a message of disarmament was going out. But, and this is absolutely in confidence, and so it is just between us girls and boys, somebody wrote a story which came out in this paper on Tuesday morning to the effect that this message, number one, was going to Geneva to Norman Davis—of course that was wrong; number two, that the message was going to contain a guaranty of security to France.[2] That went to France and I don't mind telling you that it went from here from the French people in Washington because the French people assumed that this particular paper that carried that particular story was speaking for the Administration. It got to the French Foreign Office and the French Foreign Office immediately sent for the French Press and said, "Hurrah, grand, the United States is going to guarantee the security of France." And they all believed it and at the editorial desks

190

in Paris they started in to write their editorials saying that the Americans are going to guarantee the security of France. About two hours later—about eleven o'clock their time, which is five o'clock our time—the actual message was delivered in Paris and the French said, "Oh, it is the most awful shock and disappointment we have ever had." The result was that neither the French Press nor the French Government took that peace message, the disarmament message, the way they should have taken it.

Now, the source of that information was one hundred per cent accurate and could be proved. That is one instance.

Now, I will give you the other one, also in the family. As a matter of fact, on the debt negotiations, the situation is no different from what I have told you for the last two months. Get that first. The position of this country is just what my position was last November and that is that a debtor nation has the right to come to its creditor. Now, the debtor nations have not come to us with any proposition. Now, there is no news in that, you all know it. I have told you that right along. We have made no offers. I have told you that right along. Absolutely none. We are still in the position of the creditor nation that is willing to receive conversations, offers, suggestions, from the debtor nations, and we have had nothing. Now, as a matter of fact, this is absolutely all off the record—remember that. The French Government, I think, is honestly trying to put itself in some way—we don't know how yet—into the same position that England is in by trying to do something about the old December 15th payment. Here again, this is something that is not news. You know it. I have told the French consistently that while we can say to England, "Come right along, talk to us, lay any proposition before us you want to," we cannot say quite the same thing to the French because they have not done anything about the December 15th payment. As M. Herriot said the other day in the Chamber, and as I have told you, we have told the French that the first thing we believe they should do is to do something about the December 15th payment. Nothing has come from them over here—not a thing.

Now, up to the day before yesterday, the French Government was trying, from all the information that we have had, to work out something in regard to December 15th. Yesterday morning, two papers came out with the pretty cute statements that we had made an offer to the French for some form of partial payment in June.[3] Now, that was made up out of the whole cloth. I cannot help it if you people write stories on what somebody who is a third cousin or a fifth cousin of the Administration tells you. It is not true but, in so doing, you are hurting the cause of your own Government. The result was that yesterday morning, when those stories were cabled over, the officials of the French Cabinet were seriously embarrassed because every member of the Chamber of Deputies said, "Oh, a proposition from the United States," and if what they were working on had any prospect of successful conclusion in regard to the December 15th payment, that prospect was seriously weakened by American newspaper stories. Now, that is the fact.

Now, there are two very, very good instances in the last couple of weeks of how our foreign relations, first in regard to world peace and disarmament and secondly in regard to debts, have been seriously influenced by stories made out of the whole cloth in the American papers.

Now, in regard to those stories, I have had, very reluctantly, off the record and between us, I have had to make it very clear to the French and also to one or two other nations that I specifically asked them to pay no attention from now on to stories coming out in these papers. If they want information, they can get it from this Government and, judging by the events in the past few weeks, they had better not pay any attention to that kind of story. Now, I hated to have to do that about our own papers, but that is the situation. They had seriously hurt the work we tried to carry out in international affairs.

However, coming down to domestic matters, that is all right. I am sorry to have had to say all this, but it is very serious embarrassment to our Government to have had that kind of story and I know you want me to tell you the things that worry me. Those stories that have been made up out of the whole cloth have been a source of very much worry to me where they affected our foreign relations.

Q: May I point out one case which arouses our curiosity as to whether anything is happening, particularly those of us who cover the State Department. First, these stories crop up. Then we ask the State Department if they are true or what is true and their reply is that they cannot tell us anything about it either way. The next step is to ask the White House but of course we cannot see you but twice a week so that it is difficult to check up. Then we have to believe the stories are true in view of the fact that—

The President: The only thing I can say is that Steve runs in here on the average of twice a day. Usually there is a denial. As a matter of fact, ninety-nine per cent of that stuff is not true and the odds are ninety-nine to one that there would be a denial out of here.

Q: Of course, as soon as it comes out, we have to write something from here.

Q: Mr. President, it might be helpful for your purpose if you could lift the lid sufficiently for us to inform our offices in confidence about what you said.

The President: That is perfectly all right. In other words, this should not be a thing to go beyond us, but it is all right to let the offices know about it. But it is a thing that has disturbed me, especially the French. They are easily upset—awfully upsettable—by rumors and the French Government, of course, has one of the most difficult parliamentary situations in the world to control. No human being can tell, from one day to another, what the Chamber of Deputies is going to do. Our difficulties with Congress are nothing compared to the French.

There isn't really anything new on debts, as I said before. Our position is that we are perfectly willing to receive any suggestions from the other side and we have not had any.

Q: We have a report from London saying that Ambassador Bingham said that the statement made by Mr. Davis at Geneva was a departure from traditional American principle.[4] Do you agree with that, regarding the security pact?

The President: No, I do not agree with it—that is off the record.

Q: Then he has given a wrong impression of the American viewpoint.

The President: Yes.

Q: Then you haven't anything in mind but that you are just going along with the same policy—just waiting for others to make the offers?

The President: Exactly the same position; absolutely no change at all.

Q: Couldn't we use that as background—that there is no change in the debt situation?

The President: I think you can use that as background. After all, that is not news. Of course, it depends a little bit on how you use it for background. Now, for example—you need not look through the paper I am looking at—that is neither here nor there—I want to give you an illustration of English. Here is a story that says, here is the lead (reading from the New York *Times* of May 31st, 1933), "The White House refused to concede publicly that there had been any definite program adopted by President Roosevelt for dealing with the war debt problem."[5] Now, that is a little bit like printing one day a story that I had decided this summer to make a trip to the Philippines and then, the next day, saying that the White House refused to concede that the

President was going to make a trip to the Philippines after the White House had laughed it out of court. Now, that is not good ball. It is not clean ball. It is a story one day that the President had murdered his own grandmother and the next day saying that the President had refused to concede that he had murdered his own grandmother. That is not clean ball.

Q: Is there anything new on the tariff situation in your message? Is it likely to go up this week?

The President: On the tariff? I think I will have to make this off the record because I still have not made up my mind definitely. I am working on a tariff proposal and the first draft of it has worked out to sixteen or seventeen pages. It was highly complicated. It related to possible decreases and possible increases of what might be called a temporary act; in other words, one that applied between the summer and the time the Congress comes back next winter. I have been trying to boil it down and I have got it boiled down now to three pages and a half and, if I can, I am going to try to get it down to a page and a half. I want to make it simple and as little controversial as possible. If I can get something up there that there won't be very much controversy about, not more than one day's debate, the purpose of it being made perfectly clear, I will send it up. However, that is as far as I got and I am still trying to boil it down.

[President's Press Conferences:T]

[1] May 16, 1933, above.

[2] The newspaper is not identified.

[3] Cf. the Washington dispatch to the New York *Times* of May 29, 1933 (issue of May 30, p. 1).

[4] Davis' statement of May 22, 1933, printed, *Foreign Relations, 1933*, I, 166–168.

[5] The article went on to say (p. 1) that, in spite of the denial, "it was insisted in well-informed quarters that such procedure was in contemplation," and that "what the President chiefly wanted was to have Congress out of the way before making known the details of his program, and thus escape any embarrassment which an outburst of opposition might bring."

# Breckinridge Long, Ambassador to Italy, to Roosevelt

Rome, Italy, June 1, 1933

My dear Frank: Your Ambassador to Italy has been part of a big show. The King received me yesterday, and I was taken with my whole staff. A regular procession of coaches with footmen in gorgeous uniform attended. There were four coaches, one empty carriage, like a spare tire, and one out-rider on horseback at the head of the procession. My understanding is that there were more details of formality and polite expressions of attention in the form of servants, soldiers, and salutes than any occasion the oldest resident at the Embassy remembers. It was quite a compliment to you.

I am cabling you about the Four-Power-Pact, so I will not enter into that here, as it will probably all be history before you get this letter.[1]

However, I do want to tell you about Mussolini. He is a man of comparatively short stature with a very soft, well-modulated voice and an air of quiet and dignified elegance. The long and enormous room which he uses for an office is devoid of furniture of any kind and without hangings on any wall. The only vestige of furniture is his desk, which sits across a far corner, on which there are a number of papers and several portfolios, and on the floor stacked against the wall behind the desk there are a number of other papers and files. In front of the desk are two sixteenth century Italian small chairs facing one another. Behind the desk is his own desk chair.

As I entered the room and started to walk toward him, he arose from his desk and approached me gradually. I am sure that I was looking at him much more intently than he could have been looking at me. My interest was intense. As we approached, he extended his hand at full length and said, "Your Excellency, I am very glad indeed to have you in Rome as the American Ambassador."

He was really very gracious and courteous and generous in his manner as well as in the expression of it, and he made me feel quite at ease immediately, though I must confess that I had not been ill at ease.

We turned and walked toward his desk, and I then gave him the bound copy of your Inaugural Address and explained that you had had it specially printed and specially bound and had autographed it for him.[2] He was very much pleased and said, "Oh, it is his first speech," and then said that he would read it and enjoy it and was delighted to be remembered by you in that form.

I then presented to him the autograph letter, which he received with expressions of extreme satisfaction.[3] We then sat down, and he read your letter, proceeding slowly and reading the words in a low voice to himself.

When he finished reading the letter, he said that he was delighted to have it. He said it was an excellent letter and that he appreciated it very much, and as he placed it back in its envelope and laid it on the table, he patted it with his hand and said again, "It is an excellent letter, and I am glad to have it. Will you not thank Mr. Roosevelt."

He then discussed you in highly complimentary manner. He expressed very great personal admiration. He said that you were doing a very great work in a very great way; that you were proceeding correctly from his point of view; that you would defeat the depression and that the methods that you were following would bring America back to its feet.

He then took up the Four Power Pact. He hoped you would be interested in it and would see that it meant the peace of Europe. His exact words, as I recall them were, "It will insure peace in Europe for ten years, and at the end of ten years the depression will be over."

He made some very pleasant personal references to me and seemed to know something of my past activities, which I assume he obtained from some resumé which had been prepared for him and read so recently he could not forget. At any rate, he was generously courteous.

After about fifteen minutes of conversation, he arose, and we walked together the whole length of this enormous room, proceeding very slowly and very deep in conversation. He expressed the belief that you would lead America gradually to a responsible position in international affairs and would help in the rehabilitation of a distraught world.

I told him that I had your complete confidence and the complete confidence of my Government and that I had come to Rome at a difficult time in the history of the world and had come to work and not to play; that I wanted to cooperate with him and wanted him to feel that with the confidence which I enjoyed from you that I would be able to cooperate in some substantial way.

He said, "I will cooperate. I want to cooperate. You can count upon me."

About this time we approached the door. He stopped and shook hands again firmly, and I turned and opened the door and walked out into the other room, being conscious of having been in the presence of a really unusual person.

And his whole setting is unusual. It is not only the room in which he sits and works, but it is other rooms through which you pass in proceeding to and emerging from his office which give the impression of magnificence and beauty such as I have seldom witnessed. The red waiting-room has a fourteenth century ceiling which is very high with deep red brocade silk on the walls and just enough of lovely early primitives on the walls and of sixteenth century furniture around the edge of the floor to be quite elegant. In addition, there is a blue room, which seems to be a place for council meetings, and then there is another room which I remember less distinctly. But not only the rooms themselves, but the quiet dignity with which one is met and the force indicated at the portals leave a very distinct impression of quiet but determined energy.

I am sorry to have written at such length, but I thought you would be interested to get my complete reaction from my first conversation with Mussolini, for it largely concerned you and the things you are interested in and are trying to do.

They seem to have put themselves out somewhat in their efforts to pay me courteous attention. They even sent a sleeping-car from Milan to the border for my convenience and in order that I would not have to change trains at Milan, and in every respect they have showed me extreme courtesy, and of course it only reflects the very high opinion in which you are held.

From this distance it is very hard for me to follow all you are doing. The present dispatches are meagre. No information seems to come quickly. After I get accustomed to the situation I may have some suggestion to make as to whether or not there should not be some means of keeping me closer posted as to developments at home, because it will be a great handicap to be isolated and not to have an informative background.[4]

With every expression of good will, Yours very respectfully,

Breckinridge Long

[PPF 434:TS]

[1] The Four Power Pact had been proposed by Mussolini to MacDonald and Simon on March 18, 1933 (Simon to Sir Ronald W. Graham, British ambassador to Italy, June 7, 1933, *British Documents, 1919–1939,* V, 323–330). Its object was to enable Italy, Britain, France, and Germany to take action in matters affecting them without recourse to the formal processes of the League of Nations but at the same time without departing from their obligations to the League covenant, the Locarno treaties, and the Kellogg-Briand Pact. The pact was signed in Rome on June 7 and ratified July 15, 1933, to run for ten years; see *Foreign Relations, 1933,* I, 396–425. Long had cabled Roosevelt on May 31 that the Italian government had indicated that it would be helpful if the President would express approval of the pact, not with respect to Europe but as it might affect the peace of the world (*ibid.,* 411–412).

[2] *Inaugural Address of Franklin D. Roosevelt* (Washington, 1933), one of a number specially bound by the Government Printing Office for the personal distribution of the President.

[3] May 14, 1933, above.

[4] Answered June 16, 1933; Roosevelt said he wished he could have been with Long on his visit to Mussolini (*Personal Letters, 1928–1945,* I, 351–352).

## Press Conference, Executive Offices of the White House, June 2, 1933, 4:12 P.M.

[*Excerpt*] Q: Have you approved or disapproved the Johnson Amendment to the Arms Embargo Resolution making it mandatory?

The President: No. Again off the record, Steve,[1] Secretary Hull, before he left, talked to the Foreign Relations people up there and said that in his judgment it would be a bad thing to do at this time.

Q: Mr. President, have you any plans for that resolution so far as the remainder of the session is concerned?[2]

The President: (No answer.)[3]

[President's Press Conferences:T]

[1] F. M. Stephenson of the Associated Press.
[2] See Hull to Roosevelt, May 27, 1933, above.
[3] All parenthetical words in the press conference transcripts are by the reporter unless otherwise noted.

## Roosevelt to Albert, King of the Belgians, Brussels

Washington [June 3, 1933][1]

My dear King Albert: I am asking our new Ambassador, Mr. Dave Hennen Morris, who is a very old friend of mine, to present to Your Majesty this line of personal greetings. I shall never forget the very delightful visit which I paid to you at La Panne during the war, or the two occasions on which I saw you, in Washington and in New York, after the war was over. May I ask that you be good enough to present my respectful homage to Her Majesty and cordial good wishes to your son, the Crown Prince, and to your daughter, whom I recall as reminding me so much of my own daughter when I saw her as a young girl at La Panne.

Very sincerely yours,

[*Notation*:A:FDR] Copy
[OF 14:T:Copy]

[1] This date is supplied and approximate; the letter was prepared by Under Secretary of State Phillips in response to Roosevelt's note to him of May 27 in which he outlined what he wished to say. Phillips' note sending this draft, June 1, reads: "I have prepared a draft letter to King Albert, in accordance with your instructions. In addressing him

as "King Albert" we have followed the precedents of various private letters which President Theodore Roosevelt addressed to King Edward, Emperor William and others." Phillip's draft followed the President's suggested remarks almost verbatim. The letter actually sent was written by Roosevelt in longhand (OF 14).

## Roosevelt to Arthur Sweetser, Director, Information Section, League of Nations

[Washington] June 3, 1933

Dear Mr. Sweetser: I am delighted to have your letter[1] and also the set of League of Nations' stamps which I have not got in my collection and which are a real addition to it. I am also getting the State Department to send me many of the envelopes that come from our Delegates in Geneva, but these do not bear the surcharge stamps.

We are all of us pinning great hopes to the outcome of events in Geneva and London during the next few weeks.

My sincere regards, Very sincerely yours,

[PPF 506:CT]

[1] May 23, 1933, above.

## Basil Manly, New York State Power Authority, to Roosevelt

Washington, D.C., June 3, 1933

Dear Mr. President: I am handing you herewith through Mr. McIntyre the letter from Mr. Walsh, the substance of which, as received over the telephone, I gave you at the conference yesterday with Senator La Follette.[1]

I have reported to Mr. Walsh your intention of sending a communication to the Senate on Monday. He asked me to say that this would fully meet the situation outlined in his letter.

The material on the Treaty and Joint Resolution, which you requested, was handed to Mr. McIntyre yesterday afternoon. I hope it was satisfactory.[2]

Respectfully yours,

Basil Manly

[OF 156:TS]

---

[1] Printed below. La Follette and Manly (at this time Washington representative of the New York State Power Authority) had met with Roosevelt at the White House (PPF 1-0).

[2] This material consists of: an undated letter from Walsh to Roosevelt on a plan to poll the Senate to discover the strength of the pro-treaty group; a memorandum, also undated, and presumably by Walsh, on the importance of early ratification of the St. Lawrence Seaway Treaty; and a draft presidential message to the Senate, June 5, 1933, urging ratification, presumably by either Walsh or Manly (or both). Senate Joint Resolution 43, providing for the use of St. Lawrence River power in accordance with the treaty, had been introduced by Senator Pittman on April 15, 1933, but opponents of the treaty had refused unanimous consent to bring it before the Senate (*Cong. Rec.,* vol. 77, pp. 1789–1790, 1812–1817). In his letter, Walsh reported a proposal by Pittman to poll the Senate "before finally determining whether a message should be sent urging ratification." He added that La Follette had expressed strong opposition to such a move in that it would create "the most unfavorable possible condition for determining the attitude of the Senate" and "would be taken as an implication that the St. Lawrence Treaty was not regarded as a part of the Administration's program, all the major measures of which had been supported with a strong presidential message."

## [*Enclosure*] Frank P. Walsh, Chairman, New York State Power Authority, to Roosevelt

New York City, June 2, 1933

Dear Mr. President: The Power Authority have just been advised of the intention of Senator La Follette to offer the joint resolution, providing for the division of the cost of the St. Lawrence project between the United States and the State of New York, as an amendment to the first joint resolution that comes before the Senate, and further to insist upon the treaty being considered at open executive session of the Senate.

Mr. Cosgrove[1] and I have already expressed the feeling of the Power Authority that final action on the joint resolution and active support of the treaty before adjournment of the present session of Congress seems vitally necessary.

Since our talk with you, the Trustees of the Power Authority have thoroughly canvassed the status of the project in the light of the situation in Congress, and in view of the course of action proposed by Senator La Follette I believe that I should submit their conclusions to you.

The members of the Power Authority feel that they are confronted with an increasingly difficult situation in the State as a result of the hostility of the private power interests and those associated with them. These interests are manifestly unwilling to allow a public power project on the St. Lawrence to go forward unless they can be assured in advance of getting the power on their own terms.

It is increasingly apparent that this opposition is engaged in an aggressive campaign against the treaty and that it plans to utilize the recess of Congress to push this, if possible, to the point where the position of the Power Authority as defined by the New York Statute might become untenable.

Evidences of this campaign are found in the resolutions against the treaty reported almost daily as passed by various chambers of commerce and other local bodies, which obviously have made no independent study of the proposed development. These resolutions follow very much the same line of argument as that of the Chamber of Commerce of the State of New York, attacking both the navigation and the power projects.

We are also informed by our friends in Northern New York that local chambers of commerce, legion posts, and other civic bodies are now being circularized by New York City interests opposed to the development.

As a result we may be forced to consider the necessity of devoting the months of the recess to meeting these attacks throughout the State and to reestablishing the robust public support for the project which you created. You will realize that an effort to meet the well financed campaign of interests opposed to the development of St. Lawrence power under our auspices would mean a severe strain on resources which should be conserved for our constructive work.

While appreciating the manifold difficulties which confront you and recognizing that in terms of the larger aspects of your situation you may find it inadvisable to send a message supporting Senator La Follette's effort, I felt that I should bring to your attention the present views of the Trustees as expressed at their meeting on Wednesday.

Sincerely yours,

Frank P. Walsh

[OF 156:TS]

[1] Delos M. Cosgrove, vice-chairman of the Authority.


# Prime Minister J. Ramsay MacDonald to Roosevelt

Whitehall, 4th June, 1933

*Personal*

Dear Mr. President: With the approach of the 15th our papers and public are beginning to flutter about what is to happen on that day as to debt payment, and we have been giving the matter some thought. Great pressure has been put upon us to allay uncertainty by declaring our intentions, but we do not see how that could improve matters or help you. I should like to report to you, however, what is in the minds of my colleagues as I have found it on my return from Lossiemouth[1] yesterday.

There are three conceivable ways of meeting the situation on the 15th of June.

1. Cancellation, which does not seem to be a practical possibility;

2. A postponement of payment pending the work of the International Conference, which I had hoped for;

3. A token payment pending some final debt agreement.

I am still convinced that the second method is by far and away the best and would be most helpful to both countries in their search for an amicable settlement of the whole question.

The third proposal which has occupied a considerable part of our newspaper columns during the last few days has many drawbacks, most of which arise from the fact that by making the payment, this country will be deemed once again to have admitted obligations which it said in its Notes preceding the December payment it could not continue to fulfil.

On this last point the following considerations will have to be noted:

(i) The December payment was made without serious protest on the part of our public, because there was a general desire to recognise the difficulties of the American Administration. There was also a hope that before June some agreement regarding, at any rate, the June payment would be reached—an agreement which would admit that the whole matter was in suspense and that a continuing payment of instalments was not to be made, but that the debt itself should be dealt with and settled, the December payment and the June instalment being merged in the final terms of settlement.

(ii) Public opinion here is not in a frame of mind to repeat in June what, under the above circumstances, it did in December. Even if the June payment was a token amounting to little more than a recognition of these continuing payments on the basis of old agreements and obligations, it would arouse an amount of hostility which would create a serious political situation. We should have a repetition of the unhelpful criticisms that have been gathering in volume here for years. We should be told again with added vigour that these loans were made after America had entered the war, that, as a matter of fact, they ought to be regarded as nothing more than the contribution that America made at the moment to the war effort, that, but for the pressure of war conditions, we should never have thought of taking upon our shoulders a debt which meant that we were being made responsible for financing not only ourselves but all our allies—a debt which we should have to pay irrespective of any income we might receive from Germany as reparations or from debtor allies. A renewed squabble on these lines would help nobody but do much harm. The subsequent debt arrangements which the United States made with other countries would also be raked up.

It may be said that a general settlement is now under discussion which will take this inequality into consideration. That, however, does not alter the fact that, because we had to pay these very heavy transfers of indebtedness during the past years, we have been crippled in our attempts to meet the world collapse, and that such big transfers as had to be made were one of the prime causes of the deterioration of prices. In short, for the sake of a nominal payment in June we shall be in danger of creating in this country a very serious deterioration in mutual confidence and in temper, which will have an unfortunate effect upon comprehensive debt negotiations, the International Economic Conference and, generally, upon international relations not only as between our two countries nor merely as concerns our immediate difficulties.

(iii) That, however, is not all. If the June situation is handled in the way I am now discussing, it will compel us to consider Lausanne, because the House of Commons could hardly be got to agree to any payment by us without demanding that the Government should ask from its debtors some token payment in recognition of their indebtedness to us. Nothing is more certain than that these debtors will not pay us either a mark or a franc or anything else, and our position in principle will be that once again we accept the position of being the only debtor in these days who goes on paying these peculiar war debts. If we refuse to continue in that position, as Parliament will insist that we must, we shall have to put in our claims and cause our debtors either to recognise their indebtedness, in addition to, or as a variation of, their Lausanne obligations, or default. They are quite certain to take the latter course, and once again the inter-Governmental financial relations will be thrown into disorder and difficulty, with a new financial crisis following as a possibility.

(iv) It is quite true that American public opinion is adverse to the idea of a simple moratorium in June, but our public opinion must also be considered, and unfortunately the Government has not only to face our public opinion but a serious international European situation. In deciding what action we are to take in June both of these facts must be taken into account by us. Our American creditors ought in fairness to face the whole realities and not merely a part of them. Is the little substance in a token payment worth the reactions and consequences which must follow? Strive as we may to handle the problem as being one between the United States and ourselves only, we cannot do it. We shall be forced by the circumstances into a European policy of default unless June 15th is to be got over without our having to do something which in one form or other raises the whole problem of existing inter-Government indebtedness. As I see it, the efforts we are making to move from the present evil state of things into a new relationship depend upon whether the situation which arises on the 15th June is, or is not, to be held in suspense until we see some ending to the negotiations on the whole debt in which we are now actively engaged.

That is the trend of thought here and I report it to you quite frankly.[2]

With my most sincere regards and best wishes.

I am, Yours always sincerely,

J. Ramsay MacDonald

[PSF:London Economic Conference:TS]

[1] MacDonald's home in northern Scotland.

[2] The text of this letter was sent by Simon to Lindsay in a cable of June 4, 1933 (*British Documents, 1919–1939*, V, 813–815); the letter itself was sent by diplomatic pouch. See Roosevelt's reply, June 7, 1933, below.

## Roosevelt to Senator Duncan U. Fletcher of Florida

[Washington] June 6, 1933

Dear Senator: There is no question about my standing by the Merchant Marine. Some day when we have a little more time I want to talk with you about it.[1]

Very sincerely yours,

[OF 99:CT]

[1] Fletcher, in a letter of May 27, 1933 (OF 99), urged Roosevelt to indicate his support of an adequate merchant marine as an instrument of national policy and suggested that he affirm the declaration of Congress made in the Merchant Marine Act of 1928:

that the United States should maintain a merchant marine adequate to carry the greater part of its commerce and to serve as a naval auxiliary in time of war. Rep. Schuyler Bland, chairman of the House Committee on Merchant Marine, in a letter to Roosevelt of May 2, 1933 (OF 99), saw the merchant marine as "an essential factor in national defense." Rep. John McDuffie also urged support "from the standpoint of increasing our foreign trade and maintaining national defense." Similar expressions were received from ship owners' associations, chambers of commerce, and ship company officials (OF 99). Fletcher wrote again on June 25, 1934 (OF 99). He referred to his experience in shipping matters (he had handled the Shipping Board bill in the Wilson Administration), and described the impotent and demoralized state of the Shipping Board Bureau of the Commerce Department. He recommended creation of a separate agency.

## Warren Delano Robbins, American Delegation to the London Economic Conference, to Roosevelt

London, 6th June, 1933

Dear Franklin: I have not accomplished nearly as much as I had hoped in the six days that I have been here, for the reason that we struck this lovely city just at the time of Whitsuntide, and that most of our friends and all of the officials cut off work on Friday and have only started again this morning.

I promptly went to see the Ambassador, who was as nice as he could be, but looks very badly, I think.[1] He invited us to dinner on Thursday night, and we had a quiet talk together over the general situation. Now, from what I gather from him, and after talking with a couple of newspaper men, plus Reggie Forster an American banker here, and others, I feel a little less encouraged as to the general attitude here concerning the success of the Economic Conference. They all seem to be afraid of France upsetting the apple cart, and even the British do not seem particularly optimistic as to the success of the Conference. What I can gather, about all that they hope for here is that the Conference may determine some sort of a settlement as to the payment of debts and some sort of an agreement as to the stabilization of International exchange. The papers this morning talk of your laying down the law to the Senate and take the attitude that you may insist on the Congress continuing its work for a month or so to come, commenting that should the Congress continue in session it would be very harmful to the Economic Conference. It seems to me that this is rather a gloomy way of looking at things and I don't see necessarily why the Economic Conference should not continue, and even succeed, even if our dear old Congress is in session.

The information I give you is only of value as showing that there seems to be little optimism as regards the success of the Conference.

Ramsay MacDonald is, I think, back from Lossiemouth to-day, but he has been away ever since my arrival, so also have most of the friends at the Foreign Office, including Vansittart.

I was much impressed, and I think duly honoured, to have a casual message by telephone from the King's Private Secretary (Col. Hardinge)[2] telling me that His Majesty wished to see me to-morrow at 10.45 a.m. Although I have consorted a good bit with the President of the United States, I am not entirely familiar with the workings of a private visit to the King of England; however, I shall turn up there to-morrow morning and will, of course, report to you immediately as to what went on. We have some friends here, a Mr. and Mrs. Simpson[3] (she American and he a Member of Parliament) who have invited us to dinner to-night, a dinner of eight, to meet the Prince of Wales, so within the next twenty-four hours I may have something amusing to tell you.

I had a glorious Saturday evening, Sunday and Monday with Mu[4] at her little place at Thorpe-le-Soken, and I had the particular pleasure of calling and spending about an hour with Lord Byng of Vimy.[5] He was Governor General of Canada and incidentally the General-in-Command of the Canadian troops, so I wanted particularly to see him. He is a friend of Mu's and it was very easy to arrange. We all had tea there and he and I sat in the garden for half an hour reminiscing and discussing Canadian affairs. He has aged a good deal, being about 72. He is perfectly delightful and simple, but soon gets tired. Though your family and mine do not seem to think much of 72 years as an age, he seems to show it more naturally because of the terrific strain to which he was put during the war. He seemed particularly depressed as regards the French attitude and feels that it will be difficult to take away from them that nightmare of Germany and constant fear of a new war.

This is just a short sketch of my first few impressions. I hope to give you something more worthy in a few days.

Irene, Sunny and I are blissfully happy here, and living a very satisfactory and quiet life. I imagine that once the Mission arrives, as it will on Thursday, the rest cure will be over.

With love from us all, Your affectionate cousin,

W.D.R.

[PSF:London Economic Conference:TS]

[1] Robert W. Bingham, ambassador from 1933 to 1936. He was ill during much of the London Conference.

[2] A. Hardinge, second Lord of Penshurst.

[3] Mr. and Mrs. Ernest Simpson.

[4] Muriel Delano Robbins, sister of Warren D. Robbins; they were children of Katharine R. Delano's marriage to Charles A. Robbins, and thus first cousins of Franklin D. Roosevelt.

[5] Julian H. G. Byng, first Viscount Byng of Vimy. He commanded the Canadian forces at the battle of Vimy Ridge in April 1917.

## Press Conference, Executive Offices of the White House, June 7, 1933, 10:42 A.M.

[*Excerpt*] The President: The only news is that I am getting behind in my mail. (Laughter)

Q: How does that happen?

The President: I am just one basket behind. That is all. Well, I don't think I know anything in particular this morning.

Q: Can you enlighten us in any way on these rumors coming from London on some change in the value of gold and some new debt proposition and things of that sort?

The President: We haven't had a single thing—not a single thing. Make this off the record, because it is merely the way I would write a story. Do you have to write a story about it?

Q: We have to.

The President: You might write it along these lines, that we are trying to be perfectly consistent over here in carrying out what was announced away back last November when I came down here to see the President, which was the establishment of the principle that a debtor nation can come to a creditor nation and lay its case before the creditor nation. Now, that is all, about all there is to be said. We have had from the debtor nations, as you know, in these conversations that have been going on, at the time of payment by England last December and the payment by Italy last December, we had various statements made to us as in the case of England—I have forgotten the exact language—but to the effect that they did not see how they could make the June payment. We have had what might be called unofficial representations that they did not see how they could make the June payment, but we have had no proposal, we have had no request for a formal reconsideration of the debt question. That is all there is to be said. In other words, it carries out the principle set down last November that it is up to the debtor nation, and there we are.

Q: Did you say there have been no recent informal conversations or anything on that subject within the last four or five days?

The President: No official communications.

Q: Unofficial?

Q: —The British Ambassador?

The President: I think he has been talking with the Acting Secretary of State. I have not seen him. We simply made clear to him just what I said to you—that is about all there is.

Q: You still adhere to the theory that each debtor should come individually?

The President: Yes.

Q: A large number of the British say that they cannot stabilize their currency until they know the debt situation and they claim that stabilization is the first thing that is necessary in the Conference. Do you think anything must be done about the debts first?

The President: I don't know; that is an awfully difficult question to answer. I will tell you the general position we have taken on this, and this is again off the record, merely to give you an idea about it. There have been efforts made, as you know from dispatches from the other side, to get some temporary stabilization the last two months—ever since April—and we have felt and I think the British have felt—they have come mostly from France—that the time is not ripe for temporary stabilization because we do not know as yet the status of the currency of each country in relationship to its price level. In other words, the individual currency of a nation and the individual price level of a nation. We felt that these months of April, May and June will possibly establish that internal relationship fairly well and that, having done that, having gotten the internal relationship of currency and price level fairly well fixed, then we can go ahead and discuss stabilizing currencies in relation to each other.

It is a little bit premature to go into it any further than that and our position has been that the international Government debt problem is a far less important factor in that stabilization than some of the debtor nations tried to make it out. I think—I believe I said this last week some time—I think if you will take the proportion that international Government debts bear either to the debtor nation's budget, or the proportion that they bear, let us say, to world trade, it is such a very small percentage that it is not as big a factor as some of the debtors would try to make us believe. That is about the attitude.

Q: Concerning the first part of your answer there, is it possible that conditions have progressed so that the pounds and dollars may be paid in terms of each other at the London conference?

The President: They are going to try to get some form of stabilization of the relationship between currencies. Of course there are all sorts of methods of approach. One suggestion has been the setting up of what might be called an imaginary coin that would not be coined. I don't think I would write very much about that, it is not our suggestion, it is merely one of the suggestions I use as an illustration. For example, if you and I are trying to make an international contract—you are an Englishman and I am an American—it is very difficult to make it today because you and I don't know what either the pound or the dollar is going to be a year from now when the payment is due. This particular school of thought says, "If we had an imaginary coin, you, as a Britisher, would not have to think of the dollar, you would merely have to think of the coin in its relationship to the pound and not as to the dollar. You will only have one factor to consider—the pound and the imaginary coin. I, as the American, would have only one factor to consider—the dollar and the imaginary coin. The imaginary coin would always be fixed in terms of gold or gold and silver, whereas, as it is now, you and I have to think of the pound going up and down and the dollar going up and down or of the two going up together or coming down together. You have six possibilities if you work it out with paper and pencil.

They are going to explore all those suggestions but they are going to work toward stabilization of exchange for the sake of international trade and the elimination, at the same time, of the speculative element of international exchange. In other words, get rid of those fellows in Amsterdam and Antwerp, etc., who have had in the past those very large speculative accounts, sometimes in pounds, sometimes in dollars and sometimes in francs.

Q: What would be the value of such an imaginary coin in terms of the Swiss franc or the Dutch guilder?

The President: An imaginary coin would be fixed at so many grams or grains of gold, irrespective of anything else.

Q: It would simply be a fixed weight of gold?

The President: It would simply be a fixed weight of gold and nothing more. Only they would give it a name. I don't think there is a story in that because it is only one of a great many things that have been suggested and a lot of people say that it won't work.

Q: Would you issue bonds in terms of this gold coin?

The President: I don't know; provided the total of the bonds did not exceed all the gold in the world.

Q: Mr. President, will you ask Congress this week for power to change the tariff in making the reciprocal trade agreements?

The President: I will have to give you the same answer; I don't know.

Q: Do you know whether you will do it before Congress adjourns?

The President: Again I don't know.

Q: Mr. President, has any value been suggested for the ounce of gold in these imaginary coins?

The President: No, because again it would be based on weight, not on value.

Q: I mean in the United States.

The President: You see, then the value would not have anything to do with it. It would be the weight.

Q: The relationship of the dollar toward the ounce?

The President: Yes, and that would be practically based on an international stabilization.

[President's Press Conferences:T]


# Roosevelt to Prime Minister J. Ramsay MacDonald, London

[Washington] June 7, 1933

Dear Mr. Prime Minister: I very greatly appreciate your frank and informative letter of June fourth.[1]

It is particularly useful to me to know from you the limitations and difficulties imposed upon you by public and parliamentary opinion and the external and general European situation. I, too, have certain limitations upon my course of action, which, while they change somewhat from day to day, are quite definitive and compelling. Perhaps it will clarify our course if I explain very briefly and precisely what these limitations are.

1. As the head of a creditor country I am unable to take specific action with respect to a debt until and unless a specific proposal has been made to me. I am going to consider in the light of our correspondence and conversations that we are requested to consent to a deferment of the June 15th payments for the duration of the Conference. This I refer to in paragraph #3.

2. I further understand that no proposal for final disposition of the entire debt has been made and that you desire that opportunity be given to present the broader aspects this summer and autumn. In order to clarify matters I want to express here my agreement to hear such presentation and to add that such presentation should proceed here in Washington and that your Government may select the time for its beginning.

3. I am unable, not only because of the action of Congress, but because of my plain Constitutional limitations, to extend a moratorium on the June 15th payment. Authority is Congressional.[2] As I see the business now before Congress, adjournment will take place soon, probably before the fifteenth. A number of perplexing problems must be met by the Congress before they can adjourn and the presence of these problems on their calendar makes it impossible to present to them any proposal concerning debts.[3]

4. I can acknowledge payments towards principal or interest or both.

5. I can acknowledge for my Government for the record any statement that your Government may make to me.

6. I am authorized now, in the light of legislative and executive actions taken during the past few weeks, to accept any payments in silver, under the terms of legislation enacted by Congress. Further it is my personal belief that I can accept payments in U.S. currency, because we ourselves have made American obligations payable in currency.

I am truly desirous of contributing whatever I can to the clarification of the general economic situation in order that the momentous Conference about to begin under your admirable chairmanship may succeed to the fullest degree. A great deal is at stake. I can assure you that I have seriously explored every possibility of action with regard to this debt payment and that the statement of fact I have made above is the true picture of the field of possibility. I am communicating this to you today in order that you may know how matters lie over here when you discuss the question with your ministers on Friday.[4]

With my warm regards, Faithfully yours,

[PSF:London Economic Conference:CT]

[1] Above.

[2] By joint resolution approved Dec. 23, 1931, Congress granted a moratorium for the fiscal year 1932 on foreign debts owed the United States, and provided for their repayment over a ten-year period beginning July 1, 1933. The resolution declared it against the policy of Congress that any of the debts should be canceled or reduced (47 *Stat.* 3).

[3] Roosevelt had conferred with Senator Robinson, Democratic floor leader, on May 27, and they had decided to press for the adjournment of Congress on June 10. The "perplexing problems" included the reciprocal trade program, the proposed veterans pension cuts, the National Industrial Recovery bill, and the Glass-Steagall Banking bill (New York *Times,* May 28, 1933, pp. 1, 8).

[4] Printed also in *British Documents, 1919–1939,* V, 819–820.

## Roosevelt to Mary E. Woolley, President, Mount Holyoke College, South Hadley, Massachusetts

[Washington] June 7, 1933

Dear Miss Woolley: It is good to have your note[1] and I think that things are now arranged so that the Embargo Resolution, as reported out in the Senate, will be kept safely on the table.

Very sincerely yours,

[PPF 537:CT]

[1] June 7, 1933 (PPF 537). Miss Woolley had been a delegate to the Disarmament Conference in 1932. She enclosed a copy of her letter to Senators Marcus A. Coolidge and David I. Walsh of Massachusetts of June 3, 1933. In this letter she urged passage of the McReynolds arms embargo resolution (H.J.R. 93) but without the Johnson amendment that denied the president to determine which nation was the aggressor. She said that her experience at Geneva had strengthened her conviction that the cooperation of the United States was essential if the world was to be saved from calamity.

## Roosevelt to President Rafael Leonidas Trujillo of the Dominican Republic, Santo Domingo

Washington, June 7, 1933

My dear Mr. President: I have Your Excellency's esteemed letter of February sixth before me and I beg of you to accept my heartfelt appreciation and thanks for the friendly sentiments you express.[1]

Of your communication to the Nobel Committee of the Norwegian Parliament, of which you send me a copy, I can only say that Your Excellency's action is accepted as an added evidence of the friendship and good will existing between the Dominican Republic and the United States of America.

With the earnest and confident wish that Your Excellency's administration may be fraught with great prosperity to the Dominican Republic and health and happiness to yourself, I am, with the highest consideration,

Your Excellency's Good Friend,

(s) Franklin D. Roosevelt[2]

[OF 138:T]

[1] Trujillo enclosed a copy of the letter he had written to the Nobel committee recommending Roosevelt for the peace prize (OF 138).

[2] Drafted by Under Secretary of State Phillips (Phillips to Howe, June 6, 1933, OF 138).

## Roosevelt to Senator Robert M. La Follette, Jr., of Wisconsin

[Washington] June 8, 1933

My dear Senator: I do not hesitate to tell you—and I do so with complete consistency—that I favor the resolution relating to the St. Lawrence power development passed by the House.[1] I also favor the ratification of the Great Lakes–St. Lawrence deep waterway treaty.

The joint resolution protects the people of the State of New York who own the land under water in the St. Lawrence River as far out as the International Boundary. The resolution means, in effect, that the Congress will see to it that the State of New York, in paying for the power part of the development, will pay only for that part and will thus be able to insure cheap electricity for the consuming public.

The Treaty itself has been endorsed by both major political parties. The beginning of the work of construction at an early date can be made an essential part of the national public works program and will furnish employment to thousands of people.

The above are simple facts and I have no objection to your use of this letter if you so desire.

Very sincerely yours,

[OF 156:CT]

[1] House Joint Resolution 157, to provide for use of St. Lawrence River power by New York under provisions of the Great Lakes–St. Lawrence Deep Waterway Treaty, was passed by the House April 26, 1933. Just before the final vote, James S. Parker

(N.Y.) moved to recommit the resolution to the Committee of Interstate and Foreign Commerce, and to report it back with an amendment declaring that passage should in no way be construed as an expression of the attitude of the House on the merits of the proposed treaty. This motion was lost (*Cong. Rec.*, vol. 77, pp. 2412–2414).

## Roosevelt to Augusto Rosso, Italian Ambassador, Washington

[Washington] June 8, 1933

*Personal*

My dear Signor Rosso: I have not had an opportunity before this to thank you for your note of May thirtieth[1] and to assure you that not one word of what we spoke of has been made a matter of record or even been mentioned to any other person than yourself.

Will you be good enough to tell Signor Mussolini that the whole matter remains entirely secret and also convey to him my thanks for his prompt action? It did not succeed but I am sure that it was at least worth while to make the attempt.

Very sincerely yours,

[OF 197: CT]

[1] Above.

## Press Conference, Executive Offices of the White House, June 9, 1933, 4:12 P.M.

The President: Well, what is the news?

Q: What about the tariff situation?

The President: Who has got my wire basket? I will look through it and see if I cannot tell you something about it. You go right ahead and talk while I look this up. (Laughter) . . .

The President: Well, I cannot find it. I will have to try to tell you, off the record, just for information. I am not going to send up any tariff message. That, however, does not in any way preclude the conferees—I don't mean the conferees, I mean the delegates in London—from conducting the negotiations for general tariff agreements. That can be done in London itself. Secondly, it does not preclude them in London from arranging for individual tariff conferences between us and any one other nation with the objective of arriving at reciprocal tariff agreements. These conferences are to be held as soon as possible. And then, third, there is, of course, still the right, under existing law, for either increases or decreases in existing schedules by executive order after recommendation by the Tariff Commission and in reciprocal agreements. As a matter of fact, there is very little loss of time on this thing because any agreement entered into would probably take several months to work out and can be submitted, if worked out, to Congress as soon as they reassemble in January. Any permanent reciprocal agreement or general agreement would have to go to Congress anyway.

Q: Mr. President, would that mean agreements by treaty?

The President: Well, that is the same thing.

Q: You could obtain your agreement by treaty and then submit it to the Senate, could you not?

The President: Yes, I hope so. I don't know enough about that end of the situation. I would say so, offhand.

Q: This means that the Delegation won't be able to conclude any definite agreements?

The President: Oh, yes; general agreements. That does not mean bilateral agreements because bilateral agreements have to be arrived at by this country and another specific country and obviously these people over there are not going to have six or eight conferences going at the same time with other nations. Bilateral agreements would probably be done over here.

Q: There was a big fight under your predecessor's regime on the right of Congress to pass upon any fifty per cent reduction in tariff made by the President. Assuming any reduction is not more than fifty per cent, which is within the limit of power, doesn't that bill have to go to Congress?

The President: No.

Q: That can be done by executive order, I think.

Q: That is, after recommendation for tariff revision and investigation.

Q: So that this fifty per cent reduction can be made by you upon recommendation of the Commission.

The President: No, because as I remember it the Tariff Commission's recommendations have to be based on difference in the cost of manufacture.

Q: The Tariff Commission's recommendations after investigation?

The President: Therefore it would be safer to say that any general agreement made in London could not be put into effect by a Tariff Board recommendation and by executive order unless it was based on cost of production.

Q: Then we can assume that your delegates won't make it unless justified by the cost of production and transportation and the other various things involved?

The President: At least, they would be a very important factor.

Q: Would the delegates have all that information?

The President: There is a great deal of current information on those schedules. In other words, they can get the latest information that the Tariff Commission has.

Q: It would still be subject to the Senate approval?

The President: I think they would have to go to the Senate anyway.

Q: Have you already asked for reciprocal—

The President: In other words, from the practical viewpoint, the only difference is this: The first thought was to ask Congress for what might be called "temporary authority" to put a temporary agreement into effect from some time this Fall until the Congress met and then to allow the Congress to approve it or to disapprove it. All this does is to send the signed agreements—if there are any—up to Congress in January.

Q: That is new to us. I don't think we understood that.

The President: Congress would never give me complete authority to write tariff schedules.

Q: Well, they have given you everything else. (Laughter)

The President: I never had any thought of asking for it.

Q: Have you decided not to ask for specific authority because it would delay Congress too long?

The President: No; there are whole lots of reasons and that was one factor, but only one.[1]

Q: I understood you to say that this is for background. Couldn't some of it be for publication and some of it to use for background?

The President: Yes, I think so. I don't think it is a frightfully important thing anyway. I told you all along that I was not at all certain what I would do. As a matter of fact, there was no previous intention of actually doing it. I simply decided not to do it and the effect of it is merely to cut out the temporary agreements that might last two or three months and instead of that signing treaties and submitting them to the Congress in January. It is a very unimportant thing—a matter of two or three months.

Q: It is very important in a way because when you told us some months ago that you might ask for this, we naturally wrote it up and our readers are waiting and watching for it and we would like to write an explanation of why it is unnecessary. I think it would be very helpful. It is a good story in the first place.

Q: It might be regarded in London that the fact you are not sending this up had some deeper meaning and if we could go ahead and print something—

The President: The only significance to it is the fact that we could go right on and make some agreements in London but that instead of having them go into temporary effect for a month or two, we would wait and submit them to the Senate in January. That is why it is so awfully unimportant. It merely means a matter of two or three months.

Q: Excepting that the public hasn't that view at all and I think if we could straighten them out now—

The President: There never has been any thought of asking for more than that.

Q: I had the impression there was and I think my readers have.

The President: The only thing I can think of is how well you impressed your imaginations upon your readers.

Q: You mentioned bilateral agreements. Do you plan to start soon on those in Washington?

The President: Yes, if the delegates in London can arrange for bilateral agreement meetings.

Q: That is all you have in mind as to what the delegates in London are to do on the tariff?

The President: Oh, no; the delegates in London can work on the general tariff thing—the international truce.

Q: What sort of general international agreement could you get more than, say, a tariff truce?

The President: Getting a tariff truce is a very good suggestion. They have half a dozen different proposals. Every nation has some kind of a general tariff reduction proposal. I suppose there must be thirty or forty of them along all kinds of lines such as a two per cent, five per cent, ten per cent reduction and then allowing only a certain quantity to come in. There are all sorts of things.

Q: Doesn't this mean that, as far as we are concerned, the effects and the results of the Economic Conference won't be felt until next year?

The President: Nobody ever supposed that they would be felt until next year.

Q: Don't you think we ought to be able to print this in some way more definite than as background? I mean, there has been quite a misunderstanding and if you clear it up in an authoritative way, it would be much better. Business, possibly, won't know about it. We can say that the Administration—use it in an indirect way, just as a statement of facts.

The President: The statement of facts is in the first place that there is no message going up on the tariff. Number two, that this decision in no way weakens the efforts of our delegates at the Economic Conference except that anything decided, instead of going into effect over a temporary period in the Fall, subject to action by Congress, would be submitted to Congress for action in January.

Q: Before it becomes effective?

The President: Yes, before it becomes effective. Then there is the other exception to that and that is the right to lower or raise after reports by the Tariff Commission based on the cost of production and that is always a possibility during the Fall.

Q: Can't we use that just as you say it now and say, "The Administration"? It tells all of it—just what you say.

The President: Those are the three things.

Q: Would that second exception take care of Cuba on sugar?

The President: I don't know; I have no idea at all. I have not thought of it.

Q: Talking about Cuba, there are quite a few interesting developments down there recently and, just for information and off the record, has anything been done by you or Sumner Welles with respect to the Machado regime? There has been a very definite change within the last two or three weeks.

The President: No, there isn't, really, any story on it at all. I have been so darned busy with other things that I have not read a single dispatch from Welles. All I know is that I saw him before he left and Phillips, since then, has given me a few high spots.

Q: It is a terrific move for the better and I think you ought to take credit for it if there is any bust.

The President: Not yet.

Q: Any change in the debt situation?

The President: No, nothing.

Q: Did you and Sir Ronald [Lindsay] discuss debts?

The President: Yes, among other things.

Q: Any proposals submitted?

The President: Not yet.

Q: Jap news agencies send a dispatch saying that Ishii, while he was here, made a proposal to you with which you agreed in principle or agreed with to establish an arbitration commission between Japan and the United States.

The President: Never heard of it; he may have taken it up with the State Department.

Q: No, they say no.

The President: Then he did not.

Q: The British Cabinet adjourned today without taking action on the debt.

The President: Are they meeting tomorrow?

Q: It has been postponed until Monday.

Q: It is understood there is a message here about it.

The President: I haven't had a thing.

Q: Who is going to Germany as Ambassador?

The President: It depends on how fast we can get in telephone communication with Berlin. I may know by tonight.

Q: There is a guy named Montgomery[2] who wants to go to Vienna. Does he get that job?

The President: He is going to Budapest.

Q: That is too bad; he wanted Vienna.

Q: We can get in touch with Germany right quick if you want us to do it. (Laughter)

The President: Phillips is on the phone at the present moment, I think.

[President's Press Conferences:T]

[1] Roosevelt's decision not to press for reciprocal tariff legislation was made sometime after May 31 (Hull, *Memoirs,* I, 250). Resentment in Congress over parts of the Administration's legislative program caused some Congressional leaders to urge early adjournment; on June 4 some of them informed Roosevelt that lengthening the session "might develop serious consequences" (New York *Times,* June 8, 1933, p. 1). Alarmed by these reports, Hull radioed Roosevelt on June 7 expressing his concern. Roosevelt replied the same day that the situation was "so full of dynamite" that tariff legislation seemed not only inadvisable "but impossible of achievement" (*Foreign Relations, 1933,* I, 923, 923–924). Hull was assured, however, that he had full authority to negotiate general reciprocal trade treaties based on mutual tariff concessions, because negotiation required no prior Congressional authorization. On June 11 Cox and Bullitt asked Roosevelt to send his personal assurance to Hull that he was backing him in his efforts to reduce tariffs and to remove obstacles to international trade; the President cabled Hull the same day that he was squarely behind him. He reminded Hull that if the treaties could

be signed the Senate could be called into special session in the fall to consider ratification (*Foreign Relations, 1933,* I, 633, 634).

[2] John F. Montgomery, chairman of the International Milk Co., appointed minister to Hungary June 13, 1933.

## Breckinridge Long, Ambassador to Italy, to Roosevelt

Rome, Italy, June 9, 1933

My dear Chief: The great development of the week has been the Four Power Pact.[1] Mussolini dramatized it very well. His appearance in the Senate was very well done, and he made an excellent speech. A copy of it is going in this pouch, and if you have not yet seen it, you can easily get it. The Press contains nothing else. Yesterday there was not one allusion to anything except the Four Power Pact. But the text of it has not been printed in the papers here, except that this morning there appears in *Il Popolo di Roma* the text in Italian sent from Paris in a dispatch. Apparently it has not been released by the Foreign Office for publication locally.

Mussolini and his entire official family and in fact his entire organization and all the people in Italy are very enthusiastic about it. They held popular demonstrations all over the country. His address was broadcasted by radio and was listened to in crowds wherever there was a radio amplifier.

But it was very suddenly agreed to. I was with the French Ambassador at half past five, and at that time Germany had not accepted. The next day the German Ambassador told me that he had received word at ten minutes to six. At just 6:30 Mussolini appeared before the Senate. All the arrangements had been made ahead of time, apparently relying on the fact that Germany would accept, but the British Ambassador that morning told me that he thought it was quite doubtful.

At any rate, it has been done to the enormous satisfaction of the people of Italy. It has helped to build up Mussolini to an even greater extent in the minds of his people.

The sentiment here appears to be that it makes possible some accomplishment in London. Even the Diplomatic Corps feel that without it London must have failed—but with it London may now accomplish something.

There have not been as yet any statements in the Press of reactions from the United States. Press comment from the States is lacking, though it appears from Chile, and Peru, and from all of the countries of Europe—at great length.

With every expression of admiration and affection, I am, Yours respectfully,

Breckinridge Long

I am enormously interested in this work.[2]

[OF 447:TS]

[1] Long reviewed the history of the pact in a cable to Phillips of June 6, 1933 (*Foreign Relations, 1933*, I, 413–415).

[2] An attached note, Roosevelt to Early, undated, reads: "What do you think I can reply to Breck Long about this?" No reply has been found.

## Senator Elmer Thomas of Oklahoma and Others to Roosevelt

Washington, June 9, 1933

My dear Mr. President: We, the undersigned, respectfully suggest and request that Rev. Charles E. Coughlin, of Detroit, Michigan, be designated and appointed one of the economic advisors to the American Delegation to the Economic Conference soon to be convened at London, England.

In this emergency, if funds are not available to defray the expenses of additional personnel, we advise that Rev. Coughlin is able and willing to defray all expenses connected with the mission suggested.[1]

Respectfully submitted,

Elmer Thomas
E. D. Smith
B. K. Wheeler
Huey P. Long
F. Ryan Duffy
H. Shipstead

[OF 17:TS]

[1] No acknowledgment of this letter has been found. A recommendation from Robert M. Harriss of New York that Coughlin be named to the delegation, made in a letter to Vice-President Garner of June 6, 1933, was sent by Garner to the White House for comment. McIntyre replied to Harriss June 13, 1933, that because the suggestion had come in after the delegation had been appointed it was impossible to consider it (OF 17). See Weideman and others to Roosevelt, June 10, 1933, below.

## James G. McDonald, Chairman, National Peace Conference, to Roosevelt

New York, June 9, 1933

My dear Mr. President: As Chairman of the National Peace Conference I am sending you, on behalf of ten organizations associated with the Conference, the attached expression of their enthusiastic support of your program of international cooperation. The heads of these organizations are confident that they speak for the great bulk of the membership of their groups.[1]

Respectfully yours,

James G. McDonald

[OF 2020:TS]

[1] MacDonald had been board chairman of the Foreign Policy Association, 1919–1933. In October 1933 he was appointed by the League of Nations to be High Commissioner in charge of the League's program for political refugees from Germany. This letter was acknowledged by Howe, June 12, 1933 (OF 394).

## [*Enclosure*] Members of the National Peace Conference to Roosevelt

New York, June 9, 1933

To the President: You have made the whole world your debtor. Your dramatic initiative in appealing directly and personally to the heads of fifty-four governments on May 16 disclosed to the peoples the grave danger of war that threatened them. That disclosure at once clarified the international atmosphere and permitted the hopeful resumption of the disarmament discussions at Geneva and of the preparations for the World Economic Conference at London.

But we feel that you did more than bring about a respite from haunting fear. In phrases that the masses of the people understand, you outlined a program of action, later elaborated by Ambassador Norman H. Davis, that has evoked widespread and enthusiastic support. Your proposal regarding international consultation has removed one of the most formidable obstacles to effective international action against an outlaw state. We do not interpret these suggested measures of international cooperation as depriving the United States government of independence of action in determining which state was the agressor and what penalties if any should be imposed.

Mr. President, the issues at stake could not have been put more clearly than they were by you. Before your message, it was obvious to the diplomats that the Disarmament Conference was on the verge of complete failure, that that failure would destroy the possibilities of success at the Economic Conference, and that failures at Geneva and at London would increase ominously the chances of war. Now that you have spoken in Washington and your representative in Geneva, the peoples know what is at stake—their continued existence and safety. Disarmament has ceased to be a remote technical problem. Competitive armaments are seen to be an obstacle that must be surmounted before any one can be secure. You have also shown the close interrelation between the weapons of economic warfare and those of military warfare, and have demonstrated that military disarmament and economic disarmament are intimately interdependent. You have made them real to us and to the peoples of other countries. That is an enormous gain. Now the peoples are in a position to demand imperatively that their leaders measure up to the needs of the hour.

We are confident that we speak the mind and the heart of millions of our fellow countrymen when we express to you our gratitude for your courageous and constructive leadership. We pledge you our support in the carrying through of your announced program.

Respectfully yours,

Mrs. Arthur Brin, President, National Council of Jewish Women

Valentine L. Chandor, Representative of The American Association of University Women on the National Peace Conference

Dr. Stephen P. Duggan, Director, Institute of International Education

Mrs. Kendall Emerson, Chairman, National Public Affairs Committee, National Board, Y.W.C.A.

Dr. Henry S. Leiper, Secretary, Department of Relations with Churches Abroad, Federal Council of Churches

Mrs. Daniel A. Poling, President, Council of Women for Home Missions

Mrs. E. H. Silverthorn, Chairman of the Committee on International Relations, Federation of Women's Boards of Foreign Missions

Dr. Walter W. Van Kirk, Secretary, Department of International Justice and Good-will, Federal Council of Churches

League of Nations Association, Raymond B. Fosdick, President

National Council of Young Men's Christian Association, Frederic W. Smith, President; Adrian Lyon, Chairman, General Board

U.S. Section, Women's International League for Peace and Freedom, Emily G. Balch, Consultant on Policies; Hannah Clothier Hull, President

[OF 2020:T]


## Roosevelt to Admiral Sir Lewis Bayly, Virginia Water, Surrey, England

[Washington] June 10, 1933

My dear Sir Lewis: Many thanks for that interesting letter to *The Times*.[1] I wish that you and I could have a talk about these world troubles. During the past few weeks I have been learning much, especially about the Western Pacific.

I graduated the Class at Annapolis last week and I hope to see Sims[2] in Newport this summer if I can run in there on one of our new cruisers.

Please give my regards to your niece.[3]

Always sincerely,

[PPF 218:CT]

---

[1] Bayly's letter to Roosevelt of May 31, 1933 (PPF 218), enclosed a clipping of his letter to the London *Times* (undated). The clipping was an elaboration of the idea expressed in his letter to the President: "It seems to me that our two navies could control the peace of the world if brought into play in time. With the aid of your fleet in the East, and your fleets at home, and our fleet with Hong Kong as a mutual base in case of trouble with Japan, we should be strong enough. And it would bring our two nations together in a way that no speeches will do."

Roosevelt first became acquainted with Bayly in 1918 when the latter was in command of the joint British–United States destroyer fleet based at Queenstown. He was a guest of the President at the fleet review off Sandy Hook in May 1934. Bayly says the President "talked of the great necessity of our two countries working together for the peace of the world. He gave me a message to that effect to give to the King. I wrote it down on the spot, and sent the identical paper to the King's Private Secretary" (*Pull Together*, London: Harrap, 1939, p. 277). This book is Bayly's posthumously published autobiography; the foreword, a generous tribute to his naval genius, is by Roosevelt.

[2] Admiral William S. Sims commanded the United States Naval Forces in European waters during World War I; he was a friend of Bayly.

[3] Violet Voysey.

## Breckinridge Long, Ambassador to Italy, to Roosevelt

Rome, Italy, June 10, 1933

My dear Chief: Herewith your picture in Italian. Also your statement about the Four Power Pact.[1] The papers here carry nothing else. They are having a regular orgy of enthusiastic self-appreciation. Not only have they done a very big job, but they are entirely conscious of it.

I thought the enclosure might interest you.

Yours respectfully,

Breckinridge Long

[OF 447:TS]

[1] Long enclosed a newspaper photograph of Roosevelt and a clipping from *Il Popolo di Roma* of Roosevelt's statement of June 9, 1933 (*Public Papers*, II, 221–222), expressing satisfaction at the signing of the Four Power Pact. Long had suggested that the President make such a statement in a cable to him of May 31, 1933 (*Foreign Relations, 1933*, I, 411–412).

## Representative Carl M. Weideman of Michigan and Others to Roosevelt

Washington, D.C., June 10, 1933

Dear Mr. President: The undersigned members of Congress respectfully submit for your consideration and recommendation, Rev. Charles E. Coughlin, of Royal Oak, Michigan, as an advisor to the Economic Conference to be held in London, England, beginning June 12, 1933.

He is a student of world affairs, economics and finance; and has the confidence of millions of American citizens. We believe that his presence at the Conference would instill confidence in the hearts of the average citizen of our country, and in no small manner contribute to the success of this Conference.

Respectfully submitted,

Carl M. Weideman
John D. Dingell—15th Mich.
Wm. T. Schulte—1st Indiana
B. M. Jacobsen 2nd Iowa
Fred Biermann, 4th Iowa
T. B. Werner 2nd S. Dak.
Compton I. White 1st Ida

John Young Brown, Ky at Large.
W. D. McFarlane 13th Texas
Prentiss M. Brown 11th Mich.
Edward C. Eicher, 1st Iowa
Stephen M. Young Ohio—at Large
Samuel B. Pettingill 3d Indiana

J. C. Lehr 2nd Dist. Michigan

Charles Kramer 13th California

Wm L. Fiesinger 13th Ohio.

Jennings Randolph 2nd W. Va.

Claude E. Cady 6th Mich.

Arthur D. Healey—8th Mass.

M. A. Zioncheck 1st Wash.

Abe Murdock—1st Utah

Chas. I. Faddis 25th Pa.

Harry W. Musselwhite Manistee, Mich. (9th Michigan)

Finly H. Gray M.C. 10th Ind. District

Wright Patman, 1st Dist—Texas

Otha D. Wearin—7th Iowa Dist.

Braswell Deen 8th Georgia

Finley Hamilton, 9th Ky

J. G. Scrugham Nev.

Geo. B. Terrell M.C. Texas at Large

G. Foulkes 4th Dist. Michigan

Herman P. Kopplemann—1st Conn.

Knute Hill, 4th Wash.

Emmanuel Celler N.Y.

Joe H. Eagle, 8th Texas

Ross A. Collins, Miss.

Howard W. Smith Va. at Large

Ewing Thomason—16th Tex.

Paul John Kvale at Large, Minn.

Luther A. Johnson 6th Texas

R. A. Green, 2nd Fla.

Geo. A. Dondero—17th Mich.

L. L. McCandless Hawaii

Everett M. Dirksen—16th Illinois

Frank H. Lee at Large Missouri

J. Leroy Adair Illinois

J. Mark Wilcox, 4th Dist. Florida

Virginia E. Jenckes, 6th Indiana

E. M. Schaefer 2nd Ill.

C. W. Turner 6th Dist. Tennessee

Dennis Chavez, N.M.

W. R. Thom Ohio

Louis Ludlow, Indiana

J. G. Polk Ohio

Russell Ellzey—Mississippi

Clifford R. Hope 7th Kans. District

E. W. Goss 5th Conn.

Charles D. Millard 25th District N.Y.

Brent Spence 5th Ky

[OF 17:TS]

## Robert W. Bingham, Ambassador to Great Britain, to Roosevelt

[London, June 11, 1933][1]

Dear Mr. President: On the eve of the Conference I feel I should give you some impressions I have, for what they may be worth.

I think it altogether unlikely the British will be willing to prolong the session into August; their idea being to adjourn the Conference until about October first. This was why I sent a message to you through the

State Department suggesting a possible alternative.[2] On the other hand, I feel confident the Prime Minister will do everything in his power to secure some definite achievement which will, at least, give hope for tangible results before any adjournment. I believe his idea is to secure at least a Conference agreement upon certain principles. For example, that there should be an agreement for the stabilization of currency, with some recognition of silver, and I think he will go as far as he can in securing such other general agreements as may seem practicable. In addition, I believe, that he will take advantage of any opportunity which appears to him to secure any tangible action which may appear practicable as the Conference develops.

Of course, the debt question is the shadow which hangs over the Conference and everything else. As I said to you when I last saw you, I hoped that Congress might put the control of this question in your hands because, in my judgment, it was the only way it could be handled to the best advantage, although it may very well be you have found another method.

I am hoping to see the Secretary of State tomorrow afternoon or evening, and to receive from him any information or instructions which you may have had in mind for me.

I am very glad indeed you sent Warren Robbins over, and I hope he will prolong his stay here, as I am sure he will be very helpful to the whole delegation.[3]

I understand some attack has been made by the Hearst press on the speech I made at the Pilgrims Dinner. I am enclosing a copy of it for your consideration when you may be able to look it over.[4] I should have sent it to you at once, but did not want to burden you. I am also sending a report of a telegram from the King and a letter from the Duke of Connaught, both of which were read at the dinner, and the speech made by the Prince of Wales.[5] I thought the Prince's speech was very fine, in the circumstances, and this, with the messages from the King and the Duke of Connaught, created a favorable atmosphere for my speech. Your message was most enthusiastically received.

My wife joins me in every good wish for you and Mrs. Roosevelt. As ever, Sincerely yours,

Robert W. Bingham

[OF 491:TS]

[1] An approximate date.

[2] Not present. On May 23, 1933, Roosevelt had cabled MacDonald that he could not promise to keep a delegation in London longer than two months because the delegates

would be urgently needed at home. MacDonald replied June 12 that he thoroughly understood the difficulties of keeping important ministers in London (*Foreign Relations, 1933,* I, 611; PPF 261).

[3] Robbins, State Department chief of protocol, was in charge of preliminary arrangements and protocol for the U.S. delegation.

[4] A clipping from the London *Times* of May 31, 1933, in which Bingham's speech is printed. He quoted at length from Roosevelt's inaugural address.

[5] Also in the clipping just cited.

# Press Conference, Executive Offices of the White House, June 14, 1933, 3:30 P.M.

[*Excerpt*] The President: There will be ready for you outside, as soon as we unlock the doors, copies of three documents, the British note to us—I am wrong, Steve says that there are two notes in the State Department and the third document is just a little explanatory statement from me. You will find them all out in the tender mercies of Steve.

I might just as well read the three of them to you because it will make different things clear, I believe, and then, when we get through talking about this, if anybody wants to leave, it is all right. There is a 4 o'clock release line on this by arrangement with England, the reason being that Sir Neville Chamberlain is making a speech at that time in Parliament and we have to synchronize with his speech.

The British note to us, dated June 13, is as follows: . . .[1]

Sir: In reply to the Note handed to me by the State Department on June 9th—

I can say, by way of explanation, that that is the formal notice from the Treasury Department via the State Department that the debt is due.

—I am directed by my Government to make the following communication to you:

It will be recalled that the general views of His Majesty's Government in the United Kingdom on war debts and on their relation to present world difficulties were explained in notes exchanged in November and December last. His Majesty's Government at that time decided to make payment of the amount due on December 15th but they indicated clearly that this payment "was not to be regarded as a resumption of annual payments contemplated by the existing agreement" and they announced their intention of treating this payment "as a capital payment of which account should be taken in any final settlement."

Finally they pointed out that the procedure adopted "must obviously be exceptional and abnormal" and they urged upon the United States Government "the importance of an early exchange of views with the object of concluding the proposed discussions before June 15th next in order to obviate a general breakdown of existing inter-governmental agreements."

His Majesty's Government in the United Kingdom adopted this procedure because they recognized the peculiar position in which the then United States Administration was placed, and the impossibility of their undertaking any effective discussion of the problem at that time. His Majesty's Government acted, however, on the understanding that the discussion would take place without delay, upon the provisions of the existing agreement in all its aspects, so as to arrive at a comprehensive and final settlement and in the belief that payment on December 15th would greatly increase the prospects of a satisfactory approach to the whole question.

Negotiations were accordingly started even before the new Administration was inaugurated; and His Majesty's Government in the United Kingdom have been most anxious to pursue them as rapidly as possible. On the occasion of the Prime Minister's visit to Washington the President and his advisers made preliminary explorations as to the basis of a clearer understanding of the situation. For reasons not within the control of either Government, however, it has not yet been possible to arrive at a definite conclusion of these negotiations.

All of that might be called preliminary.

A speedy conclusion is, however, urgently needed. The treatment of inter-governmental obligations must closely affect the solution of the problems with which the World Conference has to deal, because they cannot be separated from influences which have brought the world to its present plight. For instance, it is generally agreed that one of the first and the most essential of our aims should be to increase the general level of commodity prices. It may be recalled that after the Lausanne Conference there was a marked tendency for prices to rise, but that this tendency was reversed when the prospects of a final settlement of inter-governmental obligations receded, while the December payment was accompanied by a sharp fall in prices which was felt in America at least as much as in Europe. Experience, therefore, appears to show that the effect of these payments upon prices is very direct.

In the opinion of His Majesty's Government it is essential for the success of the Conference that the delegates should not be hampered and harassed by doubts about the possibility of a satisfactory settlement of war debts. Payment of a further instalment of the debt at this juncture would inevitably be judged to mean that no progress whatever had been made towards such a settlement and would, therefore, deal a damaging blow at the confidence of the delegates.

In the circumstances and in view of their action last December, His Majesty's Government had hoped that the United States Government would have been able to accede to the request of His Majesty's Government to postpone payment of the June instalment pending discussion of war debts as a whole. Since, however, this does not appear to have been found possible, His Majesty's Government are obliged to decide upon their course of action.

Such a decision must in any case be of an extremely difficult character and in considering it His Majesty's Government have felt their deep responsibility not only to their own people, but to the whole world which is awaiting the deliberations and recommendations of the Conference with the utmost anxiety.

The conclusion at which His Majesty's Government have arrived is that payment of the June instalment could not be made at this juncture without gravely imperilling the success of the Conference and involving widespread political consequences of a most serious character. In their view the instalment should be considered and discussed as part of the general subject of war debts upon which they are anxious to resume conversations as soon as they can be arranged.

This must have been written by a lady because the last paragraph has all the meat in it. That is off the record.

In the meantime, in order to make it perfectly clear that they do not regard the suspension of the June payment as in any way prejudicing an ultimate settlement, His Majesty's Government propose to make an immediate payment of Ten million dollars as an acknowledgment of the debt pending a final settlement. If, as they trust, the Government of the United States is thereafter prepared to enter upon formal negotiations for an ultimate settlement of the whole war debt question, His Majesty's Government would gladly be informed of the time and place at which the United States Government would desire such negotiations to be begun . . .

To which the Acting Secretary of State replied this morning as follows:[2] . . .

Excellency: In reply to the note handed to me by Your Excellency on the 13th instant, I am directed by the President to make the following reply:

The President understands that His Majesty's Government have concluded that payment of the June fifteenth installment "could not be made at this juncture without gravely imperilling the success of the Conference and involving widespread political consequences of a most serious character." He notes also that accompanying this communication is a payment of ten million dollars "as an acknowledgment of the debt pending a final settlement," and notes the characterization of the circumstances with which the British Government accompanies this payment, although he, by no means, concedes some of the statements concerning the world wide economic cause and effect contained in His Majesty's Government's communication, especially in so far as they affect the Economic Conference.

The President points out to His Majesty's Government the well known fact that it is not within his discretion to reduce or cancel the existing debt owed to the United States, nor is it within his power as President to alter the schedule of debt payments contained in the existing settlement. Such power rests with the Congress.

He notes likewise the suggestion of His Majesty's Government that they desire to make further representations concerning the entire question of the debt, and that His Majesty's Government requests that a time and place be indicated where such representations can be made to the President or the appropriate representative of the Executive. The President suggests that His Majesty's Government provide for such representations to be made in Washington as soon as convenient.

Any results of such a discussion of the debt question can be submitted for the information or the consideration of the Congress when it next meets . . .

And then we come down to [the part?][3] which I think might help you, and then, if we can get through with this in time, anybody who wants to ask questions may do so but remember that 4 o'clock line on this.[4]

The British Government has today announced a payment to the United States of ten million dollars with a note indicating that this payment is to be considered "as an acknowledgment of the debt pending a final settlement." It has in its accompanying note pointed out circumstances that have induced it to take this action.

Such payment does not of course in any sense prejudice the freedom of either Government in any subsequent discussion of the entire debt question which will take account of this and other debt payments. I announced in November, 1932—

Remember, that is when I came to Washington on that trip.

a policy to the effect that a debtor may at any time approach a creditor with representations concerning the debt and to ask for readjustment of the debt or its terms of payment. Under such circumstances the debtor government makes such representations as it deems of importance with respect to the desirability of any readjustment in the terms already agreed upon. The British Government availed itself of this principle following the payment of the December fifteenth payment and I had informal discussions concerning the debt with the British Ambassador even before my inauguration—

That was when Sir Ronald Lindsay came down to Warm Springs at the end of January, the 31st of January.

—On the occasion of the visit of the Prime Minister of Great Britain in April further exploration of the subject was made by us and additional discussions were held by the experts of the two Governments. Time and circumstances would not permit any definitive conclusions in these discussions because at the moment both Governments were vitally concerned in making preparation for the World Monetary and Economic Conference in London. It seems the part of fairness and wisdom to postpone formal representations on the debt subject until later.

Meanwhile the World Economic Conference is beginning under favorable auspices and it is vitally necessary that during the opening days of the Conference difficult and possibly protracted discussion of the debt be avoided.

In a spirit of cooperation I have as Executive noted the representations of the British Government with respect to the payment of the June fifteen installment inasmuch as the payment made is accompanied by a clear acknowledgment of the debt itself. In view of those representations and of the payment I have no personal hesitation in saying that I do not characterize the resultant situation as a default.

Beyond this the law and the Constitution do not permit me to go. The American public understands clearly that the settlement under which these debts are now being paid was made under the authority of Congress and that Congress alone has the right to alter the amount and method of payment of this debt. Further than this, the Congress in December, 1931, in approving the moratorium in June of that year, specifically set forth that the debt should not be cancelled or reduced.

Under my constitutional power, and in accordance with the terms of the policy which I have set forth, I can entertain representations of the British Government concerning the entire debt settlement and the British Government has requested that such opportunity be afforded. I have, therefore, suggested to them that such representations be made in Washington as soon as convenient. As a matter of information to the American public, I want to make it clear that the Economic Conference now being held in London does not include in its program any consideration of the debts owed by various governments to the United States. The American delegates have been instructed not to discuss debts with the representatives of any of the debtor governments. This is in accordance with the further principle that I have felt important, that the debts be considered on their merits and separate from other international economic questions.

I have further informed the British Government that such representations and suggestions as may be made to me by the British representatives when they discuss the problem in Washington will be submitted to the Congress for information and consideration when the Congress next meets.

And so there we are.

Q: Have you invited other nations—will other nations have to make the same offer or will they be invited?

The President: It depends on the individual nation.

Q: What about the case of Italy?

The President: I cannot tell you because as I understand it—I will have to tell you this off the record because you cannot use it yet. As

I understand it, the Italian Ambassador saw the Acting Secretary of State yesterday and told him that in all probability something will come. I don't think anything has come. I don't think any other formal note has come except the British note.

Q: Will you deal with Italy in the same terms that you have with England?

The President: Same principle for everybody.

Q: What about others that have not paid the default of that December payment?

The President: That is a different question.

Q: How will those 10 million dollars be paid?

The President: I have no information except very unofficially that it will be paid—I don't know, in pounds or dollars or something like that; not silver.

Q: There was an understanding that while debts were not part of the Agenda of the Conference, they should be discussed simultaneously with individual debtors in London?

The President: No.

Q: That understanding was never corrected, or is this to the contrary?

The President: Fred,[5] where was that understanding made, do you know?

Q: It was understood here; certainly the State Department officials at one time gave us that impression.

The President: Didn't Messrs. Day and Williams,[6] when they went over there, definitely tell them we couldn't, not long before I came in. I think they did.

Q: The last word I had on that subject was from the present Secretary of State when he gave it as his opinion at a press conference that the debts might be discussed with individual nations simultaneously with other matters in London.

The President: No, I think that Day and Williams were definitely told by Secretary Stimson that they could not agree in any way to the inclusion of debts in the Agenda and actually it does not appear in the Agenda.[7]

Q: Mr. President, the date of the meeting of Congress has been changed. Ordinarily this debt question would come up again in December, when Congress meets?

The President: Yes.

Q: But the Congress meets in January, although the debt payments are due during December, are they not?

The President: Yes.

Q: What would you do?

The President: Oh, my Lord; I haven't got as far as December. That is literally true.

Q: Congress may still be here?

Q: Have you it in mind at all that any other nation is going to follow the same line of seeking consultation? The reason I ask is that there is a bulletin in the last afternoon paper saying that the French Government had word that a new proposition for debt conference in London was about to be made. I assume they may have some information as to the British plan.

The President: Something may have come in this afternoon. Off the record, Bill Phillips told me late last night, about midnight, that he had unofficial word that the Belgians were not going to pay anything and he had word from Ambassador Rosso that a note was coming from Italy and that is all he had heard from. Oh, yes, in addition to that the Finns and Rumanians are discussing methods of payment. They are still discussing it.

Q: Mr. President, does that throw the budget out of balance for that amount?

The President: Gosh, I don't know. I would have to ask the Director of the Budget. I don't know but I don't think it does.

Q: Isn't it a fact that in preparing the tentative budgets, you excluded the debt payments from some of them?

The President: I don't think so. I am inclined to think that if you will ask the Director of the Budget you will find that a portion was included; how much, I don't know.

Q: Mr. President, is it your attitude that any debt discussion would have to take place right here?

The President: Yes.

Q: On all debts? Is that your reaction to the MacDonald speech?[8]

The President: No, that has been the rule from the very beginning— before the rule was ever made. That was my instruction to the delegates before they left Washington.

Q: Do you think it comes with good grace from MacDonald and Simon?

The President: That is an "if" question.

Q: I will withdraw it.

Q: Have you in mind how soon these discussions will begin? You said, "as soon as possible." How soon will that be?

The President: I think you had better not use this as anything except off the record because we don't know yet. It will probably be quite a long time—possibly a month or two.

Q: They will be taking place about the time the Economic Conference—

The President: Is getting over, I think so.

Q: Mr. President, would you prefer that it not take place until after the Economic Conference?

The President: We say any time that is convenient. In fact, this is off the record, we consider that there is mighty little relationship between the two, one way or the other.

[President's Press Conferences:T]

[1] Lindsay to Phillips; headings, date lines, etc., have been omitted here and below. There are no other omissions. This letter is also printed in *Foreign Relations, 1933,* I, 839–841.

[2] Phillips to Lindsay, June 14, 1933, also printed *ibid.,* p. 842.

[3] Supplied for an apparent omission in the original.

[4] The preceding exchange of letters, and the statement of the President here following, were issued to the press on June 14. The statement is also printed in *Public Papers,* II, 242–244. An abbreviated version was read by Roosevelt for the news reels and a copy is present (Speech File).

[5] Presumably J. Fred Storm of the United Press.

[6] Edmund E. Day of the Rockefeller Foundation and John H. Williams, professor of economics at Harvard. The Day–Williams cables from Geneva are printed in *Foreign Relations, 1933,* I, 452ff, beginning about mid-January 1933.

[7] The *Draft Annotated Agenda* (League of Nations, Monetary and Economic Conference, Geneva: Jan. 20, 1933), submitted by the preparatory commission of experts and used as the general program for the conference, states (p. 7): "In this programme, the problem of inter-Governmental indebtedness has not been included, because it lies outside our terms of reference." The agenda may also be found in *The Program For the World Economic Conference* (Boston: World Peace Foundation, 1933). The introduction (p. 7) states: "Silver was explicitly included in the Agenda, while reparations, war debts and specific tariff rates were excluded."

[8] At his speech opening the London Economic Conference on June 12, MacDonald raised the question of war debts although the United States had considered this subject barred from discussion (New York *Times,* June 13, 1933, p. 1).

# William C. Bullitt, Executive Officer, American Delegation, London Economic Conference, to Roosevelt

London, June 15, 1933

[*Excerpt*][1] Long before you receive this letter the fight over the chairmanship of the Monetary Commission will have been concluded.[2] I think we shall win, as I was able yesterday personally to line up a majority of the members of the Bureau to support Cox. Then, at the last minute, MacDonald postponed the meeting of the Bureau at which the matter was to be settled. This fight has grown out of the simple fact that MacDonald categorically promised us that chairmanship for Cox and at the same time promised it to Bonnet[3] for himself. Throughout the past two days MacDonald has been trying to wriggle out of the situation and has given our entire delegation the uncomfortable feeling that he is not dealing frankly with us. Our delegation felt that we should cable you in regard to this letter in plain Gray code, which we are sure the British have, so that MacDonald might know just what we think of his failure to collaborate frankly. In case we send you any further cables of importance in plain Gray, you will understand that it is for the purpose of communicating the matters contained in [them to][4] the British as well as to yourself.

A word as to stabilization. Warburg and Harrison have been working excellently together. Sprague has become somewhat of a prima donna and is doing a great deal of loose talking about London in regard to the policies of the American Government, prefaced by the statement that he is your personal representative. Jimmy is certainly the man of that trio to rely on.

Davis has been 'phoning the secretary, asking that the Secretary request him to come to London. The Secretary does not want him in London, but hates to say "No" categorically and I do not know what the issue will be; but in case Davis should come I hope you will find means to get him back on the continent before long, as nothing could be worse than divided representation for the United States at the present moment.

The members of the delegation are all working together as a delegation with excellent personal feelings and you can be sure that such brains as we have are being used not to fight each other but to fight our opponents.[5]

Every good wish to you and apologies for transmitting this sort of news. I feel obliged to let you know completely everything that is going on with the same frankness that I should if we were together in Washington. Good luck to you and a good holiday.

Yours devotedly,

(signed) William C. Bullitt

[PSF:London Economic Conference:T]

236

[1] This excerpt only is present.

[2] The Conference was organized as the Commission on Economic Affairs and the Commission on Monetary and Financial Affairs.

[3] Georges Bonnet, French Finance Minister. Cox was elected chairman of the Monetary Commission on June 15, 1933, after a stiff fight (Moley, *After Seven Years*, pp. 224ff).

[4] Supplied for an omission in the original.

[5] Bullitt's optimistic report is not borne out by the accounts in Hull's *Memoirs*, I, 254ff; Moley, *After Seven Years*, pp. 224ff; Cox, *Journey Through My Years* (New York: Simon and Schuster, 1946), chap. 21. On the other hand, Warburg cabled Roosevelt on June 16 that the delegates "were getting along excellently" (*Foreign Relations, 1933*, I, 644–645). More serious disagreements came later; see Hull to Phillips, June 27, 1933, *ibid.*, p. 659.

## Warren Delano Robbins, Protocol Officer, American Delegation, London Economic Conference, to President and Mrs. Roosevelt

[London] June 15, 1933

Dear Franklin and Eleanor: During the past week there have been few developments until yesterday and now I think we are starting. The Delegation arrived in a rather depressed condition and, very confidentially, the Secretary last Sunday became very temperamental and was on the verge of resigning.[1] To help the situation Key Pittman went on a beeno and only got back to normalcy yesterday. I think that we have him in hand now.

The big feat and the only interest I have had up to now has been to get Governor Cox in as Chairman of the Monetary Committee. The French were fighting it tooth and nail and the British showed very little interest in our desire to get the Chairmanship. Luckily I was able to get hold of Eric Gunston, who is a secretary to Neville Chamberlain, and "talk turkey" to him. I tried it out on Robert Vansittart but found him very non-committal. Gunston then came to me and asked me, after I had expressed very distinctly our desires in this matter, why we thought it was important to have one of our Delegates as Chairman of the Commission, making the comment that, after all, the Chairmanship was not so important. I replied that we considered the Chairmanship very important and that we wanted Governor Cox to get it.

I then saw my old friend LeBreton,[2] the Argentine, and got him lined up and on my return this afternoon I learned from Charlie Michelson[3] that it is okay and that the Governor will be Chairman. So far so good.

We have a long way to go and a lot of fighting to do and incidentally Bill Bullitt is a great help that way. I feel very strongly that we must stand by our guns and that if we are courteous but hard-boiled, we may accomplish something. I am doing my best to persuade the Secretary that he must fight every inch of the way. My only criticism of him is that he is a little too much of a gentleman to deal with this bunch of bandits.

Since I wrote you last I had a really delightful visit on His Majesty and I am not ashamed to tell you that I was extremely impressed. He seemed mentally extremely active and I had a good forty minutes' conversation with him alone in his library at Buckingham Palace. He wanted to know much about you both, as to how you were standing the racket, etc. He talked about former Ambassadors and said that he liked Bingham who had made an extremely good impression on him, that he liked Mellon, but that he never could stand Dawes.[4] On the tariff situation he merely said that he thought that the old English idea of free trade was impossible. I was interested to hear him comment that "we should not have been able to make that treaty with Argentina if we had not had a tariff to help us."[5]

The Conference—where the trained seals perform—did not become interesting until yesterday. Neville Chamberlain made a good speech and the Secretary of State an excellent one, followed by Litvinoff who, although he spoke in English, could not be understood. From now on little attention will be paid to speeches and they will be discouraged as the big men have already spoken.

Of course we are all thrilled, but not too well informed, as to your statement of acceptance of the debt.[6] It seems to me that the general trend of the British press is more friendly. When I got here it was not unfriendly but distinctly depressing.

Humorous comment: One of the French Delegates addressed Governor Cox thusly: "In view of the United States favoring inflation of currency, we feel that we can scarcely favor an American as Chairman of the Monetary Conference." Governor Cox: "The United States can scarcely favor as Chairman of the Monetary Conference a national of the greatest defaulting nation of the world." All seems to be friendly now.

I have just been talking with Charlie Michelson and Thurston[7]—Jung[8] is to be No. 2 man under Governor Cox and this is, I think, extremely good. The French are mad and I think our first battle is won.

I had a lot of fun breezing around London but am having still more of a thrill now sitting in on the Conference which has, as I say, only started yesterday.

I have seen Bennett and am attending the Wheat Conference with Ambassador Morgenthau and he tomorrow morning.[9] More later.

Love to you both from the three of us.

W. D. R.

[PSF:London Economic Conference:TS]

[1] Hull was depressed by Roosevelt's decision not to press for reciprocal tariff legislation, by disagreements on policy among the American delegates, and by the dispute over the chairmanship of the Monetary Commission. See Moley, *After Seven Years,* pp. 224ff; Hull, *Memoirs,* I, 252ff; Cox, *Journey Through My Years,* pp. 357–358.

[2] Tomas A. Le Breton, Argentinian representative at the London Economic Conference.

[3] An editor and newspaperman for many years, Michelson at this time was publicity director for the Democratic National Committee.

[4] Charles G. Dawes, ambassador to Great Britain from 1929 to 1932.

[5] The Roca Agreement, signed May 1, 1933; see *Foreign Relations, 1933,* IV, 722ff.

[6] June 14, 1933, above.

[7] Elliott Thurston, political editor of the Washington *Post.*

[8] Guido Jung, Italian Finance Minister.

[9] Richard B. Bennett, Prime Minister of Canada. Henry Morgenthau, Sr., and Frederick E. Murphy, publisher of the Minneapolis *Tribune,* were on the American delegation as wheat specialists.

# Press Conference, Executive Offices of the White House, June 16, 1933, 4:15 P.M.

[*Excerpt*] Q: With regard to the stabilization of currencies, you told us a while ago that we were not sure at that time that the time was ripe for stabilization, either de facto or de jure. In view of the conflicting reports from London, is there any change in our position?[1]

The President: I think the best way to talk is absolutely off the record. In the first place, our people over there obviously could not conclude any kind of an agreement without submitting it back here to the State Department and to me first. That is perfectly clear.

Number two is equally clear and that is that they have not communicated with us in any shape, manner or form.

Therefore, the third point is equally clear and that is that they have entered into absolutely no agreement on the other side, tentative or otherwise.

The reason I say this has to be strictly off the record is because it looks to me a little bit as if some of our friends belonging to the other nations in London are trying to spread around the idea that we have entered into some kind of an agreement and then, if it does not go through, try to put the blame for a failure to stabilize on us. Knowing the way things are run at those conferences, I don't think it would be above some people to do just that very thing. That, literally, is all that has happened. There hasn't been a thing done by our people about stabilization. Of course, they are talking about it but they cannot do anything without submitting it to the Secretary of State and me and they haven't let us know a thing about it except that Cox is the Chairman of that section.

Q: Here is a dispatch that they have agreed that the inflation measure should not be put in. I thought you were going to send Moley over there to look after it.

The President: No. Moley, from the very start, has been going over. He is going over a week or the week after—

Mr. Early: He expects to sail on the *Manhattan.*

The President: He expects to sail on the *Manhattan;* I didn't even know that. He will take a look-see and come back. Warren Robbins is coming back next week to report so as to give me a personal touch on things. There will be somebody else probably going over and coming back a couple of weeks later.

Q: Inasmuch as they are using propaganda of this sort, don't you think there should be some reaction of some sort?

The President: No, I am just wising you to it.

Q: Can we use this stuff, ourselves?

The President: No; just keep it in the back of your heads.

Q: Will you give us what you consider the elements of successful agreement on stabilization?

The President: Oh, my Lord; it would take me two hours and then neither one of us would know.

Q: Can the Administration enter into an agreement like that—it does not have to go to Congress?

The President: (Shakes head indicating "No.")

Q: What form does it take, the treaty form?

The President: It is too early to tell you. The thing is this, that it should take some form of gentlemen's agreement that would hold things thoroughly steady but I would not go too far about any idea of stabilization at the present time.

Q: That is in line with the question I wanted to ask: Is the Administration willing to enter into some sort of a stabilization arrangement?

The President: That sort of question again is too uncertain. It depends on what kind of a stabilization agreement and where it was and what it was. We have had nothing put up to us. It depends entirely on what was put up to us.

Q: Couldn't we use that last point, that this Government has not entered into any agreement, tentative or otherwise?

Q: That was given by Woodin?

The President: You can do that, that this Government has not entered into any agreement, tentative or otherwise, also that we have not heard anything in the way of suggestions or communiqués from the other side. Phillips told me an hour ago that nothing had come in and that nothing would be done unless submitted here and approved by the Secretary of the Treasury, the Acting Secretary of State and myself.

Q: You don't say in this case that we are not putting forward any suggestions—we are just listening?

The President: Yes.

Q: What is Harrison's function? He has gone over with the official party.

The President: No, he went over—Ernest (Lindley),[2] I don't know. I think it is on an entirely separate meeting of the Central Bank. We did not know anything about it until it was announced.[3]

[President's Press Conferences:T]

[1] On June 12, Sprague, Harrison, and Warburg had begun talks with British and French officials on some form of temporary stabilization of the dollar-pound ratio (Moley, *After Seven Years,* p. 228). On June 15 Roosevelt had cabled Hull, Sprague, and Cox that all kinds of wild reports were being circulated, and warned that any stabilization proposal would have to be approved by him and the Treasury (*Foreign Relations, 1933,* I, 641). Frederick T. Birchall's dispatch from London on June 15 said that a "somewhat vague" stabilization agreement had been tentatively drafted (New York *Times,* June 16, 1933, p. 1). In a statement in the *Times* of June 16 (p. 1), Secretary of the Treasury Woodin said that such reports were unfounded and that any proposal would first have to be submitted to the President and to the Treasury. The first draft of a proposed stabilization declaration was sent to Woodin by Sprague on June 16; on the next day Roosevelt cabled Hull his "definite policy with regard to stabilization" (*Foreign Relations, 1933,* I, 642–644, 645–646). For the succeeding exchanges, culminating in the proposal cabled to Roosevelt on July 1 (below, Phillips to Roosevelt), see *Foreign Relations, 1933,* I, 641–668, passim; Cox, *Journey Through My Years,* p. 365; Hull, *Memoirs,* I, 260–261; and Moley, *After Seven Years,* pp. 228–249.

[2] Representing the *Herald Tribune.*

[3] Moley states that in a cable received by Roosevelt on May 26 MacDonald asked that the United States send representatives to meet "apart from the Conference" to

agree on some measure of stabilization, and that Roosevelt, in his reply, agreed to send over Sprague and Harrison. Moley adds that Sprague and Harrison were given no definite instructions: "Sprague was simply told to see what he could do about negotiating some sort of arrangement designed to steady the exchanges" (*After Seven Years,* p. 216). Neither cable is in the Roosevelt papers.

## Roosevelt to William Gorham Rice, New York State Civil Service Commission, Albany

[Washington] June 16, 1933

My dear Colonel Rice: I have not had an opportunity to write you before this but I want to do so with the utmost frankness. I know that you will understand this is written in the spirit of an old friend, and also with regard to the exigencies of many matters here in Washington. The number of thoroughly competent men who are available for diplomatic service, including those who are members of the career service, far exceeds the number of embassies and legations. In the case of every one of these men there is some very definite reason for appointment. It is simply impossible to discriminate with them because after the elimination of those not so well qualified the supply far exceeds the available places.

May I also say that in going over these lists I have eliminated the names of three or four people who are actually a good deal younger than you are, on account of their age, and I have kept your name on the list because, in spite of the date of your birth, you are hale and hearty to a very unusual degree. I have told a number of those already appointed to foreign posts that I might possibly or even probably ask them to relinquish their post after one year, and in every case the appointee has been wholly willing to go along with my statement.

I can therefore only invite you to go to Holland as our minister on the same understanding which I have with many other appointees. I hope to complete the list of appointments during the next two weeks.[1]

Very sincerely yours,

[PPF 288:CT]

[1] This letter was in reply to Rice's letter of April 23, 1933 (PPF 288), objecting to the conditions placed on his appointment in Roosevelt's offer of April 20, 1933, above. Rice, who was seventy-seven at this time, wrote again June 29, 1933 (PPF 288), refusing the appointment under the conditions made. See Roosevelt to Rice, July 28, 1933, below.

## Roosevelt to Herbert Bayard Swope, New York

Washington, June 16, 1933

[*Telegram*] Would be delighted if you could accompany Raymond Moley for short visit to London.[1] I am sending him soon and feel your presence would be exceedingly helpful to him in many ways. I should be personally grateful to have you do this, having confidence as I do in your judgment and your wide knowledge of international affairs. You would be absent from this country only about a month.[2]

Franklin D. Roosevelt

[PPF 331:T]

[1] The following added words appear in the accompanying draft: "in connection with, but not a part of Economic Conference." The phrase was crossed out by Roosevelt.

[2] Moley says that Swope's appointment was urged by him over the objections of Howe, Early, and McIntyre (*After Seven Years*, pp. 231–232). Cox says that Swope went along as Moley's financial adviser (*Journey Through My Years*, p. 370). See also James A. Farley, *Jim Farley's Story* (New York: Whittlesey House, 1948), pp. 40–41.

## Robert W. Bingham, Ambassador to Great Britain, to Roosevelt

[London] June 16, 1933

Dear Mr. President: I tried to convey to you in my cable yesterday the effect of your action on the British debt.[1] The Conference was on the rocks. Your action has made it possible for it to continue hopefully, in my judgment. I have, of course, been in close touch with the delegation, and some of them had reached the point where they wanted to ask permission to leave the Conference and go home.

I was simply aghast when the Prime Minister brought in the question of debts in his opening address, and I personally regard it as a breach of faith. I do not know what pressure was brought upon him to do it, but my understanding is that after he had prepared his address, which contained no reference to the debt, he recalled copies of it which had actually been issued and inserted the paragraph. Personally, I resented it deeply, as did the members of our delegation, because we realized it would increase your difficulties at home.[2]

In addition, after promising the Chairmanship of the Monetary Commission to us, members of our delegation believed that the Prime

Minister promised it also to the French. The British with whom I have conferred agree that the Prime Minister should not have referred to the debt question, and merely offer excuses for his having done so, even going so far as to blame it upon his physical and mental condition. After the announcement of your stand upon the debt question, the atmosphere immediately cleared. They made good on their other promise that Gov. Cox should be Chairman of the Monetary Commission, and there is now hope again for specific and helpful action on the part of the Conference.

I have not attempted to burden you with details or frequent letters, and shall not do so unless you desire it.

With kindest regards, Sincerely yours,

Robert W. Bingham

[PSF:London Economic Conference:TS]

[1] Bingham refers to Roosevelt's statement of June 14, 1933, above, press conference, June 14. No June 15 cable from Bingham is present.

[2] The speech is printed in League of Nations, *Journal of the Monetary and Economic Conference, London, 1933*, pp. 8–9. MacDonald noted that the London Conference was an outgrowth of the Lausanne meeting in June 1932 and that "Lausanne indicated the subjects which ought to be dealt with." MacDonald had been the presiding officer at Lausanne, as he was now at London.

## B. H. Inness Brown to Edward M. House, Beverly Farms, Massachusetts

New York, N. Y., June 19, 1933

Dear Colonel House: Since my letter of the 17th the newspapers have carried the news of a decision in Washington which apparently means that we are not to have an attempted stabilization of currencies at this time. From what I said in my letter of the 17th,[1] with its enclosure, you will gather that I think this decision is wholly wise.

As you know, my opinion is that the price of goods (viz., "the price level"), is the expression of a quantitative equation. The true value of a dollar is the quantity of goods and services offered divided by the "number of dollars which are out." The Administration has done little as yet to increase the number of dollars that are out, viz., demand deposits, plus currency in circulation. Prices have run ahead of the facts because the public generally has anticipated a change in the "number of dollars that are out" due to a promised inflation which has not yet materialized. For the same reason the dollar has declined in terms of foreign exchange and due to a certain amount of flight from the dollar based on the fear that having lost its gold anchor, it now may be reduced to any level. To sum up, the markets are based on psychology—the wisp of hay ahead of the donkey. I have recently heard a remark attributed to Mr. O. M. W. Sprague: "The dollar being a good dollar, it is very hard to depress it in terms of foreign currencies unless we use the printing press." Whether or not he made this remark it seems to me very sound. I think we must use the printing press in order to accomplish the Administration's objective of a 1926 price level, whether or not we relate this new printing press money to gold or other metallic standard at a subsequent date at a less content of gold to the dollar than the old gold content. By printing press, however, I do not mean in the first instance the issue of greenbacks. The intelligent way of using the printing press is first to use the banking pen. I mean by this to write up demand deposits (circulation of which has historically been more than 90 per cent of all our money) on the books of the banks of the country by the open market purchase of Government bonds by the Federal Reserve Bank. When I talked with Mr. Adolf Miller[2] he assured me that I need have no concern that the Government was going to take this course in an unrelenting and large way. It has certainly not done so so far, and you will notice from the *Whirligig*[3] which I mailed to you under separate cover this morning, the general effect has not been any real inflation yet. It is true that the velocity of bank deposits is increasing, but on the other hand, so also are prices and the velocity of business, which seems to bid fair to outrun the increase in money. To put it another way, the "goods offered" would increase without any other element increasing, which eventually would mathematically result in a decrease in prices.

All this is very technical, but I think comparatively simple, and this kind of thing has been my guiding compass throughout the depression.

To state my view again: I see a dollar which is too good to be at its present low price in foreign exchange, and a price level which has outrun the amount of our money as the result of an artificial stimulation of public psychology. An artificial situation of this sort, if not changed, is bound to collapse sooner or later, since it is one of my tenets that psychology will affect the time element, but the inexorable factors eventually offset it and bring about equilibrium after an over-swing in the opposite direction.

I am afraid the President is going to have very great difficulties in mastering this matter of an expansionist policy. However able the generalissimo, I see no major general and brigadier generals scarcely at all. In the extremely important Federal Reserve Bank of New York we have George Harrison, who the President has just found it necessary to disavow to the newspaper correspondents in Washington and apparently to recall home. In the Treasury we have Messrs. Woodin and Douglas,[4] who are apparently sympathetic with the deflationists, aided by Mr. Sprague, whose attitude I do not yet know but whose prior connection would indicate a "conservative" and hence deflationist attitude. At the head of the Federal Reserve we have a gentleman named Black,[5] who is avowedly a temporary appointment and who is apparently not to be heard from in the present situation. In the smaller positions most of the men who, through the Treasury and the Federal Reserve Board, are to act, are people who were trained by the enemy. It is like Napoleon's having no marshals and brigadiers except aristocrats brought up in all of the Bourbon traditions.

All of this I emphasized in my talk with Bullitt, saying that I did not see how they could hope to get cooperation in London unless the Government first implemented itself with men in the proper positions and made its expansionist attitude clear by acts in this country before it went to London. If this had been done it would have been clear that a stabilization agreement such as was apparently under discussion last week could not take place, except on the basis of a dollar very different from the present one—a dollar decreased in value by the increase of the "number of dollars which are out." It then would not have been necessary to throw over an agreement apparently made by the experts and repudiate some of these experts and make a decision extremely distasteful to the gold-minded world, which appears to them as a personal decision of President Roosevelt. It is like his decision about the gold embargo on the 19th of April. It appeared a personal decision—almost a personal trick—to the English and French—although actually it arose out of the inexorable conditions of the American situation. If the decision had been in the early weeks of March, as I so strongly urged at that time, the question of a personal decision by the President as a political maneuver would never have arisen. It seems to me it is somewhat the same with regard to this last decision. It would appear to the outsider reading the newspapers that the President never reached his decision until French logic pointed out that the dollar could not be stabilized unless he would agree not to use the powers of inflation given him by the Thomas Amendment. To renounce those powers immediately after the adjournment of Congress in the present state of public opinion would have produced, it seems to me, an extremely difficult position politically as well as most dangerous repercussions in the markets. It seems to me, my dear Colonel, that we are in the midst of a struggle between the party of "Prices" (namely the people throughout the world who manufacture, produce and sell), and the party of "Money" (namely the banking cult, who manufacture and sell money). The banking cult, who always treated the intricacies of monetary science as a mystical knowledge, are a priesthood to whom the sovereigns have been accustomed to surrender their initiative in this province of knowledge. In the United States, due to an extraordinary spread of general interest in monetary questions and to the freedom of certain minds, the people have succeeded in overthrowing this priesthood, though its Jesuits and father confessors swarm in all households in an endeavor to restrain and modify the decision in all official places. The money cult, however, which has wished to keep its money stable in terms of a single commodity (gold) for its own convenience in transactions, has allowed such a terrific disaster to ensue upon the world that it is clear to me now that the party of Prices will win a victory in the United States, which will force a like victory in all countries.

If you should sometime find the opportunity to look through the graphs in Warren and Pearson's book on *Prices*,[6] you would appreciate what I mean. It is dangerous to philosophize, but this is my philosophy of the situation at the moment.

Forgive me for writing so long a letter.[7]

With affectionate and respectful regards, Yours sincerely,

B. H. Inness Brown

[PPF 222:TS]

[1] Not present. The "decision in Washington" refers to Phillips' cable to Hull of June 17, 1933 (*Foreign Relations, 1933*, I, 645–646), stating Roosevelt's policy on currency stabilization.

[2] A member of the Federal Reserve Board.

[3] The *National Whirligig* was a mimeographed news service of the McClure Newspaper Syndicate in New York, begun about 1932.

[4] Presumably James H. Douglas, Jr., is meant though Douglas, Assistant Secretary of the Treasury for fiscal affairs, had resigned on June 12.

[5] Eugene R. Black, governor of the Federal Reserve Board from May 1933 to August 1934, when he resigned to direct the Federal Reserve Bank in Atlanta.

[6] George F. Warren and Frank A. Pearson, *Prices* (New York: John Wiley, 1933).

Brown was a disciple of Warren and in 1934 set forth his ideas on money in a pamphlet, *A Letter of Explanation to Frank* (New York: Pandick Press, 1934).

[7] This letter was presumably handed to Roosevelt by House when he and Lewis W. Douglas came aboard the *Amberjack II* in Gloucester harbor on June 21 (New York *Times,* June 22, 1933, p. 3). Benjamin Henry Inness Brown, an old friend of House, received his law degree from Harvard in 1904 and may have known Roosevelt there. He had an office at 120 Broadway (Equitable Building), Roosevelt's business address from 1921 to 1928.

## Memorandum by Herbert B. Swope

[June 20, 1933][1]

(This is an outline of the memo I prepared this afternoon. It is largely a restatement of the obvious and intended to be merely a background for the President's decision of June 17, with reference to stabilization.[2] B.M.B.[3] is somewhat uncertain as to whether or not he wants to sign it, preferring to adhere to F.D.R.'s cable of June 17 without giving reasons therefor. Later, if it is desired, he says he is willing to prepare or to aid in preparing a more extensive precept, in which, while not departing from his agreement that nothing should be done now, he intends pointing out the need of an eventual equilibrium. There are other reasons in his mind having to do with the possible interference with the Conference that he will probably tell you about. However, as you wanted set down in writing the points I brought out this afternoon, here it is.)

It was agreed by all consulted that the present is not the time to set any limits that restrict the free movement of the dollar, although no objection is seen toward affirming our intention of eventually joining in multilateral stabilization.

Our own economic and fiscal developments are so promising that it would be dangerously unwise at this moment to erect barriers against their continuance. It would be particularly unwise from political and psychological standpoints to permit a seeming limitation to be imposed by any other nation than our own, and any stabilization sought for so eagerly by the others would be regarded as being forced.

At this time any fixed formula of stabilization by agreement must necessarily be artificial and sheerly speculative. It might easily work hardships upon us through lowered prices and heavy equalization costs.

There should be a sufficient interval allowed America to permit, in addition to the play of natural economic forces, a demonstration of the value of the price-lifting efforts you have put under way. Upon the establishment of a reasonably constant price level definitive stabilization can be undertaken. Then it could be approached on a scientific basis and also with due recognition of the factor of trade balances. That plan is preferable to attempting a premature and arbitrary process based upon guess and subject to violent fluctuations.

Always it should be kept in mind that by waiting we can value the dollar in direct ratio to the increase in domestic prices. Unquestionably that is the fairest method to ourselves and to the others.

Your attention is directed to the fact that England left the gold standard a year and nine months ago, and only now is she seeking stabilization. France did not stabilize for something like four years (verify period).

We are advancing towards a national self-containment that should be not militated against by possibly hostile influences until it has had a chance to work.

There may be a slight embarrassment caused the American Commission because of a seeming check upon their stabilization plans but perhaps that hurt can be assuaged by permitting the members to continue discussions of the project on the distinct understanding that the subject is for future decision and that at this time, because of so many uncertain factors, we are not to make even a temporary agreement. After all, as you have said, the Conference was not called solely for stabilization purposes. There are other subjects of importance that should be given consideration. Furthermore, the Conference has no mandate to reach a stabilization basis. The instructions were only to explore the subject. The position of the Delegation might be strengthened by a reaffirmation from you of this country's intention eventually to reach reasonable stabilization, but it must be borne in mind that the figures that are finally set will be of our making, based upon our experience and our needs, and not those which other nations seek to impose upon us. Were they to do that they would be exercising a partial but very real control over our internal as well as external economy.

An impression of that sort would be especially bad at this time from the viewpoint of the public which sees its distress being relieved and which regards the higher price levels as not only bringing employment and increase in wages, but also—and this is of greatest importance—sees the increase in prices as a certain means of relieving a part of their strangling debts.

The various agencies operating under the National Recovery Act have not reached a decision as to precisely what price levels we are aiming. How, then, can we impose a limitation which we have not accepted ourselves?

It is a restatement of the obvious to say that our improvement, now so definitely under way, will be the greatest contribution we can make to the good of the world.[4]

[PSF:London Economic Conference:CT]

[1] Date derived from Moley, *After Seven Years,* pp. 255–256.
[2] See Phillips to Hull, June 17, 1933, in *Foreign Relations, 1933,* I, 645–646.
[3] Bernard M. Baruch.
[4] Moley states (*After Seven Years,* pp. 255–256) that he left this memorandum with Roosevelt on the *Amberjack II* on June 20, and that the President paraphrased it and used it in preparing his message to the American delegation of June 30, 1933, below, Roosevelt to Phillips.

## Roosevelt to William Phillips, Acting Secretary of State

[Pulpit Harbor, Maine, June 23, 1933][1]

[*Telegram*] Phillips: Is Robbins on way back from London? If not think he should come as soon as convenient to him & bring any letters delegates may want to send me.[2] R.

[OF 17:AS]

[1] Pulpit Harbor is on North Haven Island, at the entrance of Penobscot Bay. The *Amberjack II* had put in here at 8 P.M. on this date, after a stormy day's sail from Chandler's Cove, near Portland. Roosevelt had been at sea a week.
[2] Phillips, in a letter to Roosevelt of June 22, 1933 (OF 17), said it was his impression that Robbins was to return after the Conference had been organized and was under way. Hull had now asked that Robbins stay until the end because of his usefulness in Latin American matters. Robbins apparently returned with the rest of the delegation in July. No letters from the delegates have been found in the Roosevelt papers.

## Press Release by Stephen T. Early, Assistant Secretary to the President

U.S.S. *Ellis*[1] [June 23, 1933]

[*Radiogram*] Recurring and widely published reports that the President will board the Cruiser *Indianapolis*[2] for a rush trip to London are without foundation in fact. The President plans to complete his vacation cruise and return to Washington as scheduled.

At no time has the President considered going to London and he sees no reason whatsoever to do so now. Reports from London, received in the last 24 hours, have been altogether satisfactory to the President.

Although the President is far up the Maine coast, he is and has been in continuous communication with Washington at all times since he left. The State Department has kept him fully advised of all developments in the Economic Conference.

Early

Note: Anchoring tonight in Pulpit Harbor.

[PSF:London Economic Conference:CT]

[1] The *Ellis* was a destroyer escort assigned to the small fleet accompanying the *Amberjack II.* The others were the destroyer *Bernadue;* the *Cuyahoga,* a Coast Guard cutter; the *Comanche,* a 70-foot motor cruiser carrying newsmen; the *Mary Alice,* a 45-foot ketch; and the *Indra,* a 90-foot schooner that carried the news and motion picture photographers (New York *Times,* June 19, 1933, p. 3). Messages were received on and sent from the *Ellis.*

[2] Confusion over Roosevelt's intentions probably arose from the fact that the published itinerary of his trip showed him planning to board the *Indianapolis* on July 1. No date was given for his return to Washington and some reporters assumed that once aboard the cruiser, he would go to London. The Columbia Broadcasting System on June 23 wired Early aboard the *Ellis:* "Appreciate collect your denial President Londonward" (OF 200-A). Early replied at once that the President had no such intention and followed this with the news release here printed. Some of this speculation had been aroused by Moley's visit to the *Amberjack II* on June 20.

# Dean Acheson, Under Secretary of the Treasury, to Marvin H. McIntyre, Assistant Secretary to the President

Washington, 6/24/33

The following dictated by Dean Acheson:[1]

1. George Harrison returned from London Friday and reported at the Federal Reserve Board and to the Under Secretary today.[2] He has a great deal of important information on the developments of the first week of the London Conference which I think the President would find very useful. This may be particularly useful in view of Warburg's cable[3] suggesting the possibility of some action on our part to prevent violent fluctuations during the next few weeks. OK[4]

2. Dr. Sprague cabled from London, asking whether he should stay or return immediately. I talked with him over telephone and we finally

agreed that subject to further instructions from the President he should stay in London until next Saturday for the purpose of conferring with Mr. Moley, it being thought desirable that everybody should be in London at one time. He now plans to sail for this country next Saturday if he can obtain permission to come on a British boat. Otherwise, he will sail on the *Manhattan*, July 4th[5] . . .[6]

[OF 17:T]

[1] Presumably over the telephone. Acheson, appointed Under Secretary of the Treasury May 19, 1933, resigned Nov. 15, 1933, in protest over the Administration's gold-buying policy.

[2] Harrison had left the delegation following receipt of Roosevelt's cable of June 17 rejecting temporary stabilization plans (Moley, *After Seven Years*, p. 232).

[3] June 22, 1933, *Foreign Relations, 1933*, I, 653.

[4] The "OK" appears in McIntyre's hand in the middle of the paragraph.

[5] Roosevelt on June 25 wired McIntyre "or Under Secretary Phillips" (both were in Washington): "Think most advisable Sprague stay London until he can see Moley" (OF 17). Moley arrived in London on June 28 and in the next few days saw Sprague, Cox, and Warburg several times (Moley, *After Seven Years*, pp. 245-251). Sprague did not return to New York until mid-July.

[6] A concluding paragraph has to do with Treasury Department matters.

## William Phillips, Acting Secretary of State, to Roosevelt

Washington, June 26, 1933

Dear Mr. President: I am anxious to carry out your wishes in regard to debt conversations.[1] Six countries have paid something in acknowledgment of their debt and have been informed that "they would be gladly heard at a date to be agreed upon between us." These countries are Great Britain, Italy, Czechoslovakia, Latvia, Lithuania and Rumania. Finland has paid in full.

Before he left for England, Moley asked me to arrange dates for these hearings, beginning with Finland and one or two of the other small countries, before we undertook to hear the British.[2] The Finnish Minister has gone away for the summer and prefers to have his business delayed until his return; the Czechoslovak Minister is ready to begin at the end of July; the Italian Ambassador early in August; I have not yet taken up the matter with any definiteness with Sir Ronald Lindsay.

The whole problem is of such far-reaching importance that I hesitate to proceed any further until I know your wishes. It would be a great help if you could let me know whether you desire me to go ahead and fix a time for each of the countries to be heard, beginning at the end of July, as Moley suggested, or whether you prefer to postpone all the "hearings" until the end of the summer, when you will be back in Washington—presumably after September 1st.

I have already sent telegraphic instructions to our representatives in the paying countries, asking them to compile the necessary information regarding the capacity to pay of the countries in question. It seemed to me important that we should have the latest information on this subject from our own representatives to check whatever may be given us by the foreign representatives.

It is a joy to think of you already in the vigorating climate of eastern Maine, as free from care as you ever will be and surrounded by the best companions in the world.

Faithfully yours,

William Phillips

[OF 20:TS]

[1] On this see Phillips to Lindsay, June 14, 1933, in *Foreign Relations, 1933,* I, 842.
[2] One of Moley's assignments in the State Department was to work on the war debt problem (*After Seven Years,* pp. 201-203).

## Dean Acheson, Under Secretary of the Treasury, to Roosevelt

[Washington] June 27, 1933

[*Telegram*] For the President from Acheson: Re your telegram of June 24th[1] referring to Warburg's 57 of June 22[2] and Cox's 58.[3] Your message 24[4] has been discussed with Secretary Woodin, Baruch, Harrison and Douglas today. Secretary Woodin is ill in New York. He was inclined this morning to think that we should do nothing now but is willing to go along with consensus of opinion. The following gives the views of Baruch, Harrison, Douglas and Acheson. We understand by telephone from London today that a message is being sent which may have an important bearing on our final judgment and we therefore feel that such judgment should be reserved.[5] Nevertheless we now wish to call attention to fact that unilateral action would consist in purchase of dollars by export of gold and would not prevent rise in dollar or fall in pound and/or franc, whereas tripartite action would, within the limits agreed upon, prevent fall in other currencies as well as the dollar. Thus unilateral action would have the effect of keeping the dollar up without an understanding or agreement on the part of the British or the French to keep the pound or the franc up while this protection to us would be furnished by tripartite action. The pound closed today slightly over $4.30, indicating exchange situation getting out of hand and increasing possibility that other countries now on gold would be forced to abandon gold, which will have the effect of putting the dollar up in relation to those countries. Our present thought, therefore, pending receipt of message from London, is that it would be better to work along the lines of the loose temporary tripartite arrangement with such further arrangements as might be mutually agreed upon and with France and England participating in the arrangement in a way that would hold up the pound and the franc, as well as the dollar. The exchange situation seems to be growing more complicated and increasing strength in commodity and security market might make it much safer now than two weeks ago to consider some form of temporary tripartite arrangement. In this connection Baruch has wired Moley to get into immediate touch with Sprague to discuss relative advantage of tripartite and unilateral action. We all feel that some brake upon speculative developments is necessary to anticipate dangerous reaction.

[*Notation*:AS] Via Naval communications in code 6/28/33 EW
[OF 17:T]

[1] Roosevelt to Acting Secretary of State Phillips, June 24, 1933 (*Foreign Relations, 1933,* I, 655). Roosevelt thought that taking steps to prevent the pound from fluctuating violently above 4.25 might be helpful; this, he thought, could be done through the Federal Reserve, "but should be limited to violent upward fluctuations."

[2] Warburg to Roosevelt, June 22, 1933 (*ibid.,* I, 653), suggesting that Roosevelt "without making any declaration whatsoever" authorize the Federal Reserve banks to take whatever action was needed to limit dollar fluctuations.

[3] Cox to Roosevelt, June 22, 1933 (*ibid.,* I, 653–654), saying that the President's cable to Hull, June 17, 1933 (*ibid.,* 645–646), in which he rejected the proposed declaration on stabilization, "hung like a pall" over the Conference, but that MacDonald had expressed the opinion that the worst crisis was now over.

[4] Meaning Roosevelt's message of June 24 to Phillips, cited above, n. 1.

[5] This reference is to Hull's cable to Roosevelt, June 27, 1933 (*ibid.,* pp. 658–659), reporting on a joint meeting held that afternoon of the British and American delegations, called by MacDonald. The British inquired whether the United States would join with others in preventing speculation in dollar exchange; they were told that no such proposal could be considered. Moley, who had arrived from New York that evening, says that on the next day Hull turned over to him and Sprague the negotiations concerning what Hull called "temporary stabilization" (*After Seven Years,* p. 246).

## Breckinridge Long, Ambassador to Italy, to Roosevelt

Rome, Italy, June 27, 1933

My dear Chief: I want to give you a picture of Italy. I was here twenty-odd years ago and formed the most distinct and lasting impressions. When I returned I expected reminiscence and revival of memories, but the landscape, a few donkey wagons, and bullocks are the only things to remind one of the Italy that was. The people have changed. Their customs and habits have changed. Their morals have changed. Their sanitary conditions have changed. The cities have changed. Rome is not to be recognized except as far as the Forum is concerned. Great avenues run through the city. The streets are clean. The people are well dressed. They move with alacrity. In the country the houses are all painted and clean. The country roads are well paved and clean. The farms are all teeming with people, just now reaping wheat by hand. The country seems as if it had been manicured every morning.

The whole temper and attitude of the people have changed. They all seem happy. They all seem busy.

I have been in Rome just four weeks. After many formalities and after the routine work of the Embassy, I have mingled around somewhat. I have accepted three luncheons and three dinners a week. The other evenings I have been in my room and tried to digest it all, except on Sundays, when I have gone forth into the country. Twice I have been west to different parts of the mountains. Once I went to Naples for lunch and back—down by the mountains and back by the sea. Once I went to Orbetello, spending the night with Senator Guglielmo at Montalto to see General Balbo[1] before his departure. So I have been north and west and south, and I have been to Ostia by the sea. I have observed the people and the country and their occupations and their little towns. I have formed an impression which is so at variance with the recollections of my former visit that there is nothing in the present reminiscent of the past. It is astounding.

They are spending large sums on public works. The campagna is being drained, and literally small cities are being built in it. Roads have not only been built but they are all being carefully attended to and swept clean even far in the country. Construction work appears here and there in every part of Italy. Many men are in uniform. The Fascisti in their black shirts are apparent in every community. They are dapper and well dressed and stand up straight and lend an atmosphere of individuality and importance to their surroundings.

The public works are very expensive. The money comes from some-where. It is hard to find out just how it is raised. Part of it comes from the Postal Savings Banks. The people deposit their savings in cash, and the Government collects the cash and gives interest-bearing Government securities. The taxes are very heavy. For instance, I bought an auto-mobile. They asked 90,000 lire. I thought it was too much. They said that I had a diplomatic privilege and could save the tax, which would be 15%. So I bought the car for about 77,000 lire. The tax was 13,000. That is a manufacturers' tax. Any Italian citizen buying the car would have had to pay the tax. The tax on gasoline is very heavy. There was a radio in the car. They wanted 4,000 lire for the radio. Christine has a radio in her car, and I like to get away from one occasionally, so I told them I did not want the radio. Afterwards the manufacturer wrote me and said that he would sell me the radio for $39.00 American money, which is about 460 lire. The difference between 460 lire and 4,000 lire represents the manufacturers' tax, the luxury tax, and the tax for the use of the radio. Everything is taxed. There is a sales tax on every article bought. There is an income tax to the Government. There are land taxes to the District, and there are municipal taxes in the cities.

In addition to these, the Fascisti pay additional taxes. For that they get privileges. They are proud, some of them, to pay the Fascisti tax. Some pay it out of obligation. Some pay it because it is advantageous and they get business from other Fascisti if they belong to the party. The Fascisti funds are spent for the education of children, not that education in the schools but in extra-curriculum education.

I hear there is much grumbling about taxes. I also hear that there is resentment in parts of Italy against the oppressive methods. I hear that the alternative is Bolshevism and that if something should happen to the Head of the Government, it would be very difficult to suppress Bolshevism, because the natural reactions of the people from the rigours of the present regime would lead them to extremes in another direction. I am not sufficiently well oriented to appraise the truth of that. Further-more, it is difficult for me to come in contact with the classes who would be Bolshevistic.

I do know that the rich have lost materially. They are renting their houses—cheap. For instance, I am offered the Villa Madama with its decorations by Raphael, a most gorgeous palace, sumptuously furnished, with great gardens, and it is a national monument, fully furnished and equipped for approximately $12,000 a year to use as an Embassy resi-dence. But the up-keep is very great beside. It is just a sample. The rich are being forced to leave their houses. Many of them have lost money in the American stock market, and conditions in Italy are not so good. The rise in value of the lire has hurt Italy's international trade. They cannot now sell automobiles abroad. The difference in exchange is about 20%. That operates as a definite barrier. Whatever Italy manufactures for export is subject to the same difficulty. In addition to that, the regular taxes are harder on the rich with their reduced incomes. Many of them complain quietly of the difficulties they have in living as they used to live.

The trains are punctual, well-equipped and fast. The running times have been decreased 20% to 30% and efficiency increased 100%. They are trying to make the people of Italy assume a national character. Instead of being Sicilians or Neapolitans or Milanese, they want them Italians. They are using the railroads to foster that. The fares have all been reduced. It is very cheap to travel in Italy today, but in addition they make a refund of 70% of the fare if you come to Rome and have your return trip ticket validated at the Fascist Exposition. That means that you will have visited the Fascist Exposition. It will educate the traveler in Fascism. It will bring him to Rome and make him see what a great city Rome is, and it will make him Italian. It will give him the national point of view.

The Fascist Exposition is a remarkable show. It is one of Mussolini's pet objects and is in charge of a Deputy named Alfieri,[2] a young, vibrant and interesting man, who is responsible for the Exposition as it exists. It consists entirely of newspaper clippings and photographs of the period from 1914 to 1932. It is the history of the Fascist Movement, its origin and its purposes. Thousands of people are there all the time. It is divided into rooms representing years or important parts of years. The clippings from newspapers are enlarged to grandiose size, as are the photographs, and there are original manuscripts of Mussolini, of editorials in his paper, for he is the expounder of Fascism. It is illustrative of all the horrors of their fight against the Bolshevics. It shows the origin of Fascism in the World War. It relates its objectives and its advantages. People are induced from all over Italy to come to the Exposition and to learn there of Fascism and to understand what it means, and they are induced to this education by a nominal railroad fare from their homes to Rome with a 70% reduction on that provided that they prove by their visit to the validating office in the Fascist Exposition that they have visited that show.

The difference in cost to the railroads must certainly be made up out of public funds. The state owns the railroads, and they have recently floated a large bond issue to electrify them.

At the end of my first four weeks, after a multitude of protocol social duties and with a very interesting period during the negotiation of the Four Power Pact, and in a strange atmosphere, and with an appreciation of grandeur somewhat benumbed by over-exercise, I can only give you my first impressions. But I think first impressions sometimes are very valuable. I have taken time to digest and with my secretary and with Randolph Harrison[3] of the Embassy whom I brought over with me, I have been quietly in my apartments about half of the time making memoranda and in conversation, gradually assorting and digesting these various experiences. I think they are valuable to me and will help me in my future better understanding, and I thought they would be interesting to you. Consequently I am troubling you at this length.

There stands out the entire change which has occurred to the country, including its people. There also stands out the enigma as to how it is all paid for. Of course there is a deficit every year, and a growing deficit, even though they have cut down for next year the expenditures in the army and in the navy. Mussolini is gambling on peace. His naval estimate is nearly $10,000,000 less (lire 170,000,000). He has changed his military policy in Albania. Their troops have been withdrawn and military administrative control has been relinquished, and their payments to Albania have not been made. They still insist upon retaining the alliance and a protectorate over Albania in order to utilize the sea coast as a defensive measure against French naval activity in the Adriatic. Of course if France could occupy those ports she would control the Adriatic, and there are no ports on the Italian side from Brindisi north to Venice. This change in policy toward Albania may be only that the expense has been too great, but it may also be the beginning of a rapprochement with France in the form of the removal of their military threat against Jugoslavia. At any rate, he is gambling on peace, and the Fascisti believe that the Four Power Pact has laid the basis for the peace which he ardently desires. We now hear that Germany may not be induced to ratify the Pact and that it will not at any rate be ratified until after the Disarmament Conference decides what the military quotas shall be. Nevertheless, they consider it as initialed as a great victory for the cause of peace, and they are conducting themselves accordingly.

I am glad you are off on a vacation and hope you come back thoroughly refreshed. You have done a wonderful job and are daily justifying the most complete confidence of even your most ardent friends.

With expressions of affection and respect, Most truly yours,

Breckinridge Long

[OF 447:TS]

[1] General Italo Balbo, at this time air marshal.
[2] Dino Alfieri was later ambassador to Germany.
[3] Appointed third secretary at Rome on April 29, 1933.


# Claude G. Bowers, Ambassador to Spain, to Roosevelt

Madrid, June 28, 1933

Dear Mr. President: In my last conversation with you before leaving Washington,[1] you asked me to ascertain from informal conversations here the reaction to a possible appeal you may make for the democratic concept of government. My relations with Fernando de los Rios, Minister of Foreign Affairs, and one of the strong men of the government, are such that I have been able to chat with him unofficially, and during the course of one of our conversations I asked him for his own reaction to such a possibility. He appeared very much impressed, and said he thought it "very important" and would like to think it over and write me his impressions. I have these now. From this reply I extract the sentences that count:

From the general point of view, the democratic form of government is attacked at the present time by the right and the left, as much by statesmen in their manifestations, as by the fact even of the existence of regimes contrary to the democratic inspiration. A manifestation which brings to universal public opinion faith in democracy and liberty, above all if it emanates from a high personality of a great Power, must necessarily produce excellent effects and, as far as I, a convinced democrat, am concerned, I would see it with the greatest enthusiasm. As far as concerns the effects of such a manifestation on Spanish public opinion, I venture to assure you that it would contribute to affirm even more the democratic faith which inspired the April revolution, and which is evident in all the political and social activities of the Republic. It would produce a movement of cordiality toward the country from which the call to universal democratic opinion emanates.

Finally, as so far as concerns the effects to be taken into consideration as regards the development of international politics, Spain, which finds itself

259

identified with the policy of security of international peace by means of the development of international institutions and, in her breast, of a firm and sure accord between England, France and the United States, democratic countries, in order to prepare themselves and the world in general against all aggression which is only possible to fear from anti-democratic regimes, Spain regards the possible manifestation with the highest interest.

Rios has lectured at Columbia and in the U. of California and in colleges in the Middle West. He is the most pronouncedly pro-American in the Government. He has a profound admiration for America, its people and institutions. As Minister of Education he used the American school system as the basis for his plan for the state schools here. A speech of mine here and an interview I gave the Spanish press on coming appears to have interested him in me; that and the fact that I write. At his suggestion to Rex Smith the A.P. man here, arrangements were made for us to lunch together at Alcala while he was Minister of Education. Just about the hour of the lunch the Government resigned and he came directly to me from the council of Ministers and gave me the story. I suggested the postponement of the luncheon because of the conferences that would begin at once and he appreciated it. In the reorganization he was made Minister of State (of Foreign Affairs) and he paid me the rather extraordinary compliment of calling on me personally at once. To everyone else he sent cards.

Thus, as you see, we have a friend in him because he is eager for the good opinion of our people.

By smashing some precedents and reversing some policies of my predecessors I have, blindly enough, made an unusual appeal to the Spanish. The press has been amazingly cordial. By meeting the representatives of the Spanish press informally I got an enthusiastic press response. It had not been done before. American newspaper men who had not been in the embassy for three years are now welcome, and the effect is good. My speech at the dinner given me by the American Chamber of Commerce in Spain, the largest ever held, with members attending from all over this country, was but a reiteration of your own statements and Hull's which are and have been in complete harmony with my own opinions, but appears to have created almost a sensation. The press response here was fine; the ovation at the dinner at the close of the speech was genuine, and I was told by Joe Flack, first secretary, that it was something entirely new in Spain, and long over-due.

Such is the atmosphere. I find the people here eager for commercial understandings with us, and, with the atmosphere friendly, think that something can be accomplished when the Administration is ready to move in that direction.

There is no possibility of a restoration. The contest is between parties of the right and left. A few snobs and the higher nobility of course are mourning for Alfonso. But just yesterday I had a conversation with Conde de Welckeck,[2] the German Ambassador, who was a boon companion of the king, and hunted with him regularly, and he told me that Alfonso has no friends; that under the dictator he degenerated, leaving everything to Primo and devoting his time to drinking and gambling.

There is not the slighest possibility of either a communistic or facist distatorship.

Azana the premier is the powerful man of Spain.[3] From every quarter here, including diplomatic circles, I hear high praise for you. Tonight Mendenez, the foreign editor of *El Sol,* the Government paper, is coming to my home to talk with me about you. He plans to write a Spanish biography or interpretation of you, and wants some background material. It will be altogether friendly.

Tomorrow I am to see Rios and intend to ask him about his plan, which is that of the Government, for an early recognition of Russia. I want to get his reasons in detail, and if they are important or especially interesting shall send you a copy of the report I shall send to the State Department.

I hear Franklin D. Jr. is coming to Spain. It will make a fine impression here. I understand he wants nothing official, but I wish I could be informed through him or Washington a few days before he comes.[4]

Oh yes, it occurs to me now what Mendenez has in mind about that book on you. He is to call it the Third Revolution. The first is that of the Jeffersonian victory in 1800; the second is that of the reaction in the Reconstruction days; and the third is that of which you are the center.

With regards and congratulations, Sincerely,

Claude G. Bowers

[OF 303:TS]

[1] Bowers saw the President on May 2 and sailed on May 10 (PPF 1-0; New York *Times,* May 11, 1933, p. 20).

[2] Count Johannes Welczeck.

[3] Manuel Azaña y Diaz.

[4] Franklin, Jr., arrived in Madrid August 10 (New York *Times,* Aug. 11, 1933, p. 13), and Bowers told Roosevelt about his son's visit with him in a long letter of Aug. 15, 1933 (PSF:Spain).

## William Phillips, Acting Secretary of State, to Roosevelt, Campobello, N.B.

Washington, June 29, 1933, 5 P.M.

[*Telegram*] The President: Secretary Hull has telegraphed in regard to a proposal concerning sugar made by the Cuban Delegation providing for no increases in production and no new subsidies during next 10 years; also that tariff duties now over 70 per cent ad valorem shall not be raised before September 1935. The Secretary says Cubans hope for our support; he asks for instructions, adding that at first glance it appears to him that the Cuban proposal is not contrary to the purposes of sugar discussions now going on in Washington.[1]

Coulter[2] informs me that the Cuban proposal, described by the Secretary, will not, in his opinion, hinder the general purposes underlying the sugar scheme now under discussion here, notwithstanding the fact that our beet interests desire to expand and Louisiana cane to restore former production.[3] He believes, however, that a safeguard should be included in proposal to protect any agreements we might make with Cuba. Taussig[4] agrees with Coulter.

Unless you perceive political objections especially in connection with the limitation on possible reductions in price of sugar which might be implied from pledge not to raise tariff rates or factors possibly affecting adversely ratification new Cuban treaty, I would be inclined to transmit Coulter's opinions to the Delegation at London.

Phillips

[PSF:London Economic Conference:T]

[1] Hull's telegram of June 28, 1933, is printed in *Foreign Relations, 1933,* I, 659–660. Roosevelt had cabled Hull on June 7 to give him "full authority" to negotiate reciprocal trade treaties; on June 8 he wrote to Welles in Cuba, approving immediate conversations for a trade treaty with that country (*ibid.,* pp. 923–924; *Personal Letters, 1928–1945,* I, 349–350).

[2] John Lee Coulter of the Tariff Commission.

[3] The conferences were being conducted by Secretary of Agriculture Wallace with representatives of sugar producers and processors to set up marketing quotas for the United States, its territories, and Cuba. The agreement finally made was disapproved by Roosevelt on recommendation of Wallace who insisted that it would have resulted in high prices without benefit to consumers (New York *Times,* July 6, p. 6; July 20, p. 13; Oct. 9, 1933, p. 1).

[4] Charles W. Taussig, sugar expert assigned to advise the American delegation. He did not go to London.

## Stephen T. Early, Assistant Secretary to the President, to Marvin H. McIntyre, Assistant Secretary to the President, Campobello, N.B.

Washington, June 30, 1933

[*Radiogram*] McIntyre for the President: Am forwarding in code extraordinarily important cable from Moley.[1] Same message, at Moley's instructions, being forwarded to Woodin and Baruch, in New York.[2] Moley anxious for the President to telephone him in London as soon as he receives his cable. Message being forwarded by land wires to Welchpool and also being transmitted by Naval Radio. Suggest you have Prince[3] at most convenient point to receive and decode.

Early

[*Notation*:A] Phoned Naval Communications 8:45 AM, with instructions to give preference over everything EWS

[PSF:London Economic Conference:T]

[1] Moley to Woodin and Baruch, June 30, 1933, in *Foreign Relations, 1933*, I, 665–666.

[2] Acheson and Baruch had gone on June 30 to Woodin's house in New York (Woodin was gravely ill) in accordance with Moley's telephoned request of the previous day (*After Seven Years*, p. 250).

[3] Kirby L. Prince was a State Department code clerk. He handled coded messages aboard the *Ellis* en route to Campobello and was on the *Indianapolis* on the return trip. The difficulties surrounding Roosevelt's reception of dispatches at Campobello were described by him at his April 8, 1935, press conference (PPF 1-0): "The State Department would not allow me to use Navy code, which is very simple. The Navy knows all about it. It is comparatively quick to decipher. We had to have a State Department code to communicate with London. So they put a State Department decoder on the cruiser. At first he was on the destroyer. Those things would come in—he would get whole groups that were entirely garbled, that did not make sense, and he would have to ask for a repeat from the State Department and it would be a number of hours before I would get a correct message. There was a terrible delay. Finally we got to Campobello and we spent two nights there—or only one. I guess it was the second day, about 1:00 o'clock in the afternoon, somebody came ashore—I guess it was you (Mr. McIntyre)—from the cruiser, the *Indianapolis*, and said, 'there is a long State Department dispatch coming in from London' and we went off on a picnic or something and came back in the evening and Mac went out to find out why we had not received the message and he found the whole thing was garbled and could not be decoded. He asked for a repeat and it was sent by wire and instead of being sent to Eastport, they sent it over Canadian Government's telegraph. It went to St. Andrews, New Brunswick. There it was taken over from one ticker and then it was sent by submarine cable to another ticker at Welchpool on Campobello. I got

the message in garbled form just before I left on the ship the following morning. Even then it was not entirely clear and I had to guess much about it. It was only then that I wrote the reply, so that you people did not miss anything on it."

## Stephen T. Early, Assistant Secretary to the President, to Marvin H. McIntyre, Assistant Secretary to the President, Campobello, N.B.

Washington, June 30, 1933

[*Radiogram*] McIntyre (for the President): Baruch, Woodin, Harrison, others recommend acceptance Moley's proposal.[1] They trying to reach the President and you. Can you contact them as quickly as possible. Moley called again and says every minute vital.[2] He most anxious to hear from President and says Economic Conference's fate is in the balance.

Early

[*Notation*:A] Phoned Naval Communications 6:15 P.   OR
[OF 17:T]

[1] Woodin, Baruch, and Harrison to Roosevelt, June 30, 1933 (*Foreign Relations, 1933,* I, 667–668), urging him to accept the proposed joint declaration on gold. Moley followed this cable two hours later with another in which he again urged acceptance of the joint declaration; he believed "success even continuance of the Conference" depended on its acceptance (*ibid.,* p. 671).

[2] In two phone calls to Woodin's house in New York, where Baruch, Acheson, and Harrison were gathered around the gravely ill Secretary of the Treasury, Moley convinced the four men that the joint declaration was not "even a remote approach to stabilization," would have no adverse effect on prices in the United States, and would not obligate the United States to ship gold abroad. They agreed with this viewpoint and so informed Roosevelt (Moley, *After Seven Years,* pp. 251–253).

## Roosevelt to William Phillips, Acting Secretary of State

[U.S.S. *Indianapolis,* Campobello, N.B., June 30, 1933, 11:55 P.M.[1]

[*Radiogram*] Phillips, Washington, Double Rush. Please send following to Hull and notify Secretary Treasury and Baruch:

Have received Hull's 80 of June thirty[2] and Sprague's 79.[3] In regard to suggested joint declaration I must tell you frankly that I believe the greater part of it relates primarily to functions of private banks and not functions of governments. Other parts of declaration relating to broad governmental policies go so far as to erect probable barriers against our own economic fiscal development.

As to paragraph one (a) of suggested joint declaration this language assumes that immediate stabilization in international monetary field will create permanent stability. This I gravely doubt because it would still allow a country to continue unbalanced budgets and other financial operations tending to eventually unsound currencies. France is an example.

As to paragraph one (b) we must be free if gold or gold and silver are reestablished as international measure of exchange to adopt our own method of stabilizing our own domestic price level in terms of the dollar regardless of foreign exchange rates.

As to paragraph three this would be possible only if we are fully free to maintain stable domestic price level as our first consideration. Also it is most advisable to insist on addition of words gold and silver to any possible currency reserve.

As to paragraph four I do not think this means anything on our part. I know of no appropriate means here to limit exchange speculation by governmental action. I am clear that this is not at the present time at least a government function but is one that could be undertaken only as a private banking function and only if governmental action is not implied or contemplated thereby. In other words, I cannot assent to private action now which might morally obligate our government now or later to approval of export of gold from the United States.

At this time any fixed formula of stabilization by agreement must necessarily be artificial and speculative. It would be particularly unwise from political and psychological standpoints to permit limitation of our action to be imposed by any other nation than our own. A sufficient interval should be allowed the United States to permit in addition to the play of economic forces a demonstration of the value of price lifting efforts which we have well in hand. These successful forces will be beneficial to other nations if they join with us toward the same end.

It would be well to reiterate fact that England left gold standard nearly two years ago and only now is seeking stabilization. Also that France did not stabilize for three years or more. If France seeks to break up conference just because we decline to accept her dictum we should take the sound position that economic conference was initiated and called to discuss and agree on permanent solutions of world economics and not to discuss domestic economic policy of one nation out of the sixty-six present. When conference was called its necessity was obvious although problem of stabilization of American dollar was not even in existence.

I have no objection to delegation using the import of this telegram as basis for a statement of American policy.[4]

Roosevelt

[PSF:London Economic Conference:CT]

[1] In *Foreign Relations, 1933*, I, 669–670, this radiogram is dated July 1, when the message was cabled from Washington.

[2] Actually, Moley's cable to Woodin and Baruch of June 30 sending the original text of the proposed stabilization declaration, printed *ibid.*, pp. 665–666.

[3] Sprague to Woodin and Baruch, June 30, 1933 (*ibid.*, pp. 664–665), urging issuance of the proposed declaration.

[4] This message was received in London at about 3 P.M. on July 1, London time, or about 8 P.M. Washington time (Moley, *After Seven Years*, p. 255). In the meantime, the delegation had cabled certain revisions in the declaration, Woodin, Baruch, and Acheson had urged acceptance, the final text had been sent, and Moley had sent a final plea (*Foreign Relations, 1933*, I, 667, 667–668, 670–671, 672). Hull proposed that he issue a statement as Secretary of State further explaining that United States policy on proposals affecting world currencies would be governed by its need to raise the domestic price level (Hull to Phillips, July 2, 1933, *ibid.*, p. 674). Moley says that this proposed statement was drafted by himself, Walter Lippmann, and Herbert Swope (*After Seven Years*, pp. 257–258). The statement was not, however, issued because Roosevelt's message to the delegation of July 2 (below, Roosevelt to Phillips) made it pointless (Carr to Roosevelt, July 3, 1933, *Foreign Relations, 1933*, I, 678–679; Moley, *After Seven Years*, pp. 257–258).

A long and circumstantial statement of the Administration's position on the stabilization issue is found in Charles Hurd's dispatch from Campobello of June 30, published in the New York *Times* of July 1, 1933, p. 1. The information was attributed to "high authority," undoubtedly the President himself.

# William Phillips, Acting Secretary of State, to Roosevelt, Campobello, N.B.

Washington, July 1, 1933, Rec'd 8:10 A.M.

[*Telegram*]
*Urgent Priority*

34, July 1, 4 a.m. The following telegram has been received from the American delegation:

"84, July 1, 8 A.M. For the President from Moley.

The complete and final text of the declaration is as follows:

Joint declaration by the countries on the gold standard and by those which are not on the gold standard.

One. The undersigned governments agree: (a) That it is in the interests of all concerned that stability in the international monetary field be attained as quickly as practicable; (b) that gold should be reestablished as the international measure of exchange value, it being recognized that the parity and the time at which each of the countries now off gold could undertake to stabilize must be decided by the respective governments concerned.

Two. The governments whose currencies are on the gold standard reassert that it is their determination to maintain the free working of that standard at the existing gold parities within the framework of their respective monetary laws. They are convinced of the importance from the point of view of the restoration of world economy and finance of such maintenance by their respective countries of the gold standard on the basis of the present gold parities.

Three. The signatory governments whose currencies are not on the gold standard without in any way prejudicing their own future ratios to gold take note of the above declaration and recognize its importance. They reaffirm as indicated in paragraph one above that the ultimate objective of their monetary policy is to restore under proper conditions an international monetary standard based on gold.

Four. Each of the governments [whose][1] currencies are not on the gold standard undertakes to adopt the measures which it may deem most appropriate to limit exchange speculation and each of the other signatory governments undertakes to cooperate to the same end.

Five. Each of the undersigned governments agrees to ask its central banks to cooperate with the central banks of the other signatory governments in limiting speculation in the exchanges and when the time comes in reestablishing a general international gold standard. Hull."[2]

Phillips, Acting

[PSF:London Economic Conference:T]

[1] Supplied from the text as printed in *Foreign Relations, 1933,* I, 670–671.

[2] The first draft of this statement seen by Roosevelt was the one sent on June 30 (*ibid.,* pp. 665–666). Just before this was sent Sprague had cabled Woodin and Baruch that the gold standard countries "insisted" that some "general statement of policy" by Britain and the United States would be helpful in the face of rumors that proposals for general devaluation would be made at the Conference (*ibid.,* pp. 664–665). The British and American delegates had therefore agreed to a proposal "for concerted action in all countries directed toward restricting speculative foreign exchange operations." The "proposal" was the statement here printed. For the circumstances back of it, see the dispatches printed *ibid.,* pp. 658ff. Moley's account should be compared with the dispatches just cited and with that of Hull in his *Memoirs,* I, 260–262.

## Stephen T. Early, Assistant Secretary to the President, to Marvin H. McIntyre, Assistant Secretary to the President, Campobello, N.B.

Washington, July 1, 1933

[*Radiogram*] Newspaper men, photographers pressing for information regarding President's return both as news matter and in order make arrangements for coverage. New York *Times* and several others have inkling of conferences aboard ship near Washington before President lands and are tying this speculatively with probable stabilization dollar fluctuation discussions between President, government officials and bankers Monday aboard *Indianapolis*.[1] Nothing has been given out from here but I think something should be given to clarify things and prevent further speculations. Any objection if I give press here such an explanation or will you do it from there?[2] Woodin, Farley, Phillips advise they will not be able accept luncheon invitation.[3] Everything here OK. Regards.

Early

[*Notation*:A] Sent by Naval Kms 12 noon EWS
[PSF:London Economic Conference:T]

[1] The *Times* of July 1 made no mention of this possible meeting but on July 2 (p. 2) announced that Roosevelt would meet with his Cabinet on board the *Indianapolis* on arrival at Annapolis on July 3. The meeting was attended by Ickes, Wallace, Swanson, Dern, Roper, and Cummings. Monetary stabilization was briefly dealt with but most of the time was taken up with economic recovery (*ibid.*, July 4, 1933, pp. 1, 3). See Harold L. Ickes, *The Secret Diary of Harold L. Ickes* (New York: Simon and Schuster, 1954), I, 58–59.

[2] Apparently no explanation was issued.

[3] Woodin could not be present because of his rapidly worsening condition. Early had warned Roosevelt on June 30 in a note to McIntyre (PPF 258), that Woodin's illness was much more serious than was generally realized; he suggested the President write or telephone him. Roosevelt wrote to him on July 3 (*Personal Letters, 1928–1945*, I, 356). Woodin offered his resignation for health reasons on July 5, 1933, but Roosevelt refused to accept it. He was obliged, however to take leave of absence in November 1933 and died early in 1934 of cancer of the throat.

## Roosevelt to William Phillips, Acting Secretary of State

U.S.S. *Indianapolis*, July 2, 1933, 6 P.M.

[*Radiogram*] Please send following to Hull as soon as possible:[1]
Herewith is a statement which I think you can use Monday morning

as a message from me to you. If you think it best not to give it out in London let me know at once and in that event I will release it here as a White House statement.

I would regard it as a catastrophe amounting to a world tragedy if the great Conference of Nations, called to bring about a more real and permanent financial stability and a greater prosperity to the masses of all nations, should, in advance of any serious effort to consider these broader problems, allow itself to be diverted by the proposal of a purely artificial and temporary experiment affecting the monetary exchange of a few nations only. Such action, such diversion, shows a singular lack of proportion and a failure to remember the larger purposes for which the Economic Conference originally was called together.

I do not relish the thought that insistence on such action should be made an excuse for the continuance of the basic economic errors that underlie so much of the present world wide depression.

The world will not long be lulled by the specious fallacy of achieving a temporary and probably an artificial stability in foreign exchange on the part of a few large countries only.

The sound internal economic system of a nation is a greater factor in its well being than the price of its currency in changing terms of the currencies of other nations.

It is for this reason that reduced cost of government, adequate government income, and ability to service government debts are all so important to ultimate stability. So too, old fetishes of so called international bankers are being replaced by efforts to plan national currencies with the objective of giving to those currencies a continuing purchasing power which does not greatly vary in terms of the commodities and need of modern civilization. Let me be frank in saying that the United States seeks the kind of a dollar which a generation hence will have the same purchasing and debt paying power as the dollar value we hope to attain in the near future. That objective means more to the good of other nations than a fixed ratio for a month or two in terms of the pound or franc.

Our broad purpose is the permanent stabilization of every nation's currency. Gold or gold and silver can well continue to be a metallic reserve behind currencies but this is not the time to dissipate gold reserves. When the world works out concerted policies in the majority of nations to produce balanced budgets and living within their means, then we can properly discuss a better distribution of the world's gold and silver supply to act as a reserve base of national currencies. Restoration of world trade is an important partner, both in the means and in the result. Here also temporary exchange fixing is not the true answer. We must rather mitigate existing embargoes to make easier the exchange of products which one nation has and the other nation has not.

The Conference was called to better and perhaps to cure fundamental economic ills. It must not be diverted from that effort.

Roosevelt

[PSF:London Economic Conference:M]

[1] This telegram is the so-called "bombshell" message to Hull, made public in London on the morning of July 3, 1933; it is also printed in *Foreign Relations, 1933,* I, 673–674, and in *Public Papers,* II, 264–266. Roosevelt's longhand draft (in the possession of Franklin D. Roosevelt, Jr.) includes a page of typed material probably prepared by Louis Howe; of this the President used only the sentence beginning "I would regard" and the two words following. The Roosevelt Library has a carbon copy of the message as sent. On that copy the date line and three minor revisions are in Roosevelt's hand.

Henry Morgenthau, Jr., describes the drafting of the message in his "Farm Credit Administration Diary" entry for July 2: "This afternoon, Sunday, the President took off his coat, sat down at his desk for a couple of hours, and wrote his message to London on money. I believe that Louis Howe had originally tried to write one for him, but as near as I could tell the President completely rewrote it. He read the whole statement to Louis Howe and me, and with a few slight changes of his own, he sent it as he wrote it the first time." (Morgenthau's "Farm Credit Administration Diary" is a record of his conversations, activities, and reflections for the period April 27–Nov. 16, 1933, while he was successively chairman of the Federal Farm Board, governor of the Farm Credit Administration, and Acting and Under Secretary of the Treasury. It is part of the Morgenthau papers in the Roosevelt Library.)

See Howe's account of the drafting of the message, July 9, 1933, below. Accounts of the impact of the message on the Conference vary somewhat. See Moley, *After Seven Years,* pp. 260–268; Hull, *Memoirs,* I, 262–269; and Cox, *Journey Through My Years,* pp. 365–367.

## Roosevelt to Dean G. Acheson, Under Secretary of the Treasury

U.S.S. *Indianapolis,* off Annapolis, July 3, 1933

Memo for Under Secretary of Treasury: Is there any way in which we could prevent what is known as "spotforward" exchange operations in this country in dollars, pounds and francs.

A friend of mine believes it can be done, making an exception of course of genuine commercial or financial transactions.

F.D.R.

[*Notation*:T] (The friend is Dave H. Morris)[1]
[PPF 1987:CT]

[1] Morris, newly appointed ambassador to Belgium, had written to Roosevelt from London (en route to his post) on June 21, 1933 (PPF 1987). He said that he believed that no matter what happened to the pound, the British would see to it that the pound would show a discount so they could keep their present trade advantage. To get currency stability, Morris recommended prohibition of the "spot forward" exchange operation except for genuine commercial or financial operations; this prohibition, however, would be effective only if the central banks of the United States, England, and France cooperated. Roosevelt dictated this memorandum while still aboard the *Indianapolis.* The reply was probably given in person at the luncheon and Cabinet meeting held on board later in the day.

## Roosevelt to Cordell Hull, Secretary of State

[U.S.S. *Indianapolis*] July 3, 1933

[*Radiogram*] for Hull. Your 91, July 2.[1] Am discussing whole tariff subject today and tomorrow and will wire you Wednesday.[2]

Roosevelt

[PSF:London Economic Conference:T]

[1] *Foreign Relations, 1933*, I, 676–678, in which Hull raised a number of questions respecting the Administration's tariff policies to which the delegation needed replies before proceeding.

[2] Roosevelt refers to the Cabinet meeting held on the *Indianapolis* on July 3. See McIntyre to Howe, July 4, and McIntyre to Roosevelt, July 4, below.

## Roosevelt to Marvin H. McIntyre, Assistant Secretary to the President

U.S.S. *Indianapolis*, July 4 [1933]

[*Radiogram*] For McIntyre, White House: Please telephone Moley and say President thinks we should oppose any adjournment because even sixty day adjournment will be construed as impossibility of practical results.[1] Tell him to read my last 2 dispatches of today, one on monetary situation and other on tariffs.[2]

Roosevelt

[PSF:London Economic Conference:T]

[1] Moley had cabled Roosevelt earlier in the day listing topics he wished to discuss over the telephone (*Foreign Relations, 1933*, I, 680). First was a recommendation that the Conference recess for from two to ten weeks "permitting formulation of your ideas into resolutions."

[2] *Ibid.*, pp. 680–681, 683–684.

## Marvin H. McIntyre, Assistant Secretary to the President, to Louis M. Howe, Personal Secretary to the President, Aboard U.S.S. *Indianapolis*, Annapolis

Washington, July 4, 1933

[*Radiogram*] Howe for President: Roper, Wallace and Tugwell have prepared memorandum you requested on Tariff in reply to Hull's communication.[1] They believe it fully accords your attitude in last message and vitally important in relation to consideration of adjournment. Also feel it will complete the picture of our whole position. They want me to get it to you at once as you may want to forward instruction to Hull immediately. Shall I get it to you or hold it until you get here tonight. They also feel it might be well if something of sort were released today.

McIntyre

[*Notation*:A] Priority—Navy Code
[*Notation*:A] Phoned Kms 12:28 P.M.
[OF 200:T]

[1] Hull's cable of July 2, 1933, mentioned in Roosevelt's message to him of July 3, above. Concerning the tariff memorandum, see the message printed immediately below.

## Marvin H. McIntyre, Assistant Secretary to the President, to Roosevelt, Aboard U.S.S. *Indianapolis,* Annapolis

Washington [July 4, 1933]

[*Radiogram*] Howe for President: Sent tariff memorandum by Navy seaplane.[1] Talked with Moley again and gave him your message.[2] Moley would like to talk with you before your conversation with Hull and I told him would ask you to telephone him tonight. He feels temporary adjournment advisable to reconstruct our delegation and says Couzens[3] would have left except for embarrassing you. Plan is to leave committees at work but final decision awaits American action. Says all other delegations favor recess or adjournment. Denies today's story that he assured Litvinoff that U.S. contemplated Russian recognition saying it was a casual two minute talk. Moley plans to leave Thursday and says he has been working with Hull staying in background.[4]

McIntyre

[PSF:London Economic Conference:TS]

[1] Roosevelt to Hull, July 4, 1933, in *Foreign Relations, 1933,* I, 685–687. The tariff memorandum was followed by a statement by Roosevelt on his stabilization policy, issued as a note from the American delegation to Secretary General Joseph Avenol under date of July 5 (*ibid.,* pp. 692–694). Moley had urged some kind of restatement to bring together the nations outside the gold bloc and to prevent immediate adjournment, and with Herbert Swope, Walter Lippmann, and John Maynard Keynes had drafted a statement and had cabled it to the President (*ibid.,* pp. 688–692; Moley, *After Seven Years,* p. 264). The cabled draft, with Roosevelt's revisions, sent July 5, is present (PSF:London Economic Conference).

[2] Roosevelt to McIntyre, July 4, 1933, above.

[3] Senator James Couzens, one of the delegates.

[4] Why McIntyre crossed out this last part is not explained. Moley left London for New York on July 6 but did not see Roosevelt until July 14 (Moley, *After Seven Years,* pp. 266–270).

## Irving Fisher, Yale University, to Roosevelt

New Haven, Connecticut, July 5, 1933

My dear Mr. President: Your message to the Economic Conference makes me one of the happiest of men. Even if it ends the Conference (which I hope you can prevent), it will do great good—abroad as well as at home. It insures the speedy coming of a new epoch with the stable unit for debts so indispensable for all.

I am writing again to ask for that long-deferred talk. I expect to be in Washington, arriving Saturday evening (at the Cosmos Club). If convenient to you I would like very much to see you Monday, the 10th. But if this is not convenient I can return to Washington the following Saturday and stay over till Monday, the 17th. I am in no hurry, so long as it can be in time to be of possible use to you in choosing the personnel and deciding on the type of organization for carrying out your proposed stabilization policy.

Very sincerely yours,

Irving Fisher[1]

[*Notation*:A:LeHand] Mac—Pres will see him at HP[2]
[PPF 431:TS]

[1] Fisher, professor of economics at Yale, was associate adviser with G. F. Warren to the Committee for the Nation. Roosevelt had known him since 1920 and after 1932 they wrote frequently to each other (PPF 431). During the campaign Fisher had sent Roosevelt an advance copy of his book, *Booms and Depressions* (New York: Adelphi, 1932). Roosevelt had thanked him and had said that the book was "going right along" with him (Fisher to Roosevelt, Sept. 10; Roosevelt to Fisher, Sept. 12, 1932, Group 12).

[2] Roosevelt saw Fisher at Hyde Park on August 9 (PPF 1-0). For Fisher's account of the interview, see I. N. Fisher, *My Father, Irving Fisher* (New York: Comet Press, 1956).

## Press Conference, Executive Offices of the White House, July 5, 1933, 12 Noon

[*Excerpt*] The President: . . . I don't think there is any particular news. I have been trying to catch up yesterday and today.[1] I have just been reading and listening to various things and of course on the international thing, I think Mac told you last night that we have been in pretty close touch with London the past week, wiring back and forth. I talked with Secretary Hull this morning on the phone and, of course, on those things any news has got to break from London, so there we are.

Q: What about these reports that you are putting forth new proposals?

The President: Anything at all has to come out of London.

Q: Will it come today, do you think, Mr. President?

The President: I don't know.

Q: Are you sending any new instructions to London, Mr. President?

The President: No, I simply cannot talk about it. Off the record, it is easy to write a story and say, "new instructions." Of course, it is not true. There have never been any instructions. We have talked the thing over by cable and telephone but there have never been any instructions.

Q: It is already off the agenda. It couldn't be anything different?

The President: Not unless taken up by unanimous consent over there.

Q: You said off the record last night that you hoped that the conference would continue?

The President: Still hope this morning.

Q: Cannot you say something that would put you on record?

The President: That is all I can say; what I told them over there and what they told me from over there. That is about all there is. I don't think you can put it one way or the other. All I can say is that I hope the conference will continue.

Q: The European nations don't think they can talk tariffs unless stabilization is taken care of first. What do you think about that?

The President: I don't know that this is the time to go into it. It is a long, long story. It comes back to the definition of the word. Suppose we talk about this off the record so it won't be attributed in any way to official sources, but just your own information. The whole question comes down to the word "stabilization." We have a very different thought about the definition of the word than do some of the Continental—not Europe, but a few of the Continental countries. In other words, they, in their economics, in those countries, they are, very properly, very much concerned with the current rate of exchange on their own currency in terms of other currency. To them that is important. To us it is not important. We are looking, fundamentally, for a different form of stabilization; in other words, a stabilization that will be based on a more or less equivalent price level in each country for X amount of goods. I hope that eventually each country in the world will have a currency which will be stable within its own domestic purchasing power.

Now, if you arrive at that objective in the world, automatically almost the exchange value of those currencies in terms of other currencies will become more or less stable. Then there is the other side of the picture: As I said, some of those countries are very much concerned with a temporary exchange value of their currencies in terms of other currencies and they seek to have us enter into a thing which is not really on the agenda at all and that is an agreement between five or six nations out of the 66 present to set up some kind of a fund, a special fund, temporarily to control the exchange fluctuation. Now, our primary objection to that method, if we are asked to participate in that fund, is that morally we would be obligated, in case that fund called for large withdrawals of gold from this country, to let down the bars on the export of gold that we have in this country. Well, we are not willing to do that at the present time. We have seen, for example, the fact that England has been, so-called, off the gold standard for a year and ten months, and they are not ready to stabilize yet. We have seen France, a few years ago, go off the gold standard and stay off the gold standard for nearly four years. We have only been off for three months. We haven't had time to turn around. We don't know, exactly like England, what to do next. There is one little item I think that is worth calling attention to. It is in one of the papers this morning. It is an A. P. story.

Q: It is all right then.

The President: (Reading) "A Government spokesman"—this is from London—"would not give a direct answer when asked in the House of Commons today"—and the House of Commons is a little like a Press Conference—"that sterling would not be advanced with gold. Mr. Hore-Belisha, Financial Secretary-Treasurer, speaking for Neville Chamberlain, Chancellor of the Exchequer, said that, 'although a return to the gold standard might be our ultimate objective'—mind you, this was said yesterday in England, this is the British Government point of view—'although a return to the gold standard might be our ultimate objective, when proper conditions were assured, we must reserve complete liberty to choose both our own time and parity.' He does not think he can usefully add anything to that statement now."

Yet, they talk on the other side about our being vague and they have been off for nearly two years. Now, that is the easiest way of explaining it. We are not ready to export gold. We are not ready to make any kind of an agreement by which we would morally obligate ourselves to export gold at this time and we are not ready to go along on the creation of some kind of stabilization fund which might obligate us to export gold. Now that, really, is the whole thing in a nutshell.

Q: It was suggested that central banks might operate in that situation independent of the Government?

The President: Central banks on the other side? I haven't the slightest idea.

Q: And the Federal Reserve Board on our side?

The President: That brings up the question whether the Federal Reserve Bank in New York legally has the authority to speculate in exchange.

Q: Do you think it has?

The President: Probably not, because the money of the Federal Reserve Banks belongs to the constituent banks that make up the Federal Reserve Bank in the district.

Q: How are we to use this?

Mr. Early: You first said it was off the record and then as not coming from any official source?

The President: Background is all right.

Q: Will you give me an explanation of how this stabilization of the dollar with reference to commodities can be brought about—this future stabilization that you speak of?

The President: I will put it this way: The easiest way is to give you an analogy. During the last Session we were all in favor, the Administration and the Congress, in favor of shorter hours of work in order to put more people back to work. Senator Black put in a bill which only had one paragraph in it and it said that nobody could work more than 30 hours a week.[2] Now, that was doing by what might be called fiat, without knowing the effect of it or without considering the effect of it, laying down definite hard and fast terms. We took the objective of the Black Bill and Congress wrote the Industrial Control Act,[3] which is so broad that it enables us in each industry to determine what the hours of work should be and to determine what the hours should be in the north and south and to determine the concentration in terms of a minimum wage. In other words, it is an elastic bill that gives discretion and authority to carry out the objective along all kinds of different lines as the need arises but with a perfectly definite principle in mind. Well, it is the same way when trying to make the dollar retain the same purchasing value when we have it to the desired point. And it will probably, as in the Industrial Control Bill, have a great many different factors and methods of arriving at the result.

Q: Would it be linked to the index price of commodities, for instance?

The President: There again you are talking in terms of the Black Bill. Not necessarily in terms of a fixed index but the objective would be to have the dollar buy substantially, in general, the same general amount of commodities. You can't say "commodities" because I can come back at you and say, "what commodities, the 10 leading commodities or the 750 commodities?" Then you get into detail. I don't know. I have a perfectly definite objective but, as to the machinery, we will probably use half a dozen different kinds of machinery.

Q: Have you the purchasing power of any particular date in mind?

The President: No. Of course we are working on that and discussing it at the present time. You cannot get any one date for everything that will be absolutely fair for every other item. Some products, along certain lines, are best averaged in 1928 and 1929; other products might go back ten or fifteen years ago. We would have to average the thing up.

Q: We used to use 1926?

The President: There again, all I can tell you on that is that there are different schools of thought.

Q: On such a basis as you suggest, Mr. President, there could not be any international standards, could there?

The President: What?

Q: On such a basis for the dollar there could not be a uniform international standard?

The President: There could not be?

Q: I am asking.

The President: Of course not. You cannot have a perfect, definite fixed range for all nations because economic conditions vary in a nation. For instance—this you will have to use entirely off the record because it relates to one specific country—Japan during the past year has undertaken a very drastic change in her economic life and they have done it because they have believed that it was worth while doing it in order to flood the markets of the world at almost any price in order to bring in the money of other nations. For instance, just to give an example, the wage scale in Japanese factories has dropped away down. They are putting out sneakers in this country at $12\frac{1}{2}$ cents a pair. They are putting out rubber boots in this country at 25 cents a pair. It is a perfectly definite national policy of cutting their own wages so low so that they can flood the markets of the world and get in outside money at any cost. Therefore, as long as any nation can do that, and nations will continue to do it when changing their economic life, you cannot have a perfectly definite fixed ratio of exchange between nations.

Q: Do you think it possible to enter into any reciprocal treaties at the present time?

The President: I hope so.

Q: Won't they work against your domestic policy here?

The President: No.

Q: Would the stability of the dollar in relation to commodities require additional shifts in the gold content of the dollar?

The President: Not of necessity. There you come down to another—all this is perfectly terrible because it is all pure theory, when you come down to it. The situation of some of the European nations is that gold in the future should be used not as a collateral behind currency at all but that it should be used purely as a medium of international exchange to pay debits and credits between countries in international trade. I think our situation is just the reverse of that and that is that gold should continue, and silver, to be used as collateral behind paper currencies and among the instructions to our delegates when they first went over there was a clause that brought out our point of view that gold perhaps should exist in the future only in the form of bullion and that that bullion should be Government-owned and kept within the nation and not shifted to and fro on steamships; that it should be kept within the nation as permanent collateral behind national currency.[4] Now you see you have two absolutely opposite thoughts for the future on that and we don't go along with the idea that gold should be used for international trade.

Q: Is this something like the Fisher Commodity Index Dollar?

The President: I haven't the faintest idea; I don't know.

Q: Well, that is the Commodity Index Dollar that seems to have been described?

The President: I don't know.

Q: You would settle international balances under the American plan?

The President: Of course we are seeking, in so far as possible, to have trade balances within any one nation as even as possible as between exports and imports.

Q: We still have a tremendous favorable balance?

The President: It is very small, in fact almost equal. For the last few years our export balance over imports has been almost negligible . . .

Q: There has been a loan made to Russia and there has been a discussion that it is the first step toward recognition. Is that in your mind?[5]

The President: I haven't heard a word about it until I saw the dispatch from London . . .

Q: Doesn't this managed currency scheme of ours result in permanent stabilization of the dollar at any time at any fixed rate?

The President: I don't know; that is a trick. It depends again on the definition of the word "stabilization."

Q: I mean fixing the dollar at a fixed price in relation to other countries.

The President: I don't know.

Q: Mr. President, under the American plan of no transfer of—

The President: That is the present stand, that is all. I don't say that possibly we will keep all the gold here. Right on that line, you will notice in my message to our delegation of July 2 that I had one sentence to the effect that we were not ready to export gold but that if and when we had a substantial stabilization of economics and currencies within other nations, that that would be time enough to talk about any re-distribution of the world's gold. You see France and ourselves have got, roughly, 7 billions out of the total of 11 billion dollars of gold. Well, suppose some country came along and said, "we are going to have a perfectly stabilized currency from now on within our own borders with a gold reserve." Is there any way in which we can get part of the French gold or our gold to help them set up such a currency? That is a perfectly safe question to ask because it will help put that country on its feet but, on the other hand, we would have to have some sort of an agreement from them.

Q: If the London conference shows definite signs of going on the rocks as a result of this stabilization, would that change the Administration's attitude?

The President: Don't put it that way. We don't think it is going on the rocks.[6]

Q: Give us a reason.

The President: Just personally hopeful.[7]

[President's Press Conferences:T]

[1] Roosevelt had returned to the White House from Annapolis the previous evening.

[2] S. 158, introduced March 10, 1933; not reported (*Cong. Rec.,* vol. 77, p. 116).

[3] National Industrial Recovery Act, approved June 16, 1933 (48 *Stat.* 195).

[4] Resolution 4 (c) of the memorandum on policy of May 30, 1933, printed in *Foreign Relations, 1933,* I, 622–627.

[5] The Amtorg Trading Corporation had just been granted a $4,000,000 loan by the Reconstruction Finance Corporation to buy American cotton (New York *Times,* July 3, p. 1).

[6] In his press conference of April 8, 1935, Roosevelt recurred to the idea that his July 2 message to the London Economic Conference (above, Roosevelt to Phillips) had caused its dissolution (President's Press Conferences). Referring to the wide differences in the theories of economists, he said:

"There is one fellow, I have forgotten who he is, an Englishman who writes for one of the weeklies like the *Spectator,* a national weekly or something like that, and he got off—it is an old story now—but I think it was the best description of what happened on the famous fourth of July, when my message went over. He said the press always looks for spot news and the only thing they could carry was that my message had busted up the economic conference, and that was the story, that my message had busted up the conference. That was all the newspapers cared about because that was spot news. But he went on to say that if they had analyzed it, they would have discovered that what the President had said was almost a repetition of what had already been announced in the Ottawa Conference in 1932, which was repeated two weeks later by the Imperial Conference in London itself—in the Imperial Conference report. Both of those passed absolutely unnoticed, although those two statements of the British colonial policy and my policy were essentially, 100 per cent, identical. Actually, in my Message to the economic conference, I had put up a brand new theory, except that the Ottawa Conference beat me by a whole year. That theory was to stabilize values, and if you once did that you would get stabilization of exchange. But that was overlooked."

[7] This press conference is printed in part in *Public Papers,* II, 267–270.

## Albert, King of the Belgians, to Roosevelt

Brussels, 5th of July 1933

Dear Mr. President, Mr. Morris, the distinguished new American Ambassador, handed me your most courteous letter and I was delighted to hear from you personally.[1]

I recollect also with great pleasure the two occasions on which the Queen and I met you at La Panne and New York. It was extremely kind of you to have a special thought for my son and my daughter, they are both, and we also, quite flourishing and I trust it is the same with you, Mrs. Roosevelt and your children.

With many of my compatriots, I am following and viewing with the greatest hope the efforts with which you are endeavouring to pull the world out of the chaos in which it seems at present still plunged, more so that I quite appreciate the difficulties with which you have, without doubt, to contend in your own country.

Thanking you heartily for your cordial message, the Queen and I send you our best greetings and I remain, dear Mr. President

Yours very sincerely

Albert[2]

[PSF:Belgium:AS]

[1] June 3, 1933, above.

[2] This letter was sent by Ambassador Dave H. Morris to Roosevelt. In a covering note to LeHand of July 10, 1933 (PSF:Belgium), Morris said: "Judging by the general unanimity of dislike by the foreign press of our present policy in the United States, I should infer that we are doing just the right thing for ourselves."

## Henry A. Wallace, Secretary of Agriculture, to Roosevelt

Washington, D.C., July 6, 1933

Dear Mr. President: I was much interested yesterday in your suggestion as to the handling of the international currency situation.[1] After I left your office, it occurred to me that it might be wise to have some one like Berle[2] and Tugwell at work on the technical details of formulating the functions of the new unit of currency which is to remain constant in purchasing power from year to year. If the world situation develops during the next three weeks as we anticipate, it will be quite essential to have something more or less definite to bring forward.

Doubtless you have already given very deep thought to this, but the matter is so extraordinarily important to the future welfare of this country as well as to the rest of the countries, that I cannot forbear writing you.

Respectfully yours,

H. A. Wallace

[OF 1:TS]

[1] Wallace had talked with Roosevelt from 2 to 2:30 P.M. (PPF 1-0).

[2] Adolph A. Berle, Jr., was at this time special counsel to the Reconstruction Finance Corporation; in 1938 he was appointed an assistant secretary of state.

## Press Conference, Executive Offices of the White House, July 7, 1933, 4 P.M.

[*Excerpt*] Q: The decision to keep Davis at home comes somewhat as a surprise to us.[1]

The President: Absolutely none at all. There is no story to it in this thing any more than there was a story over the fact that the Minister of Sweden was about to go to his post. I think, frankly, we are getting to the hot weather period. What happens on disarmament or the Disarmament Conference is very similar. Mr. Arthur Henderson has been put in complete charge during the summer of the detail work looking toward the October meeting, and it was a question when Norman Davis came back here as to whether Henderson thought that Norman Davis could be helpful, during the summer, in working out the details.[2] We got word the day before yesterday from Arthur Henderson that he did not think it necessary for Norman Davis to go over at the present time and that means he will hold himself in readiness until Henderson wants him there, and in any event, he will go over by the end of August or the first of September. Of course, he may go before.

Q: Can you tell us the significance of his presence today in this conference on the world economic discussions?

The President: What we were talking about was reviewing the original agenda of the Conference, and Norman Davis helped to make up the original agenda.

Q: Is there anything new in that connection on monetary stabilization?

The President: There was somebody, I.N.S., I think it was, had a flash that they had decided to go ahead and talk about it.[3]

Q: That was the Sub-committee?

The President: Of course, the thing comes right down to this: It is the easiest illustration and you can use it as background. There are a lot of nations there that would like to talk among themselves about fresh phases of the monetary question and they probably will do it and, if nations don't want to take part in these formal discussions about monetary matters, I suppose they won't. There is nothing very exciting about talks. It does not mean that the monetary subjects are going to be discussed among the sixty-six nations' delegates.

Q: Does this conference today—about this conference today, is it possible that the United States will have a program to carry out your ideas on raising world prices?[4]

The President: It is difficult to use "a program." After all, a conference is a conference. You go into a conference with an objective. You don't go in there with a plan saying that on such and such a date this country will do this, that or the other thing. You go in there and say, "Here is our plan for raising world prices," and you lay your plan on the table and some other nation gets up and says, "That is extremely interesting, we are going along on a parallel line." Now, you may get fifteen, twenty, thirty nations that will be interested in our plan. Some of them may be going along half way or seventy-five per cent of the way. Others may be so interested that they will say, "We may go along," and then they take it up. That is all there is. We are telling them our plan, and I think it is having quite a good deal of effect. I think, reading between the lines on what has happened before, they have a good deal more interest in our plan today than they did the day before yesterday.

Q: May we use that as background?

The President: Yes. That, on the other hand, does not mean that we are saying to the nations, "Here is our plan; you have to adopt it." It does mean that we are saying, "As a general proposition, depending in the case of each nation on the needs of that nation, we believe that an objective like ours would be a good thing for as many other nations as possible to adopt." Their methods and means of reaching the objective may differ from ours.

Q: This is the plan in your second communication of the day before yesterday? Is that the plan you are referring to now, the one Hull told two days ago, the so-called "commodity dollar"?

The President: You mean the delegation's statement?

Q: You refer to the plan?

The President: I don't quite follow.

Q: You have referred to "our plan." Is that our plan, the one contained in the Delegation's last statement to the Conference? [5]

The President: That is one way of putting it. I told of it half a dozen different ways myself. Their way was a perfectly good way of stating it.

Q: The objective of that is to raise world prices?

The President: Yes, the objective is to raise world prices.

Q: Are you discussing any new plan in this conference today?

The President: We are going ahead with the same objective.

Q: Are you discussing any new ways of attaining it?

The President: No, no new ways. There is a restatement of it in some ways, but the plan itself has not changed as far as policy goes. In other words, you have to differentiate between the two words, "plan" and "policy." In other words, the ultimate objective on the one side is that you are shooting for something, and on the other side, to come down to the question of the plan, there are half a dozen different ways of getting at that objective.

[President's Press Conferences:T]

[1] Hugh R. Wilson, delegate to the Disarmament Conference, had cabled Phillips on June 29 that the General Commission of the Conference had adjourned until Oct. 16, 1933 (*Foreign Relations, 1933*, I, 201–202). Davis had talked with Roosevelt about disarmament aboard the *Amberjack II* at Roque Island, Maine, on the previous day. On

July 5 he canceled his ship reservations and conferred with Phillips and Roosevelt in Washington. The next day it was announced that he would remain in the United States to confer with government officials on disarmament and would return to Europe in September (New York *Times,* June 29, p. 1; July 6, p. 3; July 7, 1933, p. 3).

[2] Henderson, president of the Disarmament Conference in 1932-33, received the 1934 Nobel Peace Prize for his efforts.

[3] Roosevelt had learned from Hull earlier in the day that the steering committee of the Conference had agreed to proceed with the agenda (*Foreign Relations, 1933,* I, 700–701).

[4] Phillips talked with Roosevelt on July 7 for three-quarters of an hour (PPF 1–0). What was no doubt the result of their discussion was in Phillips' cable to Hull, sent at midnight of the same day (*Foreign Relations, 1933,* I, 703–704).

[5] See Roosevelt to Hull, July 4, 1933 (*ibid.,* pp. 685–687).

## Breckinridge Long, Ambassador to Italy, to Roosevelt

Rome, Italy, July 7, 1933

*Personal*

My dear Frank: There is one question more in the minds of Italy today than any other question as far as its military and naval defenses are concerned, and that is Albania and its policy toward that small country.

Not long since Baron Aloisi, who is the Chief of Cabinet and who is Mussolini's personal man at the Foreign Office,[1] talked to me on the subject of Albania and the attitude of the American Minister there.[2] Aloisi said that the American Minister had taken a position antagonistic to the Italian policy in Albania and that he was very much surprised, because he understood that the United States and Italy were very much in accord. He spoke, no doubt, at the direction of Mussolini and expressed, not in positive language but in a very definite way, their ideas about the attitude of the American Minister at Tirana and the manner in which he had opposed the policies of Italy there.

I thought it sufficiently important to telegraph the Department, which I did. I was surprised to receive a reply to the effect that messages of that character should be sent by mail because of the expense. I was also more surprised to receive another despatch commenting upon and replying to my telegram and expressing their surprise that Baron Aloisi should have discussed the question and indicating that his remarks seemed impertinent.

While I do not care to make an issue of the manner in which the Department has received my telegram, I do think it is probably because this Embassy has not in the past informed the Department of Italy's point of view and policy in Albania and has failed to properly present the importance which Italy attaches to Albania.

As it is such an important problem for Italy today and as it is part of her foreign policy, I think it worth while for the Department to get the proper point of view, and I am having the situation studied and will send on a despatch as soon as possible which will set out the whole thing and display Italy's interest in Albania.

But as I understand your instructions, which guide my attitude toward the Italian Government and its foreign policy, I believe I would have been justified in making a recommendation to the State Department at the same time I sent the despatch about Albania. I did not make a recommendation, but in order that you may understand the situation at the earliest moment I take this opportunity to give you the important facts.

In 1925 Italy entered into a treaty with Albania by virtue of which Albania practically abandoned some of its sovereign rights and to all intents and purposes became a sort of protectorate of Italy. Under the terms of the treaty as I understand them, Italy has the right even over the objection of the King and the government of Albania to send her army into that country to restore domestic order. She had the right to direct its military operations and to supervise its army. She has the right to use certain harbors on the Adriatic. For these privileges Italy guarantees something of the independence of Albania and was to make to her certain contributions in money. There were various other provisions.

Of course it was objected to as a point of policy by Jugoslavia and she was joined by the other members of the Little Entente and by France in trying to undermine the influence of Italy at the capital, Tirana. These diplomatic activities took the form of criticism of Italy and condemnation of certain of her activities and condolences to the King[3] that he was being badly treated and all that sort of thing. It was good policy on the part of the Little Entente and on the part of Jugoslavia. Italy probably intended to use Albania for a military base in operations in case of war against Jugoslavia. That that was the original purpose seems to admit of no reasonable doubt. Military roads were built to the frontier; forts were built. The Albanian army was trained and was officered and the Italian influence permeated the country.

Since that time it has seemed either inexpedient or too expensive or impractical as a policy. It may be that Italy felt that the continuing military threat on the southern border of Jugoslavia was an irritation to France. At any rate, Italy has now changed her policy to a large extent and as regards the military. She has relinquished her control over the army of Albania; has withdrawn her own troops and most of her officers. King Zog has been antagonistic to Italy and has played an opposing policy, and Italy has for two years declined to make the monetary payments which the arrangement contemplated.

But her naval policy continues. To Italy Albania is much in the position of any important country on the Caribbean is to our policy vis à vis Panama. The Italians themselves speak of Albania as being similar to Panama in our own world. They attach great importance to the necessity of naval bases. The Straits of Otranto are only forty miles wide. Albania is on the eastern side. Adequate harbors are there. There are no harbors on the Italian side. If a French fleet should pass the Straits of Otranto, Venice and Trieste and the whole of the Adriatic world would be at their mercy. Consequently Italy insists upon holding the harbors on the coast of Albania to use them for defensive purposes against France. She stresses the defensive nature of her intentions. And they could be nothing but defensive. There is not there the possibility of an offensive movement against any nation but Albania.

Mussolini sent to Albania Aloisi himself to make the treaty. He has since had at Albania as Minister Soragna, who is practically the understudy of Aloisi and his colleague at the Geneva Conference.[4]

So that when the American Minister in Tirana apparently, or in the Italian eyes, joined forces with the Ministers of the Little Entente and with France—or in the Italian eye at least adopted the same diplomatic policy and criticised the Italians and the Italian policy, he gave evidence of a policy of the United States in opposition to Italy in her foreign policy and in the matter of what she considers to be a necessary naval defense.

Either I have wrongly construed your instructions[5] or the Department of State is still continuing to look upon Albania as a separate and independent kingdom and in possession of all its sovereign rights and powers, when as a matter of fact it has surrendered some of them to Italy.

I think that we are entirely justified in playing the game with Italy in Albania as far as her naval policy is concerned and assuming a position in Albania which would be colorless. There is no necessity of our backing up Italy there, but I do not see the necessity of opposing Italy there. Particularly is that so when one appreciates the importance which Italy attaches to her special position in that little country.

I reiterate that I do not want to make an issue of the matter, but

I do want to present the Italian political situation to your thought. As soon as I can arrange it, a despatch will be got ready to present the whole picture to the Department, but when it is presented to the Department I hope the matter will be considered in the point of view of Italian policy and not from the point of view of Albanian policy and that it will be seen that Italy's naval control of the shore of Albania is a very helpful element in maintaining the sense of security in Europe. For with Italy deprived of the possibility of a naval base near her own nerve center the sense of security in Italy cannot be as strong. And if the sense of security in Italy is lacking, there is just that additional handicap to the success which can be attained by Mussolini in his efforts to maintain peace on the Continent of Europe. It is a small thing, but it is important, and I hope that I have not troubled you with too long a letter in bringing it to your attention.

With kindest regards and best wishes, Most respectfully,

Breckinridge Long

[PSF:Italy:TS]

[1] Baron Pompeo Aloisi was at this time chief of cabinet in the ministry of foreign affairs and Italian representative on the League of Nations council.

[2] Herman Bernstein, minister from 1930 to 1933.

[3] Zog I (Ahmed Bey, king from 1928 to 1939).

[4] The Marquese A. Meli Lupi di Soragna was a member of the Italian delegation to the Geneva Disarmament Conference.

[5] No letter of instructions has been found; possibly they were verbal.

## Raymond Moley and Herbert Bayard Swope, American Delegation, London Economic Conference, to Roosevelt

S.S. *Manhattan,* July 7, 1933, 1:45 P.M.

[*Radiogram*] Your insistence on continuance of conference and outline of position make decision to go on wholly your victory. Congratulations and regards. We are returning on *Manhattan,* arriving Thursday.[1]

Moley
Swope

[OF 17:T]

[1] July 13.

## Dave H. Morris, Ambassador to Belgium, to Roosevelt

Brussels, July 7, 1933

*Confidential*

Dear Franklin: Your holographic letter to King Albert[1] was delivered in person when His Majesty received me officially on July 6th. He appreciated greatly the compliment, and of course I, as the bearer and your friend, assumed in his eyes a very special worth. In consequence my audience, so I am told, was different from the perfunctory one, and took on more of the character of a friendly interview.

His Majesty was anxious to know at first hand the trade situation in U.S.A. I told him the tide had definitely turned, and quoted him some figures Mr. Taylor, Chairman of the U.S. Steel Corporation, whom I had seen several times in London last month, had given me;[2] I confirmed His Majesty's impressions concerning the excellent demand for automobiles; and I replied as best I could to other specific questions.

He then drew me a little aside and in a low voice, apparently not heard by the others present, expressed the earnest hope that my appointment would bring about more than ever cordial relations between our countries and that he personally would be very glad to cooperate towards this end. He then dropped his voice so low that I am not certain precisely what he said, but I understood him to suggest that he hoped the pleasant relations existing between our countries would be continued (or resumed) in spite of the debt situation and that he would do his best personally. I am afraid I was taken a bit by surprise and then again I was not sure I heard him aright, so I took refuge in my reply in the generality that in America we all loved His Majesty and had the greatest possible admiration for his country.

It seems to be de rigeur that what is said in such an interview is never quoted or repeated—except to the Ambassador's sovereign, who in turn holds the message as sacred—so I assume that all there is to the matter is that you, Mr. President, have an impression of His Majesty's personal attitude on an interesting question.

In thinking over my mission here, I am wondering if you would consider the risks worth taking that I might personally try to bring about informally and not in any way officially, a suggestion from Belgium that the debts be compromised by some method which, though somewhat in the nature of a gesture, might nevertheless lead to a final settlement. Perhaps you have very definite ideas on this dangerous subject, and as it is constantly brought up, I shall hope you can give me general instructions how to handle it.

My personal letter from London is quite in consonance with subsequent developments, and I trust was of service to you.[3] Our English friends are running true to form and are past masters as ever.

With congratulations, as ever, Yours admiringly,

Dave H. Morris

[*Notation*:A] File
[OF 455:TS]

[1] June 3, 1933, above.
[2] Myron C. Taylor had sailed for Europe on May 12 to attend a business conference (New York *Times,* May 17, 1933, p. 27).
[3] Presumably Morris' letter to Roosevelt of June 21, referred to in Roosevelt's note to Acheson of July 3, above.


## William C. Bullitt, Executive Officer, American Delegation, London Economic Conference, to Roosevelt

London, July 8, 1933

*Personal*

Dear Mr. President: You will have heard from Ray and Warren[1] the news about the Conference itself and I shall not burden you with my opinions about it. There are, however, a few outside matters that have happened to come to my attention, about which I think you might like to be informed. And I am sure that you will be interested in knowing how adroitly Hull managed the very difficult situation of last Tuesday and Thursday. The Secretary was really magnificent.[2]

On Tuesday morning, July 4, MacDonald had agreed with the gold countries that the Conference should be adjourned, leaving some sort of an undefined committee or committees behind and that you should be blamed for the abandonment of the Conference. MacDonald had promised to put through this dissolution at the Bureau meeting scheduled for six o'clock.[3] When we got wind of the project, Hull sent me out to persuade MacDonald to adjourn the Bureau meeting until the following day. I argued with the Prime Minister for an hour, but could not budge him and the only way of saving the situation was for Hull to intervene at the outset of the Bureau meeting.

As usual, I went with Hull to the Bureau meeting and had the satisfaction of seeing him do a beautiful piece of work. The French, and indeed all the gold standard countries, came in roaring for blood. Mac-Donald opened the meeting with a speech that pinned responsibility for the breakdown of the Conference on your message and then read the proposals for adjournment of the Conference.

Hull got up at once and asked MacDonald a series of questions in regard to the actual situation and future work of the Conference. MacDonald, being unable to answer any of the questions which Hull had asked him, hemmed and hawed and even giggled a little in his embarrassment, and sat down after showing clearly that he was completely confused—which was just what Hull had intended.

The Secretary rose again and with great dignity pointed out that to take responsibility for the adjournment of a conference which had been called to relieve the sufferings of the world was unjustifiable, unless the actual situation and future plans were entirely clear. He said that, of course, the other representatives in the Bureau were much less well-informed than the Prime Minister himself, the President of the Conference, and since the Prime Minister's mind seemed entirely unclear it must be realized that the minds of all the other Delegates were even more unclear and it was essential that time should be taken for consideration of the whole matter. He concluded by suggesting that the Bureau should adjourn without further debate until the following day.

The Secretary's speech made a deep impression on everyone present. Bonnet became bright purple with rage and Jung was scarlet, and it was clear that the Secretary had carried the majority of the Bureau with him. Chamberlain and Bennett supported the Secretary strongly and in spite of the speeches of Bonnet and Jung, the meeting of the Bureau was adjourned until Thursday.

At the Thursday meeting of the Bureau, the Secretary again got to his feet at the first moment and made a really fine simple address on the need for continuing the Conference. We had, of course, received your telegrams, saying you wanted the Conference to go on,[4] and had lined up all the nations we could for continuance. Ishii followed Hull in support of our position and Bennett, Chamberlain and the Swedish Minister of Finance and a Chinese representative all made strong speeches supporting Hull. The gold countries and Spain were solid in opposition. Bonnet finally threatened flatly to leave the Conference at once and MacDonald appointed a committee of six to attempt to reconcile the difficulty: Hull, Chamberlain and Bennett on our side; Bonnet,

Jung and Colijn, the Dutch Prime Minister, on the other. I went with Hull and we had an extremely stiff three-hour fight before we obtained the agreement to continue, with which you are already familiar.[5] The Secretary's sincerity and distinction of character have at last begun to impress everyone impressionable. Bonnet is, of course, beyond reach. He is as cooperative as a rattlesnake.

That brings me to the question of our relations with France. Rist told me last night, under conditions which make me believe he was speaking sincerely, that the French have not the slightest intention of paying a penny on their debt to us. We should, I think, be extremely skeptical about any predictions to the contrary which may come from de Laboulaye[6] or anyone else. It seems to me that the time has almost come for us to make it clear to the French that we feel that they have rejected with contempt our effort to collaborate with them in foreign affairs, and that we should back such a statement by appropriate actions.

I have talked over the entire question with Herriot. He passed through London a week or so ago and telephoned me in advance and asked me to spend the two hours that he was in town with him. I did so. He asked me to let you know that he was continuing and would continue his fight for the payment of the debt no matter what it cost him. He stated frankly that his support of payment had destroyed his influence for the moment. He is down and out politically and extremely depressed. I know definitely that a few days ago he wrote his resignation as President of the Radical Socialist Party and as President of the Committee on Foreign Affairs of the Chamber of Deputies, and was only persuaded to reconsider by great pressure from his most intimate friends. He feels that he will not have the slightest chance to come back until November at the earliest, and it is the opinion of others that he will remain an outcast for longer than that.

Norman Davis and Dulles doubtless told you of Daladier's private promise about reducing France's airplanes and tanks. I remain extremely skeptical in regard to the French accepting any disarmament agreement whatsoever. The general opinion here is that war in Europe is inevitable; that if it comes soon France and Poland will win; that if it comes after Germany has rearmed, Germany will win. In the face of this general belief, I do not believe that the French will do any disarming worthy of the name, and I think that we should consider seriously whether or not we should withdraw our offer to consult in case of a threat of war.

The whole French attitude towards us at the moment is one of contempt and I think it would be healthy to let them know that our personal affection for them will not prevent us from refusing to support them in any way if they continue to behave as they are now behaving.

Herriot suggested very strongly that you should order our Embassy in Paris to try to bring home to the people of France the facts in regard to the French debt to us, notably the fact that what we are asking France to pay is the debt contracted after the armistice. This might be advisable and Pell, the press attaché of the Paris Embassy, is said to be a thoroughly able fellow;[7] but the matter is one of great delicacy and if you should pass along Herriot's suggestion to the Paris Embassy it should be handled with the utmost discretion.

The British position remains as usual unclear. Bennett wants MacDonald to tie the British Empire to the United States and to work with us and Latin America and China to the exclusion of Europe. There is a body of opinion in England that would favor such a policy but MacDonald seems utterly opposed to it and Simon would be violently opposed. MacDonald seems to have lost the last remnants of his prestige by his equivocal actions at this conference. Bennett turned to me at the Bureau meeting yesterday and whispered, "He is the damnedest, squirming eel in the world."

Simon continues to be chummy with the Japanese and to obstruct any possible action to restrain them. I have seen a good deal of Soong and he has told me, I think frankly, about his conversations with the French and British Governments and with Litvinov. I told Soong at the outset that we could make no move and could not participate in any move unless the British initiated it. He did his best to get action from the British and the French but failed. I am convinced that any proposition we make to the British in confidence Simon will carry at once to the Japanese as he carried the previous confidential proposals made by Stimson.

Soong and Litvinov agreed to try to get the relations of China and Russia on to a better footing for the purpose of opposing their common enemy. Before Soong had seen Litvinov, he told me that he considered that it would be decidedly valuable in restraining the Japanese if we should recognize Russia. He repeated this after seeing Litvinov and I think there is something in it. His argument was that the Japanese would be convinced that China and Russia would have the moral and perhaps the material support of the United States in case of further conflict.

Soong strikes me as an exceptionally able and straightforward fellow and I hope that when you see him you will make him talk with the utmost frankness. I am sure he hesitates a bit to let go when talking with you, because he considers a certain amount of formal politeness necessary when talking to the President of the United States. I told him that there was nothing you liked so much as plain unvarnished frankness.

I have seen Litvinov twice. At the outset of the Conference, when we were rounding up votes to elect Cox as Chairman of the Monetary Commission, I spoke to him and got him to pledge us his vote, and also asked him who was his confidential representative in America. He replied that Skvirsky[8] was his man, as I cabled you.

I then arranged a meeting between Litvinov and Ray. Ray was able to remain only a few minutes, and I continued the conversation. I asked Litvinov what Russia had to send to us in exchange for our goods. He had nothing to add to the usual list of articles. I had heard that the gold production of the Lena fields had been so increased that it now amounted to $150,000,000 a year, and I asked Litvinov if this was true. He replied that he did not have the exact figures, but that he was under the impression that the amount was much less. I am not at all sure, however, that we might not get $50,000,000 in gold a year from Russia in payment for exports and I think we should remember this in any further trade negotiations.

Litvinov said that the English argued with him continuously that it was not fair for Russia to trade with the United States since the United States had not recognized Russia, and, of course, asked whether you were contemplating recognition. I told him that your general attitude was friendly, as he could see from the fact that our representatives at this Conference, even the Secretary of State, were meeting him and talking with him as if he were a human being and not a wild man, and that trade negotiations were in progress in Washington. I told him I had not the slightest idea when you might consider it desirable to recognize Russia; that it might be soon; that it might be a long time; that he should not count on immediate recognition, but that he should not be surprised if you should recognize Russia. I told him that of course you would require an absolute pledge from the Russian Government to refrain from all propaganda directed against our institutions, governmental or economic. He said that of course Russia would be glad to give such an undertaking provided it was in bilateral form and that we agreed to refrain from propagandizing Russia. He added that Skvirsky was in a position to communicate with him privately by cable at any time.

You, of course, can judge and I cannot whether or not it is expedient to recognize Russia at this time. I feel that we ought to have a diplomatic representative not only in China, but also in Russia since the two countries will henceforth be intimately related in their policy towards Japan and if we should have first-rate men in both countries we might to a large extent control their common actions or at least prevent their acting in a way of which we disapprove.

Litvinov, of course, said that if Russia were recognized he hoped I would be sent as Ambassador, to which I replied that I could not think of a worse one for the post and that I should repeat the same remark to you. I have no idea that you would contemplate such a thing, but I should like to argue with you against it if by any chance someone should suggest such an appointment to you.

To me the most striking feature of this Conference thus far is Bennett's desire to cooperate with us and I think that if you have any plans for reciprocal tariff negotiations with Canada the time is very propitious. Incidentally, Bennett told me the other day how much he liked Warren, and I am sure that he was talking honestly. Bruce[9] of Australia talked to me with violence of the British Government in general and John Simon in particular, and I wonder if via Canada we might not make a hole in the Ottawa Agreements.

I am more than ever convinced that we can do little in Europe and should keep out of European squabbles and that our future lies in the Americas and the Far East.

Apologies for the length of this letter and every good wish.

Yours devotedly,

William C. Bullitt

[PSF:London Economic Conference:TS]

[1] Raymond Moley and Warren Delano Robbins.

[2] In his successful effort to prevent the precipitate adjournment of the Conference; see *Foreign Relations, 1933*, I, 688ff, and Hull's *Memoirs*, I, 262ff.

[3] The steering committee of the Conference, made up of delegates from the sixteen principal nations attending.

[4] See telegrams to Hull of July 4 (two) and 5 (*Foreign Relations, 1933*, I, 685–687, 688, 694–695).

[5] See Hull to Roosevelt, July 6, 1933, *ibid.*, p. 697.

[6] André de Laboulaye, recently appointed French ambassador to the United States.

[7] Robert Thompson Pell had left his post at the Paris Embassy in March for a leave of absence in the United States. In October he was named press officer of the American delegation to the Disarmament Conference at Geneva (New York *Times*, March 10, 1933, p. 20; Oct. 28, 1933, p. 17).

[8] Boris E. Skvirsky, at this time apparently connected with one of the Soviet com-

mercial offices in the United States, was Soviet chargé d'affaires in Washington from November 1933 until the arrival of Ambassador Alexander A. Troyanovsky. Skvirsky was later named counselor of embassy in Washington.

[9] Stanley Melbourne Bruce, Australian minister to Great Britain, 1932–33.

## Interview of Louis M. Howe, Personal Secretary to the President

National Broadcasting Company, Washington, July 9, 1933

For Release for Publication at 9:00 P.M. EST Sunday July 9, 1933: Interview of Colonel Louis McHenry Howe, Secretary to President Roosevelt, by Walter Trumbull, well known newspaper correspondent, as broadcast over a National Broadcasting Company network, Sunday night, July 9, 1933 . . .[1]

Mr. Trumbull: Well Mr. Howe, what were the circumstances surrounding the writing of that famous message which almost adjourned the London Conference? I understand the President wrote it in longhand.

Mr. Howe: That's right. He almost always writes important messages in longhand first. That famous document was written in the Admiral's cabin on the *Indianapolis.* The cablegrams that came in every hour or so convinced the President more and more that it was time for him to put the position of our country beyond question.

Mr. Trumbull: When did he decide on the two things which interested the public most—that we would not enter into any agreement to stabilize our currency abroad until the dollar had reached a normal level at home, and that the other matters should be taken up and gone forward with, leaving that in abeyance?

Mr. Howe: It is clear to me that you and perhaps most people do not quite understand that that was no new decision, but was merely adhering to a decision made months ago, and was in fact, in line with the policy pointed out by the committee of experts who drew up the program for this conference way back in the last months of President Hoover's administration.

Mr. Trumbull: What do you mean? Just how did this conference originate?

Mr. Howe: I suppose it has all been forgotten, Walter, that this whole conference started in 1932 by a meeting of a Commission of Experts appointed by the Governments of Germany, Belgium, Great Britain,

China, France, India, Italy and Japan, in addition to the United States, to which President Hoover had sent Mr. Edmund E. Day, Director of Social Science, Rockefeller Foundation; Mr. John H. Williams, Professor of Economics at Harvard University, and Mr. Norman Davis, acting as General Counsellor. The idea was to consider the possibilities of a general get-together meeting of all the nations to make common cause in the fight against world-wide depression. This Committee studied over all the different elements which contributed to this depression and prepared a report of some thirty-six pages which has been reprinted by the United States Department of Commerce and has been widely circulated in this country.

Mr. Trumbull: Did this report have anything to say about the gold standard?

Mr. Howe: Yes. When this committee came to take up a return to the gold standard as one of the subjects of the meeting, they carefully put in this as their conclusions on the matter, their report reading:[2]

Each Government must, of course, remain free to decide when and under what conditions it could adopt such a standard, and we do not suggest that this can or should be done without the most careful preparation. There are a great number of economic as well as financial conditions which must be fulfilled before the restoration of an international gold standard can be a practical possibility.

And in another place the report said:

The time when it will be possible for a particular country to return to the gold standard and the exchange parity at which such a return can safely be made will necessarily depend on the conditions in that country as well as those abroad, and these questions can only be determined by the proper authorities in each country separately.

This, of course, is almost the identical language employed by both the President in his message and the spokesman of the British Government in Parliament. It was not a new decision, but a firm and positive declaration of our intention to abide by the original program to which we had already tacitly agreed.

Mr. Trumbull: Do I understand you to say, Mr. Howe, that the President's message actually was in agreement with the recommendation of that original Committee of Experts?

Mr. Howe: That's it, Walter! The point the President raised in his message was really more a reaffirmation of the opinion of this committee, who also took the same ground as the President when they said that no permanent stabilization or removal of exchange restrictions could take place until, as the report says, "The governments concerned took the initial measures necessary to secure the stability of their budgets and their economic system."

Mr. Trumbull: Now that the Conference has decided to go ahead, Mr. Howe, what is it likely to do?

Mr. Howe: Of course, what will actually be done within the next few weeks at the Conference cannot be forecast, but I think you will find in a general way that the sub-committee will be appointed to consider the topics already agreed upon, and that after a short time the meetings of the full commission will be adjourned for some weeks until these committees are ready to make preliminary reports.

Mr. Trumbull: Yes, but that doesn't mean much to most of us; what are they going to report on?

Mr. Howe: There are plenty of subjects to consider. The Agenda, which is a nice diplomatic word for program, which was to guide the Conference, provided six main problems with a number of subdivisions to each.

Mr. Trumbull: What are some of these problems, Mr. Howe?

Mr. Howe: Well, there is the monetary and credit policy—then there is that of bringing the price of goods up to the cost of goods—then the resumption of the movement of capital, including the abolition of foreign exchange restrictions, and the subject of existing international indebtedness. Then the restrictions on international trade which has four subheads under it; the tariff and treaty policy, and finally, the organization of production and trade, which includes problems like the international agreement to curtail wheat production throughout the world. As I said, there are thirty-six pages of this Agenda, and the Committee will have no trouble in finding plenty of work . . .

[PSF:London Economic Conference:M]

[1] Early in June 1933 Howe had begun a series of weekly broadcasts on objectives of the New Deal; scripts for many of these are in the Howe papers in the Roosevelt Library. An account of this interview appeared in the New York *Times,* July 10, 1933, pp. 1, 2. The portion omitted above is Howe's account of the trip on the *Indianapolis* from Campobello (where he joined the President) to Annapolis.

[2] The quoted material following is from the *Draft Annotated Agenda* of the London Conference, pp. 8, 12.

## Roosevelt to Fred I. Kent, Federal Reserve Bank of New York, New York

[Washington] July 11, 1933

Dear Mr. Kent: Many thanks for your interesting letter of July fifth and for the subsequent reports.[1] I am particularly interested in your analysis of the import and export situation.

I wish you would give me a confidential guess on two things. First, what do you think will be the relationship of the pound to the franc, and second, do you think the dollar will stop at about 4.86 if nothing is done about it?[2]

Very sincerely yours,

[PPF 744:CT]

[1] Kent, director of the division of foreign exchange of the Federal Reserve Bank of New York, discussed the rise in the franc and pound sterling between June 15 and July 5, and pointed out the plight of importers who were losing money because of the price squeeze. Exporters were also tending to leave the proceeds of their exported goods in unconverted foreign currency (PPF 744).

[2] Kent, in a long reply of July 12, 1933 (PPF 744), predicted that Britain would maintain a stabilized position between the pound and the franc because it would be commercially advantageous for her to do so. He also said that the dollar value of $4.86 to the pound was largely of psychological value as a frame of reference for traders and investors. Roosevelt sent this letter to two of his current monetary advisers, George F. Warren and James Harvey Rogers, in the Department of Commerce. They replied in a joint memorandum of July 21, 1933 (PPF 744), emphasizing the dangers to the economy of a "rising dollar."

Of interest in this connection is a memorandum prepared by Warren (apparently at the President's request) entitled "Suggested Statement to the World Economic Conference," dated July 12, 1933 (PSF:London Economic Conference). The memorandum said that it was the purpose of the United States "to restore prices to such a level as will enable industry and agriculture once more to give employment to the existing masses of the unemployed and as will make possible the payment of public and private debts. It is equally the purpose of the United States to prevent any rise in the price level beyond the point necessary for the attainment of these ends." No further reference to this proposed message has been found.

## Cordell Hull, Chairman, American Delegation, London Economic Conference, to Roosevelt

London, July 11, 1933, 11:00 P.M.

[*Telegram*] By order of the Secretary of State Hull this is to be decoded only by Salmon[1] personally.

Strictly confidential for the President. No distribution to any person.

I am very grateful for your congratulatory telegram No. 111, July 6, 10 p.m.[2] It is most painful in this connection to have to report an attitude and course of conduct on the part of Professor Moley which has been utterly dumbfounding to me. I brushed aside the evident motives behind his radio speech of May which expressly discounted much or most of what you and I at the time, and all other supporters of the program for London Conference, thought could reasonably be accomplished by this Conference.[3] He sent along at least one woman from his office who according to reliable information has consistently attempted to spy on my movements and make secret reports back to Moley. After his May speech, parts of which were broadcast over England repeatedly, every reason why he should not come to the Conference while being heralded as more closely in your confidence and more entitled to speak for you than any other person, was patent. Notwithstanding, he came, with the result that for some eight days while on his voyage here the press of London and Paris, which had most unfairly assailed the American delegation, first about debts and next about temporary stabilization, with neither one of which the Delegation had anything to do, then proceeded to dramatize Moley as coming to speak and act for you and to take charge of American interests in London, with the result that the American Delegation found it impossible seriously to function in the face of great headlines morning and afternoon here about how Moley was coming to dispense salvation to every part of the world, especially as it might relate to matters immediately pending here.

When he finally arrived the high officials of the gold countries and of the United Kingdom riveted all their attention upon him, Moley. He sent Bullitt to me with the definite request that I announce to the Delegation that he, Moley, would in company with Doctor Sprague take custody of the temporary stabilization matter to the entire exclusion, again at his express request, of Warburg. Assuming that you authorized or directed statement I simply repeated the announcement he then asked me to make. And in this connection, after his failure he pretended to claim that I on my initiative directed him to assume the task. Bullitt and I agree in total refutation of this. He likewise represented to the Delegation after his failure to secure your approval of temporary stabilization proposal that he was not expressing any personal views about the matter whatever but was merely acting ad referendum.

Anyhow, he left my apartment in the forenoon and without any information on my part as to what he was doing, proceeded during the day to negotiate directly with MacDonald and other Prime Ministers or heads of treasuries from the gold countries, with the result that the first information I had came from him over the telephone near five o'clock that afternoon to the effect that "they had agreed," and requesting me to join in ratification, which I declined to do upon the ground that the Delegation had no jurisdiction and that I had expressed no opinion to you, pro or con, on temporary stabilization and that I and the Delegation had refused to MacDonald and gold countries every request to send one word to you, pro or con, about merits of temporary stabilization.[4]

After your program had thus been forced a third time on this question within a few days it was but natural that you would be somewhat emphatic in making comment.[5] This was followed by the efforts, especially of the British and the gold countries and certain other delegations controlled by the British, to adjourn the Conference and charge sole responsibility for its wrecking to you. The resolution was actually written and the gold delegates discussed it in my presence, wherein you were personally charged with wrecking the Conference. The chances seemed ninety-nine to a hundred that this course would be taken. Many of the Delegates were frozen towards me as I strove to quiet and compose them at the meeting called expressly to carry out this adjournment program. At any rate, while it so happened that I was in the position of undertaking to deal with this crisis single handed, and was lucky enough if I may say so to be the chief single factor in preserving the life of the Conference and in saving you from the outrage of being branded as its destroyer, Moley was secretly sending code messages to you about my incapacity to function here.[6] He was at the same time pretending absolute loyalty of friendship and of official attitude toward me. He does not know that I am aware of this fact and I only discovered it after he sailed. My regret only equals my amazement to discover the deliberate attempt of one I have implicitly trusted thus secretly to undermine and destroy me in my situation while openly professing both friendship and loyalty. I refer you to Senator Pittman, Governor Cox, Mr. Morrison the Texas Delegate, and others for absolute confirmation of the essentials of the statements I have herein made. Hull

Bingham

[PSF:London Economic Conference:T]

[1] David A. Salmon, chief of the Division of Communications and Records in the State Department.
[2] Printed in *Foreign Relations, 1933*, I, 698.

[3] In a radio speech made from Washington on May 20, 1933, Moley had predicted difficulties for Hull's reciprocal trade program (Moley, *After Seven Years,* pp. 208–210).

[4] From June 16 on, numerous cables dealing with stabilization were sent by Sprague, Warburg, Moley, and others to Roosevelt, Woodin, Acheson, and Phillips (*Foreign Relations, 1933,* I, 642ff). Those from London were sent, *pro forma,* over Hull's name but it is certain he did not accept responsibility for all of them and it is possible that he did not see all of them. He had made his position clear in his cable to Roosevelt and Phillips of June 21, 1933 (*ibid.,* p. 651), when he said that the delegation had not considered temporary stabilization its responsibility but rather that of Sprague and Harrison. However, see Moley, *After Seven Years,* pp. 228ff.

[5] Roosevelt's message to Phillips of July 2, 1933, above.

[6] Specifically, Moley's cable of July 4, 1933 (*Foreign Relations, 1933,* I, 680), in which he said that Pittman was the only member of the delegation able to present the President's ideas "intellectually and aggressively."

# Press Conference, Executive Offices of the White House, July 12, 1933, 11:10 A.M.

[*Excerpt*] The President: . . . And then, what is the other one—that I was having difficulty in finding enough rich Democrats to fill the diplomatic posts. Now, don't you believe it. I have in the diplomatic folder, I think there are at least two hundred and fifty or three hundred names of deserving Democrats who would like to have places under any conditions, salary or no salary. As a matter of fact, on the total thing we filled quite a lot of places and there are still quite a number going to be changed, but the reason we have not gone faster is, in the first place, I haven't had time to get around to it and, in the second place, there are quite a number of posts where the individual who happens to be there, irrespective of whether he is a political appointee, is doing special work and I want to keep him on to finish up the special work. There are half a dozen cases of that kind and, of course, those political appointees will be replaced in time. I think I told Bill Phillips to go ahead and make three or four changes, and there will be changes from time to time.[1]

Then, for instance, just to give you an example, we have career diplomats. Of course, we are going to keep them in, and if there is some political appointee carrying on special business or doing a special piece of work, I may want to keep him on until possibly the Fall and, when he goes out, I may move a career diplomat from some other place into his place. Therefore, it means that his place will be filled either by a career diplomat, or a political appointee. It will take me probably the balance of the year to get the diplomatic posts more or less permanently straightened out, but there is no difficulty in finding candidates.

Q: You said you had two hundred and fifty men of wealth. How does that compare with the vacancies?

The President: Not men of wealth.

Q: They may be able to pay their own expenses until confirmed by Congress?

The President: No; no appointments are being made because the vacancies do not exist at the present time. In fact, I think I have filled every post where there was a vacancy.

Q: I understand that on a recess appointment you have to pay your own expenses.

The President: No, if the vacancy does not occur until after Congress adjourns, then they can get their pay. It is only where the vacancy has occurred before, and I do not fill until after Congress adjourns that they cannot get paid . . .

Q: There has been a suggestion from London that after the Conference adjourns you would like to see them come over here next year.

The President: It must be hot in London, too.

Q: Have we any objection to the Conference resting for the Summer without apparently having accomplished anything?

The President: I haven't any idea what they are going to do. When the Prime Minister was here we talked about the fact that on the 12th of August every good Englishman goes grouse shooting and every good Continental goes to a Spa for two or three weeks, and therefore that undoubtedly, some time in August, the Conference, if it has not completed its labors before then, would take a recess for perhaps a month. It would be a perfectly normal thing for them to do.

Q: Did you give the Argentine Ambassador any encouragement yesterday with reference to the subject of opening negotiations for—[2]

The President: I told him we would be perfectly delighted to sit around a table and see if we couldn't find ways and means to increase trade between the Argentine and the United States.

Q: Soon?

The President: Right away. Any time they are ready to sit around a table.

Q: Does that mean a trade mission?

The President: Well, there again, I don't know whether it would be handled in that way.

Q: The Argentine has been asking to send one as soon as we are ready to receive it.

The President: And I think the Ambassador and Bill Phillips are talking over the ways and means and methods today.

Q: What other countries are you dealing with on the same basis?

The President: Quite a number. I think you had better check it with Bill Phillips. I think there are one or two with the Scandinavian countries, also Brazil, Colombia, Chile—I might have left some out.

Q: Mexico, Mr. President?

The President: I don't know.

Q: What kind of agreements are you working out with them, Mr. President?

The President: Well, for instance, let me give you an example in the case of the Argentine. We have got a very difficult situation down there on the question of meat because, in the main part of Argentina they have a hoof-and-mouth disease, and they claim it cannot be transported and given to cattle in the other countries through the exportation of beef. Our Department of Agriculture people, however, say that it can, and that Argentine beef coming into England has created outbreaks among their cattle. In any event, there is a scientific dispute there. Our Congress, two or three years ago, as you people know, passed a bill saying that we could not bring in any meat from the Argentine. Now, we are precluded by law from bringing in any meat of any kind.

Now, the Argentine Government says that down in Patagonia there has been no hoof-and-mouth disease, and we go along with them on that and say, "Yes, there isn't any." Unfortunately, however, the Congressional law used the word "country." Well, they say that Patagonia isn't really the same country as the rest of Argentina, any more than Alaska is the same country as the United States. That is a pretty good parallel. If we had some disease in this country—that is, in the continental United States—which did not exist in Alaska, Alaska would feel pretty badly if they were cut out of any exports with them down there. Patagonia is separated from the rest of the country by a very wide desert, and there is no communication by railroad across that desert, but only by sea. They are very anxious to have us ask Congress for a modification of the law, so that Patagonia mutton can come in. Well, I think it is a pretty reasonable request.

Q: Is that good mutton?

The President: What?

Q: Is that good mutton?

The President: I may have eaten it, but not knowingly. Then, here is another example of the Argentine. I talked to Senator Byrd about this. He is one of our biggest apple growers.[3] Everybody knows that American apples, by the time May comes around, are pretty poor. The cold storage apple we sometimes get in June, July and August is a pretty poor article. Now, the Argentines would like to discuss the possibility of a seasonal tariff by which we would lift the tariff on apples during June, July and August and allow fresh Argentine apples to come in here. They would not compete with our apples, and, in addition, we would have some sort of agreement under which, by the end of August, say, or the first of September, if there were any Argentine apples still in cold storage here that had not been distributed through the retailers, the Argentine Government would take them out so that they would not compete with our Fall crop. I think that is a pretty good idea to talk about.

Q: What did Senator Byrd say about that?

The President: Senator Byrd said that as far as he knew there would be no objection from the apple growers in this country. He did not think they could reasonably protest against such seasonal importations coming into this country.

Q: Flax was also mentioned as a possible exchange with Argentina.

The President: I don't know about that; it was not mentioned. I also mentioned to him that they grow down there what they call maté, which is a Paraguay tea, and it is a very interesting drink because Paraguay tea has all the pick-up qualities of coffee or tea, but, at the same time, it does not keep you awake. A great many people, when they first drink it, don't like it because it tastes like rather poor green tea, but all through South America it has become, really, as much of a drink or, rather, more of a drink than coffee itself, and I think it would be worth while in this country for them to try to sell it, or at least to let our people try it. They might like it, or they might not.

Q: Give it to the State Department reporters over here and try it out on them. (Laughter)

Q: What compensatory advantages would there be for the United States? What would they do in return for privileges at this end?

The President: Well, it would be this: Suppose, for the sake of argument, they sold us fifty million dollars more of those goods and products than they do today. The chances are that they would spend that fifty million dollars in the United States to bring American products back to the Argentine.

Q: But no special, particular activities?

The President: No.

Q: What do you think about the possibility of the hoof-and-mouth disease in the dumping of Argentine beef?

The President: Beef? I don't think it is up for discussion at the present time, because it has not been eliminated. They admit that themselves.

Q: Even to let in this Patagonia beef, it would require an act of Congress?

The President: Yes, I think we would have to have that, because the act of Congress says "country."

Q: How about the fruit fly?

The President: Have they the fruit fly in the Argentine?

Q: They won't let the grapes in and they won't let the apples in.

The President: I didn't know that.

Q: It is the Department of Agriculture's quarantine that is keeping them out, not the tariff.

The President: Does that fruit fly come on apples?

Q: It does on grapes; I am not sure about apples.

[President's Press Conferences:T]

[1] See Phillips to Roosevelt, April 8, 1933, above.

[2] The Argentine ambassador had talked with Roosevelt for fifteen minutes the preceding day (PPF 1-0).

[3] Harry Flood Byrd, appointed United States senator from Virginia on March 4, 1933, to fill the unexpired term of Claude A. Swanson, had been engaged in fruit culture all his life. He had a large fruit farm at his home in Berryville, Va.

# Cordell Hull, Chairman, American Delegation, London Economic Conference, to Roosevelt

London, July 12, 1933

My dear Mr. President: The enclosed copies of correspondence with the British Prime Minister but illustrate several similar clashes orally and more than one in writing during the recent troublous days.

Sincerely yours,

Cordell Hull

[PSF:London Economic Conference:TS]

## [*Enclosure 1*] J. Ramsay MacDonald, President, London Economic Conference, to Cordell Hull, Chairman, American Delegation

Whitehall, 5th July, 1933

My dear Secretary of State: In view of the censure implied in the President's message to you of last Friday,[1] I should like to explain what you know from your own experience but what I think should be put on record—how the work is being done.

The President seems to be under the impression that the Conference is called to do one thing and one thing only, namely to take measures to raise prices. As you know, the Conference has been called for the purpose of trying to come to agreements along the whole front of problems and actions set out in the experts' report. I understood that there was a complete agreement between the President and myself that the whole of that work should be done with the utmost expedition so that every nation should be got to co-operate, in accordance with its own conditions and position, in the world recovery. As you know, this is being done by the simultaneous setting up of a considerable number of Committees, each charged with specified problems and groups of problems. Until the later part of last week, that work was being pushed ahead with great rapidity. Some of the wider and more comprehensive problems were being negotiated quietly amongst the more important nations whose contributions to their solution were essential, and so soon as a general understanding had been reached between those nations, the whole subject was to come out for public and general settlement. The time-table plan was that by the end of this month the Conference was to have finished its work and was to leave its Bureau or some other representative committee charged with the carrying out of the Conference decisions by the Governments represented at the London meeting. The reflections that the Conference was searching for excuses for pursuing certain policies, are most unjust and can only have arisen from a lack of understanding both of the duties imposed upon the Conference and the method that it was adopting to meet them. The idea that any one delegation or combination of delegations could, without discussion or negotiation, force certain countries to do certain things, is not one which if roughly pursued could lead to anything but a world disruption. It would defeat every hope to a great co-operation of goodwill active in promoting general understanding. When the message reflecting upon the Conference was not sent to your delegation to communicate to the Conference or to guide yourself but was broadcast to the world in the first instance,[2] the most bitter resentment could not be avoided and the prospects of agreement were for the time shattered. The countries who do not agree with us in our immediate outlook have a right to be heard and have their case discussed. That is the process which has been going on and which, but for these interruptions, would have been approaching a settlement by now. At the middle of last week I was perfectly confident that I could have the work done on the projected time-table. Now I am afraid, whatever may happen during this week, my time-table will have to be extended by some return to a method which I understood that both the President and I wished to avoid, namely an adjournment of the meetings of the full Conference whilst Committees were dealing with details and negotiating agreements on them. Had I been asked before the publication of the President's censure what actually was happening, I think it would never have seen the light of day, because, as I have indicated above, it proceeds upon a complete misapprehension of how an international conference, representative as this is of sixty-six different nations who are here in the persons of Prime Ministers, Foreign Secretaries and Finance Ministers, has to be conducted if any good results are to be had from it.

With all my warmest good wishes and kindest regards, I am,

Yours very sincerely,

(Sgd.) J. Ramsay MacDonald

[PSF:London Economic Conference:T:Copy]

[1] See Roosevelt to Phillips, June 30, 1933, above.
[2] See Roosevelt to Phillips, July 2, 1933, above. This message was immediately released to the press. Because of the five hours time difference, the message, released in London in the forenoon of July 3, was published first in New York by the morning newspapers, thus giving the impression that it had been "broadcast to the world."

## [*Enclosure 2*] Cordell Hull to J. Ramsay MacDonald

[London] July 11, 1933

*Personal*

My dear Mr. Prime Minister: Your surprising letter of July 5th[1] to hand, in which you seriously criticize President Roosevelt upon the assumption or theory that there was some sort of censure of the Economic Conference by the President in a message of his to me of last Friday. Let me assure you that I find few persons who impute any such motive to the President or find any such interpretation in his message to which you refer. I assure you also that the President fully visualizes and comprehends the entire scope and purpose of the Conference.

In preparation for this London Conference the President, scores of times to my knowledge, carefully and fully examined all of the topics in the elaborate agenda prepared by the preparatory committee. You are in error, therefore, in your imputation that the President was under the impression that "the Conference seems to be called for one thing, namely to take measures to raise prices."

I am equally sure that the President is entirely familiar with the mechanics of a world conference, such as the Economic Conference now sitting in London. You may or may not recall that, at the instance of those who now criticize and insist in drawing wholly unreasonable inferences, insistent demands were made upon the President for a third decision within a few days time on the question of temporary stabilization. I have no disposition to criticize those who, in their over-eagerness, thus forced the hand of the President the third time within this brief period with the natural result that the President became somewhat emphatic in making reply to some of the arguments that have been so repeatedly thrust upon him, ɪ ot by the Conference, but by a small group, and in which he did not honestly believe.

The President evidently did not address his message about which you complain to the Conference for the reason that it was not believed that the Conference had any jurisdiction over the question of temporary stabilization—that it was not listed as any definite or concrete part of the agenda; but that it involved more of a political decision which governmental treasuries in conference with their central banks would have to make. I myself think it most unfortunate that some of our good friends, through more or less unreasoning fear, have entirely over-emphasized and exaggerated this subject and needlessly endeavored to project it into the otherwise peaceful and regular proceedings of the Economic Conference.

With the greatest respect for your usually fine judgment and to you personally for whom I entertain the highest admiration, I must respectfully but earnestly protest against the criticism contained in your letter of July 5th the entire purport of which is that the President is charged with censuring the Conference. I have thus frankly written in earnest remonstrance against the placing of record in the files of the League of Nations what I must believe was a letter written in some haste.

The President is a genuine friend of international cooperation, as you well know; has since March 4th rendered it great service; and he would be one of the last persons on earth to impede in the least the progress of this great World Economic Conference to the success of which he contributed nearly two months of earnest personal work at Washington during April and May last.

I write in the best of good feeling and with great appreciation of the fine service you are performing as President of the Monetary and Economic Conference. I am most anxious, as President Roosevelt is most anxious, to cooperate with you to the fullest extent deemed at all feasible.

With my warmest personal regards, I am, Sincerely yours,

Cordell Hull

[PSF:London Economic Conference:T:Copy]

[1] Enclosure 1, above.

# William Phillips, Acting Secretary of State, to Roosevelt

Washington, July 13, 1933

Dear Mr. President: We have received an urgent telegram for you this morning from the Delegation, No. 126,[1] saying that they doubt the advisability of offering their economic proposal which was sent to us in their No. 121[2] until they have received instructions including all material amendments you may desire.

You will recollect that in your No. 134[3] you said that you had gone over the Delegation's proposal "as carefully as time would permit and wholly approved its introduction," etc. etc. Inasmuch, however, as the Delegation in its No. 121 had asked for "concrete formulations that have been worked out in Washington" the Delegation now proposes to await the receipt of these new instructions.

I attach draft instructions which are the result of a study by State, Treasury, Commerce and Tariff Commission experts.[4] Would you be able to glance over them and to let me know whether they meet with your approval and, if not, what changes you would like me to make?

I am also enclosing copies of the three messages which I have mentioned.[5]

Faithfully yours,

William Phillips

[*Notation*:AS] OK, but it should go as the result ~~of suggestion~~ of study by the State etc experts  FDR
[OF 17:TS]

[1] Hull to Roosevelt, July 13, 1933 (*Foreign Relations, 1933*, I, 712–713).
[2] Hull to Roosevelt, July 11, 1933 (*ibid.*, pp. 706–710). This included the text of a resolution on tariffs that Hull wished to present.
[3] Roosevelt to Hull, July 12, 1933 (*ibid.*, pp. 711–712). Hull's reply is printed *ibid.*, pp. 712–713.
[4] Not present; presumably returned to Phillips. The gist of them is in Phillips to Hull, July 13, 1933 (*ibid.*, pp. 713–715).
[5] Not present.

# Press Conference, Executive Offices of the White House, July 14, 1933, 4:20 P.M.

[*Excerpt*] Q: What did you hear from Ray Moley—Secretary Moley?

The President: Nothing; he just came back, that is all. In accordance with what he went over for and what he came back for, it is just to keep me in touch with things over there . . .[1]

Q: Is there any possibility of the embargo on gold being lifted to permit the shipping of gold abroad?

The President: The only thing being talked about at the present time is, "What is bullion?" The Attorney General is working on that from the legal standpoint. In other words, it is a question as to whether gold-bearing rock which comes out of the ground in its natural state can be exported and smelted elsewhere than within the United States. Then the next question is whether smelted rock which goes through a number of processes could be refined down to, let us say, all except the final process and then exported. The question is, would that be bullion? We don't know . . .[2]

Q: I understand that somebody in the Treasury Department has recommended that either a free gold market be established or that there be permitted the exporting of mined gold.

The President: I don't know anything about it.

Q: Does the fact that this bullion question is being studied mean that you will give favorable consideration to the exportation of the unfinished product?

The President: The first thing is to determine what is bullion under the law. Probably this is just a horseback opinion before the Attorney General rules on it. I don't think that gold-bearing rock in its natural form could be considered as bullion, but it is a question as to what point in the refining process it does become substantially bullion.

Q: Have you any objection to the ore-bearing rock containing gold being exported?

The President: It is an article—

Q: Is that going to Canada?

The President: I don't know. As a matter of fact, the whole thing is, as I understand it, a very, very small matter because there are—the cost of transporting the rock in its natural state is so tremendously high that, at the present time, it is almost impossible to send out anything except rock which is right alongside the Canadian border to a smelter which is only a few miles off.

Q: How did the question come up; is there a demand for the export of this gold-bearing rock?

The President: Yes. I think it concerns merely one mine. It is a very small thing. Its total effect on the gold question is infinitesimal.

Q: That wasn't the question taken up by Senator Adams,[3] was it?

The President: Oh, quite a lot of those western senators took it up.

Q: Didn't he have more than one mine in mind when he spoke of it? He said he was speaking for all miners.

The President: A lot of senators from the gold-mining states have come in and asked whether there would not be consideration at the present time of shipping gold out of the country—gold, not the rock.

Q: Are you giving any consideration to the latter?

The President: No . . .

Q: Anything new on the managed currency? Have you anybody studying that?

The President: I suppose there are two hundred and fifty people, to my certain knowledge, studying it all the time.

Q: With an idea of bringing it down to something definite?

Q: Did you discuss that with Moley this morning?

The President: No.

Q: Did Moley give you any idea as to when the Conference might take a recess in London?

The President: No.

Q: Was that being talked about?

The President: He did not know.

Q: Reports from there today say that it is going to recess on the twenty-seventh—July 27th—I don't know how official those reports are . . .

Q: Do you care to comment on the recess of the London Conference, or have you heard of it officially?

The President: Off the record, I talked to you on Tuesday about it, about the talk I had way back last April when we discussed the possibility of their getting away by the 12th of August, grouse day, and if they did not get through by grouse day, they would probably, of necessity, recess a month or a month and a half . . .

Q: Another question about gold: I understand that there is some organization which is seeking a free market for gold or for the exporting of gold, which organization has prepared a petition stating that if this export were permitted, that many more men would be enabled to make a living in mining. Has that ever been presented to you?

The President: Yes. I don't know whether I have received the one you mention, but there have been at least five or ten petitions, and several hundred telegrams and letters, pointing out that if they could get the world rate rather than the Treasury rate it would put a lot of people to work. That is perfectly true, it would.[4]

[President's Press Conferences:T]

[1] Cf. Moley's account in *After Seven Years,* pp. 270–271.

[2] On July 27 Attorney General Cummings made public his ruling that the export of smelted gold ore and imperfectly refined ore was prohibited except under license of the Secretary of the Treasury; gold concentrates (washed ore) and gold ore could be exported (New York *Times,* July 28, 1933, p. 23).

[3] Senator Alva B. Adams of Colorado, a strong advocate of increased domestic gold production.

[4] The American Mining Congress had petitioned Secretary of the Treasury Woodin to permit increased exports of gold ore and bullion to increase employment in the mines. The Congress contended that gold mining expenses were constantly increasing, while income, based on the government-fixed price of $20.67 an ounce, remained constant (New York *Times,* July 4, p. 21). During July and August 1933, the Committee for the Nation put on an extensive publicity drive over the radio and in the press for a free market for gold and for increased gold exports (OF 5707).

## Josephus Daniels, Ambassador to Mexico, to Roosevelt

México, July 15, 1933

Dear Franklin: If you have not seen it, I hope you will read an article in the June 21st issue of *Foreign Policy Reports* (published at 18 East 41st Street, New York City) by Raymond Leslie Buell on "The Caribbean Situation: Cuba and Haiti." Inasmuch as we had much to do with Haiti in the Wilson administration, and you have had a hard nut to crack in Cuba (Welles seems to be doing finely), I am sure this article will have deep interest for you.

You know that the things we were forced to do in Haiti was a bitter pill to me, for I have always hated any foreign policy that even hinted of imperialistic control. Frank Lane[1] knew my feeling, and during the Haitian insurrection, with mock seriousness, he would rise at the Cabinet meetings and say to our colleagues "Hail the King of Haiti." The danger of that pivotal country, so near our shores, falling into the control of some European nation, added to the business of assassinating presidents, made it imperative for us to take the course followed.

Your trip of inspection (it was one of pleasant adventure too) gave to the President and the Navy Department actual knowledge of the situation.[2] I never did wholly approve that Constitution of Haiti you had a hand in framing or the elections we held by which our hand-picked President of Haiti was put in office. I expect, in the light of experience, we both regret the necessity of denying even a semblance of "self determination" in our control of Haiti, when we had to go in to end revolutions or see some European government do so. Your "Good Neighbor" policy will not, I hope, be subjected to any such emergency as we were up against when we sent General Butler, who "with the help of God and a few marines" built good roads into the interior. At least we can rejoice that we built good roads for the Haitians which they still have, or rather that Smedley made them build and paid them some good American money while they worked.[3]

I have always wanted to go to Haiti. You know I had it in mind to go the year following your visit, but was not able to make it. I hope to carry out the cherished desire one of these days unless I hear that they hold it against me that some Haitians lost their lives during the occupation of the island by the marines.

With affectionate regards to you and Mrs. Roosevelt in which my wife joins, Faithfully yours,

Josephus Daniels[4]

[OF 237:TS]

[1] Franklin K. Lane, Wilson's Secretary of the Interior.

[2] Roosevelt's inspection trip as Assistant Secretary of the Navy is described in his diary (now in the Roosevelt Library), "Trip to Haiti and Santo Domingo, 1917"; see Freidel, *Franklin D. Roosevelt,* I, 276–283.

[3] General Smedley Butler, U.S.M.C., commandant of the Haitian Gendarmerie during the American occupation of the island.

[4] A small part of the Daniels' correspondence in the Roosevelt Library has been published in Carroll Kilpatrick, ed., *Roosevelt and Daniels: A Friendship in Politics* (Chapel Hill: Univ. of North Carolina, 1952), hereafter cited as *Roosevelt and Daniels.*


# Marguerite LeHand, Private Secretary to the President, to William Phillips, Acting Secretary of State

[Washington] July 17, 1933

Dear Mr. Secretary: The President asks me to tell you that he would like to have Hampson Gary go to the South American Conference.[1]

Very sincerely yours,

M. A. LeHand

[OF 567:CT]

[1] The Seventh International Conference of American States, held in Montevideo, Uruguay, Dec. 3–26, 1933. Gary was a Texas lawyer who had served in the Foreign Service in World War I and had been minister to Switzerland, 1920–21. There is no further reference to his proposed appointment and he was not on the delegation. See Roosevelt to Hull, July 27, 1933, below.


# Sumner Welles, Ambassador to Cuba, to Roosevelt

Habana, July 17, 1933

My dear Mr. President: Your letter of June 24th made me very happy.[1] I appreciate deeply what you were good enough to write. I am more than satisfied if what I have been attempting to accomplish here in Cuba merits your approval.

The situation in general is distinctly encouraging, far more so than I had hoped six weeks ago. President Machado and the three organized political parties of the Republic have formally accepted my tender of good offices, and every important faction in the opposition has taken the same action with the exception of the small and constantly diminishing group which surrounds General Menocal.[2] I am unable to attach very much importance to the student groups. While they have not expressed their approval of what we are trying to do, they at least have declared that they will suspend all terroristic activities. It is now twelve days since we commenced negotiations and I am happy to say that the various delegates are concentrating upon questions of principle, upon the need for changing the system rather than the individuals, and have modified very distinctly the uncompromising and unreasoning attitude which many at first maintained.

I think there is now a good chance that through a reform of the Constitution and through the utilization of the new electoral code which Professor McBain[3] is helping to draft, we can work out a fair and just solution of the political problem strictly within the lines of constitutional procedure. In this connection, I feel that I must have specific and personal instructions from you. At some time within the next two or three weeks, the suggestion will be made that after a Vice President satisfactory to all parties has been selected and has taken office, the President resign and make it thus possible for the Vice President to remain in entire control of the Government until a new Constitutional Government has been elected in November 1934. This means that President Machado will have to permit the Vice President to take control about May 1934. The term which he now is filling would normally expire in May of 1935. The reason for this suggestion, which to my mind must necessarily be acceded to by President Machado, is that no opposition party will go to the national elections in November 1934 if President Machado remains in control of the Government. They are confident that fair elections cannot be held so long as he remains in the Presidency. As I have reported several times to the Department, I have every reason to believe that President Machado will agree to take this action should he be permitted to take it of his own initiative and should it not be forced upon him as a condition by the opposition. The solution in my mind, furthermore, is fair to all concerned, inasmuch as the President's own party will have just as many guaranties in the person of the Vice President, in the new constitutional reforms, and in the new electoral code as the opposition parties will have. It is perfectly possible, in fact, as I now sum up the situation, that the candidate of the President's, the Liberal, party will be elected in 1934. Consequently, the only sacrifice that the President will have to make will be to shorten his term by one year, and you will recall that the last constitutional reform which made the President's re-election possible was accomplished in such a manner as to leave very grave doubt as to its legality and as to its conformity with the articles of the preceding Constitution.

In the same last constitutional reform—that of 1928—the Senators and Congressmen extended their own terms of office. No more striking blow at the principle of representative government can be conceived. These extended terms must, of course, all be cut in the new reform so that the entire Senate and House will be renewed in the general elections of 1934.

Moreover, if the opposition parties do not go to the elections of 1934, whoever is elected in those elections will have bitter opposition to him throughout the term for which he is elected, and, in all likelihood, we will again be confronted with a situation in Cuba identical with that through which we have just been passing.

I consider the plan suggested both reasonable and eminently fair to all concerned, and I wish to urge it upon President Machado as a patriotic solution of Cuba's problem when the time comes. I wish, however, to have your specific authorization to do this and I wish, further, to be authorized to tell him that such oral representations as I make to him in this sense are being made with your full knowledge and approval.

The ground is very well cleared now for me to commence immediately the negotiations for the revision of the commercial treaty. Cuban public opinion is, in general, thoroughly well satisfied with the treatment accorded Cuba in Washington in the Sugar Conferences.[4] If, when consumption of sugar in the United States once more returns to normal, Cuba is permitted to export into the United States 2,000,000 tons of sugar at a stabilized price, and with the added preferential advantage which I hope we will be authorized to give Cuba in the new commercial treaty, she will definitely be set upon her feet again, because her exports of sugar to the world market and local consumption of sugar total another million tons, and with a production of 3,000,000 tons of sugar annually, there is no reason why social conditions in Cuba should not improve materially, providing the next Government undertakes the passage of much needed social and economic legislation. We will likewise regain an exceedingly important market for our exports.

I am, of course, keeping the negotiation of the commercial treaty as a leverage until I know definitely where I stand on the political solution.

I cabled Bill Phillips the other day that I hoped very much that I could consider my portion of the Cuban task accomplished by the end of September and then return to the Department.[5] I am particularly anxious to take up the preliminary work for the inter-American Conference at Montevideo in December, which, in my judgment, if properly handled, can result in the greatest benefit to the United States.

The overwhelming success of the Administration during these four months has given me greater satisfaction than I can express.

Faithfully yours,

Sumner Welles

[OF 470:TS]

[1] Congratulating Welles on his accomplishments in Cuba (*Personal Letters, 1928–1945,* I, 354).

[2] Mario García Menocal, former president of Cuba, at this time in the United States as leader of the anti-Machado party.

[3] Howard Lee McBain, professor of government and public law at Columbia, had been in Havana since June 1933 as an adviser to the Cuban government on revision of the Cuban constitution.

[4] See Phillips to Roosevelt, June 29, 1933, above.

[5] Welles's mission to Cuba was interrupted by the disturbances there but he remained during the early months of the Grau San Martín presidency. He returned to the State Department as an assistant secretary on Dec. 15, 1933. See press conference of Aug. 9, 1933, below. For his dispatches as ambassador, see *Foreign Relations, 1933,* V, 279ff.

# Breckinridge Long, Ambassador to Italy, to Roosevelt

Rome, Italy, July 17, 1933

My dear Chief: Arthur Henderson of Great Britain of the Disarmament Conference was here Saturday to talk to the Italian Government, and I had a long talk with him.[1] He had seen Mussolini twice, and he was definite in his statement that Mussolini had told him that he would go along with him on the modifications which he is proposing to the MacDonald Plan and that he would do everything he could to help get the Germans into line. Henderson was very pleased over the situation which exists in Italy but somewhat discouraged about France, though he has hopes that France will agree. He has tried to get the French to say any one definite thing. They talk about security and the necessity for security and the need for armament and say that they will give the minimum of disarmament for the minimum of security and the maximum of disarmament for the maximum of security. But when asked directly to name the minimum of disarmament they are evasive and non-committal. And when requested to name the maximum of disarmament they are not responsive. However, he thinks that his plan in modification of the MacDonald Plan, and which substitutes a period of eight years for the five of the MacDonald Plan and which divides the eight years into two of four each, can be worked out so as to obtain the adherence of France. The French call the first of the four-year periods the trial period. He says he prefers to call it the period of transition, because then it does not reflect upon Germany. During the first four years no actual steps in disarmament would be made but the process would begin and the preparations be undertaken. During the next four years disarmament would actually commence.

The Permanent Commission will select twenty-four men and divide them into six groups and divide the world into six geographical divisions and assign one group to each geographical division and require that it make a complete survey of the geographical division during the year and that as it visits each country it will report directly to the Secretary-General of the Commission who will be in constant touch with the Permanent President, and that the Permanent President will have the authority to convene in extraordinary and urgent session the members of the Permanent Commission in case of an adverse or alarming report from any group in any country.

As these groups visit each country there will be attached to it a fifth member by the country under inspection. The general make-up of the four members of the group would be a military man, a technical expert, a lawyer, and a man of general political experience and understanding who would probably be the Chairman of the division.

Henderson is hopeful about getting something out of France, but he feels that she is obdurate and is the main obstacle in Europe to the securement of any substantial agreement. He feels that Hitler has fortified the French position somewhat and justified it in the French mind, but he thought that his speech to the Reichstag had helped a lot.

He is very critical of the Japanese and strangely enough he proposed the same thing about which you once spoke to me—that if all the world could agree, except Japan, to have everybody sign the document and let Japan stand alone in opposition and be held responsible in the eyes of the world for having prevented disarmament.

He talked about his conversation with Sato[2] in which Sato insisted that they could not agree to anything less than 155's nor to anything less than 30-ton tanks and that they insisted on an increased naval ratio, and that he had said to Sato that he had probably made a mistake and come to the wrong Conference, that this Conference was for *dis*armament.[3]

He thinks that if you and England give the final push that France can be made to agree. Personally I do not see how you can do anything special to induce France, because you probably would not consider a guarantee of any kind to go to the aid of France. Of course that is what France is angling for. But she should not expect it and could not reasonably ask for it for the very fact of disarmament is in itself a guarantee, particularly when it is carried out under the strict supervision of an international authority.

Henderson said that he had heard in London that Norman Davis might not come back to Europe, but he said that if he was to come back he hoped that he would come in September rather than in October to the meeting because there was a lot of preparatory work to be done.[4]

Henderson is quite antagonistic to MacDonald, and I understood from his remarks that the MacDonald Plan was really Henderson's plan which MacDonald had stolen. Of course they are bitter political enemies.

I also saw on Saturday Dr. T. V. Soong of China. He feels that Japan has the ambition to absorb the whole of China and the maritime provinces of Russia and with her position solidified there that she will then embark on what he considers to be their definite ambition to dominate the world. There is no doubt about the fact that that is the definite conception in the mind of Soong. But he hopes to have the world align itself against Japan. He feels that some day the rest of the world will be forced to take an attitude to stop Japan and her aggression. He hopes it can be done by diplomatic means and he trusts that Manchuria will be evacuated under diplomatic pressure as was Shantung. But failing that, he looks to see the rest of the world lined against Japan. He said that he had been talking to the French and to the Italians and to the English. The French assured him that they would at the proper time take their stand. He told me definitely that Mussolini had told him that Italy would take its stand. He said that the British did not commit themselves and had called the Japanese trouble "an American problem" and said that they looked to us to stop Japan because we had a large interest in the Pacific.

The London Conference has been, as you know, very unpopular in all the capitals of Europe and a good many criticisms have been leveled against the American policy. But I think the sober reaction is setting in and that they see that the only sensible thing for America to do is just what you are doing. As corroborative of that change in public opinion I talked the other day to Tevfik Bey, the Minister of Foreign Affairs of Turkey on his way back from the Conference. He said that he thought that you were entirely right and fully justified from any point of view and that it would have been not only impractical but unwise for you to interrupt the process of the "experiment," as he expressed it, on which you are engaged in America and that you could not be expected to make a commitment which would have interfered with it. Present at the same time was Von Hassell,[5] the German Ambassador here and several others, and I was very glad to hear that statement definitely made in public by one other than an American and by one who had been in London and to the representatives of governments here who have themselves been hostile toward your point of view.

The Italians themselves have been very mild and quiet as compared to the others.

I am glad that Dodd has got to Germany, and I wonder if it wouldn't be well sometime, with your permission, for he and I to meet in Switzerland quietly somewhere over the week-end, not at Geneva and not at Berne, but say at Lausanne or Vevey or some such innocuous place. I really think it would help us each to a more cooperative understanding. I wrote that to him and asked him to speak to you about it, but in his answer he mentioned the probability of our meeting but didn't say if he had discussed it with you.

I am sorry to write you at such length again, but I do feel that you want me to tell you fully about some of these things.

With every good wish and with expressions of affectionate and respectful regard, I am, Yours very sincerely,

Breckinridge Long[6]

[PSF:Italy:TS]

[1] Concerning Henderson's post-conference conversations with the delegates and national leaders, see *British Documents, 1919–1939*, V, 376ff.

[2] Naotake Sato, ambassador to France, 1933–1936; delegate to the League of Nations from 1931 to 1932.

[3] The first syllable was underscored.

[4] Davis sailed for England Aug. 30, 1933, and conferred with Henderson in London on September 14.

[5] Ulrich von Hassell.

[6] Roosevelt sent this letter to Davis with a note of Aug. 14, 1933 (PSF:Italy): "I think the enclosed will be of real interest to you. Breck Long is, of course, at one of the good listening posts. Please let me have it back when you have read it."

## The Committee for the Nation to Roosevelt

New York, N. Y., July 20, 1933

[*Telegram*] The President, The White House: Referring again to our conference at White House,[1] we feel that the present emergency in the general commodity markets is such as to call for immediate and drastic action, especially inasmuch as all recent advances have reflected merely the anticipation of future governmental action to correct the country's monetary system.

Yesterday's news reports from London concerning the visit of our most prominent international banker[2] stated that he expected to see Montagu Norman and quoted him as saying, "I should not be surprised if currency stabilization were discussed." This has led the public to fear again British influence over the purchasing power of the American dollar. The public is accepting Mr. Morgan's statement as a substantiation of the rumor current over the past ten days that currency stabilization between England and the United States would be effected through the central banks of European countries cooperating with the Federal Reserve rather than by governmental action.

Our committee, having at heart the interests of the entire country and the success of your administration's program, desires to express firm conviction that immediate presidential action is needed to prevent further weakening of price structure, buying power and industrial activity.

We urge immediate establishment of open market for gold bullion, which will place the price structure under your control without relinquishing restrictions on bank withdrawals of coin or lifting of export embargo. Your administration can immediately control the open market price of gold and thereby lift and control general level of commodity prices, gradually feeling out the proper point for revaluation. You will have the enthusiastic support of the majority of business men and voters and disarm those reactionaries who advocate free play of the law of supply and demand.

Committee For The Nation,[3]
J. H. Rand, Jr.
Lessing J. Rosenwald
F. H. Sexauer
Frederic H. Frazier
Vincent Bendix

[OF 230:T]

[1] On April 13, 1933 (PPF 1-0).

[2] J. P. Morgan had sailed for England on July 13.

[3] The Committee for the Nation was formed early in March 1933 to offer advice and plans for dealing with the financial crisis. Composed largely of business executives and representatives of large concerns, the committee lobbied for an inflationary program. G. F. Warren and Irving Fisher were hired by it as economic advisers; the guiding spirit was James H. Rand, Jr., of the Rand Corporation. The group had wide support among smaller businessmen, particularly for the gold-buying program that it advocated during the summer and fall of 1933. The correspondence of the committee with the White House, extending into 1936, is extensive and includes copies of many of its publications (OF 5707).

## Press Conference, Executive Offices of the White House, July 21, 1933, 4:18 P.M.

[*Excerpt*] Q: Can you tell us when the Anglo-American debt negotiations will begin?

The President: I haven't heard a word.

Q: It has been reported that they would not begin until the first of September, since you are going to be away.

The President: I don't think there was any intention of having it before the first of September.

Q: Will Moley conduct those negotiations? The report is going around that he is going to have a definite assignment on that.

The President: No machinery has been thought of and no date has been set . . .[1]

Q: Do you care to discuss the temporary demise of the London Conference, for background?

The President: How do you mean, temporary demise? (Laughter)

Q: As the British say, "Not quite dead, but dead."

The President: No, Fred,[2] I think the only thing I can do is to talk to you off the record on that. Of course, it makes much better reading for a story to say that when the damn thing adjourns it will never come back.[3] That is news. But actually, I do not think it is correct news because they have, in the past two or three weeks, been taking up seriously a good many of the important things that are in the agenda and they seem to be getting somewhere on quite a number of things. For example, I hope they will get something on wheat that will lead, even if it does not go as far as we want, to a later and more definite agreement.[4] I hope that Key Pittman will get something out of the silver thing that will lead to better things a little later on.[5] It is my personal hope that when they do go away on the twenty-seventh, they should come back after the grouse-shooting season is over and the spa season is over and do a lot more work. They may stay through what the British call Michaelmas.

Q: Is there any prospect that it will be resumed in Washington?

The President: Not that I heard of.

Q: Have you made any decision on the gold export?

The President: That has not been talked of at all. The only thing about gold export would be that the Attorney General is giving some kind of a ruling on what is "gold" to the Treasury Department. I have not seen it yet.[6]

Q: Is that the point about ore, whether you can export it or not?

The President: Yes.

[President's Press Conferences:T]

[1] After Moley returned, Howe offered him an assignment to study the administration of criminal justice in Hawaii. Moley regarded this as an attempt to ease him out of the government gracefully and refused the job; however, he accepted another offer, this time from the President, to study the kidnapping problem for the Justice Department (*After Seven Years,* pp. 274–275). Moley finally resigned Sept. 7, 1933. His letter of resignation of August 27 and Roosevelt's letter of acceptance of the same date are printed *ibid.,* pp. 422–423, 423. He continued to serve occasionally in an advisory capacity to Roosevelt and on Oct. 18, 1933, Roosevelt, in endorsing him for membership in a New York club, referred to him as "an old friend of mine." They exchanged letters frequently until late in 1935 (PPF 743). Thereafter there appears to have been little contact, particularly after 1937, when Moley vigorously opposed the President's plan for enlarging the Supreme Court.

[2] Jesse Frederick Essary of the Baltimore *Sun.*

[3] The London Conference recessed on July 26, 1933, and was not reconvened, although some committees continued their negotiations through August. Hull delivered his closing address to the Conference on July 27 and sailed for home that evening on the *President Harding.* His report on the Conference, Aug. 5, 1933, is printed in *Foreign Relations, 1933,* I, 736–747. Before he sailed he received a cable from Roosevelt, assuring him of his regard and confidence and inviting him to Hyde Park (*ibid.,* p. 734). Roosevelt and MacDonald exchanged friendly messages on July 26 and August 5 (*ibid.,* pp. 734–735). The President said that something had been gained in the way of mutual understanding and MacDonald said that he hoped that in future it would be possible to prevent the rigid attitude of the gold bloc from stopping international agreements.

[4] A wheat agreement was signed on Aug. 25, 1933 (*ibid.,* pp. 787–825).

[5] A silver agreement was signed in London July 26, 1933, with the United States one of the signators (*ibid.,* pp. 763–764).

[6] See press conference of July 14, 1933, above.

## Esther E. Lape, Member in Charge, The American Foundation, to Roosevelt

New York, July 21, 1933

Dear Franklin: I do not know in how great detail Eleanor may have passed on my request.[1]

Let me emphasize only these points:

(1) That the group that wants to come to Hyde Park to talk with you includes, besides the members of our Committee (see this letterhead) and representatives of the Russian-American Chamber of Commerce, certain business men of the country eminently qualified to speak, not only by reason of their business weight and direct experience but also by reason of their personal calibre.[2]

(2) That your own interest in recognition is, of course, assumed by the group; what they want is not to discuss with you the general question of recognition but to present their views and their information as to general approaches to the present situation, and as to certain immediate practical possibilities which they consider to be of great importance.

(3) That the group hopes you might care to segregate perhaps two hours to discuss the question with them at Hyde Park as early in August as is practicable.

You will know, I think, that I would not suggest our coming at this time, when so many domestic measures of first importance are crowding you, if I did not believe that these men have an estimate, both practical and comprehensive, of the present situation which you will want to take into account before the matter of recognition is further advanced.[3]

Faithfully, and with good wishes always,

Esther

[OF 220-A:TS]

---

[1] Miss Lape's request was made in three letters to Mrs. Roosevelt of July 10, 12 and 18, 1933 (Group 8); she suggested that a twenty-member Committee on Russian-American Relations (of which she was one) from the American Foundation meet with the President in August or September. In her first letter she said that with the group would be "certain businessmen of authority" who were not members of the committee but who were interested in trade with Russia. The committee did not propose to urge recognition of Russia on the President but wished to make him acquainted with "certain questions of procedure and certain points of view."

[2] Among the members were Curtis Bok; Thomas S. Gates, president of the University of Pennsylvania; George H. Houston, president of Baldwin Locomotive Works; Thomas

W. Lamont, of J. P. Morgan and Co.; Dean Roscoe Pound of the Harvard Law School; and David B. Robertson, president of the Brotherhood of Locomotive Engineers.

[3] Answered July 28, 1933, below.

## James P. Warburg to Roosevelt

[Washington] July 24, 1933

Memorandum for the President: Domestic Currency Problem

The Administration has, in my judgment, never faced a more serious situation than it does today. The entire recovery program, which is the heart of its policy, is jeopardized by uncertainty and doubt in the monetary field. The National Recovery Act cannot possibly function to any useful end if there is fear of currency depreciation of an unknown amount and fear as to monetary experimentation. There has already been a tremendous flight of capital, and this flight will continue at an increasing pace so long as uncertainty prevails.

Furthermore, while the threat of inflation originally acted as a stimulus to buying of commodities, and therefore as a stimulus to production and trade, it is obvious that the rise of prices and production, stimulated by fear of money, has far outstripped reality and now constitutes a menace in itself.

In the international field, the feeling that we were embarked upon a well-ordered program is rapidly shifting into a feeling that we are fumbling about in the dark, and the result of a continuation of our present undefined monetary policy will inevitably result in further monetary chaos in other countries. The line of probable events is perfectly clear but too long a story to include in this memorandum.

I therefore urgently recommend the following:

1. That all monetary ideas, projects and studies be concentrated in one place, and it would seem to me that the logical place would be the Treasury Department (and the Federal Reserve Board.)

2. That it be decided now what authorities are to be consulted in preparing a definite monetary program; and that a commission be formed of these authorities immediately; and that this commission be given not over a month to prepare a recommendation to the Treasury.

3. That the terms of reference for the commission be defined as follows:

(a) That the United States Government desires not later than October

1st to fix the amount of devaluation which is desired in order to bring about the necessary adjustment of the price level, allowing for a subsequent variation of not over 10%.

(b) That the United States Government desires to enter into conversations as soon as possible with the other countries now off gold with a view to their likewise fixing their ratios to gold with a variation of 10% at the same time that we fix ours. (As a matter of practice it is only necessary to agree with England because the rest will fall into line. This involves at least a tentative debt settlement.)

(c) Acting on assumptions (a) and (b), the commission is asked to determine two things:

A. What amount of devaluation should be fixed for the United States dollar. For example, if a seventy cent dollar is the answer, this would mean a definite declaration that devaluation will not exceed 35% or be less than 25%, the actual figure to be determined over a period of time.

B. What should be the exact nature of the gold standard to which the United States returns in the Autumn? How can the pre-war gold standard be improved, and how can the purchasing power of the currency be rendered more stable without resorting to methods so academic and so untried that their adoption would in itself again disturb confidence?

I believe it is perfectly possible for the commission to evolve an improved gold standard, and I have a definite idea as to how a gold standard can be made more likely to provide price stability than it did in the past. I believe further that in a program such as is outlined above, we would have the active support not only of Great Britain and the Dominions, but of the Scandinavian countries and eventually even of the gold countries. The result would be that in the Autumn the off-gold countries would return to a ratio to gold on an improved gold standard and that the gold countries would very quickly adopt the new standard, some of them possibly taking this opportunity to revalue their currencies overnight without ever getting into the position of running amuck as we are doing at the present moment. If such a program is not adopted, I foresee grave danger not only domestically in the breakdown of our entire program, but internationally, in that by the time we are compelled to stabilize in the interests of our domestic picture, the present gold countries will have gone off gold and will be just where we are today.[1]

J. P. Warburg

[PSF:London Economic Conference:T]

[1] See Warburg to Roosevelt, Aug. 14, 1933, below.

## [*Enclosure*] Draft by James P. Warburg of a Proposed Letter from Roosevelt to Prime Minister MacDonald

[July 24, 1933]

[*Notation*:A:FDR] (Not sent—This was Jimmy Warburg's draft. File under Warburg)[1]

My dear Prime Minister: When you and I had our talks here in Washington only a little more than two months ago, and laid our plans for the World Monetary and Economic Conference, I little thought that I should so soon be addressing you on the subject of its adjournment. Had I been able to foresee then the march of events within my country which have necessitated so complete a change of policy in monetary matters, I should have told you in all frankness that I did not believe the time had come for the United States to participate in a conference of this sort. I should have told you that monetary stability was out of the question for some months to come, and I should not have urged upon you and the representatives of other nations that the Conference be held this summer. It has been a source of profound regret to me that events have followed the unpredictable path they have taken, and that, as a consequence, the United States has been the stormy petrel of the Conference. It is idle to deny that this is so. The Conference, so far as accomplishing tangible results is concerned, has been a failure, and the reason for its failure is that developments here have altered some of the basic premises upon which it was called into being. No one could realize this more clearly, or regret it more sincerely than I, but I should have been remiss in discharging my duty as President of the United States if I had not heeded the storm signals and altered the course of my vessel accordingly.

I am not afraid to say that in a practical sense the Conference has been a failure, because to my mind there is one thing worse that could have befallen us and that is a spurious success. If we had gone on as if nothing had happened, and had reached a series of illusory agreements, the Conference might have adjourned in a blaze of glory and the hopes of the world would have been raised to an entirely unjustifiable extent, only to be shattered irremediably by the inevitable spectacle of one agreement after another being rendered void by the inexorable progress of events.

By reason of the fact that this Conference has failed and not feared to avow its failure, it has to my mind accomplished much to redeem the self-respect and restore the courage of mankind. You, as President of the Conference, have done a heroic job under the most trying circumstances, and I am deeply grateful to you and to all the participants in the Conference for your perseverance on the one hand and your forbearance on the other. Events move at all times more rapidly in one part of the world than in another. The center of activity is constantly shifting throughout all history. It was the ill fortune of my country that it should happen to become the focal point of change at a time when rapid change anywhere spelled disaster for the deliberations of a World Conference. Your forbearance bears witness to your realization that a few months one way or the other might easily have cast some other country into this unpleasant role.

Let me say also one other thing to you and to all the nations today assembled for the last time at this session in Kensington. America is not, as so many people conclude, embarking upon economic nationalism and isolation. America will again devote herself to neighborliness when she has put her own house in order, unreservedly and, I hope, soon. We must all solve our problems and conquer our difficulties by our own will and our own strength, realizing that in putting ourselves in order quickly we are making it that much easier for others to do likewise, and realizing also that we must not achieve our own success through measures that will bring distress and disorder upon the other nations of the world.

It is my earnest hope that America will soon have found the way out of the wilderness and that she will then be able to extend the helping hand to others who have not yet reached the goal.

[PSF:London Economic Conference:T]

[1] This draft and the memorandum were probably handed to Roosevelt by Warburg when they had lunch together at the White House on July 24 (PPF 1-0). No part of the draft was used; the message actually sent (printed under date of July 26 in *Foreign Relations, 1933,* I, 734–735) was merely a brief expression of good will.

# Roosevelt to Breckinridge Long, Ambassador to Italy, Rome

[Washington] July 25, 1933

Dear Breck: I have not time to write you at length but I do want to tell you that I appreciate your letters. Your description of modern

Italy is splendid and gives me a very clear picture of the very great changes which have taken place.

As ever yours,

[PPF 434:CT]

## Roosevelt to Jesse Isador Straus, Ambassador to France, Paris

[Washington] July 26, 1933

My dear Ambassador: I am glad to have your letter of July 11th, which explains so fully and comprehensively the unhappy situation affecting members of the Foreign Service in Europe.[1]

I fully appreciate the unfortunate conditions which you describe and have already taken up with the State and Treasury Departments the question of a plan of making salary payments in gold or its equivalent. Mr. Phillips tells me that he has sent you a telegram stating that he is momentarily expecting a reply from the Treasury Department, which, with the Federal Reserve Board, has been working out a formula.[2] I confidently expect that the desired relief will be forthcoming shortly.[3]

Sincerely yours,

[OF 67:CT]

[1] Straus's letter (OF 67) was a long explanation of the effect on Foreign Service personnel of the decline in purchasing power of the dollars in which they were paid. He urged that immediate relief be given by payment of their salaries in gold as was done in the case of Navy people in the Far East.

[2] Quoted by Under Secretary of State Phillips in a letter to Roosevelt of July 26, 1933 (OF 67); Phillips said the President was sympathetic to the idea but there were technical difficulties to be cleared away.

[3] This letter was drafted by Phillips.

## Roosevelt to Mrs. Eliot Cross, Old Westbury, New York

[Washington] July 27, 1933

Dear Martha: Do please excuse this typewritten letter, but I am trying hard to catch up with my correspondence in order that I may get off to Hyde Park on Friday.

It is grand to hear from you and I do hope that you will be able to run down to Washington some day soon and see us. If you see Jean before she goes back to England do give her my love and tell her that I hope her English friends will not think my manners rough, but that a little plain conversation seemed to be the only way to make everybody understand what everybody else was driving at in the Conference.[1]

Very sincerely yours,

[PPF 673:CT]

[1] Mrs. (Martha McCook) Cross's letter (PPF 673) is undated; her husband was a Harvard friend of Roosevelt. She congratulated him on his achievements since his inauguration and quoted her friend, Jean Ward, recently arrived from England, to the same effect.

## Roosevelt to Cordell Hull, Secretary of State

[Washington] July 27, 1933

Memorandum for Secretary Hull: Will you speak to me about this when you get back?

F.D.R.

[*Notation*:CT] Letter of June 23, 1933, from Ambassador Daniels requesting that he be named a delegate to the International Conference of American States.[1]

[OF 567:CT]

[1] Daniels' letter is not present and presumably was not returned to the White House.

## Roosevelt to John S. Lawrence, Chairman, New England Council, Boston

[Washington] July 27, 1933

Dear John: It was good to get your note.[1] I don't mind telling you in confidence that I am keeping in fairly close touch with the admirable Italian gentleman.

I do wish I could have seen you on that cruise. We had a grand time.

Sincerely yours,

[PPF 101:CT]

[1] Lawrence's letter of July 18, 1933 (PPF 110), commented on the probable breakup of the London Conference. On conferences in general he said: "To get effective results a really aggressive leader is needed, and I am wondering if you could not persuade Mussolini to call one, and preside over it. He has a marvelous trading position, a united nation, full of guts and an army that talks turkey as you know . . ." Lawrence was a prominent Boston merchant and state chairman for Massachusetts of the New England Council. The Lawrences were old friends of the Roosevelts, and during the 1920's Roosevelt and Lawrence had jointly bought the houseboat *Larooco,* which they used for several winter cruises off the Florida coast.

## Roosevelt to Louis Wiley, Business Manager, The New York *Times,* New York

[Washington] July 27, 1933

Dear Louis: Many thanks for sending me those interesting quotations from Sir Robert Horne's letter.[1] I think he appreciates that orthodoxy may not be the only method for nations, any more than for individuals, to get to Heaven.

I do hope to see you one of these days.[2]

Very sincerely yours,

[PPF 675:CT]

[1] Wiley, in a letter of July 19, 1933 (PPF 675), quoted from a letter he had that day received from Horne, a member of the House of Commons. Horne quoted from his speech in Commons of July 10, 1933: "When the Chancellor said in his speech to the Conference that we must prevent wide fluctuations in the purchasing power of gold in so far as it is due to monetary causes, he is echoed by the President, who puts it thus: that we must so arrange matters in the future that a man who incurs a debt today will not find it a heavier burden when the obligation comes to be discharged because of a change in the monetary unit. Although the liturgical language is different the religion is the same. The real fact is that we cannot disassociate ourselves from the policy which the United States has adopted."
[2] Answered July 31, 1933, below.

## Roosevelt to Frederick H. Allen, New York

[Washington] July 28, 1933

My dear Allen: I have been trying to find some possible method of having the Académie over here, but government funds are, I fear, wholly out of the question.

Another thing occurs to me, and that is that this particular autumn is not a particularly propitious time to have any international gathering here in Washington![1]

With best wishes, Sincerely yours,

[PPF 692:CT]

[1] Allen, a New York attorney (Allen and Camman) with a wide acquaintance among European political figures, had written July 13, 1933 (PPF 692), about securing financial aid for a meeting of the Académie Diplomatique Internationale in the United States. He suggested that such a meeting might be of great interest in presenting the European viewpoint and in acquainting European leaders with American attitudes, and asked for suggestions on possible financial backers of such a meeting. This reply was drafted by Under Secretary of State Phillips.

## Roosevelt to Louis M. Howe, Personal Secretary to the President

Washington, July 28, 1933

Memorandum for Mr. Howe: It has been suggested that it would help us in our negotiations with Chile if we could use, say five percent of Chilean nitrate out of the total amount we buy. I understand we are buying 100 percent American nitrate at the present time. Will you look into this with the War and Navy Departments?[1]

F.D.R.

[Howe Papers:CT]

[1] Howe turned the President's suggestion over to C. J. Peoples, paymaster general of the Navy, who wrote to him July 31, 1933 (Howe papers), that neither the Navy nor any other agency was in the market for nitrate. He said the Navy had enough left from World War stocks to supply its needs for some years and the Army was also well supplied. He added that the nitrate needs of the United States could now be supplied by plants that extracted nitrogen from the air.

## Roosevelt to Esther E. Lape, Member in Charge, The American Foundation, New York

[Washington] July 28, 1933

Dear Esther: Eleanor sent me your letter[1] and I would like very much to have you come up and talk to me. However, quite frankly, I feel that I should not see the group of which you speak. I could have no group come to me at Hyde Park, or anywhere for that matter, really privately. It would be taken as an out and out announcement of recognition.

Can you come up to Hyde Park on Friday, August fourth, for lunch and we can talk at that time.[2]

I am just off, so please excuse the brevity of this note.[3]

Always sincerely yours,

[OF 220-A:CT]

[1] July 21, 1933, above.
[2] No such visit is noted in the appointments list but visits of friends were not always entered.
[3] Roosevelt left for Hyde Park that evening; he returned on August 12 (PPF 1-0).

## Roosevelt to William Gorham Rice, New York State Civil Service Commission, Albany

[Washington] July 28, 1933

My dear Colonel Rice: Do you mind if I tell you that I was somewhat surprised and much concerned at your letter of June twenty-ninth and that is the reason why I have not written you before?[1] I fear you have not understood that an Ambassador or a Minister holds an appointment wholly and solely at the pleasure of the President and there is no such thing as a "term of office."

It was only as a matter of courtesy and convenience to you and to a number of other gentlemen that, in asking them to go to a foreign post, I have told them it was entirely possible that at the end of a year or later, I might ask them to return home. In one case I told the appointee that it was possible that I might ask him to come home after an even shorter interval. Though, as a matter of fact, subsequent developments are such that he will stay at his present post for a year or longer. You were the only one, apparently, who failed to understand that diplomatic appointments are wholly personal with, and at the pleasure of, the President.

I think that I have made the situation wholly clear. If you care to go to The Hague as Minister of the United States, I shall be very glad to make the appointment immediately, but I must ask you for an immediate decision.[2]

Very sincerely yours,

[PPF 288:CT]

[1] See Roosevelt to Rice, June 16, 1933, above.

[2] Rice replied Aug. 1, 1933 (PPF 288), that he had always realized that ambassadors and ministers held their appointments at the pleasure of the President, but that he did not see his way clear to agreeing in advance to leaving a diplomatic post at the end of a year except for reason of incapacity. No further reference to the proposed appointment has been found.

## Raymond B. Stevens, Federal Trade Commission, to Roosevelt

Washington, July 28, 1933

Dear Mr. President: I am enclosing a brief memorandum I have prepared on the Corporation of Foreign Security Holders.

In the memorandum I have devoted more space to the international aspect because of my own personal experience in the last seven years in acting as an advisor for the government of a small country. In fact I consider, however, the political reaction against your administration as the more serious consequence.

Practically all of the foreign bonds now in default were issued in the last twelve years during Republican rule of "the best minds." Being certain that the machinery provided by Article II is fundamentally wrong in principle and will not produce satisfactory results, I am, as a Democrat, seriously concerned to see your administration assume an obligation for a situation which occurred under Republican rule, and for which you are in no sense responsible.

Very cordially yours,

Raymond B. Stevens

As a striking example of the public misunderstanding of the results the work of the "Corporation" will accomplish, I enclose an article published in The New York *Times* of Tuesday this week and based on an interview with Chairman March! Please read it.[1]

[OF 100-B:TS]

[1] Charles March, chairman of the Federal Trade Commission, said the corporation would deal directly with the foreign government but would not represent the United States government; rather it would act as agent for the individual holders of defaulted foreign bonds (New York *Times,* July 25, 1933, p. 27).

## [*Enclosure*] Raymond B. Stevens to Roosevelt

Corporation of Foreign Security Holders

The Corporation under Article II is in fact a government instrument. The statements in Section 210 that neither the Corporation nor any person or persons acting for it shall claim or assert or pretend to be acting for or to represent the United States Government is mere verbal denial of the reality.

All foreign debtors and foreign governments will consider and rightly consider that the Corporation represents the Government of the United States. Furthermore all holders of foreign securities will also consider and rightly consider that the Government of the United States is attempting for them to collect the interest and principal due on their foreign holdings.

Two very serious consequences will result from the fact that the Corporation is a government agency.

(1) It will complicate our foreign relations since there will be two organizations, the Department of State and the Corporation which will be dealing with foreign governments. This is certain to lead to controversies between the two organizations.

The fact that the Corporation is a government agency will in practice make it more difficult to arrange reasonable and amicable settlements or collections. On this point I speak from practical experience. For seven years I have been advisor to the Government of Siam on its foreign affairs. Whenever a foreign government has taken up with the Siamese Government matters which were not of national interest but questions of private claims and private interests of its citizens, the immediate reaction is one of suspicion, fear and resentment. Negotiations of this kind have only been successful when conducted with great tact and when there was clear and obvious justice in the suggestion, or it was obviously for the interest of the Siamese Government to accept the proposals made. Even in these cases such action still leaves a feeling of suspicion and fear. No debtor loves his creditor and when the creditor's agents appear garbed with the authority of a government even though no threats are made or no improper pressure applied, the mere fact that the authority of the government is behind the creditor makes a settlement difficult to obtain. A private organization representing bondholders can conduct negotiations more efficiently and more successfully.

(2) There are many hundred thousand holders of foreign securities. In addition many more are indirectly interested because of the holdings

by insurance companies and savings banks. Inevitably these people will expect far greater results from the operation of the "Corporation of Foreign Security Holders" than is possible to secure even with the wisest and most efficient management. The political reaction against the administration is bound to be unfavorable.

There is a marked and essential difference between the "Corporation of Foreign Security Holders" and the various organizations which have been created in European countries, notably England, France, the Netherlands, etc. The European organizations are in fact private associations of bondholders and banks. These organizations are subject to some government control and also secure the aid of the government in their negotiations but only in so far as the government deems consistent with national interest.

The purpose underlying Article II of the Securities Bill is a good one. Unfortunately the method set up is fundamentally wrong and cannot be cured by wise and efficient administration. It is far safer to postpone any action on the matter until a proper method of aiding foreign bondholders can be worked out. This is not a task of difficulty or one that should require a great deal of time.

The proposal embodied in Article II of the Securities Bill holds out little possibility of real help and is certain to have unfortunate consequences both abroad and at home.[1]

Raymond B. Stevens

[OF 100-B:TS]

[1] See Roosevelt to Johnson, July 31, 1933, below.


# William E. Dodd, Ambassador to Germany, to Roosevelt

[Berlin] July 30, 1933

My dear Mr. President: In obedience to your request for a personal report occasionally, I venture a short preliminary note.[1] There are ample documents in the files of Messrs Phillips and Carr[2] of the State Department to support what I shall say.

It is impossible as yet to say whether the new regime here is going to take a more liberal or a more ruthless direction. From conversations I have had with von Neurath,[3] the head of the Foreign Office, and Luther who returns to Washington as ambassador, both of whom had been in touch with the Reichskanzler, it is my guess they take a more moderate course. One must remember always that German statesmen and even *gelehrte männer* are quite adolescent in their analyses of international problems. The people have never learned the give-and-take group compromises which English and American leaders always apply. They are much concerned here about United States attitudes, but hardly know how to ease down off their dangerous position. This applies especially to the Jewish persecutions.

On the question of debts falling due to American citizens, the bankers of both sides have worked out a compromise fairly satisfactory to both parties. This agreement will stand as long as export-import situation holds steady. Any serious set back in foreign trade would jeopardize everything, including present ease-up in unemployment situation. This matter, like the other, is then in doubt, but leaning toward favorable outcome.

A great deal might be said about the diplomatic and consular service in which some changes are in order, but this subject will receive fuller attention after certain reports are completed. It is my judgment that war, navy and commerce personal [*sic*] can be greatly reduced and the budget considerably reduced. Many of the men are engaged in duplicating each other. We all look forward with confidence to the success of your great work.

Yours sincerely,

William E. Dodd

[OF 523:AS]

[1] Dodd had arrived in Berlin on July 13 but was not received by President Hindenburg until August 30; his status in the interval was the occasion for several exchanges between the State Department and our Embassy in Berlin (*Foreign Relations, 1933,* II, 381–385).

[2] Wilbur J. Carr, Assistant Secretary of State.

[3] Baron Konstantin von Neurath, Minister of Foreign Affairs from 1932 to 1938.


# Roosevelt to Benjamin F. Castle, New York

Hyde Park, New York, July 31, 1933

My dear Mr. Castle: Many thanks for letting me see that interesting quotation from the Belgian banker's letter. Apparently more people on the Continent are coming to the same view.[1]

Sincerely yours,

[OF 229:CT]

[1] Castle, a New York investment banker, in a letter of July 26, 1933 (OF 229), had quoted at length from the Belgian banker's letter (not further identified). The banker said Roosevelt had been right in refusing to accept the stabilization proposal made at the London Conference; that England had gone off the gold standard in September 1931 and had not yet stabilized. France had "kept francs going up and down" for four years; she and other European countries wanted to retain existing low prices on raw materials because of the advantage this gave them in the export market.

## Roosevelt to Senator Hiram Johnson, San Francisco, California

Hyde Park, New York, July 31, 1933

My dear Senator: I have been giving much consideration to the proposed Corporation of Foreign Security Holders and while I have not yet definitely made up my mind, I am inclined to agree with the inclosed personal memorandum from Raymond Stevens.[1] As you know, he is a real Progressive and talks our language. If I could get somebody thoroughly trustworthy, like George Rublee,[2] to organize a Foreign Security Holders Committee on a basis of very low cost to the bond holders and wholly nonprofit-making, we could throw the official approval of the Federal Trade Commission behind such a committee by having the committee ask the approval of the Commission for the issuance of certificates of deposit.

Because this amendment was your child I want to keep in touch with you on it.

Will you send Stevens' letter back to me, as it is wholly unofficial.

I do hope you are getting a bit of rest this summer. We have just moved to Hyde Park but I shall be back in Washington for ten days on the eleventh of August.[3]

As ever yours,

[OF 100-B:CT]

[1] July 28, 1933, above.
[2] Rublee, at this time adviser to the Colombian government, had been a member of the Federal Trade Commission under Wilson.
[3] Johnson answered Aug. 26, 1933, below.

## Louis Wiley, Business Manager, The New York *Times,*
to Roosevelt

[New York] July 31, 1933

*Personal*

Dear Mr. President: I am encouraged by your note of July 27[1] to enclose to you confidentially copies of letters received from Lord London-derry, British Air Minister,[2] and Lord Derby.[3] I send them to you, not as an agent of Great Britain or for the purpose of influencing your judgment, but to give you an impression of what leading Britishers are thinking.

I am following with the keenest interest your courageous and intelligent efforts to restore our prosperity and happiness.

With regards, Sincerely yours,

Louis Wiley

[PPF 675:TS]

[1] Above.
[2] Charles Stewart, marquess of Londonderry.
[3] Edward G. Villiers Stanley, War Secretary, 1916–1918, 1922–1924.

## [*Enclosure 1*] Lord Londonderry, British Minister for Air,
to Louis Wiley

[London] 21st July 1933

*Confidential*

Dear Mr. Wiley: If there is one fact that stands out at present, I think it is that we all hang together, and that there can be no real and lasting recovery for any of the individual nations that compose civilised society today unless that recovery is universal and world-wide.

What disquieted me in the attitude of the United States Government towards the Monetary and Economic Conference was that they appeared to be determined to adopt a purely national outlook on the subject of stabilisation; that is to say, they seemed to think that the value of the dollar should be fixed without regard to anything but the interests of the United States. That of course would be all very well were any of us self-sufficing, but the very essence of things demands that there must be give and take, and that national financial policy must take into

339

consideration the position and welfare, not only of the people of its own country, but also of the people of other countries, with whom inevitably its own people must deal if they are to prosper.

Quite apart from the reactions of your monetary policy upon the Conference, I sincerely hope and trust that reviving trade and industry will not lead to another boom, which must be followed [by] an inevitable crash when things find their real level, but that the rise in prices will be gradual and controlled, so that time may be given to the world to make the necessary adjustments without a fatal return to a wild rise of salaries and wages in an effort to keep abreast with a soaring cost of living.

With kind regards, Always yours very sincerely,

(Signed) Londonderry

[PPF 675:CT]


## [*Enclosure 2*] Lord Derby to Louis Wiley

[London, *undated*]

*Confidential*

Dear Mr. Wiley: I should be very wrong if I attempted to you, as a personal friend, to minimise the very bitter feeling there is in this country towards yours, or rather towards your President and his policy; and the reason is really not far to seek. To give you an instance within my own knowledge. I am head of the English branch of the Pilgrims, and in that capacity presided at a big luncheon for your Special Delegate Mr Cordell Hull. Between ourselves it was very difficult to organise, as on arrival at Cork he toasted the health of the "Newest Republic" in the name of the "Oldest Republic."[1] One quite realised that that was a slip of which anybody might be guilty, and though it created a certain amount of disturbance it did not prevent the success of the luncheon.[2] I cannot give you verbatim what he said, but you can take it from me that what I say is a correct representation of his remark. He spoke of the Great Economic Conference, and the words he used were to this effect: "It cannot fail; it must not fail, and I am over here on behalf of the President of the U.S.A. and my country to see that it does not fail," and within 48 hours Roosevelt had torpedoed the whole thing. Can you wonder therefore that there was, and still is, a certain amount of bitterness which it will take a very long time to allay. I deeply regret this because I, like you, think that unless there is the closest cooperation between the U.S.A. and this country the paths of peace are going to be extremely thorny.

The President's policy, as far as outward signs go is a success in your country; but is it a permanent success? Personally I cannot think that the over-production which must be the result of Roosevelt's present policy can be in the end beneficial. It may be as far as your own country is concerned, because you are by deflation and increase of wages, and the diminution of hours, given more spending power. Home consumption therefore will come probably fully up to home production, but nobody can live by taking in his neighbour's washing, and you must depend for your prosperity on a certain amount of export trade especially in foodstuffs. Now our (and I speak not only of English but of European) spending power is not increasing. There are slight signs of revival, but comparatively minute, and therefore I doubt whether you will be able to increase to any great extent your markets here. Rest assured if there is any question of dumping it will be dealt with by a very extreme tariff. It appears to me that your Middle West would have to pay far more for the labour in gathering its harvest and probably find no market for it when it is gathered.

Your Congress has not given Roosevelt the power to deal with tariffs, and to my mind a fatal blunder it was. The only way in which he can prevent the raising of tariffs against him is by mutual concessions, and if he cannot give these then there would be no sympathy with his people or wish on the part of this or indeed any European country to help him.

Nor have Congress given him the right to deal with Debts. I do not think the people in your country quite realise what it means to us to have the black cloud always over our heads. If he had been able to give a moratorium of say 10 or even more years which would have given us the opportunity to revive and therefore the ability to pay it would undoubtedly have been of enormous advantage not only to this country but also to your country.

I fear that you may think this letter of mine is full of financial fallacies. You must forgive that and believe me that I am only writing as an ignorant friend to a very highly experienced man of the world.

Yours very sincerely,

(Signed) Derby

[PPF 675:CT]

[1] This incident occurred at an impromptu talk given on June 8 by Hull in Queens-town, Ireland, on his arrival (New York *Times*, June 9, 1933, p. 4).

[2] A luncheon given by the Pilgrims for the American delegates to the London Confer-ence on June 27, 1933.

## Claude G. Bowers, Ambassador to Spain, to Roosevelt

Madrid, August 2, 1933

Dear Mr. President: I am replying to your inquiries[1] regarding the reaction to your note to the American Delegation in London respecting the Gold Bloc, and in reference to what Spain wants to sell in the American market, on a separate sheet, inclosed.[2]

The feeling here is most friendly to us. The Mallorcan incident implies no prejudice, as some American papers, ignorant of the facts, conclude. I have just sent the State Department an analysis of that incident—which was ugly in its ramifications. But de los Rios went the full length for us with unprecedented speed, and the moment the case could properly be taken to Azana he complied with my request.[3]

Just now in the Foreign Office is de los Rios, the Minister, who is pro-American, because of his intimate acquaintance with us; and the newly appointed Under Secretary is Cruze Marin,[4] who for eight years was a consul in America, the last five in Chicago. Last night he chatted with me on the terrace at the embassy for an hour, and there is no doubt in my mind of his friendly feeling for us. He pretends to enthusiasm. Both de los Rios and Marin speak English well.

Azana, the premier and the strong man of Spain, has a profound respect for us—because of our strength. He is not pro-French in my opinion. He has an ugly tongue at times. Thus when *Le Temps* of Paris made an attack upon him, he summoned the press to make reply. This he did in a sentence. "It is a strange reversal," he said. "That paper was very friendly as long as I continued to pay 200,000 pesetas." That was all—and it was enough.

Madariaga,[5] for whom I brought an enthusiastic admiration to Spain, has fallen in my estimation enormously. Here they say that he is super-ficially brilliant. He certainly is more French than the French and he is pronouncedly anti-American. He is now in Paris, ambassador there—though some of his official activities there imply that he so confuses his status that he works for France even against Spain.

Now and then some American fresh from the States drifts in, and constantly I talk with people here, in the diplomatic corps and out, and all agree that you are the only political leader in the world today who has had the vision and the courage to face realities with a realist's program. Republicans representing American business interests here are enthusiastic in their praise. My own opinion is that you are doing the biggest job in the biggest way of any President in our history. You are doing a bigger job in a more skillful and tactful way than Andrew Jackson.

I see in the Paris *Herald* that Bob Wagner is there and may visit me in Madrid. I hope he does. He grows on me constantly. Bernard Baruch sent me a radiogram from the *Olympic* saying he would be in Paris for three days and at Vichy for three weeks and would like to see me. If I see him he will have to come here. I think he wants to talk with me about the Wilson biography.

What splendid courage the Administration has displayed on the repeal issue—and what leadership! The prospect of an early repeal is making the Spanish all the keener for a commercial understanding because of their wine.[6]

With warmest regards, Sincerely,

Claude G. Bowers

[PPF 730:TS]

[1] July 11, 1933 (*Personal Letters, 1928–1945,* I, 357–358).

[2] The enclosure is present. The Spanish asked for annulment of the customs increase on cork products, moderation of the tariff on onions, olive oil, canned vegetables, and fish, and removal of the prohibition against the entry of Spanish grapes (because of the Mediterranean fruit fly).

[3] The incident referred to is the arrest and imprisonment in June 1933 of five Americans in Mallorca on charges of assaulting certain members of the police. The Americans were pardoned in February 1934, after strenuous efforts by Bowers and the State Department. Bowers had asked de los Ríos to transmit to Prime Minister Azaña his request that the prisoners be released (Bowers to Phillips, June 29, 1933, *Foreign Relations, 1933,* II, 707).

[4] Antonio de la Cruz Marin.

[5] Salvador de Madariaga y Rojo, ambassador to France, 1932–1934; chief, delegation to the League of Nations, 1934–1935.

[6] Answered Aug. 22, 1933, below.

# William Phillips, Under Secretary of State, to Roosevelt

Washington, August 3, 1933

My dear Mr. President: Minister Armour[1] in Haiti has just cabled that he has reached agreement with the Haitian Government on the text of two executive agreements, one covering Haitianization of the Garde by October 1, 1934, and withdrawal of the Marine Brigade within thirty days thereafter, and the other providing for appropriate measures of financial control until the retirement of the outstanding bonds. I enclose herewith copies of the two agreements.[2]

This is the result of months of patient negotiations. Last April Secretary Hull gave his approval to the general principles underlying the administration's policy towards Haiti. In brief this policy looked to putting an end to the special relations between Haiti and the United States at the earliest possible moment consistent with the obligations of both governments. These special relations, as you know, fall under two general heads: First, the training of the Haitian Constabulary (Garde) by American Marine officers and the presence in Haiti of a Marine brigade which has given moral support to the American officers in the Garde. Second, the fact that third parties purchased bonds of the Haitian Government in reliance on treaty obligations assumed by both Haiti and the United States to provide adequate financial control in Haiti during the life of the bonds. Under the first point we proposed to withdraw all American forces from Haiti at as early a date as could be done with proper regard for the training of the constabulary. Under the second point we proposed to reach an agreement with the Haitians, as required by the Protocol of 1919 signed by the two governments, in order to provide satisfactory measures of financial control after the expiration in 1936 of the present treaty, so that adequate provision should be made for the servicing of the bonds. This control would automatically come to an end when the bonds had been redeemed, estimated to be about 1944. At Mr. Hull's request this general plan was taken up with Senator Pittman and Senator King,[3] both of whom expressed complete approval.

The present agreements embody the principles above outlined and take the form of executive agreements rather than of a treaty, since they provide merely for carrying out the provisions of a treaty previously ratified by both governments and hence do not themselves require ratification.

I am highly gratified at the successful outcome of these negotiations. The early withdrawal of our forces from Haiti will greatly enhance the prestige of this Government throughout Latin America. It will be a signal example of practical application of your policy of the "good neighbor." Mr. Armour reports that action in the matter is urgent as President Vincent[4] of Haiti desires to publish the accords following the solution of certain political difficulties in Haiti which it is hoped will be reached within the next day or so.

May I have your approval of instructions to the Minister authorizing him to sign the agreements? We shall arrange to make the agreements public simultaneously with similar action in Haiti.

Faithfully yours,

William Phillips

[*Notation*:AS] Read & returned by the President Aug. 7th ML[5]
[OF 20:TS]

[1] Norman Armour served as minister to Haiti from 1932 to 1935.
[2] The enclosures (present) are printed in *Foreign Relations, 1933*, V, 755–761; the correspondence preceding the agreements is found on pp. 691–755. They were signed on Aug. 7, 1933.
[3] Senator William H. King of Utah.
[4] Sténio Joseph Vincent, president of Haiti from 1930 to 1941.
[5] Marguerite LeHand.

# Press Conference, Hyde Park, August 5, 1933, 3:30 P.M.

[*Excerpt*] Q: Anything on the future of the London Conference?
The President: We haven't got to that yet.[1]
Q: Anything on Russian recognition?
The President: That we have not mentioned.
Q: Do you expect to?
The President: We have only been talking for a couple of hours.
Q: You haven't got past Montevideo in that time?
The President: No.
Q: It must be a very important conference.
Q: Can you tell us when you expect the London Conference to reconvene?
The President: I don't know. I haven't any idea.
Secretary Hull: I gave the newspapermen this morning a statement in which I set forth the different agencies that are placed in charge of the recess work of the Conference with authority to call any local conference or special conference or regional conference or plenary conference at such time as their judgment may suggest in the light of the progress of the interim work that will be undertaken. They will have their

meetings—these agencies in charge will have their first meetings early in September, according to the present plans; that is, after most of the statesmen of the European countries return from their August vacations.

Q: Do they all take the whole month of August off for their vacations?

Secretary Hull: President Roosevelt first called my attention to the fact that they leave promptly on the 12th of August and shoot grouse for how many days?

The President: About a month.

Q: I think we ought to get some grouse over here. (Laughter)

The President: We have enough grousing in this country.

Well, there is one thing I can tell you literally and strictly and entirely in the family and off the record. The Secretary confirmed that one of the contributing agencies to the fact that the conference—don't put this down—one of the worst contributing agencies was the Continental and London press. It was rotten, absolutely rotten, and they gave us a dirty deal from the time we left here until we got home.

I would like to say a lot more on it. The whole press just ganged us from the start to the finish. And their press were told what to say by their governments and of course the French press is owned by anybody that will buy it, and there you are. It was a rotten situation.

Secretary Hull: I have never been accustomed to a really bad press but I did get a good dose of it over there.

Q: You are glad to be home then?

Secretary Hull: Yes.

Q: And you will appreciate us now, Mr. Secretary?

Secretary Hull: It was an impossible situation.

Q: That might make a little story. (Laughter)

The President: I said that was in the family. You see, I could not feel anything about it one way or the other out loud but I can feel very deeply about it among us.

Q: They are pretty well organized?

The President: Yes.

Q: They started off in this country before the Delegation went over.

Q: We saw some of that in the Washington Arms Conference.

Secretary Hull: They are pretty well organized. A large cross-section keeps in close touch with their governments.

Q: I have a technical question here. We had an agreement with Mac[2] before we came out that what we got from the Secretary would be held for Monday papers. That does not apply to industrial control, does it?

The President: No; it just relates to the Secretary of State.

Q: How would you write your Monday morning story? (Laughter)

Q: Tomorrow afternoon, do you think you will be across the Atlantic? You are just down in Montevideo now. (Laughter)

Q: Is there anything you or the Secretary might tell us about the progress of the trade agreements initiated by you while he was absent?

The President: I don't believe the Secretary knows anything about it at all and all I know is what there was when I left Washington. In other words, they were going ahead with the informal conversations. Bill Phillips has been talking with various ministers and ambassadors in Washington. There are five or six countries. I don't think it has got beyond that stage yet and of course Brother Espil is out of it—he is on his honeymoon.[3]

Q: Do you see a good deal of promise in that?

The President: Yes.

Q: There was a report in Washington, two or three days ago, that Secretary Hull was considering the possibility of a tour of South America before the Montevideo Conference.

Secretary Hull: I was asked this morning, down in New York, if I was going to attend the Conference and what I thought about it and I said that while I am intensely interested in anything relating to Pan-American relationships, I felt like I should get home and unpack my grip before I take up the question of another trip.

The President: I want him in Washington, right close at hand.

Q: When are you going back to Washington?

Secretary Hull: I have no definite plans. As I stated, there are two agencies that are authorized to conduct the interim proceedings during the recess. They will convene the fore part of September. They may commence subcommittee hearings on some phases of commercial policy, but until they convene and announce their plans for going forward with this recess work, naturally there will be no individual plans.

The President: Where do they meet in September?

Secretary Hull: They will meet, I think, London part of the time and Geneva part of the time. I do not mean by that that the Conference proper would be removed from London. It is just a matter of convenience when they will be attending the disarmament proceedings, some of them.

Q: What did you think of the Conference, Mr. Secretary?

Secretary Hull: Well, it was wonderfully interesting.

The President: How did you like your first view of New York Harbor? (Laughter)

Mr. Stephenson:[4] Thank you, Mr. President; much obliged.

[President's Press Conferences:T]

[1] Roosevelt referred to his talks with Hull, just returned from London.
[2] Marvin H. McIntyre.
[3] Felipe A. Espil, the Argentinian ambassador, who had recently married.
[4] F. M. Stephenson of the Associated Press.

## Raymond B. Stevens, Federal Trade Commission, to Roosevelt

Washington, August 5, 1933

Dear Mr. President: I reported the results of my conference with you on Thursday to George Rublee and Pierre Jay, the two men who had done most of the work on the creation of a Foreign Bondholders Council.[1]

As I told you in our conference, all efforts toward creating such a council ceased on the passage of the Securities Act. However, a good deal of preliminary work had already been done and five different persons had already agreed to serve on such a body, including Mr. Traphagen, Charles Francis Adams, T. Nelson Perkins, Roland S. Morris and Newton D. Baker.[2]

Mr. Rublee and Mr. Jay have immediately taken up the task of creating the Council, and I think it may be possible to set up the Council within a period of two or three weeks. Every effort is being made to keep the matter quiet so that no publicity may be given until the Council is actually created.

I will be kept informed as fast as the work progresses and will let you know of the results. Special effort of course will be made to secure the men on the list who particularly appeal to you.

Do you think it would be helpful if before the Council is created, the Federal Trade Commission would write you a letter stating its opinion that if an adequate Bondholders Committee is created, that it would be advisable not to bring into effect Article II of the Securities Act?[3]

Judge Davis[4] to a large extent shares my views on the matter, and he informs me has written a memorandum to you on the subject. I have talked briefly with Mr. Ferguson[5] and I find that he too has some doubts as to the wisdom of Article II. Chairman March[6] is favorable to the creation of the Government Corporation, but the objections to it have not been seriously presented to him. I think he has an open mind on the subject and I am hopeful that he might on reflection agree with Judge Davis and myself.

I greatly appreciated the opportunity to see you at Hyde Park and discuss somewhat at length some of the problems of the Federal Trade Commission. I hope the results of our conference will be of benefit to your administration.[7]

Cordially yours,

Raymond B. Stevens

[OF 100-B:TS]

[1] Stevens and Roosevelt conferred at 1 P.M. Aug. 3, 1933, at Hyde Park (PPF 1-0).
[2] J. C. Traphagen was president of the Bank of New York and Trust Company; Adams had been Secretary of the Navy (1929–1933), and was at this time president of the Union Trust Company of Boston; Thomas Nelson Perkins was a Boston lawyer and corporation executive; Roland S. Morris was a Philadelphia lawyer; Baker had been Wilson's Secretary of War (1916–1921) and at this time was practicing law in Cleveland.
[3] Title II of the Securities Act was, in fact, never invoked; the Foreign Bondholders Security Corporation was established in October 1933 outside the government.
[4] Ewin Lamar Davis of Tennessee, member of the Federal Trade Commission, 1933–1946.
[5] Garland S. Ferguson, Jr., of North Carolina, appointed to the Commission in 1927.
[6] Charles H. March of Minnesota, appointed in 1929.
[7] Stevens saw Roosevelt again on Aug. 18, 1933 (PPF 1-0); see Roosevelt to Hull, Morgenthau, and Roper, Aug. 31, 1933, below.

# Press Conference, Hyde Park, August 9, 1933, 11 A.M.

[*Excerpt*] The President: Frankly I don't know if there is any news.
Q: Anything on Cuba?
The President: I haven't anything. There may be something later on. As far as I know, there is no change from what the press dispatches have.

Q: That is a very delicate situation down there and we realize it is hard for you to say anything.

The President: It really is; I haven't any word at all.

Q: Is there any way you can let us know or guide us as to what your policy is?

The President: As far as policy goes, you have it perfectly straight and that is that we are acting as *amicus curiae* to the Cuban people.

Q: What is that?

The President: He would. (Laughter)

Q: I don't know whether he is starting a new war down there or not. (Laughter)[1]

The President: We are using our good offices to help them straighten things out.

Q: Does that mean a concrete proposal or a definite suggestion?

The President: That I don't know. Welles is talking to them all the time to help them out in the nature of personal suggestions. There is no government action on our part. It is simply saying to Welles, "Go ahead and help all you can."

Q: I think the point is whether or not we believe that Machado's retirement is absolutely necessary to help things out.

The President: I don't know. In other words, that is a thing that they know in Havana better than we do. And, certainly, we cannot be in the position of saying to Machado, "You have to get out." That would be obvious interference with the internal affairs of another nation.

Q: The stories say that Ambassador Welles has suggested that he take a leave of absence.[2]

The President: I don't believe that is accurate. I think you will probably find that those suggestions came from people down there in one of the parties or all three of the parties.

Q: Assuming that Machado did go out, would that mean a special election in advance of 1934?

The President: I do not know; I am not familiar enough with the Cuban situation.

Q: Is there any Vice President?

The President: No, there is not; that is the trouble. I think the Secretary of State becomes Acting President and I think one of their questions is whether the Senate or the Courts would have the right to elect a Vice President to become Acting President during the balance of the period. Now, that is the thing I cannot say anything about because I have never read their Constitution.

Q: Isn't there also a question as to the eligibility of the present Secretary of State? He is not Cuban born.

The President: Yes.

Q: The election now is due in 1934, is it not?

The President: Yes.

Q: Would this leave of absence of Machado last until the regular election?

The President: I have no idea. It is one of the things I am not talking about at all because I have no information on it. I have to be terribly careful not to be in a position of intimating that the Cubans get rid of their President.

Q: Is it still critical down there?

The President: Yesterday things were apparently quiet. Nothing in this morning's paper.

Q: Has the general strike extended, or have you any information on that point?

The President: I did not get anything on that at all . . .

Q: Again on Cuba, some time ago Machado was going to seek an American authority on election laws to go down there and prepare the way.

The President: That has all been done.

Q: Do we know who it is?

The President: I cannot remember offhand.[3] It has all been done and they put in an excellent report and everybody was pleased about it.

Q: That was on the election laws?

The President: Yes.

Q: It is a revision of them?

The President: As I understand it, the general objective of it was a general revision of the election laws so that they will carry out their election in approximately the same way the last election was held, where they asked us to come in and supervise it. Of course the object was to have a perfectly fair election without supervision.

Q: We did not go in with troops the last time?

The President: No. I think it was old man Crowder who did it.[4]

Q: What would have to happen in Cuba before we would send troops down there? Just what extremity?

The President: Was it in the *Tribune* this morning—there was an editorial which stated pretty well Elihu Root's definition. It would require a case of complete anarchy.

Q: Complete disorder?

The President: The *Tribune* had it right. They quoted Root and that seems to be a pretty good definition of the Platt Amendment.

[President's Press Conferences:T]

---

[1] This and the preceding two sentences are as in the original. It is possible that the stenographer omitted something.

[2] On Aug. 7, 1933, Welles informed Hull that on August 6 he had had an interview

with President Machado and had urged "this entirely constitutional and dignified solution" upon him (*Foreign Relations, 1933*, V, 336–337).

[3] Dr. Howard Lee McBain, professor of government at Columbia.

[4] Major General Enoch H. Crowder, American ambassador to Cuba, 1923–1927. Crowder had helped revise the Cuban electoral laws in 1919, and it was these laws that McBain had been called in to amend; see Welles to Hull, Aug. 22, 1933, *Foreign Relations, 1933*, V, 372.

## John F. Coar to Roosevelt

Berlin, August 9, 1933

My dear President Roosevelt: Within the last five weeks I have had many, often lengthy talks with influential personages over here. The general substance of these talks I communicated the other day to our Ambassador because a final conference with the Chancellor impended, and through his kind offices this letter goes forward to you now.

In the aforesaid talks my chief effort has been to impress those close to the "Führer" with the very serious nature of our own people's attitude toward the German Government's antisemitic policy. One of my last talks (of nearly two hours) was with the "leader's" personal representative and most influential adviser, Mr. Hess. I believe, and have also been told by his intimates, that he is now greatly disturbed. Hence, I am inclined to take certain suggestions made by him somewhat seriously. The substance of my talk with him and of his suggestions to me were communicated by him to the "leader" and arrangements have been made for a similar meeting between the latter and me. This meeting will probably take place this week, on invitation of the "leader," at Berchtesgaden (Bavaria). As one of the prime conditions of this conference I have insisted on its strictly private and frank character. On the other hand, the condition has been made that this conference is to be treated by me as absolutely confidential except that its substance may be communicated to you. I shall impress on the Chancellor the resentment we Americans feel toward the antisemitic policy, and also give him my views of the probable consequences. I shall not discuss with him the merits or demerits of any suggestions he may make that are diplomatic in character. If these shall make it possible to bring the very ticklish problem of antisemitism within the range of diplomatic discussion, practical results may be achievable. Without disclosing Mr. Hess's suggestions I have discussed this point with our Ambassador, who feels that I can say things to the "leader" and say them in a way, his own diplomatic position prohibits. Ambassador Dodd is a wonderfully fine selection for the extraordinarily difficult "job" and I hope to have the pleasure of putting him in personal touch with some of my friends with whom he can talk frankly and who can and will talk as frankly to him.

It is possible that I may be obliged to return next week on the Hamburg-American liner *Deutschland,* arriving in New York August 25. If I can have word from you at my home in Kingston, Mass., I shall be glad to run down to Washington at your convenience, or to do so immediately on my arrival in New York if word to that effect reaches me on arrival of the steamer.[1]

With all best wishes, Loyally yours,

John F. Coar

[PPF 3716:TS]

[1] Coar, born in Berlin of American parents and educated at Bonn and Harvard, had corresponded with Roosevelt during his governorship (Group 12). Coar had sent him two of his books: *The Old and the New Germany* (New York: Knopf, 1924) and *The Peace of Nations* (Plymouth: Memorial Press, 1928) shortly after the 1932 election. He had tried to see Hull in May 1933 but Hull's departure for the London Conference prevented a meeting (Durand to Howe, no date, PPF 3716). He knew Hitler well enough to be accorded interviews; how he became acquainted with him and what were his political views does not appear from the correspondence. See Dodd, *Diary,* pp. 20–21, 23–24.

## Roosevelt to William W. Hoffman, New York

Hyde Park, New York, August 10, 1933

Dear Bill: I am delighted to see that clipping from *The Times.*[1] I was a little afraid that they still felt that I was a sort of pirate who had torpedoed their pet schemes at the Economic Conference!

I do hope to see you one of these days soon.

Very sincerely yours,

[PPF 705:CT]

[1] Hoffman, in a letter of Aug. 7, 1933 (PPF 705), had sent an editorial from the London *Times* of July 26, 1933, which commented approvingly on Roosevelt's address of July 24, 1933, and reviewed the accomplishments of his Administration (*Public Papers,* II, 295–303).

## Press Conference, Hyde Park, August 11, 1933

[*Excerpt*] Q: The morning papers, at least one of them, published an interview with President Machado which said that if the Liberal Party would request him to get out, he would.[1]

Q: What sort of reaction are you getting from other Latin-American countries, if any?

The President: Nothing at all, not a thing. The only thing they had was the protest of the Spanish Ambassador down there and the inquiry of the British Ambassador.

Q: Here is a dispatch from Santiago, Chile, which came into our office. It seems to represent the attitude down there.

The President: (Looks over dispatch.) I think they are getting it down there, through the Latin-American countries, all right. I think they are getting it all right.

Q: Hamilton Fish gave a pretty story and also lined up the successful and possible steps that might be taken on the Cuban situation.[2] And the first one concerned economic and financial and political pressure. Now, it is my understanding that Machado has really lost the support of the big financial interests, the support he did have, ever since he lost the interest on the bonds. Do you have any comment, on or off the record?

The President: Entirely off the record, here is the real situation on the financial end of it. It is far, far less important than one would suppose. Take the Chase and the National City Banks, they have just about given up hope of getting any part of their investment back and they are in the position of saying that anything they can get back is grand. They are not in a position to dictate or to ask for terms or anything like that. The major part of the investment is gone, hook, line and sinker, for all time and they know it. Therefore they are not much of a factor.

On the other hand, during the past four months, I have been talking with Cubans about trying to put the country back on its feet economically. There are various factors in that. I don't think you can use this unless you can use it without any possible connection with me—leave me out entirely. I don't know how you can do it but I think you can say this: That for the past four months the State Department and the friends of Cuba in this country—leaving out all reference to the White House or the Administration—have been interested in doing everything they possibly can toward the economic rehabilitation of Cuba for the sake of the Cuban people and that that seems to involve perhaps three factors. The first factor is a land policy and, on the land policy, one of the difficulties has been that the tendency of the past ten or fifteen years has been to eliminate the small planter of tobacco and sugar. The small planter always gave a little piece of ground to his employees to cultivate. Therefore, they were almost immune from starvation. However, the centralization of the small planters into big units has tended to take the Cuban farmer off the land—I mean off a little piece of acreage—and concentrate him in the villages. Hence, when sugar or tobacco get in a bad way economically and they lay off people, those people are subject to starvation. Therefore our thought and the most intelligent Cuban thought has been to get people back on little pieces of land where they will be able to grow their own food supply.

The second phase relates to the Cuban debts, the Cuban National Debt. That is altogether too high. The external debt and the internal debt is too high, the rate of interest is too high and the amortization payments are too high and probably there should be, for the sake of the tax situation in Cuba, a complete reorganization of the Government debt, putting it on a lower interest basis and extending the period of payment, lengthening out the annual amortization, which would make the Government finances far easier to work out and enable them to reduce taxes.

Then, of course, the third factor is what we have been working at both in London and Havana and Washington, which is the original sugar agreement, which would tend to stabilize the Cuban situation. I think you can say that the State Department has been seeking a larger quota than the quota of 1,750,000 tons, which has been the figure discussed.

Q: For Cuba?

The President: For Cuba. Of course even a larger quota, such as 2,000,000 tons would be away below what their output was six or eight years ago.

Q: Before the Hoover tariff?

The President: Yes.

Q: Was that 1,750,000 tons actually agreed on at that conference?

The President: No. Nothing was agreed on. It was merely a figure for discussion.

Q: Are you considering admitting that amount under the preferential tariff?

The President: It would come under the preferential tariff.

Q: Possibly the 20 per cent preferential might be increased?

The President: I don't know; we have not discussed that at all. The whole sugar quota business is getting on pretty well. The Philippines are involved in it, of course, to a certain extent but they are coming along in pretty good shape with it.

Q: Would this quota mean anything unless you did get the Philippines in on it?

The President: Yes and no. We ought to get the Philippines in on it because, after all, the Independence Bill, if it is agreed to, puts the time for the 850,000 tons from the Philippines at five years. It is not a very long time that we have to worry about.

Q: How about the Dutch? Would they come in under it?

The President: In a sense, it is an original agreement. It means the United States, on the consumption end, and Mexico, on the consumption end, and then the producing countries that are in the neighborhood, Puerto Rico, Cuba, Mexico, which is also a producing country, the Philippines and Hawaii and then the beet sugar growers.

Q: Is Mexico willing to go in on it?

The President: Yes. We are getting excellent cooperation from Mexico on everything. First rate. Josephus Daniels is doing a good job and they like him a lot.

Q: That is pretty good.

The President: Do not connect me up with that because it should not come from me.

Q: It is a good story.

The President: And then, of course, the fourth factor in that is the continuation of the reciprocity tariff studies which we are engaged in at the present time.

Q: I am not quite clear about the tariff on Cuban sugar. Under this sugar agreement, would a certain amount of Cuban sugar be admitted duty-free?

The President: Not that I know of. I think you have a continuation of the present preferential tariff. I don't think there is any question about admitting it free. It is an attempt to equalize consumption and production.

Q: This may be a stupid question but, if we do establish a quota of 1,750,000 or 2,000,000 tons for Cuban sugar, it would mean that amount could come in under the preferential tariff?

The President: Yes. It means, in fact, limiting the amount of sugar production in Hawaii, limiting the amount of beet sugar production here, limiting the amount of production by general agreement in Puerto Rico and Cuba.

Q: At present Cuba is free to send in anything she can?

The President: Yes. It is trying to do for the sugar crop, beet and cane, which comes in here, what we are doing with wheat and cotton within our own borders.

I think there is one other thing to be said about it. It is interesting because really for the first time it sets up a logical geographical region for a geographical portion of the world and eliminates entirely the bringing of sugar, let us say, from the Dutch East Indies, which is distinctly uneconomical.

Q: Is Secretary Hull in agreement with that?

The President: Very much. You see, it is not an economic thing to bring sugar from the Dutch East Indies to the United States.

Q: Thank you, Mr. President.

The President: I will see you all tonight at 11 P.M.

Q: And you will sail for Cuba on the 31st?

The President: No. The only person I am worried about is Sam (Schulman, the photographer, who was reported to be operating in the fighting area).

Q: Have you had any protest on that?

The President: No.

Q: What makes matters worse is that the heaviest fighting is concentrated around Sloppy Joe's.[3]

The President: I haven't had a protest from the *Herald Tribune*.

Q: He is probably living with Sumner Welles.[4]


[President's Press Conferences:T]


[1] Machado made this statement August 8 (printed in the New York *Times*, Aug. 11, 1933, p. 8) and resigned August 11.

[2] Fish, ranking member of the House Foreign Affairs Committee, saw Roosevelt in Hyde Park on August 10. After his talk he issued a statement to the effect that if Machado refused to vacate his office, the United States should use its rights under the Platt Amendment to force his retirement by political and economic measures (*ibid.*, p. 8).

[3] The famous Havana bar.

[4] At this time ambassador to Cuba. (The press conference ends here.)

## William E. Dodd, Ambassador to Germany, to Roosevelt

Berlin, August 12, 1933

Dear Mr President: There are a few points in the situation here and in Europe which I venture to impose upon you as briefly as possible.

1. The tension is still very sharp. The British-French protest last Monday[1] added to feeling of the Germans that they must arm; and all the evidence that comes to this office tends to show that armament and training men for war are major interests. Last night my son was driving a small party of guests home and the car was stopped twice and searched before he had time to show his status and persuade the Nazi police to look at his license tag, showing Embassy rights. I have no objection to submitting to anything the Germans (except Jews) submit to; but I cite this as revelation of the spirit and temper of official Germany. And I must add that the treatment of the Jews continues, though not in quite so drastic form. We have one of the best residences in Berlin at $150 a month—due to the fact that the owner is a wealthy Jew, most willing to let us have it. Not insignificant is the fact that the house was originally a Warburg home (the Hamburg-New York family).

2. I have said war sentiment is sharp. I ought to add that the British Military Attaché reports a conversation a few days ago with Winston Churchill to the effect that their Government is ready, on the request of France, to apply utmost force against Germany; and reports come to me from trustworthy sources that the British authorities here allow letters and messages from the Jews to be forwarded in their pouches. And this has resulted in the most effective boycott of German goods in England and something of the same thing in the United States. I have letters from the Boston *Herald* and the New York *Times* in proof of this tendency. This is given not in defense of German armament and anti-semitic attitudes (both contrary to all liberal philosophy), but to explain the tense situation and the possibility of worse things ahead. Fundamentally, I believe a people has a right to govern itself and that other peoples must exercise patience even when cruelties and injustices are done. Give men a chance to try their schemes.

3. We have watched the situation here as closely as possible and, as suggested in former letter,[2] the authorities tend to more generous attitudes and especially to a cultivation of more friendly attitudes towards the United States. I could give you three official decisions the last ten or twelve days in proof of this. There are two reasons: the general

tendency of all revolutionary movements is to swing a little to the right as soon as they are firmly fixed, and the stern economic reason that Germans must have increasing exports if they are to avoid catastrophe. They are not always wise in their methods, as revealed in the telegram last evening of the Consul General here[3]—but when the bearings of a move are made perfectly clear, they listen and even reverse themselves in some cases. The grain and meat import attitudes now under discussion in London.

Let me close by giving one or two more items. A Professor John F. Coar, of remarkable background, came to me a few days ago. Rudolf Hess, Hitler party chief who sits in all Cabinet meetings, wished to take him (Coar) to Hitler to talk American attitudes. He wrote you a letter which we put into the pouch. He and Hess are with the Reichskanzler this week-end. He speaks German perfectly. I declined any connection, but am to be informed as to attitudes. Yesterday, August 11, Winthrop Aldrich came to see me.[4] He reports, what we knew, that private debts are fairly secure, if German exports continue. He and Schacht are to be with the Reichskanzler Monday, talking American attitudes. There is to be a report. Aldrich was delighted to know Morgans had fallen into line. If you can restrain English and French, I think situation here will ease off.

Yours,

William E. Dodd

P.S. My opinion is: Another world economic conference next year, if Congress will co-operate; one point, cease offensive armaments (if not agreed to before); second, reciprocal trade concessions; third, revision of immigration barriers—aimed at opening undeveloped regions to European unemployment. Let Luther[5] explain, if considered. WED[6]

[OF 523:TS]

[1] The protest to Germany of Aug. 7, 1933, over the Nazi propaganda attacks on the Dollfuss regime.

[2] July 30, 1933, above.

[3] George S. Messersmith to Hull, Aug. 11, 1933 (*Foreign Relations, 1933,* II, 474-475), reporting issuance of restrictions on ship travel prejudicial to non-German steamship lines.

[4] Aldrich, chairman of the board of the Chase National Bank of New York, was one of the delegation of bankers in Berlin negotiating with Hjalmar Schacht in an attempt to prevent repudiation of German bonds (Dodd, *Diary,* pp. 21-22, 31).

[5] Hans Luther, German ambassador to the United States.

[6] Answered Sept. 13, 1933, below.

## Roosevelt to Edward B. Krumbhaar, University of Pennsylvania, Philadelphia

[Washington] August 14, 1933

*Private*

Dear Ned: I am delighted to enclose a note to Ambassador Dodd in Berlin and I know that he will do everything possible to help you in your work.

Because of the fact that you will have access to many scientific men in Germany I hope you will on your return run down to Washington to see me and to give me your slant on the situation there. Do not, of course, say anything to anybody about this but I should much like to have your opinions.[1]

With best regards, Always sincerely yours,

[PPF 720:CT]

[1] Krumbhaar, professor of pathology at the University of Pennsylvania, had asked for a letter of introduction to Dodd in connection with a trip to Germany to secure reductions in the cost of imported German scientific periodicals (Aug. 9, 1933, PPF 720). A copy of Roosevelt's letter of introduction, Aug. 14, 1933, is with the letter here printed; in it he referred to Krumbhaar as his "old school and college classmate and . . . one of the really most eminent doctors in the country." Krumbhaar asked for an appointment after his return from Germany but none is noted in the White House appointments list. He saw Roosevelt the following June at the Groton commencement (Krumbhaar to Roosevelt, June 8, 1934, PPF 720).

## Roosevelt to William E. Dodd, Ambassador to Germany, Berlin

[Washington] August 14, 1933

My dear Mr. Ambassador: It is good to get your letter of July thirtieth[1] and I am glad to note that you do not seem quite as pessimistic as some other people.

Things here are going well and the reemployment program is in full swing. Also the price level is not only keeping up but increasing, the bank situation is better and the usual seasonal slump has been transformed into additional employment.

I hope all goes well with your living arrangements. I was glad that we could work out the transfer of gold.[2]

Let me have any news.

Always sincerely yours,

[OF 523:CT]

[1] Above.
[2] To lessen the hardships on Foreign Service personnel caused by the lowered value of the dollar, arrangements were made to draw on gold transfers for salary payments.


# Roosevelt to William Phillips, Under Secretary of State

[Washington] August 14, 1933

Memorandum for the Under Secretary of State: I wish you would talk this over with the Secretary. I am inclined to think that we should say that if by the end of September or early October it then seems advisable for Sir Frederick Leith-Ross to come to Washington I shall be delighted to see him but that any definite decision or announcement might well be held up for a few weeks.

F.D.R.

[*Notation*:T] Letter to Pres. from William Phillips, Under Secretary of State, dated 8-5-33, re inquiry from British Gov't as to whether it would be convenient for Pres. to have Sir Frederick Leith-Ross come to Wash. early in Oct. to enter into preliminary discussions.[1]

[OF 48:CT]

[1] This letter is present (OF 48). It was decided that Leith-Ross should see Roosevelt on October 5 (Roosevelt to Hull, Sept. 13, 1933, OF 48). Leith-Ross reached Washington on Oct. 4, 1933; see memoranda by Hull, Oct. 4, Nov. 6, 1933, in *Foreign Relations, 1933,* I, 842–843, 843.


# Roosevelt to Herbert S. Welsh, Sunapee, New Hampshire

[Washington] August 14, 1933

Dear Herbert: Many thanks for that nice note of yours.[1]

You are right that Secretary Hull's whole appearance in London stamped him as a great statesman and even the countries that were hostile have come to that realization.

I hope to see you one of these days soon.

Sincerely yours,

[PPF 724:CT]

[1] Welsh, in his letter of July 28, 1933 (PPF 724), said that Hull's address at the last session of the London Conference had affected him profoundly and that he spoke as a great statesman when he sought to show that any lasting recovery in the United States had to rest on closer cooperation with the rest of the world. (Hull's speech was printed in the New York *Times* of July 28, 1933, p. 5.)

## James P. Warburg to Roosevelt

August 14, 1933

### Suggested Agenda for Monetary Group

There are two major uncertainties in the monetary field today which act as a deterrent upon business recovery. These uncertainties are:

1. What kind of a dollar are we going to have in the future?

2. How big a dollar are we going to have in the future?

It is the task of the commission to eliminate these two uncertainties without in any way hindering the Administration in the other elements of its recovery program.

I. What kind of a dollar are we to have? A gold dollar such as we had prior to March, 1933? A gold and silver dollar (symmetalism)? A commodity dollar? Or a dollar based on gold but with an element of flexibility greater than was inherent in the old gold standard?

If the latter, then how is this greater flexibility to be attained, so that, on the one hand, we shall have a dollar with a more stable purchasing power than in the past without, on the other hand, exposing ourselves to the risk of mismanagement which is implicit in any managed currency?

II. (a) How big a dollar are we to have? Are we to return to the original parity with gold? Are we to reduce the gold content? And, if the latter, by how much?

(b) Is it possible at this moment to fix the exact amount of devaluation desired, or is it necessary merely to establish an experimental range of say 10%, within which the final new gold point will be established after a certain amount of experimentation?

(c) What should be the procedure during such an experimental period? How often should it be permissible to change the gold price? In whom should the power to change the gold price be vested?

III. What should be done about newly mined gold? Should miners be allowed to export, or should nothing be done about the gold mining industry until the Government is ready to fix new gold points for all gold?

IV. (a) At what point in the determination of the qualitative and quantitative features of the new dollar should consultation with foreign countries take place? What foreign countries should be consulted? To what extent should our policy be determined entirely independently of the attitude of foreign countries, and to what extent should it be influenced by the attitude of other countries?

(b) What will be the probable effect upon other countries if we continue our present undefined policy? What will be the effect if we establish a new gold point or an experimental range? What will be the effect if we merely establish a price for new gold, maintaining the present gold embargo?

V. What changes, if any, should be made in the legal minimum gold requirements of the Federal Reserve System? What changes, if any, should be made in the Federal Reserve System itself? If any changes are recommended, are they dependent upon similar action by other countries or are they recommended irrespective of the attitude of other countries?[1]

J.P.W.

[OF 229:T]

[1] With this memorandum is a list of names in Roosevelt's hand, presumably persons whom he thought should make up the "monetary group": Dean Acheson, Lewis Douglas, O. M. W. Sprague, Eugene R. Black, George L. Harrison, Walter W. Stewart (former adviser to the Bank of England), and Warren R. Burgess (vice-president of the Federal Reserve Bank of New York). See Woodin to Roosevelt, Sept. 28, 1933, below.

# Roosevelt to Cordell Hull, Secretary of State

[Washington] August 15, 1933

Memorandum for the Secretary of State: Will you bring this when we talk over the setting up of the delegation and staff of Montevideo.

F.D.R.

[*Notation*:T] Letter from Warren Delano Robbins about Delegation in Montevideo—gives list of personnel. Dated July 24, 1933.[1]

[OF 567:CT]

[1] Not present; presumably retained by Hull. See Roosevelt to Hull, Oct. 20, 1933, below.

## Roosevelt to Cordell Hull, Secretary of State

[Washington] August 19, 1933

Memo. for the Secretary of State: In considering possible imports from the Argentine please investigate possibilities of increasing linseed from 40 to 50 per cent of our requirements if increase can be limited to coast crushers.

Also tin corned beef on which there is now six cents a pound duty. Also wine. On this I think we should study a possible set up providing wine quotas.

F.D.R.

[OF 20:CT]

## Roosevelt to Cordell Hull, Secretary of State, and William Phillips, Under Secretary of State

Washington, August 19, 1933

Memo. for Hon. Cordell Hull, Hon. William Phillips: Here is a new debt settlement plan which was talked over with the President of France.

F.D.R.

[OF 212:T]

## [*Enclosure*] Memorandum on War Debts by Clarence K. Streit

[*Notation*:T] C. Streit[1]
*Confidential*

[*Excerpt*] Annex.[2] Sketch plan for hitching war debts and reparations to public works.

Plan meets American political requirements of keeping debts structure intact, neither annulling or reducing it, provides as much token money as now received, and solves the problem of arranging a synchronized international public works program.

Plan meets French political requirements of not transferring debt, of not losing the Lausanne reparations payment, and of providing funds for public works.

Plan meets British requirements of removing debt transfer pressure on budget and currency, involves no public work expenditure out of their budget.

Plan allows everyone hope for elimination of debt problem while giving United States a chance to prove whether the argument that this will bring good times is really sound, without in the course of the experiment losing any of its legal rights to the debts.

The debtors would pay their debt annuities in monthly installments into the World Bank where they would remain on deposit for a specified term, say five years at least. It would be agreed in advance that the greater part of this annuity, say 80 or 90 per cent, would be reinvested by the Bank in public works back in the debtor country. The transfer in each case would thus be reduced to ten or twenty per cent of the annuity, which would go into a common pool to be invested by the Bank for common purposes, such as in currency stabilization funds or in the development of backward non-debtor countries as China, Turkey, etc., or in mandated areas. This ten or twenty per cent of the annuity would be a token that the debt structure was being kept intact and that this was more than a matter of encouraging public works.

The interest on the investment of the annuity would be paid to the United States, as a further token.

Under the Balfour principle this plan would involve no public works in England, in practice. Just as the French and Italian annuities to us would be spent on public works in France and Italy, so the French, Italian and other annuities to England, which cover England's debt to us, would be spent on public works in France, Italy, etc.

The second feature of the plan is that at the start it would be agreed that the position would be reconsidered at the end of five years, and if at that time American exports had returned to a certain level—say to that of 1929—we would reduce the remainder of the debt accordingly and continue the same system for another five years with what was left, and would then again reconsider the position.

In other words, we would hitch the debts to prosperity as well as to public works. What the American public wants is good times more than anything else. If we can return to our exports of 1929 that means an increase in them, over 1932 of $3,600,000,000—or more than 15 times the debt annuity—and since our exports then were only 10 per cent of our production, it really means an increase of prosperity through the country of 150 times that prevailing today. If we could get that back no one would object to paying for the privilege the trifling sum the debts annuity amounts to beside it.

This, of course, seems heretical because it is the reverse of normal procedure with private debt which makes the object of the recovery the ability then to pay the debt, instead of attaining freedom from debt. The reverse process is used in this case because the war debts are essentially a political matter and cannot be handled on ordinary debt lines. For all practical purposes the debt is really being paid by the increase in our exports under this plan, but to get the increase started you have got first to remove the poisoning part of the debt question and soothe the political susceptibilities on both sides of the Atlantic, by contriving to prejudice neither the American position of no sacrifice of legal rights, nor the French position of no transfer or no commitment to pay in full for fifty years after they have renounced most of reparations. Each side holds his ground, but meanwhile they set the debts to work on the common interest they have—public works.

The same principle of course would be applied by France, etc., to Germany as regards the $750,000,000 lump sum Lausanne arranged on reparations, which would be divided into annuities.

It would be easy to hitch this plan also at one stroke more directly to our exports and to European peace. The French worked out in connection with the plan for European Union a scheme of pan-European automobile express highways and electric power lines. If this money was spent on these public works it would encourage our automobile and copper exports while providing a very useful means of binding Europe together peacefully. As an example of the many possibilities, there is now a well-advanced plan for an automobile toll tunnel under Mont Blanc connecting France and Italy, which both governments are said to approve and which is technically easy to construct. This should be one of the first of these works because it would greatly shorten the trunk line between Paris and Rome, would make for better feeling between France and Italy, would stimulate the automobile industry, while the idea of riding through the biggest mountain in Europe which tourists already flock to see would grip the world's imagination and stimulate the tourist trade on both sides of the frontier. And Americans would be the first to want to go through the tunnel they had really built.

Most Americans know that they cannot force Europe to pay that debt. Most of them fear that the debt money if not paid will be spent on arms and war. None of them seem to realize that it is easy to put that debt money to work constructively in Europe and change it from a poisonous into a most useful purpose. When they do realize it they will be all in favor of it for it will restore them to their own conception of themselves as a generous and constructive people. The way to solve the debts problem is to put the debts to work as we did the Boxer indemnity.

And when the world sees what can be done for the benefit of everyone by assuring the world this constant flow of funds into a common agency for work that is of common benefit it may be hard to get the debtors to stop paying their debt. For they will then perhaps have realized that the world is going to be more and more in need of such a constant flow of credit. We have the reparations question to bless for the existence of a World Bank. We can bless the debts for something even more valuable, if we set ourselves to this problem constructively.

Notes on the war debt plan. Budget position: The U.S. would have on her credit side the money she had on deposit in the B.I.S. as debt payments; England's credits and debits in the B.I.S. would about balance; France's debits there to the U.S. and England would be compensated by her credits from reparation deposits by Germany.

Later future: It could be arranged that at the end of the first five years, the annuities that had been paid in that period would be reinvested, say for a period of ten years, and on a basis of say fifty per cent in the paying country and fifty per cent in the common pool at the end of the next period, the process could be continued until finally the whole amount became a common fund, free from any national earmark. The interest-drawing owners of the deposits would not, of course, change.

It might be arranged that as soon as a certain export figure was reached, all the interest payments on the original debt funding agreements we made would be cancelled. It could also be arranged so that when a certain higher export figure was reached, the remaining principal due on the war debts would be automatically reduced by a certain degree or cancelled. This would simplify the thing, and add to the incentive everywhere to pull together to bring back prosperity, since the sooner prosperity came, the sooner the debt burden would be removed.

In good times, in 1928, the debts were paid and we had a budget surplus of $600,000,000 with low taxes. If the debts had not been paid, we would still have enjoyed a $350,000,000 surplus with the same low taxes.

In bad times, in 1932, we face a $2,000,000,000 deficit, despite high taxes. Even if the debts were paid, nine-tenths of that deficit would still remain to be met by taxation. The payment of the debts in bad times simply means the transfer of what now amounts to about one-third of Europe's power to buy the goods our workmen make, to the U.S. Treasury to be paid out in aid to the unemployed.

In short, in good times we wouldn't miss the non-payment of the debts, and in bad times, we cannot get them paid and they would not save us if they were paid.

Think of the psychological effect on business if it were assured in the next few months that for the next five years the world could be sure of $20,000,000 being spent every month on public and other productive works. It is not so much the sum that matters, but the fact that it will be spent constantly, for 60 months.

Just as the President put forward his public works program as a $3,000,000,000 one, and thus seized the popular imagination by merely capitalizing at the outset the total to be eventually spent, so one could treat this as a billion and a quarter program—for it will amount to that in five years. The three billion, no more than billion and a quarter program, is not going to be spent in a lump, but in instalments over a period of time.

By putting the debt payments on a monthly basis, it makes it easier to pay and budget, and it also makes it easier to arrange to invest the money wisely and to organize the spending of it well.

It is a very lucky thing that both France and the United States agree in desiring to relieve unemployment and stimulate business through public works. That greatly simplifies the debt question politically.

It is also very lucky that the debts are spread over a good many countries and that their heaviest incidence is in the most wealthy ones, France, Italy, Belgium. That allows the stimulus of public works to be applied at once broadly in Europe, and deeply. There is nothing so easily at hand for arranging a synchronized international public works program as the fact that so many countries owe us money which we can't collect but which they don't want to default. If we really believe that a synchronized program will raise prices, we should play this debt card to the limit.

If we are wise we will use this situation also to the utmost to help the French promote Briand's[3] scheme of European Union. That is the only real cure of the German problem, and the only way to peace and prosperity in Europe. And the way to promote this union is to get the

Europeans to working together on roads, electric lines, etc., that bind them closer and closer together and make frontiers and nationalism less and less important—until the Polish corridor becomes of no more political importance than the New York corridor between New Jersey and Connecticut. And the richer and more unified Europe is the better market it will be for us. We have only poverty and discord to fear in our neighbors as in our own country.

[OF 212:T]

[1] Clarence K. Streit was New York *Times* correspondent in Geneva and founder and head of Federal Union, an organization working for immediate union of fifteen "Atlantic Democracies" along the lines established by the United States constitution. The object was to combat the rise of totalitarianism. His ideas are presented in detail in his book *Union Now: A Proposal for a Federal Union of the Leading Democracies* (New York: Harper, 1939). The memorandum here printed may be compared with his "A Plan for World Recovery Based on Use of War Debts," in the New York *Times,* Sept. 24, 1933, IX, 3.
[2] Presumably this refers to another document but none other than the one here printed is present.
[3] Aristide Briand, four times prime minister of France, in 1930 proposed a "United States of Europe" as a means of preserving peace.

# Roosevelt to Ruth Bryan Owen, Minister to Denmark, Copenhagen

[Washington] August 19, 1933

My dear Ruth Owen: I am delighted to have your letter and I have heard from many people of the splendid reception you have had in Denmark and the excellent way in which you have undertaken your task.[1]

You are right about making the trade balance more even and I am working on that with the State Department experts.

I am glad that we have been able to equalize the monetary difficulties by the export of gold. We had much trouble in finding a legal way of committing this act of justice.

Always sincerely,

[OF 437:CT]

[1] In her letter of July 27, 1933 (OF 437), she urged that Denmark be included among the countries with which new trade agreements were to be made. Although the Danish public liked and wanted American goods, Denmark was refusing to buy from countries that did not reciprocate.

## Roosevelt to the Reverend Malcolm E. Peabody, Northeast Harbor, Maine

[Washington] August 19, 1933

Dear Malcolm: It was good to get that nice letter of yours and I do wish I could have a chance to talk with you one of these days.[1]

Things on the whole are progressing fairly well. That Navy program was wholly mine—I must confess—for the very good reason that under the Treaty of 1921, as modified by the London Treaty of 1930, the naval ratios were set up as Great Britain, ten; United States, ten; Japan, seven. This Treaty was fortified by the allocation to each nation on the above ratio of a definite number of ships or a definite tonnage for each class of ships. Somewhat to my dismay I discovered that as a simple mathematical problem of self-defense the Japanese had built and kept their Navy up to the Treaty provisions. Great Britain had done so in large part but we had not kept up at all, with the net result that our Navy was and probably is actually inferior to the Japanese Navy.

All this I tell you in confidence of course, and also the further fact that the whole scheme of things in Tokio does not make for an assurance of non-aggression in the future.

As a matter of fact our building program, far from building us up to our Treaty quotas, will barely suffice to keep us almost up to the ship strength of the Japanese Navy and still, of course, far below the British Navy. I am not concerned about the latter, but I am about the first.

As ever yours,

[PPF 732:CT]

[1] In his letter of Aug. 14, 1933 (PPF 732), Peabody protested Roosevelt's program to enlarge the Navy. Peabody, son of Endicott Peabody, headmaster of Groton, was an Episcopalian clergyman and later became bishop coadjutor of the diocese of central New York.

## Roosevelt to William Phillips, Under Secretary of State

[Washington] August 19, 1933

Memorandum for the Under Secretary of State: I have read your memorandum about Liberia with the greatest interest.[1] I think we should continue the present policy with, however, the clear understanding that we are not guaranteeing monies due Firestone or making our continued interest depend on Firestone's financial interest.

At all times we should remember that Firestone went into Liberia at his own financial risk and it is not the business of the State Department to pull his financial chestnuts out of the fire except as a friend of the Liberian people.

F.D.R.

[OF 476:CT]

[1] In this memorandum (Aug. 16, 1933, *Foreign Relations, 1933*, II, 924–926), Phillips said the State Department was being accused of "selling out Liberia" for the benefit of the Firestone interests; however, he pointed out, the Department was cooperating with the League of Nations in a plan whereby the League would supervise the rehabilitation of the country. For the pre-Roosevelt background and the State Department's difficulty with the Firestone interests in January-February 1933 see *Moffat Papers*, pp. 80–87.

# Louis M. Howe, Personal Secretary to the President, to the Right Reverend John Francis Noll, Bishop of Fort Wayne, Indiana

[Washington, August 19, 1933]

My dear Bishop Noll: The President has asked me to reply to your letter of July 6, 1933, drawing attention to the fact that no invocation was made at the opening session of the Monetary and Economic Conference at London; and suggesting that, should this Government find it advisable to recognize the present regime in Russia, the declaration of recognition clearly stipulate that this Government does not thereby approve of either the communistic or the atheistic creed of the Soviet Republics.[1]

The contents of your letter have been carefully noted, and appropriate consideration will be given to your suggestion with respect to Russia when the question of the recognition of a Russian Government is under consideration.

Your kind expressions with respect to the President are very much appreciated.

Very sincerely yours,

[OF 17:CT]

[1] Bishop Noll said (OF 17) that though he was sure there were millions of people who honestly believed that the Conference had failed because of the differences between the gold standard countries and the United States, he believed that it had failed "because the great Ruler of Nations was completely ignored." This reply was drafted in the State Department.

## Roosevelt to Cordell Hull, Secretary of State

Washington, August 21, 1933

Memo. for the Secretary of State: I think you will be interested in reading this. Make a note of what Claude Bowers suggests in regard to Spanish exports to the United States. Will you let me have this back when you have read it.[1]

F.D.R.

[PPF 730:CT]

[1] This refers to Bowers' letter of August 2, above. Hull returned it with the comment that he had made a note of Bowers' "interesting suggestion" (Sept. 26, 1933, PPF 730).

## Roosevelt to Claude G. Bowers, Ambassador to Spain, Madrid

Hyde Park, New York, August 22, 1933[1]

My dear Claude: It is good to have your interesting letter[2] and from all sides I hear of the excellent work you are doing. I think the Mallorcan incident was generally accepted in this country as being at least half the fault of some very bumptious Americans who would not conform to the customs of the country and who made the mistake of making fun of the local people. That never pays.

I am glad to have your suggestions in regard to possible exports from Spain to the United States. That is just the kind of thing that we must cultivate. I hope you can counteract the French propaganda in every way possible because, as you and I know, the French press simply declines to tell the truth or to print the real news.

I have read with delight of your goodness to my boy Franklin. He seems to have had a marvelous time and I hope that he will bring back a photograph of himself dressed as a matador.[3]

In a sense we are at the crisis of the development of the new program but I think that if we can get these codes for the main industries signed up in the next week we shall be definitely on the way.

My best regards. Keep me in touch.

Very sincerely yours,

[PPF 730:CT]

[1] Roosevelt was in Hyde Park from August 20 to 31; over the Labor Day week end he was cruising off Montauk Point on the Astor yacht *Nourmahal*. He returned to Washington September 5.

[2] Aug. 2, 1933, above.

[3] See Bowers to Roosevelt, Aug. 15, 1933 (PSF:Spain).


# Roosevelt to Leo S. Rowe, Director General, Pan American Union

Hyde Park, New York, August 22, 1933

My dear Rowe: I had hoped to be able to have a talk with you during these two weeks but, as you know, the new codes have taken every moment.[1] I hope you will run in and see me as soon as I get back in September. Meanwhile I trust you will keep in touch with the Secretary of State in regard to organizing for the Montevideo Conference.[2]

Very sincerely yours,

[OF 480:CT]

[1] This letter was in reply to Rowe's letter of July 25, 1933 (OF 480), asking for a conference with Roosevelt and enclosing a memorandum of June 1, 1933, on the state of affairs in Latin America. Rowe said the attitude of Latin American governments and peoples toward the United States was friendlier than it had been for some time, and that the President's speech before the Pan American Union governing board of April 12, 1933, and his world message on disarmament of May 16, 1933 (*Public Papers*, II, 129–132, 185–191), had had far-reaching influence.

[2] The Seventh International Conference of American States was originally planned for December 1932; circumstances of its postponement to the following December are explained in *Foreign Relations, 1932*, V, 1–7. Documents relating to the 1933 meeting are printed *ibid., 1933*, IV, 1–227. See also *Seventh International Conference of American States, Montevideo, Uruguay, December 3, 1933. Special Handbook for the Use of Delegates* (Baltimore: Pan American Union, 1933); and *Report of the Delegates of the United States of America to the Seventh International Conference of American States* (Washington, 1934). Hull devotes two chapters of his *Memoirs* to the conference; his important speeches and statements relating to it have been published as *Addresses and Statements by the Honorable Cordell Hull in Connection with His Trip to South America 1933–1934 to Attend the Seventh International Conference of American States, Montevideo, Uruguay* (Washington, 1935).

## William Phillips, Under Secretary of State, to Roosevelt

Washington, August 23, 1933

Dear Mr. President: At the last meeting of the Cabinet[1] you asked me a question with regard to the number of American citizens in Germany who have been subjected to assault or mistreatment and I promised you a report thereon.

I enclose a brief memorandum showing that there are twelve cases on record of mistreatment by Germans wearing the uniform of the National Socialist party. Of course, this does not mean that there may not have been other cases which have not, as yet, been brought to our attention officially.

Faithfully yours,

William Phillips

[*Notation*:AS] OK  Return    FDR[2]
[OF 198:TS]

[1] On August 18.
[2] Meaning: return the memorandum to Phillips.

## Press Conference, Hyde Park, August 25, 1933, 3:55 P.M.

[*Excerpt*] Mr. Early: Davis[1] called up last night to say what a splendid reaction he had had abroad and to say that already he had received three invitations to start work in Washington. The first came from the German Embassy.

The President: I love it.

Q: Particularly in Mr. Davis' talk to us he said that you were subscribing more or less to what he termed "the French plan" for setting up—

The President: That is Eddie's question.[2]

Mr. Roddan: We have been battling for three days about that.

The President: Here it is as I understand it, although I don't understand it as well as Norman does. The thing in a nutshell is this: Away back last April I became more and more convinced that I ought to put myself in the other fellow's place and I tried to put myself in the place of the Frenchmen. Keep this off the record because we really can't write anything about it, even coming under the Hyde Park date line. If I were a Frenchman and were certain in my own mind that Germany was not living up to treaties, I wouldn't scrap a thing and neither would any of us. And there is a general feeling in France that Germany has not been living up to them. In other words, we know that the Germans are drilling, the school children are drilling and there are all kinds of reports and rumors from the French border that Germany has been manufacturing 75 guns secretly and so forth and so on. I felt last April, when they were all over here, that France would never agree to any kind of disarmament unless she could be persuaded that Germany was not re-arming in the meantime, and I talked to MacDonald about it and Herriot and Jung, and they all agreed with the general proposition that there would have to be some kind of continuous inspection and that if that continuous inspection proved to the satisfaction of France and Italy and Germany and England and the rest of the world that Germany was living up to its treaty obligations and not re-arming, in that case France would not have a leg to stand on—she would have to agree to disarm. I put it up to them and out of that conversation came the first—when the Conference met again about the first of May came what was called "The French Plan for Continuous Inspection." In the beginning, the British were rather hostile to it and their reason for being hostile to it was, I think, that other nations might find out how weak they were in certain lines. Well, probably the other nations know how weak you are in certain lines anyway, just as well as you do yourself, and the British are coming around to the principle of continuous inspection.

Now, the French plan has been changed in various details from time to time and what it is at the present time, I don't know. I don't know what the present French plan is. It may be different today from what it was a month ago. I don't think anybody but Henderson could say what the present French plan is, but we do know the principle, and that is expressed by using the words "continuous inspection." That means, of course,—Eddie Roddan please quote to W. R.[3]—that means, if we go along, that a bunch of foreign officers will come here and look into our Navy Yards and arsenals *if,* if American officers can go into Germany and France and everywhere else and see what they are making. In other words, it is sauce for the goose and the gander.

That is the French Plan in a nutshell and it is dependent on getting everybody to do it, and I consider it of great importance because, as I say, I would not disarm unless I had assurance that the other fellow is going to disarm.

Q: That is the proposition of continuous inspection in your message and what Norman Davis did out in Geneva, and there is nothing new in it. But the French Plan is to turn over these big offensive weapons that these countries give up—turn them over to the League of Nations and make that an independent state.

Q: That is part of the original proposal.

Q: A part of it, but it is pretty big.

The President: I never heard of it.

Q: The French proposed it.

The President: They propose something every day but I don't think anybody attaches any importance to that.

Q: They always do.

The President: I don't think so.

Q: If it is part of the plan, are you for it?

The President: No.

Q: It is a League of Nations Commission under the French Plan.

The President: To do what?

Q: This continuous inspection will be done under the League of Nations.

The President: That is not under the MacDonald plan?

Q: Under the French plan.

The President: It is to be carried on by the Committee on Disarmament, the Permanent Committee on Disarmament, which will be the same Committee which, in case somebody goes across somebody else's border, will call all the heads of states and see whether it can be stopped.[4]

[President's Press Conferences:T]

[1] Norman H. Davis conferred with Roosevelt at Hyde Park on Aug. 30, 1933, just before sailing for Europe to resume discussions preliminary to the reconvening of the Disarmament Conference on October 16.

[2] Edward L. Roddan, a reporter for Universal News Service.

[3] William Randolph Hearst.

[4] At his Aug. 23, 1933, press conference, Roosevelt had said that he did not know what the "French Plan" was, that it changed every week. He referred again to it in the press conference of August 30, complaining that the wording of an Associated Press dispatch from Geneva on August 23 gave "entirely the wrong slant," in that it left the impression that the League, under the "French Plan," would be armed to move against aggressor nations. He said: "Now, that is an erroneous lead because what actually happened—well, I talked to Norman Davis about this on the 'phone yesterday . . . The French Plan as we mean it—the French Plan, which I think is our plan and I think we sold it to the French and to the British, is to implement disarmament by constant inspection of every nation's armaments. That is what we mean by the French Plan."

# Senator Hiram W. Johnson of California to Roosevelt

San Francisco, California, August 26th, 1933

My dear Mr. President: I very humbly apologize for not having sooner answered your letter dated at Hyde Park, July 31st.[1] I know that you will pardon me when I tell you that before the receipt of your letter here Mrs. Johnson and I received a terribly tragic blow, which has kept me from my office until just recently.[2]

It was very kind of you to write me about the Foreign Securities Act,[3] and Title II which you designate as my child.

I read with the utmost interest the letter of Mr. Raymond Stevens which you enclosed,[4] with the statements of which you are inclined to agree. Of course, your ultimate decision in the matter will be accepted by me without demur; but although I have the same high opinion of Mr. Stevens and Mr. Rublee that you express, I am unable to accept their conclusions. Your representatives presented Title I of the Act to prevent in the future the shameful misrepresentation and fraud which had exploited American investors. Title II was added to aid those who in the past had been deceived and robbed by the very practices Title I denounced. The government with its strong arm sought by your proposed law to preclude a recurrence of what it had, in some measure at least, been responsible for; and as complementary of this, some of us thought it should endeavor to aid those who had been wronged. The second title seemed to me the logical consequence of the first.

You will recall that after the investigation which I conducted into the sale of foreign securities, an investigation carried on without assistance of any kind or character and without expense of any sort save for stenographic fees, and in the teeth of the opposition of the State Department as then constituted, belated efforts in behalf of American investors were made by that Department, the exact nature and character of which have really never been disclosed. Certain gentlemen were called into consultation, among whom perhaps the most active was Mr. Rublee. Eighteen months of effort and investigation resulted in a decision, as I understand it, by these gentlemen, designated for some reason "the secret six," that at some time, somewhere under some circumstances in the far future, a private corporation would be organized by a selected group of citizens, and this private corporation would have as its executive officer with a very high salary, Mr. Norman H. Davis! This represented a year and a half of a private activity, in conjunction secretly with the

State Department, on the part of those who do not believe in any governmental effort in behalf of bewildered citizens who admittedly have been swindled, and who have only their government to look to for protection, comfort and aid.

For some years now there has been complete accord among those familiar with the subject, that some method should be devised by which the ordinary citizen who held foreign securities might have some representation. At least it was thought that an endeavor should be made to salvage something from his wretched investment. Various organizations have been formed for this purpose. Some of these in good faith have tried to help; some have been a mere "racket," designed to wring a little more money from the already impoverished investor; some, while ostensibly seeking to protect the exploited investor, have in reality been for the protection of those guilty of the misrepresentation and fraud. But the important thing concerning these private efforts, not only those of organizations such as have just been referred to, but of the "secret six" working at the State Department, is that the results accomplished by them have been exactly nothing. For reasons, unnecessary to discuss, their efforts have been unavailing, and wholly fruitless. The results of the investigation I conducted, and a knowledge of the utterly futile efforts of various private organizations and the subsequent eighteen months of unavailing travail of the "secret six," led some of us whose sole thought was of the unhappy investor, to conclude that the only way in which anything could be accomplished for him was by a public corporation whose activities would be along the lines of those of the corporations of Great Britain and some of the continental countries.

I turned to Mr. Stevens' letter with no small degree of surprise. He says that as a Democrat he is seriously concerned to see your Administration assume an obligation for a situation which occurred under Republican rule and for which you are in no sense responsible. I might paraphrase his statement and say that as an American I would be seriously concerned to see an Administration for which I have such enthusiastic regard refuse to assume an obligation to try to remedy a situation which occurred under Republican rule, and in which our people suffered grievous wrong and great financial loss. Of course you are not in any way responsible for what has happened, and you are not in any sense responsible for the laissez faire doctrine of Mr. Hoover under which the Administration preceding this occupied itself with weeping and wailing and gnashing its teeth, and had not the courage or the patriotism necessary to undertake remedial measures even though empirical. It is the glory of this Administration, of which all of us are so proud, that it has dared to do and has gallantly embarked upon an economic adventure the most astounding the world has even seen; and that it has gone forward without fear though the end no human being can foresee. Today, and for some weeks past, in just this one community, thousands of home owners have been registering under one of the laws passed, and not the most important, and are asking the government to intervene and save their homes. By far the greatest percentage of these will be disappointed ultimately but unquestionably a very great good will be accomplished for many. The disappointed naturally will react politically; but I am very glad to see that such an obvious result neither frightened nor deterred this Administration from acting for the benefit of some. If Mr. Stevens' view had been followed and if the one thought of the Administration had been only political results, no attempt would have been made to save the homes of unfortunate American citizens.

Of course there is muttering and grumbling beneath the surface concerning the National Recovery Act, and its effect on some businesses may be injurious, but who would tremble and hesitate and timidly falter in this vast undertaking? We are endeavoring to correct a situation which occurred under Republican rule, and for which you are in no sense responsible, but who would exchange this Administration's high purpose for the do nothing preachment of Mr. Stevens. The doctrine of Mr. Stevens is not a doctrine of progressivism; and, thank God, it has not been yours in the terrible economic crisis of this Nation.

I cannot for one moment concede the serious consequences which Mr. Stevens seems to feel will result from the formation of the public corporation provided for by Title II. To my mind it is perfectly absurd to say that it would complicate our foreign relations, or that we are bound to have controversies between the Department of State and the corporation. I spent an afternoon talking of this situation with Mr. Feis of the State Department. I thought I left him convinced that the formation of a corporation by law was quite appropriate and that our differences had finally developed into the mere mode of selection of the directors of the corporation. He was insistent that some should be chosen by the National Chamber of Commerce, some by the Carnegie Foundation and others by semi-public bodies. I very emphatically declined to acquiesce in any such method of procedure. Bitter experience has taught those whose sole object was to aid Americans who had been swindled, that little dependence could be placed upon an organization chosen by chambers of commerce or other semi-public bodies; and we believed that within a brief period after such a selection the control of the directors would be with the very men who had originally perpetrated the wrong. I told Mr. Feis that I preferred no law at all to a law which, in my opinion, would be likely to be manipulated and directed by the international bankers and investment houses which with their high-powered salesmen had induced the unwary American public to invest their savings in foreign securities. I have thought from the beginning, and I still think, that the only organization from which any results may be expected is an organization over which, if it ever be desirable, the government itself may exercise absolute dominion and control. Personally I am not interested in any other kind, and any other kind, I think, will be as barren of results to the general investing American public as have been the combined efforts of the private organizations now existing, the State Department and its "secret six."

The essence of Mr. Stevens' objection, under his point marked (1), is that a private organization can conduct negotiations more efficiently and successfully. The answer is before us in the realities. Private organizations have neither been efficient nor successful. They have utterly and absolutely failed. The question presented, therefore, is: shall we decline to attempt any other method, acknowledging that we are beaten; and say to those who look so longingly to this present government, which has feared no experiment in behalf of its people, it hesitates to take a perfectly plain and logical course in an endeavor to salvage something for its citizens who have lost much. I have yet to hear of any government taking offense at the operation of the English public corporation which has its far flung committees in nearly every debtor country on earth. It is rather difficult for me to regard the English corporation as a private association. It was created by an act of Parliament and subsequently amended by an act of Parliament. Mr. Stevens says concerning this organization and that of other governments that they "are subject to some governmental control and secure the aid of the government in their negotiations, but only in so far as the government deems consistent with national interest." I am sure that those who are interested in our public corporation do not ask more—indeed less. I cannot quite fathom this statement of Mr. Stevens when his objection is so emphatic to having the government connected at all with the corporation we created by Title II. It seems to me that one part of his argument is the direct antithesis of the other.

In the last analysis, the argument of Mr. Stevens is the gospel of timidity and fear. Nothing has yet been done, although years have elapsed, for the protection or the aid of those holding defaulted foreign securities in this country. Private endeavors have been lamentably lacking any results. We have endeavored to adopt now what other nations long ago did, as the sole means of salvaging something. These foreign governments, as Mr. Stevens says, aid in the negotiations of their public corporations which are subject to some governmental control. Of course if these foreign governments, as Mr. Stevens states, lend their aid "only in so far as the government deems consistent with national interest" naturally all the dreadful consequences adverted to by Mr. Stevens are perfectly certain to occur. What the English believe consistent with their national interest needs no elaboration. When Great Britain, for instance, "so far as the government deems consistent with national interest," aids its public corporation, the delicate sensibilities of countries like Siam, as Mr. Stevens points out, are at once offended and "the immediate reaction is one of suspicion, fear and resentment." And so, we may readily conclude that all debtor countries, where their defaulted obligations have been sold in England, look upon that tight little isle with "suspicion, fear and resentment." This awful fate our government may suffer if it dare even permit the creation of a public corporation for the benefit of our citizens, and this may be so even though that corporation is hedged about with every conceivable safe-guarding provision.

I apologize for the length of this communication. I would not take it amiss if it were never read. I want it, however, to complete the record upon the subject; and if possible to prevent those who have little and who have been grossly swindled by those who have much, from fading from our memories into those forgotten.

How heartily I congratulate you upon the work you are doing I cannot adequately express! May your heart continue strong in your good deeds and your high achievement, and may you have from all of our people the same emphatic and enthusiastic support that you have from—

Yours most sincerely,

Hiram W. Johnson

P.S. I am enclosing herein, as you requested, the letter of Mr. Stevens. HWJ[5]

[OF 100-B:TS]

[1] Above.
[2] This reference is not explained by the information available.
[3] The Securities Exchange Act of 1933 is meant.
[4] July 28, 1933, above.
[5] Roosevelt asked Stevens to read Johnson's letter and to talk with him about it (Sept. 6, 1933), OF 100-B). Stevens replied Sept. 26, 1933, below.

## Roosevelt to Cordell Hull, Secretary of State, Henry Morgenthau, Jr., Acting Secretary of the Treasury, and Daniel C. Roper, Secretary of Commerce

Hyde Park, N.Y., August 31, 1933

Memo . . . I wish the Secretary of State would have a little talk with Commissioner Stevens, the Acting Secretary of the Treasury and the Secretary of Commerce in order to set up the small committee of four which Commissioner Stevens and I discussed two weeks ago.[1]

The object of this committee of four is to work out something definite in regard to the protecting of the interests of American holders of foreign securities, and I think that within a week or ten days a recommendation could be made to me.

F.D.R.

[OF 100-B:CT]

[1] Stevens and Roosevelt had conferred at the White House on Aug. 18, 1933 (PPF 1-0). The "small committee" eventually became the Foreign Bondholders Protective Council, Inc., with more than a dozen members; see *Public Papers,* II, 411–415, and memorandum by Feis, Sept. 15, 1933, below.

## James Harvey Rogers to Roosevelt

New York, August 31, 1933

My dear Mr. President: When our conversation ended yesterday you had just raised the question of the potential strength of the dollar. I agree with Governor Norman that it is very great.[1] The reasons are three:

(1) The huge balances held abroad by Americans are apt to be withdrawn at any time.

(2) The large recent short-sales of dollars by foreign speculators are apt to be covered at any time.

(3) The approach of fall with its usual increase in our exports will likewise stimulate a demand for dollars.

In my opinion it is largely the fear of further depreciation that is holding these strengthening influences in check. For this reason I think it would be unwise to remove the present uncertainty regarding the future course of the dollar until after our October discussions with the British.[2]

For similar reasons I think it is at present inadvisable to make any definite devaluation of the dollar or to open a free gold market. Either course would, I think, precipitate a large inflow of funds to this country and the resulting large gold imports would very likely bring immediate difficulties in the Gold Bloc countries. On the character of these difficulties I hope to be able to give you more specific information upon my return from Paris on September 24.

I am sending to Miss LeHand a list of addresses for the entire period of my absence from this country.[3]

Yours very sincerely,

James Harvey Rogers

[*Notation*:A:FDR] File
[OF 229:TS]

---

[1] Rogers, professor of political economy at Yale, had been appointed on July 10, 1933, to survey federal finances. A disciple of Irving Fisher, Rogers was committed to the inflation idea propounded by Fisher, Warren, and others. He had talked with Roosevelt at Hyde Park on August 30 (PPF 1-0). On August 28 Roosevelt had conferred in Hyde Park with Montagu Norman, governor of the Bank of England, and George L. Harrison, governor of the Federal Reserve Bank of New York, who had been conferring on gold policy and stabilization (New York *Times*, Aug. 29, 1933, p. 25).

In this connection, a telegram from Emerson Bigelow, of the Foreign Exchange and Trade Institute, to Roosevelt is perhaps relevant. The telegram was received at Hyde Park on August 28 at 12:37 P.M., in ample time for the President to have read it before his talk with Norman and Harrison at 5:15 P.M., the same afternoon (OF 230). Bigelow, arguing that British opposition to American price-raising efforts was weakening, urged Roosevelt to push the price-raising program. He added: "Either Montagu Norman is still promoting the inflation of gold or he is ready to abandon that highly dangerous policy. If his purpose is unchanged his failure to induce you to come to his rescue will mean the collapse of gold corner and those in England willing to cooperate with us would have their chance." Early acknowledged the telegram on August 30, saying that the President had read it "with a great deal of interest" (OF 230).

[2] On war debts.

[3] Rogers had been appointed to the Economic Commission of the League of Nations and was going to France in this connection. His associate, Warren, also went abroad in August to study financial conditions in northern Europe.

# William E. Dodd, Ambassador to Germany, to Roosevelt

[Berlin] September 1, 1933

Dear Mr. President: My reception on the 30th by the Reichspresident was extraordinarily cordeal[1] and the fifteen minutes conversation that followed showed a keen interest in and appreciation of your great undertaking.[2] I inferred from all that was said that he is in full sympathy with your attitudes as to the futility of war and the nessity of freer international exchanges. His health seems to be good . . .[3]

Yours sincerely,

William E. Dodd

[OF 523:AS]

[1] Dodd's letters, both the holograph (as this one) and the typed, show a cavalier attitude toward spelling that no doubt was owing more to haste than to anything else.
[2] For this meeting, see Dodd, *Diary,* pp. 30–31.
[3] The rest of Dodd's letter deals with personnel problems at the Embassy.

## John F. Coar to Louis M. Howe, Personal Secretary to the President

Kingston, Mass., September 2, 1933

My dear Col. Howe: I am just back from Germany where I had an opportunity for very intimate conversations with Chancellor Hitler. In a general way, Ambassador Dodd has been informed of the purpose and the results and I believe the information I was at liberty to convey to him was forwarded to Washington. It is now most desirable that I should have a personal talk with the President, for the purpose of carrying out the promise I made the Chancellor and of submitting to him, wholly unofficially, Mr. Hitler's views and what he is prepared to do provided a personal understanding can be reached between him and our President.

Can you not arrange for me to have a talk with Mr. Roosevelt sometime next week. Upon the outcome of this talk will depend the issuance of temporary orders in respect to the anti-Semitic policy, and eventually a solution of that particular problem wholly in line, I believe, with our President's desires. Mr. Dodd agrees with me that this preliminary personal understanding must be reached before the matter is taken up diplomatically, and I cannot urge too strongly that the desired opportunity for a personal talk with Mr. Roosevelt be arranged at the earliest moment. I can only assure you that I have succeeded in obtaining the agreement to concessions that were regarded as utterly unobtainable not only by extremists like Wise, Untermyer and "cohorts," but even by such men as Baruch, Kahn, Finley and others.[1] It seems to me (if Ambassador Dodd interpreted the President's wishes correctly), that what

384

I shall have to say to Mr. Roosevelt will be of singular help to him in eliminating certain international problems from the crazy picture puzzle he is trying to put together. More than this I cannot say without violating confidences. Before I saw Mr. Hitler for the final interview I communicated with Mr. Roosevelt indicating, in a general way, what I had in hand, and forwarded this letter through the kind offices of Ambassador Dodd, after letting him read it, to the President. My return, as announced in that letter, was delayed chiefly because it seemed wise to allow Mr. H. an opportunity to "cool off," for he is a man of impulse, and I feared he might not, after second thought, adhere to his promise. However, he has done so, and just before sailing, I received confirmation, by long distance from Munich, to this effect.

May I not hope that you will present this matter in the strictest confidence to the President, adding that the least suggestion of a "diplomatic" move will enrage Mr. Hitler, and that the first move of that kind must come from him and will come from him under certain conditions. Mr. Dodd agrees absolutely with me in this respect. I shall be glad to go to Washington or any other locality after receiving word from you, but would suggest that the latter part of next week will conflict least with engagements and duties that my two months absence now make pressing.[2]

Very sincerely yours,

John F. Coar

[PPF 3716:TS]

[1] Rabbi Stephen S. Wise, founder of the Zionist Organization of America; Samuel Untermyer, a distinguished New York liberal lawyer; Bernard M. Baruch, financier and businessman; Otto H. Kahn, partner in banking firm of Kuhn, Loeb and Co.; John H. Finley, associate editor of the New York *Times.*

[2] An accompanying note from Roosevelt to McIntyre, Sept. 11, 1933, reads: "In view of this letter I think I should see John F. Coar." Roosevelt's illness later in the month prevented this and on September 21 Coar wrote again (PPF 3716): "Whatever personal influence I may be able to exert on a certain 'person' in Germany will, of course, be greater the more speedily I can re-employ it." There is no further mention of an appointment. Coar went to Germany again in 1934 (Dodd, *Diary,* p. 183).

# Press Conference, Executive Offices of the White House, September 6, 1933

[*Excerpt*] The President: I don't know that there is any news at all today. I am keeping in touch with the Cuban situation. Then we had a birthday party last night. There has very little happened where Cuba is concerned. You probably know as much as I do.

Q: What is the status this morning?[1]

The President: I have just talked with the Secretary of State. He talked with Ambassador Welles this morning. You will have to get it from him. There isn't any news. That, of course, is a good sign things are quiet in Havana, the only disturbing element apparently coming from the many outlying places, Cienfuegos and Guantanamo, etc. The trouble there seems to be fairly wide-spread over the island, and for that reason we have ordered a number, I don't know how many, four or five, additional small ships down there to be within steaming distance, for the protection of American lives in the various outlying places in case of need.

This is merely a precautionary measure and the Secretary of the Navy is leaving this afternoon on the *Indianapolis,* from Annapolis, for the West Coast. Of course, that means in case of a crisis of some kind the *Indianapolis* will be in the neighborhood of Cuba in about two days. But that trip was a scheduled trip. As you all know, he was going anyway. The only other ship movement is also a part of the thing that was done a month ago or more. The *Mississippi* is leaving for the West Coast.

Q: Where is she leaving from?

The President: Norfolk.

Q: Will she sort of hesitate down around Cuba?

The President: It is too early to tell. She wouldn't get there for two or three days. There might be a hesitation—might not. She might keep on going.

Q: Mr. President, there are reports this morning that marines are being concentrated at Quantico and at different points along the Eastern Seaboard.

The President: Not that I know of.[2]

Q: Mr. President, in that connection, I was talking to the Marine Commandant just today. He said he had ordered 1106 of them concentrated at Quantico, pulling them in from Philadelphia, Norfolk, Washington, ten companies from Annapolis—told us we should inquire direct for the reason for that.

The President: I suppose the Navy Department may have gotten them down, and it is probably perfectly true. But merely again as a precautionary measure, saving twenty-four hours in case of need. Lay off on this intervention stuff. As you know, that is absolutely the last thing we have in mind. We don't want to do it.

Another thing, on the general Latin-American policy: You can't say that the Cuban situation is the keynote of Latin-American policy, because there is no other American nation that is in the same status as Cuba. In Cuba we have treaty obligations—in other nations we haven't. In other words, don't intimate anything we do in Cuba is the same as we will do in Haiti, Santo Domingo, etc.

Q: Under the Treaty of Paris we have obligations to foreign governments in regard to Cuba, in addition to the Platt Amendment, which says we have the privilege to intervene for the purpose of carrying out the provisions of the Treaty of Paris. I tried to find the Treaty of Paris but couldn't and haven't read it. I have the impression there was something in the Treaty that the United States preserve—

The President: I don't know. Ask the State Department.

[President's Press Conferences:T]

---

[1] The government of Carlos Céspedes, which had taken power August 13, was overthrown on September 5 and a junta of five civilians took over all authority. Four destroyers were sent to Cuban waters for the protection of Americans (New York *Times,* Sept. 6, p. 1; Sept. 7, 1933, p. 1).

[2] The concentration of Marines at east coast bases began on September 6 (*ibid.,* Sept. 7, 1933, p. 1).

## Press Conference, Executive Offices of the White House, September 6, 1933, 5:45 P.M.

The President: I told them[1] three things: First, that I wanted them to have complete and constant information about the Cuban situation to the full extent that we have that information. Yesterday morning the State Department commenced keeping them informed—all the American Republics—of what was going on just as fast as it came in and we are continuing that and will continue to let them have everything we know.

The second point that I explained to them, as I did to you gentlemen this morning—that the United States had absolutely no desire to intervene and is seeking every means to avoid intervention.

And the third point was that I expressed to them the very definite hope on the part of the United States, that might be called the key to our policy, is that the Cuban people will obtain as rapidly as possible a government of their own choosing and, equally important, a government that will be able to maintain order and, of course, if a government is constituted as quickly as possible, that will maintain order, it will have the happy effect of eliminating altogether any preparation or thought of the necessity for intervention. And then finally—this is not one of the points but the way I would write it would be this: That the object of calling these gentlemen in is to give them full information and to make perfectly clear to all other American Republics what the position of the United States is in regard to Cuba, yet making clear to the other American Republics that we believe that they have just as much interest as we have in the preservation of order and orderly government.

Q: Is there anything new on Cuba that you care to tell us?

The President: Let me read this: "Conditions in Cienfuegos are not as good as they were. There seems to be a good deal of disquiet—" that is a grand word, "—in a number of other places—especially apparent on the southern coast."

That is from Welles.[2]

[President's Press Conferences:T]

[1] Roosevelt had just talked with the Argentinian, Brazilian, Chilean, and Mexican ambassadors, together with Secretary of State Hull and Assistant Secretary Jefferson Caffery (New York *Times,* Sept. 7, 1933, p. 1). This was the reason for the second press conference on the same day.

[2] Not further identified.


## Cordell Hull, Secretary of State, to Louis M. Howe, Personal Secretary to the President

Washington, September 6, 1933

*Strictly Confidential*

My dear Mr. Howe: From the foreign point of view I see a serious disadvantage to the President sending a message to the testimonial dinner given to Mr. Untermyer in recognition of his work against the persecution of the Jews in Germany. Mr. Untermyer has been a leader of that school of thought among the Jews which has been advocating the use of an unofficial boycott against German goods. It would be hard to frame a message that would not be interpreted as at least an implied endorsement of such a boycott, which is contrary to this Government's beliefs. There may, of course, be political advantages which would make the sending of a message desirable but, if so, it should be framed with the utmost care so as not to inflame public opinion further either in Germany or among the Jews in this country; such inflammation of opinion would only react further on the Jews in Germany whose lot we have been endeavoring to improve without giving ground for resentment in Germany.[1]

Sincerely yours,

Cordell Hull

[*Notation*:A:FDR] File
[OF 198-A:TS]

[1] Samuel Untermyer, a distinguished New York lawyer, was president of the World Jewish Economic Federation and had been chosen to represent American-Jewish war veterans in an appeal to the League of Nations to aid German Jews. Ezekiel Rabinowitz, secretary of the American League for Defense of Jewish Rights, had asked Roosevelt for a message to be read at the League's dinner for Untermyer in New York, Sept. 10, 1933 (Rabinowitz to Roosevelt, Sept. 2, 1933, OF 198-A). Rabinowitz said that such a message would "hearten American Jewry as well as all other forces who believe in the principles of liberty and justice." Howe asked Hull for advice on the day the telegram was received (OF 198-A), but apparently no reply was made to Rabinowitz and Roosevelt sent no message to the Untermyer dinner. Alfred E. Smith gave the major address at the dinner, and James W. Gerard, former ambassador to Germany, and Bainbridge Colby, former Secretary of State, also spoke.

# Press Conference, Executive Offices of the White House, Sept. 8, 1933

The President: I guess you know all the news I do.

Q: Is Mr. Gore going to leave the Governorship of Puerto Rico?[1]

The President: Not that I have ever heard of.

Q: Is there anything on Cuba?

The President: There has not been anything today.

Q: There is a report out that the Cubans have agreed to a peaceable landing of sailors and bluejackets.

The President: Not unless it happened in the last three minutes and a half.

Q: There is word that an inspection party of sailors was landed.

The President: Not that we have any information on.

Q: There is a paragraph out of Paris today saying we made overtures to reopen debt negotiations. Can you comment?

The President: Not that we know of.

Q: Can you tell us anything about the Sugar Conference yesterday?

The President: There isn't very much to tell except we went over tentative allocations. There have been a number of changes made and they are being taken up with the various other people who are concerned in them.

Q: Is Dr. Coulter[2] to work it out?

The President: Yes . . .

Q: What time are you leaving today?

The President: I am not going until tomorrow.[3]

Q: Are you going in the morning or afternoon?

The President: I don't know.

Q: How come you are not going tonight?

The President: To tell you the truth I was afraid that going to Quantico somebody would write a story that I was reviewing the Marines before they started on their way to Cuba.

Q: Are they going down to Cuba?

The President: I am going, in that connection, to tell you a famous old story about Mr. Bryan.[4] In the old days he came into my office in the Navy Department and said, "I have to have a battleship right away—I have to have it by this afternoon."

I said, "Mr. Bryan, I am awfully sorry, battleships are few and far between, and to get it by this afternoon is impossible; I have a good gunboat in Quantico."

Mr. Bryan said, "That's all right; that's all right."

I said, "I thought you wanted a battleship."

He answered, "No, when I say a battleship I don't mean anything technical. I mean just something that floats."

You people are all absolved, but the headline writers are not. Some of the editorial writers are not. They think we have sent a large armada to Cuba. As a matter of fact, as you know, we have only twelve ships in Cuban waters at the present time. I think we have another ten or fifteen that are on their way down in that general direction.[5] Some of them may go into Cuban waters. But there are two things—but this is just for background—there are two things I do think ought to be in your stories.

In the first place, what are these ships? Outside of the *Mississippi* and the *Richmond,* that is now in Havana Harbor, all of them are little bits of things—destroyers, Coast Guard boats, etc. Because of the length of the Cuban coastline—there are a great many harbors in Cuba—one of our problems has been the fact that there have been potential threats against American lives. For instance, in a good many different places, for instance on the Isle of Pines (this is off the record)—just one of those things and no use writing a story about it—anything may happen on the Isle of Pines—there are a good many Americans down there, two or three hundred, also a Cuban Penal Colony with 2,008 prisoners and most of them pretty rough prisoners, and the officers in charge of the Penal Colony were asked to step aside and the Colony came into the control of Major Benitez. He realized after he had gotten control that they only had supplies of food for two days and he didn't know any way of getting any more supplies. Some Americans were told by Major Benitez that if he didn't get supplies in two days he would let the prisoners loose. So we sent a destroyer in there. It got in this morning, probably took a look-see and will go on.

You see, Cuba is nearly seven hundred miles long and there are cities, fairly important cities, on both coasts, practically the length of both the northern coast and the southern coast. It takes a great many vessels to cover that area. This talk about it's being a large armada and a great display of strength is sort of silly. The great majority of these boats are operating all alone, one boat all by itself. A destroyer with perhaps a crew of ninety people on board might land thirty or forty men from that ship, so you see it is not a very serious military occupation on that basis.

Q: The last word that you received from Cuba—was the situation better than in the last couple of days?

The President: That is always a relative term, Fred.[6] I'd hate to say better or worse. I should say the best way to describe it is that it is still somewhat tense and that a final solution doesn't appear to have been arrived at yet.

Q: I am just curious—would that be called a "flotilla"? Or what is an armada?

The President: No, neither, because a fleet, a flotilla, an armada, or anything like that, means a lot of ships together. Where you have twelve or twenty ships all scattered along twelve hundred to fourteen hundred miles of coast, I don't think there is any particular word for it.

Q: It's the copy reader's problem.

The President: That's it—your headline men know the word to describe it.

Q: Somebody suggested a "cordon" . . .

Q: How long will you give Cuba to get a stable government down there?

The President: Really, Stevie![7]

Q: Is it a fair view to say that you think they ought to have something a little more stable than the crowd that is there now?

391

The President: Off the record—here's the difficulty with the Cuban situation at the present time—it is this: You have down there a committee of five gentlemen[8] who are the last people that have been chosen by the Army, and no government has been set up. You simply have a committee that has been set up by the Army. That is as far as they have gone. Now we are waiting for some new step. You can't call that a government. There isn't any very serious rioting, but so far as a permanent or stable government goes, I haven't got the faintest idea what may happen between now and six o'clock. This committee may become the government or it may decide to turn things over to some other committee to become the government, or some individual. We don't know. It is awfully hard to describe a situation like that where the only thing is a Committee of Five that has been set up by the Army. They have been holding almost a continuous conference since last night, and again at eleven o'clock today, and we haven't had any report since that from that eleven o'clock meeting.

Q: If you hear anything will you let us know?

Q: Do you anticipate any communication with Ambassador Welles tonight?

The President: Yes, we hear from him quite constantly. The Secretary of State, for instance, has telephoned him a couple of times today.[9]

[President's Press Conferences:T]

[1] Robert H. Gore of Florida had been appointed governor on April 28, 1933; he was unpopular in the island and resigned Jan. 12, 1934, to be succeeded by Blanton Winship. Gore had seen Roosevelt on Sept. 8, 1933 (PPF 1-0).

[2] John L. Coulter of the United States Tariff Commission, an authority on sugar.

[3] Roosevelt spent Saturday and Sunday, September 9–10, on a cruise on the Potomac (New York *Times,* Sept. 11, 1933, p. 12).

[4] William Jennings Bryan, Secretary of State from 1913 to 1915.

[5] By September 8 twenty-nine American vessels had been alerted for Cuban waters.

[6] J. Fred Storm of the United Press.

[7] Francis M. Stephenson of the Associated Press.

[8] The civilian junta composed of Porfirio Franco, Sergio Carbo, Guillermo Portela, Ramón Grau San Martín, and José M. Irezarri on Sept. 10, 1933, proclaimed Grau San Martín provisional president of Cuba.

[9] *Foreign Relations, 1933,* V, in the section dealing with Cuban affairs, contains no transcripts or other reference to these telephone calls on September 8, but does print (p. 410) a memorandum of the three-way conversation at 11 P.M. on September 9, between Welles, Hull, and Roosevelt.

## Roosevelt to Nathan Straus, Jr., National Chairman, American Palestine Campaign, New York

[Washington] September 8, 1933

My dear Mr. Straus: I regret that official duty prevents me from accepting your cordial invitation to attend the presentation of the Jewish pageant, "The Romance of a People," at the Polo Grounds, New York City, on September fourteenth. On various occasions in the past I have expressed my sympathy with the purpose of the Jewish people in the rebuilding of their homeland. I welcome this opportunity to endorse again the establishment of a homeland for the Jewish people through a reconstruction of Palestine.

I am glad to know that the Pageant this year is to chronicle four thousand years of Jewish history and to facilitate the further development of Palestine. Because of my utter inability to participate with you in this celebration, I am asking Postmaster General Farley to attend as my personal representative and to extend to all my best wishes for the Jewish New Year. I hope very sincerely that the New Year will bring greater peace, understanding and good fortune to all.[1]

Very sincerely yours,

[PPF 19:CT]

[1] The pageant was postponed from its planned opening at the New York Polo Grounds on September 14 because of rain. It opened on September 30 and ran for three weeks, raising $200,000 to help settle German Jews in Palestine (New York *Times*, Sept. 14, p. 19; Sept. 16, p. 15; Oct. 20, 1933, p. 21). During the 1932 campaign Roosevelt had endorsed Zionism and the Balfour Declaration of 1917 in a letter to Morris Rothenberg of the Zionist Organization of America, dated Oct. 28, 1932 (PPF 19). (The United States had recognized the British mandate in Palestine in the U.S.-British Mandate Treaty of 1924, which upheld the Balfour Declaration.) The violence of American protests and counter-boycotts (by Jews and non-Jews alike) against anti-Semitic outrages in Germany had made difficult the Administration's position with respect both to aid for Palestine and for Jews within Germany; for this reason, extreme caution was used in issuing public statements about the Jewish problem. Early telegraphed Straus on September 12 that Farley had to go to Chicago and could not attend the pageant; Senator Wagner took his place. The letter here printed was published in the New York *Times* of Sept. 12, 1933, p. 26.

## Roosevelt to Breckinridge Long, Ambassador to Italy, Rome

[Washington] September 11, 1933

Dear Breck: Just a line to tell you that T.R., Jr., lunched with us at the White House on Friday and was most cordial in every way. F.D.R., Jr., came back on the steamer with him and apparently everything was lovely![1]

I hope all goes well. Signor Mussolini has a wonderful chance to force through an agreement at the Disarmament Conference. Frankly, I feel that he can accomplish more than anyone else.

As ever yours,

[PSF:Italy:CT]

[1] The Roosevelts had just returned from traveling in Persia, Turkey, and Italy, following Theodore, Jr.'s, resignation as governor general of the Philippines in March 1933. In Italy they had visited Long who had arranged an audience with Mussolini for them (Long to Roosevelt, Aug. 2, 1933, PSF:Italy). Franklin, Jr., had spent the summer in Europe.

## Press Conference, Executive Offices of the White House, September 13, 1933

[*Excerpt*] Q: Have you had any communication from Havana that the new government down there is becoming sufficiently stable to merit recognition?[1]

The President: I haven't read the dispatches this morning. I haven't anything you haven't got.

Q: Do you know anything about withdrawing Naval forces yet?

The President: That's sort of a cagey, catch question. Some of them have left and some of them have gone. [*sic*] Some of the coal-burning ships have come away and others have taken their places, and somebody suggested a cordon. I said it was a good word and then looked it up and found it was a rotten word because "cordon" presupposes a connection between every link of the cordon, and of course down in Cuba there is no connection between the different outlying boats. So try and find a new one.

[President's Press Conferences:T]

[1] Ramón Grau San Martín became president Sept. 10, 1933.

## Roosevelt to William E. Dodd, Ambassador to Germany, Berlin

[Washington] September 13, 1933

My dear Mr. Ambassador: I have not had a chance to thank you for yours of August 12th,[1] for, as you know, I have been at Hyde Park, and, of late, Cuba. Henry Ford and the Coal people have kept me working eighteen hours a day.[2]

I can only send you this brief note to suggest you do everything possible to pave the way for the possibility that France and England, and indeed most of the rest of Europe, will try to put it up to Germany at the Disarmament Conference. The crux of the matter will be some form of continuous international inspections. That is a sine qua non on the part of France, and, I think, a reasonable one. Perhaps the German Government could use as a face saver the claim that they would have equal rights to full knowledge of what the French were doing.

Very sincerely yours,

[OF 523:CT]

[1] Above.
[2] Ford had been opposing the National Recovery Administration automobile code with great vigor, and the bituminous coal producers and miners had been unable to agree on a coal code.

## Roosevelt to Cordell Hull, Secretary of State

Washington, September 13, 1933

Memorandum . . . I think you will be interested in this letter from Mr. Daniels.[1]

FDR

[OF 237:TS]

[1] Sept. 9, 1933 (*Roosevelt and Daniels,* pp. 145–147), discussing Mexican opinion toward the United States in light of the Cuban troubles. Daniels urged that any overt action be in concert with Mexico and the principal South American powers. Hull said he had read the letter "with a great deal of interest" (to Roosevelt, Sept. 21, 1933, OF 237). The great concern of the Administration was that any semblance of American intervention would threaten the success of the coming Montevideo conference (telephone conversation between Hull and Daniels, Sept. 9, 1933, *Foreign Relations, 1933,* V, 412–413).

## Roosevelt to Louis M. Howe, Personal Secretary to the President

[Washington, Sept. 14, 1933]

Hull & Roper & Treasury
O'Brien & Page—[1]
Arrange conference (at least 1 hour) to work out some co-ordinating
Tariff machinery—a clearing house—[2]

F.D.R.

[OF 61:AS]

[1] Robert L. O'Brien was chairman, and Thomas W. Page a member, of the Tariff Commission.

[2] No entry for such a meeting appears in the White House appointments list (PPF 1-0), but that fact does not necessarily mean it was not held. The memorandum here printed was in reply to Howe's memorandum to Roosevelt of Sept. 14, 1933 (OF 61), enclosing a note from O'Brien dated Sept. 11, 1933. This note submitted a number of questions for Roosevelt's decision: did the President consider the "tariff moratorium" still in effect; did he wish to take action on a number of completed investigations for adjustment of duty?

## Herbert Feis, Economic Adviser to the State Department, to Cordell Hull, Secretary of State

[Washington] September 15, 1933

[*Notation*:A:FDR] Stevens[1]

Again in Regard to Defaulted Foreign Securities: The agitation concerned with the condition of the American holders of foreign securities in default appears to be rising again; it becomes urgent to consider whether some positive action cannot be taken to put an end to this agitation.

There have been two alternative positives: (a) the fostering by official action of the creation of an adequate and disinterested private body (one entirely independent of all special interests, and particularly of banking interests); (b) the creation of an official body under Title II of the Federal Securities Act.

I remain strongly of the opinion that the first development is far more desirable from the point of view of administration than the second—if it is feasible. May I repeat my reasons again in briefest summary:

(1) The reduced volume of international trade and the very much controlled exchanges continue to make it increasingly harder for governments to meet foreign debts. The prospect that any body will within the next twelve months effect beneficial settlements of importance for any group of bondholders is very small. There are minor opportunities as regards one or two situations like Colombia, within which I think the State Department can act informally (but ineffectively). If the Administration brought the official body into existence and the official body failed to achieve any quick results, the Administration would come in for criticism and complaint on the part of the bondholders.

(2) The embarrassments and difficulties of governmental debt collection are shown by the experience of the American Government in regard to intergovernmental debts. I should not think that the Administration would want to add to its already great embarrassment in this field.

(3) I have the opinion that the proper private body will turn out to be a more efficient debt collector than any official or semi-official body.

(4) I believe there will be a grave danger that any semi-official debt collecting body would complicate our foreign relations, especially in Latin America.

Other reasons could be added to this list, but these appear to me to have enough weight to show that it is advisable to try first to aid in the creation of a suitable private body to protect the now widely scattered bondholders against further neglect of their interests. The small organizing group that has been at work trying to carry forward this task has temporarily suspended its operations. The partial list of a board of directors which the members of this group prepared, has been submitted, I believe, to the President and he thought the personnel excellent.[2] To the partial list others should be added of perhaps a slightly less conservative character. The completion of the personnel and the selection of the directing secretary (a very vital step) could be carried through, I think, if the organization knew how it was to finance itself. It is important that during the first few years of its existence this body should not have to call for deposits of bonds, and it therefore needs a fund of perhaps $150,000 to carry it through its early existence. Mr. Rublee told me when I last discussed the subject with him, that the New York issuing houses and banks would be willing to put up the money, but I think this would defeat the whole idea. It seems to me logical that these funds might be provided on loan either by the Federal Reserve System or by the Reconstruction Finance Corporation (I do not know whether either of these bodies at the present moment has the legal authority to make such an advance, but I should think that if there were a will to do so a way could be found).

The defaulted foreign bond situation is an important element in the whole banking situation, and on this ground alone the aid of one of these two institutions would be well justified. Something of a precedent is to be found in the close connection between the British Corporation of Foreign Bondholders and the Bank of England (the Chairman of the Corporation is a Director of the Bank of England). It is furthermore quite possible that either or both of these bodies might find it advisable to cooperate with this organization in various situations.

I therefore recommend as immediate measures:

(1) That the partial personnel, a list of which has already been presented to the President, be brought together in the near future in an informal discussion with representatives of the State and Treasury Departments and of the Federal Reserve Board or the R.F.C. (such a meeting might be arranged casually, as a dinner meeting of, say, the Council on Foreign Relations). The question of completing the personnel and of bringing the organization into existence might then be thoroughly canvassed.

(2) That the Federal Reserve or the R.F.C. be consulted on the question of making the necessary loan to the organization.

While this plan is being executed, it should be made clear to those composing the organization that it should be regarded as private and independent in character, that it would act on its own responsibility, and that the Government would retain full freedom of action in regard to its negotiations on all debt situations.

If this effort should again fail, it will probably prove only a matter of time when it will become advisable to invoke Title II. If that is so, the most careful thought should be given to two questions:

(a) The wisdom of endeavoring to revise Title II so as to reduce the official connection between the debt collecting organization and the Government. This might be done particularly by leaving the nomination of the directing board to private organizations, instead of giving it to the Federal Trade Commission (the members of the Council of the British Corporation of Foreign Bondholders are so nominated by various private bodies). However, it might prove very difficult and perhaps impossible to get Congress to amend Title II, unless the rest of the Act should come up for reconsideration in Congress.

(b) If Title II is carried out the selection of personnel (the six directors and the directing secretary) becomes the highest importance. The individuals selected must be entirely above suspicion of special interest or special connection. They should be persons with some knowledge of foreign affairs and great discretion. Their remuneration should be moderate and strictly limited (the Act leaves rather wide margins). Finally, the Administration should make it completely clear that it took no responsibility for the actions of the organization.

[OF 100-B:T]

[1] Raymond B. Stevens of the Federal Trade Commission.
[2] See White House statement of Oct. 20, 1933, in *Public Papers,* II, 411–413, and Roosevelt to Steiwer, Nov. 6, 1933, below.

## Dave H. Morris, Ambassador to Belgium, to Roosevelt

Brussels, Belgium, September 19, 1933

My dear Franklin: This letter is personal and confidential. It ventures to suggest a possible solution to one of your many problems. If you can properly do so, I should greatly appreciate receiving either by cable or letter an indication of your general reaction to the idea offered.

In personal letters I have written of the mortification and regret expressed to me privately by various Belgian leaders at their country not having met its American debt payments, how Belgians were an honest people in heart and fact, and that they felt that if some way could be found to liquidate their American obligations they would be happy to make any sacrifices politically and socially possible. You know my answer has always been that I have no authority officially to discuss debts and that was a matter you reserved to yourself, and indeed Congress was the final authority.[1]

A family dinner, including the ladies, was recently given by Mr. Paul van Zeeland,[2] the "Directeur de la Banque Nationale de Belgique," in his country home and my bride, Jack Gade[3] and I met there Count de Broqueville who is the Prime Minister in the Government here.[4] The four of us men after dinner talked over the situation along the lines just indicated and to make a long story short, concluded that if informally and unofficially it could be ascertained that you would recommend the acceptance of the following plan in broad outline and principle, the Belgians believed it could be presented to you officially very soon and in about any form you might indicate, namely:

399

1. Belgium would pursue these unofficial negotiations with us in strict secrecy, without informing any other power, including France.

2. Belgium would first of all acknowledge in principle her obligation to America.

3. Belgium feels very strongly her right to a privileged position in the consideration of her pre-armistice debt, and that she should receive special treatment in our consideration of it to which no other power is entitled.

4. The post-armistice debt itself consists of two portions, capital and interest. Owing to the present crisis, the Belgians feel that the interest could and should be cancelled.

In regard to the capital, this would be paid and in ninety-nine equal instalments instead of the fifty-six agreed upon in the present Belgian debt settlement.

5. In order to meet the President's wishes and contribute to world credit expansion, the Belgians suggest the following arrangement:

I. The actual value of the ninety-nine annuities would be calculated.

II. The sum (called "n") would at once be paid the United States in the following manner:

(a) Twenty per cent in gold. (b) Twenty per cent in silver, calculated at $15\frac{1}{2}$ in its relation to gold. (c) Sixty per cent in Belgian Government Treasury notes payable in installments to be agreed upon and paid in to a trust fund held by the B.I.S. These notes would serve as the basis of a flotation of one or several international loans, the proceeds of which would be paid to the U.S.A.

6. The previous suggestions lend themselves to many combinations of figures. They could and should result in a total actual debt reduction of about 70 per cent, this figure varying according to what may be agreed upon in the actual negotiations.

7. It must be understood that no power should receive more favorable treatment in regard to the post armistice debt than Belgium, but if such should be the case, Belgium would receive proportional consideration.

It was believed the President could for various reasons with propriety recommend to Congress such a settlement and particularly because of the present stalemate. It was further believed that Congress would realize how little Belgium could or would pay. She has just been forced to float an internal loan of one and a half billion francs largely so as to balance past budgets, supply work for unemployed and repay foreign short-term maturities. It was believed that a large cash payment to the U.S.A. would aid in balancing its budget. From the Belgian point of view nothing more quickly could turn strained relations into friendly ones than settling the debt once and for all. Increases in our mutual trade would naturally result. We could probably tie into the settlement a Belgian promise not to raise tariffs against American products nor to damage our commercial interests by quota regulations, matters which now are of perplexing concern to us in the Embassy and Consulate.

The Belgians believed lastly that their government could with equal propriety recommend the settlement for reasons just as cogent. It should, however, be recognized that the Prime Minister has as yet not consulted any of the members of his Cabinet.

Particular emphasis was laid upon the urgent necessity to keep absolutely confidential, informal and personal among you and those previously mentioned the suggestions herein made. Should our informal talk become known and merely result in failure, it would only make all the more difficult, if not impossible, any future satisfactory negotiations.

If you are at all in sympathy with the plan, please let me know how you wish the next step taken. Of course, Mr. Van Zeeland with or without Jack Gade could at any time cross and call at the White House without causing comment.[5]

Yours as ever,

Dave H. Morris

[PSF:Belgium:TS]

[1] See Morris to Roosevelt, July 7, 1933, above. On Aug. 15, 1933, Frank Walker, director of the National Emergency Council, wrote to Roosevelt, quoting from a letter he had received from Morris: "I suppose you know that Franklin told me to side-step the question of debts, but that is a very hard thing to do over here, because everybody is thinking about them and talking about them, so the best I can do is to say that officially I am not allowed to discuss the matter" (OF 455).

[2] Van Zeeland, banker and economist, was later Foreign Minister of Belgium.

[3] John Allyne Gade was naval attaché at the American Embassy in Brussels. Gade's appointment, July 12, 1933, was arranged at the request of Morris, his classmate at Harvard (Morris to Howe, May 26, 1933, OF 455).

[4] Charles de Broqueville, prime minister of Belgium from 1932 to 1934.

[5] No reply has been found. Belgium again defaulted when her Dec. 15, 1933, debt installment came due.

# Cordell Hull, Secretary of State, to Roosevelt

Washington, September 21, 1933

My dear Mr. President: Since my memorandum to you of August 15[1] on our Liberian policy, some changes have taken place in the situation there. General Winship[2] returned to Monrovia, accompanied by Doctor Mackenzie[3] representing the League of Nations, in the hope that jointly they might persuade Barclay[4] to accept the plan of assistance as prepared on June 27, and to call a special session of the Legislature for its ratification. This he has declined to do as he considers certain of the features objectionable. He has been supported and encouraged in this position by the more aggressive groups in the United States opposing the plan. He has, therefore, returned the plan to Geneva for discussion before the Council of the League, giving his representative there full power to accept provided the objectionable features are removed or materially modified. General Winship informs me that the principle Liberian objections are:

(First) Too wide authority for League officials, which would result in "virtually destroying the sovereignty of the Republic."

(Second) An American, the chief adviser.

(Third) Increase in debt to Firestone interests represented by issue of $150,000 Finance Corporation bonds to provide working capital fund.

(Fourth) Alleged excessive cost of plan, coupled with reduction to $300,000 (recommended by Ligthart) of the budget for annual ordinary operating expenses of government.

We are still convinced that from our point of view some form of international cooperation is the best solution of this problem and we believe that there are certain modifications in the plan which we can accept and still retain its general form. General Winship is en route to Geneva, and while events there may alter the situation considerably, we should like your approval in principle to the following line of action. To instruct General Winship:

(1) To oppose modification of the powers granted the Chief Adviser since any weakening of these will destroy the effectiveness of the plan. (The fact that the Chief Adviser will be responsible to the League and that the term of the proposed plan is five years would seem to dispose of the sovereignty objection.)

(2) To acquiesce on behalf of the United States Government in the appointment of a neutral adviser, i.e., one from a nation not having special interests in Liberia or territory contiguous thereto.

(3) To support a larger budget estimate for Liberia with a clearly specified sum for education.

I am, my dear Mr. President, Faithfully yours,

Cordell Hull

[*Notation*:AS] Sec State—I entirely approve  FDR
[OF 476:TS]

[1] Not present; cf. Phillips to Roosevelt, Aug. 16, 1933, in *Foreign Relations, 1933,* II, 924–926, prepared at Hull's direction.
[2] General Blanton Winship, special commissioner to Liberia.
[3] Not further identified.
[4] Edwin J. Barclay, president of Liberia from 1930 to 1934.

# Press Conference, Executive Offices of the White House, September 22, 1933, 3:53 P.M.

[*Excerpt*] Q: Any progress in the negotiations to sell cotton to the Russians?

The President: Not that I know of.

Q: Any negotiations with regard to France?

The President: What about France?

Q: There is a report that somebody is coming over here to negotiate the purchase of three million bales of cotton, which is about four times France's annual consumption.

The President: I think that fellow got a lot of free advertising, off the record. I never heard of him.

Q: Speaking of the debts, have you given any consideration as to who will handle the preliminary discussions for the State Department?

The President: The State Department, that is all . . .

Q: Any changes in the last couple of weeks, bringing Russian recognition closer?

The President: No, not a thing. I will have to tell you this off the record: On that story about Morgenthau there is really nothing in it because over the last three months there have been all sorts of people, some of them thought they had the right to speak for Russia and others did have the right to speak for Russia, and they have been running around to various people in the Administration and about three months ago we tied it all up and told them to go in to see Henry Morgenthau and nothing has happened since then.[1]

Q: The general impression got around that Morgenthau had been designated by you.

The President: No. It was merely because the State Department was being bothered by Chicago people and Boston people and New York people, who all claimed they had that or this or the other right to buy three million bales of cotton, and they were being so bothered that we told the State Department people and the Agriculture people to refer them all to Henry Morgenthau. That was three months ago . . .

Q: There is an impression in some quarters that you may get around to the question of Russian recognition before January first.

The President: People have been saying that since the fourth of March. I cannot give any more specific answers now than I could on the fourth of March . . .

Q: Anything new on the Cuban situation?

The President: Not a thing today.

Q: Anything on Fred Greene of New York State going to China?[2]

The President: No.

Q: The dope was that the Chinese Minister wanted to borrow somebody to build roads and Greene was recommended.

The President: I can only tell you off the record to check up because I know the Chinese Minister did get in touch with Greene, but that is all I heard. That was when he visited Hyde Park with Soong about a month and a half ago.

Q: That is off the record?

The President: Yes, I don't know anything about it.

[President's Press Conferences:T]

[1] On September 20, 1933, Roosevelt appointed Henry Morgenthau, Jr., Farm Credit Administrator, to direct Russian-American trade negotiations and to assist American business firms seeking trade contacts with the Russians in anticipation of American recognition (New York *Times,* Sept. 21, 1933, p. 31).

[2] Colonel Frederick Stuart Greene, New York state superintendent of public works for a number of years in the Smith, Roosevelt, and Lehman administrations.

# Herbert Feis, Economic Adviser to the State Department, to Cordell Hull, Secretary of State

[Washington] September 25, 1933

Skeleton Outline of Alternative Approaches to Possible Debt Agreement with Great Britain

Section I. It is generally agreed that three courses are open in regard to the handling of the impending debt discussions with the British: (a)

Standing on the letter of the bond, taking a passive attitude, and letting the matter go to default; (b) Devising some further temporary make-shift formula to carry past the next few debt payments—that is, some continuation of small token payments (the danger in this, besides the political difficulties, is that these small payments may come to be regarded as normal and the debt will become dead except for these small payments); (c) *An equitable offer or counter-offer for a permanent settlement.*[1] Up to the present neither side may be said to have made a fully equitable offer to the other. The British now are likely to make another inequitable offer (for example, payments intended to fit into the Lausanne settlement). We might then be prepared to put up to them an equitable counter-offer for reducing the debt, refusal of which the British Government would find it extremely hard to defend throughout the world.

The third course is certainly the most beneficial, if it is possible. The suggestions below are merely intended to illustrate the number of alternative lines along which such an equitable offer might be worked out.

Section II. Any offer that would be widely recognized as equitable in the present circumstances will call for a reduction of the British debt. A reduction merely by writing down the interest rate or even by completely wiping out interest is, I think, virtually certain of refusal by Great Britain and will not be convincing enough in general.

Of course, in considering any of these suggestions the reception by American public opinion and the political attitudes that have to be reckoned with have to be considered.

In addition it would be desirable that it have some features that would facilitate transfer.

The following are merely possible elements that are worth consideration:

(1) The principal might be written down in accordance with an index in the change in gold prices since the period 1917–19 so that it can be claimed that Great Britain was only being asked to pay back in commodities and services exactly what had been loaned them.

(2) Against the principal might be credited the interest payments which the British have already paid ($1,912,000,000, reducing the principal from $4,277,000,000 to $2,365,000,000).

(3) The principal could be divided into two parts: (a) one part to be paid over a short period of years; (b) a part that is to remain merely as a claim by the United States collectible in kind under special circumstances, such as war, crop failure, or monetary disturbance in the United States.

(4) More complicated applications of the same idea whereby, for example, the principals contained in the schedules might be divided into three parts: (a) the part payable in a short number of annuities; (b) the part giving us an indefinite claim on the special circumstances; (c) a part which could be used to finance the travels of American tourists in the British Empire under special arrangement; (d) a part that could be used to carry out various projects such as a scheme for seadromes for transatlantic aviation.

(5) Still another idea that could be introduced to cover a small part of the debt is that it should be collected by having Great Britain turn over to this Government certain property in kind such as cable and radio rights, fuel oil bunker stations. This would be extremely difficult to arrange but it is worth consideration as a minor element in the settlement.

(6) (a) An agreement containing any one of the preceding elements might also have a feature increasing or decreasing the amounts paid in accordance with the degree of trade between this country and the United Kingdom or between this country and the British Empire, or (b) alternatively, some index of prosperity in Great Britain.

This list could be greatly lengthened. There are all possible elements of discussion that might be brought into the arrangement if once the basic contention is defined.[2]

[*Notation*:A:FDR] File
[PSF:Great Britain:T]

[1] Italics indicate underscoring in the original.
[2] This memorandum is unaddressed but was presumably prepared for Hull. There is no covering document; Hull and Phillips talked with Roosevelt on October 5 and possibly brought the memorandum with them at that time (PPF 1-0).

## William Phillips, Under Secretary of State, to Cordell Hull, Secretary of State

[Washington] September 25, 1933

Dear Mr. Secretary: I understand that the President is going to speak before a meeting of the Catholic Charities on or about October 4th. It occurs to me that possibly he might feel that it would be worth while to utilize this occasion to say something about our concern with respect to the situation in Germany. The following statement is given merely as a suggestion. It could, of course, be improved and if the President likes the idea perhaps we could round it out for him. Following some reference to our own national economic recovery it might be said that:

"We expect from other nations a friendly avoidance of any steps which might hinder or delay our own economic recovery. On our part we shall avoid any action which might interfere with the economic programs which other governments have adopted. When, however, such programs of national recovery are accompanied by measures which give rise to fears of a policy of aggression, we cannot remain indifferent to them and we must exert our peaceful diplomacy to mitigate the evils which they cause. Nor can the American people watch unmoved the carrying out of a program which includes measures of racial and cultural persecution. Our sense of justice, our deepest sympathies, are aroused. I sincerely hope that this persecution will cease before it has caused such profound resentment as to make difficult that international cooperation on which so largely depend the maintenance of peace and the revival of prosperity."[1]

WP

[Notation:A:FDR] File
[OF 198:TS]

[1] Phillips' suggested remarks were not used; see the speech as given, in *Public Papers,* II, 379–382.

# Roosevelt to John Lee Coulter, United States Tariff Commission

Washington, September 26, 1933

Memorandum for Commissioner Coulter: Referring to your memorandum to me of September 15th, in regard to the sugar quotas: What should we do about protests being received from Mexico, Peru and perhaps other Central and South American countries? Are they provided for in any way?[1]

[OF 241:CT]

[1] Coulter, economic adviser on sugar to the Tariff Commission, had written to Roosevelt Sept. 15, 1933 (OF 241), enclosing a proposed plan of agreement on production and export quotas signed by representatives of the sugar industry from the Virgin

Islands, Philippine Islands, and Hawaii. A quota was assigned to Cuba although Coulter had not been able to talk with its representatives because of the state of affairs there. According to Coulter, the memorandum of agreement was in reply to a request made by the President and Executive Council, meeting at the White House on Sept. 7, 1933. Coulter replied September 29, below.

## Raymond B. Stevens, Federal Trade Commission, to Roosevelt

Washington, September 26, 1933

Dear Mr. President: I am returning herewith Senator Johnson's letter[1] and also Mr. Haskell's letter,[2] with regard to bringing into force Article II of the Securities Act.

I have had no hope that Senator Johnson's views could be changed or influenced. Both Mr. Rublee and Dr. Feis talked with him at the time Article II was under consideration. He is convinced of two things, first, that no private Bondholders Council can be created that will function, and two, that any such council would be sure to be dominated by the investment bankers. Also he cannot or will not see the difference between the British Bondholders Council and the Corporation set up under Article II.

In fact the British Corporation is an entirely private one. Every corporation must receive a charter from a government either under a general act or special act. Whether or not the corporation when created is a private one or a government agency depends entirely on control. In the British Corporation not a single director is selected by the government or responsible to the government. The only control exercised over the Corporation by the government is the provision in the charter fixing the maximum salaries which may be paid to the president, vice president and directors.

Under Article II the Corporation is not merely created by a special act but every director is appointed by the Federal Trade Commission, and the Commission must approve every appointment and salary of all officials of the Corporation, and the Corporation must report annually to the Federal Trade Commission and Congress. This makes the Corporation a government Corporation and thereby the government directly and formally assumes the obligation of collecting for its citizens their debts against foreign governments and foreign companies.

My political argument against bringing into effect Article II was based upon the belief clearly stated in both the memorandum and my letter, that Article II was "fundamentally wrong in principle," would not produce satisfactory results, and would complicate our foreign relations. If I thought the Corporation under Article II was the only way in which bondholders could be given assistance, and that its creation was not contrary to the public interest, I should not advise you against bringing it into effect merely on the ground that the results might prove disappointing and therefore hurt you politically.

It is clear, however, from Senator Johnson's letter, that the creation of a private corporation should be connected in no way with efforts begun under the Hoover Administration.

Last week I had a conference with Secretary Hull and Dr. Feis. Dr. Feis and myself have worked out a plan to have the Council of Foreign Relations sponsor the Bondholders Council. Secretary Hull is in accord with both our views in general and the proposed method of getting a private Council started. I think most of the persons selected by the former group should be retained. Some new persons of liberal reputation should be added from the far west and middle west. I am confident that Dr. Feis and myself can get the Council of Foreign Relations to proceed in the matter. All that is needed at the moment is your approval of this plan. I would be glad to be of assistance in the matter, and I can do so just as well as a private citizen as I could if I still were a member of the Commission.[3]

Yours sincerely,

Raymond B. Stevens

[OF 100-B:TS]

[1] Aug. 26, 1933, above.
[2] Not present.
[3] See Stevens to Roosevelt, Oct. 5, 1933, below.

# Press Conference, Hyde Park, September 27, 1933, 3:30 P.M.

[*Excerpt*] Q: What do you hear about Cuba?

The President: I have not heard since yesterday afternoon. This is entirely off the record although you know about it as much as I do. The situation is that Mr. San Martin is sitting there in the Presidential Palace and he has his local army with him, which consists of about fifteen hundred men and a bunch of students. Apparently they are not collecting any taxes anywhere on the Island and, of course, their government cannot go on there forever without taxes. Something is bound to happen. They might start collecting taxes—that might solve it—but if they do not collect taxes—

Q: Did you ever see students collecting taxes.

The President: So we are just sitting and waiting.

[President's Press Conferences:T]

## Prime Minister J. Ramsay MacDonald to Roosevelt

Whitehall, September 27th, 1933

*Purely Personal and Unofficial*

My dear President: I was very glad to have your letter delivered to me by Mr. Norman Davis.[1] I watch from day to day, so far as newspapers and reports will allow me, the valiant struggle you are putting up to straighten things out in the United States, and I pray that you will secure a great success. You have opportunities for experiment which we do not have here. Our margins are very narrow; the equipoise of our economic life is very delicate; to pull out a brick, to see what is behind or to get at some rotten bit of structure, is as dangerous in the State as I have just found out it is in my own delightful old house which is beginning to show signs of its two centuries of years. But with care, exercised in carrying out a very clearly defined policy aimed at increasing both prices and consumption, we are steadily effecting improvements.

Every day, however, I come across decisive proofs that, unless we get the world in a healthier condition, we are going to be able to do very little that is to be permanent and is to remove the awful poverty of our day. Every stream of international commerce is as parched as our Scotch rivers have been this summer on account of the drought. No fish have been able to get up and the reservoirs of water-supply upon which hundreds of villages depend, are almost down to their mud bottom. To spend a quiet half-hour musing over the unity of things is very profitable; but how few such half-hours have you or I got?

I saw the Dutch Prime Minister[2] this week and had a patient survey with him over the field. You know, we really must try and get some means of imparting some degree of certainty to international exchanges. You can help us enormously and we can help you, if our exchanges were a bit more steady. I do not dream of anything that is permanent. I do

410

not think that you can settle rock foundations or anything of the kind; but if we could just patch something up to keep going from day to day, I am sure that both your general aim and mine would be enormously facilitated. Please do not imagine I am butting in on your province. I am just venturing to impose upon our mutual relationships and mention to you one of my biggest troubles in getting things going on this side of the world.

I saw Leith Ross before he left and told him that, apart from his official work of discussing Debts, if you show any disposition to have a general talk with him on how matters stand, he must withhold nothing from you but tell you exactly what is passing through my mind; and nobody knows what that is better than he does.

The Disarmament situation is becoming increasingly difficult. On this side here there can be no doubt at all but that the conduct, the pose and the spirit of the German Government have raised fear and unsettlement where, largely owing to us, calmness and confidence had begun to operate.[3] And, in addition to that, the same unfortunate hesitations arise from the more remote country, Japan. I cannot honestly say to you that we can get such a good agreement to-day as we could have got twelve months ago. This letter has been interrupted by a telephone communication from Sir John Simon at Geneva. He reports no great achievement as yet by reason of the private negotiations, but he does say that our efforts are getting the more troublesome powers a little closer together. I am seeing him here in a few days and he says he will give me a more complete report.

Now, I must not take up any more of your very crowded moments. I just send you all my best wishes and, with kindest regards to Mrs. Roosevelt and yourself, believe me to be

Yours always sincerely,

J. Ramsay MacDonald

P.S. I hope that your indisposition of which I saw has now completely gone.[4] JRM

[PSF:Great Britain:TS]

---

[1] Aug. 30, 1933, printed in *Foreign Relations, 1933,* I, 210–211. Roosevelt said that he felt "an insane rush to further armaments" in Europe was far more dangerous than squabbles over gold or stabilization or tariffs. He sent this letter to Davis with a personal note and a formal letter of instructions, both of the same date (*ibid.,* pp. 208, 209–210). Roosevelt and Davis had conferred on disarmament in Hyde Park on August 22 (PPF 1-0).

[2] Hendrick Colijn.

[3] Germany withdrew from the Disarmament Conference on Oct. 14, 1933, and in effect, from the League of Nations at the same time; see *British Documents, 1919–1939,* V, 655ff, and *Foreign Relations, 1933,* I, 211ff. Norman Davis had a two-hour conference with MacDonald on Sept. 10, 1933; the conference is summarized by Davis, *ibid.,* pp. 214–217.

[4] The newspapers had reported on September 18 that Roosevelt was suffering from a cold, but he recovered from it within a few days.

## Jesse Isidor Straus, Ambassador to France, to Roosevelt

New York, September 27, 1933

Dear Mr. President: You suggested that I put in writing the plan I proposed to you as to debt settlements.

It is somewhat along the line that you yourself expressed to me, but is different in mechanics. I base it on the assumption that most governments would like to pay if a possible method could be devised; one not too onerous.

I mentioned to you that Dave Morris had asked me to tell you of his conversation with the King of Belgium who expressed a desire to find a way out.[1] I believe France would not be averse though I have not specifically touched on the subject with any French authority. My opinion is based on impression. I have not available information as to maturities or amounts of United States bonds outstanding so I cannot be very specific, nor can I make any detailed plan as I am quite in the dark as to what the actual computations might show if the settlement was effected on this basis. Of course, in the State Department there are many men who have specialized on this problem and their judgment of the mathematical side of the matter will be of the greatest importance.

The general plan is as follows: Extend the period of completion of payment of foreign debts to one hundred years. From each government ask for serial bonds or notes maturing 1% a year at a low rate of interest, say $2\frac{1}{2}\%$. Issue, by refunding our own bonds at $2\frac{1}{2}\%$ tax exempt, serial bonds or notes, each of our own issues to mature thirty or sixty days after the foreign bonds due date. Funds received from the foreign maturities would pay our own maturing obligations. Each foreign bond maturity would have a United States bond maturity practically coinciding.

The plan would set up assets against our present United States maturities to the amount of over ten billion dollars and would ultimately reduce our national debt by that amount.

The loss to our Government would be the difference made by the tax exempt clause in the refunded bonds, but at the present low interest rates, there would be an economy against rates now being offered—say, on the Fourth Liberty $4\frac{1}{4}$'s for instance. Perhaps the administration might be willing to make these bonds eligible for payment of estate taxes at par, if held continuously until at least one year prior to death of decedent.

Yours faithfully,

Jesse Isidor Straus

[OF 212:TS]

[1] See Morris to Roosevelt, July 7, 1933, above.

# William H. Woodin, Secretary of the Treasury, to Roosevelt

Washington, September 28, 1933

My dear Mr. President: I am enclosing herewith report of the special group appointed to advise you on monetary matters.

This report has been unqualifiedly agreed to by, and carries the strong recommendation of, every member of the group except Doctor Sprague, who was not present.

Respectfully yours,

W. H. Woodin

[PPF 258:TS]

# [*Enclosure*] Report for the President

The group unanimously and unqualifiedly recommends that:

1. The Treasury Department be immediately instructed to prepare itself for discussions with Great Britain, having as their objective the stabilization of the dollar in terms of sterling and looking toward the return of both currencies to some such modernized gold standard as the type suggested in the group's interim report.

2. In the meantime the Federal Reserve Bank of New York be authorized to take such steps including the export of gold as may be necessary to prevent the dollar from depreciating below the 4.86 sterling rate and the present gold rate.

3. Open market operations, which were recommended in the interim report as a method of preventing the strengthening of the dollar, would under the present circumstances seem unnecessary, both from the point of view of the exchange situation and from the point of view of the banking and credit position. This recommendation is made without consideration of any factors other than economic ones.[1]

[PPF 258:T]

---

[1] After the London Conference, the issue on fiscal policy was drawn between the anti-inflation group, led by Warburg, Sprague, and Acheson, and those who favored inflationary measures, among them Warren and Rogers. While returning from the Conference, Warburg had prepared a "Memorandum on Domestic Currency Problem," printed in his book, *The Money Muddle* (New York: A. A. Knopf, 1934), pp. 124–127, under date of July 24, 1933. A revised and expanded version of this memorandum, dated Aug. 2, 1933, is in the Roosevelt papers (OF 229); very likely Warburg gave this to the President when he saw him in Hyde Park on August 8. On that day Warburg, Warren, and Rogers discussed financial policy with Roosevelt, and on the next day he went over their recommendations with Irving Fisher (PPF 1-0); I. N. Fisher, *My Father, Irving Fisher*, pp. 276–281); Warburg, *The Money Muddle*, pp. 137–140.

## John Lee Coulter, United States Tariff Commission, to Roosevelt

Washington, September 29, 1933

*Subject: Sugar Agreement*

My dear Mr. President: Referring to your memorandum of September 26,[1] it is true that the first draft of the sugar agreement which got into circulation and was used as the basis for the first public hearing was not entirely clear as to phraseology, and was, I believe, subject to very definite protest by Central and South American countries, since it implied what might be interpreted as an embargo on refined sugar from other foreign countries than Cuba, and very extreme restrictions on raw sugar from other foreign countries than Cuba.

The final draft as filed with the Honorable Secretary of Agriculture has been gone over with the most extreme care not only by the Assistant Secretary of State (Mr. Caffery), Dr. Feis, and other experts of the State

Department, but also by several of the experts of the Department of Agriculture. Several of these gentlemen made most valuable suggestions, especially on the very point of your memorandum. All of the suggestions made by the experts of the several government departments have been accepted unanimously by the Committee representing all branches of the sugar industry. The agreement is, therefore, now ready for approval by Secretary Wallace.

The sections of the agreement bearing upon the subject of your memorandum set forth—

(1) that foreign refined sugars may enter the American markets without restriction up to an amount equal to the average performance of the last five years;

(2) that raw sugars may be imported to be refined and reexported;

(3) that imports may be brought in without limit for the use of manufacturers for reexport in manufactured commodities such as canned fruits, vegetables, candied fruits, confectionery of all kinds, etc;

(4) that additional raw sugars from full-duty countries may be brought in at any time in any amount when there is a shortage in the producing areas which are parties to the agreement, or when the price reaches the world price, plus the duty, and, in any event, without restriction, may be offered in the American Market in an amount equal to the average of the last five years.

A further section provides that "this agreement shall terminate * * *[2] on reasonable notice upon the order of the President of the United States". This section was inserted in order to make sure that if any foreign protest had merit, or if any manipulation were attempted, the President could at any time dissolve the agreement.

As already noted, the State Department has advised me that these provisions are more than liberal and fully cover any possible international situation.

Respectfully,

John Lee Coulter

[OF 241:TS]

[1] Above.
[2] Asterisks in the original.

## Roosevelt to William H. Woodin, Secretary of the Treasury

At Hyde Park, New York, September 30, 1933

*Private and Confidential*

Dear Will: I do not like or approve the report of the special monetary group.[1]

1. They have failed to take into consideration the United States, and look at things, I fear, from the point of view of New York and banking. The first recommendation for discussions with Great Britain is premature; Great Britain is not ready to enter into this discussion.

2. The effort to prevent the dollar from depreciating below 4.86 is unsound from the American point of view unless the pound weakens with the dollar in its relationship to gold. If the pound and gold remain at substantially the present price I should hope to see the dollar go to $5.00 or more in relation to the pound.

3. Open market operations should most certainly continue, both from the point of view of the exchange situation and the banking and credit position.[2]

Tell the committee that commodity prices must go up, especially agricultural prices.

I suggest that the committee let you and me have the recommendation of how to obtain that objective and that objective only.

You and I understand this National situation and I wish our banking and economist friends would realize the seriousness of the situation from the point of view of the debtor classes,—i.e., 90 percent of the human beings in this country—and think less from the point of view of the 10 per cent who constitute the creditor classes.[3]

[PPF 258:CT]

[1] Woodin to Roosevelt, Sept. 28, 1933, above.
[2] The special monetary group had urged open market operations in an interim report to Woodin of Aug. 29, 1933 (OF 229). With this Roosevelt agreed; see his letter to Woodin of Oct. 9, 1933, in *Personal Letters, 1929–1945,* I, 361.
[3] Printed also *ibid.,* 360–361.

## Raymond B. Stevens, Federal Trade Commission, to Roosevelt

Washington, October 5, 1933

Dear Mr. President: I desire to report the latest developments with regard to the creation of a private adequate Bondholders Council.

When I saw you on the train on Tuesday, the 26th,[1] I made the recommendation, suggested to me by the State Department, that the Council of Foreign Relations should be requested to sponsor the creation of a private council. When Dr. Feis and I examined, however, the list of the present officials of the Council of Foreign Relations, we decided that it would be inadvisable to ask them to act in the matter. Unfortunately among the present officials are two of the counsel for J. P. Morgan, to wit, John W. Davis and Frank Polk, Mr. Leffingwell,[2] a partner of Morgan's, and among the other directors are Norman Davis and Paul Cravath. Not only would this organization appear to represent Wall Street, but above all, the House of Morgan.

I have had a conference with both Secretary Hull and with Mr. Acheson. We are all of the opinion that the private Council cannot be set up without the approval of the Government, and that that approval might as well be direct as indirect, and that accordingly the most effective and quickest method of getting a private organization created would be for the Secretary of State and the Secretary of the Treasury, and the Chairman of the Federal Trade Commission to invite to Washington for a conference the group of men whose names have already been considered and approved by you.[3] If this were done this group should be informed that the Government considers that the creation of a private corporation is necessary and that they would be rendering an important public service if they would proceed to form such an organization. It should, of course, be understood that once formed the Government would not be responsible for it.

Our views with the reasons therefor are embodied in the form of a draft letter to you, which of course would not be sent unless you approved in advance.

I think there ought to be a conference with you as soon as possible, and the conference should be attended by Secretary Hull, either the Secretary of the Treasury himself or Mr. Acheson, and the Chairman of the Federal Trade Commission and myself. At this conference the whole question could be discussed and I hope a course finally agreed upon. The matter is becoming urgent because of the pressure which is being brought to bear to bring into force Title II of the Securities Act.

I have therefore asked Col. McIntyre for an appointment for Secretary Hull, the Secretary of the Treasury, the Chairman of the Federal Trade Commission and myself. I have written this letter to give you in advance some idea of what we intend to propose for your decision.

Yours sincerely,

Raymond B. Stevens

[OF 100-B:TS]

---

[1] Between Washington and New York, en route to Hyde Park. Roosevelt returned to Washington on October 5 (PPF 1-0).

[2] Russell C. Leffingwell.

[3] See Roosevelt to Steiwer, Nov. 6, 1933, below.

## Roosevelt to Cordell Hull, Secretary of State, and Homer S. Cummings, Attorney General

[Washington] October 6, 1933

Memorandum from the President for the Secretary of State and the Attorney General: In regard to the correspondence relating to the closing of the work of the Mixed Claims Commission, United States and Germany, I can see that it is impossible to set a definite date for the closing of the work of this Commission at this time.

Nevertheless, I hope that both the Department of State and the Department of Justice will press for such final action as may enable the Commission to wind up its work in the very near future.[1]

[OF 198-C:CT]

---

[1] Roosevelt here referred to Attorney General Cummings' memorandum to him of Sept. 13, 1933 (OF 198-C), enclosing two memoranda on the status of the Mixed Claims Commission he had received from Assistant Attorney General Frank J. Wideman, July 25 and Aug. 9, 1933. (The German-American Mixed Claims Commission was established in 1922 to adjudicate claims of American civilians for damages incurred in consequence of the war with Germany.) Under the Appropriation Act of June 16, 1933 (48 *Stat.* 278–279), the State Department was directed to bring the business of the Claims Commission to a close. When the State Department thereupon directed that the Commission close its work on or before Oct. 1, 1933, various objections were raised; these are discussed in the Wideman memoranda. Regular appropriations for the Commission continued to be made until 1940.

# Press Conference, Executive Offices of the White House, October 11, 1933, 10:40 A.M.

[*Excerpt*] The President: . . . I asked the President of Panama to come in today and told him that this would be a unique experience for him.[1] From my point of view we have had a very satisfactory talk—

President Arias: And from mine also.

The President: And the President says, from his also. I think his visit does illustrate the practical way of taking up problems that occur between different countries and I think we are making very satisfactory progress.

There are a number of matters such as, for instance, the present condition in that the Republic of Panama cannot have its own radio station. Well, that seems like a perfectly absurd situation. It has been created because of the military problems of the Panama Canal, but we are trying to work out something which will enable the Republic of Panama, like any other nation, to have its own radio station. Then, there are other matters such as, for instance, the competition of certain supplies—competition created by the Canal Zone authorities which affects the merchants of the Republic.

Those are all matters which probably can be ironed out satisfactorily.

Then, of course, there is the other thing which we have talked about. It is a rather interesting parallel, although I think I will have to say this almost off the record because you cannot say that it comes from me—the parallel—you can invent that yourselves. Panama has a corridor problem. Right across the middle of Panama there is a corridor belonging to somebody else and yet we are perfectly convinced that through mechanical means and through cooperation and talking things over, we can make the life of the Republic of Panama perfectly practical and satisfactory so that the corridor which splits the Republic in two will not interfere with the orderly development of the Republic. In other words, the lesson I draw from it is the fact that the President of Panama comes here and talks things over and makes a solution of our problem, a perfectly peaceful and practical solution, possible. I am not saying that other nations ought to do the same thing, but!

So, we are getting on very well and it is delightful to have Señor Arias here. I told him that some time, when and if I can get away from Washington, I hope to go down through the Canal, stop in Panama and visit him . . .

Q: Can you tell us anything about the British Debt negotiation?

The President: Only what I read in the papers and that was inaccurate.[2] No, they have only just begun to talk on it and, as I understand from Steve, there won't be any news during the preliminaries unless it is handed out in the form of a joint statement.

Q: Might it involve the question of stabilization of currency?

The President: Not that I know of.

Q: Wouldn't it be natural to stabilize—

The President: Not necessarily.

Q: How would they pay?

The President: As a matter of fact, on this debt thing it would be best not to speculate because it would be pure speculation and the chances are 99 to 1 that the speculation would be wrong and, in the third place, it frankly doesn't do an awful lot of good in international relations to get the trend of the public mind one way or the other before there has been any meeting of the government minds.

I know you people won't mind my saying this, but the more I look at it the more true I think it is—and this doesn't affect us people over here so much—but if anybody would ask me what was the greatest single factor that contributed to the London Economic Conference not accomplishing more than it did—and this is off the record and between us—I would say it is the Continental press. They established a public and publicity background that necessarily concentrated the attention of that London Economic Conference on just one subject when they had twenty subjects. The Continental press and, to a large extent, the British press were responsible for that.

Of course, it is also equally true that people concerned in that London Economic Conference got a great deal of their own personal slant from the press. It not only had a public influence but a serious influence on the delegates themselves and an influence on the publicity out of London. Of course, the delegates were, in large part, responsible too, but the publicity that came out of London and concentrated that Conference on just the one question of stabilization did a very serious hurt to good results.

On this debt thing, we are a little bit the same way. We are merely engaged on the preliminary conversation and in those conversations they will take up twenty different formulas and each one will have its ramifications of all kinds. They will explore them for a long, long time and nothing will come to me until they have explored them all. Then they may come to me and the Prime Minister of the Cabinet in London and say that such and such method is out of the question and another method is out of the question, but "we do think it is worth going ahead with discussions" on this line or that or on three different alternative lines. And then the British Government may consider it and I will consider it and then we may get to the second stage or may not.[3]

It is as vague as that and any story that says we are engaged on this particular proposition at this time just isn't so and will tend to stir up not only public opinion in England and the United States on an issue which is not an issue, but will also tend to crystallize the point of view of the government officials and the negotiators themselves.

That is why I hope very much on the debt negotiations that there won't be any categorical stories one way or the other because the thing is frankly and definitely completely up in the air. It is in the preliminary, exploratory stage.

Q: You expect this will take some time?

The President: Yes. And all we can say is we hope there will be some meeting of the minds on it, but we don't know. I will tell you all just as soon as there is anything tangible to go on, but there isn't yet.

Q: Will you be good enough to clear us up in the same general way about the situation at Geneva?

The President: Well, I may—I would love to do it if I can do it off the record—completely off the record. The difficulty is this: Any story coming out of Washington to Geneva might have a pretty bad effect on the negotiations there. No matter what the story was, it might look like interference by Washington.

Now, the real situation in Geneva is, as I see it, this:—Keep this entirely off the record, literally off the record. The real situation is this: That the Conference started in a long time ago, around a year and a half ago, with all the nations sitting around the table and all interested and all trying to work toward a practical solution of disarmament.

Gradually, and unfortunately, the whole thing has narrowed down to a very small number of great powers so that today, before the session begins on what—the 16th?—before it begins, it has, I am sorry to say, ceased to be a plenary meeting of all the nations and has come down, virtually, to a consideration of the European political problem in which Italy, France, Great Britain are involved and we are, in a sense, sitting on the outside but with access to what is going on. And Norman Davis is trying to act as *amicus curiae*—he is not trying to tell them what to do but when they get in a jam, Norman Davis is talking to them and getting them to suggest ways and means of getting out of that particular jam.

Now, at the end of last week, it got into this kind of a jam: The French position was predicated on some form of—I have forgotten what the exact expression is—a trial period during which Germany would not re-arm and if Germany proved that she was not re-arming during the trial period, then France, at the end of the period, would start disarming herself and Italy would do the same thing, and so on. Germany felt that she couldn't, with self-respect, agree to being put into the position of everybody watching her during the trial period; that it was against her national honor.

I think at the present time that they are engaged in finding a new way of stating somewhat the same thing; in other words, perhaps, of starting immediate disarmament but that during the trial period—they won't mention the word trial period—during the first few years the disarmament would not be very great or very effective. In other words, as practical people realize, it would really amount to the same thing, but actually it would help Germany to have it set out in a less brutal way than being given an ultimatum for a trial period.

That is what they are working on at the present time and if they can find a method of stating it that will save everybody's national honor on the continent, the thing will work out. If they cannot find a method of stating it, it doesn't look very favorable to an actual signing up for disarmament. That is the situation as it is today.

Q: Will that preclude manufacture by Germany of this armament she is talking about?

The President: I don't know. I didn't talk to Davis about that at all.[4]

[President's Press Conferences:T]

[1] President Harmodio Arias was in Washington from Oct. 9 to 18, 1933, and a guest at the White House from October 9 to 11 (New York *Times,* Oct. 10, 1933, p. 23). See joint statement issued on Oct. 17, 1933, *Public Papers,* II, 407–409.

[2] See New York *Times,* Oct. 11, 1933, p. 18, which carried rumors of a debt settlement with the British.

[3] These talks had been going on since Oct. 5, 1933; see Hull's memorandum of October 4 on plans for the meeting the following day with Sir Frederick Leith-Ross, chief economic adviser of the British government, with Under Secretary of the Treasury Acheson and Frederick Livesey of the Economic Adviser's Office of the State Department (*Foreign Relations, 1933,* I, 842–843). The October 13 Cabinet meeting was largely devoted to the debt conversations (Ickes, *Diary,* I, 106–107). Ickes says that Acheson appeared "willing to make the utmost concessions to Great Britain," Budget Director Douglas "vigorously argued for an agreement on such terms as Great Britain might be willing to submit," and Hull thought the debts should be used "as a club" to force reasonable trade concessions. (See also Hull, *Memoirs,* I, 381.) Roosevelt's view was that the British had not yet made a proposition and that we were waiting for one.

[4] Printed in part in *Public Papers,* II, 389–393.

## Cordell Hull, Secretary of State, to Roosevelt

Washington, October 11, 1933

Dear Mr. President: Secretary Wallace is very earnestly urging that the State Department designate a suitable outstanding person as a delegate to the Third International Conference for the Roerich Peace Pact,[1] which meets here in December. He also is very insistent that I send a message to the meeting.

He having been over the matter more or less repeatedly with you, I am wondering if you have any suggestions relative to the foregoing which you would care to pass on to me.

Sincerely yours,

Cordell Hull

[*Notation*:AS] C.H.   Will you speak to me about this?   FDR
[OF 723:TS]

[1] The peace pact was the idea of Nicholas K. Roerich, a Russian-born artist, archeologist, and explorer. The United States and the other members of the Pan American Union signed the pact on April 15, 1935; European nations, however, largely ignored it. Wallace was deeply impressed by the plan. There is a long letter from him to Roosevelt of Sept. 18, 1933 (OF 723), concerning it. At Roosevelt's request, Wallace drafted a message to be sent to the Conference but it is not clear whether the message was actually sent (Wallace to Roosevelt, no date, OF 723).

## Roosevelt to the Third Annual Women's Conference on Current Problems, Waldorf Hotel, New York, October 13, 1933, 10 P.M.

[*Excerpt*] I am glad to have the opportunity of greeting those who are attending the Third Annual Women's Conference on Current Problems.

I note that the subject of this Conference is "This Crisis in History," and this leads me to suggest that the short space of ten minutes will scarcely allow me to do more than congratulate you on your courage in seeking fully to discuss "This Crisis in History" in the space of two days.

May I, however, touch very briefly on two matters which are much in my mind—two problems which can be helped by public interest and public discussion.

423

One of them relates to the peace of the world. The danger to world peace certainly does not come from the United States of America. As a nation, we are overwhelmingly against engaging in war. As a nation we are seeking no additional territory at the expense of our neighbors.

The United States does not seek to annex Canada or any part thereof, to annex Mexico or any part thereof, or to annex Cuba or any part thereof. It is this attitude of the overwhelming majority of our people towards their neighbors—this complete lack of a national desire for territorial expansion—which makes the rest of the world begin to understand that the United States is opposed to war.

I will go one step further in saying that the very great majority of the inhabitants of the world feel the same as we do about territorial expansion or getting rich or powerful at the expense of their neighbors. It is only in the case of such people in the world as still have imperialistic desires for expansion and domination in their minds or in their hearts that threats to world peace lie. And, finally, it seems clear to me that it is only through constant education and the stressing of the ideals of peace that those who still seek imperialism can be brought in line with the majority.[1]

[Speech File:T]

---

[1] Roosevelt spoke to the Conference from the White House over a nationwide network. (For the entire text see *Public Papers*, II, 393–395.) The text here printed is that of the stenographic transcript; the Roosevelt Library also has a draft, the signed reading copy, and the White House press release of the reading copy. Roosevelt made a few changes in the draft, none significant; it is not certain that he composed it. The Conference was sponsored by the New York *Herald Tribune*. Helen Rogers Reid, wife of Ogden Mills Reid, editor of the *Tribune,* thanked Roosevelt for his speech in a letter to him of Oct. 17, 1933 (PPF 897). She said that his voice was as clear as if he had been speaking from the platform. Roosevelt replied Oct. 20, 1933 (PPF 897): "Many thanks for your note. It gave me the greatest of pleasure to speak to the Conference, and I am sure that those fine meetings did much good."

## William E. Dodd, Ambassador to Germany, to Roosevelt

[Berlin] October 13, 1933

Dear Mr. President: After the long delay in my official recognition here,[1] the engagements for public appearances piled up a little. Oct. 5, I spoke before American Society here on The Dilemma in the United States and on October 12, Columbus day, I used the occasion to point out the hazzards of arbitrary and minority government under the subject of Economic Nationalism. Since some criticism has been cabled back by some of the Hearst press people and thinking, therefore, that some embarrassing interpretations may have been put out at home I [am] taking the liberty of enclosing verbatim copies.[2] In case you do ever get time to rest yourself by reading (as I have the habit of doing), I hope you will look over these pages.

I was informed beforehand that members of the Foreign and Economic ministries would be present; and consequently, I grouped subjects of my discussion so that all industrial countries might have due attention. I also endeavored to be absolutely non-partisan as between countries, giving Germany a little less implied criticism than any other. The result was in both cases extraordinary approval of Germans present, as also of our own business people. Copies of Ms were supplied to German as well as our own press. As the second address was to be attended by Dr. von Schacht and others of the Reischbank and Foreign Office, I submitted ms. to Counsellor here (very strongly protokol) and he agreed that no one anywhere could reasonably take offense. And would add that Schacht publicly agreed and applauded extravagantly and all other Germans present. I have never noted more unanimous approval. Nearly all the press here (except extreme Nazi organ[3] which ignored occasion) gave fair and favorable comment next day. My interpretation of this is that all liberal Germany is with us—and more than half of Germany is at heart liberal.

Pardon so long a story. In case State Department protokol people make complaint, I wish you to know that it was my purpose to put forward in best way possible American ideals as you, Wilson, Lincoln and Jefferson interpreted them. It is my view that Europe, especially eastern Europe, needs to have American principles put before their peoples as clearly as possible—the educated and even uneducated people are in the main with us, only they are forbidden to say anything.

This has been the hardest day I have yet had here. The Kanzler and the cabinet have been in session nearly all day. You probably know the outcome. I hope Germany is entering Geneva pact.[4]

Yours sincerely

William E. Dodd

[PSF:Germany:Dodd:AS]

[1] Dodd arrived in Germany on July 13 but was not received by President von Hindenburg until August 30.

[2] Present; concerning the speeches, see Dodd, *Diary,* pp. 43–44, 46–47.

[3] Presumably the *Voelkischer Beobachter,* a Berlin daily, considered the Nazi party organ.

[4] Hitler announced Germany's withdrawal from the League of Nations and the Disarmament Conference on Oct. 14, 1933; see Dodd, *Diary,* pp. 47–48.

## Breckinridge Long, Ambassador to Italy, to Roosevelt

Rome, Italy, October 13, 1933

My dear Chief: While your mind is absorbed with internal developments and the operations of the N.R.A., and while mine is almost exclusively devoted at the present time to disarmament movements that are now centering in Rome, I will steal a few minutes and try to project for your attention a phase of foreign activity which is quite apparent here and which is not very pleasant.

I refer to the news emanating from America. It is very unfavorable. Just how it gets into the Press abroad and just why I am not able to guess, nor am I able to make any suggestion as to how it could be cured, because we lack a censorship or any control over outgoing messages. No doubt there has been a great deal of gambling on the dollar. It has been forced down in Italy and France to a point far below its value. In order to support the movements there are published in papers stories about the probability of cutting the gold content and of the imminence of inflationary measures. It has been going on for months. I had it markedly called to my attention a few weeks ago when I was in Northern Italy. At Milan I met a number of the most prominent industrialists of Italy and a number of Americans. Almost every one of them had received that Monday morning cables from their brokers or bankers in New York to the effect that inflation was imminent and that the dollar would be cut to fifty-five cents gold content value. If that many cables were received in Northern Italy, the number sent out to France, England, and Germany must have run to a considerable number.

The Paris-English papers are not trustworthy as sources of information. They color their own news to suit themselves. The British Press is more or less hostile. The Italian Press is entirely controlled and so nothing appears in it except an occasional little item such as one which appeared in this morning's edition of the *Popolo di Roma*—a short telegraphic item to the effect that you were immediately proceeding to cut the gold value of the dollar. While in the Italian Press, there is very little comment, and while most of that which appears is complimentary, the other papers are far from being the same. I have discussed the situation with several newspaper men and they are convinced that there must be some reason back in the United States for persons to send out false or misleading statements. It applies not only to finance, but it runs the whole gamut of political activity. You cannot always say that the contents of any one article in the Press is bad for some particular reason, but the tone of them is bad when there is not some particularly antagonistic statement.

I have no suggestion to make in connection with it, but I think you ought to know that there exists a situation in the Press abroad, and consequently in popular opinion abroad, which has its source in some few persons, or comparatively few persons, in the states, whether they be reporters or newspaper correspondents or propagandists I know not.

Perhaps Louie Howe with his keen perception and his intimate contacts with the leaders of the newspaper world could find out what the trouble is and devise some means to offset it. There is a young man named Fumasoni-Biondi, who represents in Washington the *Corriere della Sera* of Milan. He is quite conscious of the situation here from the point of view I have mentioned. I have talked to him on several occasions. He is about to return to Washington, if he has not already left. I think he would talk frankly to Louie Howe or to whomsoever else you might suggest. He is friendly to the United States and a very keen young man. While he can offer no suggestion as to cure, he can tell him a good deal of the impressions of the United States which are created in the minds of the readers of the European Press of today.

I call the matter seriously to your attention. It is hurtful to American prestige and is detrimental to the development of a friendly popular attitude toward the United States on the part of the people of Western Europe.

With every good wish and with affectionate and respectful regards, I am, Very sincerely,

Breckinridge Long

P.S. I am looking forward to seeing Jimmie and his wife[1] here next week and will have McAdoo[2] with me tomorrow. BL[3]

[OF 447:TS]

[1] The President's eldest son, James, and his wife Betsy.

[2] William Gibbs McAdoo, Secretary of the Treasury, 1913–1918, at this time senator from California.

[3] An attached memorandum, Roosevelt to Early, no date, reads: "What do you think I can reply to Breck Long about this?"

## Raymond Robins to Roosevelt

New York City, 14th October, 1933

Dear Mr. President: Enclosed are some items upon the two points—"freedom of worship and guarantees against propaganda"—that you emphasized in our talk of yesterday afternoon.[1]

Should you desire more or other assurance on these points, I am confident that they can be secured and if advised by you of the substance and method of this further assurance, I would gladly undertake to secure such.

On these or any other points regarding conditions in the Soviet Union on which I may have or can secure the facts I will be glad to serve your wishes.

My present plans bring me to Washington on the 20th or 21st inst. and a word from Mr. McIntyre would secure my presence at your convenience.

A telegram sent to the above address, or a telephone message here—Regent 4-4041—will reach me promptly.

I have a copy of the book *First To Go Back* and will read it with interest.[2]

May I say that in common with many millions of your fellow citizens, I regard your address to the Convention of the American Legion as the most courageous, wise and true utterance made by any political leader for long years.[3]

With appreciation and every good wish, Faithfully yours,

Raymond Robins[4]

[OF 220:TS]

---

[1] Robins had talked with Roosevelt at the White House at 4:45 P.M. (PPF 1-0). A lecturer and writer, he was identified with numerous liberal causes and at this time was actively urging recognition of the U.S.S.R. by the United States. The enclosures he refers to consist of typed copies of Stalin's statement of Jan. 28, 1929, promising noninterference in the internal affairs of other countries; a report by E. L. Keen, European manager of the United Press, of his interview with Alexsi Rykov, president of the Soviet of People's Commissars, published in the New York *Sun* of Feb. 26, 1930; Maxim Litvinov's statement of Feb. 11, 1932, avowing the Soviet Union's peaceful foreign policy; and a statement on the 1924 recognition of the Soviet Union by France which appeared in the *Russian Review* of Dec. 1, 1924. With the enclosures is a memorandum by Roosevelt: "Send this material to Mr. Bullitt and Mr. Morgenthau Jr. FDR."

Robins was in Russia from April to June of 1933 studying Soviet industry, agriculture, and education; on his return he went at once to Washington to attempt to persuade the Roosevelt Administration to recognize Russia. His talks with government leaders are mentioned in Ickes, *Diary,* pp. 62, 63, and are discussed at greater length in Sister Anne V. Meiburger's *Efforts of Raymond Robins Toward the Recognition of Soviet Russia and the Outlawry of War, 1917–1933* (Washington: Catholic University Press, 1958), pp. 175ff. The latter book describes Robins' interview with the President.

[2] Irina Skariatina (Mrs. Victor Blakeslee), *First To Go Back: An Aristocrat in Soviet Russia* (Indianapolis: Bobbs-Merrill, 1933), a sympathetic account of the U.S.S.R. in 1933. Presumably Roosevelt had mentioned the book to Robins at their White House talk. In a letter to the President of October 28, 1933 (OF 220), Robins said: "You suggested my reading—'The First To Go Back' by Irina Scaritina, which I have done with genuine interest. It is a little too favorable, i.e. not enough of the costs in hunger, death and bitterness in uprooted folks that has been paid for the extraordinary achievements by the Soviet regime in the past fifteen years, but it seems to me an honest picture . . . "

[3] The speech before the American Legion in convention in Chicago, Oct. 2, 1933 (*Public Papers,* II, 373–378).

[4] Answered Oct. 17, 1933, below.

# Roosevelt to Representative Arthur P. Lamneck, Columbus, Ohio

[Washington] October 15, 1933

Dear Mr. Lamneck: Your confidential letter was duly delivered into my hands without having been opened, and I am glad to have it. I wish that Mr. Janney could have a talk with Secretary Woodin. There is no question that this is no time to tie ourselves to European currencies.[1]

Very sincerely yours,

[PPF 889:CT]

[1] Lamneck's letter (PPF 889) was undated. He asked Roosevelt to talk with Janney who, he said, was an expert in international finance who had evidence of an international financial conspiracy against the United States. Janney appears to have been the John Janney who, as head of the American Society of Practical Economists, testified before the Senate Committee on Banking and Currency on Jan. 22, 1934, on the Gold Reserve Act of 1934. In his statement, Janney said that should the United States resort to a managed currency by changing the gold content of the dollar, an agreement with Great Britain would necessarily follow and that nation would then control our price level (*The Gold Reserve Act of 1934,* Hearings Before the Committee on Banking and Currency, U.S. Senate, 73d Cong., 2nd sess., on S. 2366, A Bill to Protect the Currency System of the United States, to Provide for the Better Use of the Monetary Gold Stock of the United States, and for Other Purposes, Jan. 19–23, 1934, Washington, D.C., pp. 364–381).

## James M. Cox, Dayton, Ohio, to Roosevelt

Washington, October 16, 1933

Taken over phone from Governor Cox:

My dear Frank: A group of fine citizens, internationally minded, asked me by 'phone this morning whether I would join it in a visit to Sec. Hull for the purpose of presenting its view as to what our country ought to be doing in the situation developed by Hitler's latest move.[1] I told them that no such plan on the part of the group could proceed except upon the theory that the President himself intended doing nothing as I was convinced that he would not only do something but do the very best "something" possible. For the time these gentlemen will be doing nothing.

It was my feeling that if they went to the State Dept. there would be publicity and then the public might gain the idea that your hand had been forced.

I impressed upon the gentlemen in question that you were in closer touch with things than we could possibly be and no one could deny your grasp of psychological developments.

What they have in mind is that you should make a statement to the effect that this country would not look with unconcern or indifference upon the development of a grave situation abroad. We are interested in amicable adjustment, fair to all interests, but we cannot be expected to be sympathetic with any nation which at this critical juncture makes an aggressive or overt move.

I give all of this to you for what it is worth.

Kind regards,

[*Notation*:A:LeHand] Mac: Prepare letter of thanks.    FDR[2]
[*Notation*:AS] Ackd 10-17-33 MWD[3]
[PPF 53:T]

---

[1] Presumably Germany's withdrawal from the Disarmament Conference and the League of Nations.

[2] In this and similar notations, the secretary's name has been given to indicate that the entire notation is in her hand.

[3] Maude W. Dwyer, a White House stenographer. Roosevelt's reply to Cox of this date (in its entirety) reads: "Thanks very much for your telephonic letter. I have every hope that events in the near future will amply justify your course" (PPF 53).

## Roosevelt to Raymond Robins, New York

[Washington] October 17, 1933

My dear Robins: Many thanks for those notes.[1] I shall be glad to talk with you further about this general subject a little later on. It was good to see you the other day.

Sincerely yours,

[OF 220:CT]

[1] See Robins to Roosevelt, Oct. 14, 1933, above.

## Roosevelt to Dean Acheson, Under Secretary of the Treasury

[Washington] October 19, 1933

Memorandum . . . re marking of imported articles: I am inclined to believe that the statute requirements that they be marked so "as to indicate the country of origin" is not carried out by a mere indication of cities or provinces.

Whereas, to you and me or anyone engaged in foreign trade, geographical names of cities and provinces mean something definite at first glance, we must remember that many millions of people do not know just where these places are located.

For example, if you go into a community of one thousand people, how many of them could tell you what country Bohemia is a part of? How many people could tell you what country Berne is located in?

For these reasons, I believe that Article 509 (b) of the Customs Regulations of 1931 should be amended so as to state definitely that the name of the political entity known as a nation would be marked on the goods imported. I do not think that the present Article indicates "the country of origin."[1]

[OF 21-T:CT]

[1] Roosevelt had asked Acheson, at the Cabinet meeting of October 13, 1933, "to investigate the legality of importations from Germany of goods bearing the name of the German state in which they were made rather than of Germany itself." Acheson reported that the Tariff Act of 1930 did not require the use of the name of the country of origin but permitted the names of principal cities, regions (such as the Rhineland),

and provinces (Acheson to Howe, Oct. 14, 1933, OF 21-T). The act referred to was interpreted the next year, by Treasury Decision 46978, to require the name of country of origin (Acting Secretary of the Treasury Coolidge to Howe, Sept. 25, 1934, OF 21-T). The new interpretation created another customs problem into which the President was drawn because importers of rare books objected to the marking. One protest was from a bookdealer friend of Roosevelt, Hubert Burgess of Boston, who wrote: "Imagine stamping a first edition of Browning or Burns, Keats, Shakespeare, or any other first edition with indelible ink? This ruling is not logical nor in any way necessary—to this idea I know you will agree" (Burgess to Roosevelt, Sept. 5, 1934, OF 21-T). Roosevelt directed that the matter be looked into (Roosevelt to Howe, no date, filed with the above), and it was discovered that the tariff act did not require stamping where this would cause damage.

## Roosevelt to Senator W. Warren Barbour, Locust, New Jersey

[Washington] October 19, 1933

My dear Senator Barbour: Thank you for your letter of October 17th.[1] I have held up the allocation of public works fund moneys for Army and Navy aircraft, because of the possibility that some agreement might be reached in regard to aircraft quotas at the Disarmament Conference. Because of the new situation,[2] however, I expect to make an allocation both for the Army and the Navy within the next week or two.

With my sincere good wishes, Faithfully yours,

[*Notation*:T] Copy of this letter sent to the Secretary of the Interior. M.D.[3]
[OF 249:T]

[1] Senator Barbour said (OF 249) that representatives of the New Jersey aviation industry had asked him what they might expect concerning future government expenditures on aircraft.

[2] The withdrawal of Germany from the League and from the Disarmament Conference.

[3] Margaret Durand, secretary to Louis Howe.

## Roosevelt to Cordell Hull, Secretary of State

[Washington] October 20, 1933

Memorandum from the President for the Secretary of State: Will you speak to Miss Perkins about this and afterwards to me? Do you think we should include a woman?

[*Notation*:T] (Letter dated Oct. 12 from Secretary of Labor re delegation to Pan-American Conference in Montevideo)[1]

[OF 567:CT]

[1] The letter from Secretary of Labor Frances Perkins is not present. Presumably it was retained in the State Department. One of the delegates appointed was Miss Sophonisba P. Breckinridge, a professor in the Graduate School of Social Service of the University of Chicago. She was recommended by Senator Edward P. Costigan of Colorado, who also suggested the appointment of Mrs. Grace Bryan Hargreaves (Howe to Costigan, Oct. 2, 21, 1933, OF 567). John Bassett Moore, judge of the Permanent Court of International Justice, recommended the appointment of Stephen P. Duggan, director of the Institute of International Education (Moore to Phillips, Aug. 8, 1933, OF 567). Moore said that Duggan represented the cultural side of our relations with South America and that his appointment would help counteract the general impression there that the United States was interested only in commercial matters. Phillips thought the suggestion "a good one" (Phillips to Roosevelt, Aug. 14, 1933, OF 567). Duggan was also proposed by Henry N. MacCracken, president of Vassar College, and by John H. Finley, associate editor of the New York *Times;* Roosevelt acknowledged both recommendations (MacCracken to Roosevelt, Aug. 30, and the latter's reply, Sept. 20, 1933; Finley to Roosevelt Sept. 3, and the latter's reply, Sept. 12, 1933, OF 567). Ickes proposed the appointment of Simon J. Lubin of San Francisco, president of the Pan American Institute of Reciprocal Trade (Roosevelt to Ickes, Oct. 13, 1933, OF 567). The delegation as finally constituted consisted of Secretary of State Hull, Alexander Weddell, ambassador to Argentina, J. Reuben Clark, former ambassador to Mexico, J. Butler Wright, minister to Uruguay, Spruille Braden, a New York financier with wide experience in South America, and Miss Breckinridge, mentioned above. The staff of the delegation included James Clement Dunn, secretary general; Ernest H. Gruening, adviser; R. Henry Norweb, Walter C. Thurston, and Benjamin Muse, counselors; Wallace McClure, Anna A. O'Neill, Alexander V. Dye, and James C. Corliss, technical advisers; and Ulric Bell, press officer (*Report of the Delegates of the United States of America to the Seventh International Conference of American States, Montevideo, Uruguay, December 3–26, 1933,* State Department Conference Series No. 19, Washington, 1934, p. 1; hereafter cited as *Report of the Delegates to the Seventh International Conference*).

## Frank L. Polk to Roosevelt

New York, October 20, 1933

My dear Mr. President: I am taking the liberty of writing you on the subject of Russian recognition which seems to be receiving serious consideration at this time. I fully appreciate that there are economic and diplomatic reasons for recognition and therefore confine myself to the respectful suggestion that careful consideration be given the rights of Americans who were doing business in Russia before the Revolution.

A recognition, without some specific protection of the just legal rights of such Americans, individuals and corporations, would, as has been the case in other countries, result in grave injustice. I think it might be useful for me to cite an example in order to make my point: An American bank at the time of the Revolution had, let us say, a million dollars on deposit in this country in the name of the Imperial Russian Government. It had also on deposit with various Russian banks rubles which even at the time of the Revolution were worth on the market well over two million dollars. In the event of an unconditional recognition of the Soviet Government, that Government could claim in the American courts the one million dollars which had been deposited by the Imperial Russian Government prior to the Revolution and would leave the American bank entirely without remedy as to the rubles confiscated by the Soviet Government. This is one of many examples I could give and I feel sure that the Department of State have a long list where the result would be the same.

With all that you have on your mind I hesitated to write you direct but the experience of the business men of Great Britain, where careful provisions were not made by the terms of recognition, has put the American business man very much on notice as to what his fate may be.[1]

Again with many apologies, and with all good wishes, believe me, Yours faithfully,

Frank L. Polk

[OF 220:TS]

---

[1] Polk was a partner in the law firm headed by John W. Davis. For the exchanges resulting in resumption of diplomatic relations, see *Foreign Relations: The Soviet Union, 1933–1939,* passim, especially Roosevelt's letter of Oct. 10, 1933, to Mikhail Kalinin, proposing the opening of discussions, and the latter's reply, Oct. 17, 1933, accepting the proposal, pp. 17–18, 18. Some of this correspondence is also published in *Public Papers,* II, 415–417, 471–487, 498–499. The exchanges of October 10 and 17 were given out at the President's October 20 press conference; his principal comment on them to the reporters was: "I don't think there is much to add to that except this: This won't fall on you people, but there is a certain difficulty which the press always has and that is the headline fellow. And he is very apt to copy your leads. I hope that before you send your stories in that you will read both of these letters. They describe the situation 100 per cent. This is a request and an acceptance of the thought of sitting together at a table to see whether we can devise means for settling various problems that exist between two great nations, two great peoples. That is as far as it goes. And that is all it is." The President was asked to indicate some of the problems that needed solution and replied: "I wish I could. You know, there are a lot of them that have come up

in the past sixteen years, some of them are very old problems and some new. If I were to start listing them for you I would have to consult the State Department first." Roosevelt answered Polk, Oct. 28, 1933, below.

## Press Conference, President's Bedroom, The White House, October 25, 1933, 10:45 A.M.

[*Excerpt*] Q: The question of the constitutionality of having the RFC doing the gold trading has been raised. Do you have any question in mind about that?

The President: The Attorney General has ruled on it.[1]

Q: There seems to be some difference of opinion among the—

The President: The Attorney General has ruled on it.

Q: Will there be an Executive Order? Jesse Jones indicated there would be this morning at the Treasury.[2]

The President: No. They fixed the price this morning.[3]

Q: 31.36. The London price is 30.99. Is that news to you?

The President: I knew it had gone up a couple of shillings.

Q: Any discussion or further illustration of the monetary policy?

The President: I thought the speech covered that all right.[4]

Q: I came over here burdened with questions, none of which seem worth while asking unless you want to discuss it in a general way.

The President: Here is the thing. Of course everybody in New York would like to have from me a schedule for sixty days or a year ahead saying exactly what will be done every morning before breakfast. It is perfectly natural that they would like to have it. But what we are aiming at is an objective.

Q: Is this off the record?

The President: No. You can use this for background. And, of course, when it comes down to an announcement of what will be done tomorrow or a week or a month ahead, that is perfectly impossible. Great Britain doesn't do it and no nation does it in their governmental financial operations. Nobody knows what the British Treasury or the Bank of England is going to do tomorrow or what the Bank of France is going to do.

Q: Of course it is perfectly impossible to say now when or if any foreign operation may be engaged in?

The President: No.

Q: In that connection, I wonder if you are ready to say yet whether the Treasury gold, already held by the Treasury, will be revalued in any sense or in connection with the purchases by the RFC at higher prices?

The President: That is like asking a question: "Are you going to issue a proclamation?", which I have power to do under authority of Congress.[5] But, of course, I can't say anything at all. That is what lots of people would like to know.

Q: Do you consider it a favorable sign the way foreign exchange markets have discounted the mere announcement of this new policy?

The President: There again you are bringing in a factor which should not be over-emphasized, and that is the foreign exchange value. It is the same thing that appeared a little bit in that AP dispatch a week or ten days ago in which the very excellent phrase was used about the 4% tail wagging the 96% dog, which is a peach.

Q: (Mr. Stephenson) I wish I could take credit for it. (Laughter)

The President: That is the difficulty of over-emphasis of what happens in regard to foreign exchange, except there you find a single factor of the American Government's policy. You have the other factor of British and French stories, etc., over which we have no control.

Q: Can't that be fairly interpreted as a pretty definite reaction to the single policy of which you speak?

The President: Not necessarily, because I haven't the vaguest idea of what they are going to do. They may reverse the trend this day, this moment.

[President's Press Conferences:T]

[1] No opinion was published; see the New York *Times,* Oct. 27, 1933, p. 1.

[2] Director, Reconstruction Finance Corporation, 1932–1939.

[3] The President may have misunderstood this question. Executive order 6359, authorizing United States mints and assay offices to receive and the Reconstruction Finance Corporation to acquire and dispose of newly minted gold, was issued Oct. 25, 1933. The executive order and the new Treasury regulations on gold may be found in the New York *Times* of Oct. 27, 1933, p. 15.

[4] The speech of October 22, printed in *Public Papers,* II, 420–427, in which Roosevelt restated the Administration's determination to restore commodity price levels to "enable agriculture and industry once more to give work to the unemployed." Roosevelt had been under continual pressure since the middle of October to check the deflationary movement caused by falling farm prices. Warren had written to him on October 16 from Cornell University (OF 229) that a definite increase in the price of gold was necessary. Among other measures, he urged the purchase of newly mined gold at prices that would be gradually advanced until the desired price level was reached; as a start it might be well to relax control on the flight of capital and to give out rumors of inflation to get gold to $35 an ounce as soon as possible.

[5] Under authority of the Thomas Amendment to the Agricultural Adjustment Act.

## Frank C. Walker, Executive Secretary, The Executive Council, to Roosevelt

Washington, October 25th, 1933

To the President of the United States from the Executive Secretary of the Executive Council: There was delivered to you yesterday a copy of a recommendation made by the Administrator of Agricultural Adjustment[1] in respect to coordinating efforts with reference to the development of foreign trade. For your convenience this recommendation is herewith quoted:

Agricultural exports are more important to the nation than are industrial exports. In the twenty-three years from 1910 to 1932 the total income from all exports averaged 7.45 percent of the whole national income, but the proportion of agricultural income attributable to agricultural exports was 17.85 percent, while the proportion of industrial income attributable to industrial exports was only 5.21 percent. The importance to industry itself of buying power in farm areas has been demonstrated and now is admitted generally.

A certain amount of special machinery already has been created to study foreign markets. An inter-departmental board on reciprocity treaties has been acting for several months past and has been doing good work. The Agricultural Adjustment Administration has a small unit, the purpose of which is to negotiate wherever possible the sale of agricultural commodities. Other institutions of the Government have been doing a certain amount of basic research work that should be very helpful in laying the ground work for an approach to the solution of the problem. While all of these efforts are worth while, I believe that more vigorous and better coordinated effort with reference to the development of our foreign trade is imperatively needed.

It has occurred to me that the designation by the President of a special committee to deal with this problem, and through which the activities of all Government departments and institutions would be coordinated, would be most helpful. I would suggest that this committee have no other duties. I suggest further that any statistical data utilized should be set forth on two bases—(1) measured by the volume of the commodities, and (2) measured by value expressed in dollars.

I have studied this recommendation, and in my judgment this problem merits early action.[2]

Frank C. Walker

[OF 20:TS]

[1] George N. Peek.

[2] An accompanying memorandum from Roosevelt to Hull, Oct. 27, 1933, reads: "Will you and the Secretary of Commerce let me have a definite set-up to carry this into effect, if you approve?" See Hull to Roosevelt, Oct. 27, 1933, below.

## Roosevelt to Hugh Gibson, Ambassador to Brazil, Rio de Janeiro

[Washington] October 26, 1933

Dear Hugh: I am delighted to have your letter and the memorandum.[1]

I am taking up the United Press matter immediately, but I doubt whether the A.P. could or would spend the money for increased service in Latin America.

What to do about American financial relations is beyond me for the moment. We Americans were such fools when we had the chance a few years ago that we dread the fire.

You are absolutely right about the steamships. I hope to get a new policy through this coming Congress. I am glad to hear about the Embassy, for I had an idea that it was modern and a credit to us. You might look around and see what it would cost to buy—rather than build—an existing house; also whether the Embassy offices could be in the same place. It is in most cases a wasteful practice to have two completely separate establishments, one for business and the other for the Ambassador. For example, how much more practical and economical it would have been if in Paris we could have got rid of the Ambassador's house and given him a complete section of the new building on the Place de la Concorde!

It is good to get your letter. I hope all goes well with you and yours. Very sincerely yours,

[OF 405:CT]

[1] Not present, but Roosevelt quotes from it in the letter following. A memorandum from Roosevelt to Hull, Oct. 26, 1933 (OF 405), indicates that the Gibson letter and memorandum were sent to Hull. Gibson, a Foreign Service officer since 1908, was appointed ambassador to Brazil in May 1933 and held the post until July 1937, when he retired.

## Roosevelt to Roy W. Howard, Chairman of the Board, Scripps-Howard Newspapers, New York

[Washington] October 26, 1933

*Personal and Confidential*

Dear Roy: A friend of mine in Brazil writes me as follows:[1]

The Havas Agency is notoriously anti-American, and plays up all our doings in an unfriendly way and now and then goes in for really low intrigue in order to stir up bad blood. The United Press plays a considerable role here but is only second to Havas in its harmful presentation of American news.[2] They give little serious news, but a steady stream of kidnapping, racketeering, gangsters, scandals, graft, Hollywood divorces, and other similar stuff. I religiously read through the papers every day in my back-firing Portuguese and my only surprise is that the Brazilians are not filled with contempt for us. If my opinion of the United States were based on Havas and United Press despatches, I should think we were a thoroughly contemptible outfit. The Associated Press distributes a limited service, but it is issued by the Havas people and is not much better than it or the United Press in its handling of the news.

The remedy for this situation would seem to be in two parts—first, to have somebody in authority appeal to the heads of the United Press as presumably good patriotic Americans to modify the character of the news they send to these countries with a view to getting news more representative of American life and less concentrated on the aspects that we ourselves deplore. The second step would be to devise some method of getting an independent and full-scale Associated Press service in this field. Of course, an Associated Press franchise is an expensive thing in this part of the world and there are very few papers that could afford it.

This is something about which you know more than I do, but I thought you would be interested in reading it.[3]

Very sincerely yours,

[OF 405:CT]

[1] Hugh Gibson, ambassador to Brazil.
[2] The United Press, unlike the Associated Press, was not a member of the Havas syndicate, and was thus in competition with Havas.
[3] Answered Oct. 28, 1933, below.

# Press Conference, Executive Offices of the White House, October 27, 1933, 4:08 P.M.

[*Excerpt*] The President: I was just saying to the front row that I am afraid it is a sort of dull day today. The Secretary of State, I think, told you this morning that he is not pushing off until the 11th of November.[1] He asked me to emphasize again to you that this is not caused by any one thing but by a multiplicity of problems that he cannot finish by the 5th of November. In other words, do not write the story that it is Russia, because it is a lot of other things too.[2] Russia is merely one of the incidents; he has his commercial negotiations still going on with five nations, he still has the British representative over here on the debts, and there are quite a number of other things which he has got to clean up before he goes on account of the fact that Congress will be in session before he gets back. He has to go over his budget, have that all finished or the highlights of it before he goes away.

Q: Does that mean that the British negotiations are likely to be cleared up before he goes away?

The President: That I don't know. There are a good many ramifications, not only there but also with respect to other countries.

[President's Press Conferences:T]

[1] For the Montevideo Conference.
[2] Litvinov arrived November 7; see Hull, *Memoirs*, I, 292–307.


## Cordell Hull, Secretary of State, to Roosevelt

Washington, Oct. 27, 1933

Dear Mr. President: I directed that the enclosed memorandum (which is somewhat prolix) be drafted in order to emphasize the need for unifying this commercial policy situation.[1]

Sincerely yours,

Cordell Hull

[OF 970:TS]

[1] The memorandum is in reply to Walker's of Oct. 25, 1933, above.


## [*Enclosure*] Herbert Feis, Economic Adviser to the State Department, to Cordell Hull

October 26, 1933

The urgent necessity of working out an adequate and coordinated method for dealing with commercial policy questions: In the past, the handling of the commercial policy of this Government required relatively little Executive action, and that largely of a routine nature. There was a single column tariff extended to all countries. The Treasury and customs authorities administered this simple tariff, the State Department undertook to protect American trade against injuries and discrimination and to handle complaints from foreign governments in regard to the administration of the American tariff.

The course of economic development throughout the world and the movement of American policy is making the field of commercial policy much more complex and has created a very urgent and important need for developing and improving our handling of it. We now have the following scattered branches of commercial policy either in being or in prospect, each of which is being dealt with somewhat independently of the rest, with resultant ineffectiveness, confusion, and loss of opportunity:

(1) The State Department is engaged in steady day to day handling of situations throughout the world, involving American trade interests—the whole paraphernalia of discriminations under tariff laws, quota laws, exchange controls, et cetera.

It likewise is undertaking a series of bilateral treaty negotiations with Colombia, Brazil, Cuba, Argentina, Portugal and Sweden.

(2) It is contemplated that admission to the American wines and spirits market will be placed on a bargaining basis and the State Department in collaboration with other interested Departments is likely soon to be engaged in another series of bargaining negotiations in this field.

(3) Section 3 (e) of the National Recovery Act just effectuated by an Executive Order contemplates a process of study by the NRA and by the Tariff Commission and action by the President in regard to imports which threaten the effectiveness of codes.

(4) Under the agricultural marketing provisions of the Agricultural Adjustment Act, the Secretary of Agriculture is empowered to license importers and dealers in imported agricultural products.

(5) The Reconstruction Finance Corporation is authorized to make loans for the export of American products. It has done so and has extended several such loans, as for instance that to China.

(6) The whole problem of possible interchange of goods between this country and Russia will soon be up for consideration.

(7) The Tariff Commission has duties both under the Tariff Act and under the National Recovery Act.

It is apparent that all these activities will have great bearing upon each other and that a unified policy should be worked out among them. For that reason it is suggested that there be established somewhere in the Government one head authority over whose desk must pass all matters arising in the field of international commercial policy. The State Department is entrusted with the duty of conducting the foreign relations of this country and it is the channel through which foreign trade negotiations ordinarily pass. It is likewise the normal channel of communication with foreign governmental authorities. For that reason it is suggested that a separate branch of the State Department be designated to unify Government action in the field of commercial policy, under a specially qualified head. This branch would of course have to work every hour and every day in conjunction with all other interested branches of the Government and likewise be in close touch with the President.

It is therefore suggested that this matter receive immediate attention and study.[1]

H.F.

[OF 970:TS]

[1] See Roosevelt to Hull, Oct. 30, 1933, below.

## Roosevelt to Frank L. Polk, New York

[Washington] October 28, 1933

Dear Frank: Many thanks for yours of October 20th.[1] We shall do everything possible to see that justice is done in the matter of the old claims and counter-claims.[2]

I do hope to see you one of these days soon.

Very sincerely yours,

[OF 220:CT]

[1] Above.

[2] Documents relating to the resumption of trade and diplomatic relations with the Soviet Union, the Russian debt to the United States, the revolutionary activities of Soviet nationals, and the rights of Americans in the Soviet Union are printed in *Foreign Relations, 1933,* II, 778–840, and in *Public Papers,* II, 415–417, 471–487. Hull devotes a chapter in his *Memoirs,* I, 292–307, to the subject. Efforts to make an arrangement with the Soviet government on debts dragged on until early in 1935 when Hull announced that the United States had given up hope of arriving at an agreement (Hull to Wiley, Jan. 30, 1935, *Foreign Relations: The Soviet Union, 1933–1939,* pp. 172–173).

## William E. Dodd, Ambassador to Germany, to Roosevelt

Berlin, October 28, 1933

Dear Mr. President: Senator Bulkley[1] on his way home met a good and reliable friend in Holland who said: "Fritz Thyssen* said to me at dinner a day or two ago that he had forced the German Government to withdraw from Geneva." Since this fits into some other information that has come to me, I venture to report it to you. I am afraid other great ammunition manufacturers in Europe have played their parts too.

Since my long talk with the Reichskanzler October 17,[2] events have been a little disconcerting. The Kanzler stressed peace to the limit; but he, Goebbels and Göring (a little out of favor) go on arousing common men's ire against the outside world in a way to defeat his promises to me. Liberal and intellectual Germany is very uneasy, but it dares not speak out. I told Hitler that Germany is the best educated country in the world, that it is not Italy, and the people of the United States sympathized with its people—and hoped above all things that no war would be allowed here. Perhaps I was too frank, but I had to be honest. I am hoping against hope. The election here is a farce.

Your ruling about paying salaries in gold prevented the necessity of resignation on my part. We simply can not get on here on less than the legal salary; and I am afraid I shall have trouble even then, if we give even a minimum of attention to the proper claims of people here or those who come here and are entitled to attention. I wish to thank you most heartily, and to add that there are some rulings of the staff here (approved by myself) which involve resort to the complicated Registered Marks. The State Department has all needful information, but it is easy for misunderstandings to arise. In case the thing should be brought to your attention, I wish to say that I have explained the matter as best I could to Mr. Phillips.

I hope your great work goes on successfully. No man in all history has ever had so great a problem to solve.**

Yours sincerely,

William E. Dodd

* Great ammunition and steel man in the Ruhr region.

** Information here to the effect that Japan is trying to make entente with Germany. It came to me confidential. I have heard several remarks from Germans showing same tendency. The failure of Stimson two years ago, perhaps inevitable, in Far East policy is going to be calamitous, I fear.

W.E.D.[3]

[PPF 1043:TS]

[1] Senator Robert J. Bulkley of Ohio, chairman of the Senate Committee on Manufactures and member of the Senate Committee on Banking and Currency, had visited

France, England, Belgium, and Germany in October and November discussing world currency matters with the leading statesmen of these countries (New York *Times,* Oct. 13, 1933, p. 32; Nov. 5, 1933, II, 16).

[2] See Dodd to Hull, Oct. 17, 1933, *Foreign Relations, 1933,* II, 396–397, and Dodd, *Diary,* pp. 48–50.

[3] Answered Nov. 13, 1933, below.

## Roy W. Howard, Chairman of the Board, Scripps-Howard Newspapers, to Roosevelt

New York, October 28, 1933

*Personal*

My dear Governor: I appreciate very much your passing along to me the comment from your friend in Brazil.[1] As this is definitely and specifically Karl Bickel's proposition, I am passing it along to him with an admonition to observe its personal and confidential nature.[2] While I am somewhat out of touch with the present-day South American activities of the United Press, your friend's misinformation is so palpable that I know that Bickel, as President of the United Press, will be keenly interested in getting the actual facts to you.

The suggestion that "an Associated Press franchise is an expensive thing" in South America is a bit amusing in light of the fact that the Associated Press, functioning along entirely legitimate lines, of course, is making a constant drive on the United Press clients, there being, of course, no expense whatever attaching to membership in the Associated Press down there, beyond the weekly charge for the service.

While I have not heard of any complaints of this sort relative to American press reports in South America in recent years, they used to be frequent in the days when I was on the United Press, both the AP and the UP being object of the kicks which were invariably based on the consistent refusal of both of these organizations to turn themselves into American propaganda bureaus and thereby discredit themselves with South Americans and foreigners alike, as completely and as thoroughly as the European agencies have done.

I am sure Bickel will appreciate your kindness and co-operation in passing this comment along.

Cordially yours,

Roy

PS: I have been strongly tempted to offer you a telephonic earful on this local political situation into which you have been dragged more deeply than you may suspect, and certainly entirely contrary to the thought you expressed to me on Primary Day.[3] Possibly as an evidence that I am getting old, I have, however, restrained myself from butting in, even with a suggestion which I know you would not construe as otherwise than friendly. RWH

[OF 405:TS]

[1] Oct. 26, 1933, above.
[2] See Bickel to Roosevelt, Oct. 30, 1933, below.
[3] Howard referred to the mayoralty campaign in New York, in which Fiorello LaGuardia was elected mayor on a Fusion ticket. Roosevelt had been noncommittal about the several candidates, but Joseph V. McKee, running as an independent Democrat, had claimed to have his support.

## Karl A. Bickel, President, United Press, to Roosevelt

New York City, October 30, 1933

My dear Mr. President: I am exceedingly grateful to you for your thoughtfulness in passing on to Roy Howard—and permitting him confidentially to pass on to me—the very interesting comment upon our service by your friend in Brazil.[1]

Every press association executive who is engaged in the international distribution of news is keenly aware of the fact that the national living abroad is most sensitive in his reactions to news from home. In our experience in serving the newspapers in some forty-two different nations we frequently find ourselves under the critical fire of Americans in the diplomatic and consular service and those who are engaged in private commercial endeavor. The principal source of trouble rests in the fact that the average American abroad—or at home, for that matter—does not understand that, if the United Press is to deliver each day an honest picture of the world's events, it must be, above every other thing, utterly and completely objective.

Neither does the reader seem to understand that the United Press does not create the news and that our only discretion in the use of the various items before us is limited to the exercise of our judgment on which of the stories are the most important or which possess the greatest qualities to the news consumers of the country to which the dispatches are directed. Obviously, we would much rather report on a world of sweetness and light, but the world we are reporting is the world of our fellow human beings. A very small part of those human beings are gangsters, kidnapers, municipal grafters and others with a blunted social and ethical sense, and at times their activities bring them into the scope of our work.

I know that you well understand that the United Press is not a propaganda service, and that we cannot delete or suppress news because that news deals with some phase of civic or social ugliness. Long ago we discovered that there is no man so wise, so tolerant and so understanding as to deserve to be given the power to censor a news service and to be capable of ruling justly that "this item shall go and this item shall be suppressed."

The fact that the United Press does not attempt to do that sort of thing has been the corner-stone of its successful delivery of service to more than ninety percent of the substantial daily newspapers south of the Panama Canal. Because the nations of Latin-America (and of Asia and Europe, as well) have come to understand, over the past twenty years, that a United Press dispatch represents, so far as it is within our power, an impartial and objective picture of an event, without nationalistic coloring, without private commercial or financial bias, it is of inestimable service to our country. It is of infinitely more value to the United States, in the most selfish and materialistic sense, than the efforts of governmentally subsidized services, such as Havas of France, Wolff of Germany, or Rengo of Japan.

Before leaving this general question of crime, graft and scandal news that your friend brought up, there is one point that I want to make exceedingly clear: When I am talking about crime news I am talking about the gangster, the bank robber, the kidnaper, etc. I am not talking about political graft and about certain forms of "racketeering" which have assumed a position in our national life that is of much more significance than mere "crime" of the police court variety. I know many well-intentioned and often indignant gentlemen, abroad and at home, who grow choleric over United Press reports on Congressional investigations such as that into the Stock Exchange, international banking, packing house and stock yards, election expenses, etc. In the heat of their denunciations they sometimes refer to all this as "scandal and crime" news and feel that we are both unwise and unpatriotic in handling it for what we think it is worth, in the international field, as news.

There are any number of men and women who feel that we should "play" these things "down"; that they "are not properly understood abroad," etc. We have very little sympathy for that point of view. We carry these items, if they are news, because it is our business to carry them, because we would be simply short-weighing our clients and delivering a dishonest package of goods if we did not. But beyond that, these people do not seem to realize that there is no longer the remotest possibility of doing a job of national dirty linen washing in secret. Such items, if they are of any interest to the Brazilian, the Japanese or the German, cannot be suppressed. If the United Press does not carry them fairly, justly and in honest balance with the rest of the world's events, they will be carried by one of the foreign governmentally subsidized agencies and carried, you can be sure, with every unfortunate or harmful element super-stressed.

Touching directly upon the complaint of your correspondent regarding our general South American service and our Brazilian service in particular, it is a matter of fact that, out of a general service of from 8,000 to 10,000 cabled words per day to Buenos Aires, where our Brazilian service is made up, we carry but a trifling amount of crime. Of American crime we do not average 50 words per day. In our Brazilian service, of course, the average is not nearly that much.

The newspapers of South America as a rule care less about "crime" than almost any other general group of newspapers in the world. *La Prensa* of Buenos Aires, which is one of the two or three greatest newspapers in the world, and which receives about ninety percent of all its foreign news through the United Press, prints practically no crime.

When I received the inclosure in your letter covering the report on our Brazilian service, I cabled our Buenos Aires bureau for a report on exactly what we had carried to Rio Janeiro over the past three days as a fair sample of service into Brazil. The reply reads as follows:

Replying to yours October 28th report contains only general worldwide information basis exactly same service as that which we make up Buenos Aires report plus the usual advance mail services. Fine (our Rio Janeiro manager) cables me that very little scandal and crime is published in Rio Janeiro from United Press except an occasional Hollywood divorce and news of the importance of the recent convictions and life sentences under the Lindbergh law which generally briefest. An examination of the 169 cables sent Rio during the last three days fails to show single item remotely connected with crime or scandal, unless a story on mid-western farm strike is crime. Principal items were on the trip of the Graf Zeppelin, U.S. gold prices, French-German politics, Uruguayan political disturbances, Pan-American Conference, Franco-Brazil tariffs, Geneva disarmament, Havana riots, Chaco war, Fascist anniversary, Arab-Jewish struggle, Portuguese revolt and general Lisbon stuff, Mexican unrest, Panter's arrest[2] and U.S. farm strike.

Now that farm strike story, which we do not regard as "Scandal" or "crime" might be just exactly the sort of a news item your friend referred to. News definitions depend a great deal on the point of view. Shortly after we went into the business of supplying a South American report, during the Wilson administration, we carried daily stories covering the Federal Trade investigation into the Chicago packing houses' operation and we were almost overwhelmed by a flood of protests from American business men in Buenos Aires interested in the United States plants who regarded our handling of the story at all as a gross betrayal of American interests. We were publicly denounced in many foreign cities by American Clubs for carrying what seems to us to be entirely routine and colorless stories relating to the Sacco-Vanzetti trials and execution. We were blamed for carrying "too much Lindbergh" at the time when world-wide interest in the kidnaping was at its height. During the Coolidge administration an American business man in South America, representing a great American interest, vigorously criticized us for carrying an extract of an address of the President of the United States; and shortly afterwards an American diplomat objected because we were carrying extracts from the Senate addresses of Senator Borah,[3] then chairman of the Senate Foreign Relations Committee, on American policy in regard to Nicaragua.

These instances merely serve to illustrate how easy it is for the most well-intentioned critic to fail to grasp the fact that an honest news report must be objective and that it cannot "select" its items with the view of keeping its service in line with a diplomat's opinion or a business man's desires.

In this connection the following extract of a recent report on American news services serving the Latin-American press made by the Council on Inter-American Relations after a considerable study and investigation, might be of interest to your friend. The report, after discussing the relative differences in organization between the United Press and the Associated Press, states:

Material sent out by these services is treated in an objective way, propaganda is avoided and every effort is made to concentrate upon news values. It is, however, inevitable that in the course of work of this sort, certain material may be sent out which appears critical of the United States. If this occurs it is generally due to the conditions of the work itself.

I want to make it very clear that the comments of the gentleman from Brazil have not been received in this office in any light or derisive fashion. What growth the United Press has enjoyed over the past twenty years it has largely gained from the criticism of its friends, and we regard this criticism as honest, well intentioned and informative. I have asked our Buenos Aires filing office to make a most careful study of the service going to Brazil, and we are again going over our daily file to South America in the light of the suggestions and criticisms advanced in the letter to you.

Brazil is a difficult field—one of the most difficult in South America. Its entire newspaper structure is built up on a basis very different from that of the United States, or even of the Argentine or Chile. We are very frank in our acknowledgment that we can learn a great deal and have yet to learn a great deal before we will feel that our Brazilian business is on the sound and permanent footing that we are striving for, and any help that we can receive from any resident of that country is genuinely and sincerely welcome.[4]

Very sincerely yours,

(S) Karl A. Bickel

[OF 405:T]

[1] Roosevelt to Howard, Oct. 26, 1933, above.
[2] Noel Panter, a British newspaperman, had recently been arrested in Munich on espionage charges.
[3] Senator William E. Borah of Idaho.
[4] The President asked that Bickel be given an appointment (Grace Tully to Early, Nov. 3, 1933, OF 405); his name does not, however, appear in the White House appointments list. With his letter Bickel sent a brief note, of the same date. He said he had written in considerable detail because Roosevelt might wish to send a copy to his "correspondent" (Ambassador Hugh Gibson). He asked if he might send a copy to James I. Miller, the United Press vice-president in charge of South America. Answered, Nov. 7, 1933, below.

# Roosevelt to Cordell Hull, Secretary of State

Washington, October 30, 1933

Memorandum from the President for the Secretary of State: Confirming what I have already suggested to you, will you and the Secretary of Commerce please work out a plan for executive machinery and, if necessary, executive orders or directions coordinating all matters relating to tariff and foreign trade in such a way that the various Federal agencies will clear through some one individual.

Such a tying in of existing agencies will affect:

1. State Department
2. Treasury Department
3. N.R.A.
4. A.A.A.
5. R.F.C.
6. Tariff Commission[1]

[OF 970:CT]

[1] See Hull to Roosevelt, Nov. 2, 1933, below.


# Henry M. Kannee to Marvin H. McIntyre, Assistant Secretary to the President

Washington, October 30, 1933

Memo for Mr. McIntyre

The following are State Department requests:

1. The Japanese Ambassador is leaving. Jimmy Dunn[1] says that the advisable thing to do is to have the Secretary of State say that the President told him that he wanted to see the Japanese Ambassador before he goes. They are not going to play it up as a news item, but it would be a very nice gesture. The date can be fixed later on. Also, after the Ambassador has seen the President, it would be advisable for the President to send him an autographed photograph. *Tea later*[2]

2. Irwin B. Laughlin, former Ambassador to Spain, has returned to Washington, where he lives, and feels that he should report to the President. *OK.*[3]

3. The State Department feels that the President should see Arthur B. Lane, recently appointed Minister to Nicaragua, and until recently Counsellor of the American Embassy at Mexico City. *OK*[4]

4. Br. Admiral here on November tenth. *5:30.* Vernou spoke to the President about a luncheon. The State Department also recommends it. Is that O.K.? *Tea*[5]

5. The retiring South African Minister[6] is leaving Washington on Thursday. Does the President want to see him? The State Department does not think it is essential. *Out*

6. Litvinoff.[7]

H.M.K.[8]

[OF 197:T]

[1] James C. Dunn, chief of protocol.
[2] This and the other italicized words are in Roosevelt's hand. The Japanese ambassador, Katsuji Debuchi, apparently did not call.
[3] Laughlin was at the White House on November 2 (PPF 1-0).
[4] November 2 (PPF 1-0).
[5] Rear Admiral Reginald A. R. Drax; Walter N. Vernou was naval aide.
[6] Eric H. Louw.
[7] With Secretary of State Hull on November 10 (PPF 1-0).
[8] Henry M. Kannee was secretary to McIntyre.

# Senator Frederic C. Walcott of Connecticut to Roosevelt

Norfolk, Connecticut, November 1, 1933

My dear Mr. President: These are strenuous times and the whole world is looking at you and placing upon your broad shoulders greater responsibilities than ever rested on any one man before.

I have made several speeches during the last four months, supporting the N.R.A. and your program, and have had excellent editorial comments, showing the general feeling of the public in the East, but I am receiving disturbing letters from the Mississippi valley, some from Republicans and others from Democrats, which indicate a serious conflict this winter in Congress between the agricultural interests of the Middle West and the manufacturing interests of the East, the latter very largely, and in some quarters enthusiastically, supporting your program.

I hesitate to take even a moment of your time to read a letter, but I have recently received some interesting letters from Francis E. Powell, the chairman of the International Sugar Council and for many years chairman of the board of the Anglo-British Oil Company, now retired, a brilliant man, who, although an American, knows intimately the leaders of thought in England and therefore speaks, I believe, in a semi-official way. You may recall that he came over last May with a proposal which, while not official, he was sure would be acceptable to

England and to France, based upon prompt cash settlements, to be extended, perhaps, over two or three years. The figures in May were, for Great Britain, 200,000,000 pounds sterling, and, for France, $850,000,000 in gold. I handed you a signed memorandum to this effect, feeling that it was well worth keeping in mind in view of possible conversations. Now that the last attempt has apparently been inconclusive, I am quoting the contents of one of Mr. Powell's letters, which tell their own story:

I especially avoided contact with the members of the American Delegation to the World Conference as I did not want them to feel that their experience here would be colored by any American opinion, but I am still of the view that no successful World Conference can be held and no international stability can be established until the British-American debt matter is settled and out of the way.

To refresh your memory, the suggestion which I made while I was in Washington is still unchanged. I am fortified in this by the opinion of competent British friends I have talked with here, and I believe that the British delegation has the main points of this kind of a settlement in their minds.

My thought is that if the British delegates after due discussion are prepared to make a definite proposal to the United States to settle their war debts by a cash payment of approximately 200,000,000 pounds, that this will give a basis for the President to make a definite recommendation to Congress. So long as there is no proposal before Congress, one cannot say whether they would finally refuse a reduction or not, but my own feeling is that the above sum is all that the British Government can pay. Even then they would have to raise it by getting their British nationals to patriotically deposit with the Government American securities which could be used in the payment of the debt and for which the British holders would accept a British Government bond at a low interest rate, say $3\frac{1}{2}\%$.

If payment was made in this way, the American Government could cash in these American securities and by depositing the resultant amount in the Federal Reserve could issue against it $2\frac{1}{2}$ times that amount of currency. This would give all the inflation possibilities that the country needs or could absorb.

In putting forward the proposal to Congress, my idea would be for the President to say that it should have due and careful consideration but that perhaps it is a little less than the United States could afford to accept. Congress or the President might then consider as a countervailing proposition 250,000,000 pounds and eventually a settlement might come about through adjustment to say 220,000,000 pounds.

The main point is to get this very controversial matter out of the international picture. It would have a tremendous effect in encouraging international trade and to that extent would materially assist in the success of the N.R.A. program. Believe me when I say that this country is not in a position, and never will be in our time in a position, to either pay more than this capital sum or even to continue the instalments of interest as provided under the original agreement.

A settlement now would prevent all the controversy and trouble of discussions that would arise in connection with the payment due in December and would so restore good feeling and confidence between the two countries as to more than compensate the United States for any apparent loss in the capital of the debt. I say apparent because it is only that and not real. It is not real because it will never be available.

I know how deeply you feel on this subject and this is my excuse for writing you again at length as I have done.[1]

With highest esteem, Faithfully yours,

F. C. Walcott

[OF 212:TS]

[1] Answered Nov. 8, 1933, below.

## Roosevelt to Governor Tom Berry, Pierre, South Dakota

[Washington] November 2, 1933

My dear Governor Berry: Replying to your letter of October eighteenth[1] regarding an embargo on blackstrap molasses: if we should take such action in this case, we might equally well take similar action in the case of many other products now imported which compete directly or indirectly with American farm products, such as bananas, silk, etc.

Over the past five years every country in the world has been taking steps to improve its position in the world by seeking to reduce its imports and increase its exports. Obviously, all countries cannot do this at the same time. The net effect has been to reduce both imports and exports from all countries. As a result of a Senate Resolution, the Department of Agriculture submitted in June a voluminous report on *World Trade Barriers in Relation to American Agriculture* (Senate Document No. 70). This report shows very clearly that the attempts to raise trade barriers have made conditions constantly worse.

By and large, I am of the belief that our farmers have much more to gain by restoring as rapidly as possible the foreign markets for our products than by attempting to seize more of the domestic market with the inevitable result of narrowing still further the export outlet. As you know, negotiations are now in progress with many different countries for mutual reductions of trade barriers. Definite progress in this direction has already been made in the case of the International Wheat Agreement. We hope that further concessions along this line may be obtained in return for some concessions to foreign countries when the wine and liquor traffic is restored. Negotiations for the removal of trade barriers will, we may hope, go forward in the next year or two and gradually remove some of the halters which have been slowly but effectively strangling world trade.

Three of our great farm products—wheat, cotton, and hogs—depend on world markets for a considerable part of their sale. Unless we restore these world markets many people will have to be taken out of farming permanently and a great deal of fertile acreage will have to be withdrawn. I do not believe that anyone in this country is prepared to face the difficulties which would be involved in such a drastic transformation of our agricultural and industrial structure.

I am well aware of the fact that a current emergency situation can be urged in support of the step which you suggest. Similar emergency situations were urged for each successive step that nations have taken during the past decade, yet the cumulative effect of these steps has been to almost completely eliminate all international trade.

I believe that the only way real prosperity can be restored will be by each nation taking steps which lead to its own prosperity without damaging the prosperity of the other countries. Steps such as this one can only lead to temporary improvements of conditions in one country at a cost of poorer conditions in other countries which are its customers. The world depression is sufficient evidence that such short-sighted policies do not pay in the long run.

In general, our relations with other nations might be seriously impaired by such action as you propose, and therefore the attitude of the State Department would have large influence in any determination of policy.[2]

Appreciating the sincerity of your interest, I am, Very sincerely yours,

[OF 307:CT]

[1] Berry (OF 307) urged an embargo on the importation of blackstrap molasses, used in making industrial alcohol, as a means of creating an additional market for surplus corn.

[2] Drafted in the Agriculture Department, possibly by Wallace (Wallace to Roosevelt, Nov. 1, 1933, OF 307).

## Cordell Hull, Secretary of State, to Roosevelt

Washington, November 2, 1933

My dear Mr. President: I understand that you are giving thought to the idea of assigning to the Department of Agriculture the duty of regulating imports of wines and spirits during the period prior to the enactment of permanent legislation. I believe it is also your further idea that admission to the American market during this period should be exchanged for opportunities for American products in foreign markets, particularly for American agricultural products. As you know, I am in thorough accord with this policy.[1]

The Department of State is of course continually engaged in the conduct of commercial relations with the rest of the world and is the treaty-negotiating agency. If it is to carry out its duties effectively, it must be in a position to be able to deal with all elements in the import and export trade. I therefore respectfully suggest in order to avoid possible misunderstanding and the crossing of wires that the Department of Agriculture be informed that the negotiations dealing with entry of wines and spirits will, like all other international trade questions, be executed through this Department. I have drafted a suggested letter for this purpose.[2]

May I take this occasion to follow up one of the thoughts expressed in the memorandum which I have already forwarded to you dealing with the question of policy in this field of wines and spirits? When permanent legislation is passed dealing with the whole subject, would it not be advisable to have first a tariff scheme that will make bargaining possible and second, to have the power reserved to the Executive to make use of other means of regulation of the import trade? When this is done, may I suggest that in the law this reserved power be assigned to you directly rather than to the Department of Agriculture? My thought is that as our whole idea for the coordination of the commercial policy work of this Government is developed and applied, the conduct of negotiations in this field will be one branch of the work of the chairman of the interdepartmental Executive Committee.

I hope that shortly we shall be able to carry out the appointment to the Department which has already met with your approval. The individual in question, if he accepts, might well act as Chairman of this interdepartmental Executive Committee. However, as there should be no delay in setting up the contemplated machinery, Mr. Phillips could, if you approve, undertake the duties as temporary Chairman.

I enclose a draft of a circular letter which you might care to use in connection with a communication to the heads of departments and Government organizations on this subject.

It would be of great help to me to know whether this general idea meets with your approval.

Faithfully yours,

Cordell Hull

[OF 614-A:TS]

[1] Wine and liquor imports were at this time under embargo. The embargo was lifted Dec. 2, 1933, with the signing by Roosevelt of the National Recovery Administration Code for the Alcoholic Beverages Importing Industry, which set up quotas. The prospective flood of French wines and liquors resulted in a number of letters to the newspapers from persons who urged that the United States permit importations only from such countries as had made an effort to pay their debts to us; see New York *Times*, Sept. 14, 1933, p. 22.

[2] The draft enclosed was prepared by Herbert Feis, economic adviser to the State Department. Extensively revised in the White House (presumably by Roosevelt), it was sent to Peek and other agency heads as the letter of Nov. 11, 1933, below.

# Press Conference, Executive Offices of the White House, November 3, 1933, 4:10 P.M.

[*Excerpt*] Q: Any debt developments you can tell us?

The President: Nothing new on that.

Q: Can you tell us whether the conversations have narrowed down?

The President: No, because I am not taking part in those conversations. Just the British and Acheson . . .[1]

Q: Can you give us any information or background on the results of your new gold program, without going into it?

The President: I don't think so, because, after all, on this gold thing, it is as Jesse Jones told some of you yesterday.[2] For instance, you take the stabilization fund in England. The results and figures are never given out on that. Nor do they do it in France or in any other nation which is conducting anything in the way of central banking operations or government operations.

Q: Has either of those countries made anything in the nature of a protest to us?

The President: No.

Q: They will know over on the other side, where the purchases are made, in the Banks of England or France?

The President: Oh, yes.

Q: They will know what your purchases are?

The President: I suppose they disclose it just the way they would any other purchase or sale through their own banks.

Q: They refused to yesterday.

The President: Did they?

Q: The Bank of France said that they do not disclose the dealings with customers.

The President: Then it does not get disclosed.

Q: There are back stairs there, too. They let it out to their friends.

The President: Yes?

[President's Press Conferences:T]

[1] The negotiations ended Nov. 6, 1933, without accomplishment; see Lindsay's exchange of notes with Hull of that date in *Foreign Relations, 1933*, I, 844, 844–845. See also Roosevelt's note to George V of Nov. 5, 1933, in *Personal Letters, 1928–1945*, I, 370–371, and his statement of Nov. 7, 1933, below.

[2] Probably in connection with announcement to the press of the beginning of the Reconstruction Finance Corporation's gold-buying program; see New York *Times*, Nov. 3, 1933, p. 1.

## Spencer V. B. Nichols to Roosevelt

New York, November 3, 1933

Dear Mr. President: Last night a group of your fellow members were gathered at the Century Club. The conversation that ensued gave me courage to address a personal letter to you in spite of the many problems that I know demand your attention.

All of us have been workers of the first hour in the cause of international affairs. Many of us have been your personal friends through the years and have been associated with the many causes for which you have stood in the past and the present.

Some of us were present in the development of the political future of Woodrow Wilson, remaining close to him in life and since prizing the distinction of being leaders of Wilsonian democracy. We have spent of our time and substance since Woodrow Wilson retired from the White

House to keep alive his principles. We have welcomed and furthered every agency that developed his program and through the period of Republican administration we kept the faith.

Today we are uncertain of our duty. We have faithfully accepted your inspired leadership and we have tried to uphold your hand in public addresses and in giving you support through recognized agencies.

At the moment Raymond Fosdick and a small group of us are trying through the League of Nations Association to further, not membership in the League or even the hope for appointment of a Commissioner General to the League to strengthen its prestige at this crisis, but rather to make articulate the vast number of citizens who see in the League's principles of international interdependence, the sole function upon which we may build for the future.

The pendulum has swung to the left—nationalism and isolation are only articulate and we desire to strive to publicize the inarticulate voice of America in order that once you have achieved your high purpose in our domestic concerns, we may have prepared an enlightened public opinion upon which you may depend in your efforts to guide our international relationships however synonymous the two may obviously be.

My query is, how may we, your friends, best serve you? We have too long remained inarticulate. I have been personally asked to deliver several addresses on the new deal. I enclose an address that I have prepared for delivery in several sections of the country.[1] May I express the hope that consideration may be given to its contents and if possible an expression from you if it would prove helpful or not. I pledge you that any communication will be considered as highly confidential if so addressed to me at 850 Seventh Avenue, N.Y.C. We would serve you if you would show us the way.

With warmest personal greetings, believe me, Mr. President, Cordially and faithfully yours,

S.V.B. Nichols

[OF 184-A:TS]

[1] An 11-page typed speech entitled "The New Deal." Nichols, a lawyer, was for a short time an assistant secretary of state in the Wilson Administration. He was active as an officer in the League of Nations Association, the Woodrow Wilson Foundation, and like organizations, and was the author of a number of articles on international relations. McIntyre replied Nov. 12, 1933 (OF 184-A), that all the President could ask for was intelligent cooperation and support; if this carried with it criticism that was constructive, "it would still be helpful and not unwelcome." See Roosevelt to the Woodrow Wilson Foundation, Dec. 28, 1933, below.

# William Phillips, Acting Secretary of State, to Roosevelt

Washington, November 4, 1933

My dear Mr. President: I am enclosing herewith for your consideration and approval certain of the draft instructions to our delegates to the Conference at Montevideo covering the more important items on the Agenda. These include the subjects under Chapter I of the Agenda, the so-called "Organization of Peace" questions, and those under Chapter IV on commercial and financial policy. I also attach draft instructions on the subject of the Monroe Doctrine; non-recognition of the Martinez regime in El Salvador; external loans of the Latin American countries now in default; and participation in the Pan American Conferences.[1]

As you may recall, the question of "Intervention" has always been a thorny subject for us at these Pan American Conferences. Our record in the matter, particularly in late years, has been so fine and straight-forward—e.g. withdrawal from Nicaragua, the agreement with Haiti providing for withdrawal of Marines next October, our attitude towards Cuba—that I think we can make a good showing on the subject and one that should command the respect and admiration of all fair-minded Latin Americans. However, we of course cannot renounce our right, recognized under international law, to protect our citizens in foreign countries in the event of complete breakdown of government. Nor can we renounce certain special rights and responsibilities granted us under treaties with certain Latin American countries, e.g. Cuba, Haiti, Panama, and the Dominican Republic. The question of intervention is likely to arise under various guises at the Montevideo Conference, probably chiefly in connection with the chapter of the Agenda on the codification of international law, one item of which covers the subject "The Rights and Duties of States." In this connection we propose, if possible, to avoid discussion of the matter through laying emphasis on the fact that codification of international law obviously can take place only when there is general agreement upon the principles involved, and that it would therefore be advisable to concentrate effort for codification on subjects concerning which there appears to be such general agreement as would give hope of making progress in this field. For instance, subjects which might be treated with some hope of constructive accomplishment in the way of codification would be: Extradition; Territorial Sea; and Nationality.

In addition to the topics mentioned hereinabove, the Agenda covers many other items of a more or less routine nature; I do not feel it necessary to take your time for a consideration of the instructions concerning them.

In connection with the instruction on the Monroe Doctrine, I should like to invite your attention particularly to the statement therein that there would be no objection on the part of the United States to the adoption of a resolution, if desired by the Latin American Republics, that in the event the rights of an American nation are threatened by an aggressive action of a non-American power, the American Republics should communicate with one another fully and frankly in order to reach an understanding concerning the measures to be taken, jointly or separately, to meet the exigencies of the particular situation, provided always that freedom of action on the part of the United States under the Monroe Doctrine were completely reserved. This statement is taken bodily from the instructions to our Delegates to the Fifth and Sixth Pan American Conferences. I am in favor of the proposal, and feel that, as stated subsequently in the instruction, it might be advisable for our Delegation to put forward such a proposal in an effort to forestall action by other Delegations seeking to limit the scope of the Monroe Doctrine. I might add that in general the proposal to communicate with one another in the event of threat of aggressive action is similar to the obligation undertaken in the treaty of December 13, 1921, between the United States, the British Empire, France and Japan, relating to their possessions in the region of the Pacific Ocean.

The draft instructions covering the Monroe Doctrine and external debts refer to statements which, under certain contingencies, it might be advisable for the head of our Delegation to make at Montevideo. I am having these statements prepared and shall submit them to you later for your approval.[2]

Faithfully yours,

William Phillips

[*Notation*:AS] OK    FDR
[PSF:State:TS]

---

[1] The draft instructions are present; see the formal "Instructions to Delegates" of Nov. 10, 1933, signed by Hull, in *Foreign Relations, 1933,* IV, 43–155.
[2] See Howe to Hull, Nov. 9, 1933, below.

## William Phillips, Acting Secretary of State, to Roosevelt

[Washington] November 4, 1933

My dear Mr. President: I am in receipt of a communication from the Secretary General of the League of Nations inviting the appointment by this Government of American representatives to sit on the Special Temporary Committee for Assistance to Indigent Foreigners and the Enforcement of Maintenance Orders Abroad, the first meeting of which will be held at Geneva on December 4, 1933.

The Secretary of Labor has expressed interest in the work of the Special Committee and desires that this Government be represented thereon in view of the particular problems confronting her Department with regard to destitute aliens in the United States.

The members of the Committee, while representing their respective Governments, will exercise merely a deliberative function in their expert capacities without making decision in behalf of their Governments or otherwise acting in a manner binding upon their Governments.

Upon the recommendation of the Secretary of Labor, I respectfully submit for your approval as this Government's representatives in an expert and advisory capacity on the Special Committee, the names of Professor Joseph Perkins Chamberlain, of Columbia University, New York, and Mr. George L. Warren, Director of the International Migration Service. Also, upon the recommendation of the Secretary of Labor, I solicit your approval for the designation of Miss Florence W. Hutsinpillar, of the Department of Labor, as Technical Adviser to the American representatives.

The Secretary of Labor has informed me that her Department will defray the expenses of the American representation on the Special Committee.

Faithfully yours,

[*Notation*:A:Tully] OK    FDR
[OF 184:CT]


## Roosevelt to General Gerardo Machado, Montreal

[Washington] November 6, 1933

Excellency: I have received and read with interest Your Excellency's letter of October 19, 1933, informing me of your deep concern with regard to the establishment in Cuba of a Court of Sanctions.[1] I may say that the latest advices I have received do not indicate that this Court has as yet started functioning.

As you know, no one more than myself desires peace and happiness for the Cuban people. To be lasting, and not ephemeral, however, national peace and happiness must be the product of the efforts of a people themselves. It is needless for me to add that I am most anxious that the several problems facing Cuba be solved at the earliest possible moment, as the continuance of the political disturbance and economic distress naturally works great hardship on the population of the Island.

I am pleased to learn of Your Excellency's appreciation of the courtesies extended to you by the public officials of this country on your recent visit here.[2]

Very truly yours,

[PSF:Cuba:CT]

[1] Machado said (PSF:Cuba) that only Roosevelt could prevent the excesses certain to follow establishment of a court of sanctions, set up to try the chief figures of his ousted regime. His party, he said, had accepted the mediation of Ambassador Welles not because of the advice he could give ("inasmuch as Your Excellency's high representative was a new arrival in our country and unfamiliar with its psychology") but because of the guarantee this mediation gave to the agreements that might be entered into. Roosevelt's reply (here printed) was drafted in the State Department, probably by Phillips.

The suppression of the Nov. 8, 1933, revolt against the Grau San Martín government was accompanied by execution of prisoners; the executions led to demands for United States intervention from both Cubans and foreigners in Cuba (Welles to Hull, Nov. 10, 1933, *Foreign Relations*, V, 519–520). Welles then arranged to meet with the President at Warm Springs on November 19 (Welles to Phillips, Nov. 13, 1933; Phillips to Welles, Nov. 14, 1933, *ibid.*, pp. 520–521, 521). A statement, drafted by Welles and Phillips and issued by Roosevelt on Nov. 23, 1933, expressed the concern of the United States over the trouble in Cuba and indicated that no provisional government set up there would be recognized unless it had general support (*ibid.*, pp. 525–526). Carlos Mendieta was made provisional president of Cuba on Jan. 18, 1934; see press conference of Nov. 24, 1933, below.

[2] After fleeing from Havana to Miami, Machado sought asylum in Montreal, Canada, remaining there until mid-November 1933.

## Roosevelt to Senator Frederick Steiwer of Oregon

[Washington] November 6, 1933

My dear Senator Steiwer: I beg to acknowledge your letter of October 30, 1933 inquiring whether it is planned to establish the Corporation of Foreign Bondholders in accordance with Title II of the Securities Act of 1933.[1]

On October 20, 1933, I conferred with a group of persons who had been invited to Washington to discuss the creation of an organization for the protection of American holders of foreign securities. These persons consisted of Laird Bell, Hendon Chubb, W. L. Clayton, John Cowles, Herman Ekern, Ernest M. Hopkins, Phillip La Follette, Mills B. Lane, Frank O. Lowden, Orrin K. McMurray, Roland S. Morris, Thomas D. Thacher, J. C. Traphagen, and Quincy Wright. Messrs. Charles Francis Adams, Newton D. Baker, and J. Reuben Clark had also been invited to come but, though they were unable to do so, expressed their willingness to help in such an effort.[2]

Under the sponsorship of this representative group of American citizens, an organization is, as I understand, to be effected which shall be entirely independent of any special private interest and have no connections with the investment banking houses that originally issued the loans. Such an organization could, I hope, act effectively to protect the interests of American bondholders. Furthermore, such action would be entirely in accord with the traditional policy of our government, which has been to regard loan and investment transactions as private transactions to be handled by the parties primarily concerned.

The course of conduct of this organization will be closely watched by the officials of those departments of this government primarily concerned with the questions involved. It might, indeed, be added that that course of conduct will come under my personal scrutiny. An effort so promising in character should have the implicit support of our government. It would be unfortunate if at this stage my powers should be exercised to bring into existence the Corporation of Foreign Bondholders, since such action would necessarily doom a hopeful effort of this kind to failure. For that reason it seems to me that the government should be slow to act directly until we shall be assured that an organization of this character cannot adequately protect what is our common interest— the rights of American holders of foreign securities.[3]

Faithfully yours,

[OF 100-B:CT]

[1] Steiwer (OF 100-B) urged that the Foreign Bondholders Corporation be established to do away with the great inequities in the settlements being made by foreign countries with American bondholders, and the inordinate fees being collected by the independently organized bondholders committees.

[2] The President's conference followed a meeting at the Treasury Department to which the persons named had been invited by letters dated Oct. 12–13, 1933, signed by the Secretary of State, the Secretary of the Treasury, and the chairman of the Federal Trade Commission (OF 100-B). The invitation stated that the creation of an organization for the protection of American holders of foreign securities was of "such public significance as to make its proper handling a public service." Before the meeting, Raymond Stevens of the Federal Trade Commission went to New York to get financial assistance for the organization "from other sources than investment bankers" (Stevens to Roosevelt, Oct. 15, 1933, OF 100-B). Organization of the Foreign Bondholders Protective Council was completed at a meeting in Washington on Dec. 18, 1933; all those named above were made directors excepting Lane and Traphagen whose names do not appear in the published account (New York *Times,* Dec. 19, 1933, p. 31). Stevens was elected president.

[3] Drafted by James M. Landis of the Federal Trade Commission (Landis to Roosevelt, Nov. 6, 1933, OF 100-B, enclosing the draft).


## Roosevelt to Karl A. Bickel, President, United Press, New York

[Washington] November 7, 1933

My dear Bickel: Many thanks for yours of October 30th.[1] I am sending it to the friend in Brazil.[2]

It is all right to let Mr. Miller have a copy of the comments—in confidence, of course—without advising him as to the source.

Very sincerely yours,


[OF 405:CT]

[1] Above.
[2] Ambassador Hugh Gibson.


## Roosevelt to Hugh Gibson, Ambassador to Brazil, Rio de Janeiro

[Washington] November 7, 1933

Dear Hugh: I took up the matter with the United Press, without advising Mr. Bickel as to the source, and I now inclose a copy of his letter.[1]

I think the United Press wants to do the right thing, and on the whole they have far more influence in Latin America than the A.P. has.

Always sincerely,

[OF 405:CT]

¹ Oct. 30, 1933, above.


## Statement by Roosevelt on the British War Debt

[Washington] November 7, 1933

For some weeks representatives of the British Government have been conferring with representatives of this government on the subject of the British debt to this country growing out of the World War. The conversations were requested by the British Government in its notes of last June and December, a request to which I gladly acceded in view of the policy which I announced in November, 1932, that a debtor may at any time approach a creditor with representations concerning the debt and ask for readjustment of the debt or its terms of payment.

The conversations, now concluded, have in no sense prejudiced the position which either government has taken in the past or may take in any subsequent discussion of the entire debt question. They have, however, given an opportunity for a full and frank discussion of the representations which the British Government has made.

These discussions have made clear the great difficulty, if not impossibility, of reaching sound conclusions upon the amounts of international payments practicable over any considerable period of time in the face of the unprecedented state of world economic and financial conditions.

It has, therefore, been concluded to adjourn the discussions until certain factors in the world situation—commercial and monetary— become more clarified. In the meantime, I have as Executive noted the representations of the British Government. I am also assured by that Government that it continues to acknowledge the debt without, of course, prejudicing its right again to present the matter of its readjustment, and that on December 15, 1933, it will give tangible expression of this acknowledgment by the payment of seven and one-half million dollars in United States currency.

In view of these representations, of the payment, and of the impossibility, at this time, of passing finally and justly upon the request for a readjustment of the debt, I have no personal hesitation in saying that I shall not regard the British Government as in default.[1]

[White House Press Releases:M]

[1] Printed also in *Public Papers,* II, 450–451. The text had been previously agreed upon by the negotiators, according to Hull's memorandum of Nov. 6, 1933, in *Foreign Relations, 1933,* I, 843.

## Henry A. Wallace, Secretary of Agriculture, to Roosevelt

Washington, D.C., Nov. 7, 1933

Dear Mr. President: As you of course are aware, one element which may come up in your conversations with the Russians is the question of Russian wheat exports.

The situation is that Russia signed the International Wheat Agreement with the understanding that her export quota this year would be settled by subsequent negotiations with the four over-seas exporting countries, Argentina, Australia, Canada, and the United States.

When the first meeting of the International Wheat Advisory Committee was held at London the latter part of September, negotiations were resumed with Russia to determine the amount of her export quota. Prospective wheat exports for this year had left room for Russian exports of roughly one million tons (37 million bushels). The export quantity offered Russia was 37 million bushels as a tentative quota. At the negotiations in September, the exporting countries proposed an alternative scheme by which Russia would be entitled to an additional quota of 8 million bushels, or 45 million bushels in all, if the world demand took a larger quantity than had previously been estimated. The Russian representative at London refused to accept this modified quota, emphasizing its conditional character; and the matter was left open for subsequent discussion.

We feel that it is desirable that a final agreement be reached with Russia as to the maximum quantity of wheat she will export during the current crop year. Her exports to date (as shown by the table enclosed herewith) have not been in sufficient volume to indicate a great likelihood that she will export materially more wheat than she did last season when her exports totaled only 19 million bushels. The quota of 37 million bushels originally offered would allow considerable expansion of exports above what they were last year. At the same time, our confidential reports from observers in Europe indicate that, except in the Ukraine, the Russian crop this year is not nearly so large as claimed in newspaper dispatches, and is deficient in other regions which have ready access to water transportation on the Black Sea. For these reasons, we are inclined to feel that the Russians would be more willing to concede a reasonable export quota at this time than they were two months ago.

We do not feel that there is any great danger of Russian exports being so large this season as to upset the International Agreement. Furthermore, during the discussions at London, the Russian representative indicated informally that even though they did not accept an export quota they would not throw wheat on the market in a deliberate attempt to break the market, but would endeavor to live up to the spirit of the Agreement.

In view of these facts, I would state that my feeling is that it would be desirable if they would agree to limit their exports this season to a reasonable figure, but there is no need for us to make material concessions to secure their cooperation.

This is, of course, a matter in which final agreement will have to be reached with the other three exporters at the next session of the International Wheat Advisory Committee in London in the last week of November; but any preliminary understanding we can reach with the Russians at this time will be a major contribution to such a final agreement. It might be desirable to consult with Canada as to any wheat quota proposals suggested by the Russians, since Canada and the United States would be the principal countries concerned in any concessions made to the Russians on this year's marketings.

I am sending a copy of this communication to Secretary Hull and Mr. Morgenthau for their information.[1]

Sincerely yours,

H. A. Wallace

[OF 220-A:TS]

[1] Wallace enclosed a table showing exports of wheat and flour from Russia for the period 1925–1933. An attached note, Roosevelt to William C. Bullitt, special assistant to the Secretary of State, undated, reads: "Read and return at your leisure."

# Press Conference, Executive Offices of the White House, November 8, 1933, 10:55 A.M.

[Excerpt] Q: Can you tell us anything about the delegations in Montevideo?

The President: Hasn't that been given out?

Mr. Early: It will be given out late today.[1]

The President: It is going to be given out late today. I think the only possible change, and that has not been decided on definitely, is whether we can spare Caffery to go down there at this time.[2] This is for background. As you all know, the original plan away back last summer was that Sumner Welles would come back and go down to Montevideo, and that Caffery would take the place of Sumner Welles in Cuba. Of course, that arrangement had to be thrown overboard and Welles is staying in Cuba and it is possible that Caffery will stay here.

Q: Can you give us any background on the conference with Litvinoff?

The President: No, except that they are coming to lunch. As you all know—and this is for background—on anything of that kind, both sides arrange three or four hundred pages of material of all sorts, details and figures, and then they start to go through this large volume of things and they use the process of elimination. The first part of it is rather mechanical, it is rather a mechanical procedure, keeping in very close touch, personally, at all times. Of course, there is no use sitting in when going into the details and figures. Litvinoff is coming to lunch, and I will probably have a talk with him after lunch and see him again, probably tomorrow evening.[3]

[President's Press Conferences:T]

---

[1] This press release on the Montevideo Conference was issued the next day. It is printed in *Public Papers,* II, 459–463, with a note on the accomplishments of the conference.

[2] Jefferson Caffery, a career Foreign Service officer, was at this time an assistant secretary of state. He was appointed personal representative of the President, with the rank of ambassador, on Dec. 5, 1933.

[3] The two conferred at noon on November 10 and for three hours on the evening of that day (PPF 1-0).

## Roosevelt to Senator Frederic C. Walcott, Norfolk, Connecticut

[Washington] November 8, 1933

Dear Fred: I was much interested in your letter[1] and when I see you I will tell you confidentially of the actual progress of the negotiations which have ended in a deadlock. I think you will be a bit horrified, first, at the suggestions that were made to us, and secondly, as to the extremely adamant position that was taken in regard even to suggestions of some kind of compromise.

When are you coming to Washington? Be sure to run in and see me. I go to Warm Springs the 17th but will be back December 4th.

Always sincerely,

[OF 212:CT]

[1] Nov. 1, 1933, above.

# Roosevelt to Governor Robert Gore, La Fortaleza, Puerto Rico

[Washington] November 9, 1933

My dear Governor: I am in receipt of your letter of October 26, 1933, suggesting the appointment of a Puerto Rican to serve on the American Delegation to the Seventh International Conference of American States shortly to be held at Montevideo.[1]

I have given this matter the careful consideration which it merits and feel that there is much to recommend it but after weighing all the factors that are involved I have arrived at the conclusion that it would not be advisable to make such an appointment.

There are two important reasons underlying my decision. In the first place, I find that it is not anticipated that there will arise during the sessions of the Conference any questions of importance in the solution of which a Puerto Rican would be of particular assistance. Secondly, it is desired, for reasons of economy and efficiency, that the personnel of the American Delegation be reduced to a minimum.

Therefore, while I agree with you that good grounds exist why a Puerto Rican should be appointed on the American Delegation, I do not feel that in view of the special circumstances outlined above I would be justified in naming such an individual at this time.[2]

Believe me, my dear Governor, Sincerely yours,

(s) Franklin D. Roosevelt

[OF 567:T:Copy]

[1] Gore thought that the fact that Puerto Rico had been a part of the United States for twenty-five years should be recognized (OF 567).

[2] Drafted by the State Department.

## Cordell Hull, Secretary of State, to Roosevelt

Washington, November 9, 1933

My dear Mr. President: In accordance with my letter of November 4, 1933,[1] I am enclosing herewith for your consideration and approval drafts on the Monroe Doctrine and Pan American Debt Problem, which might be used by our Delegates at the Montevideo Conference in formulating a statement, should the occasion arise which would necessitate a pronouncement on either of these subjects.

Faithfully yours,

Cordell Hull

[*Notation*: AS] OK    FDR
[OF 567:TS]

[1] Not found.

## [*Enclosure*] Cordell Hull to Roosevelt

Monroe Doctrine. The Monroe Doctrine was conceived and brought forth by President Monroe more than one hundred years ago to forestall the designs and ambitions of Europe against the new and struggling Republics of this hemisphere. It served its purpose then; since then it has more than once, and successfully, been brought to bear to the same end. As originally conceived and as actually applied, it has had to do only with aggressive designs of Europe against the Americas, certain popular ideas and conceptions to the contrary notwithstanding. It has primarily in view the protection of the United States against non-American aggression, but it incidentally has operated to the benefit of other American States. The doctrine has nothing to do with inter-American relations and has never been so invoked by the Government of the United States. Being thus a doctrine having to do with the integrity and preservation of the United States, it is a unilateral principle of high policy which the United States can neither abandon nor curtail.

If other nations shall see fit to adopt and announce a similar or equivalent principle, such an action would lie entirely within their power and rights as sovereign states.

Pan American Debt Problem. In periods of economic depression there inevitably arise stresses on the relations between debtors and creditors which tend to provoke distorted views and recriminations. It becomes difficult to see debt transactions in true perspective during such periods. This situation arises both within every country and across many frontiers. In the latter case it may affect international relations and it is important that the feelings natural to debtor or creditor be not confused or accentuated by an admixture with national feeling.

As an economic phenomenon foreign loans have normally represented the financing of relatively undeveloped territories by the investment of funds which the people of such territories were unable themselves to supply. This is or should be a mutually beneficial transaction enhancing the wealth both of debtor and creditor and of the world. The great example of this use of credit is the United States, whose development moving rapidly across the country from the original States on the Atlantic coast was financed in part by the savings of the people of the original States but in large part by the investment of European savings in railroads and other development projects in the United States. At times of depression in the United States there has been throughout its history a considerable agitation by the debtors against creditors but this has not involved nationalistic feeling. Creditors foreign and domestic have shared the same vicissitudes without prejudice as to nationality. Despite large losses during the numerous recurring periods of hard times, European investors have continued to supply funds for American development so that up to the cataclysm of the World War the United States was the great debtor nation of the world and was paying annually very large sums to creditors across the Atlantic.

The other countries of this hemisphere have similarly benefited from foreign loans in spite of the unfortunate circumstances attending many of the first ventures of newly-freed Latin American States as borrowers.

During the 1820's London floated loans to many of the Latin American Republics, which had just achieved their freedom from Spain; in many instances only minor fractions of the borrowed funds ever reached the treasuries of the borrowing countries; in almost every case, the debtors maintained interest payments for only a year or two and then defaulted.[1]

The financial histories of the twenty Latin American States are of course chequered with the vicissitudes and difficulties which have attended the development of their territories and peoples, but the inflow of foreign capital has been almost a continuous process essential to their development. When the European nations to whose investors Latin American countries were accustomed to look had been financially crip-

471

pled by the great World War, the American bankers and investing public naturally stepped forward to assume the vacant role, to seek the profits and assume the risks of foreign investment.

The sudden tremendous outflow of American capital in foreign loans in the years 1923 to 1929 was a great factor in the prosperity of those years, but the optimism of that time has now given way to the severest depression. Two-thirds of the $1,500,000,000 of Latin American loans outstanding in the United States are in entire or partial default on interest payments, as are a large part of American loans to other foreign borrowers. It is natural that all the parties to transactions which have so quickly proved unfortunate should be dissatisfied. It is also natural that so far the strongest current of dissatisfaction is that flowing from the holders of the bonds and directed in the first instance against the sponsors of these securities, that is, principally against the American bankers charged with having recommended improvident loans. In some instances which have achieved wide notoriety, the general charge of unwisdom has been supplemented by evidences of unethical and greedy practices.

In these circumstances there is danger of overlooking the essential elements in these transactions. In a few instances there may have been an abnormal spread between the amount paid by the bond purchaser and the amount received by the borrower but this should not conceal the fact that in general the dollar loans have represented actual transfers of purchasing power from the lenders to the borrowing treasuries much more directly than loans of the 1820's and subsequent decades. In these earlier periods it has been frequent that the nominal value of the issued bonds was much greater than the actual amounts which the lenders advanced or which the borrowers received. This has not been the characteristic of our American lending. The typical original American purchaser of a Latin American bond paid 96% of the par value of the bond, the borrower received some 4% or 5% less. The bankers' share should not obscure the reality of the transfer from the investor's pocket to the borrower's treasury.

The dollar loans have preponderantly served two purposes for Latin America: the financing of the first recovery after the World War and the financing of public works developing the economic capacity and the amenities of civilization in Latin America.

In European countries used to issuing their own bonds at a discount and bearing a low rate of interest, it has been customary to float foreign bonds bearing 4% or 5% coupons at 60% or 70% of par. The Haitian

5% franc loan of 1910 was bought from the Haitian Government at 72.3 less gratuities, etc. and was offered to the public at 88½. This is of course an abnormal spread. In Europe, the Ottoman debt includes 6's sold at 62½, 5's at 50 and 52; a Greek 5% loan of 1884 was sold at 68½.[2]

Perhaps one-half of the loans now outstanding represent the refinancing in the United States of previous existing debt of the borrowers whether internal and floating or external funded debt. Such loans were floated in many instances with the hope of regularizing the debt structure of the borrowing Government, converting multitudinous short term or maturing debts into funded debts repayable over a generation, thus relieving budgets and establishing, it was hoped, a basis for future sound financing and the credit standing of the borrower. Loans of this refinancing type would commonly include some provision for the immediate financial needs of the borrower in respect of public works. Some $525,000,000 of Latin American bonds were sold exclusively for the purpose of debt retirement and refunding; some $765,000,000 for public works and debt retirement jointly; and some $530,000,000 for the exclusive purpose of public works. These figures refer to the portion of dollar loans taken by Americans only. If those portions sold outside the United States are included, these totals would be $560,000,000, $845,000,000 and $570,000,000.

The American loans of 1925 to 1929 were compared at the time by foreign observers to a Nile flood enriching the lands over which they flowed. They placed at the disposal of borrowers New York funds which could be availed of for payments in any part of the world, as it was not the American practice to require that borrowers use loan proceeds for purchases in the United States. These availabilities have enabled debtor countries to meet obligations or satisfy their current import requirements in all external markets. Thus the loan proceeds have for the most part flowed to the borrowing countries commingled with the usual flow of commerce as the borrowers have sold New York drafts to their citizens and used the proceeds of these sales for expenditures within their own territories. In part the proceeds are directly traceable in public works which will subsist permanently, railroads, subways, highways, port improvements, irrigation works, city improvements, waterworks, etc. while in part they replenished the funds of banks in the borrowing countries and thence flowed out in farm and urban credits. These were not loans for war-time destructions but were an extension to foreign countries of the peace-time credit facilities which, based on the resources and activity of the United States, have aided its own domestic development.

In a time of depression and credit collapse it becomes easy for the debtor to denounce his creditors and for the creditor to denounce the intermediary who recommended the debt transaction. Several periods of this kind have occurred during the century or so in which international loans have been of importance but after each period the States which need foreign capital to develop their resources have again sought credit of the peoples in a position to save over and above their own current capital needs. Foreign financing obeys the compulsion of strong economic needs. States which have not developed sufficient capital markets in their own countries to assure purchase of the necessary national equipment for development of natural resources must again have recourse to those who are able to advance such equipment against the promise of the borrower to repay with interest over a long period of years. It is therefore in the interest of such countries not to overlook the feelings or the rights of the honest creditor, the individual who trusting to the credit of the borrower has purchased for investment a solemn obligation of the debtor. This is not a matter of a transaction between a borrower and a banking intermediary nor is it a transaction between governments. In the United States, at least, foreign bonds have been widely distributed by sale to individual investors. It is these individual investors who have to be considered. Governments cannot dispose of their rights. This has been universally recognized and all recent international discussions of the matter have taken the same position taken most recently by the Monetary and Economic Conference at London that when adjustments of debts are necessary, they should be made by direct negotiations between debtors and creditors.

The London Conference went further and recommended that Governments encourage the establishment of organizations in a position directly to represent bondholders. In the spirit of this unanimous recommendation the President of the United States, after much preparatory work had been accomplished by interested citizens, recently announced the formation of a committee of distinguished citizens charged with establishing an organization entirely independent of investment bankers but which should directly represent the thousands of actual American holders of foreign securities.[3] It is this organization of disinterested citizens charged solely with safeguarding the rights and interests of American bondholders that foreign debtors must satisfy if they are to conserve vis-à-vis the American public the standing of honest debtors. The problem is not inter-governmental.

In the present unparalleled depression defaults of various degrees on foreign debt services have occurred in all quarters of the globe. European as well as American countries have found it necessary to decree suspensions of transfer or of payment of interest and amortization on foreign bonds. Conferences have discussed the problem and found no general solution. Each country's problem is individual and solutions can be found only by discussions with creditors in which each recognizes the rights and difficulties of the other. Furthermore, it has been the judgment of such conferences that it is not yet time to negotiate permanent debt adjustments in view of the unsettled economic and financial condition of the whole world. The question is not peculiar to the Americas and our treatment of it cannot greatly vary from the solutions found by the world in general.

[OF 567:T]

[1] In the original, this paragraph is typed in the margin.
[2] This paragraph is also in the margin of the original.
[3] See *Public Papers*, II, 411–413.

# Louis M. Howe, Personal Secretary to the President, to Cordell Hull, Secretary of State

[Washington] November 9, 1933

Dear Mr. Secretary: In accordance with our talk, I am sending you some rough notes in regard to the coming conference.

I would suggest that your opening speech be modeled somewhat along these lines:

First—the usual kind words about good neighbors, band of brothers, etcetera. Secondly—a statement of the anxiety of the present administration to do everything in its power to hasten closer relationship between the people of the two Americas which is the fundamental purpose of these international conferences; that the United States has carefully studied the problem of not only how to do something but how to do something quickly, and is convinced that all better understandings and relationships between the nations, their governments, their commercial interests and between their nationals as individuals, hang primarily on far better means of communication between the two Americas than those that exist at present. We cannot know each other better until we can meet each other oftener; until we can have a daily intercourse, almost.

Then I would elaborate a little on the four methods of transportation (steamship, railway, auto, airplane) and point out how slow they are at present and how greatly they can be improved. I would then point out that this is something that can be immediately undertaken, and in view of all this it is the desire of the United States to move that the program be so arranged that the subject of "Transportation," which is now the next to the last item of the list of topics published as the agenda, be taken up on either the first or second day in order that full time may be given for discussions and that the necessary permanent committees to carry on the work be appointed and get a chance to get acquainted. (But, of course, I would endeavor at a preliminary informal conference to get an informal agreement that this be done by unanimous consent.)

I would then say it is the purpose of the United States to suggest that the subject of a great highway between the two continents, the development of air communications and improved radio facilities be definitely added to the list of topics, and that where separate agencies are already established in consideration of these subjects there will be a consolidation of such individual agencies and the general conference, for the expedition of the work. Then I would touch with regret on the present international economic situations and the conditions of the world which makes it impractical at this time to reach definite conclusions on several of the suggestions which, two years ago, seemed ready for action as well as discussion.

I would list such as those you and the President deem wise, and I would certainly cite as an example as to why this is impossible, the changing French quotas and particularly the recent announcement of Great Britain that she will discontinue the present tariff truce, as evidence that fixed commercial relationships cannot be gone forward with during the present state of flux in regard to the internal commercial policies of the different nations, but that this is, of course, only a temporary condition and that we of the United States at least are hopeful that the world is rapidly on its way to regaining its economic equilibrium.

I would carefully stress the willingness of the President to urge on the Congress of the United States such financial assistance towards the preliminary surveys and other matters which can be immediately taken up as it seems practical and possible for us to give.

I would call attention to the fact that for the first time, through the creation of a quasi governmental committee by the last Congress of foreign bondholders, an authoritative voice for our nationals has been provided and the whole question of such obligations of the different

476

governments as are not intergovernmental debts can now be taken up in an earnest effort to adjust all such obligations on a fair and reasonable basis, and that the United States is willing to immediately proceed to discuss the preliminary form of organization and method of procedure for later conferences upon these lines, of course, resisting any attempt to discuss them now, on the grounds that the proper procedure is to arrange our machinery first before we try to use it.

In regard to the particular subjects to be avoided like the plague—the particular list I made out—using the headings, beginning on page 36 of the "Special Handbook"[1] for the use of delegates—are as follows:

Any part of Topic 1,[2] which may draw us into the discussions of the present struggle between Paraguay and Bolivia or the present conditions in Cuba; Chapter 2—"Problems of International Law" seems safe, although Section A—"The Rights and Duties of States" should be carefully studied for possible trouble. Topic 7—under this head on page 55, has also a possible snag, inasmuch as the control of the river is part of the Paraguay fight.[3] Chapter 3—on the "Political and Civil Rights of Women" is safe; and if you don't want to talk about anything else, you can just let the women go to it for the rest of the conference.

Chapter 4—on "Economic and Financial Problems"—Topic A[4] should be avoided on account of the resolution in reference to necessity of custom tariffs and discriminatory internal taxes on national products. Although the recommendation is not necessarily trouble making. But the whole topic is built up largely on the world economic conference in Geneva in 1927. Our position here, of course, is that the time has not yet come owing to the economic troubles of the last two years.

Topic 9B—on Currency Stabilization, of course, is to be avoided for reasons already given. Topic 9C[5]—seems safe, but wants to be studied with some care. Topic 9D[6]—seems perfectly safe. Topics 10, 11 and 12[7] cannot be taken up until we have settled down. Topic 13[8] must be handled carefully as it is dangerous in Items 4, 5, and 7 on page 77 of the subjects treated, and we must avoid getting into a discussion on indirect embargo by quarantine. Topic 14 seems safe for discussion only.[9] Topic 15 seems safe not only to discuss but perhaps to reach conclusions on.[10] The same is true of Topics 16[11] and 17.[12]

Chapter 5—"Social Problems"[13] seems safe and we can talk a lot about what we have done on the child labor end of it. Chapter 6 on "Intellectual Cooperation" is safe, but we must watch that the wild students do not slip something over on us. Topic 24 on page 103 seems safe.[14] On "Transportation" I have already written in full. I would urge, however, on Topic 26,[15] page 109—immediate and careful study of the new plan to run a line down the inside of the Andes rather than along the coast as first proposed. This would keep the steamship people quiet. Topic 27 is, of course, safe.[16] Chapter 8 is perfectly safe to discuss.[17]

I think this covers the printed agenda.

We will try up here through our own news service to magnify everything that is done about transportation in order to build this up as the big achievement of the conference. It looks like the only thing of importance that we can brag about when we come home even if all goes well.

I hope you have a nice trip and I cannot tell you how much I appreciate your kindness about Hartley.[18] Incidentally, the young man is rather good at analyzing material if you get hard put to it for somebody to help out.

I have sent a copy of this to the President, and you can take it up with him. His views may be widely diversive from mine.

As ever,

Important Note: The more I think of it the more I think it good ball, if practical, to add to those going down, Videll[19] of Air Craft, McDonald[20] on Highways and someone from the Railway Committee, and list them as speakers on the subjects, as they have all the technical knowledge needed to get things really moving.

Saranoff[21] is sending a radio man down unofficially whose name will be given to you, and with whom you can consult on radio. In addition Pettey[22] or someone else on the Radio Commission might also go along.

[OF 567:T]

---

[1] *Seventh International Conference of American States, Montevideo, Uruguay, December 3, 1933. Special Handbook for the use of Delegates* (Baltimore, 1933), compiled by the Pan American Union. The agenda is printed in the *Handbook* and also in Hull's instructions to the delegates of Nov. 10, 1933, in *Foreign Relations, 1933,* IV, 43–155.

[2] "Methods for the prevention and pacific settlement of Inter-American conflicts."

[3] "Report of the Permanent Committee on Public International Law of Rio de Janeiro on the general principles which may facilitate regional agreements between adjacent states on the industrial and agricultural use of the waters of international rivers . . ."

[4] "Customs Duties."

[5] "Commercial Arbitration."

[6] "Promotion of Tourist Travel."

[7] "Import quotas"; "Import prohibitions"; "Collective Commercial Treaties."

[8] "Report on the resolutions of the Inter-American Conference on Agriculture." The items Howe refers to have to do with problems relating to forestry, to plant industry, and to agricultural economics.

[9] "Report on the establishment of an Inter-American economic and financial organization under the auspices of the Pan American Union."

[10] "The Inter-American protection of patents of invention."

[11] "Consideration of the draft convention on customs procedure and port formalities formulated by the Pan American Commission on customs procedure and port formalities . . ."

[12] "Consideration of projects of uniform legislation relative to such topics as: (a) Bills of Exchange, Checks and other Commercial Paper; (b) Bills of Lading; (c) Insurance . . ."

[13] Improvement in working conditions, improvement in housing, unemployment insurance, child welfare, pure food and drug legislation.

[14] "International cooperation to make effective respect for and conservation of the national domain over historical monuments and archeological remains."

[15] "Report of the Pan American Railway Committee."

[16] "Study of the penal provisions and of the regulations of the Convention on Commercial Aviation signed at the Sixth International Conference of American States."

[17] "International Conferences of American States."

[18] Howe's son, who had been given a place on the United States delegation staff as an assistant secretary.

[19] Eugene L. Vidal, director of the Bureau of Air Commerce of the Department of Commerce.

[20] Thomas H. MacDonald, chief of the Bureau of Public Roads of the Department of Agriculture.

[21] David Sarnoff, president of the Radio Corporation of America.

[22] Herbert L. Pettey, secretary of the Federal Radio Commission.


# Press Conference, Executive Offices of the White House, November 10, 1933, 4:10 P.M.

[*Excerpt*] Q: The dispatches from Moscow this afternoon state that the terms of the recognition agreement have reached there and have been given to Soviet leaders for information. The White House statements have not indicated that discussion had reached that far.[1]

The President: I think the White House statement is the correct one.

Q: Mr. Litvinov is coming in tonight for a friendly discussion, is he not?

The President: I don't think there will be any news. I think it will be the usual communiqué to the effect that we are making progress. I can almost tell you in advance that the communiqué will report progress.

Q: How much? (Laughter)

Q: You say there will be one coming out tonight?

The President: I don't think it is necessary because it is a personal talk between Mr. Litvinov and myself. I think it will save everybody's time—I know and he knows that there won't be anything coming out so why not let it go at that.

Q: Will you talk alone?

The President: I think so.

Q: Will Secretary Hull be there?

The President: I don't think so. He is sailing tomorrow morning. Of course we may ask people to come in with figures and things like that.

Q: It is beginning to look as though there won't be recognition before next week.

The President: Well? (Laughter)

Q: Will there be recognition?

The President: I think you had better put it this way, that some of the stories written were premature.

[President's Press Conferences:T]

[1] The reference is presumably to the first joint statement issued, Nov. 10, 1933 (*Public Papers*, II, 465), which merely said that the conversations were continuing. The statement was issued following Litvinov's morning conference with Hull at the State Department and with Hull and the President at the White House at noon.

# Roosevelt to Arthur Bliss Lane, Minister to Nicaragua

[Washington] November 11, 1933

*Personal*

Dear Mr. Lane: Many thanks for yours of November 7th.[1] Nothing further will be said or done about the suggested "free port" in the Gulf of California. As a matter of fact, the Arizona people are not at all keen for it, and the suggestion was only advanced on the theory that it might bring development and money to that section of Mexico.

I do hope to be able next year to stop on the Mexican Border if I come back that way from the West Coast.[2] As I remember it, President Taft did very much the same thing.

Always sincerely,

[OF 617:CT]

[1] Lane, newly appointed minister to Nicaragua, was from 1930 to 1933 counselor of the United States Embassy in Mexico. He wrote (OF 617): "When I saw Dr. Puig in New York immediately subsequent to his interview with you, he said that you had mentioned to him the desirability of establishing a free port on the Gulf of California; that he had been disturbed by this suggestion; and that in order not to arouse any antagonism within the Mexican Government, he had not even reported the matter to

his Government." Dr. José Manuel Puig y Casauranc was at this time Foreign Minister of Mexico; he had talked with Roosevelt and Hull at the White House, on Oct. 18, 1933 (PPF 1-0).

[2] Lane had conveyed President Abelardo L. Rodríguez' invitation to meet Roosevelt if he should visit the West, and had suggested as a meeting place the bridge between El Paso and Ciudad Juárez.

# Roosevelt to Richmond P. Hobson, President, World Narcotics Defense Association, New York

[Washington, November 11, 1933]

Dear Captain Hobson: I refer to your letter of October 19, 1933,[1] in which you suggest that the United States Government send a good will commissioner to various Latin American, Far Eastern and European countries which have not yet ratified the Geneva Convention of 1931 for Limiting the Manufacture and Regulating the Distribution of Narcotic Drugs, with the object of endeavoring to create public sentiment in those countries in favor of early ratification of the Convention to which reference is made.

While this idea undoubtedly has intrinsic merit, I feel that, in view of various considerations, it would be impracticable of application. As I am sure you realize, the Administration is exerting itself actively and effectively through already constituted agencies, including representatives of the United States abroad, towards seeing that the United States does its part in the international campaign against the illicit trade in narcotic drugs, not only by controlling the production and distribution of narcotic drugs within its own territories, but also by urging adherence to the various narcotic drug pacts, and especially to the 1931 Geneva Convention, by those nations not yet parties to these pacts.

Sincerely yours,

[OF 431:CT]

[1] Hobson (the Spanish-American War hero who had sunk the *Merrimac* in Santiago Harbor) wrote that Russia had announced its intention not to ratify the convention and was engaged in developing the opium trade on a large scale (OF 431). The Japanese were building opium factories in Japan, Korea, and in China. It had been proposed that the World Narcotics Defense Association send a mission to Russia and the Far East, and also to Latin America, to promote public sentiment in favor of ratification. The finances of the Association did not, however, permit this and Hobson therefore urged that the United States government send someone to the areas mentioned.

## Roosevelt to George N. Peek, Administrator, Agricultural Adjustment Administration

[Washington] November 11, 1933

My dear Mr. Peek: It appears to me that the growing complexity of American commercial relations with foreign countries requires a new step in the systemization of the handling of these relations. This new step in systemization is dictated by two sets of circumstances:

(1) Under the Administration's program of recovery, numerous departments are assigned powers or duties which directly touch upon trade relations with other countries. It is plain that the acts of each of the separate branches of the Government must be brought into a coherent policy system with the acts of all the rest.

(2) The changing policies of other governments and the changing methods of regulating international trade greatly complicate the Government's task of proper direction of American trade.

I therefore have decided to designate one officer in the Department of State to carry the primary responsibility of supervising the international commercial policy of this Government into a coherent whole. Hereafter may I ask that you give the necessary instructions in your Department that before any acts are taken under legislation or otherwise which directly affect the export and import trade in this country, this official should be consulted concerning the action and his approval secured.

It is my idea that this official should be the chairman of an Executive Committee for the coordination of commercial policy and the negotiation of commercial treaties and trade agreements, and that in his decisions he would be very largely carrying out the judgment of the Committee. Upon this Committee your Department will be represented.

It is my further expectation that as this Committee develops its work, all subordinate interdepartmental committees engaged in the work of negotiating commercial treaties, the elaboration of trade agreements, et cetera, will report to the responsible official and through him to the governing Committee.

I also request that you instruct your Department that this official, as chairman of the coordinating Committee, should be the regular channel of communication with all foreign governments on all policy matters affecting American export and import trade.

The arrangements contemplated in this order will be elaborated in further directions which will be transmitted later.

I have asked Mr. Phillips, Under Secretary of State, to undertake these duties as chairman of the coordinating Committee until such time as a permanent selection is made. Therefore, pending further notice, he will be chairman *pro tem.*[1]

Sincerely yours,

[OF 970:CT]

[1] Peek was an Illinois farm machinery manufacturer whose advocacy in the twenties of higher prices for farm products, and whose campaign to get the McNary-Haugen farm bills through Congress in 1927 and 1928, had made him an important spokesman for the farmers, especially the cotton, corn, and wheat growers. He believed in unlimited production of these commodities at a guaranteed parity price and government subsidies in the sale of the surpluses abroad. Appointed the first head of the Agricultural Adjustment Administration, his ideas on the control of crop surpluses were completely opposed to those held by Wallace and Tugwell. He resigned (at the President's request) on Dec. 15, 1933, not over a question of major policy but because Wallace objected to his carrying matters to the President for decision. See Gilbert C. Fite, *George N. Peek and the Fight for Farm Parity* (Norman: Univ. of Oklahoma, 1954), and Peek's *Why Quit Our Own* (New York: Van Nostrand, 1936).

This letter is also printed in *Public Papers,* II, 466–467. See Roosevelt to Phillips, Nov. 14, 1933, below.

# Edward M. House to Daniel C. Roper, Secretary of Commerce

New York, November 12, 1933

Dear Dan: Something of a crisis has arisen which I think the President should know.

I am not sure that you know Professor Sprague or how much confidence you have in him, but Europe and financial America have the greatest possible faith in him and he is the only one of the so-called brain trust that they think knows what it is all about.

He sent me word from Boston Friday that he would like to see me today and although I was in bed with fever I saw him this morning at ten o'clock. I had some inkling in advance as to what he wanted and was prepared for what he told me. He said that he had not seen the President for three months and that he is getting all his financial advice from others—most of which he considers bad. This is the impression here and generally in the East.

Dr. Sprague told me frankly that unless the President asked his advice he would resign. I asked him not to do so for a week or ten days until I could communicate with the President through you.

The most serious phase of the situation is that Sprague is planning to let the President know why he is resigning and that he will publish a letter giving his reasons for withdrawing. He feels that he has some reputation to maintain and that is the only way in which he can do it.

This is only a part of the trouble. He wondered whether I would be willing to come out in the open with Newton Baker and other party leaders and state my disagreement with the President's financial policy. I told him that in no circumstances would I be willing to do so, that I was a friend of the President and all the advice I had to give would be given him privately.

In investigating the matter from others this morning, I find that it is tentatively planned to hire Carnegie Hall for a mass meeting and to get such men as Al Smith, Newton Baker, David F. Houston, Carter Glass and other leaders of the party to make speeches of protest. This, of course, would be very serious and would raise a terrible racket both in this country and in Europe.

If I were in the President's place I would send for Sprague and have a talk with him. He can tell him if he likes that I asked him to see him.

If you want to talk with me further please ring me up Tuesday or Wednesday and let me know if there is anything I can do to help. It seems to me to be an alarming situation and one that Al Smith and others would welcome.[1]

Yours always,

E. M. House

[PPF 222:TS]

[1] Roosevelt wrote to House Nov. 21, 1933 (*Personal Letters, 1928–1945,* I, 371–373). He said that Sprague had failed to contribute a single concrete proposal "which would help us to lift the price level and therefore the debt burden"; that all he had suggested was open market purchases and stabilization of the dollar with the pound. See Roosevelt to Sprague, Nov. 22, 1933, below.

## Roosevelt to William E. Dodd, Ambassador to Germany, Berlin

[Washington] November 13, 1933

My dear Dodd: I need not tell you that I welcome your letters,[1] and I am glad that the gold transfers help. Possibly by early in the year we can restore the 15 per cent cut in part or in whole; I know that would help. I am glad you have been frank with certain people. I think that is a good thing. Walter Lippmann was here last week and made the interesting suggestion that about 8 per cent of the population of the entire world, i.e., Germany and Japan, is able, because of imperialistic attitude, to prevent peaceful guarantees and armament reductions on the part of the other 92 per cent of the world.[2]

Recent actions in New York on the part of Nazi agents have not helped the cause of Germany, and I feel the situation is even more serious than the papers have discovered it to be.[3]

I sometimes feel that the world problems are getting worse instead of better. In our own country, however, it spite of sniping, "chiseling" and growling by the extreme right and by the extreme left, we are actually putting people back to work and raising values.

Keep up the good work!

Always sincerely,

[PPF 1043:CT]

[1] The most recent one was that of Oct. 28, 1933, above.

[2] Lippmann's visit was not noted in the appointments list.

[3] The newspapers had recently been full of reports of alleged Nazi propaganda activities, and on November 11 Rep. Samuel Dickstein of New York announced that the House Immigration Committee, of which he was chairman, would open hearings on the reports (New York *Times,* Nov. 12, 1933, p. 3).

## Roosevelt to William Phillips, Acting Secretary of State

[Washington] November 14, 1933

Memorandum . . . In accordance with your letter of November 10th[1] I have signed and sent the letters referring to coordination of all matters relating to tariff and foreign trade, to the Secretaries of State, Treasury, Commerce and Agriculture, and also to General Johnson,[2] Mr. Robert L. O'Brien and Mr. George N. Peek.

I do not think it is necessary at this time to add Mr. Jesse Jones or Mr. Morgenthau, because if a matter involving financing should come up I can refer it to this new committee.[3]

[OF 970:CT]

[1] Enclosing drafts of letters to be sent to the persons named here (OF 970).

[2] General Hugh S. Johnson, administrator of the National Recovery Administration.

[3] On Nov. 22, 1933, the President sent the file on the coordinating committee to Acting

Secretary of State Phillips and asked him to serve as temporary chairman (OF 970). Shortly thereafter Phillips turned the chairmanship over to Assistant Secretary of State Francis B. Sayre. As of March 15, 1934 (OF 970), the Executive Committee on Commercial Policy was constituted as follows: Sayre, chairman; Marriner S. Eccles, special assistant to the Secretary of the Treasury; John Dickinson, Assistant Secretary of Commerce; Willard L. Thorp, director of the Bureau of Foreign and Domestic Commerce of the Commerce Department; Rexford G. Tugwell, Assistant Secretary of Agriculture; H. R. Tolley, assistant administrator of the Agricultural Adjustment Administration; Oscar B. Ryder, chief of the Imports Division of the National Recovery Administration; Robert L. O'Brien, chairman of the Tariff Commission; Thomas W. Page, a member of the Tariff Commission; and Harry F. Payer, of the Reconstruction Finance Corporation. Payer, special counsel in charge of foreign trade matters, was appointed at Roosevelt's suggestion (Roosevelt to Phillips, Jan. 9, 1934, OF 970). George N. Peek was an ex officio member.

Following the establishment on March 23, 1934, of the Office of Special Adviser to the President on Foreign Trade, Roosevelt issued executive order 6656 directing that the Executive Committee on Commercial Policy "continue to exercise its present functions." Subsequently Miss Perkins asked that the Labor Department be represented on the committee and that Isador Lubin be the representative (Perkins to Roosevelt, June 29, 1934, OF 970). Sayre, however, told her that he thought it unwise to enlarge the membership to a point where it would cease to be a committee and would become more like a debating club (Sayre to Perkins, July 9, 1934, OF 970).

# Marvin H. McIntyre, Assistant Secretary to the President, to Roosevelt

Washington, 11/15/33

Memo. for the President: Jesse Jones telephones, says Harrison[1] wants instructions before twelve o'clock about gold selling.

Jesse says Cummings agrees that they have the right to do it.

Jesse thinks Harrison should be permitted to go ahead.

M. H. M.

[*Notation*:A:FDR] Tell Jesse to talk with HM Jr. before going ahead

Bullitt thinks five minutes with Litvinoff as soon as possible would be very helpful. They are still at White House. Shall I bring them over and let him wait in Cabinet Room?

M.H.M.

[*Notation*:A:FDR] 2 PM[2]
[OF 229:T]

---

[1] George L. Harrison, governor of the Federal Reserve Bank of New York.

[2] The White house appointments list notes an appointment for Litvinov, Bullitt, and Morgenthau from 2 to 4 P.M.

## Breckinridge Long, Ambassador to Italy, to
## Louis M. Howe, Personal Secretary to the President

Rome, Italy, November 16, 1933

My dear Louie: I am enclosing herewith a copy of a despatch on the proposed changes in the structure of the Government of Italy. I think it would be of particular interest to the President if he has time to read it. The last page or so of it is highly confidential, so that it cannot be scattered around, but I think some of the leaders in our Government ought to be informed of the change which is going on here. It is highly significant and of fundamental political interest. I think Homer Cummings as the law officer of the Government and the Secretaries of Commerce and Labor ought to be advised. Also I believe a few of the Administration's friends in both the Senate and the House ought to know the fundamental constitutional changes impending here and their significance. If I could go outside of the official family, I would also suggest that Ernest Lindley and even David Lawrence or other of your trusted friends in the Press fraternity be informed.

Things are probably moving so fast there at home that your mind is probably occupied with things there to the exclusion of political changes in Europe, but the particular changes here are of such revolutionary and novel significance that they will merit the study on the part of responsible officers of our Government—particularly those who are politically minded. And I am also a believer in the discreet use of the Press—but that is up to you. If the President should be at Warm Springs and have a little more time on his hands, he might have an opportunity to read this despatch, and if it is at all possible for him to do so without tiring him or wearing him out, I suggest that you might send it to him.

I wrote the President about my lack of contacts at home, and I hope you saw the letter and can do something about it. It really is getting to be a serious matter.

I wish you would write me or have some one else write me some of the background of developments there.

With every good wish, Yours as ever,

Breckinridge Long

[OF 447:TS]

487

## [*Enclosure*] Breckinridge Long to Cordell Hull, Secretary of State

Rome, November 16, 1933

Sir: I have the honor to transmit herewith copy of speech delivered by the Chief of the Government before the National Council of Corporations on November 14th, 1933, as well as a copy of the resolutions adopted by the National Council of Corporations on November 13th, with regard to the creation of the corporations of category and the substitution of the National Council of Corporations for the present Chamber of Deputies.[1]

Since Thursday of last week, November 9th, there has been in session in Rome the General Assembly of the National Council of Corporations, the session of which is destined to be a political landmark. From the point of view of history as it will be written, the deliberations and proceedings of these few days will lay the basis for a new political era in Italy. For that reason I have succumbed to the temptation to send this despatch to draw attention to a few hypotheses which are not yet on a factual basis, but which already are of such substance as to cast definite shadows across the future political paths of Italy.

The historic session of the General Assembly of the National Council of Corporations now drawing to a close has some of the characteristics of a Constitutional Convention—at least it is exercising the functions usually vested in such a body in the United States. It is debating the reasons for and the general program of effecting changes in the organic law of the country. While it has refrained from making any specific proposals in the form of constitutional amendments it did adopt yesterday a resolution the text of which "defers to the Grand Council of Fascism the decision as to the further developments of a constitutional political character ("in senso politico-constituzionale") which must be determined as a consequence of the actual constitution and practical operation of the Corporations."

The subject matter of discussion has revolved around the unfeatured thought that the Chamber of Deputies is antiquated, purely political, incapable of legislating for or administering the complicated affairs of a truly Fascist State, and consequently ought to be abolished.

Continuity of the thought supplants the Chamber of Deputies with the General Assembly of the National Council of Corporations.

The thought is not articulated for the first time in Italy. Since 1926,

I believe, there have been occasional references to the general objective of making the state as a whole really Fascist—including the supposition that the Chamber of Deputies should conform in structure. But this is the first time steps have been taken which permit the deduction that changes of a structural nature are imminent. Consequently the possible historic significance.

To abolish the Chamber of Deputies would be a revolutionary step. Taken in time of peace and after years of deliberate experimentation rather than in time of war or during the sudden eruption of political upheavals, it assumes added importance and greater dignity. But revolutionary as it may be and important as it may become, it is not, according to Fascist doctrine, a step backward. Rather, from their point of view, it is a step forward in the direction of the final realization of representative government.

The Fascists have realized, as we have, that the State is a collection of individuals whose life, liberty and property is to be protected, but they frankly go farther and admit that each of these individuals is dependent for peaceful and lawful enjoyment of that life, liberty and property on their opportunities to engage in commerce and industry. Therefore, the Fascists believe that commerce and industry are also objects of concern for the State, which, in the complicated affairs of modern civilization, is obligated to regulate and control them in order that one large corporation may not by unfair practice destroy a small competitor and deprive of employment those working for the latter. In the same spirit capital is denied the right to lock out Labor; and Labor is prevented from "striking" against Capital. Each must cooperate, if necessary under the mediation of the representative of the State. But they must cooperate.

So that the Fascist State is inextricably involved with production, industry, commerce and credit as a guarantor of the partnership of Capital and Labor. And being involved, it has determined on a policy to treat these activities of its citizens in the same manner and to the same extent it treats the citizens themselves.

They believe that a Chamber of Deputies composed of members elected from certain geographical districts is not necessarily representative. They believe that just because a man lives in a certain town and receives more of the votes as a member of a political party than another man, he is not necessarily a true representative of that locality.

On the other hand, they affirm that when all the people of that district are organized into corporations of production, commerce, industry and credit—one category for employees, another for employers—and when each submit names of their own choosing as prospective representatives, the ultimate composition of the national body will be representative in fact, not only of geographical subdivisions but also of Capital and of Labor and of every line of commerce and industry.

Inculcated with this philosophy the specific steps to abolish the Chamber of Deputies and to erect a structure composed of commercial and industrial elements have been slowly and carefully taken and are now, I believe, on the verge of realization.

The resolve to defer decision to the Fascist Grand Council is, to all intents and purposes, to place it directly in the lap of Mussolini.

Mr. Mussolini, speaking to the meeting, referred to the Chamber of Deputies as "an Institution which we found here and which is foreign to our mentality and to Fascist sympathies. The Chamber presupposes a world which we have demolished; presupposes a number of political parties and their specious and violent attacks on the Government. From the day in which we abolished this plurality of political parties the Chamber of Deputies lost the real reason for its existence."

And later he said: "Today we take anew a decisive step along the road of the Revolution."

So there is no doubt of the attitude of the Chief of the Government on the subject of the futility of the Chamber of Deputies in Italy. It will cease to exist as soon as the regular requirements of constitutional procedure are complied with.

Under this procedure the lower house would be compelled to pass resolutions effacing itself.

Whatever form the Fascist Grand Council decides to propose will be passed by the Chamber, adhered to by the Senate, approved by Mussolini, and decreed by the competent authorities.

The general elections will be held in the spring of 1934. It is now scheduled to hold the elections to choose members of the existing Chamber of Deputies. The change will not be made before that election but the House then chosen will during its life decree its own demise as an institution. And when that is accomplished the national political structure of Italy will have undergone a renovation which will keep it in character with the economic concept of the State. The new lower house will be composed of members of the executive departments, of the Fascist Party, of Capital invested in all industries, of Labor in all categories, and of the technical sciences, authorized to regulate production, control industry, offer state guarantees of credit, coordinate capital and labor, limit production to consumptive capacity, and develop the wealth and political power of the Italian people.

It will be a new departure in government. It will be representative of all activities in the state. It will be the lower rung on the ladder of a centralized power in government such as our civilization has not visualized, for in the hand of the State will be held the reins of all productivity, of all commerce, of all credit, of all political powers. One man will be able to speak effectively and with authority for a nation. And it will have been accomplished not only without war, without any opposition, but with the help and enthusiastic support of all classes, in an orderly, systematic manner and through the prescribed procedure of constitutional government.

It would be a mistake to interpret this structural change of the government as of purely political significance. It is the expression of an economic philosophy which uses political apparatus for its realization. It aims at the metamorphosis of production; from that of unbridled capitalism to that of rational coordination, from concentrated industrial control of the forces of the State to a State control of the evils of over-production, from the concentration of the wealth of the masses in the hands of an uncontrolled few to a subordination of massed capital and its activities to the desires of the State. "Today we are burying economic liberalism," said Mussolini.

The movement to impregnate the Army and Navy with Fascism proceeds gradually and with the accomplishment of that object and the change in the character of the lower house the State of Italy will be practically a Fascist State.

There will be, however, several inconsistencies in that structure. The Senate, now shorn of real power, will remain so if it continues as a body. Because of its historic background and name it probably will continue as it is, a body composed of life appointees, as a decoration and a rostrum of honored citizens, whose advice might be formally asked on state occasions but whose voice would be raised only in agreement. Or, it may be that the Senate might itself be reformed and reappear as the Fascist Grand Council, which is in reality today the upper house of the structure. But that change does not appear to be imminent. However, it is in the category of distinct possibilities.

### Confidential [2]

Another inconsistency is the Royal Family. In a state of the character to be assumed by the eventual complete Fascist State, it is hard to visualize the continuing importance of a King and a large coterie of royalty. That the matter was once given some thought is testified by the provision in the Constitution whereby the Supreme Fascist Council is given a veto over the succession to the throne. For the time being there will be no movement to eliminate the King. Certainly the present King will continue through his life. After that it will remain to be seen how the Supreme Council will approach the use of a power so frankly stated, which, though frequently exercised in the events of history, has not been announced as a power of government and has usually found the reason for its use in some untoward circumstance and by power of some extra-formal opposition.[3]

Respectfully yours,

Breckinridge Long

[OF 447:CT]

[1] Mussolini's speech is present; the resolutions are not. The speech was reported in the New York *Times* of Nov. 15, 1933, p. 1.

[2] This word was added by Howe.

[3] Howe placed Long's letter and its enclosures before Roosevelt with a memorandum, Dec. 4, 1933 (OF 447), asking whether copies should be sent to Cummings, Roper, and Perkins, as Long suggested. He also questioned the advisability of sending copies to Lindley or Lawrence. Roosevelt replied (undated note, filed with Howe's memorandum): "I have been very glad to read it and I think you might ask Phillips if it is all right before sending it." Phillips thought the dispatch should be shown to the Attorney General and to the Commerce and Labor secretaries but not to the press (Phillips to Howe, Dec. 20, 1933, OF 447). The upshot was that copies were sent to the officials mentioned but not to Lindley or Lawrence (Howe to Long, Dec. 28, 1933, OF 447).

## William Phillips, Acting Secretary of State, to Roosevelt

[Washington] November 16, 1933

My dear Mr. President: I have just been informed that, according to tentative plans, the first meeting of the Governing Body of the organization which has been set up by the League of Nations to assist German refugees, will take place at Lausanne, Switzerland, on November 28th. This Government, while it has accepted the invitation of the League of Nations to appoint a member of the Governing Body, has not yet selected its representative in that capacity.

Would you care to consider the designation of Mr. Raymond Blaine Fosdick, or Mr. Leland Harrison, or possibly Professor Joseph P. Chamberlain,[1] to act in behalf of this Government as a member of the Governing Body? As it is not intended that the expenses of its representation will be assumed by this Government, it will be necessary for the American representative to bear his own traveling and subsistence expenses.

Faithfully yours,

William Phillips

[*Notation*:A:LeHand] W.P.   Yes, in the order named.   FDR
[OF 184:CT]

[1] Fosdick, under secretary of the League of Nations, 1920–1921, was a New York lawyer. Harrison had been a career Foreign Service officer; in 1935 he was appointed minister to Rumania. Chamberlain was professor of public law at Columbia University.


# Roosevelt to Robert T. Crane, Executive Director, Social Science Research Council, New York

Washington [November 17, 1933]

My dear Mr. Crane: At your request, the Secretary of the Interior has submitted to me a communication from the Social Science Research Council with reference to its proposal to institute two commissions of inquiry on subjects of major significance in the life and welfare of the American people, namely, National Policy in International Economic Relations, and Public Service Personnel.[1]

I approve of the plan as outlined. I believe that in making the result of their studies available to the Government these commissions will be able to make a distinct contribution.

Sincerely yours,

[OF 868:CT]

[1] In a letter of Nov. 15, 1933 (OF 868), Crane said the proposed inquiry would deal with the relation of nationalism and internationalism to American national policy in international economic relations. The Council proposed that the study be made by Harold W. Dodds, president of Princeton, Isaiah Bowman, director of the American Geographical Society, and Monte Lemann, a New Orleans lawyer.


# Stephen T. Early, Assistant Secretary to the President, to Roosevelt

Washington, 11/17—2 p. [1933]

Memo for the President: Sen. William H. King phoned asking that this message be given to you immediately. The Senator says he speaks for himself, Sen. Swanson[1] and a group of other Sens. in asking that you, in announcing recognition of Russia or proclaiming recognition by proclamation, shall reserve the right of prior recognition of Armenia made by the U.S. King points out that he recently was in Armenia, that Soviet Govt. officials told him they ultimately would recognize Armenia's independence but that he understands Litvinoff refused to give you any assurances on this point during the negotiations just concluded.

King says that he and the other Sens. would be very happy if you made a reservation in the recognition announcement, making it clear that this Govt. reserved prior recognition of Armenia, including that part of Armenia in Russia.[2]

STE

[OF 220-A:CT]

[1] Secretary of the Navy Claude Swanson, formerly senator from Virginia.

[2] The exchanges of letters between Roosevelt and Litvinov resulting in the resumption of diplomatic relations between the United States and Russia are published in *Public Papers*, II, 471–487. The letters were made public at Roosevelt's press conference of Nov. 17, 1933; the transcript of the conference consists largely of lengthy excerpts from the letters. The President explained that he was asking the reporters to read the documents because he was "not going to comment officially or personally on the record in regard to these negotiations." When asked, near the end of the conference, whether the exchange meant "automatic recognition" or whether it depended on an exchange of ambassadors, he replied, "Oh, my Lord; that is a technical question to which I don't know the answer. I should say, as a horseback opinion, that we resumed relations with Russia at ten minutes before midnight last night and that ambassadors will be exchanged as soon as convenient to both countries. But the relations were established at about ten minutes before midnight." He was also asked if an American ambassador had been selected and he replied that the Russian government would be asked if William C. Bullitt would be acceptable. Roosevelt devoted several paragraphs of his Savannah, Georgia, speech of Nov. 18, 1933, to the successful conclusion of the negotiations; this speech is printed in *Public Papers*, II, 489–493.

# Roosevelt to Mrs. Russell William Magna, President General, Daughters of the American Revolution, Washington

At Warm Springs, November 20, 1933

Dear Mrs. Magna: Thank you for sending me your letter of November 15th. In case you have not seen a copy of the interchange of letters with the Foreign Minister of Russia, I am asking the State Department to send a copy to you, referring especially to the letters regarding propaganda.[1]

Very sincerely yours,

[OF 220-A:CT]

[1] Mrs. Magna said that the D.A.R. opposed recognition of Russia because of the Soviet government's declared intention to overthrow the government of the United States (OF 220-A). She acknowledged receipt of the letters mentioned (printed in *Public Papers*, II, 471–487) in a letter to the President of Nov. 24, 1933 (OF 220-A).

## Memorandum by Roosevelt, Warm Springs, November 22, 1933

(The President dictated the following to be given to the Press in the event there was any necessity. It was never released, to my knowledge.)[1]

The President: With respect to the money going out, you can tell them what the answer would have been. It would have been off the record, but that there has been a great deal of talk ever since last April of the flight of capital from the United States and that the people responsible for this talk have been privately going around New York City and other places in a mouth-to-mouth campaign, charging that between four billion and five billions of capital had left this country and last week I had a very careful check-up made by two different agencies. One was the Federal Reserve Bank itself and the other was through the representatives of private bankers in London, Paris and other European centers. Both of these check-ups agree, and the total amount from April to date is probably not more than six or seven hundred million dollars, which is a drop in the bucket, and that most of that amount is not money sent out of this country at all, but is credit balances which Americans, instead of bringing back home, have left in London, Paris, et cetera, primarily for speculative reasons, hoping that by leaving it there they could eventually bring more money home than they originally got for the sale of American products. For instance, the best example is this: A raw cotton exporting firm, exporting ten millions worth of cotton to Liverpool, would be paid ten millions in Liverpool and instead of buying dollars with that ten million, they have left it on deposit in British banks.

Mr. Early: Unless you have a reason for getting that out sub rosa, I would never give it out, not even as background.

The President: Kannee, write it out and you and I keep it, because it is a pretty good explanation.

[President's Press Conferences:T]

[1] Note by Henry M. Kannee, secretary to McIntyre.

## Roosevelt to O. M. W. Sprague, Special Adviser to the Secretary of the Treasury, Washington

[Washington, November 22, 1933][1]

My dear Professor Sprague: I have received your letter of resignation.[2]

Information received by me since I talked with you on Nov. 16th leads me to tell you that if you had not resigned you would have been dismissed from the Government service.

You have every right to disagree with the Treasury Dept. policy, to resign your position under the Gov. and thereafter as a private citizen to make any statements you choose.

But for many weeks prior to your resignation and while still a gov. servant for you to make addresses and seek to call public meetings of protest was close to the border line of disloyalty to the Government you were serving at the time. If other any employees in the departments followed your course we would have chaos, not government.

You have intimated that you have not been consulted of late—That is true, for the very good reason that when I did consult you you offered no suggestion towards the immediate alleviation of unemployment or of the debt burden. Even when I talked with you on Nov. 16th you could only suggest some vague plan of building a lot of suburban homes.

If the Gov. had followed your do-nothing advice the nation would have slipped back to the conditions of last March. You place a former artificial gold standard among nations above human suffering and the crying needs of your own country.

What you say or do after your resignation is your own affair: what you said and did while you were still an employee of your Government stands out as an act of disservice to the people of the U.S.

FDR

[OF 21:AS]

[1] An approximate and supplied date. This letter, a draft in Roosevelt's hand, was not sent.

[2] Not found in the Roosevelt papers. Sprague's letter, dated Nov. 16, 1933, was, however, made public by him and appeared in the newspapers of Nov. 22, 1933; see the New York *Times* of that date, p. 2. Sprague said he was in such fundamental disagreement with Roosevelt's monetary policies that he had decided to resign. He opposed the Administration's policy of depreciating the dollar because it would be ineffective in bringing about a speedy price rise and because it threatened a complete breakdown in the credit of the government. The President, he said, was faced with the alternative of either giving up the present policy or of meeting government expenditures with additional paper money. This would no doubt bring about a price rise but only through a distrust of the currency. He concluded: "I have now reached the conclusion that there is no defense from a drift into unrestrained inflation other than an aroused and organized public opinion. It is for the purpose of contributing as I may to such a movement that with feelings of profound disappointment I sever my connection with your administration."

## Roosevelt to Monsignor Robert F. Keegan, New York

[Washington] November 22, 1933

Dear Monsignor Keegan: That was such a nice letter which you wrote me and I know I have no need to tell you how happy I was to receive it.[1]

I feel that we have really accomplished much in regard to the difficult question of religion in Russia. I would be so interested to know what you hear officially.

My best wishes to you.

Always sincerely,

[PPF 628:CT]

[1] Keegan, in his letter of Nov. 18, 1933 (PPF 628), congratulated Roosevelt on the outcome of the Russian negotiations.

## Theodor H. Hoffmann, Chairman, National Council of the Steuben Society of America, to Roosevelt

New York, N. Y., November 22, 1933

Sir: Permit me to thank you for your willingness to receive a Committee of the Steuben Society of America, including myself, on last Tuesday, the fourteenth, enabling us to place before you our invitation, and to solicit your attendance at the forthcoming German Day Festival, to be held in commemoration of the 250th Anniversary of the first organized

German Settlement on the North American Continent, to take place on the evening of December 6th, at Madison Square Garden, New York.

The Committee was delighted with friendly comments and the valuable suggestions you were kind enough to give us.

I am glad to report that Admiral Yates Stirling, Commandant, Brooklyn Navy Yard and Major General John F. Preston, Inspector General of the United States Army, have both consented to be with us upon the occasion in question and to address the audience.

If we understood you correctly, you intended to consider the possibility of your presence with us on December 6th.

In venturing to remind you of your thought at the time and in wishing this to be a renewal of our invitation, we need hardly say that your acceptance would be considered by all of us and our friends as giving to the Festival its crowning significance and glory.

In anticipation of your giving this, our most sincere request, your thoughtful consideration, I beg to remain, Sir, on behalf of the Committee,

Yours sincerely,

Theo. H. Hoffmann[1]

[OF 198-A:TS]

[1] The Steuben Society had had a long and honorable history but about this time it was charged with having been taken over by pro-Nazi elements. (Ickes comments on this in his *Diary*, I, 111–112.)Roosevelt decided not to appear at the German Day Festival and Miss Perkins was asked to go. She, however, thought it would be "extremely unwise" for her to participate in the program: "It would certainly be misconstrued by the Jews and it would be difficult to dissociate the Immigration Service of this Department from the Nazi problem and immigration from Germany" (Perkins to McIntyre, Nov. 22, 1933, OF 198-A). She suggested that Secretary of Commerce Roper should go; he could discuss something unrelated to the political situation. Roper agreed to speak but before he did so Ickes had been invited and had declined (Hoffmann to McIntyre, Nov. 24, 1933, OF 198-A). At the meeting in Madison Square Garden, Roper presented the greetings of the President and spoke of the higher duties of citizenship under the New Deal.

## Laurence A. Steinhardt, Minister to Sweden, to Marvin H. McIntyre, Assistant Secretary to the President

Stockholm, November 23, 1933

Dear Mac: I am enclosing herewith copy of a despatch which I have sent to the Department to-day and which I believe the President should see.

While it deals with conditions in Sweden, he will, of course, appreciate that the situation is general and exists to substantially the same extent throughout most of Europe. He may even find it useful in answering certain important corporate interests of the United States which have been so free of late in their criticism of some of his policies. It seems to me that they might spend their time to better advantage in criticizing their own policies and business practices.

The enclosed despatch was not hastily dictated. It represents several months of intensive investigation that I have conducted personally to find out why leading American products can only be purchased in Europe by multi-millionaires, why cheaper European merchandise undersells superior American merchandise in the European markets and why the United States is only obtaining a small fraction of the market that should and could be ours.

Affectionate greetings to all of you.

Cordially yours,

Laurence A. Steinhardt

[Notation:A:LeHand] Mac    Give to Peek    FDR
[OF 462:TS]

## [Enclosure] Laurence A. Steinhardt to Cordell Hull, Secretary of State

Stockholm, November 23, 1933

Sir: I have the honor to enclose herewith copy of an interview given by me under date of November 17, 1933, to *Svenska Dagbladet* (Conservative, Stockholm) which was published in full by that paper—generally regarded as the leading daily newspaper in Stockholm—after first having been translated into Swedish.[1]

This interview was intended by me to counteract to some extent at least the somewhat hysterical news items and conclusions which the Swedish press has drawn during the past two or three weeks from the erratic movements of the dollar in the foreign exchange markets. Important Swedish business, commercial, and banking circles, and particularly the Swedish press have during the past three weeks been concentrating their entire attention on the foreign exchange value of the dollar to the virtual complete exclusion of other important balancing factors in the

American economic and financial situation. A continuation for any length of time of this one-sided point of view is bound to affect Swedish-American trade adversely.

While Swedish exports to the United States continue to expand, Swedish imports from the United States continue to contract—the exact opposite of what might be expected from the depreciation in the foreign exchange value of the dollar. It is rather difficult to explain this phenomenon. Some of the large pulp and newsprint exporters have recently expressed doubts as to the advisability of continuing shipments to the United States without some assurance as to the proceeds in Swedish crowns to be received by them arising out of such sales. It is a fair statement that if there were any other markets to which they could turn they would hesitate to continue shipments to the United States unless payment were guaranteed in Sterling or Swedish crowns. Having no other market to turn to and recognizing that it is only a matter of time before the dollar is stabilized, they are continuing their shipments to the United States, invoking a fairly satisfactory method recently inaugurated whereby payment in Swedish crowns at the prevailing rate of exchange is assured them by the sale of the equivalent amount of dollars at the time of making the contract instead of the conversion of dollars into crowns at the time of payment as has been the practice heretofore. I believe this method will satisfactorily bridge the gap until stabilization takes place.

The continued shrinkage of American exports to Sweden in spite of the great advantage to American manufacturers and exporters occasioned by the depreciation of the dollar, is being caused in my opinion almost exclusively by the ignorance, carelessness, and actual stupidity of important American business interests. While decrying Government interference with business on the one hand and beseeching the Government for assistance and relief on the other, American manufacturers and exporters in so far as the Swedish market is concerned are daily losing opportunities the like of which they will not see again for a generation. The principal vice of which American manufacturers and exporters are guilty is placing their products in the hands of an agent who is given Stockholm or Sweden as an exclusive territory. This American practice is by no means confined to the Swedish market but is prevalent throughout the world with the result that the total volume of export business being lost to the United States is enormous. Sweden affords the best example of this situation by reason of its extremely moderate tariffs and the fact that there are comparatively few trade impediments such as licenses, quotas, and other restrictions. These exclusive agencies operate almost universally as follows:

The General Motors Corporation, for example, has for years given the exclusive agency for the sale of all of its products in Stockholm to a Swedish agent. It is in the interest of this individual to make as much profit as possible without exhausting his limited market. He endeavors to obtain the maximum profit to himself per automobile sold. The result is that he sells General Motors' automobiles in Stockholm for more than double—as to some cars two and one-half times—their retail sales price in the city of New York. As the tariff on automobiles imported into Sweden varies from a minimum of 15 per cent to a maximum of 20 per cent ad valorem, and as the ocean freight and insurance averages considerably less than $100 per car, a General Motors automobile which retails for $1,500 in New York City should sell for not much more than $2,000 in Stockholm, as against which the agent demands $3,000 and even $3,500. If the prospective purchaser is intelligent enough to ascertain this huge and unjustifiable discrepancy, and endeavors to purchase the car in New York and order shipment to Stockholm, he is advised that the General Motors Corporation or its subsidiary in New York is not permitted to fill the order as it has given an exclusive sales agency to an agent in Stockholm.

The cost of the car to the agent being the American price F.O.B. factory the General Motors Corporation does not share in the additional $1,000 or $1,500 extorted from the purchaser. What the American corporation desires therefore is the maximum possible unit sales because the price which it receives per car is the same regardless of the retail price charged by the agent in Stockholm. By permitting the agent to demand an extortionate retail price the corporation destroys its volume of sales in Sweden and grants to the agent an exorbitant profit on a small volume of sales. Thus the agent profits excessively and preserves his limited market at the expense of the corporation's volume of sales. The agent's course in this respect is marked with great shrewdness for his market in Stockholm being a limited one he seeks to make the greatest possible profit per car sold. As the General Motors Corporation receives only a fixed number of dollars per car sold regardless of the retail price received by the agent, it does not benefit by the exorbitant price charged by the agent but on the contrary permits its foreign market to be destroyed by causing the public to buy automobiles manufactured in other countries which undersell the General Motors products in Stockholm—although these foreign cars are much more high-priced products in their respective domestic markets than are General Motors'. Accordingly we see the absurd situation of a Buick automobile which sells for $1,200 or $1,500 in New York being sold in Stockholm for more than a French, German, Italian, or English automobile which costs $2,000 in its domestic market. All these cars are subject to the same rate of duty into Sweden.

As all of the American automobile manufacturers engage in the same practice, the Swedish purchaser has little choice as between American cars. If a single one of the leading American automobile manufacturers would take the trouble to investigate this situation and deal with it properly, that manufacturer would within 90 days have the Swedish market for American automobiles in his hands, and would encroach upon the sales of European cars which cannot meet the competition of American cars at fair prices, reflecting American costs plus import duty, ocean freight, and insurance.

Virtually the same situation exists in so far as the so-called Big Four cigarette manufacturers are concerned, radio manufacturers, producers of canned goods, fruits and a vast number of other American manufactured products which are popular and in urgent demand in Sweden and which the Swedish public find prohibitively priced in the hands of an exclusive agent. I can find not the slightest justification between the prices demanded here by the exclusive agents and the prices paid by me in New York for the same products after adding the Swedish tariff, ocean freight, insurance and expenses of distribution and retail sale.

The situation with respect to gasoline, crude oil, and other petroleum products is quite different. The Russian Naptha Syndicate is continuously increasing its percentage of sales at the expense of the Standard Oil Company of New Jersey and the Texas Corporation. The problem in this field is one of price-cutting and entirely different from the situation outlined above.

Having spent the greater part of my life in the midst of American industry within the United States I have reluctantly come to the conclusion during the past four months that the recognized ingenuity, initiative, intelligence, and general capability of American business is confined to the Continental United States, and that the very same corporations which have made American industry a by-word of competitive efficiency, when it comes to their foreign markets are nothing less than a complete failure, due more to the indifference of the executive heads in failing to recognize their potential markets in Europe than to their inability to cope with the situation if they would once realize that these markets are either being neglected, are in the hands of incapable individuals or under the control of selfish foreigners.

Respectfully yours,

Laurence A. Steinhardt

[OF 462:CT]

[1] A long statement on the accomplishments of the Roosevelt Administration.

# Press Conference, Warm Springs, November 24, 1933, 4 P.M.

[*Excerpt*] Q: Any reaction on your Cuban statement?[1]

The President: I haven't heard a peep.

Q: There is a lot of discussion as to whether that meant an invitation to the Grau San Martin Government.

The President: Just what was said. It is a repetition of what was said before.

Q: To get back—

Q: There is a great division among these gentlemen on your statement. Some say it is an invitation and the majority think not.[2]

The President: The majority is right. Only, use that as background. From the very beginning, we have said all along that we are not taking sides in any way. It is up to the Cuban people to decide and so far it appears at the present time that we haven't yet got a provisional government that clearly has the support of the majority of the Cuban people. What can we do? We can't do anything. The matter rests.

Q: You seem to have pretty good confidence that we may get a good government down there, from that statement.

The President: And then the only other thing there—the only real bit of news in that statement was that we are going to do shortly what we were planning on for some time, and that is to swap Welles and Caffery. Of course that has been planned for some time.[3]

[President's Press Conferences:T]

[1] Nov. 23, 1933, printed in *Foreign Relations, 1933,* V, 525–526.

[2] An invitation for Grau San Martín, the provisional president, to resign. See Welles to Phillips, Dec. 7, 1933, *ibid.,* 533–536.

[3] Welles left his post December 13 and was replaced by Jefferson Caffery, at this time an assistant secretary of state, on December 18 (Matthews to Phillips, Dec. 13, 1933; Caffery to Phillips, Dec. 18, 1933, *ibid.,* pp. 541, 543).

## Roosevelt to James M. Farley, Postmaster General

At Warm Springs, Georgia, November 27, 1933

Memorandum from the President for the Postmaster General: You can tell this man that the Administration is in favor of ratification of the St. Lawrence Seaway Treaty and that we hope the Senate will ratify it this winter.[1]

[OF 66:CT]

[1] Farley, in a note to Miss LeHand, Nov. 20, 1933 (OF 66), enclosed an inquiry (not present) about the Seaway from P. H. Falter, President of the Massena, N.Y., Chamber of Commerce.

## Roosevelt to William Phillips, Acting Secretary of State

At Warm Springs, Georgia, November 27, 1933

Memorandum from the President for the Acting Secretary of State: I forgot to send this to you when Sumner Welles was with me.[1] He seems to have had excellent support from all Americans in Cuba, regardless of the fact that they have been almost all put out of business.

[OF 470:CT]

[1] The enclosure has not been identified.

## George H. Earle, Minister to Austria, to Roosevelt

Vienna, November 27, 1933

My dear Mr. President: Following your instructions, I have called on the American Ambassador in Berlin, and the American Ministers to Prague and Buda Pesth.[1]

I have also just completed a journey through the nine Austrian provinces in which I interviewed the Governors, Commanding Generals and Chambers of Commerce. Chancellor Dollfuss has talked frankly to me many times, as did President Masaryk when I was in Prague and I have utilized every opportunity possible to learn the sentiments of politicians and business men in Austria, Germany, Hungary and Czecho Slovakia.

The last four years have been bad ones for prophets, but since your orders were to send you my impressions, I am doing so.

Economically, Central Europe is barely holding her own. The people to a man in these countries are watching your progress in America, feeling that if a turn for the better is to come it must originate in America.

In Austria, the economic situation is slightly better. If only trade relations with other countries could be but slightly improved, Austria would be on the road to much better things and the Dollfuss Government firmly established. If foreign trade does not improve, the Dollfuss Government will fall.

In Germany, there is a slight improvement in business since June, but conditions are much worse than a year ago. Her shipping and foreign trade have suffered tremendously due to the Jewish boycott.

Politically the whole situation in Europe centers on Hitler. In my opinion, he is a paranoiac, with a gift of eloquence of a kind about half way between Bryan and Billy Sunday. He is opportunist enough to capitalize the German reaction against the Versailles Treaty, magnify the Communist threat and stir up the latent racial antipathy of the Germans to the Jews, a thing easy to do since the Jews still have a little left, in contrast to the utter impoverishment of the Germans.

He has made the militaristic spirit today in Germany the most intense in her history.

What a paranoiac will do when he feels his power waning, and whether Germany is adequately armed, are questions I can not answer.

Hitler is an Austrian and more than anything he wants Austria as part of the German Reich. The crude tactics he has used to break the Austrian resistance has resulted in the growth of a real Austrian Nationalism, that never existed before. In the past, the Austrian children were taught that the history and traditions of Austria were inseparably linked with the Hapsburgs. With the fall of the Hapsburgs, the Austrians were bewildered and hopeless and ready to become a province of Germany. Now, thanks to Hitler's methods, only the Nazis want the Anschluss.

Of one thing I am sure. Hitler has surrounded Germany with a ring of enemies bound together by a great fear of the ruthless military efficiency of the Prussian.

The Hitler virus injected into the German veins is well exemplified by the German Minister Rieth[2] here.

He takes the most insolent attitude toward the Austrian Government, ignoring the invitations of the President and Chancellor to their receptions, saying that the Austrian Government is purely a makeshift affair and will end at any moment.

When he returned my call, he asked me if I would frankly tell him my impressions of my trip through Austria.

I then told him I had found the Nazi sentiment had decreased.

Rieth became very angry, said that he had agents in every class and occupation in Austria, that Austria was 50% Nazi, that a Nazi putsch would sweep Dollfuss out at any moment and then would come a pogrom such as Europe had never seen, that every Jew of every nationality would lose their property and be lucky to escape from Austria with their lives.

There are several hundred American Jewish doctors, students and their families here that I feel personally responsible for.

If this putsch comes, as most of the foreign diplomats and newspaper men believe it will, I am afraid there would be little I could do or say to help them in the hysteria of that time.

For this reason in telling the press about the beauties and resources of Austria that I saw in my trip, I injected the statement that we Americans were purely observers and what Austria did internally was her business and not ours, but that since 90% of Americans were descended from people who had come there to escape racial or religious persecution, that the sympathy of the American people would not likely remain with a nation that indulged in such persecution.[3]

The Austrian is like a college freshman who desires popularity above all else and members of the foreign office have told me my statement would have great influence, and Dollfuss said that it had not only not embarrassed him but had helped him in dealing with this issue.

I understand there has been criticism of my statement in America.

Please believe me, Mr. President, that I regret more than I can say if sentiments of humanity on my part and a desire to protect American citizens have caused me to commit a diplomatic blunder and embarrass you in any way. I assure you I shall be very careful of what I say in the future.

In summarizing the situation, I believe the peace of Europe depends upon the independence of Austria and that Austrian independence depends entirely on her economic welfare.

Before I left America, I talked with prominent business men, publicists and bankers.

All were willing to do everything in their power to promote trade with Austria. Dollfuss is enthusiastic about such a plan and wants me to go back with a business representative of the Austrian Government in January to discuss the matter and get action if possible.

In the last three years America has lost millions of dollars of exports to Austria in meats, automobiles, etc., which could be replaced if we would take her wines, cheese, etc.

In closing, may I quote the words of Sir Walford Selby, British Minister to Austria: "If the Nazis come to power and attempt the Anschluss, some army will march!"[4]

Respectfully and loyally yours,

George H. Earle III

[PSF:Austria:TS]

[1] George H. Earle was a wealthy Pennsylvania sugar manufacturer; this letter is apparently his only communication with Roosevelt as minister.

[2] Dr. Kurt Rieth.

[3] Earle also told the State Department this. He said he could suggest measures to improve Austrian-American trade relations and asked for permission to come home to do this (Earle to Moffat, Nov. 21, 1933, *Foreign Relations, 1934,* II, 3-4). He arrived in New York on January 25 and returned to Europe on Feb. 15, 1934, thus missing the Socialist uprising that broke out in Vienna on February 12 (New York *Times,* Jan. 26, p. 11; Feb. 16, 1934, p. 2). Earle submitted his resignation on Mar. 14, 1934.

[4] Answered Dec. 22, 1933 (*Personal Letters, 1928–1945,* I, 379–380). Among other things the President said he hoped that "the present very real danger will not extend to Vienna."

# William E. Dodd, Ambassador to Germany, to Roosevelt

Berlin, November 27, 1933

*Confidential*

Dear Mr. President: I am preparing a somewhat careful analysis of the ruling trio here with a view to more accurate understanding in the State Department as to the situation. As I can not get the report off in today's pouch, I am taking the liberty of summarizing it to you.

Your remark in your letter of the 13th[1] about the eight percent of the world's population defeating ninety-two percent in their peaceful objectives leads me to think that you might possibly profit from this summary.

The Hitler regime is composed of three rather inexperienced and very dogmatic persons, all of whom have been more or less connected with murderous undertakings in the last eight or ten years. It is a combination of men who represent different groups of the present German majority (not an actual majority). Hitler, now about 45, was an orphan at 13, went through the war without promotion or decorations, so much worshipped here, and who had very curious experiences in Munich between 1919 and 1923. He is romantic-minded, half-informed about great historical figures in Germany, and he was for a number of years a strict imitator of Mussolini. He rose to power by organizing elements in Germany which were partly unemployed and wholly indignant because Germany had not won the great war. His devices are the devices which men set up in ancient Rome, namely, his flag and salute. He has definitely said on a number of occasions that a people survives by fighting and dies through peaceful policies. His influence is and has been wholly belligerent. The last six or eight months he has made many, many announcements of peaceful purpose, and at the time being, and I think he is perfectly sincere and is consequently willing to negotiate with France. However, in the back of his mind is the old German idea of dominating Europe through warfare.

Hitler's first lieutenant is Joseph Goebbels, some ten years younger, a miniature figure who was not engaged in the war but who imbibed the bitterness against France and the rest of the world during that long struggle. After the war he engaged in organizing belligerent groups in western Germany and took every possible occasion to challenge the old Socialist regime which submitted to the Treaty of Versailles. He joined Hitler and made constant declarations that the German people, once united, would domineer the world. While Hitler is a fair orator as German oratory goes, Goebbels is a past master. He makes a point of stirring animosities and hatreds whenever there is opportunity, and he has combined all the newspaper, radio, publications and art activities of Germany into one vast propaganda machine. Through these agencies he is bent upon forcing all Germans into one solid phalanx. He is far cleverer than Hitler, much more belligerent, and, I am told, always refuses to have contacts with foreigners.

The third member of this triumvirate is Hermann Goering, about forty, who comes from South Germany, and who was involved, as Goebbels also, in the early Putsch movement in Munich; was a fugitive from justice for some months while Hitler was in jail, and became intensely violent against all democratic and socialist groups. His wife died as a result of exposure while they were both fugitives from justice. The liberal-socialist government issued pardons for Hitler and Goering about the same time and they recommenced their belligerent agitations about 1926–27. While Goebbels represents something approaching a communistic body of German opinion (mobilized against official Communism), Goering represents a more aristocratic and Prussian Germanism. He is not without support amongst the larger business interests. He had a marvelous experience during the war as an aviator and became as intensely war-like as either Goebbels or Hitler. He is the Prussian Minister President, and has mobilized all the old Prussian extremists and militarists on behalf of the existing regime.

You have, therefore, a unique triumvirate. Hitler, less educated, more romantic, with a semi-criminal record; Goebbels and Goering, both Doctors of Philosophy, both animated by intense class and foreign hatreds and both willing to resort to most ruthless arbitrary methods. Each of the three has a body of support necessary for the maintenance of the present regime. They do not love each other, but in order to maintain their power, they have to sit down together. I do not think there has ever been in modern history such a unique group. There was such a group in ancient Rome, and you probably recall what happened. You may see, therefore, something of the problem you have to deal with, and also some of the reasons why a man of my background might be doubtful of any early success.

Sincerely yours,

William E. Dodd

[PSF:Germany:TS]

[1] Above.

## Robert W. Bingham, Ambassador to Great Britain, to Roosevelt

[London] December 4, 1933

Dear Mr. President: Your letter[1] made me quite happy and I am looking forward eagerly to seeing you on December 22nd.

I did not deliver the packages to the King in person, as I should have liked so much to do, because he has not been well, and I did not want to delay the delivery. Therefore, I delivered them to Sir Clive Wigram.[2] I am sure both your letter and the interesting and very amusing envelopes will be heartily appreciated.

I am glad that you have gotten rid of Sprague. Through his pomposity and vanity he made a fool of himself here during the Economic Conference. I should have written you directly about him except that I was assured the facts would reach you through two men whom we both could trust, and thought that was a better method than writing you about him.

The conditions in our country have been persistently misrepresented in the press here, especially by Wilmott Lewis.[3] When you established the method of gold purchases he sent a dispatch to the *Times* to the effect that you had adopted a policy of "Suicide or murder." I communicated with Sir Campbell Stuart,[4] whom I have known for a long time, and he came out at once to see me, and before I had said a word, he told me how disturbed he was over Lewis's dispatches. I told him that, through Lewis, his newspaper was persistently and constantly misleading the British public, and he agreed with me. Two or three days later Lewis sent over a dispatch in which he rather lamely climbed down from his position, and since then his dispatches have not been so bad, but there is an underlying hostility in all that he sends over here. In addition, the financial newspapers publish a lot of stuff they get out of the Mellon-Mills den in New York. As a result, on Thanksgiving night, when I had to speak to the American Society, I took occasion to deal with the subject of conditions in America since your inauguration, and apparently with some good results.

Ramsay MacDonald has lost out completely here, I think and is a mere figurehead, and many of the Conservatives, with their large majority in the House of Commons, are opposed to continuing the pretense of the national government (which is a mere pretense). They are split among themselves on the question of continuing MacDonald as Prime Minister, and Simon and other Liberals in Cabinet positions, but they are nervous and frightened over the great increase in the labor vote, and they attribute their own losses and labor's increases to the fear on the part of the public that the Conservatives may adopt a war-like policy, which the British people, as a whole, seem determined to avoid. This attitude, of which the government is completely conscious, should result in their making much greater efforts to cooperate with you in the only policy which holds out real assurance for peace, namely, in the abolition of offensive armament, leading on, as it will inevitably do, to reduction even in defensive armament.

Referring again to Wilmott Lewis, whose misrepresentations I deeply resent, I have had two more talks with Sir Campbell Stuart on the subject, and one with Mr. Brand,[5] who married Phyllis Langhorne, and is a director of the *Times,* and have discussed the subject also with Lord and Lady Astor, who perhaps have more influence with Geoffrey Dawson, the Editor of the *Times,* than any one else. All four of these people with whom I have discussed the subject, are disturbed over it, and seem to resent it as much as I do. I saw Geoffrey Dawson at a luncheon given for me by the *Times* management, and he said to me, "I don't understand your President's policy," and I told him that from what had appeared in his newspaper, it was perfectly obvious he did not understand it, as otherwise he would not have permitted the foolish and misleading things to appear in the *Times* which he had allowed to be printed.

On the whole, however, I believe practically everybody here wants to see you perform your great task successfully. Some of this feeling grows out of a decent, friendly attitude, but most of it is due to the fact that they are afraid a failure would have a bad effect on themselves.

I must thank you again for your letter. It makes me happy to feel that you think I am getting on with my job here. As I shall see you soon, I shall reserve some of the things I might write about until that time.

My wife joins me in cordial greeting to you and Mrs. Roosevelt.

Very sincerely,

Robert W. Bingham

[PSF:Great Britain:TS]

[1] Nov. 13, 1933 (*Personal Letters, 1928–1945,* I, 369–370), expressing his concern over the situation in Germany.

[2] Private secretary to King George. Roosevelt had sent the king some stamps for his collection in a letter of Nov. 5, 1933 (*ibid.,* pp. 370–371).

[3] London *Times* correspondent in New York.

[4] Chairman of the Imperial Communications Advisory Committee.

[5] Robert Henry Brand.

# Press Conference, Executive Offices of the White House, December 6, 1933, 10:50 A.M.

[*Excerpt*] Q: Mussolini has suggested that the Covenant of the League of Nations be revised in order to make it easier for the United States, among other nations, to join it. Have we given him any grounds for belief that we would be prepared to do so?

The President: No, no indication on the subject at all . . .[1]

511

Q: Can you give us any indication of what the attitude of the United States Delegation at Montevideo will be towards the proposal for a six-year moratorium on all debts?

The President: I think it has been made very clear on that, that it is primarily a subject between the Republics which have sold bonds to investors outside of their own borders, between them and the investors. In other words, the easiest way of putting it is that the United States is not owed any money by any of the South American republics and it is therefore a matter between those republics and any of the bond-holders, the holders of their bonds.[2]

[President's Press Conferences:T]

[1] See Long to Roosevelt, Dec. 15, 1933, below.

[2] Before the opening of the Montevideo Conference, Mexico had proposed certain additions to the agenda, including a moratorium on debt payments of from six to ten years, stabilization of currencies, creation of central banks, use of silver in monetary systems, and control of the exchange market (Daniels to Hull, Sept. 14, 1933, *Foreign Relations, 1933,* IV, 11–14). Hull then told the Mexican ambassador that he hoped the debt question could be avoided at Montevideo and that Mexico would be agreeable to the methods offered by the Foreign Bondholders Protective Council. The head of the Mexican delegation, José M. Puig, finally gave up his effort to add to the agenda before the Conference met but reserved the right to propose additions there (Hull to Daniels, Sept. 28; Daniels to Hull, Sept. 29, two letters; memorandum by Caffery, Oct. 2, 1933, all *ibid.,* pp. 17, 17–18, 18–19, 19). On Oct. 19, 1933, Hull informed Ambassador Gibson in Brazil of the Mexican move (*ibid.,* pp. 31-32). He said the United States would "deprecate any discussion" of the debt and other questions at Montevideo but if the other nations insisted the United States would not oppose it. Mexico, on December 4, did ask for inclusion of the additional questions but the Conference referred the proposals to the Third Pan American Financial Conference, to meet in Santiago, Chile. See *Report of the Delegates to the Seventh International Conference of American States,* pp. 26–31.

# William Phillips, Acting Secretary of State, to Roosevelt

Washington, December 6, 1933

Dear Mr. President: You have already indicated that you would be willing to receive the payment of $1,000,000 on account of the Italian debt due the United States on December 15th. The offer of this amount was made to me informally by the Italian Ambassador.[1] It has now been confirmed by a resolution of the Fascist Grand Council passed last night and reading as follows:

The Grand Council of Fascism, in view of the further installment of the war debt to the United States which falls due on December 15th, and although it is forced to note that the course of events has not permitted of negotiations on the question as the Grand Council had augured in its session of June 11, 1933, resolves: to make a payment of $1,000,000 as renewed proof of Italy's good will pending a definitive settlement which will close this item of the accountancy opened by the war.

Would you be so good as to glance through the enclosed proposed exchange of notes with the Italian Government and indicate whether they meet with your approval?[2]

Faithfully yours,

William Phillips

[*Notation*:AS] A few slight changes    FDR
[OF 233:TS]

[1] Phillips reported this to Roosevelt in a letter of Nov. 23, 1933 (OF 212). He noted that the payment due from Italy was $2,133,905 but that the Treasury was in favor of accepting the token payment here offered. He also noted that the June 15, 1933, installment of $12,545,416 was still unpaid.

[2] Rosso to Phillips, Dec. 7, 1933; Phillips to Rosso, Dec. 12, 1933 (*Foreign Relations, 1933,* I, 892, 892–893). Phillips told Rosso that the President had pointed out that it was not in his discretion to reduce or cancel the debt; however, in view of the Italian government's acknowledgment of the debt it would not be considered in default.

## Roosevelt to Ruth Bryan Owen, Minister to Denmark, Copenhagen

Washington [December 7, 1933]

My dear Mrs. Owen: I have received your letter of November 17th and have noted your remarks concerning the depreciation in the purchasing value of your income and the incomes of other officers and employees of this Government serving in Denmark, on account of the decline in the exchange value of United States currency.[1]

While it has been possible for the Treasury to arrange to cash dollar salary and expense checks and drafts at the mint par rate in certain countries where the dollar sells at a discount, it is of course impossible to apply this plan with advantage in Denmark, so long as the dollar commands a premium at Copenhagen over its mint par value in terms of local currency.

I am informed that the arrangement which has been worked out by the Treasury is the best that can be made under the existing law, but the whole question is being studied by the Bureau of the Budget in order that appropriate recommendations may be made to Congress when it convenes.

I have been pleased to refer your statements to the Secretary of State, so that he may use them, along with data submitted by other officers throughout the Foreign Service of his Department, in preparing his recommendations of remedial action.[2]

Very sincerely yours,

[OF 437:CT]

[1] Mrs. Owen pointed out that the recent arrangement to pay Foreign Service salaries in gold applied only to gold standard countries, and that as soon as the dollar had begun to depreciate Mexico had arranged to pay her minister in Denmark in French francs (OF 437).
[2] Drafted in the State Department.


## Roosevelt to Raymond Robins, New York

[Washington] December 8, 1933

My dear Mr. Robins: I was glad to receive your kind letter of November 29th, and to know that you are in such complete agreement.[1]

If we follow a logical procedure I am sure that a great deal of good will be derived, and that it will be helpful to both countries.

With kindest regards, Very sincerely yours,

[OF 220-A:CT]

[1] Robins congratulated the President on his "great move for international peace, economic recovery and control of price levels in the international market by the recognition of the Soviet Union" (OF 220-A). He enclosed newspaper clippings of recent talks he had made in support of the Administration's Russian policy.


## Press Conference, Executive Offices of the White House, December 8, 1933, 3:40 P.M.

[Excerpt] Q: One of the Latin American countries has proposed at the Pan-American Conference that tariffs be restored to the 1928 level for a period of five years. What do you think about it?

The President: I did not even know it.

Q: Mr. President, Mr. Welles has had a conversation with the Grau San Martin government in Cuba lately. Is there any change in our aspect toward the Cuban situation at all—any change in our policy?

The President: No. I spoke to Phillips at Cabinet meeting[1] and asked him whether he had heard anything about the talk that same day with Grau San Martin and he said that he had had a dispatch come in this morning.[2] It is somewhere in the ante-room. I have not read it yet. However, he told me that there was no change in the situation . . .

Q: There was a story printed two days ago or three days ago, on December 6th, that the Administration was letting it be known privately that the Johnson Bill, which is pending in Congress, might be recommended for passage if there were further defaults of foreign debts. That is a very vague bill which will prohibit the sale or purchase of foreign securities.

The President: The only thing I know of is what I read in some paper. I never read the bill itself. I don't know what it is. Is it absolutely a prohibition on the sale of foreign securities?

Q: It is a prohibition on the sale of securities of foreign governments whose securities are in default, or any subdivision thereof. In other words, it would affect the French Government.

The President: How about private firms?

Q: No, not private firms.[3]

[President's Press Conferences:T]

[1] Just before the press conference.

[2] Welles to Phillips, Dec. 7, 1933 (*Foreign Relations, 1933*, V, 533–536). Welles said that there was strong reason for thinking that Grau San Martín's renewed attempt to seek a compromise was in the hope that an opportunity would arise for the seizing of the provisional government "by a dictatorial government composed solely of elements of the extreme Left."

[3] Senator Hiram Johnson of California had introduced S. 682, to bar financial transactions with any country that was in default on its obligations to the United States, on March 22, 1933. It was reported favorably but did not come up for vote during the session (*Cong. Rec.,* vol. 77, pp. 705, 1323, 2968). The bill was an outgrowth of disclosures of the 1931–32 Senate hearings on the floating of foreign bonds in the United States.

Johnson had been the prime mover in the investigation; see his speech in the Senate of March 15, 1932 (*Cong. Rec.,* vol. 75, pp. 6052–6062). The Administration was fearful of the effects of the bill on its coming reciprocal trade negotiations (and on the operations of the Export-Import Bank), and after the measure passed the Senate on Jan. 11, 1934, Senator Robinson, the floor leader, moved to reconsider (*Cong. Rec.,* vol. 78, pp. 441, 446–448). The Administration then sought approval of certain amendments. See Moore to Hull, Jan. 22, 1934, below.

## Beckinridge Long, Ambassador to Italy, to Roosevelt

Rome, Italy, December 8, 1933

My dear Frank: The Duce is saying in an article which he has written and which is for publication next week in the Hearst papers in the United States that Italy is committed to the gold standard and that Italy will not leave it. While I have not seen the article I have been informed by one who has seen it that it is a definite statement. Jung says the same thing. Beneduce,[1] who is a financial genius of Italy, says the same thing: "Italy is definitely and positively committed to the gold."

Nevertheless, Italy has paid in silver the interest on the Morgan Loan and has paid in silver such sums as she has paid to the United States on her War loans. Gold is impounded in Italy and is prohibited from export except under permit.

None of them say that Italy will not revise the value of the lira, and the position of the Government in regard to that movement in that the Duce fixed it at 90 to the pound. That gave the lira the value of approximately $5\frac{1}{5}$ cents when the pound was at 4.87 and our dollar at about par.

Since then the pound has shrunk and the dollar has shrunk so that there are about 60 lira to the pound and the lira is worth $8\frac{1}{4}$ cents in dollars.

I am now told by an Italian by the name of Ruggieri, who is the representative here of the Chase National Bank, that he had just had a conversation with the head of the Bank of Italy. He says that official told him that Mussolini had never intended to fix the gold content of the lira at a definite quantity of refined gold and that he only pegged it in its relation to the pound; that the Duce announced it would be of the value of about 90 to the pound; that the pound has now shrunk to the point where the lira is only about 60 to the pound; and that Mussolini can easily readjust the value of the lira by fixing its value again as of 90 to the pound; that that action would not be considered as going off the gold; and that he has had some recent conversations with the Duce as a result of which he has reason to believe that that may take place.

This was told me in great confidence. Ruggieri was much impressed with this conversation. Of course the Bank of Italy did not say Mussolini was going to adopt this particular policy, but his statements were such as to impress Ruggieri with the thought that it possibly would be done.

At least Ruggieri is of that opinion. After all, a statement by the head of the Bank of Italy to a responsible financial agent in Rome is significant.

Of course the manufacturers and exporters have been clamoring for a readjustment of the value of the lira because they are losing their export business. But in addition to the lira and irrespective of its relation to the pound, they are suffering here by reason of Japanese importations. The Japanese are laying down silk and rayon in Italy cheaper than it can be manufactured here. They are selling bicycles in Rome for 50 lira each—$4.00 at the present rate of exchange. They have flooded Eritrea, the Red Sea colony, and Italian Somaliland with their manufactures and with their population. Tripoli and the Italian insular possessions they supply with manufactured goods from here after having imported them into Italy.

So between Japanese importations and the lack of Italian exports they are soon to be confronted with some drastic decision, and I would not be surprised to see them devalue the lira and to do it by readjusting its value to the pound—and still continue the fiction of the gold standard. This will probably be expedited if France goes off the gold—which is persistently rumored here.

I tried to listen to your radio address on the sixth, but we couldn't even find out from the Italian press what day it was to be delivered, and I have only seen it referred to since as having been delivered. In about three weeks I will get a copy of it from the Department of State.[2]

With every good wish, Affectionately and respectfully yours,

Breckinridge Long[3]

[OF 447:TS]

[1] Presumably Alberto Beneduce, vice-president of the board of the Bank for International Settlements.

[2] Roosevelt's speech before the Federal Council of Churches of Christ in America, meeting in Washington, is printed in *Public Papers,* II, 517–520.

[3] An attached memorandum, Roosevelt to Morgenthau, Dec. 27, 1933, reads: "For your information and return." On this Morgenthau wrote: "Thanks for letting me read this."


# Speech by Roosevelt to the Gridiron Club, Willard Hotel, Washington, December 9, 1933

[*Excerpt*] And now, my friends, I want to tell you in the sacred confidence of this room of the one disturbing thought that comes to me day after day. Here is this great Nation of ours with dollars that maintain a useful purchasing power; with a currency that is sounder than it has been in many years; with gold reserves greater than any Nation has ever held; with people going back to work literally by the millions; with a recovery program that is an accepted success. And yet with this stable dollar—with this sound currency, we in America are disturbed by the fluctuations and the uncertainty of the currencies and the exchanges of other nations. We see our dollar constant, permanent—a rock of Gibraltar—and our good friend the Pound gyrating up and down in comparison with our dollar, and our friend the Franc turning hand springs in relation to our good old stable dollar.

We wonder when we wake up in the morning where the Pound and the Franc & other currencies are going to go to in the course of the day. Our importers and exporters when about to make a contract in foreign lands cannot be sure what kind of money they will be paid in on the fulfillment of the contract. It is a hard problem. Here we sit, making good! Here we sit, with our vast resources—resources of population and resources from Mother Nature. We know our own future for the very simple fact that this good old dollar of ours is the sole yardstick of 93 per cent of everything that we grow or make or own, or buy or sell in this country—93 per cent of all that we deal in in this country. But, of course, we do feel concerned for that other little 7 per cent of things that we grow or make or use that is affected by foreign exchange.

We should like to see this 7 per cent made stable even as the other 93 per cent is stable. We should like it not only for our own concern in this 7 per cent but also because we honestly wish and hope that the other Nations of the world will so stabilize themselves that we can all be stable—they as well as ourselves.

Here again it is not just a question of whose baby has the measles— that is a selfish thought—but it is again the application on a broader scale of what I have said before about trying to get a perspective of the whole of the Nation and not just a little part of it. We in America seek a perspective of the world as a whole and the relationship, the true relationship, of every part of the world to every other part. We hope for the stability of world currency, we hope for an increase in the exchange of goods and products between nations—not with the thought of making one Nation rich at the expense of another but of letting all nations participate in the profits of world trade.

We who are the guests of the distinguished Members of the Gridiron Club know that in the quips, the skits and the satire there is much solid gold and that more than one true word has been spoken here tonight in jest. I am grateful to all of you for another happy evening—and may I say in bidding you goodnight that I hope the charming brides to whom I have referred will soon be feeling better.[1]

[Speech File:T]

[1] This excerpt is from the last third of the speech; in the preceding part Roosevelt defended the Administration against the charge that its policies (respecting the newspaper code of the National Recovery Administration) infringed on freedom of the press. The text is that of the ribbon copy of the last of three drafts; it bears the notation: "Gridiron Speech Dec 1933. As delivered FDR." This draft contains numerous revisions in Roosevelt's hand. See Harrison to Roosevelt, Dec. 12, 1933, below.

## White House Press Release on Foreign Trade, December 11, 1933

Creation of a temporary committee to recommend permanent machinery to coordinate all government relations to American foreign trade was announced today at the White House.

The report of the Committee and final action thereon is expected within two weeks.

George Peek, Agricultural Adjustment Administrator, having completed the organization period of the A.A.A., is designated to head this Committee as special assistant to the President on American trade policy.

The Committee will include the members of the two departmental committees, the Interdepartmental Advisory Board on Reciprocal Treaties, Interdepartmental Trade Policy Committee, and such other individuals as Mr. Peek may select.

As far back as last March, in his discussions of the agricultural policy, the President discussed with Mr. Peek the possibility and the advisability of reopening foreign markets for agricultural surpluses. It was decided at that time that the immediate domestic supply should be restricted, in view of the fact that foreign markets were closed temporarily by tariffs, quotas, etc., so that the immediate task was to restrict production until the machinery for the limitation of burdensome surpluses could be put in operation.

Now the time has come to initiate the second part of the program and to correlate the two parts, the internal adjustment of production with such effective foreign purchasing power as may be developed by reciprocal tariffs, barter, and other international arrangements.

Mr. Peek will head the new organization when it is created.[1]

[White House Press Releases:M]

[1] See Roosevelt to department heads, Dec. 20, 1933, below.

## William Phillips, Acting Secretary of State, to Roosevelt

Washington, December 11, 1933

My dear Mr. President: We have been requested by the authorities of the League of Nations informally to suggest two American nationals suitable for service as member and alternate member of the League Financial Committee. Mr. Norman Davis is the present American member, but due to the difficulty attendant upon one individual from overseas attending all meetings, the system of official alternates has been set up.

I have been in touch with Mr. Davis, who suggests the following: (a) that he remain the American member with the understanding that when arrangements are made for an American member (probably George Harrison) to go on the B.I.S.[1] Board at Basel, Mr. Davis would step aside in his favor; (b) that we suggest an alternate member Mr. George E. Roberts of the National City Bank.[2] The latter has not been consulted, but if you approve the idea, Mr. Norman Davis will approach him through Mr. James H. Perkins, President of the Bank.

Faithfully yours,

William Phillips

[*Notation*:AS] W.P. Better do nothing at this time. FDR.
[OF 184:TS]

[1] Bank for International Settlements.
[2] At this time economic adviser to the Bank; formerly, a vice-president. Author of numerous works on finance, in 1895 Roberts published *Coin at School in Finance,* widely read during the great silver debate of the nineties.

## William Phillips, Acting Secretary of State, to Roosevelt

Washington, December 11, 1933

Dear Mr. President: Upon thinking over the problem connected with Mr. Peek,[1] it has occurred to me that possibly the following solution might appeal to you, i.e. to create Mr. Peek Special Assistant to the President on the Formulation of American Foreign Commercial Policy charged with the duty:

(a) of advising the President from time to time upon questions of foreign commercial policy;

(b) of preparing a special report upon this matter to the President, and

(c) of sitting as an ex-officio member of the Executive Committee on Commercial Policy.

There are, as you know, already two inter-Departmental Committees at work with respect to foreign trade:

(1) For the negotiation of reciprocal bargaining treaties and

(2) on commercial policy, which was set up by Executive Order on November 21.

(I have been chairman pro-tem under your directions and have recently turned the chairmanship over to Frank Sayre.)

I am sure a place can be found for Mr. Peek as a member ex-officio of both committees and at the same time give him the broader field which you have in mind.

Faithfully yours,

William Phillips

[*Notation*:A:FDR] File
[OF 971:TS]

[1] Peek's differences with Secretary of Agriculture Wallace over administration of the Agricultural Adjustment Administration; see Fite, *George N. Peek,* pp. 264–266.

# George L. Harrison, Governor, Federal Reserve Bank of New York, to Roosevelt

[New York] December 12, 1933

Dear Mr. President: On November 27, following his return from Warm Springs, Secretary Morgenthau asked me to inquire of Governor Norman of the Bank of England, whether he thought the British government would be willing to join the United States government in de jure stabilization of their currencies in terms of gold either at once or following a short period of de facto stabilization.

While I have reported to you orally the substance of my conversations with Governor Norman on this subject, I am enclosing herewith a memorandum, as you suggested, recording the essence of these talks with respect to the specific question which Secretary Morgenthau presented to me. This memorandum has been prepared from contemporaneous and detailed notes of my conversations with Governor Norman.

Respectfully yours,

George L. Harrison

[PSF:Treasury:TS]

## [*Enclosure*] Memorandum of Certain Conversations Between George L. Harrison, Governor of the Federal Reserve Bank of New York, and Montagu C. Norman, Governor of the Bank of England

On November 28, 1933, I telephoned Governor Norman to inquire whether he thought the British government would be willing to join the United States government in de jure stabilization of their currencies in terms of gold either at once or following a short period of de facto stabilization. I told Governor Norman that while I had no assurance that the United States government would agree to prompt de jure stabilization of the dollar in terms of gold, nevertheless I would take the matter up with the Administration if Governor Norman thought there was a prospect that the British government would be willing to undertake an early de jure stabilization of the pound, if at the same time the United States government took similar action with respect to the dollar.

On December 1, Governor Norman advised me on the telephone that he had discussed the matter with Sir Frederick Leith-Ross of the British Treasury, and that he (Governor Norman) was quite certain that the British government would not now be willing to consider de jure stabilization of the pound in terms of gold in the near future whether by their own action alone or jointly with the United States government, nor would they be willing to give any commitment as to a minimum rate of stabilization in the future. Governor Norman went on to say, however, that they would be glad to consider an arrangement for de facto stabilization of the dollar-sterling exchange rate for a temporary period through the use of an agreed amount of gold. He asked me to ascertain, if possible, whether Washington would be interested now in considering such an arrangement.[1]

[PSF:Treasury:T]

[1] See memorandum by Roosevelt, Dec. 16, 1933, below.

## William Phillips, Acting Secretary of State, to Roosevelt

Washington, December 12, 1933

My dear Mr. President: I beg to enclose a telegram from the Secretary dated December 9th referring to representations which may possibly be made to you on behalf of the National Woman's Party with regard to treaties covering nationality of women and equal rights for women. You will note that Mr. Hull asks me to keep you fully advised.

These representations will perhaps be made to you through one or more of four channels, namely; (a) questions at your press conference; (b) direct telegrams from Miss Doris Stevens[1] or others at Montevideo; (c) similar telegrams to Senators and others of prominence, urging them to approach you or to make public statements; (d) associates of Miss Stevens in Washington.

May I refresh your memory as to the reasons why the State Department has not been in favor of the writing of treaties on nationality at Montevideo:

1. By Executive Order of April 25, 1933, three members of your Cabinet[2] were designated as a Committee to draft a revision of the nationality laws of the United States; nationality is largely a matter, not of international law, but of domestic law.

2. Under Resolution 6 of the Hague Conference of 1930 (which was largely based on a proposal made by the American Delegation) studies of the Governments are proceeding (to be submitted by 1935) which are to take particularly into consideration the rights of children; and the derivative and other nationality rights of children present some of the most difficult problems in the field of nationality.

In addition we have also been opposed because:

1. Questions of sex equality are matters of internal concern in all countries.

2. This Government should not enter into treaty engagements in respect of (for example) property rights or voting rights of women in other countries.

3. Here such questions are in part for Congress and in part for the states to determine; but they are no business of foreign nations.

4. Treaties binding us in such questions would go directly counter to beneficent provisions of recent codes in favor of women in industry and would be opposed to our own national policy.

Faithfully yours,

William Phillips

[Notation:A:FDR] File
[OF 567:TS]

[1] Miss Stevens (Mrs. Jonathan Mitchell), women's suffrage leader, was the first United States representative on, and also the first chairman of, the Inter-American Commission of Women, created by the Sixth Pan-American Conference of 1928.
[2] Hull, Perkins, and Cummings.

## [Enclosure] Cordell Hull, Chairman, American Delegation, Seventh Pan-American Conference, to William Phillips

Montevideo, December 9, 1933

[Telegram] The following is strictly confidential for Phillips. Miss Breckinridge[1] has been told by representative here of New York Times that his paper desires to know why she opposes treaties covering nationality of women and equal rights for women.

Doris Stevens, who is here as Chairman of the Inter-American Commission of Women, has probably inspired this request. Miss Stevens is apparently on intimate terms with the representative of Times.

Secretary of Labor, Miss Perkins, can fully explain relationship between National Woman's Party, to which Miss Stevens belongs, and the balance of women's movement in United States.

A member of our delegation has been told by Miss Stevens that in 1930 at the Conference on Codification held at The Hague she went over the heads of the delegates directly to the White House in order to secure favorable action to her cause. (Consult Hackworth[2] on this point.)

As far as it can be obtained unofficially, the general view of Latin American delegates here is one of opposition to the treaties on nationality of women and equal rights for women which are being put forward by Miss Stevens.

Apparently the other powers do not wish to make such treaties which would make it unfortunate if the Stevens tactics of 1930 were repeated and existing instruction on these matters were changed.

Please consult Miss Perkins and also communicate with the President fully, in order that he may have all the facts in the case.[3]

Hull

[OF 567:T]

[1] Sophonisba Breckinridge, a member of the delegation.
[2] Green H. Hackworth, legal adviser of the State Department.
[3] See National Association of Women Lawyers to Roosevelt, Dec. 13, 1933, below.

## Press Conference, Executive Offices of the White House, December 13, 1933, 10:40 A.M.

[*Excerpt*] Q: Can you give us any background on the statement of Secretary Hull at Montevideo yesterday and on the general plans which Peek is going to carry out for the building up of foreign trade?[1]

The President: I don't think there is anything that you do not know already. Of course the general thought is that—this is for background —that if we can take care of our surpluses in that way, it is going to aid in the general working out of the situation with respect to the agricultural surplus problem and possibly other surpluses.

Q: Do you anticipate that the time is approaching in the near future for a general—when a general reduction in tariffs will be either advisable or practically possible?

The President: I would not put it that way because you can have an objective on that but, at the same time, not feel particularly optimistic about getting very far with it. At the present time, under the present world conditions—frankly, I think you had better keep this off the record or use it as background—I don't think there is very much in sight except through bilateral treaties, which might be extended to take in a few other countries. But any general agreement among nations on tariffs today is pretty slim as to prospects for the next few months.

Q: What is the situation with regard to the most-favored-nation clause? How far can it go in tariff trading without infringing on the most-favored-nation-clause?

The President: Have you had anything on the Colombian Treaty yet?

Q: Not yet; no details.

The President: I don't know whether I can say anything about it. At any rate, the Colombian Treaty has been finished and the Treaty is a straight reciprocal treaty with Colombia, but it has in it the clause that if any other nation wishes to do the same thing, they are at liberty to do it . . .

Q: Can you give us some background on foreign debts?

The President: Foreign debts? You don't need background there; you have the facts.

Q: They are just debts.

Q: Are we going to do anything on France, telling them to come across?

The President: No, what can we do?

Q: Just go to war.

Q: Tell them they can't sell us champagne.

Q: In the recent White House conference, was there something looking toward a merger of communications companies—anything on that?

The President: That is one of the things we have been studying of late. The whole communications problem is a pretty involved one. The Government has got to get a policy. We haven't any communications policy at the present time.

It falls into really four fields. The first three relate to the domestic field and the fourth relates to the foreign field. In the domestic field are voice communications by wire—that is the telephone; symbol communication by wire, which is the telegraph; and voice and symbol, which is radio . . .

Then, in the foreign field, the suggestion is made that all foreign communications, whether they be by cable or voice radio or symbol radio, should all be brought into relationship with each other and make one picture out of the whole foreign field.

That report has been made in tentative form—only tentative form so far—by this Committee of the Department of Commerce and the next step will be to talk with the two Chairmen up on the Hill, Sam Rayburn and Clarence Dill. It is only a tentative report without any final recommendations and we will take it up with the Committees before we have a final policy . . .

Q: Can you tell us how far your plan goes for revision of the Treaty with Cuba, particularly the Platt Amendment?

The President: I have not done a thing on that except what I said in Warm Springs. You remember that statement in Warm Springs.[2] I have no new information except what I read in the papers. Evidently what happened the day before yesterday, when Sumner Welles saw the President, the President said something to him—I don't think that Sumner initiated the conversation—said something to Sumner about the possibility of the modification of the existing treaty and I think that Sumner's answer was in the words of my statement from Warm Springs and I think that is as far as it has gone.

Q: Mr. President, is there any talk of reopening or re-negotiating any phase of the St. Lawrence Waterway Treaty?

The President: Not that I know of.

Q: The Mississippi Valley Conference at St. Louis stated that there was consideration of some such re-negotiation?

The President: Not that I know of. The only thing I can think of on that, that you might have heard, is that there was some thought on the part of the Chicago and Illinois people with respect to the present clause in the Treaty. That clause, as I remember it, says that if the amount of water allocated to the Chicago Drainage Canal proves to be insufficient—something along those lines—that then we would have the right to ask for arbitration on an additional amount. Some of the people do not think that that language is quite clear enough, although they go along with the general purpose of it. As far as I know, there is no definite plan or proposal to change the present language because the other side believes the present language is sufficient.

Q: That could only be done if Canada consented?

The President: Yes, that could only be done if Canada consented.

[President's Press Conferences:T]

---

[1] Hull proposed the "immediate adoption of the policy of bilateral reciprocity commercial treaties based on mutual concessions," and an "understanding with other important countries . . . to bring down these trade barriers to a level dictated by a moderate tariff policy." The proposal was adopted by a resolution of the Conference, printed, with Hull's statement, in *Report of the Delegates to the Seventh International Conference of American States,* pp. 55–56. Hull's statement is also printed in State Department, *Press Releases,* Dec. 16, 1933, pp. 342–343, and in *Addresses and Statements by the Honorable Cordell Hull In Connection with His Trip to South America 1933–1934 to Attend the Seventh International Conference of American States, Montevideo, Uruguay* (Washington, 1935), pp. 27–29.

[2] Nov. 23, 1933, printed in *Public Papers,* II, 499–501.

## Claude G. Bowers, Ambassador to Spain, to Roosevelt

Madrid, December 13, 1933

Dear Mr. President: . . .[1] Over here your activities are followed with keen interest. The other day I was talking with de los Rios, former Minister of State and a profound student of economics and political science, and he said that if your policies work out as he thinks they will, it will mean a world-wide revolution in government.

The American colony here, as elsewhere, composed largely of the agents of American businesses and Republicans, are affected by the propoganda[2] of the European press. The other day I spoke at a luncheon of the American Chamber of Commerce, and availed myself of the opportunity to meet this propoganda both at home and abroad, by sharply reminding them of the miraculous improvements wrought since I addressed them five months ago. Purposely I made it an assertive, arrogant speech and touched unkindly upon "the prophets of pessimism and paralysis who sat for four years twirling their thumbs in masterful inactivity, and waiting like Macawber for something to turn up." It was amusing. The expression of astonishment which continued throughout the speech and the thunder of applause at the close delighted me. It created something of a sensation. Capt. Rock head of the Telephone Company was effusive afterwards in his commendation of what you are doing.

The recent elections mean a more conservative republican policy and they indicate nothing like a restoration of the monarchy. American papers imply that the Agrarians are monarchists. I have been informed in Spanish circles that 80% of them are republicans, and Sir George Graham, the British Ambassador, has the same figures. Lerreux will go in as Prime Minister in a few days.[3] He is a typical American politician. We are very good friends. The syndicalists have tried to terrorize the country with a few bombs but no one is worried.

The other day I had a letter from Ruth Bryan Owen who is much distressed over the failure of the State Department to prevent the disaster which is falling upon us generally outside of France and Germany where our people are being paid in gold. She suggested that I write you. I understand that when Congress meets something will, or may be done. The situation in this country is very serious. The cost of living is going up, and unlike in most European countries it never has gone down since the war as in other nations. The peseta is pegged with the franc and has been for three years, arbitrarily held there by the Spanish Government. Every penny an American official loses in France by the fall in the dollar is lost here. The result is that in pesetas my salary instead of being reduced 15% is reduced 51% from that of my predecessors. It is possible to live and meet absolutely necessary obligations on the $17,500 less the 15% but not on 49% of the original salary.

The vice consul at Bilboa has had to borrow money to send his wife and child home to live with her people while he lives in a cheap furnished room. He is an excellent man. Several of the consuls have had to put up their cars. Our Commercial Attaché has had to move into cheaper quarters, have his telephone removed, store his car, and drop his membership in clubs that are important in his work. Some girl clerks' salaries, reduced to pesetas, brings them wages below those permitted by the law here for such work on the ground that it is below the Spanish standard of living. Everyone who comes here—Krock of the *Times*, Call[4] who represented us at the International Parliamentary Union, is shocked and has reported the conditions to the State Department. Of course it is an impossible situation and must be corrected in some way as soon as possible. The Associated Press and the representatives of private businesses here have had salary readjustments to meet the conditions.

Am sorry Farley did not come to Spain from Paris. I went to France annually for seven years and Spain is far more interesting, the people infinitely more friendly.[5]

With regards, Sincerely,

Claude G. Bowers

[OF 303:TS]

[1] Omitted is a long paragraph on party politics in the United States.
[2] Misspellings here and below as in the original.
[3] Alejandro Lerroux became premier on December 16.
[4] Arthur Deerin Call, editor of *World Affairs*.
[5] Roosevelt replied Feb. 5, 1934 (*Personal Letters, 1928–1945,* I, 389–390), saying that financial aid for the embassy staffs was expected from Congress.

## The National Association of Women Lawyers to Roosevelt

[Washington] December 13, 1933

Memorandum: The National Association of Women Lawyers, consisting of lawyers throughout the country, is deeply interested in the events at Montevideo, particularly in relation to the treaty concerning the nationality of women as follows:

"The Contracting Parties agree that from the going into effect of this treaty there shall be no distinction based on sex in their law and practice relating to nationality."

Cables from Montevideo inform us that this treaty has been recommended for adoption by the subcommittee of the third Commission consisting of representatives of the following countries: Brazil, Chile, Cuba, Mexico, Peru, Uruguay. We understand that it is to be voted upon by the full Commission on Friday.

Speaking for the National Association of Women Lawyers we earnestly request that you instruct the American delegates in Montevideo to exert their influence to have this treaty recommended by the full Commission and adopted by the Conference.

Such action would be in harmony with the position taken by the United States on nationality matters on previous occasions and in harmony with the expressed ideals of this country looking toward justice to all. At the Hague in 1930 the United States voted against a proposed international Convention on nationality because it contained discriminations against women. In May 1930 the House of Representatives adopted a resolution commending the action of our delegates to the Hague and approving the principle of equality in nationality matters, in the following language:

Resolved further, That it is hereby declared to be the policy of the United States of America that there should be absolute equality for both sexes in nationality, and that in the treaties, law and practice of the United States relating to nationality there should be no distinction based on sex (H.J. 331).

On March 3, 1933, a bill removing the few remaining discriminations in the United States laws of nationality was unanimously passed by the Senate (*Congressional Record*, Mar. 3, 1933, p. 5524). On May 15, 1933, the same bill was reported favorably to the House of Representatives by the Committee on Immigration and Naturalization of the House of Representatives, and is now awaiting passage.[1]

The United States has always been proud of its leadership in dealing fairly with women and with all classes of its population and the only consistent position that can be taken now is the exertion of every effort to secure the adoption of the proposed Nationality treaty.

On behalf of the National Association of Women Lawyers

Olive Stott Gabriel, President
Ellen Spencer Mussey, Member of Advisory Council
Grace Hays Riley, Vice President for the District of Columbia
Rebekah S. Greathouse, Member of Executive Committee
Laura M. Berrien, Chairman of the Committee on International Relations[2]

[OF 567:T]

[1] H.R. 3673 was not passed until the next year. It was approved May 24, 1934 (48 *Stat.* 797).

[2] After leaving this memorial at the White House, the delegation called on Acting Secretary of State Phillips who told them that the matter was entirely in Hull's hands (Phillips to Hull, Dec. 14, 1933, *Foreign Relations, 1933,* IV, p. 187). Phillips, in a letter to the President of Dec. 19, 1933 (*ibid.,* pp. 197–198), noted that the United States nationality laws were being reviewed by a Cabinet committee and that until the committee reported and Congress acted the view of the State Department was that no general international agreement should be made. Roosevelt, however, decided to withdraw objections to the treaty and authorized Hull to sign it with the reservation that agreement was subject to Congressional action (Phillips to Hull, Dec. 19, 1933, *ibid.,* p. 201). Further explanation of the Administration's change in position on the treaty was made by Phillips (quoting the President) in a cable to Hull of Dec. 20, 1933 (*ibid.,* p. 203). The text of the convention as adopted Dec. 26, 1933, is printed *ibid.,* pp. 212–214. It was ratified by the United States on July 13, 1934, and proclaimed by the President Jan. 18, 1935 (*ibid.,* p. 214*n*).

# William Phillips, Acting Secretary of State, to Roosevelt

Washington, December 13, 1933

Dear Mr. President: I am sending you a copy of the note which I received late yesterday from the Belgian Ambassador, in which the statement is made that the Belgian Government finds itself unable to make the payment falling due on December 15th.[1] I also enclose a draft acknowledgment which, of course, in view of the length of the Belgian note, will be regarded as somewhat curt.[2] However, this reply merely follows the reply which we have already sent to Estonia,[3] which, as you will recollect, has already defaulted.

Faithfully yours,

William Phillips

May I have an indication of your views?

[*Notation*:AS] OK   FDR
[OF 212:TS]

---

[1] *Foreign Relations, 1933,* I, 851–852.
[2] This draft, in its entirety, reads: "In acknowledging the receipt of the note transmitted under your No. 4095 of December 12, 1933, I take note of Your Excellency's statement that the Belgian Government finds itself unable to make the payment falling due December 15, 1933, on account of the indebtedness of Belgium to the United States." The reply is printed in State Department, *Press Releases,* Dec. 16, 1933, p. 351.
[3] Dec. 9, 1933, printed *ibid.,* p. 352.

## William Phillips, Acting Secretary of State, to Roosevelt

Washington, December 14, 1933

Dear Mr. President: With reference to the exchange of telegrams with Ambassador Dodd which has already been brought to your attention,[1] I am enclosing a copy of another confidential telegram regarding Germany's position on disarmament which I have just received.[2]

It does not seem that this calls for any reply. I have sent a copy, in paraphrase, to Norman Davis in New York.

Faithfully yours,

William Phillips

[PSF:Germany:TS]

---

[1] Dodd to Phillips, Dec. 9, 10, and Phillips to Dodd, Dec. 11, 1933, *Foreign Relations, 1933,* I, 327–328, 330, 330–332.
[2] There are two of December 14 (*ibid.,* pp. 335–336, 336–342; the second enclosed a copy of Hitler's note to British Ambassador Sir Eric Clare Edmund Phipps of Dec. 11, 1933).

## Press Conference, Executive Offices of the White House, December 15, 1933, 4:05 P.M.

[*Excerpt*] The President: Well, what is the news?

Q: I wish to ask you a question about that State Department release you have on the desk.[1]

The President: Steve said you were going to. If you won't connect the White House up with this, I will give you the background on it. It is in that kind of diplomatic language that nobody can understand. It does not say directly one thing or the other but there are two sentences in here. The first is that "The French Government has never contemplated the unilateral violation of undertakings freely entered into," and that is saying that when the French Government has made a bilateral contract between itself and one other government, it has never violated it. Then it goes on into the next sentence and says, in perfectly foggy language, something to the effect that decisions were taken on both sides in 1931 and 1932, which modified conditions that formerly existed. Well, that is a unilateral statement on their part. I take it that certain things they did over there at Lausanne had changed conditions. Of course that does not bind the United States in any shape, manner or form. In other words, our position has not altered at all.

Q: Do you construe those dates, 1931 and 1932, as relating to the Hoover moratorium?

The President: It is just guess on my part, but I should say so, off-hand.

Q: Any suggestions in there of an agreement with President Hoover and Secretary Stimson with regard to what the countries might do if the powers omitted reparations?

The President: Not that we were able to find out.

Q: We were not able to find out anything from the communiqués the night Laval left town either.

The President: The only answer is that our position does not change a bit.

[President's Press Conferences:T]

---

[1] This press release consisted of an exchange of notes between Ambassador André de Laboulaye and Hull of Dec. 15, 1933, and Phillips and Laboulaye, of the same date; the notes are printed in the State Department's *Press Releases* under date of Dec. 16, 1933, pp. 356–357. Laboulaye announced his government's inability to meet the De-

cember 15 debt payment and referred to the resolution of the Chamber of Deputies of Dec. 13, 1932. He said his government had "never contemplated the unilateral violations of undertakings freely entered into." But economic changes since 1932 now justified new arrangements. Phillips' reply was a one-sentence acknowledgment.

## Breckinridge Long, Ambassador to Italy, to Roosevelt

Rome, Italy, December 15, 1933

Dear Frank: I am really sorry to trouble you so much with these letters. The subject matters however are so important I see no other course. I can't talk. You ought to know what I think. So—I have to write.

As seen from Rome, the attitude of Italy toward the current political situation in Europe, including disarmament and the League of Nations, is as follows:

Disarmament:

(a) Italy sincerely desires disarmament, is and has been ready to agree to drastic reductions provided other governments do likewise. She has even diminished appropriations for both army and navy;

(b) Italy views the German attitude toward armament in a practical way, believing it better to concede something in the way of controlled armament rather than see the alternative, a Germany stealthily but effectively armed;

(c) Italy has been engaged in efforts of reconciliation and mediation with the hope of effecting some semblance of disarmament now and holding out the hope of more satisfactory reductions in the next few years.

Accompanying the desire for disarmament is the question of the vitality of the League of Nations and its continuing existence. Italy approaches the League and the disarmament problem as a united objective. Without the League disarmament progress will cease. Supervision, coordination and unanimity will be lacking.

So the League becomes the most important of the two questions.

Italy views the League as:

(1) An agency under control of France and operated through alliances with Belgium, Poland and the governments of the Little Entente;

(2) An agency for the enforcement of the sanctions of the Versailles and other post-war treaties;

(3) A body composed of representatives of small countries who have no real power but whose positions on the governing organs of the League permit them to confound confusion and to become the objects of seductive gestures from other powers for the purpose of using their votes;

(4) A body overgrown with bureaucracy, enmeshed with detail and encumbered by committees;

(5) A body too costly for its usefulness;

(6) A body ineffectual in world situations because of its preoccupation with European politics—vide, especially Japan, Manchukuo, China.

With valid objections to the League, as it exists and as it is operated, Italy has determined to move for change in structure and change in objective—to make it more practical.

Failing, Italy will withdraw.

With Italy out—with Germany, Japan, Russia and the United States out—the League cannot survive even as a European influence. The withdrawal of Italy would, in all probability, be followed by those of Austria, Hungary, Turkey, possibly Bulgaria and Greece.

The consequence would be a return to the old system of alliances.

Visualizing the possibility, Italy is proceeding to lay the groundwork for possible alliances. She has maintained close relations with Germany. She has augmented cordial relations with Turkey, Russia and Greece and has been instrumental in assisting them to closer cooperation, between each other and with them individually and Bulgaria. She has strengthened her ties with Austria and Hungary, both politically and economically.

The result is that Italy is in a position to surround the Little Entente. Germany, Austria, Hungary and Italy on the west; Greece, Albania and Turkey on the south; Bulgaria and the Black Sea on the east; and Russia on the north, provided they were coordinating, would effectually surround the Little Entente and Poland and might render it more advisable for them, in circumstances short of war, to cooperate with the "Eastern Bloc"—east of the Rhine—rather than with France. In case of war they could be over-run.

The same alliance would cut France away from her Little Entente by drawing a straight line north and south—Germany, Austria, Italy.

In diplomatic moves it might leave France alone, to face world opinion if she blocked disarmament and reconstruction of the League.

In war it would cause France to face Germany and Italy with the strong probability of air assistance from Russia.

535

The maneuvers centering in Rome lead me unmistakably to the opinion that Italy is—

(1) Trying, sincerely, to reform the League for peaceful purposes;

(2) Laying the basis for extensive, encircling alliances for possible development in case France blocks either disarmament or reform of the League—and they are inseparable.

The position of England is enigmatic. Her position in case the League fails is unknown here but her power is discounted in Italian circles. They feel the British Empire is losing cohesion; that centrifugal forces are at work; that the growing independence of the dominions detracts from the centralized power of England; that England would probably take sides with the group opposed, fundamentally and in the long run, to excessive armament in Europe.

Of course Italy does not forget who controls the Mediterranean and her dependence on free ingress and egress. But her opinion of England as a military power on the continent is decreasing.

The German proposals: 300,000 men, adequate armor, no offensive weapons, no gas warfare or bombing planes, gradual allied reduction, inspection of factories, and non-aggression pacts with each contiguous neighbor—with sanctions—will appeal to Italy, England, Italy's "allies." France will oppose—and her allies.

It has the color of increasing armament instead of decreasing. It will take a lot of explaining to convince the man on the street it is "reduction."

Nevertheless—Germany has a *sine qua non.* Some armament is necessary to satisfy her national self-respect. The non-aggression pacts will lend substance to her professions of peaceful intent. And the program offers a practical solution of the impasse in Europe.

The English think a French government with Paul-Boncour, Daladier, and Herriot could hold the country in line for acceptance.

If she does accept. O. K.

If France and her allies continue opposition—the show is over.

Germany will arm anyway. There will be no supervision and no agreement of any kind. France cannot attack. It is too late. Germany is a tough nut today—and France knows it. Chemical warfare would be the result of invasion. It would be a difficult task indeed to penetrate Germany, even on the pretext of preventing armament.

So, while the German proposals may look like a program for armament, it is the best Europe can produce today. It seems the only practical step to get somewhere on the road to armament reduction during the next ten years.

And if it fails—disarmament and the League may both be memories of the past.

If you can lead the way out—consider it. But, the political penalties of failure, even of partial success, are severe—as we have learned.[1]

With kindest regards and best wishes, Sincerely and respectfully,

Breckinridge Long

[PSF:Italy:TS]

[1] An attached note, Roosevelt to Phillips, Jan. 3, 1934, reads: "Will you speak to me about this some day?" J. Pierrepont Moffat, chief of the Division of Western European Affairs in the State Department, was apparently called upon for comment; his note to Phillips of Jan. 6, 1934 (with the letter here printed), characterizes Long's analysis as interesting but "too much simplified." He thought that Long underestimated the ability of Great Britain to hold Italy in line and he doubted that Italy could hope to draw Germany and Russia together; the evidence appeared to indicate that Russia was "playing far more with the French bloc than with the German." Moffat concluded that if, however, Long's view was the correct one, then the prime lesson to be drawn from it was that any armaments agreement on an upward basis was a purely European adjustment in which the United States should not become involved, and that the traditional American policy of promoting disarmament but "disinteresting ourselves in rearmament" was the only sound one.

## Memorandum by Roosevelt on the Gold Standard

The White House, Dec. 16, 1933

*Private*

This memorandum[1] requires elucidation for the *historical record.*

During the last three weeks of November, a very definite drive was made by New York bankers and by political forces led by Ogden Mills and by pressure originating from British sources, to create definite sentiment in this country to have the gold content of the dollar definitely fixed by the United States. As a part of all this, assurance was given by the same sources that if the United States would go back on gold that Great Britain would follow.

My advices were (a) that England would not go back on gold simultaneously with us; (b) that England would like to have us go back on gold but would not follow herself, thereby keeping her favorable trading position absolutely liquid.

In order to place England on record, and solely for that purpose, and not because we intended or expected to go back on gold standard, George

Harrison made this unofficial interrogation of Montagu Norman. As we expected, it was turned down by the Bank of England and the British Treasury.[2]

FDR

[PSF:Treasury:TS]

[1] Harrison's memorandum of December 12, above.
[2] Also printed in *Personal Letters, 1928–1945,* I, 376.


# Roosevelt to William E. Dodd, Ambassador to Germany, Berlin

[Washington] December 19, 1933

My dear Dodd: I shall be very grateful if you will give the inclosed to Dr. Helmut Magers.[1]

It was very good of you to write the preface, and I appreciate it.

As ever yours,

[PPF 1043:CT]

[1] Below.


# Roosevelt to Dr. Helmut Magers, Berlin

[Washington] December 19, 1933

My dear Dr. Magers: I want to send you my thanks for the copy of your little book about me and the "New Deal."[1] Though, as you know, I went to school in Germany and could speak German with considerable fluency at one time, I am reading your book not only with great interest but because it will help my German.

Very sincerely yours,

[PPF 1043:CT]

[1] *Ein Revolutionär aus Common Sense* (Leipzig: R. Kittler Verlag, 1934). The book is in the Roosevelt Library. Dr. Magers' inscription on the flyleaf reads: "To the President of the United States, Franklin D. Roosevelt, in profound admiration of his conception

of a new economic order and with devotion for his personality. The author. Baden, Germany, November 9, 1933." The introduction is by Ambassador William E. Dodd, and is in German. Dodd said that Roosevelt and his program were of imperative interest to every informed European, and especially to every German who was aware of the tremendous problems confronting German leadership. He said that Roosevelt had a deep interest in European questions and understood clearly that a great country could not live in isolation and that any progress in civilization had to be based on vastly greater cooperation and general peace.

## Roosevelt to Mrs. Roosevelt

Washington, December 19, 1933

Memo for Mrs. Roosevelt: Tell her in confidence that politically speaking and judging by the present time, it would be unwise to do anything about the World Court.[1]

F.D.R.

[OF 202:T]

[1] Esther Lape had written to Mrs. Roosevelt on Dec. 10, 1933, to ask her help in arranging an interview for her and Curtis Bok with the President to urge American adherence to the World Court. She said ratification of the three pending World Court treaties might have a stabilizing influence internationally out of all proportion to the issue itself. (A copy of Miss Lape's letter is with the note here printed.)

## Clark Howell, Publisher, The Atlanta *Constitution,* to Roosevelt

Atlanta, Ga., December 19, 1933

Dear Mr. President: You will recall my conversation with you regarding Japan, both at Warm Springs the week before you left there and on the train trip with you to Atlanta.

As I explained to you my interest in the situation arose solely out of the fact that newspaper friends of mine in Japan, evidently impressed with *The Constitution's* criticisms of the Stimson policy as regards Manchoukuo had written me along the line of my talks with you, asking me to take up with you the matter of how you would receive an overture suggesting a non-aggression understanding, the effect of which would be to counteract the hostile propaganda being pushed by extremists of both countries.

539

I felt sure that should such an overture be made you would receive it in the spirit in which it was sent.

I am informed now by one of these newspaper friends that such an overture is contemplated, but they want to be certain that it would not be sidetracked if sent.

It seems that John Bassett Moore has been quoted somewhere as saying that the only thing for this country to do is to recognize Manchoukuo, but he is reported to have said that Stimson holds that you made a commitment to him last March that the administration would make no change in the policy of non-recognition regarding Manchoukuo.

It appears that this observation whether true or not, is still fresh in the memory of the Japanese foreign office.

I do not believe you made any such committal. In my opinion Stimson made an awful bungle of the whole Manchoukuo affair and placed our country in an entirely untenable position, largely as the result of the pro-Chinese and anti-Japanese attitude of our Far Eastern department as then constituted.

The new Japanese ambassador, Saito, is said to be a splendid man and he is very fond of this country. He is particularly anxious that all possible cause of friction between the two countries be removed and is willing to do anything he can to that end.

I believe this to be your attitude.

You will note that recently the Hearst papers have started again their anti-Japanese propaganda with a half page cartoon showing Japan reaching her arms across the sea to grasp the Philippines. The talk of such extremists on both sides fans the flame of discontent.

If there is any country in the world that should be friendly to the United States it is Japan. I have every reason to believe that the government of that country is willing to go the limit toward reaching a complete understanding that will perpetuate the friendly relations between the two countries, and a step of this kind would contribute wonderfully to the peace of the world.

That the Manchoukuo situation is an accomplished fact there can be no doubt, but even if we should not be in a position now to formally recognize that government, there is no reason why we should not send to Manchoukuo a commissioner to represent this country, which would not be recognition de facto.

This was done in substance in Korea when the United States was the first country to recognize the Japanese position there by withdrawing our legation from Korea.

You understand of course that what I have said on this subject has been of my own accord, and without in the slightest degree committing you further than to say that I believed you would welcome such an overture as that above suggested.

I do not know how far you would be willing to go in a letter to me as bearing upon the situation, but if you could send to me a message that will have the effect of easing the Japanese mind on the point that any overture that may be made by that government would not be favorably received, I think I can assure you that such an overture will reach you.

There never was a more propitious time than now for such a step. With best wishes for a Merry Christmas for you and yours, I am

Sincerely yours,

Clark Howell

[*Notation*:A:FDR] Take up with Philips[1]
[PPF 604:TS]

---

[1] See Hornbeck to Phillips, Jan. 2, 1934, below.

## Roosevelt to Heads of Departments and Independent Agencies

[Washington] December 20, 1933

To the Heads of the Executive Departments and Independent Establishments of the Government: I have appointed George N. Peek as the Chairman of a committee to make tentative recommendations with respect to our foreign trade. Will you please make available to Mr. Peek or any representative he may designate such information as he requests relating thereto.[1]

[OF 971:T]

---

[1] This letter was drafted by Peek who sent it to Roosevelt in a note of Dec. 15, 1933 (OF 971). Peek submitted a report on Dec. 30, 1933, not found in the Roosevelt papers but printed in part in Peek's book, *Why Quit Our Own*, (New York: Van Nostrand, 1936), pp. 181–183. In this report he recommended the appointment of a foreign trade administrator, responsible only to the President, whose main duty would be to make effective the "non-political and non-diplomatic" aspects of foreign trade policy. He also recommended a system of bookkeeping for foreign trade transactions (to determine whether

there was a "balance" of exchange between the United States and each country with which it exchanged goods and services) so that the President would have the facts in bargaining on tariff rates, "or otherwise protecting the agricultural and industrial interests" of the country. Peek said his report was completely disregarded (*ibid.*, p. 183). See Roosevelt to Peek, March 23, 1934, below.

## William Phillips, Acting Secretary of State, to Roosevelt

Washington, December 21, 1933

Dear Mr. President: The Treasury Department has been studying the proposed new schedule of payments with respect to the Finnish debt to the United States based on your penciled memorandum attached hereto.

The Treasury has taken as a basis the Italian debt settlement which required only arbitrary payments of $5,000,000 principal per annum for the first five years, interest payments beginning in the sixth year at $\frac{1}{8}\%$, increasing to $\frac{1}{4}\%$ in the 16th year.

As you will note, the Treasury table carries the principal payments which have actually been made by Finland. It charges no interest during the first five years, and $\frac{1}{8}\%$ interest thereafter. Subtracting the excess interest actually paid over what would have been paid on this basis leaves a new principal amount of $5,854,903.25. The Treasury figures that this amount, if paid in 30 years without interest, would require equal annual payments of $195,163.44; if in 40 years at 1% interest, $178,313.77 per annum; if in 50 years at $1\frac{1}{2}\%$ interest, $167,285.30 per annum.

I should be very grateful if you would let me know whether we are proceeding along lines which have your general approval.

Faithfully yours,

William Phillips

[OF 212:TS]

## [*Enclosure*] Memorandum by Roosevelt on the Finnish Debt

Finland

| | |
|---|---:|
| Original loan . . . . . . . . . . . . . . . . . . . . . . . . . . . . . . . . . . | 8,000,000 |
| Payments to date | |
|     Principal . . . . . . . . . . . . . . . . . . . . . . . . . . . . . . . . . | 1,000,000 |
|     Interest . . . . . . . . . . . . . . . . . . . . . . . . . . . . . . . . . . | 1,000,000 |
| New plan | |
|     Orig loan . . . . . . . . . . . . . . . . . . . . . . . . . . . . . . . . | 8,000,000 |
|     Deduct prin. paid . . . . . . . . . . . . . . . . . . . . . . . . . . | 1,000,000 |
|     Balance due on orig loan . . . . . . . . . . . . . . . . . . . . . . . | 7,000,000 |

Deduct

Formula. Int paid             1,000,000

If Ital plan followed $= \frac{1}{4}\% = $ 250,000

750,000

| | |
|---|---:|
| Excess Int over lowest Ital plan . . . . . . . . . . . . . . . . . . | 750,000 |
| Due . . . . . . . . . . . . . . . . . . . . . . . . . . . . . . . . . . . . . . . . | 6,250,000 |

If paid in 30 years    no int.
If paid in 40 years    1%
If paid in 50 years    $1\frac{1}{2}\%$[1]

[OF 212:A:FDR]

[1] Answered below.

## Roosevelt to William Phillips, Acting Secretary of State

[Washington] December 22, 1933

Memorandum from the President for the Acting Secretary of State: These Treasury Department figures carry out my thought precisely.[1] Do you think that the lesser annual payments on the forty-year plan and the still smaller payments on the fifty-year plan are counterbalanced by the reduction in the total amount to be paid under the five-year plan? In other words,

| | |
|---|---:|
| 30 years—no interest—equals | $5,854,903 |
| 40 years—1% interest—equals | 7,132,550 |
| 50 years—$1\frac{1}{2}\%$ interest—equals | 8,364,265 |

In your judgment, if you were representing Finland, would you recommend the thirty-year-no-interest-plan even though this involves larger annual payments? I want the Finnish Government, of course, to accept the thirty-year plan.

If you think this will attract them and that they will go through with it, I take it the next step will be a tentative agreement, and you can tell them that I would submit such an agreement to the Congress for approval.

[OF 212:CT]

[1] Tables showing the Finnish debt computed according to the terms of the Italian settlement, sent to Roosevelt by Acheson Nov. 14, 1933 (OF 212), and referred to in Phillips' letter above. The next reference to the Finnish debt is found in Roosevelt's press conference of Feb. 16, 1934, below.

## William Phillips, Acting Secretary of State, to Roosevelt

Washington, December 22, 1933

My dear Mr. President: The Executive Committee on Commercial Policy, under the chairmanship of Francis B. Sayre, has completed a report on commercial policy, which I transmit herewith with the hope that you will find an opportunity to read it. The report represents the unanimous viewpoint of the representatives of the various departments concerned. Secretary Wallace and Mr. Peek have been sitting with the Committee during the last few meetings and have given their approval to the conclusions reached.

Secretaries Wallace and Roper and Mr. Sayre and I would be deeply grateful if, at your convenience, you could set a time to discuss the matters submitted in the report because it is essential for all of us to have your instruction with respect to these all important matters.

Faithfully yours,

William Phillips

[OF 614-A:TS]

## [*Enclosure*] Report of Committee on Commercial Policy

[Washington] December 22, 1933

Part I. Summary of Conclusion: Our foreign trade has decreased about two-thirds in value from its peak and faces trade barriers which are unprecedented and still rising. This means on the one hand that the solution of the problems facing various fields of economic life without some recovery of export trade is difficult to foresee; while on the other hand it means that our total balance of payments with the rest of the world is only being settled at a very low level of interchange involving the loss of a great part of American foreign investment.

Thus a broad reconsideration of our commercial policy is compelled.

(1) It is essential and urgent that there be framed and applied a coherent commercial policy. This policy should be formulated in a governing plan which should control:

(a) The exercise of all powers affecting import and export trade now in the hands of the Executive (the A.A.A., N.R.A., R.F.C., Tariff Commission, and Treasury powers);

(b) The direction of treaty negotiations;

(c) All special international trade financing and/or trade exchanges in which the Government might engage, or in which it might have an interest.

The application of such a plan would appear to be the only alternative to confused action by many departments and the only effective means of achieving a satisfactory integration between the different branches of our domestic economic life and between the whole of our domestic economic life and that of other countries.

The formulation of this policy is not a problem in blacks and whites; it is not a matter of deciding between "nationalist" and "internationalist" policies; it is an intricate task of judging how best a sound domestic situation may be attained and retained by a proper marking off and fitting together of the field of American economic activity and the field of foreign economic activity.

The Committee presents below a summary outline of the main principles which it believes would form a satisfactory guiding policy.

(2) It is agreed that a satisfactory comprehensive commercial policy, based on national needs and advantages, can best and most expeditiously be carried out if Congress confers a certain measure of authority on the Executive to modify existing tariff rates upward and downward and to inaugurate as far as it may be wise and necessary other forms of trade terms and trade arrangements.

(3) It is to be expected that the Executive would proceed only gradually with the exercise of the power conferred upon him, adjusting its actions to circumstances in this country and abroad and exploring particularly the possibility of reciprocal agreements with other governments.

(4) It follows that steps should immediately be taken to frame a new commercial policy bill to be introduced into Congress. This bill might fall into three parts:

(a) The general introductory preamble would set forth the general principles of the commercial policy scheme which it is intended to develop (see below) and then enumerate the findings of fact on which the Executive would proceed to exercise its power.

(b) It would provide in its main substantive provisions for a grant to the Executive of the power necessary to carry out this policy to be used when and as the Executive deems it advisable with reference to the state of facts enumerated, among which would be of leading importance the securing of adequate concessions in connection with reciprocal negotiations with other countries (the Committee believes that the grant permitting Executive action should be drawn as broadly as possible).

(c) It should provide for the designation of the necessary governmental agency or agencies to furnish the factual material, to analyze and classify the same in reference to a policy to be followed, and to advise on the application of this policy; in connection herewith the reorganization of the Tariff Commission should be considered.

Whether or not the bill should provide that action by the Executive should become effective only after having been laid before Congress for a specified period is a question which the Committee deems the President alone is in a position to decide.

It will be noted after study of the policy proposed below that if the Executive were given the power to execute that policy there will be no further need of Section 336 of the present Tariff Act; and indeed the principle of that Section might run in contradiction to the policy outlined.

(5) It seems feasible to the Committee to continue to go forward with the actual treaty negotiations in which the American Government is engaged at the present moment. But it is clear that it will be difficult if not impossible to make the process of reciprocal treaty arrangement important in the sense of opening up a considerable volume of trade until and unless some coherent commercial policy is devised and applied.

(6) The question of whether this policy would require a revision or denunciation of some or all of our existing commercial treaties can be left to later determination . . .[1]

[OF 614-A:T]

[1] This "Summary of Conclusions" is the first part of the report; the remainder amounts to over 5,000 words. See Sayre to Roosevelt, Dec. 27, 1933, below.

## Richard J. Walsh, Editor of *Asia*, to Stephen T. Early, Assistant Secretary to the President

New York, N.Y., December 22, 1933

Dear Mr. Early: You may not identify me as the president of the John Day Company. I am now dividing my time between that company and the editorship of *Asia*.

First of all, I want to add my thanks to those of Mr. Rimington[1] for the great courtesy which you and everybody else there showed to him in his negotiations with the President for the new book. And we are delighted that you and the President like my suggestion for the title, *On Our Way*.[2]

Now a bit of *Asia* business:

I have just been looking at an article which the President wrote for *Asia* Magazine and which was published in July 1923, under the title "Shall We Trust Japan?" It has occurred to me that it would be both useful and interesting to reprint this article in our April issue. Of course it should not be done without making very emphatic display, both at the top of the article and on the contents page, of the fact that it is a reprint of an article written ten years ago. Nor should a word be changed. I suppose it is ordinarily within our rights to reprint anything that has appeared in our columns. But obviously in this case we should not do so without the President's consent. Accordingly I am applying for that consent. I will undertake if you wish to submit proofs showing exactly how the article would be set up, with indication that it is a reprint.

I am enclosing photostatic copies of the pages from the July 1923 issue on which the article appeared.[3]

With all best wishes for a Merry Christmas.

Sincerely yours,

Richard J. Walsh

[OF 197-A:TS]

[1] Critchell Rimington, associate editor of the John Day Company.

[2] Published in April 1934.

[3] In this long article Roosevelt traced the growth of the mutual apprehension and hostility of the American and Japanese peoples. He pointed out that naval specialists had long agreed that in the event of a war the Philippines could not be held by the United States nor could our West Coast be threatened by the Japanese. A war would be profitless to both. The Japanese had faithfully carried out their obligations under the Washington Naval Agreement but our government had given the American people totally inadequate information on these vitally important matters, and a magnificent

opportunity to improve relations had been let slip. He concluded: "If, instead of looking for causes of offense, we in all good faith confidently expect from Japan cooperation in world upbuilding, we shall go far toward insuring peace."

The editorial note introducing the article begins: "That an Assistant Secretary of the Navy, one of whose chief duties during a large part of his term of office was to prepare to fight Japan, can now write as Mr. Roosevelt does in this plea for a pacific attitude on the part of the United States toward Japan, must bring a new conviction of the possibilities for a permanent and increasing strong bond of friendship." Early replied Dec. 28, 1933 (OF 197-A), that there was no objection to republication of the article provided that Walsh made it clear that it dealt with "conditions prevailing at that time, which conditions differ substantially from those now prevailing"; also, that republication was made on Walsh's own authority, "without approval of the President."

The article appeared in the March 1934 issue of *Asia*, pp. 170–175. The editorial note introducing the article said, in part: "We venture to reprint it, on our own responsibility, in view of the special interest at this time in the forthcoming naval conference. It is important, however, to bear in mind that the article dealt with the conditions in 1923, which differ substantially from those which now prevail."

## William E. Dodd, Ambassador to Germany, to Roosevelt

[Berlin] December 23, 1933

Dear Mr. President: Perhaps you won't object to a belated New Year's greeting from this centre of arbitrary government. You must know you have our ardent good wishes. You have already done a great work; but it's going to take more than four years to apply your system—and as usual leadership is seriously handicapped, perhaps necessarily on the whole, by fixed elections. My prophesy is that you will have no difficulty on that score.

If you do not object I hope you will recaste State Department groupings a little. There are cliques who jeopardize the service by favoring rich personal friends and kinsfolk. We are suffering from such a ruling here now. I would like to know you had given a mandate to the Secretary to stop favoritisms and if necessary re-assign persons who make trouble. In my judgment new recruits should not be taken in upon any but bases of merit; perhaps new folks kept off till the present service people can be arranged according to merit; and after this let some of the higher posts go to very best service men, with new blood at critical centres. This might over-come present social stunt nuisance. I am not opposed to normal social contacts, but against making ourselves rediculous imitating Louis XIV. I believe budget might be reduced by one-fourth and service improved.

As to present status of German-French armament negotiations, I want to say: I do not fall for English propositions without consideration. They made unwise commitments in Far East from which leaders—at least the Ambassador here—wish to escape. The French are standing too stubbornly against all concessions to Germany—especially Herriot. Strangely the German Foreign Secretary expresses great concern over danger of Japanese attack upon Russia.[1]

About January 7 to 10 English will be making tentative proposition to you.[2] My analysis is that if you could get English and French together and put through present ten year pact tied on to similar pact for Far East, you might do what our great friend, Wilson, failed to do: actually start world on road to peaceful negotiations in place of old road to war. You can perhaps bring Borah, Johnson and McAdoo to agree if they understand imminence of war in Far East.

If you can not get actual agreements from England and France, Italy, Germany, Poland and Russia, autocratic powers, will unite on French-Balkan problems and leave Far East to us alone. Change of German attitude as to Poland and Russia is obvious here. If this sort of a pact is agreed to, it won't be peaceful very long. Perhaps I am wrong; but such is my mature judgment—nor am I either "German" or "British."

Yours Sincerely,

William E. Dodd

[PSF:Germany:AS]

[1] Cf. Dodd to Phillips, Dec. 19 and 22, 1933, in *Foreign Relations, 1933,* I, 347–348, 348–349.

[2] January 10 was the date of the first 1934 meeting of the British Cabinet, "when important decisions regarding disarmament policy" had to be made (Atherton to Phillips, Jan. 2, 1934, *ibid., 1934,* I, 1–4). Dodd presumably refers to this meeting but the "tentative proposition" is not further explained.

## Norman H. Davis, Chairman, United States Delegation, Disarmament Conference, to Roosevelt

New York, December 26, 1933

My dear Mr. President: With reference to our recent telephone conversation I have endeavored to give a brief analysis of the disarmament situation and I have also added to this, for your consideration, something which I think it might be useful for you to say.

It occurs to me that in connection with any statement on disarmament it might be well for you to say something about the naval building program which has been so misunderstood in certain quarters. I would, therefore, suggest for your consideration that you say something to the following effect:

Until there is a general disarmament agreement or until there is a modification in the existing Treaty for Naval Limitation I have deemed it wise to keep up our naval strength, but well within the limits of the Treaty. We shall, nevertheless, be glad to consider with the naval powers still further reductions in the present naval limitations.

I now plan to get to Washington on next Thursday morning and hope to see you some time during the day.[1]

With warm regards, I am, Faithfully yours,

Norman H. Davis

[OF 29:TS]

[1] No indication that Davis saw Roosevelt on Thursday (December 28) has been found; however, appointments were not always noted in the appointments list.


## [*Enclosure*] Memorandum by Norman H. Davis to Roosevelt on Disarmament

At the General Disarmament Conference in Geneva we have played an active role and have endeavored in every proper way to achieve success. Progress has been slow for, although all countries have recognized the menace to international peace and the drain on world economy, of excessive armaments, they have hesitated to reduce them because of fear. Anything that lessens the danger of attack or that reduces the power of offense in case of attack, and correspondingly strengthens the power of defense, serves to diminish this sense of fear and insecurity. With this in mind, I telegraphed on May 16th to the Chiefs of State of all nations suggesting an agreement to abolish all weapons of peculiarly offensive power and also a general pact whereby, subject to treaty rights and limitations, no nation should move its armed forces across its own frontiers. With these two propositions I still hold.

On October 14th Germany withdrew from the Disarmament Conference and soon thereafter from the League of Nations. Since then the discussions have centered in two fields. In the one, which is peculiarly European in scope and involves considerations of a primarily European character, we are not participants. In the other, however, which is universal in aspect and concerns measures of disarmament, we have constantly taken part and shall continue to exert our full effort towards ultimate success.

While the effort to secure agreement for a general reduction and limitation in armaments has received what many regard as a serious set-back, it may well be that the recent crisis in the disarmament negotiations may prove to be a stepping stone to a later agreement. It forces a choice between two courses, one leading to another race in armaments and war, the other to a limitation in armaments and peace. Surely the disastrous experience of the last War, from which the world has not yet recovered, should have a determining effect in preventing such a recurrence.

While some governments may still be pursuing policies which do not promote peace, and while manufacturers of armaments in certain countries may be fomenting international discord and strife, from which they expect to profit, the peoples of the world are becoming more and more averse to war and more than ever desirous of peace. The peoples, who so earnestly desire peace, know instinctively that rivalry in armaments is a sure road to war. They also know that if the states of the world should recognize by Covenant that armaments are of mutual concern and are no longer based alone upon autonomous decisions, mutual suspicion will be diminished and good neighborliness will be increased. I am persuaded that public opinion will continue to press governments towards this happy issue.

[OF 29:T]


# William Phillips, Acting Secretary of State, to Roosevelt

Washington, December 26, 1933

*Confidential*

Dear Mr. President: In case this confidential telegram from Bullitt has not come to your personal attention, I venture to send you an additional copy. May I point out the marked passage on page two in which he refers to a joint attack by Poland and Germany acting in concert with Japan, which is something so new and unexpected that I thought it worth while to make sure that you had noted it. The last part of the telegram dealing with personnel matters is being taken care of in accordance with Bullitt's request.[1]

Faithfully yours,

William Phillips

[PSF:Russia:TS]

[1] The telegram from Bullitt, Dec. 24, 1933, is printed in *Foreign Relations: The Soviet Union, 1933–1939*, pp. 53–54. He reported that on December 21 Litvinov had asked him to tell the President that his government was "under great pressure" from France to join the League of Nations; he wanted to know if the United States would have any objection. Litvinov had explained this reversal in Soviet policy by saying that France had insisted on League membership by the Soviet Union in return for a mutual defense pact against Germany and Japan. The marked passage stated that Litvinov did not fear an immediate attack by either Poland or Germany but in case the expected war with Japan lasted two years "he anticipated a joint attack by Poland and Germany, acting in concert with Japan." On the Soviet expectation of war with Japan, see also Bullitt's dispatch to Phillips, Jan. 4, 1934, *ibid.*, pp. 55–62.

# Leo S. Rowe, Director General, Pan American Union, to Roosevelt

Montevideo, 26 of December 1933

My dear Mr. President: The Conference comes to a close this afternoon with a real measure of accomplishment to its credit. The outstanding characteristic of the Conference has been the far reaching influence of your declaration of Latin American policy and the personal influence of Secretary Hull, who, from the first session gained the good will, the confidence and the cooperation of all the delegations. The result has been that in addition to its specific achievements, the general atmosphere of the Conference has been more friendly toward the United States than at any time since the assembling of the First Conference at Washington.[1] In sending Secretary Hull as Chairman of the Delegation of the United States you did a great service to the cause of Pan Americanism.

I am planning to remain here until the end of the week and will then visit Argentina, Chile and Peru, reporting to you as soon as I reach Washington in February.

I beg to remain, my dear Mr. President

Sincerely yours

L. S. Rowe

[OF 480:AS]

[1] Hull commented on this repeatedly after his return; see *Addresses and Statements by Cordell Hull,* pp. 83–103, particularly his speech before the National Press Club of Feb. 10, 1934, pp. 90–103.

## John Cudahy, Ambassador to Poland, to Roosevelt

Warsaw, Poland, December 27, 1933

My dear Mr. President: I am taking this first opportunity of writing you direct, as you requested, after conferring with my colleagues at our diplomatic missions in Bucharest, Belgrade, Budapest, Vienna, Prague, Berlin, and Paris.

I started on my tour of these capitals with a prejudice that Germany was engaged in large-scale war preparations threatening the peace of Europe. This prejudice was entirely dissipated after my visit to that country, my conferences with the Ambassador at Berlin, members of his Staff, and our Military Attaché. There is a unity in Germany, an intense feeling of national solidarity and patriotic buoyancy, which strikes one almost immediately. And the allegiance to Hitler borders on fanaticism. But the reports of training large bodies of troops for war, and assembling huge supplies of war materials are, in my opinion, entirely baseless.

These reports have been founded on scraps of information, such as the importation of copper, manganese, zinc, and nickel during the past six to eight months in excess of Germany's industrial needs. Also the production of airplanes in greater proportion than produced by the factories of England. But as our Military Attaché has so sensibly pointed out there is no marked evidence of an increase in muskets and small arm ammunition, nor of any accumulation of large projectiles and armament which would be impossible of concealment. This does not gainsay the fact that the country is being organized on a military basis. Besides the authorized regular army—the Stahlhelm of 100,000—there are marching clubs—The Brown Shirts (Sturm-Abteilung), The Black Shirts (Schutz Staffel) and the Arbeitsdienst—all told nearly 2,000,000 men in uniform. Also the drilling and discipline of youth is proceeding rapidly under the Reich's Jugend Führung. By January 1, 1934, half the contingent of young men born in 1914 will be inducted in the labor service.

This appears menacing unless one is on the ground to realize that there is nothing essentially belligerent or alarming about these activities. They are really only a manifestation of Germany, affording an outlet for the peculiar social need of a country which loves display and pageantry. Half of the Brown Shirts are unemployed and the organization provides relief and cheap meals for the needy members. These marching clubs are essentially social. The German feels important and distinguished in a uniform and what has been taken for a blatant display of militarism is merely an expression of the unique German gregarious instinct, accountable on the same grounds that our Elks, Eagles, Woodmen, etc., are accountable.

The present leaders of the government are well aware of the impotent military position of the country, and how success against France enforced by Poland and The Little Entente would be unthinkable.

This attitude is not inconsistent with Hitler's ambition to achieve by political methods the Anschluss with Austria. The Anschluss is not a dead issue. The present government of Austria is in the precarious hands of a minority dictator. Probably 40 per cent of the electorate is Nazi and the Social Democrats control 25 per cent of the remaining votes, giving the Christian Democrats, the Party of Dollfuss, a striking minority. Upon the death or removal of Dollfuss, Austria might well go Nazi and fall under the domination of Hitler's strange hypnotic leadership. But instead of being an unsettling influence throughout Europe this should clarify the alignment against Germany by bringing Italy definitely on the side of the nations opposed to further relaxation of the Versailles Treaty in favor of Germany. Dismembered Austria has a population of only 6 million and no capital resources for war. The Anschluss should weaken rather than strengthen Germany's position in Europe.

The Little Entente—Rumania, Yugoslavia, and Czechoslovakia—with a combined standing army of nearly 1 million men, would unquestionably side with France in the case of hostilities with Germany; although how aggressively would likely depend upon their prospects for material benefits. Poland, regarding Germany as a constant menace to the territory she acquired by the Versailles Treaty, would likely take an aggressive part in case of such a war.

The most disturbing element at the present time is France, which regards the growing power and unity of Germany with mounting fear and distrust. It is France which has inspired in most part this propaganda of German military preparation.

Concretely, the only constructive step to allay this fear and control this agitation is for all the leading powers to concentrate on the formation of a Board of Arms Control to function under the jurisdiction of the League of Nations. Such a Board, dominated by impartial, judicial nations, such as Great Britain, the United States, Switzerland, and the Netherlands, might be a body of effective and far-reaching influence. At least it should be given a trial. It should be far more effective than any international court, for it would go upon the theory of preventing preparation for war, instead of attempting to intervene when hostile countries fully ready are determined upon force.

There are, Mr. President, other comments I have in mind as a result of my observations and discussions with my colleagues, but I fear already the length of this memorandum has trespassed upon your patience. If, in your opinion, what I have said here is of any weight or moment, I shall write further at a later time.[1]

I am, Mr. President, with profound respect and esteem, Obediently yours,

John Cudahy

[PPF 1193:TS]

[1] Answered Jan. 8, 1934 (*Personal Letters, 1928–1945*, I, 383). Roosevelt said he hoped Cudahy was right in his estimate of the German war preparations. "The chief problem is, of course, whether the marching of the general spirit of things is heading consciously or sub-consciously toward an idea of extension of boundaries."

# Francis B. Sayre, Assistant Secretary of State, to Roosevelt

Washington, December 27, 1933

My dear Mr. President: On October 5, 1933, the Argentine Ambassador presented to the State Department a memorandum containing a list of the concessions which the Argentine Government desires in the commercial agreement to be negotiated between the United States and Argentine governments.[1] Argentina has asked tariff reductions on a number of agricultural products the most important of which are flaxseed, corn, casein, canned beef, turkeys, cattle hides, wool and grapes. Our Inter-Departmental Advisory Board on Reciprocal Treaties, in cooperation with the Department of Agriculture and other interested Departments, has been giving intensive study to the Argentine requests as a result of which the enclosed draft reply to the Argentine Government has been prepared.[2] This reply has the general approval of the representatives of the various Departments serving on the Inter-Departmental Board. It is agreed that substantial reductions could be offered on hides and skins, casein, coarse wool, and grapes, and moderate reductions on canned beef and turkeys, without serious injury to domestic producers.

The negotiation of this treaty presents a fundamental problem of policy, however, which arises in more or less acute form in most of the reciprocal bargaining treaties, i.e. whether our attempt shall be to negotiate a series of real exchanges embodying concessions of substantial value or a series of shadow treaties without real substance.

The Argentine treaty presents this question in an aggravated form inasmuch as Argentina competes in many of its products with the United States.

The problem is presented concretely in the case of flax. Of the Argentine requests, a lowered tariff on flaxseed is the one of largest if not of vital importance to the Argentine Government. The present American duty on flaxseed is sixty-five cents per bushel and the Argentine Government has requested that the duty should be reduced to twenty cents per bushel, the rate which was in effect under the 1913 Tariff Act. In the United States, flaxseed accounts for less than one-half of one per cent of the total farm income. Even in North Dakota, the state in which flax is of the greatest relative importance, flaxseed accounts on the average for only about six and one-half per cent of the gross farm income. On the other hand, flaxseed is a major crop in Argentina and constitutes one of the principal exports of that country. From the purely economic viewpoint it would seem wise to grant to the Argentine Government a moderate reduction in flaxseed in order to purchase therewith corresponding concessions from the Argentine Government covering the exportation of American goods such, for instance, as fresh and preserved fruits. But from the purely political standpoint, whether or not it is wise to grant a concession on flaxseed is open to question. Would such a concession kill the ratification of the treaty? In the proposed draft a reduction on flaxseed from sixty-five cents to fifty cents is proposed provided, however, that the total importation of flaxseed into the United

States from all sources during any year should not exceed fourteen million bushels. Whether or not the United States should grant a concession on flaxseed, which is the vital thing which Argentina desires, is a question of underlying policy which you yourself will doubtless wish to decide.

Similar questions in less aggravated form arise in connection with the other requests of the Argentine Government. In the enclosed draft reply a compromise has been reached by the Inter-Departmental Committee which seeks to meet the Argentine requests with concessions which are real but which are not radical nor unduly injurious to American producers. In all cases the concessions proposed seem advisable economically. The real question is as to political expediency.

I have discussed this matter at some length with the Secretary of Agriculture. He feels that the decision involves so important a question of policy that he requested to be present when the matter is discussed. I should greatly welcome an opportunity for the Secretary of Agriculture, the Under Secretary of State and myself to discuss this matter with you before presenting our draft reply to the Argentine Government.[3]

Faithfully yours,

Francis B. Sayre[4]

[OF 366:TS]

[1] A long memorandum on the Argentine request, prepared in the Treaty Division of the State Department, is present.

[2] Not present.

[3] This letter was sent to Roosevelt by Phillips in a note of Dec. 27, 1933 (OF 20); Phillips also indicated that it was important for him and Sayre to know the President's views "in respect to the broad lines of policies involved, as well as on the more particular items involved in the negotiations with the Argentine."

[4] This document is representative of many in the Roosevelt papers having to do with tariff matters. The President's particular powers in tariff negotiation lay in the provision of the Tariff Act of 1930 (46 *Stat.* 701) that authorized him, under certain circumstances, to raise or lower a duty as much as 50 per cent of the statutory rate. This power might be exercised if it should be found that existing duties did not equalize the costs of production of the domestic article over the foreign import. The President first requested the Tariff Commission to investigate and make a report; if a rise (or, less likely, a reduction) was recommended, this was done by proclamation. This authority was continued by the Reciprocal Trade Agreements Act of 1934 (48 *Stat.* 943), enacted as an amendment to the 1930 act.

The authority of the President was greatly enlarged by the provision of the National Industrial Recovery Act of June 16, 1933, that permitted him, under certain conditions, to limit or bar altogether importation of articles the introduction of which was endangering the maintenance of a code (48 *Stat.* 196–197). This authority ended with the invalidation of the NIRA act on May 27, 1935.

Aside from tariff matters involving large issues of foreign policy such as would normally be submitted by our officials abroad, or by the State Department, or by the Congress, the President daily received communications from exporters, manufacturers, industrialists, and their organizations protesting alleged inequities in import duties and asking that investigations be made. The subjects of the correspondence covered virtually the entire import list, from avocados and asbestos to wool and zinc. The issues presented ranged from the difficulties of small manufacturers, who urged higher duties, and the problems of importers, who wanted lower tariffs, to the problems of whole regions, the latter involving domestic political issues as well as international difficulties. (An example is the outcry from Washington and Oregon following the lumber importation agreement with Canada in November of 1934.) Complaints or inquiries were referred by the White House to either the Tariff Commission or to the State Department or other department for reply, or the President replied on the basis of a draft prepared by the appropriate agency. Where the Tariff Commission made a formal inquiry, a report was sent to the President who sent it to the State Department for recommendation. The President then noted his approval or disapproval of the State Department recommendation (see Hull to Roosevelt, May 19, 1934, OF 61-R; and Jan. 11, 1935, OF 61-S). After November 1933 these matters were handled in the State Department by the Executive Committee on Commercial Policy. Sometimes the State Department asked the President to withhold action on a Tariff Commission recommendation until pending negotiations were completed. Sometimes also, the State Department delayed action on a Tariff Commission recommendation "with a view to the use of the reduction in . . . duty in bargaining with other governments under the program of reciprocal trade agreements" (Hull to Roosevelt, Dec. 7, 1934, OF 61-A).

## Speech by Roosevelt at the Woodrow Wilson Foundation Dinner, Mayflower Hotel, Washington, December 28, 1933

Mr. Morris, Mrs. Wilson, friends of Woodrow Wilson here in Washington and throughout the land:[1] Today, on the birthday of President Wilson, I received a very delightful thing, a little memorandum sent to me by Woodrow Wilson's old secretary, Tom Brahany. The memorandum is dated August, 1919, and it is from the President's secretary and it reads, "For the President: Acting Secretary of the Navy Roosevelt would like to see the President on some urgent matters." And below that there is a pencilled memorandum, "Friday, 15, at 2.30 at the House." Evidently I was told about Friday the 15th at 2.30 and this young Assistant Secretary of the Navy had an engagement in Newport on that date. So, below that again, in typewriting, are these words: "Mr. Roosevelt is leaving tomorrow night for Newport on an inspection trip. He hopes that the President can give him two minutes tomorrow, Thursday, August 14." Then, in pencil again, in the President's handwriting, he struck out the words, "Friday the 15th," and substituted the words, "Thursday, the 14th, at 12.30 at the White House. W.W., OK."[2]

"Comprehension must be the soil in which shall grow all the fruits of friendship." Those words, used by President Wilson in the Mobile speech in 1913, twenty years ago, can well serve, I think, as a statement of policy by the Government of the United States. That policy applies equally to a comprehension of our internal problems and our international relations.

Woodrow Wilson was a teacher, and when he used that word "comprehension" he meant it not in terms of the statesmen and political leaders and business executives and financial kings; he meant it rather in its application to the peoples of the world who are constantly going to school to learn simple truths in order that they and their neighbors can live their lives more safely, more happily, more fully.

In every continent and in every country Woodrow Wilson accelerated comprehension on the part of the people themselves. It is, I believe, true that the events of the past ten months have caused a greater interest in government, the problems of government, and the purposes of government than in any similar period in our American history; and yet this recent interest and comprehension would have been impossible for the American people had they not had from Woodrow Wilson the original stimulus, the original understanding of which he spoke twenty years ago.

In that speech in Mobile, President Wilson first enunciated the definite statement "that the United States will never again seek one additional foot of territory by conquest." The United States accepted that declaration of policy. The President went further, pointing out with special reference to our Latin American relations, our neighbors, that material interests must never be made superior to human liberty.

Nevertheless, we know that largely as a result of the convulsion of the World War and its after effects, the complete fruition of that policy of unselfishness has not in every case been obtained. And in this we, all of us, in all of these American nations have to share the responsibility.[3]

I do not hesitate to say that if I had, for example, been engaged in a political campaign as a citizen of some other American republic I might have been strongly tempted to play upon the fears of my compatriots of that republic by charging the United States of North America with some form of imperialistic desire for selfish aggrandizement. As a citizen of some other republic I might have found it difficult to believe fully in the altruism of the richest American republic. In particular, as a citizen of some other republic, I might have found it hard to approve of the occupation of the territory of other republics, even as a temporary measure.

It therefore has seemed clear to me as President that the time has come to supplement and to implement the declaration of President Wilson by the further declaration that the definite policy of the United States from now on is one opposed to armed intervention.

The maintenance of constitutional government in other nations is not a sacred obligation devolving upon the United States alone. The maintenance of law and the orderly processes of government in this hemisphere is the concern of each individual nation within its own borders first of all. It is only if and when the failure of orderly processes affects the other nations of the continent that it becomes their concern; and the point to stress is that in such an event it becomes the joint concern of a whole continent in which we are all neighbors.

It is the comprehension of that doctrine—comprehension not by the leaders alone but by the peoples of all the American republics, that has made the conference now concluding its labors in Montevideo such a splendid success. A better state of feeling among the neighbor nations of North and Central and South America exists today than at any time within the memory of this generation. For participation in the bringing about of that result we can feel proud that so much credit belongs to the Secretary of State of the United States, Cordell Hull.

In the wider world field, however, a chain of events has led, we fear, of late, away from rather than towards the ultimate objectives of Woodrow Wilson.

The superficial observer charges this failure to the growth of what the superficial observer calls the spirit of nationalism. But, in so doing he suggests a nationalism in the wrong sense, a nationalism in its narrower, restrictive sense; he suggests a nationalism of that kind supported by the overwhelming masses of the people themselves in each nation.[4]

I challenge that description of the world population today.

The blame for the danger to world peace lies not in the world population but in the political leaders of that population.

In this place about fifteen years ago, the imagination of the masses of world population was stirred, as never before, by President Wilson's gallant appeal to them—to those masses—to banish future war. His appeal meant much to them, but it meant little to the imagination or the hearts of a large number of the so-called statesmen who gathered in Paris to assemble a treaty of so-called peace in 1919. I saw that with my own eyes. I heard that with my own ears. Political profit, personal prestige, national aggrandizement attended the birth of the League of Nations, and handicapped it from its infancy by seeking their own profit and their own safety first.[5]

Nevertheless, through the League directly, or through its guiding motives indirectly, the states of the world, in the years that have gone by, have groped forward to find something better than the old way of composing their differences.

The League has provided a common meeting place; it has provided machinery which serves for international discussion; and in very many practical instances of which you and I know it has helped labor and health and commerce and education, and last but not least, the actual settlement of many disputes great and small between nations great and small.

Today the United States is cooperating openly in the fuller utilization of the League of Nations machinery than ever before.

I believe that I express the views of my countrymen when I state that the old policies, the old alliances, the old combinations and balances of power have proved themselves inadequate for the preservation of world peace. The League of Nations, encouraging as it does the extension of non-aggression pacts, of reduction of armament agreements, is a prop in the world peace structure, and it must remain.

We are not members and we do not contemplate membership. We are giving cooperation to the League in every matter which is not primarily political and in every matter which obviously represents the views and the good of the peoples of the world as distinguished from the views and the good of political leaders, of privileged classes and of imperialistic aims.

If you figure the world's population at approximately one billion and a half people, you will find it safe to guess that at least 90% of all of that billion and a half of people are today content with the territorial limits of their respective nations and are willing further to reduce their armed forces tomorrow if every other nation in the world will agree to do the same thing. Back of the threat to world peace lies the fear and perhaps even the possibility that the other 10% of the people of the world may go along with a leadership which seeks territorial expansion at the expense of neighbors and which under various pleas in avoidance are unwilling to reduce armament or stop rearmament even if everybody else agrees to non-aggression and to arms reduction.

If that 10% of the world population can be persuaded by the other

90% to do their own thinking and not be so finely led, we will have practical peace, permanent peace, real peace throughout the world. As you know, our own country has reduced the immediate steps to this greatest of objectives—reduced those steps to practical and reasonable terms.[6]

I have said to every nation in the world something to this effect:

1. Let every nation agree to eliminate over a short period of years, and by progressive steps, every weapon of offense that it has in its possession and to create no additional new weapons of offense. That, of course, does not guarantee a nation against invasion unless at the same time we allow the nations to implement that fact with the right to fortify its own border with permanent and non-mobile defenses; and also with the right to assure itself through international continuing inspection that its neighbors are not creating nor maintaining offensive weapons of war.

2. A simple declaration that no nation will permit any of its armed forces to cross its own borders into the territory of another nation. Such an act would be regarded by humanity as an act of aggression and, as an act, therefore, that would call for condemnation by the world as a whole.

3. It is clear, of course, that no such general agreement for the elimination of aggression or the elimination of the weapons of offensive warfare would be of any value in this world unless every nation, without exception, would enter into such an agreement by solemn obligation. If then such an agreement were signed by a great majority of the nations, an overwhelming majority in my opinion, on the definite condition that it would go into effect only when signed by all the nations, then, my friends, it would be a comparatively easy matter to separate the sheep from the goats, a comparatively simple matter to determine which nations in this enlightened time are willing to go on record by refusing to sign that pact, willing to go on record as belonging to the small minority of mankind which still believes in the use of the sword for invasion of and attack upon their neighbors. I did not make this suggestion until I felt assured, after a hard-headed practical survey, that the temper of the overwhelming majority of all men and women in my own country as well as those who make up the world's population, the large majority subscribes to the fundamental objective I have set forth and to the practical road to that objective.[7] The political leaders of many of these peoples interpose and will continue to interpose argument, excuse, befogging amendment—yes, and even ridicule. But I tell them that the men and women they serve are so far in advance of that type of leader-

ship that we could get a world accord on world peace immediately if the people of the world could speak for themselves.

Through all of the centuries of recorded history and down to the world conflict of 1914 to 1918, wars were made by governments. Woodrow Wilson challenged that necessity. That challenge made the people who create and the people who change governments think. They wondered with Woodrow Wilson whether the people themselves could not some day prevent governments from making war.

It is but an extension of the challenge of Woodrow Wilson for us to propose in this newer generation that from now on war by governments shall be changed to peace by peoples.[8]

[Speech File:T]

[1] Roland S. Morris, president of the Wilson Foundation, and Mrs. Woodrow Wilson. Others at the speakers' table included such distinguished "Wilsonians" as Supreme Court Justice Pierce Butler, William Phillips, Francis Sayre, Cary T. Grayson, Mrs. Emily Newell Blair, Hamilton Fish Armstrong, and Norman H. Davis. Roosevelt had helped organize the Foundation and had served it as vice-president and as trustee.

[2] This text is that of the stenographic transcript and includes a number of additions made by Roosevelt in reading the speech. Of these, this first paragraph is the most important; it does not appear in the text as released to the newspapers nor as printed in *Public Papers* (I, 544–549). In addition to the transcript and reading copy, the Roosevelt Library has a draft and the mimeographed press release containing the White House reporter's shorthand notes of the changes made. The typed draft, apparently composed by Roosevelt, has a number of additions and deletions in his hand; the more significant of these are noted below. The only other draft of which mention has been found is referred to in a letter from Under Secretary of State Phillips to Roosevelt of Dec. 26, 1933 (OF 184), asking that he make some reference to the League at the Wilson dinner. "Since the withdrawal of Germany and Italy the League's prestige is at a low ebb, and, of course, any word from you in support of its usefulness would be greatly appreciated. Hugh Wilson, who has just returned to Washington from Geneva, has drawn up this reference, which I venture to send you merely as a thought which you might care to consider." Wilson's "reference" has not, however, been found.

Here, a letter from Herbert S. Houston, distinguished editor and publicist and a founder of the Woodrow Wilson Foundation, is of interest. Houston wrote to Roosevelt Dec. 18, 1933 (OF 404-A), to suggest that he accept Litvinov's Geneva proposal for complete disarmament, or if that was too extreme, "progressive disarmament with complete disarmament as a declared objective." "Such a declaration from you, at this moment, would 'save' the Disarmament Conference and put fresh hope in a disheartened and disillusioned world. Moreover, it would make the Good Neighbor stand forth, much as Secretary Hull presented the symbol at Montevideo the other day, but in greater stature . . . challenging the whole world to sanity and a new confidence."

[3] In the reading copy this paragraph originally read: "Nevertheless . . . the will of that policy of unselfishness has not in every case been followed by the deed. And those who were leaders in almost all of the republics of the new world must in part at least share the blame."

[4] The reading copy has: "The superficial observer calls the cause of this Nationalism;

the use of that term connotes nationalism in its narrower, restrictive sense and above all a nationalism which in that sense is based on, and supported by, the over-whelming masses of the people themselves in each nation."

[5] Reading copy: "Political profit, personal prestige, national aggrandizement launched the League of Nations, an over-burdened ship with a crew the members of which sought their own safety and their own profit first."

[6] Reading copy: "Our own country has reduced the means to the peace objective to practical terms."

[7] Reading copy: "It is not a pipe dream of mine—it is assurance based on a hard-headed survey of what I believe to be the temper of the over-whelming majority of all men and women who make up the world's population—when I say that the people of nearly all nations subscribe today to the fundamental objective I have set forth and the practical road to that objective."

[8] Editorial comment on the speech was favorable; analyses of domestic, European, and South American newspaper opinion are found in digests sent to Early by K. C. Blackburn, Press Intelligence director, Jan. 5 and 8, 1934 (OF 1275), and by Welles to Roosevelt, Jan. 15 and 23, 1934 (PPF 107). The New York *Times* approved but at the same time took occasion (editorially) to refer to Roosevelt's speech to the New York State Grange of Feb. 2, 1932, in which he repudiated the League (Dec. 30, 1933, p. 12).

## Robert Underwood Johnson, Director, Hall of Fame, New York University, to Roosevelt

New York, December 28, 1933

Dear Mr. President: I have not before written to you on the very important subject of this letter, which is the opportunity which we now have to accept the great benefits to creators of copyright property offered to us by the Berne Union, and of which we can avail ourselves by entering into that body.

Several attempts have heretofore been made to accomplish this most desirable purpose, but they have always been in the form of an entire revision of the Copyright Law, and such revision has awakened so much controversy that the secondary interests have fought over details and the original idea has been lost sight of.[1]

Will you do me the honor to read the petition to the Senate which I herewith enclose, presented on the 12th of June by Mr. Cutting, in support of his bill called the "short bill," a copy of which I also enclose herewith.[2]

I should be very glad if you could see your way to recommending such legislation to Congress in your message.

I am asking Mr. Thorvald Solberg, late and for many years Register of Copyrights, who drafted this bill, to request an interview from you on the subject so that you may be absolutely sure of your ground in taking this desired step which would be greeted I am sure with approbation in all the countries which are members of the Berne Union. My position is that once we have entered the Union, this bill will be no obstacle to a further revision of the general law, whereas if we attempt the whole problem now, the result will be the same deplorable failure and delay that has attended similar attempts heretofore.[3]

I am, indeed, Very respectfully and faithfully yours,

R. U. Johnson

[OF 699:TS]

[1] Johnson, for many years editor of *Century Magazine,* had long been in the forefront of the effort to improve American copyright laws and to bring the United States into the International Copyright Union; see his *Remembered Yesterdays* (Boston: Little, Brown, 1923). The Union secured to nationals of the member countries equal rights of copyright; based on the Berne Convention of 1886, it had been most recently revised in Rome in 1928 and it was to this agreement that Johnson and other editors and writers were urging adherence. Under the Copyright Law of 1909 bilateral and other treaties prescribed the rights of foreigners but the British were still required to print their books in the United States to secure copyright. Cutting's bill (S. 1928) was intended to bring United States statues in conformity with the International Convention, following ratification of the convention by the Senate. Introduced June 10, 1933, it was referred to the Senate Foreign Relations Committee but was not reported, and efforts of its supporters to get it reported in the 1934 session also failed (*Cong. Rec.,* vol. 77, p. 5622). The situation as it was at the beginning of the 1934 session is succinctly described in a pamphlet prepared by Thorvald Solberg, United States Register of Copyrights from 1897 to 1930, and also a leader in the copyright fight: *The Present International Copyright Situation* (Washington, 1934). This pamphlet contains a copy of the Cutting bill.

[2] The petition, May 17, 1933, signed by Johnson, is printed in *Cong. Rec.,* vol. 77, p. 5716; the copy enclosed is from the *Record.* The copy of the bill enclosed is the committee print.

[3] Acknowledged by McIntyre Jan. 23, 1934 (OF 699). See Johnson to Roosevelt, April 16, 1934, below.

# William Phillips, Acting Secretary of State, to Roosevelt

Washington, December 29, 1933

My dear Mr. President: In accordance with an informal arrangement with the Secretary General of the League of Nations, this Department has, for the past eight years, transmitted copies of the United States

Treaty Series and Executive Agreement Series to the League for printing in the League of Nations Treaty Series. Following prolonged study of this matter in the Department, I am now writing to suggest your approval of the formal registration with the League of all future treaties or executive agreements entered into by the United States.

Article 18 of the League Covenant reads as follows:

> Every treaty or international engagement entered into hereafter by any Member of the League shall be forthwith registered with the Secretariat and shall as soon as possible be published by it. No such treaty or international engagement shall be binding until so registered.

With respect to registration on the part of Non-Members, the Secretary General, in a memorandum approved by the League Council on May 19, 1920, proposed, "although the registration will be for this part absolutely voluntary, to accept applications for the registration of treaties, et cetera, even though none of the parties is at the time a Member of the League of Nations."

Voluntary registration in accordance with this memorandum would, of course, involve no obligation such as is contained in the second sentence of Article 18 and would represent a mere administrative act on our part and the League's part, carrying with it no legal consequences. On the other hand, it would serve to regularize a practice which is now followed by virtually every country in the world and assist the Secretariat in the publication of the uniform League Treaty Series which is one of the League's most useful activities. While in the past, the voluntary registration of treaties might possibly have proved politically unwise, I believe that our present League relations and public opinion on this subject are such that the step can now be taken with little publicity and without unfavorable reaction.

In this connection, it might be of interest to point out that Secretary Stimson, shortly before leaving office, expressed his approval of the action now proposed.

Faithfully yours,

William Phillips

[*Notation*:AS] W.P.   OK   FDR
[OF 184:TS]

## Stanley K. Hornbeck, Chief, Division of Far Eastern Affairs, State Department, to William Phillips, Acting Secretary of State

[Washington] January 2, 1934

*Confidential*

Mr. Phillips: Herewith certain notes by way of comment on Mr. Howell's letter—as something in the nature of an aide memoire in case you should care to discuss with the President the contents of the letter in question.[1]

Incidentally, Mr. Norman Davis informed me the other day that a friend of the President had suggested to the President the conclusion of a non-aggression pact with Japan and said that the President had replied that he had no intention of acting upon that suggestion. He also said that the President had said to that friend that he looked with high regard upon the principle of "non-recognition."

SKH

[PPF 604:TS]

[1] Dec. 19, 1933, above.

## [*Enclosure*] Stanley K. Hornbeck to William Phillips

Comments on Mr. Howell's letter of December 19:

First paragraph. Nothing.

Second paragraph: In an earlier letter, addressed to Mr. Hull, Mr. Howell stated that he had been talking this matter over with Mr. K. K. Kawakami—who is a Japanese press correspondent located in Washington. Mr. Kawakami has recently published an article (or articles) in Japan advising the Japanese Government to the effect that the way for it to obtain its objectives in relations with the United States is to have its representatives talk first and only with the President. It has long been felt that Mr. Kawakami wishes to play the role of a self-appointed diplomatist. It now looks as though he were attempting to instill in Mr. Howell a similar aspiration. In this paragraph and the third to last paragraph of the letter, Mr. Howell virtually asks the President to inform him—for communication by him to his Japanese contacts—whether the

President's reaction to their overture suggesting a non-aggression understanding between the United States and Japan would be favorable or unfavorable. It is believed that no response should be made to such a request. With regard to counteracting "the hostile propaganda being pushed by extremists of both countries," Mr. Howell is somewhat out of date. There was a few months ago a great deal of hostile propaganda, emanating principally from Japan; there is at present little, and at no time has there been much which originated in this country. What we need most at present in relations between the two countries is a period of peace and quiet in which for the most part Nature may be allowed to take its course.

Third paragraph. If such an overture is made it should be made openly and above board by duly constituted agents and through authorized and recognized channels.

Fourth paragraph. If the Japanese Government wishes to make such an overture informally and tentatively, it knows well that it can do so without fear of official betrayal in this country; it does not need to have its inquiry made through underground channels and by self-appointed go-betweens.

Fifth paragraph. It is not believed that John Bassett Moore has said the things attributed to him in this paragraph. If he has said them, what difference does it make? The decisions and acts of the present Administration should be and will be made on the merits of situations as they are and problems as they come before it, in the light of law, treaties and express commitments.

Sixth paragraph. Same.

Seventh paragraph. Here also it is not believed that the President made any such commitment. Whether the previous Administration "made an awful bungle of the whole 'Manchukuo' affair" and so forth is a matter of opinion. This paragraph sounds as though it had been inspired by Mr. Kawakami who has long made it his practice to affirm —for propaganda purposes, we assume—that the Far Eastern Division of the Department of State is "pro-Chinese and anti-Japanese." With regard to commitments, the present Administration informed the Secretary General of the League of Nations, in September last, after Mr. Hull had submitted the matter to the President, that our policy with regard to non-recognition "remains unchanged."

Eighth paragraph. Mr. Saito[1] cannot possibly be more anxious than was his predecessor, Mr. Debuchi, or than are officers of the American

Government who are concerned with the conduct of relations between Japan and the United States, including officers of the Division of Far Eastern Affairs, "that all possible causes of friction between the two countries be removed"; nor will Mr. Saito work any harder toward that end than will they.

Ninth paragraph. Correct.

Tenth paragraph. The conclusion of a non-aggression pact would not put an end to this type of cartooning or to the talk of extremists.

Eleventh paragraph. Nor would it, in fact, contribute much toward a "complete understanding."

Twelfth paragraph. It is true that "the 'Manchukuo' situation is an accomplished fact." It does not follow that we need to or should give it or those who brought it about our blessing. What advantage would accrue to the United States from sending "to 'Manchukuo' a commissioner to represent this country?"

Thirteenth paragraph. Have we ever profited from, and have we not always been a little ashamed of what we did in reference to Korea in that connection?

Fourteenth paragraph. Nothing.

Fifteenth paragraph. It is believed that the President should not make any commitment either by letter or orally to Mr. Howell on this subject. As stated above, if the Japanese Government wishes to bring forward such a proposal or to do any reconnoitering in connection with its desire to do so, it can and will take the initiative, and recognized agencies and methods are available to it.

Referring to the question of a bilateral non-aggression pact on its merits, it may be remarked that there already exists between the United States and Japan a non-aggression pact: namely, the Kellogg-Briand Pact—to which not alone these two countries but more than sixty others are parties. It is believed that there is neither need nor place for a bilateral non-aggression pact between the United States and Japan; but in case this Government should come to the conclusion that the making of such a pact would serve a useful purpose, it is believed that assent on the part of the American Government to enter upon the negotiation of such a pact should be given only on the understanding that there should be negotiated and be concluded simultaneously between and among all of the major powers which possess interests in the Far East a complete group of such pacts. This subject has been discussed in other memoranda which are available; and a considerable amount of data with regard to projects for and possible contents of non-aggression pacts is on file in the Far Eastern Division.

[*Notation*:A:FDR] File under Clark Howell
[PPF 604:T]

[1] Hirosi Saito's appointment as ambassador to the United States was announced Dec. 16, 1933. He succeeded Katsuja Debuchi who had been called home for consultation in October (New York *Times,* Dec. 16, 1933, p. 3).

## Francis B. Sayre, Assistant Secretary of State, to Roosevelt

Washington, January 2, 1934

My dear Mr. President: At our conference at the White House on the afternoon of December 28,[1] I spoke of the desire of the Swedish Government to negotiate with the United States a commercial bargaining treaty covering the importation into this country of wood pulp and newsprint from Sweden and of the Swedish Minister's position that to make the treaty satisfactory to Sweden he must request the United States to give an assurance that the duties on such commodities imported from Sweden should not be increased during the life of the treaty through the application of Section 3 (e) of the National Industrial Recovery Act. You told me, if I understood you correctly, that inasmuch as the United States was interested in securing cheap wood pulp and newsprint we could safely give such assurance to Sweden in return for adequate compensations from the Swedish Government. In accordance with your statement, I have prepared a memorandum which I should like to lay before the Swedish Minister as a preliminary to our negotiations.

Perhaps I should call your attention to the fact that Canada produces and exports to the United States all three of the products mentioned in the statement. Sweden is the chief source of our imports of unbleached sulphite and sulphate wood pulp but Canada is the chief source of our imports of newsprint by a very wide margin. However, a guaranty to Sweden of continued free entry of these products would not prevent the imposition of duties or restrictions on imports from Canada since we have no most-favored-nation treaty with Canada. The assurance which it is proposed to give to Sweden would not, therefore, in any way weaken our position for negotiating a reciprocal trade agreement with Canada at some later time.

I should appreciate it if you would O.K. the enclosed memorandum, if it meets with your approval, before I show it to the Swedish Minister.[2]
Faithfully yours,

Francis B. Sayre

[OF 167:TS]

[1] From 3 to 5:15 P.M.; with Sayre were Secretary of Agriculture Wallace, Assistant Secretary of Agriculture Tugwell, Acting Secretary of State Phillips, Herbert Feis, economic adviser to the State Department, George Peek, special adviser to the President on foreign trade, and Assistant Secretary of Commerce Dickinson (PPF 1-0). Those present refused to comment on what was discussed. The New York *Times,* however, said that it had learned that "general principles regarding an increase in exports were discussed" (Dec. 29, 1933, p. 3).
[2] Answered Jan. 6, 1934, below.

## [*Enclosure*] Francis B. Sayre to Roosevelt

Memorandum. As a preliminary step in exploring the possibility of concluding a reciprocal trade agreement between the United States and Sweden the Minister of Sweden has raised the question as to the relation of the National Industrial Recovery Act to imports of wood pulp and newsprint from Sweden and has inquired regarding the nature of the assurances which the United States would be prepared to give on this subject.

The United States would be prepared, in return for acceptable provisions regarding the treatment of American commerce by Sweden, to give assurances that unbleached sulphite and sulphate wood pulp and standard newsprint paper would be exempt from import duties or restrictions, including charges or restrictions to which these products might otherwise be subject under the provisions of the National Industrial Recovery Act.

[OF 167:T]

## Robert P. Skinner, Ambassador to Turkey, to Roosevelt

Istanbul, January 2, 1934

Dear Mr. President: I cannot adequately express to you the pleasure which my associates and I have derived from your Christmas letter of

November tenth.[1] In the course of my experience of thirty-six years nothing of the sort has occurred before. It fills us with exhilaration to follow a leader who leads, in whose success we have faith, and whose efforts we propose to second as circumstances permit. I send you the grateful thanks of my staff and myself for your kind remembrances.

Here in Turkey within the past ten days we have been fortunate in breaking down Turkish resistance to the importation of American goods to the point that we have now obtained a list of permissible imports which doubles the preceding list, and thus opens the opportunity to our people to increase their sales proportionately. Whether or not they do so (and I believe they will) depends upon themselves. This is our small contribution to your reconstruction campaign.

I congratulate you upon having reached a fair arrangement with the Russians. It was time that something of this sort was done. No doubt there must emerge a commercial treaty, and in this connection I venture to remind you of the draft which I laid before you last July. Among other important points, the draft provides (Article XII) that the Russian Government shall not directly act in a mercantile capacity in the United States, but may set up commercial companies amenable to our laws like any others. It would be unfair and would lead to a repetition of difficulties encountered here and elsewhere if members of the Russian Mission, entitled to diplomatic privileges and paying no taxes, were permitted to compete as merchants with private concerns in the United States enjoying no such fiscal and other immunities. There are several points of this kind, all of which must be considered most carefully.

Please do not think that I have forgotten the stamps. In this matter I am in the hands of the Turks who, if they have adopted Western methods in many respects, certainly have not adopted the practice of doing things rapidly. However, you will hear from me eventually, I am sure.

I close these lines with every wish from myself, and those by whom I am surrounded, that the New Year may preserve you in health and strength for the continued carrying on of your efforts to guide our country to a well-ordered prosperity.[2]

Sincerely and respectfully yours,

Robert P. Skinner

[OF 502:TS]

---

[1] A note of greeting and appreciation for his "loyal and intelligent cooperation with us in Washington"; similar notes were sent to all Foreign Service officers. (See *Public*

*Papers*, II, 543–544.) Skinner had previously been minister to the Baltic states. In his note to Roosevelt proposing him, Under Secretary of State Phillips referred to the fact that Skinner had been in the Foreign Service for over thirty years and had done excellent work, and that his promotion "would round out a very useful career to the Government" (May 26, 1933, OF 502).

[2] Answered Jan. 22, 1934, below.

## Roosevelt to the Congress, January 3, 1934

[*Excerpt*] I cannot, unfortunately, present to you a picture of complete optimism regarding world affairs.

The delegation representing the United States has worked in close cooperation with the other American Republics assembled at Montevideo to make that conference an outstanding success. We have, I hope, made it clear to our neighbors that we seek with them future avoidance of territorial expansion and of interference by one nation in the internal affairs of another. Furthermore, all of us are seeking the restoration of commerce in ways which will preclude the building up of large favorable trade balances by any one nation at the expense of trade debits on the part of other nations.

In other parts of the world, however, fear of immediate or future aggression and with this the spending of vast sums on armament, and the continued building up of defensive trade barriers, prevent any great progress in peace or trade agreements. I have made it clear that the United States can not take part in political arrangements in Europe but that we stand ready to cooperate at any time in practicable measures on a world basis looking to immediate reduction of armaments and the lowering of the barriers against commerce.

I expect to report to you later in regard to debts owed the Government and people of this country by the governments and peoples of other countries. Several nations, acknowledging the debt, have paid in small part; other nations have failed to pay. One nation—Finland—has paid the installments due this country in full.[1]

[Speech File:T]

[1] This excerpt is but a small part of the 1934 annual message; for the entire text see *Public Papers*, III, 8–14. The Roosevelt Library has two drafts, the reading copy, and a copy of the official press release. There is also a summary of Roosevelt's foreign policy prepared in the State Department and sent to McIntyre by Phillips under cover of a note of Dec. 22, 1933 (PPF 1820). The text of this excerpt is from the reading copy.

## Press Conference, Executive Offices of the White House, January 3, 1934, 10:50 A.M.

[*Excerpt*] Q: You said in the Message[1] that some of the sister nations were not ready to stabilize. Does that mean that we are?

The President: I do not think I need to elaborate on the language at all. It is perfectly clear and speaks for itself.

Q: Mr. President, do the other Messages make specific recommendations?

The President: I haven't any schedule at all. I don't know. There will be, of course, during the course of the session, other messages. I don't think that I will adopt the attitude of sending a message up on every specific subject. Some of the legislation will probably originate in committees. In other words, there will be a pretty close liaison between the White House and the committees and there will be substantial agreement. A good many things will not be—will not take the form of messages to Congress at all. There probably will be a message, as I said the other day, on tariffs but there isn't any regular schedule of messages or even a determination of what things will take the form of messages and what won't.

Q: Tentatively again, isn't every nation going to stabilize if it could name the parity figures?

The President: If it could name its own figure? I don't know. I think you had better use this—I suppose you can use it as background. There are a good many nations whose entire financial set-up is so weak that it makes it awfully difficult for them to do anything—unbalanced budgets, things of that kind. It is a little bit as if you and Stevie[2] and I were to agree to enter into a partnership and each put in $100,000. And then you and I were to discover that while Stevie had $100,000, he was living away beyond his means. Well, the chances are that you and I would go ahead without Stevie and that is a perfectly good illustration of one of the international problems relating to permanent stabilization.

You will notice that when I used the word "stabilization," I also used the word "permanent" which is a very different thing than "temporary" and also the term "world-wide." In other words, we are looking a long ways or to the time when we can get it world-wide.

Q: Are there any countries that just want to stay away from stabilization and stay away from gold and go on a managed currency entirely?

The President: For instance, Sweden has a managed currency today.

Q: Would Sweden have preferred to stay away?

The President: Great Britain has a managed currency.

Q: And there is some sentiment toward keeping it that way?

The President: Yes.

[President's Press Conferences:T]

[1] Roosevelt to the Congress, Jan. 3, 1934, above.
[2] F. M. Stephenson of the Associated Press.

# William E. Dodd, Ambassador to Germany, to Roosevelt

[Berlin] January 3, 1934

*Confidential*

Dear Mr. President: I do not like to add to your administrative difficulties; but Secretary Hull is away and there are two or three things that require some attention:

1. The Blücher palace deal ($1,700,000 involved and another $1,000,000 necessary if use is to be made of the property) will be reviewed by Foreign Relations committees of the two houses—as it ought to be. The thing was bought when Governmental people thought the kingdom of heaven was at hand, everybody about to be rich. I have studied whole problem and think I have found a solution at lowest possible cost. I have discouraged all discussion here lest it defeat possibility of disposing of part of the property to German government for money enough to reduce cost of needful improvements to a sum we can afford. This is one of the reasons I have asked State Department for leave about March 15.[1]

2. The condition of the Foreign Service requires some attention—some points not best to commit to paper. I will illustrate by saying that I have no real private secretary and have written more letters by hand the last six months than I wrote in Chicago the last six years. The thing can be corrected without costing the Department a dollar—at same time proper transfers and readjustment would save $12,000 to $15,000 a year here. Pardon me if I add, in all confidence, the appropriate officials in Washington cannot be induced to see the situation aright without some very positive pressure from above. If Mr. Bullitt will leave three assistantships on his staff vacant till he comes this way in February I can supply him good people: a code-room man who knows Russian, a typist and a clerk. If he already has enough people of this type ask him to keep some vacancies on Consular staff. It would help all round.

3. The European situation has been improved by your 28 December address.[2] The French saw your point and the Germans got your "boundaries" rebuke. It was a good and a timely thing. But in view of coming negotiations and especially new tariff adjustments, we need very active men in London and Paris. I fear present incumbents are not going to be able to function actively. In case of vacancies, will you excuse me if I say I believe Phillips would function well in Paris and it would then be easier for some shifts in State Departments that would limit a little the favoritisms that prevail there. But the greater thing would be vigorous co-operation between London, Paris and Berlin and possibly better international relations. I can not help thinking whole world situation might be more closely articulated and war rendered far less likely.

Pardon these adventurous suggestions. Do not think I have any personal axe to grind or any personal grievances about anything. I hope it is the public service alone that motivates letter. If, in view of circumstances, you could authorize return to Washington for a week or two in March I would be glad. I would then ask brief extension of time in order to get a little outdoor vacation on my farm near Bluemont, Virginia. Work here has been such that some let-up is necessary. As Hull can not now pass on such matters and part of the problems mentioned involve policy, I trust you will pardon appeal to you. Ask State Department to wire me in case you see sufficient reason in what I have presented for a return to Washington.[3]

Yours sincerely,

William E. Dodd

[OF 523:AS]

[1] Concerning this statement, see Dodd, *Diary,* pp. 15, 297, 324.
[2] Speech by Roosevelt at the Woodrow Wilson Foundation dinner, above.
[3] Roosevelt sent this letter to Bullitt with a note, Jan. 22, 1934 (OF 523): "Will you read this confidential letter and return it to me?" He also sent it to Hull who said he had read it with interest (Hull to Roosevelt, Jan. 31, 1934, OF 523).

# Press Conference, Executive Offices of the White House, January 5, 1934, 4:03 P.M.

[*Excerpt*] Q: What can you tell us about liquor?[1] . . .

The President: I got a darned good story about Scotch whisky but I cannot tell you. Go to the British Embassy and ask them.

Q: Going to be cheaper Scotch?

The President: No, less.

Q: How about Canadian Rye?

The President: Well, we are letting quite a lot of that in.

Q: Have the British come forward for any other request for additional quota?

The President: I might tell you this, off the record. I cannot tell you the results but I can tell you off the record entirely what the situation is. We are trying, quite frankly, to get rid of certain agricultural surpluses, especially hog surpluses and butter surpluses and our good friends, the British, are now getting about sixty-five per cent of all their hogs and a good part of their butter from Denmark and, out of the kindness of their hearts, they have been allowing us to send in six per cent of their consumption. They, very generously, have offered to raise that to seven and a half, and they think it is very generous, but we have not yet decided how much Scotch whisky we are going to allow in. And, for the story itself, I am only going to give you a lead as to where to go. For the story itself, consult the British Embassy and the State Department.

Q: So there won't be any misunderstanding, the International News had it in their story this morning.[2]

The President: That is all right. (Laughter)

Q: May we have it as background or off the record?

The President: Off the record, because it is not in my jurisdiction yet.

Q: Would you care to discuss the subject of the French wine and liquor quotas in connection with the same thing?

The President: I think that is all settled up.

Q: I thought there were still some matters in connection with the wine to be settled?

The President: I do not know, I had an idea it was settled up.

Q: When do you intend to make your tariff proposals to the Congress?

The President: Probably not for some time.

Q: Can you tell us anything about war debts?

The President: About war debts?

Q: Yes.

The President: I am going to say something to Congress later on but I do not know when.[3]

Q: Have you anybody preparing material for you on the subject?

The President: Not for me. I think the Senate passed a Resolution; they wanted the data from the Treasury Department to be given them.

[President's Press Conferences:T]

[1] Roosevelt had just said that he had been conferring with Secretary of Agriculture Wallace on negotiations then under way with Great Britain on an American proposal to increase imports of Scotch whiskey in exchange for a British increase in pork imports. At this time no agreement had been reached but on January 8 it was announced that Great Britain had raised its pork import quota from 6.3 per cent to 7.6 per cent in exchange for a doubling of the whiskey quota (New York *Times,* Jan. 6, p. 9; Jan. 9, 1933, p. 1).

[2] See *ibid.,* Jan. 6, p. 9.

[3] See message to Congress of June 1, 1934, below.

## Roosevelt to Francis B. Sayre, Assistant Secretary of State

[Washington] January 6, 1934

Memorandum . . . I think the enclosed memorandum for the Swedish Minister is all right but, of course, it should be made clear that a commercial bargaining treaty should definitely increase the exports of the United States to Sweden by approximately the same amount of money as the increased imports from Sweden.[1]

F.D.R.

[OF 167:CT]

[1] Enclosed in Sayre to Roosevelt, Jan. 2, 1934, above.

## John Franklin Carter to Roosevelt

Washington, D.C., January 6, 1934

My dear Mr. President: In accordance with your suggestion, I made an opportunity to lunch with Sir Wilmott Lewis in order to explore his general journalistic attitude towards the Administration and its various experiments. Naturally, it was an entirely casual and indirect discussion as between newspapermen, without any implication of official interest in the subject. The sum and substance of my conclusions is that there is no malice in Lewis but that he is the victim of two contradictory impulses; one, a strong moral belief in the necessity of a spiritual regeneration of American life, and, two, inability to resist an epigram or an ingenious metaphor.

He has long contended that America needs a Savonarola, both to reform the many evils of our business system and to reform our national life. Politically, he believes that we should evolve a real two-Party system based on political convictions and a system of government approaching the Parliamentary, with initiative vested in the Executive and veto power in the Legislature, especially in budgetary matters. Economically, he believes that the only hope of the world lies in the resumption of international trade and hence he deplores the nationalistic tendency here, as well as in Great Britain. For you personally he expressed the warmest admiration and maintained that it was absurd and preposterous for any one to expect anything from the Hoover-Wadsworth-Mills group in the Republican Party. They were politically dead in his opinion.

So far as concerned the British attitude towards this Administration, he said it was one of lively and apprehensive interest. He said that there was fear lest our monetary policy should drive France off the gold standard, thereby occasioning a rush of funds to London for "safety," which would drive up the exchange value of the pound and compel the British either to devalue or force up the international commodity price level. He said that the Beaverbrook press favored the Administration, partly because of Beaverbrook's investments in this country and in Canada and also because Beaverbrook was using your vigorous policy as a political weapon against MacDonald and Baldwin, i.e. in a demand for more vigorous and courageous British leadership. He also said that the British felt that our change in stabilization policy at the London Conference proved that you "weren't a good man to go shooting with." I suggested that Mr. MacDonald's action in bringing up the war-debts the first day of the Conference proved that he "wasn't a good man to play ball with."

On the whole, I came to the conclusion that his political views were matters of deep conviction and that—barring his occasional seduction by a telling metaphor or a piquant epigram—he should be regarded as a man who is both worthy of confidence and able to expound the economic policies of this Administration. If those policies happen to inconvenience British interests, it can be taken for granted that British opinion will be unsympathetic towards them.

So far as French newspapers are concerned, I also had lunch this week with Comte Raoul de Roussy de Sales, who represents *Paris Soir* and several other publications whose names elude me. I found him practical and sympathetic in his attitude towards the Administration. He said that French opinion towards this country was just now dominated by fear lest our monetary policy should drive France off gold and thereby impair French political prestige. He said that no French Government could take the political responsibility for further devaluation but that Paris opinion no longer inclined to the opinion that the essential purpose of our monetary policy was to drive France off the gold standard. He said, however, that for several months France had been deluged with letters from individuals in New York, warning French citizens that France would be forced off gold by our policy and that this had stirred up some political resentment against us. He corroborated Lewis's opinion that nothing much could be expected from the conservative wing of the Republican Party and he regarded the attitude of the New York bankers towards the Administration as both comic and tragic.

I think that the essential problem is the diverse nature of American and European journalism. Our journalism aspires to be general, factual and objective. European journalism tends to minimize the facts and to concentrate on interpretation, especially in matters of foreign correspondence. Moreover, European newspapers address a selective public and tend to reflect the personal fears, interests and prejudices of the particular group addressed. This means that European correspondence from this country will contain far more critical passages than would be true of American journalism from Europe, with the important exceptions of the early days of the Russian experiment and the initial period of the Hitler movement in Germany. On this account, I think it must be taken for granted that, depending on the political and social viewpoint of the publications involved, British and European correspondents in Washington and New York will not generally present a sympathetic or an objective picture of your Administration. In the case of Great Britain, I believe that until British opinion is convinced that our economic policies are not calculated to injure what they regard as British interests, there will be considerable reserve and an occasional hyper-critical flare-up with respect to our general economic behavior.

I also believe that, until the present monetary and credit control is cleared up in this country, there will be a certain amount of denationalized wigwagging back and forth between our private bankers and the

European banks of issue, but that this will represent common financial interests rather than anything in the nature of an international political intrigue.[1]

I am, my dear Mr. President, Respectfully yours,

John Franklin Carter

[OF 4514:TS]

[1] With this letter are filed two undated memoranda. One, Early to LeHand, reads: "John Franklin Carter has left a very interesting report for the President which I think he will want to read." The other, Roosevelt to Early, reads: "Thank John Franklin Carter very much for that very interesting report and that I think it is a very fair summary of the attitude of the British and French." Also present is Early's note of acknowledgment of Jan. 16, 1934. Carter was at this time writing a syndicated newspaper column of political comment under the name of Jay Franklin. He had served in the Foreign Service and in the State Department.

# Roosevelt to Senator Joseph T. Robinson of Arkansas

Washington, January 8, 1934

*Confidential*

Memorandum . . . The World Court advocates have given me the enclosed in confidence.[1] I wish you would check on the probable Senate vote. If we get a lull it might, of course, be possible to carry out what is actually a platform pledge in both party platforms.[2] Will you keep this in confidence and let me have it back when you are through?

[OF 202:CT]

[1] The enclosure, not present, is identified in a note to this memorandum as printed in *Personal Letters, 1928–1945,* I, 384, as "a private poll of the Senate in which 65 senators were reported as favorable to adherence, 16 opposed, and 15 doubtful."

[2] The reference to the World Court in the 1932 Republican party platform reads in part: "The acceptance by Americans of membership in the World Court has been approved by three successive Republican Presidents and we commend this attitude of supporting in this form the settlement of international disputes by the rule of law." The reference in the 1932 Democratic party platform reads: "We advocate . . . adherence to the World Court with the pending reservations" (New York *Times,* June 16, p. 15; June 30, 1932, p. 15). The "pending reservations" are those incorporated in the protocol for the accession of the United States of Sept. 14, 1929; this may be found in Manley O. Hudson, *The World Court, 1921–1934* (Boston: World Peace Foundation, 1934), pp. 249–251. It was this protocol that was before the Senate. Roosevelt and Senator Robinson had, however, already decided not to press for its ratification. Fol-

lowing a conference on Jan. 4, 1934, Robinson announced that he and Roosevelt felt that the situation in Europe was not opportune (New York *Times,* Jan. 5, 1934, p. 16). The Senate Foreign Relations Committee held hearings during the session but the strength of the opposition led Robinson (in a committee meeting on May 30) to move for postponement until the next session (New York *Times,* May 31, 1934, p. 8).

## William Phillips, Acting Secretary of State, to Roosevelt

Washington, January 8, 1934

My dear Mr. President: On receipt of the Secretary's message from Montevideo with respect to the unfortunate Havas despatch,[1] which you have specifically called to my attention, I was on the point of taking the matter up with the French Ambassador when I received a further message that the Secretary wished to make a study of the whole matter when he returns in order to see whether he could find grounds on which he could make a complaint to the French Government.

There are several incidents of equal seriousness and I can assure you that we shall have a good case to present. In the circumstances I feel that I ought to await the Secretary's return.

Faithfully yours,

William Phillips

[OF 20:TS]

[1] Secretary of State Hull's message of Dec. 21, 1933 (OF 20), quoted a Havas dispatch as follows: "The North American warship *Wyoming* has arrived [in Cuba] with 1800 men on board. It is thought that the North Americans are taking precautions in order that in case of necessity they may comply with the stipulations of the Treaty of Paris obliging the United States to protect the lives and interests of Spaniards residing in Cuba." Hull added: "From my experience this is typical of the usual Havas method of distorting news items in a manner which will be detrimental to the United States and I think the Department should take particular note of this form of anti-American propaganda which is being carried on by an organization now receiving a direct subsidy from the French Government and which is really in effect a semi-official agency."

## Roosevelt to William Phillips, Acting Secretary of State

[Washington] January 9, 1934

Memorandum from the President for the Under Secretary of State, Mr. Phillips: In regard to pay of the Diplomatic and Consular Services, I am inclined more and more to the thought that it should be based on cost of living in each country. Would it be possible to take a normal period, say 1909 to 1914, as the basis for index and from that work out the amount of variation in exchange rates necessary today to arrive at a fair scale? There are undoubted inequalities at this time which the gold payments do not correct. Perhaps Congress would go along with this thought.[1]

[OF 20:T]

[1] Filed with this letter is a copy of Secretary of State Hull's statement of Feb. 21, 1934, before the Senate subcommittee holding hearings on the State Department budget for the fiscal year ending June 30, 1935, urging increased appropriations for living expenses and post allowances of Foreign Service employees. For the printed statement, see Senate, *Hearings . . . on H.R. 7513, A Bill Making Appropriations for the Departments of State and Justice . . . for the Fiscal Year Ending June 30, 1935 . . .* (Washington, 1934). See also Roosevelt to Oliver, Feb. 24, 1934, below.

# Roosevelt to the Senate, January 10, 1934

TO THE SENATE: I request the consideration of ratification by the Senate of the so-called St. Lawrence Treaty with Canada. Broad national reasons lead me, without hesitation, to advocate the Treaty. There are two main considerations, navigation and power.

Canada and the United States are possessed of a natural flow of water from near the center of the continent to the ocean—a flow which throughout the greater part of its length is today available for navigation by large-size vessels. A system of locks at the eastern end of Lake Superior, a dredged channel between Lake Huron and Lake Erie, and another series of great locks between Lake Erie and Lake Ontario provide free and adequate navigation to a point well down the St. Lawrence River. From there, a series of three rapids, all of them within a distance of 120 miles, now impede navigation by ocean-going vessels; but a Canadian canal already provides facilities for smaller ships. This Canadian canal now is used substantially up to its capacity.

Two of the three rapids are wholly in Canadian territory; the other is in the so-called international section. A great power development at the Beauharnois rapids in Canada is already nearing completion and locks for ocean-going ships have been planned for and could readily be built at a low cost as part of the plan. This means that only two additional series of locks are required for a complete and continuous seaway from Duluth to salt water. I call your attention to the simple fact that Canada alone can, if desired, build locks at the Lachine rapids and at the international sector and thus provide a seaway wholly within Canadian control without treaty participation by the United States. This, however, would be a reversal of the policy of cooperation which the United States and Canada have continuously maintained for generations.

I want to make it very clear that this great international highway for shipping is without any question going to be completed in the near future and that this completion should be carried out by both Nations instead of by one.

I am sending you herewith a summary of data prepared at my request by governmental agencies. This summary, in its relation to the economic aspects of the seaway, shows from the broad national point of view, first, that commerce and transportation will be greatly benefited and, secondly, local fears of economic harm to special localities or to special interests are grossly exaggerated. It is, I believe, a historic fact that every great improvement directed to better commercial communications, whether in the case of railroads into new territory, or the deepening of great rivers, or the building of canals, or even the cutting of the Isthmus of Panama, have all been subjected to opposition on the part of local interests which conjure up imaginary fears and fail to realize that improved transportation results in increased commerce benefiting directly or indirectly all sections.

For example, I am convinced that the building of the St. Lawrence Seaway will not injure the railroads or throw their employees out of work; that it will not in any way interfere with the proper use of the Mississippi River or the Missouri River for navigation. Let us be wholly frank in saying that it is better economics to send grain or other raw materials from our Northwest to Europe via the Great Lakes and St. Lawrence than it is to send them around three sides of a square—via Texas ports or the Mississippi, thence, through the Gulf of Mexico and thence, from the southern end of the North Atlantic to its northern end. In this illustration, it is well to remember that a straight line is the shortest distance between two points.

I am satisfied that the treaty contains adequate provision for the needs of the Chicago Drainage District and for navigation between Lake Michigan and the Mississippi River. A special report from the Chief of Engineers of the War Department covers this subject.

On the affirmative side, I subscribe to the definite belief that the completion of the seaway will greatly serve the economic and transportation needs of a vast area of the United States and should, therefore, be considered solely from the national point of view.

The other great objective provided for in the treaty relates to the development of electric power. As you know, I have advocated the development of four great power areas in the United States, each to serve as a yardstick and each to be controlled by government or governmental agencies. The Tennessee Valley plants and projects in the southeast, the Boulder Dam on the Colorado River in the southwest, the Columbia River projects in the northwest are already under construction. The St. Lawrence development in the northeast calls for action. This River is a source of incomparably cheap power located in proximity to a great industrial and rural market and within transmission distance of millions of domestic consumers.

The legislature of the State of New York by unanimous vote set up the necessary State machinery during my term as Governor of New York and the State stands ready to cooperate with the Federal Government in the distribution of power in accordance with what I believe is today a definite national policy.

Power in the international sector of the St. Lawrence cannot be developed without a treaty between the United States and Canada. On the other hand, Canada can develop a huge block of new power at the two other rapids which lie wholly within Canadian territory. Here again, as in the case of navigation, it is better in every way that we should maintain the historic principle of accord with Canada in the mutual development of the two Nations.

I have not stressed the fact that the starting of this great work will put thousands of unemployed to work. I have preferred to stress the great future advantages to our country and especially the fact that all of us should view this treaty in the light of the benefits which it confers on the people of the United States as a whole.[1]

Franklin D. Roosevelt

THE WHITE HOUSE, January 10, 1934.

[*Notation*:A] VP: Read   ordered printed as Sen Doc with illustrations and accompanying data. Table

[Speech File:TS:Microfilm]

---

[1] This text is from a microfilm copy of the original in the National Archives. It bears certain changes in capitalization made by the printer in preparing the message for publication; the text here printed, however, is in the form as signed. The Roosevelt Library also has the final draft, with a number of revisions in Roosevelt's hand, and a copy of the White House press release of the message. It is also printed in *Public Papers,* III, 29–31.

## Claude G. Bowers, Ambassador to Spain, to Roosevelt

Madrid, January 10, 1934

*Purely Personal*

Dear Mr. President: I called on Lerreux personally to express appreciation of his message to you on your Wilson Day speech.[1] He was plainly pleased and expressed the hope that better trade relations may soon be established between the two countries.

Some important developments regarding our trade relations with Spain come within the category of things concerning which you requested that I write you personally. During the last eight months the people here have been keenly interested in the readjustment of these relations. Concerning all of this I have kept the State Department fully informed. On September 27, No. 150, I reported that unless some disposition should be shown to consider these proposed readjustments we would ultimately be confronted with a policy frankly aimed at the great advantages we now have in the trade of the two nations.[2]

We are now face to face with that situation, for Spain has announced her adoption of the contingent system, with a battle cry—"We trade with those who trade with us." I have just learned on good official authority that within six weeks or two months we shall be up against the operation of this system.

I also learn that despite their inability to agree on many things, 90% of the Cortes will support the Government in this policy as it relates to us. This does not mean an anti-American sentiment. The Spaniard wants nothing so much as better and closer relations with us. This week in a two day speech in the Cortes, Badia of Catalonia discussed the trade relations of the two nations, without manifesting the slightest animosity. His purpose was to show that we have a tremendous advantage and to persuade the Cortes that unless some concessions are made to Spain to improve her position in the trade of the two nations, Spain will have to take steps to protect herself.

You may be interested in the reason for the concentration of this attention upon us at this time. Spain has suffered a great loss in her exportations and 50% of this loss comes from the United States. The feeling, as I find it here, is that we have a great advantage, and are entirely unsympathetic and cold toward any suggestions that we increase our trade with Spain.

There is no doubt that the first reaction to the wine quota was very bad. I refer not so much to the Government here as to the public generally. The basis for the quota was not understood, nor its temporary nature, and the great advantage given France and Italy was resented. They had pinned their hope of doing something worth while toward reducing the unfavorable trade balance through wine. They had sold a great amount on faith; the purchase money was in Spanish banks; and they were unable to deliver. This misunderstanding has been cleared, but unless we show a generous disposition in the negotiations now on in Washington I expect a flare-up.

We are selling $26,000,000 worth of American goods to Spain and are buying $11,000,000 worth—an unfavorable balance of $15,000,000. I am reliably informed that in the determination of our advantages later it is the intention to make full use of the vast sums of money annually sent from here to the United States from the Telephone Company, the film companies, the General Electric etc. I learn confidentially that the Tel & Tel is sending home $5,000,000 a year. We are all convinced here that unless we manifest a disposition to consider the trade desires of Spain which I sent you some time ago, we are in for rough weather within two months. If nothing is done until the contingent system is applied to us it will be difficult to change the quotas fixed. If we show a disposition to discuss these matters in Washington soon we may be spared more serious trouble in the future.

We are all agreed that the problem now is to hold the trade we have.

Your Wilson Day address made a profound and favorable impression here which is not reflected in the Spanish press for reasons I have indicated before. Everything I hear from home, from Republicans as much as Democrats, indicates that the popularity of your policies has not waned.

It must annoy our friends, the enemy, to have Mr. Hoover giving them advice publicly.

With regards and best wishes, Sincerely,

Claude G. Bowers

Apropos of American sentiment in Spain. The other day there was a two day festival in honor of Washington Irving in Granada and I was asked to attend and make a short speech at the dedication of the finest road in the Granada woods to him. A committee of leading citizens went out thirty miles to meet us and to conduct us in; it accompanied me thirty miles out on the return. The town was aflutter with our flag. At the theatre when we reached our box, draped with the flag, the players who were spouting their lines left the stage, the orchestra played "America," the 3000 people rose and gave us an ovation. When the play was over, the orchestra played "The Star Spangled Banner," and the ovation was repeated. Spain is pro-American—no doubt of that.

[PSF:Spain:TS]

[1] Alejandro Lerroux, president of the Council of Ministers, had cabled Roosevelt on Dec. 31, 1933, to express the pleasure of his government at Roosevelt's Wilson Day speech of Dec. 28, 1933 (above); his cable is printed in State Department, *Press Releases*, Jan. 6, 1934, p. 3.
[2] This dispatch does not appear in the State Department's *Foreign Relations* but see the 1934 volume, II, 687–708, in this series for correspondence on efforts of the United States and Spain to resolve their trade disagreements.

## Representative Samuel Dickstein of New York to Roosevelt

Washington, D.C., January 12th, 1934

My dear Mr. President: I have the honor to enclose herewith for your earnest consideration, a copy of the printed hearings held before the Committee on Immigration and Naturalization, on Nazi Activities in the United States, which I promised to send you.[1]

You will note that only a few hearings were printed and each one numbered, in order that they might not get into other than responsible hands. The hearings sent you are numbered one.

I have been very cautious during the entire examination and have come to the conclusion that it is most essential to have a complete Congressional investigation, and I most urgently request that I have an opportunity to personally discuss the matter with you along these lines. I tried to communicate with the White House, but found it a little difficult. No doubt you have been overworked.

I shall appreciate the opportunity at the first available moment to have the honor to converse with you and to bring before you some additional information, and I am sure you will agree with me that action is necessary and that Congress should immediately investigate the matter, pursuant to House Resolution number 198, a copy of which I am enclosing.[2]

With kind personal regards, I am, Respectfully yours,

Samuel Dickstein

[OF 3552:TS]

[1] *Nazi Propaganda Activities by Aliens in the United States* . . . (Washington, 1934).
[2] The resolution is present; see Roosevelt's reply, Jan. 31, 1934, below.


## Arthur Sweetser, Director, The Secretariat, League of Nations, to Roosevelt

Geneva, January 15th, 1934

Dear Mr. President: To-day, after fourteen years in the League, I am starting in on a new position.[1] My first action I very much desire to be to report the fact to you for two reasons. First, I have long had an instinct to have my somewhat special situation known directly to the Chief Executive of my own country. Secondly, during recent weeks has come a more immediate urge to express my profound enthusiasm for what you are doing at home; the changes in American society seem to me to be deep, salutary and permanent, a guide and inspiration for other nations as well.

It was a strange, and for me a very happy, coincidence that your speech on Woodrow Wilson,[2] to whom indirectly I owe my original appointment with the League, should have come just an hour before the close of a long phase of my work here. You would be gratified, I am sure, to know what a profound impression it made on those who have followed the League all these years; they welcomed it as the most direct and unequivocal declaration on the League by any President since Mr. Wilson, a flash of clarity and frankness which, in its balanced phrases, they feel will be one of the most important new guide-posts on the road to meeting the world's underlying problem of effective international organization for peace.

Hardly had I passed on its good news to a few of my friends in the Secretariat than I received a letter from the Secretary-General concluding my 14-year membership in the Information Section and appointing me Director hors section to serve with him and a special Committee for the reorganization of the system of general information and liaison necessitated by recent changes in the Secretariat. Within this would also fall the particular interest I have had all these years in the co-operation between the United States and the League which is now so mutually helpful and fruitful.

We face into a difficult period. The League is struggling under a double pressure, first the profound conflicts of governments, which render general agreement very difficult; second the agitation for possible reform, which inevitably creates a temporary unsteadiness. Both are likely, I think, to come to their climax in 1935/36.

The underlying international problem through 1935 will increasingly be, I think, that of organized international co-operation which will be ruthlessly thrust into the foreground through the forthcoming completion of Japan's and Germany's withdrawal from the League and its methods of co-operation and peaceful settlement. Early in 1935, also, the European area may be still further complicated by the Saar plebiscite which, if in itself a small thing, is sufficient to focalise the whole Franco-German controversy. Finally, throughout that period the Pacific area will be profoundly disturbed by the approaching termination of the Washington and London Naval Treaties and perhaps the reopening of the whole political situation there.

Nevertheless, I profoundly believe that out of all this will come eventual good. These very crises provide the best argument for a strong mechanism for peace and co-operation. The agitation for reform has at the same time forced world opinion to pull the League up by the roots, to appreciate that its machinery is better and more supple than thought, and to realise that it is the policies of governments rather than the structural form of the League that most need reform. A great deal of support has been brought out, either from unexpected quarters, such as certain British Conservative elements, which, when actually faced with a threat to the League, have rallied rather strongly towards it, or from quarters hitherto somewhat inarticulate, such as the smaller nations, as for instance, in the excellent Dutch statement. Most discussed of all, however, has been the fact that, on the same day as your Wilson speech, Molotoff, later backed by Stalin and Litvinoff, made Russia's first friendly declaration on the League.

It is not surprising, then, that amidst these vast currents, proposals for League reform have been postponed; nevertheless, they have been all to the good in stimulating much useful study and suggestion and demonstrating that the League is not intangible or untouchable but freely capable of adaptation and improvement. Clearly the League has not yet reached its final stage either in form or composition. There would seem every hope that, as its foundations have proved so solid, something stronger, more universal, even if looser, may reasonably soon be erected on them. Despite the present black clouds, President Wilson's ideal seems to me nearer consummation than ever.

In sending you this brief word, may I assure you both of my desire to be of any possible service in this work and of my devotion and admiration for the tremendous program you are putting through at home?

I have the honour to be, my dear Mr. President, Most respectfully yours,

Arthur Sweetser[3]

[PPF 506:TS]

[1] As director of the League Secretariat.
[2] Dec. 28, 1933, above.
[3] Answered Feb. 6, 1934, below.

# Roosevelt to Lincoln MacVeagh, Minister to Greece, Athens

[Washington] January 16, 1934

Dear Mr. MacVeagh: I have not had a chance before this to tell you how much I appreciate your letters and also that I hear from very many sources of the fine work you are doing.

That court decision in the Insull case certainly belongs under the title of "curiosa."[1]

I wish you would drop me a line to give me your own opinion as to the present and future ability of the Greek government to pay us a little more on the debt. I rather envy you being in Athens and I wish I could run over to visit you.

Very sincerely yours,

[PPF 1192:CT]

[1] Presumably the rejection by the Greek Supreme Court of the application of the United States for extradition of Samuel Insull.

## Press Conference, Executive Offices of the White House, January 17, 1934, 10:45 A.M.

[*Excerpt*] Q: Mr. President, is it a good guess that the war debt message will contain a recommendation for reduction of armaments?

The President: I have no idea. I have not taken it up at all.

Q: Mr. President, can you tell us the status of negotiations with England?

The President: I have not talked with Phillips about it for ten days. I do not know exactly how far they have got.

Q: Are you seeking any understanding with Great Britain on the currency and monetary program?

The President: No.

Q: Or on trade?

The President: No. The only thing I know about is the big whiskey deal. (Laughter)

Q: Is the whiskey coming in?

The President: Yes, and the pigs are going out.[1]

Q: There have been reports published this morning to the effect that the Administration has undertaken conversation with Great Britain to avoid any sort of possible conflict of stabilization funds?

The President: No, nothing on it. No communications at all . . .

Q: Ireland is sending over the head of its Department of Commerce to talk the possibility of reciprocal trade agreements with us. Can such an agreement be drawn by you or must there be a tariff Message to the Congress?

The President: I do not know. That is the first I heard of it.

Q: I wonder if the Administration has any objections to the State Department going ahead with it?

The President: No. Tell me, can we enter into a trade agreement with Ireland without the consent of Great Britain?

Q: I think so. Ireland claims they can. (Laughter)

Q: Would you care to discuss Senator Johnson's bill for trading with countries who are in debt with us?

The President: I think you had better lay off that for a while.[2] (Laughter)

[President's Press Conferences:T]

[1] See press conference, Jan. 5, 1934, above.
[2] See Moore to Hull, Jan. 22, 1934, below.

## Press Conference, Executive Offices of the White House, January 19, 1934, 4:18 P.M.

[*Excerpt*] Q: Mr. President, what do you think of today's president in Cuba?[1]

The President: Well, I think if I were writing the story—just a background story, let us say—I would put it this way: that we do hope that the election—don't bring me into this at all—of Mr. Mendieta looks very hopeful towards a realization of the two points that we have hoped would be fulfilled. The first was a government in Cuba which would have the substantial backing of the Cuban people; and the other, a government that would be able substantially to maintain law and order.

Of course, you cannot, within twenty-four or forty-eight hours, determine that this new government will be able to fulfill those hopes. I do not call them conditions, I call them hopes. I think you can make it a guess that if in perhaps a week from now or ten days from now there seems to be a carrying out, a fulfillment of those hopes—in other words, if things go along all right—that probably I will converse with some of the other American republics and have an interchange of views in regard to recognition, making it clear that recognition would not be in any way dependent on an agreement in any way between the various American republics; but, having talked things over with them before, I think that probably we should have a general talk about the situation as we hope it will be a week or ten days from now.

Q: Mr. President, will any of our ships be withdrawn in the meantime, or will things stay as they are?

The President: It depends entirely. I couldn't tell you yet. If the people down there seem to think that things are quite normal the thing to do would be to withdraw the ships, but we have no report on that yet . . .

Q: Can you tell us anything about the Johnson Bill that would prevent the issuance of bonds of a defaulting country?

The President: Yes. That question came up Wednesday. I am not ready to shoot on it. I am studying the bill with great care . . .

Q: Mr. President, can you tell us anything about your talk today with Whitney and the other railroad men? They were very silent when they went out of here today.[2]

The President: We talked about two things. One was, tentatively about the 10% railroad pay reduction, which does not come to a head until sometime in the spring. We just talked about it in very general terms. The other subject was the St. Lawrence. I pointed out, in the case of the St. Lawrence, that whether the Treaty was ratified or not the seaway without any question would be built, and that it could be built by Canada without entering into United States territory at all and without building a dam. All they would need would be some locks.

[President's Press Conference:T]

[1] Carlos Mendieta became provisional president of Cuba on Jan. 18, 1934.
[2] C. F. Whitney is the only member of this group identified by the White House appointments list.

## Clark Howell, Editor, The Atlanta *Constitution,* to Roosevelt

Atlanta, Ga., January 20, 1934

Dear Franklin: I am attaching herewith Associated Press news report of an address recently delivered by Mr. Hornbeck, Chief of Division of Far Eastern Affairs of the Department of State.[1] Hornbeck is a hold-over from the Stimson Administration and he takes this occasion to reassert the Stimson policy as regards Manchuria.

You will recall that you and I talked over this question on our way up from Warm Springs, and from what you said to me I do not think that Hornbeck is authorized to commit you as he is apparently doing to the so-called "Stimson policy" which, in my opinion, has done more to disrupt the friendly relations between this country and Japan than anything else. Hornbeck you know is intensely pro-Chinese and is antagonistic to Japan. He lived and taught school in China and his attitude is largely controlled by his former affiliations there.

I repeat my opinion as expressed to you that the most forward step that could possibly be taken to bring about a complete understanding between this country and Japan, and incidentally which would lead to a peace agreement between Japan and Russia, and the assurance of peace in the Pacific, would be along a line of such procedure as that of which we talked and of which I wrote you sometime ago.

I am sure that you will be receptive to such a step. The Japan government will make the overture but it hesitates to do so until it knows that such an overture will be favorably received.

You recall that you told me that you would not only receive it in the spirit in which it may be sent but that you would welcome it. I, of course, did not commit you in replying to my Japanese newspaper friends but I told them that I felt this would be your attitude.

I am now informed confidentially that Otohiko Matsukata is now on his way to this country in an unofficial capacity. He is a Harvard graduate, is a descendant of one of the oldest families in Japan, and I understand has been a guest several times at your Hyde Park home. Evidently his coming bears upon the ascertainment of your position in the matter referred to.

The jingoes of both countries are active in the effort to stir up trouble between the two countries. They are intensifying the situation. You can stop it, and thus contribute to world wide peace along the line of your talk with me.[2]

Sincerely yours,[3]

[PPF 604:T]

[1] This unidentified clipping quotes a Japanese Foreign Office spokesman as saying that his government regarded "as unfortunate and untimely" a speech made by Hornbeck in Washington on Jan. 18, 1934. The Japanese objected particularly to Hornbeck's assertion of the Stimson policy of "non-recognition of governments made by swords."

[2] Answered Jan. 25, 1934, below.

[3] Howell failed to sign this letter.

## Roosevelt to Robert P. Skinner, Ambassador to Turkey, Istanbul

[Washington] January 22, 1934

My dear Mr. Ambassador: I am delighted to have your letter of January second[1] and I want to congratulate you on the excellent work you are doing, especially in the building up of reciprocal trade with Turkey. Our definite efforts toward this end with many countries, plus the cheaper exchange value of the dollar, is building up our foreign trade in a way which I think is very satisfactory.[2]

I hope all goes well with you.

Very sincerely yours,

[OF 502:CT]

[1] Above.

[2] On this subject, see the section on Turkey in *Foreign Relations, 1934,* II.

## Roosevelt to Henry Morgenthau, Jr., Secretary of the Treasury

Washington, January 22, 1934

Memorandum for the Secretary of the Treasury: If you have not seen this it will interest you. All advices from Europe go to prove that the International bankers to whom I have referred in the past, in somewhat uncomplimentary terms, are making their last fight for the theory of central banks which will be controlled largely by bankers, rather than by governments.[1]

F.D.R.

[OF 229:T]

[1] Roosevelt enclosed a note from Réne Léon, Jan. 18, 1934, who enclosed a copy of a letter he had sent to Viscount Hailsham (Douglas McGarel Hogg), British Secretary of State for War, Jan. 17, 1934. Léon said that the only British interests that were profiting from the low silver exchange rate were those industrialists (chiefly in textiles) who had factories in China and who were benefiting from the low cost of production there. Thus the interests of a comparative handful of people were being put ahead of all other British and American interests. The President's statement on silver in his last message to Congress, Léon said, offered the two countries a wonderful opportunity for an agreement on silver before the situation in the Far East and in Central Europe deteriorated beyond control.

## Roosevelt to Senator George W. Norris of Nebraska

[Washington] January 22, 1934

My dear Senator Norris: I have had a conference with the Railway Labor Executives[1] and I pointed out to them that in my judgment the ship canal will not injure the railroads of the country and furthermore, that it will be built anyway by Canada alone if we fail to ratify. I am inclined to think that this is a very strong point to stress, because in such a case Canada could discriminate against American ships by charging higher tolls, etc.[2]

Very sincerely yours,

[OF 66:CT]

[1] Jan. 19, 1934 (PPF 1-0).
[2] Roosevelt was replying to Norris' letter of Jan. 18, 1934 (OF 66), reporting on the organized drive of the railway union heads against ratification of the St. Lawrence

Waterway Treaty. Norris wondered if these leaders could be induced to stop their campaign: "The officials of these labor organizations should realize that they are going too far when they undertake to control the votes of their own friends in matters of this kind."

## Roosevelt to William Phillips, Under Secretary of State

[Washington] January 22, 1934

Memorandum for Honorable William Phillips: Suydam Cutting and Kermit Roosevelt are most anxious that I should send some kind of message to the Dalai Lama.

What do you think?[1]

F.D.R.

[PPF 1224:CT]

[1] Cutting, a friend of Roosevelt, had traveled widely in Tibet and other parts of Asia (in 1940 he published an account of his travels: *The Fire Ox and Other Years,* New York: Scribners). He had received word from Lhasa of the death of the Dalai Lama and had suggested to his friend Kermit Roosevelt that the President send a message to his successor (Kermit Roosevelt to Roosevelt, Jan. 18, 1934, PPF 1224). Phillips advised against this, though Miss LeHand wrote to Kermit that personally the President "would love to do it" (Feb. 2, 1934, PPF 1224).

## Members of the California Delegation in Congress to Roosevelt

Washington, D.C., January 22, 1934

Dear Mr. President: From time to time we hear disquieting rumors as to efforts to induce your Administration to favor the abolition of the Japanese Exclusion policy adopted by the Act of 1924,[1] and to support a quota law as a substitute policy.

As Members of the California Delegation we are vigorously opposed to such action and sincerely hope your Administration has no such purpose.

We believe in the Exclusion policy based on ineligibility of citizenship as the wise policy to be maintained and the one which, when accepted as a permanent policy, will contribute most to the maintenance of friendship between this country, Japan and other oriental countries whose people are likewise ineligible to citizenship.

The ineligible list probably includes the majority of the world's population.

We regard the proposed quota system as only an entering wedge to destroy the Exclusion policy and then to be followed by many years, if not decades, of agitation and contention to place Japan on an actual equality with favored European nations instead of the technical equality on which the quota basis is founded.

It would be absurd to accept the contention that a nation which really insists on a status of "equality" as to immigration with white countries would long be satisfied with the nominal, arbitrary and juggled equality of the present quota rule.

Confident that we represent the best and overwhelming sentiment of our State, and of your supporters therein, we express our earnest hope that your Administration will not become responsible for renewal of an agitation that we believe will be undesirable, persistent, and unhappy in its consequences.[2]

Respectfully submitted,

| | |
|---|---|
| Clarence F. Lea | W. E. Evans |
| Harry L. Englebright | J. H. Hoeppel |
| Frank H. Buck | Charles Kramer |
| Florence P. Kahn | Thomas F. Ford |
| Richard J. Welch | Wm I. Traeger |
| Albert E. Carter | John F. Dockweiler |
| Ralph R. Eltse | Chas. J. Colden |
| John J. McGrath | John H. Burke |
| Denver S. Church | Sam L. Collins |
| Henry E. Stubbs | Geo. Burnham |

[OF 133:TS]

[1] 43 *Stat.* 153.
[2] See Hull to Roosevelt, Jan. 31, 1934, below.


# R. Walton Moore, Assistant Secretary of State, to Cordell Hull, Secretary of State

Washington, January 22, 1934

My dear Judge: The enclosures relate to two measures introduced in the Senate.[1]

In addition, I may say that the Senate is now debating the St. Lawrence Waterways Treaty, which was favorably supported by the Committee at the special session of Congress. This Department is doing what it can to support the President's effort to have the Treaty ratified, but my information from Senators Robinson and Pittman, and other members of Congress, is that the result is in very grave doubt, with the chance against ratification.

As you perhaps already know, the President has determined not to ask for the ratification of the World Court Treaty at this time.

I think you will wish to consider what the President should do in the way of advising action on the Pan-American Arbitration Treaty. You will recall that that treaty, when heretofore considered, was subjected to a destructive reservation and that before you left Washington there was prepared here a modified reservation which it is thought the Senate may be willing to accept.

As you may wish to know what other measures, besides those specifically referred to, have been introduced, I have had a compilation made including all measures which is herewith enclosed.

Yours very sincerely,

R. Walton Moore

[Moore Papers:Johnson Bill:TS]

---

[1] No enclosures are present other than the one printed below and a committee print of S. 682 as it passed the Senate on Jan. 11, 1934; the essential part of this bill reads:

"Be it enacted . . . That hereafter it shall be unlawful for any person within the United States . . . to purchase or sell the bonds, securities, or other obligations of any foreign government issued after the passage of this Act, or to make any loan to such government, including any political subdivision thereof, while such government or political subdivision is in default in the payment of its obligations, or any part thereof, to the Government and/or to any citizen of the United States or to any corporation organized in the United States."

## [*Enclosure*] R. Walton Moore to Cordell Hull

January 19, 1934

Memorandum for Secretary Hull with respect to Senate bill 682 introduced by Senator Johnson of California, which passed the Senate but is now under a motion for reconsideration made by Senator Robinson of Arkansas:

Senator Robinson is in touch with the President about this measure. I understand that if it is to be further dealt with, he will endeavor to have Senator Johnson agree to amending it so as to simply vest in the

President authority to do what is contemplated. But I have suggested that in all probability should the President call in Senator Johnson he might succeed in persuading him to abandon any effort to pass the Bill.[1]

The passage of the Bill in anything like its present form would irritate many governments; would probably prevent many desirable transactions; and would raise difficult questions of interpretation. While it may be supposed that the intention is to penalize the purchaser of securities issued by governments that have absolutely refused to make any payment on account, nevertheless it is hard to understand how a court could interpret the word "default" so narrowly.

Since the above was written the bill has been further considered. Last night (the 21st inst.) Bullitt & I talked with Senator Johnson.[2]

RWM[3]

[Moore Papers:Johnson Bill:TS]

[1] There is nothing to indicate that such a meeting took place.
[2] This last paragraph is an autograph postscript.
[3] See Moore to Robinson, Jan. 27, 1934, below.

# William Phillips, Under Secretary of State, to Roosevelt

Washington, January 22, 1934

My dear Mr. President: In connection with the German Ambassador's visit to you at noon today, it occurs to me that you may be interested to glance through a telegram which Mr. George Rublee has just handed me and which comes from Laird Bell, representative of the Bondholders Protective Council, addressed to Pierre Jay. I also enclose a brief memorandum which contains what seems to us to be the two most important points in connection with this matter.[1]

Faithfully yours,

William Phillips

[OF 198:TS]

[1] On Dec. 18, 1933, the Reichsbank announced that bond interest payments due American creditors on loans to German states, municipalities, and corporations (other than the loans under the Dawes and Young plans) would be sharply reduced (Phillips to Dodd, Dec. 29, 1933, *Foreign Relations, 1933*, II, 459–460, and preceding correspondence). Acting Secretary of State Phillips instructed Dodd to make joint protest with the British (who were similarly discriminated against) and urged Roosevelt to take up the matter with Ambassador Luther (Phillips to Dodd, Jan. 15; Phillips to Roosevelt, Jan. 19, 1934, *Foreign Relations, 1934*, II, 334–335, 335–337).

Roosevelt and Luther met on January 22; a brief statement by the White House said merely that the President had asked that American creditors be given the same treatment as other nations (*Public Papers,* III, 61). The Dutch and Swiss governments had succeeded in getting preferential treatment for their nationals because of the state of their trade balances with Germany. Representatives of American and British bond issuing houses had arranged to meet in Berlin on Jan. 22, 1934, to confer with German officials on the interest reductions, and on Jan. 24, 1934, Hull cabled Dodd that the German authorities should be informed that the State Department regarded, for all practical purposes, the Foreign Bondholders Protective Council as the official agent of American holders of foreign bonds (*Foreign Relations, 1934,* II, 344–345).

Laird Bell and John Foster Dulles, as representatives of the Council, sailed for Europe on January 13 (New York *Times,* Jan. 14, 1934, II, 7). Bell had been in Roosevelt's class at Harvard. A distinguished Chicago lawyer, he had, early in the Roosevelt Administration, declined an offer of appointment as Under Secretary of the Treasury (Bell to Roosevelt, May 17, 1933, PPF 472). He wrote to the President about the conference on March 20; in this he endorsed Ambassador Dodd's view that the basic problems confronting the German economy were the growth of the idea of self-sufficiency, the great fear of financial collapse, and the great expenditures on unemployment relief (PPF 472). Dulles, a Washington lawyer, had held a number of important posts connected with the Hague Peace Conference of 1907, the War Trade Board and the Reparations Commission.

## [*Enclosure 1*] Laird Bell to Pierre Jay

[Berlin] January 20, 1934

[*Telegram*] Jay. On arrival here find situation developing very critically. Understand Dutch and possibly Swiss will decline attend conference on ground they cannot participate in private groups meeting to discuss agreements made by their governments with German Government. Dutch position is furthermore one of indifference. They apparently do not press for special arrangement, but merely take position that if Switzerland gets such an arrangement they must have comparable treatment. Swedes have determined not attend conference as protest against nonpayment Kreuger loan. They oppose special preferential arrangements and advocate equality but insist equality implies payment Kreuger interest since this only direct Government obligation where interest not fully paid.[1] British declined attend Monday on ground proposed Swiss arrangement only today in their hands and Dutch agreement not yet available and conference cannot therefore be had until these proposed agreements can be more closely studied. Dulles also asked before leaving New York that conference be somewhat adjourned to permit our consideration before meeting of proposed Swiss Dutch agreements and exchange views thereon between creditors. Just learn Reichsbank has postponed meeting until twenty-fifth and we have arranged meet Berlin Wednesday with British and probably Swedes who willing attend creditor meeting as they wish evidence full cooperation with English ourselves and make clear their nonattendance at Reichsbank meeting is only protest against Kreuger treatment. Swedish Parliament within last few days enacted law under which clearing can be established and apparently strong English pressure in same direction. There is therefore increasing risk that eventuality which has always been feared might occur namely countries with whom Germany has favorable trade balance will secure full or at least preferential payment with serious results to American bondholders. In face this critical situation we greatly embarrassed by reported failure State Department to lay our position before Swiss Dutch Governments as we understood had been promised at State Department conferences January tenth. Postponement conference affords breathing space for our Government still lay matter before Swiss Dutch which consider absolutely essential. Think situation so critical strongly urge council take matter up in Washington on Monday. Dulles will meanwhile use best efforts avoid open break on registration issue. Dulles concurs in foregoing. Request you give copy his office.

Bell

[OF 198:T]

---

[1] The Ivar Kreuger Swedish Match Company loan. By agreement reached between Germany and Sweden on Aug. 30, 1934, the interest rate on the Kreuger loan was reduced from 6 to $4\frac{1}{2}$ per cent (New York *Times,* Aug. 31, 1934, p. 24).

## [*Enclosure 2*] William Phillips to Roosevelt

[January 22, 1934]

Suggestions

1. That the only government that seems to be pressing with determination for special treatment is Switzerland. The Swiss Government is the one determined to press the demand for special payment. If, however, Germany gives in to Switzerland, it appears that the Dutch Government, the Swedes and the British will follow with clearing agreements likewise leading to special treatment, and leaving the United States, the main creditor, in a position of securing poorer treatment.

2. The German Ambassador may argue that these special agreements are not discriminatory because the special payments arise merely out of special extra purchases of German goods. An adequate disproof of

this claim would require long technical argument. It may simply be said in substance that it is impossible to segregate a small segment of bilateral trade from the rest of the whole international trade process and to base special debt payment upon it without being discriminatory. It is a direct inducement for countries to shut off German trade so that in return for permitting "extra trade" they can demand extra debt payment.[1]

[OF 198:T]

[1] See Dodd to Roosevelt, Feb. 8, 1934, below.


## Raymond B. Fosdick to Roosevelt

New York, January 23, 1934

My dear Mr. President: Here is a copy of a letter which has just come in from Malcolm W. Davis who is attached to the Secretariat of the League of Nations in Geneva. It relates to the reception of your Woodrow Wilson speech[1] in Europe and it may be that you will be interested in some of the points of view which it reflects. The last long paragraph on page two is, to my way of thinking, particularly significant.[2]

With best wishes, Faithfully yours,

Raymond B. Fosdick

[PPF 328:TS]

[1] Dec. 28, 1933, above.
[2] Answered Feb. 1, 1934, below.


## [*Enclosure*] Malcolm W. Davis to Raymond B. Fosdick

[Geneva] January 12, 1934

It is possible to give you now a better impression of the response to Roosevelt's Woodrow Wilson day speech than when I wrote in first reply to your cablegram. On the whole, it is one of appreciative encouragement. At the same time, this is offset somewhat, as you would expect with your knowledge of Europe, by the attack on the peace treaties—in quarters representing the sentiments of countries benefited by the treaties and wanting to maintain them unrevised—and as an aftermath of the postponement of action on the World Court. This second decision, comprehensible to us in terms of our politics, is inevitably felt in Europe as a cold dash following the cordial tone of the speech. The feeling will pass, however; it is due to the constant fact that Europeans tend to be interested only in our actions which affect matters that are on their own minds, rather than in those which we may put foremost for our own reasons.

Avenol (the new Secretary-General of the League), having digested the actual text of the remarks about the League and disarmament, expressed much pleasure and satisfaction in the attitude taken. Frank Walters (head of a Division in the Secretariat) considered the speech "constructive, helpful, and timely." Other officials in the League Secretariat voice similar views. Butler, at the Labor Office, with whom I talked, considered the speech "excellent" and was of course particularly pleased by the mention of what has been done for the benefit of labor.

Lord Cecil[1] (whose committee meeting I attended in Brussels) was evidently cheered by the fact that the President had chosen this moment not only to reaffirm the American proposals for disarmament but also to emphasize cooperation with the League. (As one of the "so-called statesmen" who was at Paris to draft the "so-called peace of 1919" he could hardly be much delighted by the reference to the war settlement.) Philip Noel-Baker was enthusiastic. He had been talking in Paris also with Boncour and Pierre Comert and Pierre de Lanux, whom he reported as all heartened by the things that the President had said and as disposed to take the address as a basis for development of policy. Ruyssen, the French Secretary-General of the Federation of League of Nations Societies, took the same line. None of them, I was interested to note, took exception to any parts, evidently considering it better to accept the criticism of the peace treaties along with the praise of the League and build on the foundation of the positive program outlined in regard to international cooperation. Henri Rolin (Belgian) felt the same way. They all spoke of the portions of the speech appealing to the peoples as the mainstay of peace, and condemning use of force for invasion. These, naturally, are the portions that fit in with Belgian and French policy. Von Bodman, the German Assistant Secretary-General of the Federation of League Societies, talked more about the portions of the speech that condemned the Treaty of Versailles, with satisfaction that a distinction was drawn between it and Wilson's program for peace; he said that his friends were much impressed with this section of the speech, and with the American insistence on real reduction of armaments. So there you are—different passages in the speech pleased both sides, and they all feel the President is a statesman who can see their point of view. It was an astute, clear, honest statement (in my opinion now), of great use and value in relation to the mediatory role that the United States has to play, with the emphasis on the essential sound truth that we favor the settlement of questions, whatever they are, by peaceful means.

Another thing that has struck me, in these talks, is the way in which the President is gaining ground in English and European esteem. There is a great change from the summer and autumn when, after the Economic Conference and the fight about gold, he was regarded with resentment and suspicion. A shift of sentiment is occurring, I think, partly due to the progress of the reconstruction and recovery program, partly due to American policies at the Pan American Conference, partly due to this new pronouncement on international policies generally. Both confidence and interest in him are on the increase again, and there is a kind of faith, or feeling, that if and when he does turn around to international questions he will do it in a big sweeping way, with convictions and courage, and carry Americans with him. As you know, Europe's question always is whether the people and the politicians will support the President in any proposal. The belief is growing here that the people will make the politicians go with the President. That will be important in creating reliance upon any proposals that may be made in his name, because he is thought too sagacious to put forward any plan that he does not know he can put through.

Romm, just back from Moscow, says that the Soviet officials liked the President's speech.[2]

[PPF 238:T:Copy]

[1] Robert Cecil, first Viscount Cecil of Chelwood, long active in League of Nations affairs, was at this time a member of the League Committee on the Composition of the Council.

[2] Vladimar Romm, special correspondent of the Moscow newspaper *Isvestia.*

## William Phillips, Under Secretary of State, to Roosevelt

Washington, January 23, 1934

Dear Mr. President: The other day at the Cabinet Meeting[1] you asked for information in regard to a cotton concession which might be granted to Japan in Ethiopia.

As I did not have the facts at that time, I have since looked the matter up and find that, in a recent despatch from Addis Ababa, reports to this effect cannot be confirmed although they were current for several weeks in Ethiopia towards the end of the past year.

Mr. Southard,[2] our Resident Minister, expresses the opinion that it is very doubtful that the Japanese will seek any such concession, in view of the present undeveloped condition of the country, where roads practically do not exist and where the government and courts are ineffectual. It is possible that the Ethiopians might offer Japan certain inducements and liberty of operation, but we regard this as rather improbable at the present time. In this respect Mr. Southard points out that Japan appears to be following in the earlier steps of many foreign countries in much over-estimating the economic and trading potentialities of this little and backward empire. Some, at least, of the European countries are pretty well disillusioned by this time and others, including Japan, will inevitably come to the same conclusions.

Faithfully yours,

William Phillips

[PSF:Japan:TS]

[1] January 19.
[2] Addison E. Southard, minister resident in Addis Ababa since 1927.


# Press Conference, Executive Offices of the White House, January 24, 1934, 10:45 A.M.

[*Excerpt*] Q: Yesterday Senator Tydings, after his Committee had acted on the Hawes-Cutting Bill, issued a statement favoring the extension of seven months on the Hawes-Cutting Treaty.[1]

The President: There again, it is first in the basket. I have a written memorandum from Manuel Quezon, who is, I think, talking with the Secretary of War about it this week.[2] And I won't do a single thing until I have talked with the Secretary of War. I haven't said yes or no to any proposal. I have not even talked to Senator Tydings about it except that I did talk to Senator Cutting last week in regard to extending the life before last Wednesday, the day it was to expire, and we both agreed it was not necessary to extend the life before last Wednesday, that it could be done later if we decide to do it.[3]

Q: Among other things that Senator Tydings said yesterday was that after the new election if the Legislature again failed to take action, or action adversely, it would be notice to Congress that the Filipinos do not desire independence and would be willing to continue under their present status.[4]

The President: No, nothing to say . . .

Q: Dispatches from Tokio indicate the Japanese Government has approached our Government with a view to settling disputes which will occur in the next two years, meaning the naval question. Have you received any information to that effect?

The President: Nothing done on the preliminaries of the naval conference at all . . .[5]

Q: Your statement, issued at the time the German Ambassador was here, mentioned the German trade.[6] Can you explain that for us?

The President: Only as a matter of theory. I told him just what I told a great many other people, that the ultimate ideal, the ultimate objective was for every nation's trade to be on a balanced basis, so that the total income from foreign ports equalled the total outgo to foreign ports, with the world objective of eliminating these large favorable or unfavorable trade balances that have to be paid in gold from time to time. That being so, in the case of Germany, for example, we would be perfectly willing to discuss with them the question first as to whether the trade between Germany and America, both ways, is out of balance or not. The thing has never been studied. We don't know until we actually make a complete study whether we actually export more goods to Germany than we receive from Germany. We have never explored the other side of the picture—the invisible exports of money from this country to Germany through the tourist trade, remittances by immigrants, and so forth.

The first step is to get figures along that line and then, if it appears that there is a balance, favorable or unfavorable, one way or the other, the time will come to try to correct that through purchases on the debit side of the ledger.

Q: Mr. President, is the Government giving its support to the American representatives to the Debt Conference?

The President: Yes and no. They are private individuals; one of them is a classmate of mine.[7] They are private individuals but, at the same time, we have said perfectly clearly to the German Ambassador and also to our Ambassador on the other side that we are anticipating the same kind of treatment, without discrimination, that other nations are getting.

There has been a great deal of complaint, as everybody knows, about discrimination. Switzerland and Holland are being paid approximately 100% on the debts that are due their citizens by German municipalities and states and corporations, as against other nations that are getting only 50% in cash and scrip for the other 50% which, when you come to cash it, only works out at 25%. We were disturbed, Great Britain was disturbed, and other nations, by the suggestion from Berlin that this 50% cash payment would be further reduced to 30 or 35%. That is all we have done.

Q: Mr. President, the special treatment to Holland and Switzerland followed threats of retaliation by them. Have we gone as far as that?

The President: No.

Q: Can you tell us what the German Ambassador said in reply to your representations concerning discrimination against Americans?

The President: I think you had better ask him.

Q: We did, Mr. President. (Laughter)

The President: Of course, off the record—I think you had better use it as background as long as you do not attribute it to me in any way—the theory of the German Ambassador and German Government is a theory which is somewhat difficult to understand. It goes along this line: That if they pay 100 cents on the dollar to Switzerland and Holland creditors, eventually, some day in the future, the general economic situation will be so much better that they will be able to pay 100 cents on the dollar to other people. The best word to use is an unbalanced theory that does not bring much cash into one's pockets.

Q: In that connection, is there anything to be said on the rumor that the German Government is buying bonds at the present low prices?

The President: That has been stated. It has been stated that as high as five hundred million dollars of German bonds in this country have already been bought up at away below par. I don't know whether that is true or not. I don't know whether anybody has checked.

Q: It has been checked, and the statement has been found to be accurate. In the last year, 1932, they are supposed to have bought up a good deal more than the equivalent interest payments would have been had they met their various payments due on obligations.

The President: Yes?

Q: In connection with the debts, Secretary Morgenthau, at the hearing, is quoted as saying that the responsibility has been transferred back from the Treasury to the State Department.[8] Is there any significance in that?

The President: No . . .

Q: Did you get a chance to read Prime Minister MacDonald's speech this morning in which he suggested stabilization of the currencies?

The President: Off the record, I have read it; on the record, I have not.[9] (Laughter)

[President's Press Conferences:T]

[1] The Senate Committee on Territories and Insular Affairs, of which Millard F. Tydings of Maryland was chairman, had approved an extension of the Hawes-Cutting Act of Jan. 17, 1933 (47 *Stat.* 761), which extended independence to the Philippines provided that it was ratified by the Philippine legislature before Jan. 17, 1934. Quezon's party opposed the enabling act as not sufficiently generous to the Philippines and it was not ratified.

[2] Quezon's letter to Roosevelt of Jan. 15, 1934, is not present but is referred to in a letter from Secretary of War Dern to Roosevelt of Jan. 30, 1934, enclosing a draft reply (OF 400). No White House copy of this draft has been found and presumably it was not sent.

[3] An appointment is noted for Tydings (on Jan. 22, 1934) but not for Cutting (PPF 1-0).

[4] Quoted in the New York *Times* of Jan. 24, 1934, p. 12. The Hawes-Cutting Act was extended until Oct. 1, 1934, by the act approved March 24, 1934 (48 *Stat.* 456).

[5] See the section, "Negotiations preliminary to the London Naval Conference of 1935," in *Foreign Relations, 1934,* I, 217–259.

[6] Statement of Jan. 22, 1934, in *Public Papers,* III, 61.

[7] Laird Bell; see Phillips to Roosevelt, Jan. 22, 1934, above.

[8] In his testimony of Jan. 24, 1934, before the House Appropriations Committee on the Treasury-Post Office appropriation bill (New York *Times,* Jan. 25, 1934, p. 16).

[9] Reported *ibid.,* Jan. 24, 1934, p. 1.


# Roosevelt to William Phillips, Under Secretary of State

Washington, January 24, 1934

Memorandum from the President for the Under Secretary of State: What can I say to Claude Bowers in regard to the Spanish Wine quota? The Ambassador is much concerned.[1]

[PSF:Spain:CT]

[1] Roosevelt refers here to Bowers' letter of Jan. 10, 1934, above; see Phillips to Roosevelt, Jan. 29, 1934, below.

## Roosevelt to Clark Howell, Editor, The Atlanta *Constitution*, Atlanta, Georgia

[Washington] January 25, 1934

Dear Clark: Many thanks for your letter of January twentieth. I am happy to know that Otohiko Matsukata is coming here. He was in college with me. I shall be delighted to see him again.[1]

As ever yours,

[PPF 604:CT]

[1] See Howell to Roosevelt, Jan. 20, 1934, above. Howell wrote again Feb. 2, 1934 (PPF 719), to say that he had told Matsukata that the President would be pleased to see him. He said also: "Sooner or later we will have to abandon the Stimson policy, which caused unnecessary friction between two countries which have been traditional friends. The Far Eastern Division of our State Department is unquestionably anti-Japanese and it seems determined to commit you to the Stimson policy, which I think is unfortunate."

## Norman H. Davis to Roosevelt

New York, January 25, 1934

My dear Mr. President: As recently suggested by you, I have prepared a memorandum on our so-called Neutrality Policy. I regret that I have not been able to make this more concise but I could not well cover the subject in fewer words.

In a day or so I shall also send to you, for your consideration, a memorandum on the Arms Embargo Resolution.[1]

Faithfully yours,

Norman H. Davis

[OF 29:TS:Photostat]

[1] Not found in the Roosevelt papers.

## [*Enclosure*] Norman H. Davis to Roosevelt

### Memorandum Regarding Neutrality Policy

During the course of the disarmament negotiations France, and also other Powers, made various proposals for the organization of peace in

Europe, which were opposed by the British, partly on the ground that Great Britain could not commit herself to any program of action for the maintenance of peace in Europe because of the danger that the United States might consider such action a violation of its rights as a neutral and thus bring Great Britain into conflict with the United States. The United States, which had fathered the Kellogg-Briand Pact, was, accordingly, put in the position of appearing to block a solution of the disarmament problem and a promotion of peace by maintaining the indefensible position that there should be no distinction between an aggressor nation that violates that Pact and an innocent nation that may be attacked.

For us there were two questions of prime importance to consider. First, to what extent could we wisely assist, directly or indirectly, in bringing about a universal reduction and limitation of armaments, which is of vital importance to us; and second, how could we best avoid being drawn into war in case of a violation of the Kellogg-Briand Pact and the Disarmament Convention.

In discussing this matter with you last March you wisely decided that, while the United States should not make any commitments to take action against any nation that breaks the peace in violation of its Treaty obligations, it should not aid and abet such nation by insisting that there was no difference between such a nation and the nation that was the victim of the violation, in case it is possible to determine the guilty party. It was, furthermore, felt that if the United States should continue to adhere strictly to the traditional policy of neutrality, which did not succeed in preventing us from being drawn into the last war, and in fact, brought us to the verge of war with Great Britain, we would be blocking the organization of peace and doing nothing constructive to avoid being drawn into another war. It was also felt that if the Kellogg-Briand Pact has any significance it must affect the rights of belligerency, from which the rights and obligations of neutrality flow.

This general subject came up for discussion during the visits of Prime Minister MacDonald and M. Herriot to the United States in the spring of 1933 and a suggestion as to the American attitude under certain circumstances was set forth by you to the British and French representatives. This was subsequently communicated to me with authorization, at the appropriate time in the disarmament negotiations, to state publicly the attitude of the United States.

This I did on May 22, 1933 when, in the course of a speech before the General Commission, I made the following statement:

In addition I wish to make it clear that we are ready not only to do our part toward the substantive reduction of armament but if this is effected by general international agreement, we are also prepared to contribute in other ways to the organization of peace. In particular we are willing to consult the other states in case of a threat to peace with a view to averting conflict. Further than that, in the event that the states, in conference, determine that a state has been guilty of a breach of the peace in violation of its international obligations and take measures against the violator, then, if we concur in the judgment rendered us as to the responsible and guilty party, we will refrain from any action tending to defeat such collective effort which these states may thus make to restore peace.

Shortly thereafter in the course of a general debate in the General Commission, I stated that at the appropriate time and as a part of a General Disarmament Agreement, the United States would make a unilateral declaration along the following lines:

Recognizing that any breach or threat of breach of the Pact of Paris (Kellogg-Briand Pact) is a matter of concern to all the signatories thereto, the Government of the United States of America declares that in the event of a breach or threat of breach of this Pact, it will be prepared to confer with a view to the maintenance of peace in the event that consultation for such purpose is arranged pursuant (a) to Articles one to five of Part I of the Disarmament Convention, or (b) pursuant to the machinery for general consultation which now exists or may hereafter be constituted.

In the event that following a decision by the conference of the Powers in consultation in determining the aggressor with which, on the basis of its independent judgment, the Government of the United States agreed, the Government of the United States will undertake to refrain from any action and to withhold protection from its citizens if engaged in activities which would tend to defeat the collective effort which the States in consultation might have decided upon against the aggressor.

It was made clear at this time that the foregoing declarations indicated in a general way, but without commitment as to phraseology, the position which the United States Government would be disposed to take.

This declaration has been variously misinterpreted in Congress and in the Press as indicating a willingness to abandon neutrality and as constituting a binding commitment as to future action. This misconception of the purpose and intent of the declaration might be cleared away by bringing out the following points:

(1) The declaration does not involve any attempt to predetermine the action of the United States. The decision would be taken when the emergency arose. It would thus depend upon the recognition by the

United States that there was a breach, or threatened breach, of a treaty to which we were a party (the Pact of Paris) and, consequent upon that breach, action by other Powers against the treaty violator whom we agreed with them in recognizing as such.

(2) The obligation under the declaration is a negative one, involving no participation in collective or punitive action against a treaty violator; it would call for no trade or other embargoes on our part.

(3) The declaration does not imply an abandonment of neutrality. It does imply that we would not intervene to protect the trade of our nationals who might endeavor to carry on that trade in spite of restrictive measures imposed by the states, other than the United States, which had joined together in collective action against the treaty violator.

(4) In effect the declaration indicates a policy on the part of the United States not to intervene rather than any support of a policy of intervention; it is a convenant to keep out of trouble, not to involve us in trouble.

(5) Finally, the declaration is contingent upon the conclusion and ratification of a general disarmament agreement satisfactory to the United States; that is to say, until the nations of the world have themselves taken steps for the preservation of peace by reducing and limiting their armaments, there would be no occasion for a declaration to be made.[1]

[OF 29:T:Photostat]

[1] See Roosevelt to Hull, Jan. 30, 1934, below.

# Press Conference, Executive Offices of the White House, January 26, 1934, 4:05 P.M.

[*Excerpt*] Q: Reports are printed today that you have named or will name individual experts for virtually each major country on foreign exchange when the stabilization fund becomes operative.[1]

The President: That is a new one on me.

Q: It is on the front pages of the papers today.

The President: Probably what that story arose from was that somebody was down here a couple of days ago and wanted to know about the proposed monetary commission and I think I casually remarked that of course we would have people to keep us in touch with the actual facts on exchange in probably a dozen different centers of exchange including, I think I used the words, "including Shanghai." And probably whoever I told it to—I have forgotten who it was—announced that I was going to have fifty experts centered all over the world . . .

Q: The recognition of Salvador has started talk of the possibility of the United States going into Pan America and recognizing revolutionary governments as set up in—

The President: There isn't anything on that at all. The only thing, as I remember it, is that the three Central American Governments, which were still bound by the old non-recognition treaties—you see, Costa Rica had withdrawn and Salvador practically had taken itself out, and the three that were still bound decided to make this recognition of the present Salvador Government immediately, and then call together a conference of the five republics in order to discuss a new agreement relating to recognition. Of course, our policy there has been to go along with the Central American policies. We were not a signatory of that previous treaty but we said as long as that is the general rule in Central America, we would adopt the same policy. That is all that happened.

Q: No change.

The President: No. There is, as I understand it, going to be a meeting of the five governments after recognition of Salvador.[2]

Q: Are you any nearer the tariff Message to the Congress?

The President: No.

Q: How about war debts?

The President: The only thing we are nearer on is that I have to ask the Secretary of State to bring himself up to date on the reports that were made during his absence.

Q: I have one more inquiry on money here. The dollar, you know, is getting stronger every day and closed at 4.94 to the pound in London today. Is there anything of special significance on our monetary program?

The President: Not that I know of.

Q: We have reports that unusually large amounts of foreign money are coming into this country presumably for investment purposes and there is a report that one company is offering $60,000,000 in securities on the London market. Has that any particular connection?

The President: I think probably you had better ask Henry Morgenthau about it. I think that some of the gold that we have been purchasing on the other side is coming back to this country in the form of bars.

Q: Paris is clearing out fifteen millions a day, mostly sent to this country.

[President's Press Conferences:T]

614

¹ The stabilization fund set up by the Gold Reserve Act of 1934, approved Jan. 30, 1934 (48 *Stat.* 337).

² By a treaty signed in 1923, Nicaragua, El Salvador, Costa Rica, Guatemala, and Honduras agreed to withold recognition from any Central American government attaining power through force. In December 1931, Maximiliano Martínez became president of El Salvador through a military revolt. The other Central American republics refused to recognize him and the United States also refused to do so. El Salvador and Costa Rica thereupon denounced the 1923 treaty under procedures provided by it, and on Jan. 1, 1934, recognized the Martinez government (Welles to Roosevelt, Jan. 8, 1934, *Foreign Relations, 1934,* V, 218–219). In view of the circumstances, the State Department then recommended that the United States also recognize El Salvador, and this was done Jan. 26, 1934 (Welles to Roosevelt, Jan. 25, 1934, *ibid.,* pp. 255–256).

# R. Walton Moore, Assistant Secretary of State, to Senator Joseph T. Robinson of Arkansas

[Washington] January 27, 1934

My dear Senator: Enclosed is a copy of Senator Johnson's bill, marked "A," which follows the copy marked "B" which was used by Secretary Hull in his recent conference with the President.[1] The latter was approved by the President, except that he was most urgent that the obligations should be confined to those due the Federal Government. I am handing you a copy of memorandum made by the President himself, giving his view on that point and also suggesting alternative proposals relative to foreign governments to be affected. You will notice that draft "A" incorporates his second proposal by applying the bill to any country that has failed to pay in part or in whole. The Russian situation, we believe, is saved by the amendment of Section 2 as indicated in the draft "A."[2]

I am handing you a copy of the bill marked "C" showing a notation made by Senator Johnson when I talked with him the other day.

We do not think that the amendment desired by Mr. Butler[3] should be accepted. It seems pretty clear that any situation such as he describes is taken care of by the exception with reference to a renewal or adjustment of existing indebtedness made on page 2, Section 1. I am returning Mr. Butler's letters and also your copy of the bill marked "D" handed me this morning.

I have shown Secretary Hull the copy of the bill marked "A" and also this letter.

Yours very sincerely,

[Moore Papers:Johnson Bill:CT]

[1] No enclosures are present except the memorandum printed below. For texts of the bill (S. 682) as it passed the Senate the first time on January 11, and as it was approved following reconsideration and amendment on February 2, see *Cong. Rec.*, vol. 78, pp. 446, 1824. Hull had had tea with Roosevelt on Sunday, January 21 (PPF 1-0).

[2] Financing of trade with the Soviet Union through the Export-Import Bank would have been barred by the bill as it stood at this time.

[3] Not further identified.


# [*Enclosure*] Memorandum by Roosevelt on the Johnson Bill

The White House, Washington

A. Make it apply only to those countries who have failed totally to pay anything on installments due United States Government.

(Except Russia.)

E.g.—France—

B. Make it apply to any country who has failed in part or in whole.

But eliminate anyway everything except debts due the Federal Government.[1]

[Moore Papers:Johnson Bill:CT]

[1] These ideas were elaborated in a memorandum of Jan. 31, 1934, prepared for Senator Robinson by Green H. Hackworth, legal adviser to the State Department, and sent to Robinson by Moore in a note of Jan. 31, 1934; both are printed in *Foreign Relations, 1934*, I, 525, 525–526. During this time Senator Johnson had been in consultation with Robinson and the State Department; the amendments he offered on Feb. 2, 1934, largely met the Administration's wishes (*Cong. Rec.*, vol. 78, pp. 1822–1824). Johnson said at the time that it was immaterial whether he was "in wholehearted accord with some of the amendments" but that he was willing to consent to their addition so that there might be "immediate action" (*ibid.*, p. 1823). Refunding issues and private debts were exempted from the prohibition, as were public corporations created by Congress or corporations in which the government of the United States had a controlling interest (48 *Stat.* 574). This last amendment removed the operations of the Export-Import Bank from the penalties of the bill. The bill then went to the House; see Moore to Roosevelt, March 12, 1934, below.


# William Phillips, Under Secretary of State, to Roosevelt

Washington, January 29, 1934

My dear Mr. President: With reference to your inquiry of January 24th regarding Ambassador Bowers' concern over the Spanish wine quota,[1] the situation at the moment is as follows: As you know, our negotiators are attempting to persuade Spain to purchase some of the excess tobacco crop in this country in return for which we have expressed a willingness to increase the Spanish quota on wines.

During the course of the negotiations the Spanish Government told us they would be willing to buy $150,000 worth of tobacco more than they had originally intended, if we purchased wine at the ratio value of three for one to help balance trade between the two countries. We have replied that we were not concerned regarding the formula of equivalence which Spain desires to use if we are able to obtain a concrete proposal satisfactory to our tobacco growers. Consequently we have requested them to state the definite amount that they intend to purchase, but we have not had any word from the Spanish Embassy during the past few days.[2]

Faithfully yours,

(S)William Phillips

[OF 303:T:Copy]

[1] Roosevelt to Phillips, Jan. 24, 1934, above.
[2] This letter was sent to Bowers; see Roosevelt's letter to him of Feb. 5, 1934, in *Personal Letters, 1928–1945*, I, 389–390.

## Roosevelt to Mrs. Albert L. Deane, New York

[Washington] January 30, 1934

My dear Mrs. Deane: Thank you much for your letter.[1] Frankly, I do not know how to effect a permanency in American foreign policy. My own experience is that advisory boards soon drift into oblivion. At least we have a permanent democratic and consular service and most officials in the State Department are drafted from this service.

Very sincerely yours,

[PPF 359:CT]

[1] Mrs. Deane had written to Roosevelt on Jan. 25, 1934 (PPF 359), to congratulate him and Mrs. Roosevelt on their talks to the Women's Conference on Current Problems on Oct. 13, 1933, above. To ensure permanency for the Administration's Latin American policy she proposed the creation of an advisory board in the State Department to act as a kind of general staff.

## Roosevelt to Cordell Hull, Secretary of State

Washington, January 30, 1934

Memorandum for Secretary of State: I think you and I should have a talk about this general subject. It affects the embargo resolution which is still before the Senate.[1]

F.D.R.

[OF 29:T:Photostat]

[1] Roosevelt's memorandum refers to the Davis memorandum of Jan. 25, 1934, above.

## Roosevelt to Henry Moskowitz, New York

[Washington] January 30, 1934

Dear Henry: I am delighted to read the words of Mr. Ernest Franklin. I have heard of his great ability and knowledge—and he seems to understand our situation much more clearly than most Englishmen.[1]

I do hope to see you one of these days soon.

Always sincerely yours,

[OF 229:CT]

[1] Franklin was head of the London banking house of Samuel Montague and Company and an authority on foreign exchange. Moskowitz (husband of Belle Moskowitz, Al Smith's secretary when Smith was governor) had sent a page of quotations from a speech by Franklin at a recent dinner of the Lombard Association, made up of managers of the foreign departments of important London bank and trust companies. Franklin said that no better way to raise commodity prices could have been found than to do what Roosevelt did: raise the dollar price of gold. However, he asked, did the President know that there was a limit to the lengths he could go without driving France and Holland off the gold standard?

## Homer S. Cummings, Attorney General, to Roosevelt

[Washington] January 30, 1934

My dear Mr. President: In response to your oral request made some days ago for suggestions as to the possibility of offsetting German assets now in the control of the United States against the unpaid debts due the United States from the Government of Germany, I submit herewith a study of this question, made by Mr. Holtzoff, of the Department of Justice.[1]

I have refrained from writing a formal opinion on the subject in view of possible questions of policy involved, and the necessity for having Congressional action, should it be decided to carry out the plan. Moreover, it occurred to me that you might wish to discuss the subject with the Secretary of State.

I think the attached memorandum is very helpful, and I am prepared to carry the study of the subject further, whenever you may desire.

Respectfully yours,

Homer Cummings

[OF 198:TS]

[1] "Memorandum for the Attorney General re offsetting German assets in control of the United States against the indebtedness of the Government of Germany to the United States, Jan. 15, 1934." Alexander Holtzoff was at this time a special assistant to the Attorney General; in 1945 he was appointed judge of the United States District Court for Washington, D.C. Holtzoff described the various funds in the control of the United States from which payments could be made and the procedure to be followed. He concluded that, "in applying assets belonging to German Nationals in its control as against monies due it from the German Government, the United States would be acting pursuant to express treaty provisions and would not be violating any legal rights of Germany or her Nationals." See Roosevelt to Cummings and Morgenthau, Feb. 5, 1934, below.

# Roosevelt to Representative Samuel Dickstein of New York

[Washington] January 31, 1934

My dear Mr. Dickstein: Since receiving your letter of January 12th, I have not had sufficient time to form any definite opinion as to what action might properly be taken on the Resolution enclosed therewith.[1] However, I have no doubt it will be carefully considered by the Committee having jurisdiction, and by the House of Representatives in the event of its being brought before that body.

Very sincerely yours,

[OF 3552:CT]

[1] Roosevelt sent Dickstein's letter (above) to Under Secretary of State Phillips for comment. Phillips replied Jan. 29, 1934 (OF 3552), that he and Assistant Secretary

of State Moore had had several conferences with Dickstein and had examined some of the evidence that had been submitted to his committee; Dickstein hoped that the President would indicate his interest in getting the resolution out of the Rules Committee. Phillips said that he and Moore thought it would be better for the President not to do this and enclosed a draft reply to Dickstein, the letter here printed. H.R. 198, providing for the appointment of a special committee of the House to investigate Nazi propaganda activities, had been introduced by Dickstein on Jan. 3, 1934. The resolution was reported on March 7, debated (at some length) on March 20, and passed. On April 5 the speaker of the House appointed a special committee headed by John W. McCormack to carry out the resolution (*Cong. Rec.,* vol. 78, pp. 13–14, 25, 3929, 4934–4949, 6160). The anti-Nazi demonstrations in New York and Dickstein's investigations were the subject of a number of memoranda and letters to and from Ambassador Luther and his Berlin office as published in *Documents on German Foreign Policy, 1918–1945,* II, 252–255, 467, 492, 552–554, 565–566, 574–575.

## Cordell Hull, Secretary of State, to Roosevelt

Washington, January 31, 1934

My dear Mr. President: There has been brought to my attention the letter here attached of January 22 addressed to you by some twenty members of the California Delegation in the House of Representatives.[1] In this letter, the signers express the earnest hope "that your Administration will not become responsible for renewal of an agitation that we believe will be undesirable, persistent, and unhappy in its consequences" directed toward alteration of the Immigration Act of 1924 to the end that immigration from Japan be placed on a quota basis.

To the numerous suggestions and inquiries which have been addressed to me on this subject, I have made it a practice to reply to the effect that we regard this question as one to be dealt with by the legislative branch of the Government. In view of the circumstances above indicated, I have not expressed to the various inquirers and persons offering suggestions any opinion favorable or unfavorable with regard to a change in the law; but I have suggested that proponents of a change in the law should direct their efforts to converting to their views a sufficient number of members of Congress to insure the passage of amendatory legislation, if and when introduced in Congress, of the character which they advocate. I have further suggested that in the interest of good relations between this country and Japan it is desirable that this matter be not made the subject of acrimonious discussion and that no chances should be taken by putting forward proposals for legislation adverse action upon which, if taken, in Congress, would make matters worse than they have been.

Might it not be feasible, by way of action upon the letter under reference, for you to call in some member of the signatory group and inform him for communication to the others that it is no part of your intention under existing circumstances to take any step with regard to the matter.[2]

Faithfully yours,

Cordell Hull

[OF 133:TS]

---

[1] Above.
[2] See Oregon and Washington members of Congress to Roosevelt, Feb. 10, 1934, below.


## Cordell Hull, Secretary of State, to Roosevelt

Washington, January 31, 1934

My dear Mr. President: Concern over the conditions in our Foreign Service compels me to bring to your attention again the necessity for some additional provision for the members of that Service over that which you have already recommended. The estimate submitted to Congress last week will, if adopted, remedy the future losses resulting directly from the depreciation of the dollar. That, however, will only insure to employees abroad the normal foreign currency equivalent of the remaining eighty-five per cent of their salaries, fifteen per cent having been cut off by the Economy Act. It will reimburse them for none of the losses which they sustained during the past ten months due to the decline of the dollar and before the so-called gold payments were begun, and in countries to which the gold payments were not applicable.

The employees of the Foreign Service have suffered losses out of all proportion to those which other employees of the Government have suffered. It seems to me that if we are to succeed in maintaining abroad a body of men capable of furthering our trade relations, protecting the interests of our people, and carrying out successfully our foreign policy, we must place the men in a position to enable them to accomplish these tasks. Probably the speediest and best way to do this, in addition to preventing losses through the decline of the dollar on the exchanges, would be by restoring the rent, heat and light allowances to the amounts provided in 1932 and by providing also a reasonable sum for post allowances. To do this would require for rent, heat and light an additional amount of $300,000 for 1934 and $775,000 for 1935, and for post allowances $100,000 for 1934 and $200,000 for 1935. Estimates of these amounts, which are understood to have your approval, were presented to the Bureau of the Budget, but have not been transmitted to Congress. My impression is that failure to transmit them was due to the fact that they did not meet with the approval of Representative Oliver.[1]

I believe that if you were to request that these estimates be transmitted to Congress, and at the same time explain to Mr. Oliver and to the Chairmen of the Committees on Appropriations of the House and Senate that you consider these amounts essential to the proper maintenance and efficiency of the Foreign Service, they would be willing to recommend them to the two Houses of Congress. I very much hope that this may be done, and venture to enclose drafts of letters which, if you approve, might be sent by you to the gentlemen mentioned.[2]

Faithfully yours,

Cordell Hull

[OF 67:TS]

[1] William B. Oliver of Alabama, chairman of the House Subcommittee on Appropriations for State, Justice, Commerce and Labor.

[2] Hull's letter was sent by McIntyre (on Feb. 1, 1934) to Budget Director Douglas, with drafts of proposed letters from the President to the chairman of the Senate Appropriations Committee, the chairman of the House Appropriations Committee, and to Representative Oliver (OF 67). Douglas then submitted to Roosevelt, in a letter of Feb. 21, 1934 (OF 67), supplemental estimates of appropriations for the State Department amounting to $954,000 for office and living quarters for the Foreign Service, and $300,000 for cost of living allowances for Foreign Service Officers. See Roosevelt to Oliver, Feb. 24, 1934, below.

## Roosevelt to Raymond B. Fosdick, New York

[Washington] February 1, 1934

Dear Ray: Thank you for letting me see the message from Davis.[1] In the present European situation I feel very much as if I were groping for a door in a blank wall. The situation may get better and enable us to give some leadership.

Very sincerely yours,

[PPF 328:CT]

[1] Enclosure with Fosdick to Roosevelt, Jan. 23, 1934, above.

Press Conference, Executive Offices of the White House,
February 2, 1934, 10:50 A.M.

[*Excerpt*] Q: Can you tell us something about the conversation late
yesterday with Mr. Jones and Mr. Bullitt?[1]

The President: I do not think I can. I think you are a little ahead
of time. The machinery—we have not decided on what kind of machinery we are going to use for a certain purpose yet.

Wait a minute, I think I can—I don't know, you had better see Jones
about it but I can tell you what it is about. There is no reason why
I should not tell you, off the record, what it is about. Don't print the
thing until you have seen Jones. We are probably going to organize some
kind of corporation, which may be a District banking corporation, in
order to establish certain—I cannot think of what the word is—endorse-
ments of loans to Russia. It is not straight credit.

Q: Confined entirely to Russia?

The President: That is the primary purpose. But you had better get
that from Jesse because there was not a final decision on the form of
the corporation yesterday afternoon.

Q: Do you mean by that endorsement of loans a Government guarantee of the loans to the American exporters?

The President: Portions, yes. It means, of course, the American
exporter would take some of the risk himself. That is the general
theory.

Q: Would that entail an amendment to the R.F.C. Act with respect
to export credits?

The President: I do not think so.

Q: Mr. President, how much credit is contemplated, exactly?

The President: That has not been discussed.

Q: Would it come under the Federal Reserve System? There is a
provision in there?

The President: I should think so. I think it is the kind of bank that
the R.F.C., if I remember it, can take stock in. But, as I say, you must
check with Jesse Jones on that first because I do not know enough about
the actual details.[2]

Q: In view of the fact that they are trying to get unanimous consent
to vote on the St. Lawrence, is there anything you can say with reference
to it?

The President: Only that Senator Robinson told me yesterday that they are trying to get a unanimous consent vote in about a week. That is all right, so far as I am concerned.

Q: Norman H. Davis is in town studying disarmament over at the State Department. In view of the fact that the British and Italians have made proposals, have you anything to say?

The President: So far as I know, there has been no date set for the reconvening of the conference. There is a committee meeting which will decide on a date. I think that committee meeting is to be held on the fourth of February, day after tomorrow.

Q: The thirteenth.

The President: It has been put off? Ask Davis.

Q: In connection with that, both the British and the Italian proposals provide that—our position as outlined by Secretary Hull is that we are opposed to any rearmament by any nation at the present time but in view of these other proposals, is it a safe proposition that if Europe agrees to let Germany rearm, we won't object?[3]

The President: I cannot say anything about it for the reason that since Geneva adjourned there have been at least six different proposals and you can never tell whether they are coming through as definite and final proposals, and also the fact that they seem still to be in the realm of European politics rather than world disarmament. We made our position pretty clear on that. We draw the line and distinction between European political adjustments and world disarmament.

Q: Now that you have recognized Cuba, is there anything you can tell us on sugar?

The President: I am talking with several people about that this afternoon. Of course the Philippine situation is also somewhat involved. We have not made any decision or found any plan different from the one we had a month ago or a week ago.

Q: Are you still working on the idea of quotas?

The President: Yes, in general.

Q: Can you tell us with whom you are going to talk?

The President: I think I am talking with—I am having two talks, one with the Secretary of War around noon and with Señor Quezon around fifteen minutes later and, this afternoon, I think I am talking with Secretary Hull and Sumner Welles.[4] This is just developing, that is all.

Q: To return to Russia, will this banking corporation handle any arrangement for mutual exchange of goods as well as credit?

The President: That I do not know; I have not got as far as that at all.

Q: To clarify that a little bit more, is this along the lines of the plan suggested by Peek to you in his report?[5]

The President: It all ties in together.

Q: We still do not know what the Peek report is. That is the reason for the question.

The President: That was only a very preliminary report, that is all. It ties in with so many departments, Agriculture, Commerce, State, et cetera. Probably over the week end or early in the week we will get to it.

Q: Have you had any conversations about Stock Exchange regulations?

The President: No.

Q: Have you had any protests from the Japanese or others on the naval situation?

The President: No, I have not heard a word.

Q: In that connection, Pan Pacific[6] asks that you come to Tokio when and if you go to Hawaii?

The President: That is still perfectly vague. It depends on Congress and a lot of other things.

Q: I think he was saying that you have an invitation to go to Japan when you go to Hawaii.

The President: No. It is a very grave question as to whether I can take enough time to go to Hawaii. You have to go straight up from the Canal to San Diego.

Q: This morning I noticed that in London the gold price has gone to $34.85. In view of that and the fact that they have substituted the American dollar in place of the French franc—

The President: Now you are getting on the subject we called "verboten," Fred.[7]

Q: Do you care to say whether we are having any negotiations with Great Britain—(Laughter)

The President: Stevie,[8] we will consider that question as duly asked and a "No" answer made from now on.

Mr. Stephenson: The sky is the limit.

[President's Press Conferences:T]

---

[1] Jesse Jones, chairman of the Reconstruction Finance Corporation, William C. Bullitt, ambassador to the Soviet Union, and John Wiley, counselor of embassy at Moscow, had talked with Roosevelt the day before on a proposal to extend credits to American exporters to Russia (PPF 1-0).

[2] Jones described the proposed bank to the reporters after this news conference (New York Times, Feb. 3, 1934, p. 19). Capital was to be furnished by the Reconstruction

Finance Corporation and all stock was to be owned by the government. Such a bank had for some time been urged by American importers and exporters so that they could finance foreign sales under conditions comparable to those available to their foreign competitors. A plan for a bank similar to the one now proposed had been drawn up early in 1934 by a committee of businessmen headed by John Abbink, general manager of Business Publishers International Corporation; the plan, however, contemplated private financing. This plan had come before the R.F.C. unofficially some time before Jan. 22, 1934. Establishment of the bank as the Export-Import Bank of Washington, D.C., was authorized by executive order 6581 of Feb. 2, 1934, and Peek was named president (New York *Times,* Jan. 21, II, 6; Jan. 23, p. 35; Feb. 13, p. 1; Feb. 27, 1934, p. 27; *Public Papers,* III, 76–78). Peek did not definitely accept his appointment until February 26; on that day he met with Roosevelt, Hull, Wallace, Roper, and other officials at the White House. After the meeting Peek announced that although the export of industrial products would be encouraged by the bank, its chief concern would be agricultural exports (New York *Times,* Feb. 27, 1934, p. 27). See press conference of Feb. 28, 1934, below.

[3] The British proposal was sent to the principal European powers under date of Jan. 25, 1934 (*British Documents,* VI, 314–324), and to Washington under date of Jan. 29, 1934 (State Department, *Press Releases,* March 3, 1934, pp. 110–121). Among other things, it proposed: (1) immediate consultation among the signators on infraction of the disarmament convention; (2) reduction of the average daily effective force of the British, French, Italian, and Polish armies to 200,000 men; (3) no military training outside armies; (4) agreement on the maximum caliber of guns in frontier fortifications; and (5) gradual reduction to a determined figure of air forces. The State Department's reply of Feb. 19, 1934 (*Foreign Relations, 1934,* I, 22–23), noted that in many respects the British proposals were the same as those offered by the United States since the opening of the Disarmament Conference in 1932 but in some respects did not go so far. The American Government was "not in any way a participant in the European problems" but it was vitally interested in maintenance of peace and therefore welcomed this effort. The Italian proposals of Jan. 31, 1934, to permit Germany an army of 300,000 men and providing for abolition of chemical warfare and the banning of bombardment of civilian centers are summarized in the New York *Times* of Feb. 1, 1934, p. 1. See press conference of March 2, 1934, below.

[4] It was decided at this meeting to increase the Cuban sugar import quota to 1,944,000 tons, an increase of 244,000 tons over the quota rejected by Wallace the previous year (New York *Times,* Feb. 3, 1934, p. 26). On Feb. 8, 1934, Roosevelt asked Congress for an amendment to the Agricultural Adjustment Act that would give the Secretary of Agriculture authority to license refiners, importers, and handlers, thus making possible enforcement of the quota mentioned. This was done by the act approved May 9, 1934 (*Public Papers,* III, 86–88; 48 *Stat.* 670). See Roosevelt's statement on signing the act in *Public Papers,* III, 219–222.

[5] Presumably the report of Dec. 30, 1933, printed in part in Peek, *Why Quit Our Own,* pp. 181–183.

[6] The Pan Pacific Club of Tokyo.

[7] J. Fred Storm of the United Press.

[8] F. M. Stephenson of the Associated Press.

## Mary E. Woolley, President, Mount Holyoke College, to Roosevelt

South Hadley, Massachusetts, February 2, 1934

My dear Mr. President: The proposed building up of the navy to treaty strength alarms me because of its psychological effect upon possible disarmament. Is it not going to make the way more, rather than less difficult? Will it not weaken the effect of the "good neighbor" attitude which you have so splendidly endorsed?[1]

Very sincerely yours,

Mary E. Woolley

[PPF 537:TS]

[1] Answered Feb. 13, 1934, below.

## Roosevelt to Henry L. Roosevelt, Assistant Secretary of the Navy

[Washington] February 2, 1934

*Private and Confidential*

Memorandum for Colonel Roosevelt: The R.F.C. and Treasury would have quite a large sum in gold on the other side—London and Paris. To ship it to this country in commerical ships would cost a lot of money. Have we any Navy ships going to Europe this spring or summer which could bring some of it home—for instance, is the midshipmen's practice cruise going to European waters. We can insure only ten million on any one ship.[1]

F.D.R.

[OF 18:CT]

[1] Assistant Secretary Roosevelt sent this memorandum to Morgenthau, who replied Feb. 9, 1934 (OF 18): "Thank you for forwarding to me the memorandum upon the matter of transporting gold, as brought to our attention by the President. Personally, I believe that we should be very seriously misunderstood if we brought back gold from Europe in United States battleships." Assistant Secretary Roosevelt sent Morgenthau's note to the President on Feb. 16, 1934 (OF 18); with this the idea was dropped.

## Roosevelt to Homer S. Cummings, Attorney General, and Henry Morgenthau, Jr., Secretary of the Treasury

[Washington] February 5, 1934

Memorandum . . . To the suggestion of offsetting German assets now in control of the United States against indebtedness of Germany to the United States.[1]

I suggest that an informal order be issued by the Secretary of the Treasury and the Attorney General, preventing any payments by the United States without specific approval by you two gentlemen.

F.D.R.

[OF 198:CT]

[1] See Cummings to Roosevelt, Jan. 30, 1934, above.

## William C. Bullitt, Ambassador to the Union of Soviet Socialist Republics, to Roosevelt

Washington, February 5, 1934

*Confidential*

My dear Mr. President: In accordance with your instructions I submit herewith some thoughts on the attitude to be adopted by the United States in case of a war between Japan and the Soviet Union.

(1) An attack by Japan on the Soviet Union this spring seems less likely than it did a few weeks ago. (It now seems probable that Japan will turn her attention this year to the domination of North China, Mongolia and Chinese Turkestan.)

(2) In case war seems imminent the Government of the United States should call the attention of the Japanese and Soviet Governments to their obligations under the Kellogg Pact.

(3) As soon as war is declared the President should announce the neutrality of the United States.

(4) In the event of war, Navy expects Japan to confine operations to Far Eastern waters. (An Atlantic blockade would be illegal. A blockade to be legal would have to be established in Russian territorial waters in the Gulf of Finland and the Black Sea. The physical difficulties of maintaining such a blockade and the danger of involving neutrals make such a blockade improbable.)

(5) Japan could and would establish at once a legal and effective blockade of the Pacific coast of the Soviet Union.

(6) As the Soviet Government is the only purchasing agency in the Union, all exports to Russia in time of war technically will be contraband.

(7) It would be physically impossible for American vessels to run the blockade of the Pacific ports of the Soviet Union.

(8) American vessels unmolested could reach the Black Sea ports and Leningrad.

(9) In view of (7) and (8), the risk of our being involved in the war would not be diminished by forbidding American ships to trade directly with the warring powers and such prohibition would inflict unnecessary hardship on the U.S. Merchant Marine.

(10) In case Navy should be mistaken and Japan should attempt to blockade Leningrad and the Black Sea ports of the Soviet Union, it would be advisable to forbid American ships to trade directly with either of the warring powers.

(11) In that event we should make certain that our trade with the Soviet Union via Helsingfors, Tallinn, Memel, Koenigsburg, Danzig, Gydnia, Hamburg, et cetera, will not be molested.

(12) We should insist, therefore, from the outbreak of hostilities that contraband goods if destined to a neutral port shall not be interfered with (under the doctrine of continuous voyage) in the absence of clear proof that they are immediately destined to a warring state. If it can be shown that the goods are to become part of the common stock of the neutral country, the right of seizure shall not exist.

(13) This policy would not interfere with Japan's blockade in the Far East as there is now no communication by land between China and the Soviet Union.

(14) In order that we may not be isolated in taking this position, it seems advisable to agree in advance with Great Britain that in the event of an attempt by Japan to establish an Atlantic blockade the United States and Great Britain will declare that while they are neutrals they will insist that their commerce with other neutral states be unmolested unless it can be shown clearly that the immediate destination of the cargoes is one or another of the warring powers. (As in the case of the Kellogg Pact, other powers should be invited to adhere to this agreement.)

(15) The advance discussion of naval ratios which the British Government has proposed seems to offer an appropriate opportunity to feel out

the British in regard to future joint action of this sort. (In this connection, as a long-time policy, it seems advisable for the United States and Great Britain to adopt a strict definition of "contraband"—vis-à-vis each other at least—such definition to be that adopted by the London Naval Conference of 1908–09.)

(16) The best insurance against the United States being drawn into a war between Japan and the Soviet Union is a large navy. In the event that Japan begins to build above her present ratio, we should speak softly and build three ships to her one.

I append memoranda from Navy, Mr. Hackworth and Mr. Hornbeck.[1]

Yours very respectfully,

William C. Bullitt

[PSF:Japan:TS]

[1] Not present. Green H. Hackworth was legal adviser of the State Department; Stanley K. Hornbeck was chief of the Division of Far Eastern Affairs.

## Roosevelt to Arthur Sweetser, Director, The Secretariat, League of Nations, Geneva

[Washington] February 6, 1934

*Personal*

Dear Arthur: I was glad to get your letter, more so because of the optimistic note you sound.[1]

You, who are so close, know that many phases of the international situation are related, and that sincere effort toward the elimination of key obstacles will go a long way toward clearing the whole situation.

I congratulate you on the promotion that has come to you. I know it was deserved and merited through long and efficient service.

Very sincerely yours,

[PPF 506:CT]

[1] Jan. 15, 1934, above.

## Press Conference, Executive Offices of the White House, February 7, 1934, 10:40 A.M.

[*Excerpt*] Q: As a result of your conversations with Bullitt, have you anything further to say on Russian relations?[1]

The President: There isn't any news on that except this new Import-Export Bank which is in process of organization. We have not even discussed the people to run it yet . . .

The President: Of course, on other debts, I think everybody is working towards the same end. You take, for instance, foreign debts. Let us take foreign debts of foreign governments that are owed to American citizens. Let us take them from the practical point of view. Suppose, for the sake of argument, I had bought ten bonds of some other government a few years ago. They are eight per cent bonds. I know of quite a lot of eight per cent bonds. It is an unconscionable rate. Now, what I do want is to get my $10,000 back and, in order to get it back, I ought to be entirely willing to reduce that eight per cent to four or five per cent if, in so doing, it will enable the foreign government to pay me back my $10,000. What I want is my principal back and certainly it would be very foolish on my part to insist on eight per cent if that jeopardizes the $10,000. I think that is the easiest way of putting it. Now, that applies all the way through. If we can reorganize the debt structure—foreign, private, agricultural, real estate, industrial, everything else—by reducing interest, we automatically make the payment of the principal more probable and we reduce the fixed charges of the country at the same time, thus increasing the probable value of the equities . . .

Q: Have any of the foreign nations indicated their willingness to pay up if you reduce the interest payments?

The President: No.

Q: Could you reduce those interest charges much further?[2]

[President's Press Conferences:T]

---

[1] See press conference of Feb. 2, 1934, above.

[2] The press conference was brought to a close at this point and no reply was made to this question.

## Louis M. Howe, Personal Secretary to the President, to Roosevelt

Washington, February 7, 1934

Memo to the President

Dear Boss: The attached was given to me, and it is something I would like back. It is most interesting as it tells about Mussolini before he became the master he is today.[1]

L.H.

[*Notation*:AS] LH   This is good!   FDR
[Howe Papers:T]

[1] This memorandum refers to an article, "Gambetta Calls on Signor Mussolini," by Sir Thomas Barclay, originally published in the *Fortnightly Review* of December 1923. Barclay had sent it to Howe in a letter of April 13, 1933 (Howe Papers), in which he said: "I may mention that though I considered it prudent to warn the readers of the *Fortnightly* that the Interview was imaginary, it nevertheless gives the gist of my conversation with Mussolini and is still as true today as it was eleven years ago." The main point of the article was that Mussolini saw no profit for Italy in membership in the League of Nations; instead she would rely on friendship with England who would act as a counterbalance to France.

## Breckinridge Long, Ambassador to Italy, to Roosevelt

Rome, February 7, 1934

*Highly Confidential*

Dear Frank: I would like to talk to you a few minutes about a situation developing in Europe which may not amount to anything but which has such possibilities that it is well worth keeping in mind and watching. I am not sending a despatch to the Department because there are no facts. So I take this means of bringing directly to your attention a situation which may develop and have wide-spread consequences.

There is a well defined movement to restore the monarchy in France. Strikes and rioting in Paris, which have now spread to various of the outlying cities, are being carried on under the direction of the *Action Française* with communist support. The *Action Française* is the royalist organ. There are possibilities of a Bonapartist restoration—which I discount. The other possibility is the restoration of the house of Orléans-Bourbon, now united in the person of the Duke de Guise. He is the Pretender to the throne of France.

His daughter is Francoise of France. She is married to Prince Christopher of Greece whose nephew is the Pretender to the throne of Greece. Françoise is a very clever young woman. She is in Rome and from Rome is intimately in touch with developments in France.

I know her very well and have talked to her about this matter very guardedly on several occasions. Her brother is the Count de Paris and as such is the heir apparent to the Pretender to the French throne. However, he is well known to be an illegitimate son and therefore is not considered by circles which are backing the royalist cause to be eligible. He has his headquarters in Brussels. Francoise has a sister who married the Duke d'Aosta. He is the second in line to the throne of Italy. The Crown Prince in Italy is not at all well liked and has made remarks critical of the Duce. He is presumably not in favor with the Fascist chiefs and certainly is not popular with the people of Italy. On the other hand, the Duke d'Aosta is on intimately cordial relations with the Fascist officials and is the most popular of all the figures in connection with the royal family.

Because of the stigma attached to the brother of Françoise and naturally the odium in which her mother would be held by the legitimists, it is quite possible that she might figure in the picture rather than her brother and rather than her father, who is himself the actual Pretender. She is shrewd, careful, well educated, intelligent and politically minded. She has conducted herself very well in Rome where she has been given the royal rank.

The situation in which France finds itself today is lending itself to the furtherance of the royalist schemes. There is intense dissatisfaction with the Government there. In fact it goes farther. There is wide-spread discontent with the parliamentary system. This is fostered of course by the royalists and also by the communists, but it is being helped by the idea of Fascism, which has some ardent supporters in France. The theory of a monarchy is not far removed from the dictatorial principle of government so prevalent in Europe. In both systems power is concentrated and almost absolute. In one, it is transmitted by heredity. The other lacks that element. But both represent a high concentration of power in the hands of an individual. The continent of Europe is pretty well committed to that idea for the time being. Vide Russia, the Balkan states, Germany, Austria and Italy.

When people attain a nervous pitch, somewhat more exaggerated than actually exists in France today, and labor under the impression that they are against a principle of government or against a set of men who symbolize in their minds a principle of government, they are apt to run off at any tangent. The French are notoriously and historically that way. There was the Revolution of 1789, the Triumvirate, Napoleon, the Republic, the Restoration, another Republic, another revolution, and now the Third Republic. They are not committed to any form of government. They are excitable, emotional and possessed of great power under the influence of mass psychology. If they increase their nervous tension there might easily be an opposition to the present government carried on by various elements which in themselves are incompatible except in their opposition but which would result in the adoption of one or the other of the ideas held by those temporarily in opposition to the existing government. It might more easily be, and much more easily, a restoration of the monarchy than the revival of the Bonapartists or an accession to power of communism.

But there are several other elements, which indicate that some persons in the government itself are parties to the possibilities of a restoration. Chiappe has just been dismissed as Chief of Police. His name has been associated with the restoration movement. His dismissal no doubt was partly responsible for the increased manifestations of rioting. Last night they were worse than at any other time. He has declined to go to the colonies and continues in France, where in spite of his dismissal he has many political and official connections.

Our friend Tardieu[1] has lost some of his political power and is not now considered to be one of the leaders of French political thought but the fact is that he lost it because he declined to cooperate with his successors in office and has been considered to be something of an opportunist and playing with the royalists.

Our friend Charles de Chambrun is the French Ambassador in Rome. He is leaving tonight for Paris. He is a member of the Cincinnati. He even wears his Cincinnati medal on his uniform when they wear medals. The Cincinnati are considered to be part of the royalist group, at least amongst the anti-parliamentary elements, in Paris. They are distinctly of the right—of the extreme right—and have given reason to be suspected of being sympathetic to a restoration. Whether de Chambrun partakes of the political theories of his colleagues in Paris, I do not know. However, he has now as a house guest for whom he gave a big dinner the other night, Marquis de la Ferronnays, who is a royalist member of the Chamber of Deputies. Françoise was at the Embassy that night and something must have transpired there because to one or two of her intimates she manifested great excitement and perturbation and left the

Embassy under a considerable emotional strain as soon as she could politely and courteously do so, though not as soon as she wanted to do so.

I bring de Chambrun into this picture only on suspicion. But if he is in it, no doubt his two brothers are in it; the Marquis is a member of the French Senate and one of its influential members; the other brother, as you know, is a general in the army.

The Princess Françoise and the royalists generally lack money. It is hard to see how they could finance a coup. I have strong reasons to suspect—though this is all a fabrication of conjecture and thin filament—that a man by the name of Fummi, who is the representative in Rome of J. P. Morgan and who has access to all the financial circles in Europe, is acting with Françoise and within her entire confidence. I am morally certain of the last statement. What his function is—I can only assume that it is as a financial agent in addition to being a close personal friend. That Morgan could be brought into such a movement, I seriously doubt, but his French banking connections might find it to their political advantage to be on the inside of a movement if they had any idea that it was going to succeed.

Fummi has access to the Italian authorities. The Italian authorities have been very courteous, to say the least, to Francoise. Italy looks with grave apprehension upon the continuance of an unsettled situation in France. France can make no commitments. Nobody can speak for her. With France in the shadow of a political revolution, the hand of Germany is strengthened and the delicate situation in Austria becomes more acute because Italy cannot rely upon French aid in preventing Anschluss or even a Nazi coup with some German assistance. So that the lack of responsibility in the French Government—or what goes by that name—is upsetting the picture and the balance in Europe and it is a matter of serious concern to Italy. Consequently Italy would be glad to see something happen in France which would put the government in control of a definite group who could speak for France and could re-enter European politics on the side of Italy. There is also the well-known thought that Mussolini would like to see dictatorial governments throughout Europe.

Given these elements, you have this possibility—that Italy, under cover and without showing her hand, would give some clandestine support to the cause of Françoise whose own sister might easily soon become the Queen of Italy. Françoise and her crowd would be willing to make any concession. They want the throne. They would accept a dictator under them and themselves retain the nominal function of sovereignty. If Mussolini could find in France a satisfactory person to cooperate with him and Françoise would accept—and no doubt she would—Italy might be very glad to help in such ways as she could, even financially—particularly in view of the fact that the Fascist Grand Council has authority under the Italian system of government to pass upon the succession to the throne and to veto the accession of the Heir Apparent. The Fascist Grand Council is Mussolini's mouthpiece. Since they do not like the Prince of Piedmont, the Crown Prince, and do like the next in line, his cousin the Duke of Aosta, they might easily exercise their power and declare him king when this one dies. Then Françoise's sister would be on the throne of Italy and if Françoise or her father or even her brother were on the throne of France, each of them rendering authority to a dictator to exercise functions of state in their name, it would be a development which would be very pleasing to Italy no doubt.

How much of this you will hear from other places I don't know. I have no way to find out. I cannot write about it, nor can I talk to anybody here—except possibly to Françoise herself. It is not a matter one could talk about with members of the Fascist Government or with any other element in Rome. There are very few people in Washington who ought to know that I have written such a letter. But the political possibilities of the situation are so interesting, and the movements in France are so corroborative of my suspicions that I feel there is some substance to my intuitive sense. It all may come to nothing. However, while the elements are before our eyes and some of them working, I think it is the part of wisdom to watch it, and I bring it to your attention just so that it will be somewhere in the back of your head. You have enough things to worry you at home but this won't worry [sic].

Apologies again for the length of this, but it didn't seem possible to make it much shorter.

With every good wish and expressions of affectionate and respectful regard, I am, Yours as ever,

Breckinridge Long[2]

[PSF:Italy:Long:TS]

[1] André Tardieu, former premier.
[2] See Roosevelt to Hull, Feb. 28, 1934, below.

# William E. Dodd, Ambassador to Germany, to Roosevelt

[Berlin] Feby. 8, 1934

Dear Mr. President: The daily and almost hourly conferences and calls due to the presence of American, English and Swiss Bond delegations caused me to overlook the opportunity of wiring our congratulations on the occasion of your 52$^{nd}$ birthday. But you must know that I am now, as I have long been, grateful as a citizen and a co-worker to you for what you are and the monumental work you have done this last year. If there is a moment of time to spare let me dwell for a moment on some points of common concern.

The German Finance and Economics authorities here are now and have been quite aware of the wrong involved in their rulings. I have had "set-tos" with all responsible parties. Schacht finally declared to me that he had never favored the discriminations. There are really two groups functioning here: one is composed of Foreign Office, Reichsbank and Wirtschaftsministerium: the other of the curious combination of Hitler, Göring and Goebbels who hardly know there is an international opinion to reckon with. The President stands aloof, but he is fully conscious of international trends and casts his influence the right way, as I think, when decisions are left to him—as happens quite often now.

In view of above facts, I feel that the Bond matter was decided as well as we could have hoped for.[1] One thing went a long way: your announced personal attitude which was promptly published here.[2] However, the 6% and 7% interest rates which our New York bankers fixed are regarded here as far too high; and our tariff rates of 1922 and 1930 are regarded as largely responsible for existing state of things: all other countries having imitated them.

I am enclosing a clipping from Paris *Tribune* just to show you how your suggestions are taken on this side.[3] It is my opinion that is the only real solution to our economic dilemma, i.e. a slow transfer of some millions of people from the industrial centres, artificially built up by too protective tariffs and corporate railway misconcentration. We forgot Jefferson's dictum that no man or group must be allowed to profiteer and now the profiteers, as well as the rest of us, are paying the penalty. However, it is no easy job to transfer unwilling and miseducated city folk to small farms all about the country. You can do it by degrees and especially after you carry the election of 1934 overwhelmingly, as you will. And you must also carry the election of 1936. That will put you where Jefferson was in 1805–06 when he attacked in very cautious way two great problems: the pretensions of the courts [Marshall][4] which were already lined up for commercial privilege and the slavocracy, suddenly grown powerful, due to 30¢ cotton. He delayed his great task till he had all power; but even he was defeated [reasons never made clear in our history]. The reasons were new, war in Europe [Napoleon at Austerlitz] and the revolt of Democrats in the south who should have agreed to gradual abolition! One of the greatest of leaders, every state but two behind him, was defeated in one of the greatest and wisest of moves!

You will say: Why so discouraging? I reply that under our unique system Presidents of the greatest sincerity and highest talents have lost in their 6th and 7th years: Jefferson and Wilson; Jackson, Lincoln and Cleveland never able to carry their purposes. You have what Jefferson had: perfect confidence of the masses. You have even more difficult problem, nobody in all history a more difficult one. The United States must stabilize on fair economic basis; it must then become a world leader. If you can redistribute population, open world markets, put all banks under control and then show Europe how to stop barbarism of war, you will have won the gratitude of the ages. I think you can do it, if no war breaks out and you manage next two elections successfully. Pardon so long a story. All good wishes.

Yours Sincerely,

William E. Dodd

[PSF:Germany:AS]

[1] The German government on Jan. 31, 1934, informed the conference of creditors in Berlin that it would be obliged to continue the preferential treatment of its Dutch and Swiss creditors until June 30, 1934. It proposed a meeting in April to make a permanent settlement of the problem and said that during the six-month period it would "purchase at 67 percent of par (stead of 50) conversions kasse scrip covering interest maturing during this period other than Dutch and Swiss" (Dodd to Hull, Jan. 31, 1934, *Foreign Relations, 1934,* II, 346). Following this arrangement for a higher conversion rate of scrip, the German government asked for assurances from the State Department that the United States would not in the future rule that the use of scrip to promote German exports would afford grounds for invoking anti-dumping or anti-bounty penalties. Hull refused to give such assurances on the ground that the system was liable to change by Germany at any time (Hull to Roosevelt, Feb. 9, 1934, OF 198).

[2] See press conference of Jan. 24, 1934, above.

[3] Not present.

[4] These brackets, and those following, are in the original.

## Members of the Oregon and Washington Delegations in Congress to Roosevelt

Washington, D.C., February 10, 1934

Dear Mr. President: In view of the effort being made to induce your Administration to favor the abolition of the Japanese Exclusion policy and adoption of the quota law as a substitute policy, we, as Representatives from the States of Washington and Oregon, take this means of protesting against such action.

We are vigorously opposed to the abolition of the Exclusion policy and feel that even the revival of agitation on the subject would be unfortunate.

We believe in the Exclusion policy based on ineligibility of citizenship as the wise one to be maintained and the one which, when accepted as a permanent policy, will contribute most to the maintenance of friendship between this country, Japan and other oriental countries whose people are likewise ineligible to citizenship.

Respectfully submitted,

Charles H. Martin, 3d, Oregon
Mon C. Wallgren, Wash., 2nd.
Martin F. Smith, 3rd Wash. Dist.
James W. Mott, 1st District, Oregon
Walter M. Pierce, 2nd Dist. of Oregon
Sam B. Hill, 5th Dist., Washington
Wesley Lloyd, 6th Dist., Washington
Knute Hill, 4th Wash.[1]

[OF 20:TS]

[1] McIntyre sent this letter to Under Secretary of State Phillips who recommended that the petition be handled as was the similar one of Jan. 22, 1934, from the California delegation (above). Phillips said (OF 133): "It is the understanding of this Department that the President intended to call in one or more of the representatives from California and inform them in confidence that it was no part of the intention of the Administration to bring this question up." An attached note, Roosevelt to McIntyre, undated, reads: "Mac: Ask the most responsible of California Congressmen to come and see me and let me have this letter when he comes." The White House appointments file shows that appointments were made for Representatives Charles H. Martin of Oregon and Clarence F. Lea of California for Feb. 26, 1934, at 11:15 A.M.

## Jesse Isidor Straus, Ambassador to France, to Roosevelt

Paris, February 10, 1934

*Personal*

My dear Mr. President: I am just in receipt of your letter of January 22nd, in which you sent me the message that I am to convey to the members and guests of the American Club of Paris at their Washington's Birthday dinner.[1]

I appreciate that in the press of the many matters which claim your attention, you should not have forgotten my request for such a message, and I am certain that the American Club will be equally appreciative.

Conditions here have been rather unfortunate and though the reports of the rioting in the streets may have been exaggerated, as I understand it has been by our press at home, there has been considerable disorder not only in various parts of Paris but also in many of the other cities and towns of France. It would appear now, however, that with the announcement this morning of the Doumergue Cabinet, tranquillity, at least for a time will be restored though the French press is not unanimous in its praise of the members of the new cabinet.[2] It was rather hoped and expected that certain younger men might be brought in, but the Cabinet is certainly one of personalities, that is, names that carry weight for past performance throughout the country.

I hope that you continue to enjoy the same good health and spirits as when last I saw you, and beg to remain, with kindest regards, Very sincerely yours,

Jesse Isidor Straus

[PSF:France:Straus:TS]

[1] Inviting Americans abroad to emulate the first president (PSF:France).

[2] The disturbances resulted from disclosure that high government officials had been implicated in the Stavisky scandals. One consequence was the recall to office of Gaston Doumergue, president of France from 1924 to 1931, who served as premier from February to November 1934.

## Roosevelt to Clark Howell, Editor, The Atlanta *Constitution*, Atlanta, Georgia

[Washington] February 13, 1934

Dear Clark: Just a line to tell you that I hope to see my old friend Matsukata very soon.[1] All goes well.

Always sincerely yours,

[PPF 604:CT]

[1] At the White House on February 20 (PPF 1-0). See Roosevelt to Hull, Feb. 26, 1934, below.

## Roosevelt to Mary E. Woolley, President, Mount Holyoke College, South Hadley, Massachusetts

[Washington] February 13, 1934

My dear Dr. Woolley: Thanks for your little note. I hope some time to have a talk with you in regard to disarmament in general, and the Navy in particular.

Very sincerely yours,

[PPF 537:CT]

[1] Feb. 2, 1934, above.

## Hamilton Fish Armstrong, Editor, *Foreign Affairs,* to Roosevelt

New York, February 15, 1934

Dear Mr. President: You often have shown a quite undue regard for opinions I have expressed about events abroad. I am sailing for Europe in a few days. Before I go, may I send you the following thought?

What has been happening in Austria is very tragic. The social democracy of Austria, the only element sincerely devoted to the Austrian Republic, has been rooted out; hundreds of people, whose only fault is to believe in what most Americans believe in, have been killed. I am afraid that Dollfuss has killed Austria. To please the Heimwehr and its

Italian backers he undertook to fight Austrian social democracy at the same time that he fought the Nazis. He differed from the Nazis not at all in social theory, in economic theory, or in anti-semitism, but only on whether or not to join Germany. He has now killed the strongest Austrian element opposed to joining Germany; he has diminished his prestige enormously, at home and abroad; the Nazis will inherit the broken pieces of his rule.

The American people cannot be uninterested in this result, either on general grounds of principle or on grounds of national interest. It is symptomatic of something which is happening on a much wider scale. I therefore venture to make the following suggestion.

The Administration's social, economic and financial program (incidentally, I believe in it thoroughly) has unfortunately been interpreted in Europe as putting you in the ranks of "dictators." I know that is not at all the case. I know you are imbued with American traditions and are endeavoring to adapt them to the exigencies of social reconstruction and economic recovery. But the fact remains that in Europe it is commonly said that the American citadel of democracy has capitulated. I know from personal experience that this has had a profoundly discouraging effect.

I suggest that you take an early opportunity to re-affirm publicly and emphatically, your belief in liberalism and democracy. The incidental effect on domestic political affairs might well be good, in dispelling misconceptions and fears of some of our own people. I believe that abroad the effect would be reinvigorating and that it would serve the long-range interests of the United States. The peoples of Europe need to be reminded that the most powerful nation in the world has not yet decided that the only alternatives to choose between are communist dictatorship or fascist dictatorship.

With kindest regards, Yours ever sincerely,

Hamilton Fish Armstrong

Wouldn't Washington's Birthday, or March 4th, be a suitable occasion?[1]

[PPF 6011:TS]

[1] Armstrong wrote to Roosevelt several times a year, sending him copies of his writings and commenting on foreign affairs. He returned from Europe in May and was asked to the White House on May 17 to report on his visit (Armstrong to Roosevelt, May 8, 1934, PPF 6011; PPF 1-0). His book, *Europe Between Wars?* (New York: Macmillan, 1934), was based on his 1934 trip.

## Senator Clarence C. Dill of Washington to Roosevelt

[Washington] Feb. 15, 1934

My dear Mr. President: After the conference of myself and Congressman Rayburn with you, I talked with Mr. Irwin Stewart of the State Department and Commander Hooper[1] of the Naval Communications Service about your suggestion for having a provision in the Communications bill to require American ownership of all our foreign communication systems. We found there would be no difficulty at all so far as requiring American ownership of international radio systems is concerned, but when it comes to the cables we find a most perplexing situation.

There already is a French cable with offices in this country and the Commercial cable at San Francisco is three-fourths foreign owned. It is the fear of Mr. Stewart that if we were to attempt to require American ownership of all cables with offices in this country we would invite such retaliation in the twenty-two foreign countries in which our American cables have landing rights that the retaliation might be extremely damaging to these cable companies.

I am enclosing herewith a memorandum prepared for me by the Clerk of the Senate Committee on Interstate Commerce after consultation with Mr. Stewart, who gave him most of the detailed information this memorandum contains. I am sending it to you for your consideration, because I doubt the wisdom of attempting to write such a section into the bill requiring American ownership of cables with landings in this country. In light of the fact that there probably will not be any more long cables laid in the world, I doubt the wisdom of such a provision in the law.

I shall be glad to have your own reaction to the facts in the memorandum.

Sincerely yours,

C. C. Dill

[OF 859:TS]

[1] Stanford Hooper.

## [*Enclosure*] Albert Stephen, Clerk, Senate Committee on Interstate Commerce, to Senator Clarence C. Dill

[Washington] February 15, 1934

Memorandum to Senator Dill: Effect of extending to cable companies the prohibition against alien ownership.

Foreign owned cables have landings in the United States in only five instances, three at New York, one at San Francisco, and one in the Philippine Islands, as follows:

(a) New York.

1. French Cable Co.—1 cable,

2. Anglo-American Cable Co.—2 cables, leased to Western Union for 99 years from April 1, 1911.

3. Ex-German cable—1. Title in Principal Allied and Associated Powers (including U.S.); may be operated by French Cable Co.

(b) San Francisco.

Commercial Pacific Cable Co.—owned $\frac{1}{4}$ by Commercial Cable Co. and $\frac{3}{4}$ by English and Danish companies. Cable operated by American Company.

(c) Philippine Islands.

Eastern Extension, Australia and China Telegraph Co.—1 cable.

On the other hand, American owned cables have landings in 22 foreign countries, as follows:

1. England; 2. Irish Free State; 3. France; 4. Portugal; 5. China (Commercial Pacific Cable; $\frac{1}{4}$ American owned; American operated); 6. Canada; 7. Newfoundland; 8. Mexico; 9. Cuba; 10. Haiti; 11. San Domingo; 12. El Salvador; 13. Nicaragua; 14. Costa Rica; 15. Colombia; 16. Venezuela; 17. Ecuador; 18. Peru; 19. Chile; 20. Argentina; 21. Brazil; 22. Uruguay.

The prohibition to alien ownership of cables which are presently laid would doubtless invite retaliation by some or all of the 22 countries at which American cables touch, and would only achieve a 100 per cent American ownership in the 5 instances shown. Furthermore, nearly every North Atlantic cable touches Canadian territory also on this side of the waters and the prohibition might result in diverting these cables to Canada for subsequent transmission from Canada to the United States.

If the limitation is applied only to future cables, it is probable that no such future cables will be built because of the improvement in the art of radio, and yet the inclusion of such a prohibition in a bill as introduced or passed would doubtless breed ill feeling, internationally.

If the provision were made applicable to present cables, it would have the following results:

(a) Invite retaliation;

(b) Force I.T.T. to do one of three things:

(1) Acquire 75 per cent control of Commercial Pacific Cable;

(2) Divert their cable to Vancouver, B.C.; or

(3) Cease the operation of this cable;

(c) Force the French cable out of the United States, which probably would result in France excluding Western Union and Commercial from France; and

(d) Force Anglo-American cable out of United States, which cable although foreign owned, was in 1911 leased for 99 years to Western Union; and this in turn would probably result in Western Union and Commercial being excluded from European countries.

For these reasons it is submitted that it would be inexpedient to extend the prohibition against foreign ownership of radio to include cables.[1]

Respectfully,

Albert Stephen

[OF 859:T]

[1] Roosevelt acknowledged receipt of Dill's letter and its enclosure in a note of Feb. 17, 1934, below.

# Press Conference, Executive Offices of the White House, February 16, 1934, 4:10 P.M.

[*Excerpt*] Q: There is a report on the Hill that either in the war debt Message or in a separate Message you are expected to ask legislation in order to make a concession to Finland because it has kept up its payments. Anything to that?

The President: You are two months ahead of time.

Q: Does that mean a debt Message is not going up in two months?

The President: Maybe. Frankly, I have not given any consideration either to the tariff Message[1] or the debt Message,[2] any more than I had two months ago.

Q: You received the new Japanese Ambassador this week and exchanged greetings in which you said that you thought that any problems should be settled amicably. Do you care to go into that at this time?

Q: Are there any discussions coming up on that?

The President: Not that I know of. The State Department is the place to ask.

Q: We noticed he told you that anything done in the Far East would be in the interests of peace.[3]

[President's Press Conferences:T]

[1] March 2, 1934, below.

[2] June 1, 1934, below.

[3] Hirosi Saito, on Feb. 13, 1934 (PPF 1-0), in a formal exchange of greetings, said that Japan had been obliged to take decisive steps "for the consolidation of stability and good order" in eastern Asia, but that the "abiding aspiration" of the Japanese nation was peace in this area (State Department, *Press Releases,* Feb. 17, 1934, pp. 92–93).

## Roosevelt to Cordell Hull, Secretary of State

[Washington, February 16, 1934][1]

Dear Cordell: The offer by the Moscow Soviet of the building site in the park which we discussed with Bullitt seems to me so favorable that we should be sure not to delay our acceptance of it. I understand that Bullitt had a further conversation with Troyanovsky on Saturday, and that Troyanovsky said that he hoped to have word from his Government on Monday that the lease could be renewed at the end of the ninety-nine-year period. If the Soviet Government refuses this extension, I think we should accept the ninety-nine-year lease and trust to the skill of our successors to retain the property if we should wish to retain it at the end of that period.

I suggest that you should call a meeting of the Foreign Service Buildings Commission as soon as possible to consider the matter and that you should consult the Chairmen of the Congressional Committees on Appropriations and the Chairman of the Committee on Foreign Affairs of the House and the Committee on Foreign Relations of the Senate with a view to having an amendment to the present State Department appropriations Bill added in the Senate.

I understand that there is an unappropriated balance of $1,250,000 in the $10,000,000 authorized by the Foreign Service Buildings Act of May 7, 1926. A similar sum of $1,250,000 was appropriated, I believe for Tokyo and as much, I think, will be needed for Moscow, in view of the unusual problems there: e.g. hospitalization. I should not recommend the expenditure of such a sum at the present time if I were not convinced that it is essential for our Government to construct in Moscow as soon as possible permanent offices and living quarters for our officials. The site which has been offered us seems to me to present an opportunity to do in the finest manner what necessity compels us to do. We can build an embassy on that hill in the city park overlooking the river which will be as simple and beautiful as Monticello and I myself should like to see a modern version of Monticello built there with subsidiary buildings patterned after those which fringe the lawn of the university of Virginia. I like the idea of planting Thomas Jefferson in Moscow. For this particular job I know no one so well fitted as Harrie T. Lindeberg of 2 East 47th Street, New York, and I hope that it will be found possible to employ him. I suggest that as soon as possible he should be requested to prepare preliminary sketches and draw up the final project. I understand that there is an unspent balance in the Foreign Buildings Fund already appropriated which might be used for this purpose. It occurs to me that since there are no American contractors doing business in Moscow, as there were in Paris when the Government building there was constructed, you might wish to have the Foreign Service Buildings Commission authorize you to manage the construction without regard to American statutes, which is permissible under the Act of May 7, 1926 (c.250.3 44 *Stat.* 404).[2]

Yours very sincerely,

[PSF:Russia:CT]

[1] A supplied and approximate date.
[2] According to an accompanying note this letter was drafted by Bullitt.

## Roosevelt to Cordell Hull, Secretary of State

Washington, February 16, 1934

Memorandum from the President for the Secretary of State: In regard to the whole matter, it should be remembered that when the President of Panama was in Washington, the United States had not legally or in any other way devalued the content of gold in the dollar. At that time we were off the gold basis except that we permitted balances of Foreign Governments' gold in New York to be exported to those Foreign Governments. All that was said by me to the President of Panama in October was that I believed we could pay the amount due Panama in gold. Since that date an entirely different situation has arisen. The content of the gold dollar has been greatly reduced. Obviously I think there can be no question of bad faith. The conversation of October related to one thing and the situation today is wholly different.

In view of this—what do you recommend?[1]

[OF 110:CT]

[1] See Hull to Roosevelt, Feb. 21, 1934, below.


## Roosevelt to Senator Clarence C. Dill of Washington

Washington, February 17, 1934

Memorandum . . . In view of your very interesting memorandum of February 15th,[1] about the cables, I am inclined to agree with you in doubting the wisdom in writing a section requiring American ownership of landing cables in this country.[2]

[OF 859:CT]

[1] Above.
[2] Roosevelt had earlier raised the security problem with John K. Roosevelt, vice-president of All American Cables, Inc., at the White House on Feb. 1, 1934 (John K. Roosevelt to Roosevelt, Feb. 2, 1934, OF 589). See press conference of March 16, 1934, below.


## Roosevelt to Senator Elbert D. Thomas of Utah

[Washington] February 17, 1934

My dear Senator: I have received your letter of January 15, 1934, in regard to your Bill (S. 2399) for the amendment of certain provisions of the laws relating to the extraterritorial jurisdiction of the United States in China and have noted your references to the present Judge of the United States Court for China and his predecessor in that office, and have read the letter from the Honorable John Bassett Moore in regard to the latter.[1]

I have referred your letter to the Attorney General and the Secretary of State and I am now advised that a copy of your bill was recently referred by the Chairman of the Senate Committee on Foreign Relations to the Secretary of State for his recommendations.[2] I attach hereto a copy of the Secretary of State's letter to Senator Pittman[3] expressing the opinion that the enactment or public discussion of the bill would be inopportune and inadvisable because of treaty negotiations requested by the Government of China which will involve consideration of the extraterritorial jurisdiction of the United States in China. When you introduced your bill you, of course, had no knowledge of this situation and I am sure that you will agree that the consideration of legislation materially affecting our extraterritorial jurisdiction in China should be deferred until the conclusion of the forthcoming negotiations with the Government of China.

I greatly appreciate your interest in the administration of the extraterritorial jurisdiction of the United States in China and I do not need to assure you that I fully share your views on the importance of having as judge of the Court a person who is not only fully qualified technically, but whose administration of the important duties of the Court will reflect credit on the United States.[4]

Very sincerely yours,

[OF 151:CT]

[1] The letters were sent to the Attorney General and were not returned to the White House. Thomas' letter and Moore's letter of Jan. 13, 1934, urged the reappointment of Charles S. Lobengier as judge of the United States Court for China (McIntyre to Cummings, Jan. 17, 1934, OF 151).

[2] S. 2399, to amend the act creating a United States Court for China approved June 30, 1906, was introduced Jan. 18, 1934 (*Cong. Rec.,* vol. 78, p. 851). It was not reported.

[3] Not present.

[4] Drafted in the office of the Attorney General (Cummings to Roosevelt, Feb. 16, 1934, OF 151).

# Roosevelt to Cordell Hull, Secretary of State

[Washington] February 20, 1934

Memorandum for Secretary of State: For your information.

F.D.R.

[*Notation*:T] Copy of telegram to Pres. from "Frankfurter": London advices from Vienna indicate serious danger of excesses, particularly anti-Jewish. Deeply hope it will commend itself to you to make appropriate representations to Austria if indeed you have not already done so. International usage and our own precedents amply support such action. We joined in protest to Roumania in 1872; in 1891 President Harrison declared quote Suggestions of humanity unquote warranted protest to Russia. In 1902 T.R. invited powers to make representations to Russia. None in better position than you to make such appeal. Time of essence, may be too late to await Earle's return. Frankfurter.[1]

[PPF 140:CT]

[1] Felix Frankfurter. George Earle, minister to Austria, was en route to Vienna after a leave in the United States.

## Roosevelt to William Phillips, Under Secretary of State

[Washington] February 21, 1934

Memorandum for Under Secretary of State Phillips: I think this is an excellent idea. Perhaps you and the Secretary would take it up with Mr. Child and proceed with it.

F.D.R.

[*Notation*:T] Letter to the Pres. from Under Sec. of State 2/17/34 Re: A question of a trip throughout Europe to be made by Mr. Richard Washburn Child. Suggests the appt. of Mr. Child as special adviser to the Sec. of State in his capacity as Chr. of the Delegation of the U.S. to the London Economic Conference, with instructions to make his report to the Sec. in that capacity.[1]

[OF 20:CT]

[1] Child's appointment as special adviser to Hull was announced March 5, 1934; his assignment was to investigate the economic situation in Europe and the status of the resolutions and other projects left pending by the Economic Conference (New York *Times*, March 6, 1934, p. 4). Stephen P. Duggan, en route to Moscow to promote Soviet-United States cultural relations, wrote to Roosevelt from Stuttgart on March 9 to protest Child's appointment as "startling and disappointing" (PPF 1404). Duggan said that Child was "a pronounced believer in fascism" and would be regarded as directly representing the President. Roosevelt replied March 26, 1934 (PPF 1404), inviting Duggan to come in to see him after his return from Europe and not to worry "about the gentleman in question."

Child conferred with MacDonald and Sir John Simon in London on March 22 and then went to Dublin to talk with Eamon de Valera. While in Dublin the newly appointed American minister, William Wallace McDowell, died suddenly (on April 9) and Child offered himself as his successor. In a letter to Roosevelt of April 11, 1934 (OF 218-B), he said that he was qualified to deal with the Irish "on something more than a fox-hunting basis." (Child has misdated this letter March 11.) Roosevelt thought well of the idea; a note to Hull accompanying the letter just cited reads: "What do you think of this rather happy thought?" The proposal is not mentioned further in the Roosevelt papers. Child went on to call on national leaders in Paris, Warsaw, Rome (where he talked with Mussolini), Brussels, and Amsterdam. See his letter to Roosevelt of Aug. 30, 1934, below.

## Cordell Hull, Secretary of State, to Roosevelt

Washington, February 21, 1934

Dear Mr. President: Referring further to demand of Panama Government for payment of the Canal annuity of $250,000 by the United States Government "in gold coin of the United States," the Panama Minister here presented this demand to Mr. Edwin Wilson, head of the Latin American division here in the Department.

It occurred to me that it would emphasize the matter much less to let Wilson rather casually send for the Minister and make reply to him, in substance as set out in the attached manuscript, by doing so orally and making no written record.

I wish you would read this over and offer any comment or suggestions, and return as soon as convenient.[1]

Cordell Hull

[Notation:AS] C.H.   Yes, grand idea   FDR
[OF 110:TS]

[1] Hull's enclosed memorandum pointed out that the devaluation by the United States of the dollar had reduced by 40 per cent external debts payable in the United States and that financial conditions were therefore now quite different. Hull again referred to the Panama Canal annuity in a note to Roosevelt of March 20, 1934 (OF 110). His view was that: (1) the legal obligation to pay Panama in 1904 gold dollars was "very doubtful"; (2) if, however, the United States insisted on this stand, Panama would probably insist on arbitration of the question, which, "for obvious reasons," was undesirable; and (3) "it would be likewise unwise, because of its effect upon other obligations of the United States, either to admit Panama's contention or to make any settlement which would appear to imply such admission." He therefore suggested that Panama be told that the matter would be dealt with in the new treaty to be negotiated between the two governments. Roosevelt endorsed this memorandum: "C.H. OK FDR."

## Felix Frankfurter to Roosevelt

Oxford, England, 22.II.34

Dear Mr. President: 1. If the enclosed editorial from *The Times* has not already reached you, it may interest you because of the indication it furnishes that *The Times* has been made aware of the need of more accurate and sympathetic interpretation of American affairs.[1]

2. The enclosed editorial from the *Manchester Guardian* regarding the Viennese situation[2] puts in English English some of the considerations which, in the light of some authentic information, led me to cable you about the Austrian situation.[3] Things are not what they might seem from the Austrian Government's communiqués. That Dollfuss in his own feelings is trying to avoid and avert excesses, I believe. If he were a wholly free man he would go in for a policy of appeasement. But he ceased to be a free man from the time that he surrendered to the Heimwehr. The evidence is, I believe, conclusive that the advances made by the Socialists for an alliance with Dollfuss and his Party, on condition that the minimum requirements of a democratic state should be observed, were rejected by him. I need not tell you that Austria is really the football between the rivalries of Hitler and Mussolini. And that's where the matter now stands. The victimization which the Germans have made so familiar is proceeding and will continue to proceed in Austria in all sorts of ways, though much less fiercely—Austria being Austria . . .[4]

With warm regards, Faithfully yours,

F.F.

[PPF 140:TS]

[1] The editorial (the clipping is undated) approved legislation for the control of speculation, and Roosevelt's efforts, as in the case of the air mail contracts, to get rid of graft in government.

[2] From the issue of Feb. 20, 1934. The editorial deprecated the summary death sentences handed out by the Dollfuss regime following the Socialist revolt of February 12–13 and urged the British Home Secretary to make strong protest. The *Guardian* feared a Jewish pogrom in Vienna.

[3] See Roosevelt to Hull, Feb. 20, 1934, above.

[4] The rest of this letter is about domestic affairs.

## Roosevelt to Representative William B. Oliver of Alabama

[Washington, February 24, 1934]

My dear Mr. Oliver: After giving further consideration to the needs of the Foreign Service of the Department of State, I am convinced that the appropriation which I recently recommended for the prevention of further losses through the decline of the dollar in international exchange will not insure the maintenance of that Service during the fiscal year 1935 upon a plane essential to its efficiency in protecting the interests of our people abroad and carrying out effectively the foreign policy of this Government. It therefore seems to me that something more must be done and I can think of no more speedy or convenient way of accomplishing the desired result than by restoring the rent, heat and light allowances to the amounts granted in 1932 and providing an appropriation for post allowances. We cannot have an efficient Foreign Service unless we can lift from the minds of the men in it the burden of anxiety over the financial condition of themselves and their families which now interferes materially with the discharge of their duties. I am quite sure it is not sound economy to fail to make adequate appropriations for this purpose.

I am enclosing for your information copies of supplementary estimates which, for the reasons above stated, I have transmitted for the consideration of the Congress.[1]

Very sincerely yours,

[OF 67:CT]

[1] This letter was also sent to James Buchanan, chairman of the House Appropriations Committee, and to Carter Glass, chairman of the Senate Appropriations Committee. Additional funds were provided in the Legislative Branch Appropriation Act approved May 30, 1934 (48 *Stat.* 817).

## Roosevelt to George K. Briggs, Boston

[Washington] February 26, 1934

Dear George: That Uncle of yours is a grand fellow.[1] Incidentally he is lucky to be looking down on the world from the heights above Geneva. He is not the only one who is a bit shivery about the international situation, East and West. I am particularly glad to have those figures in the addenda.[2]

I hear rumors of a reunion of the crew some day soon and it sounds good to me.[3] If this weather keeps up you and Hazel will have to come on skis.

As ever yours,

[PPF 402:CT]

[1] Sinclair Kennedy. Briggs (a Boston insurance broker and old friend) had written to Roosevelt Feb. 23, 1934, enclosing Kennedy's letter of Feb. 6, 1934 (PPF 402).

[2] The figures showed Japan's mounting exports to various countries. Kennedy said that Japan's foreign policy was governed by her need to provide work for her increasing population: "But the land, certainly, and the commerce, in large measure . . . must be taken from somebody else who will be loath to part with it. I do not picture Japan as obsessed by her military and naval strength, but as building it up as a means and assurance of attaining these (for her) essential ends. Unless the rest of us give up peacefully, the test of arms is bound to come."

[3] Roosevelt here referred to the cruise he and Briggs had taken the summer before (from July 11 to 16) from Port Jefferson on Long Island Sound to Portsmouth, New Hampshire, in the forty-foot yawl, *Myth II.* They were accompanied by James, John, and Franklin, Jr., and Robert Delano, a cousin (New York *Times,* July 12, 1932, p. 3; "Log of Myth II," PPF 402).

# Roosevelt to Cordell Hull, Secretary of State

Washington, February 26, 1934

*Personal and Confidential*

Memorandum for the Secretary of State: I think you and Mr. Hornbeck will be distinctly interested in seeing this letter which was handed to me in person by Mr. Otohiko Matsukata the other day. After you have read it please let me have it back.[1]

F.D.R.

[OF 197-A:T]

[1] In his letter of Feb. 26, 1934 (PPF 1589), Matsukata thanked Roosevelt for having received him and said that he had sent on to his friends in Japan the "friendly thoughts" the President had expressed. He later asked for another appointment in a letter to Roosevelt of March 17, 1934 (PSF:Japan). With this letter is a note from Roosevelt to Miss LeHand: "Should love to see him and suggest to him after President gets back from the South on the 8th or 9th." The State Department, however, advised against another appointment in the belief that the Japanese ambassador, whose house guest Matsukata was, hoped to use him as a channel of communication between the Embassy and the President (Dunn to McIntyre, March 28, 1934, enclosing Hornbeck to Dunn, March 28, 1934, PSF:Japan).

## Stanley K. Hornbeck, Chief, Division of Far Eastern Affairs, to Cordell Hull, Secretary of State

[Washington] February 26, 1934

Mr. Secretary: Herewith the memorandum which Mr. Matsukata gave the President, together with certain comments (superimposed).

The President asks that you please return the memorandum to him.

SKH

[PSF:Japan:TS]

## [*Enclosure 1*] Otohiko Matsukata to Roosevelt

New York [February 20, 1934]

I am grateful to you for this honor and privilege you have accorded me. I have no intention to lay before you any plan for the improvement of our relations with America, for that is the task for our Ambassador, but I wish to convey to you some of my personal views and sentiments.

It has long been my conviction that the peace of the Far East and the Pacific depends largely upon friendly relations between America and Japan. I believe also that this view is shared by all of our statesmen.

Perhaps some of the things which have happened in Japan during the past few years have seemed to you strange and inexplicable. For instance, the assassination of Premier Inukai by officers and cadets in uniform must have been a shock to Americans.[1] We ourselves were deeply shocked, but we could at least understand the circumstances which led up to the tragic event. For some years our army and navy men had felt that our government had been in the hands of corrupt, inefficient, self-seeking party politicians. They had felt that political corruption had been leading the nation into degeneration and ultimate ruin. It was while they were in this defiant and rebellious mood that the London Naval Treaty was signed which they resented for two reasons. First, the treaty was accepted by our Government without the full consent of those who were directly responsible for national defense. Secondly, the treaty gave our naval men a sense of insecurity. Personally, I feel that if the London Conference considered just a little more sympathetically the contentions of our naval men, the cause of peace would have been served much better.

655

It was a combination of such circumstances which caused intense unrest among our military and naval men, culminating in the assassination of the Premier. They sacrificed the Premier in the hope that this drastic action might serve to awaken the dormant conscience of the politicians and to convince the nation of the imperativeness of purging politics and government of corruption and ineptitude. They thought that the aim justified the means.

It goes without saying that neither the army nor the navy has any intentions of usurping the powers of the Government. All they want is honest, patriotic, and efficient government. They are not opposed to party Government, provided party government is not dominated by corrupt politicians.

No one can fail to see that under the cautious guidance of the present Cabinet Japan has been gradually regaining normalcy. This desirable tendency will be all the more accelerated if other nations will show a willingness to cooperate with Japan for the improvement of her foreign relations.

The abnormal and unfortunate condition which had prevailed in Japan before the assassination of the Premier explains, at least partly, the "explosion" in Manchuria. In a sense, it was a protest of the officers on the spot against the "corrupt" party government which, they thought, permitted Chinese anti-foreignism and Soviet influence to undermine the Japanese rights and interests established at a sacrifice of untold life and treasure in two wars, which, as they saw it, had been forced upon Japan.

I presume that the officers on the spot, already restive and resentful, acted on the spur of the moment, without asking for instructions of the home Government or the General Staff. I admit that this was regrettable, but we were simply swept into where we are by force of circumstances which none could avoid.

Many foreigners say that Japan will make of Manchuria a second Korea. This view ignores a certain essential fact. Korea is peopled by Koreans, and not by alien races. Therefore, Japan, by annexing Korea, invited no foreign complications. On the contrary, Manchuria is peopled largely by Chinese. Should Japan annex Manchuria, the Chinese in Manchuria, who are now friendly to us, might change their attitude and fraternize with China, which would cause endless trouble to us.

Since my arrival in America I have heard so much about the impending crisis between Russia and Japan. This is rather a surprise to me. I can confidentially say that our Government has been making sincere and strenuous efforts to maintain peace with Russia. That at least was my conviction before I left Tokyo. It seems to me highly significant that all the war talk that has been heard has come from Russia, while Japan maintains a dignified silence. I am afraid that this constant harping upon the possibility of war, will serve no good purpose. Certainly it is not calculated to promote peace.

Our Foreign minister, Mr. Hirota,[2] has more than once proposed that both Russia and Japan remove military forces from along their respective sides of the Manchurian-Siberian border line. This he thinks will dissipate the tension between the two countries, and will pave the way to amicable settlement of pending questions. But Russia somehow has been cool to this proposal.

About China, I regret to have to repeat what has been said a hundred times by critical observers of all nationalities—namely, that China, though potentially great, has shown no signs of becoming an organized, stable nation in the conceivable future. Moreover, disruptive and destructive influence of the communist movement is far more serious than is commonly known abroad.

I regret to have to say that the American attitude has always seemed to us partial in favor of China and biased against Japan. I feel that this has been an obstacle to perfect understanding between America and Japan. Please do not misunderstand me. Japan does not ask America to be favorable to her. We simply ask you to be impartial as between Japan and China.

I am exceedingly happy to assure you that since your assumption of the Presidency, our national sentiment toward America has signally improved. I wish you could visualize how happy we were when you ordered the major force of your fleet back to the Atlantic. It was an event which the Japanese will long remember.

I am also happy to be able to report that your Ambassador, Mr. Grew, is exceedingly popular in Japan. Our leaders have both admiration and confidence in him, because they know that he is sincere and doing his best to promote good understanding between America and Japan.

We also think that the appointment of Mr. Saito as Ambassador to the United States is a very happy one. Only after our Government had considered a number of candidates, did it come to the conclusion that Mr. Saito was best qualified for this post and to handle the problems which are awaiting adjustment.

I am grateful to you for your kindness in allowing me this opportunity of laying before you certain facts and views which I consider essential.

Although the opinion I have expressed is my personal opinion, I believe that it is shared by a very large number of our leaders, both in and out of the Government.

Perhaps it is needless to assure you that my absorbing desire is peace and friendship between the United States and Japan. The happy years which I passed in America among my American friends have ever been fresh in my mind, and I have been deeply pained as I have watched the recent trend of events which have conspired to estrange our two nations. That is what has brought me to America after an absence of seventeen years. Nothing could make me happier than to see American-Japanese relations restored to their former state of cordiality.

[PSF:Japan:T]

[1] Prince Tsuyoshi Inukai was murdered in May 1932 by a group of extreme nationalists.

[2] Koki Hirota, Foreign Minister from 1932 to 1936.

## [*Enclosure 2*] Stanley K. Hornbeck to Cordell Hull

[Washington] February 26, 1934

There is not much in Mr. M's memorandum which calls for discussion or comment.

Mr. M's desire is to promote good relations between Japan and the United States, and he feels that, toward that end, it is necessary for the United States better to "understand" Japan. Toward enabling us to "understand" he offers certain items of "explanation."

Taken at face value, the statements which Mr. M. makes would indicate that there are some things badly out of joint in Japanese internal politics. After that, Mr. M. thinks that, in Japanese-Russian relations, Russia is unreasonable, and that, in Japanese-American relations, the United States is prejudiced in favor of China and against Japan.

Mr. M. states that Mr. Grew is popular in Japan and has the confidence of Japan's leaders. He thinks that Japan's choice of Mr. Saito as Japanese Ambassador here was a happy one.

Only two items in the memorandum seem to call for special comment. Such comment is submitted in the pages here attached.

One of the most striking paragraphs, as illustrating the confusion of reasoning with which the Japanese approach and endeavor to explain certain of their problems and acts, in the text of his memorandum, is the paragraph (on page 5) which reads:

Our Foreign Minister, Mr. Hirota, has more than once proposed that Russia and Japan remove military forces from along their respective sides of the Manchurian-Siberian border line. This he thinks will dissipate the tension between the two countries, and will pave the way to amicable settlement of pending questions. But Russia somehow has been cool to this proposal.

As we well know, the Japanese contend that Manchuria is now an independent state, "Manchukuo." A proposal that both Russia and Japan remove their military forces from along their respective sides of the Manchurian-Siberian border line should contemplate withdrawal of Japanese forces from positions south and east of the southeastern boundary of Manchuria. But this is not at all what the Japanese have in mind: what they propose is that the Russians should withdraw from positions north of the northern boundary of Manchuria and the Japanese from positions south of the northern boundary of Manchuria. In other words, they regard North Manchuria as the Japanese "side" of the Manchurian-Siberian border line, while at the same time affirming that "Manchukuo" is an independent state and in no way governed or controlled by Japan. Naturally the Russians are "cool to this proposal" for a withdrawal by them from positions on their own soil in return for a withdrawal by the Japanese from positions not on but far removed from Japanese soil.

Mr. M. says (on page 6):

I regret to have to say that the American attitude has always seemed to us partial in favor of China and biased against Japan. I feel that this has been an obstacle to perfect understanding between America and Japan. Please do not misunderstand me. Japan does not ask America to be favorable to her. We simply ask you to be impartial as between Japan and China.

The view that "the American attitude had always" been "partial in favor of China and biased against Japan" is historically inaccurate. There have been, during the eighty years since relations or contact between the United States and Japan began, several periods when Japan was in high favor in this country and China in disfavor. However, since 1894 (beginning of Chino-Japanese war) and especially since 1906 (when, after the Russo-Japanese war, Japan embarked upon a course of discrimination against other nations in Manchuria) "the American attitude" has been most of the time more favorable toward China than toward Japan. This is easily explainable: the human animal is inclined to be favorably disposed toward those with whom he finds it easiest to get on, those who are not in competition with him, those who do not get in his way, those who do not threaten him either in word or in fact, those who cannot harm him, those who are soft-spoken and easy-going, etc., etc., and to be unfavorably disposed toward those whose attitude and/or actions are the reverse. Generally and comparatively speaking, the Chinese have been and are easy-going and complacent, whereas the Japanese have been and are active, aggressive and inclined to be bellicose.

With regard to official action, however, as contrasted with popular opinion and attitude, I am inclined to believe that the American Government has been much more conciliatory and given to making concessions toward Japan than toward China.

Given a situation such as began with developments in Manchuria in September 1931, the position taken by the United States in defense of and insistence upon respect for treaty obligations inevitably threw the United States onto what happened to be the "side" of China and therefore ranged the American Government, along with that of all the other powers, in opposition to the country which was disregarding treaty obligations, which country happened to be Japan. Thus, as between China and Japan, we "favored" China. That fact, however, was accidental.

To say that we are "partial in favor of China" and "biased against Japan" is a good deal like saying that parents and teachers and friends and judges and administrators, etc., are partial in favor of good boys and biased against bad boys.

As a matter of fact neither China nor Japan behave at all well in international relations. Both cause other countries a great deal of unusual and unpleasant bother. But the Chinese delinquencies are comparatively petty and are for the most part those of inefficiency and ineptitude, whereas the Japanese delinquencies are on a large scale and involve important consequences and are deliberately planned and efficiently carried out. Naturally, in American psychology, the reaction is comparatively favorable to the Chinese and unfavorable to the Japanese.

The thing most noticeably missing from practically all of these Japanese statements which urge in this country the improvement of friendly relations between Japan and the United States is any evidence of consciousness or concern on the part of the authors with regard to the fact that Japan has broken treaties and has defied (and vilified) all who remonstrate. It happens that the United States attaches definite and great importance to the existence, the spirit and the substance of the treaties.

The thing most noticeably present in practically all of these Japanese statements and similar statements made by American "friends of Japan" is the suggestion or implied suggestion that, in order to improve relations between Japan and the United States, the one of the two countries which has done least in the way of unfriendly manifestation toward the other (that is, the United States) make some concession(s) or free gift(s) to the one that has most offended (that is, Japan). But nowhere are there offered any suggestions that Japan make any concessions or free gifts.

There is in fact in the situation as it stands today no real "tension" between the two countries. The United States has not done nor have we any intention of doing Japan any injury. There is no reason whatever why we should proceed as though we had been in the wrong, no reason why we should send Japan flowers or pay her compliments as a peace offering: we certainly do not owe Japan anything in connection with Manchuria or in connection with immigration or in connection with naval ratios or in connection with the Mandated Islands, nor would the conclusion of a bilateral non-aggression pact amount to anything other than a present by us to Japan at the expense of China and of the general principles of our foreign policy as applicable and as hitherto applied in reference to the Far East.

It is believed that an appropriate reply to all suggestions that the American Government should do something definite and concrete and involving concessions toward improving and signalizing friendly relations between this country and Japan is: What about Japan's doing something definite and concrete and involving concessions toward demonstrating that she desires and values the friendship of the United States and that she intends to show some regard for her treaty obligations to the United States (and to other powers).

SKH

[PSF:Japan:TS]

## Jesse Isidor Straus, Ambassador to France, to Roosevelt

Paris, February 27, 1934

*Personal*

Dear Mr. President: The enclosed clipping from the *Matin* of a few days ago I thought would interest and amuse you.[1] It is written by Pierre Lyautey who has just returned from America full of enthusiasm for you and the U.S.A. He is a nephew of Marshal Lyautey.[2]

After all the excitement of the 6th and 7th of February Paris and, in fact, France, are quiet.[3] Parliament seems to have taken a leaf out of your book and has granted the Prime Minister powers far beyond those that are normally granted him. The result may be the balancing of the budget by decree through a cutting of expenditures. It is expected that Parliament will then take a recess of from four to six weeks. In the meantime, there is to be a convention of the Radical-Socialist Party and an investigation of the various scandals will also be proceeding, though I think the expectation as to the latter is that not much will come of it.

What may happen when Parliament reassembles in April nobody seems to be willing to prophesy. Some think the Cabinet may again be in trouble and that a directorate or possibly even a dictatorship may ensue. The difficulty with the dictatorship is, however, that there seems to be no one single strong man of youth and vigor to take the helm.

Since my return I have not been able to do very much, first, because of the cabinet upsets, and, second, because of the pressure of work on all the new Cabinet Ministers to get through the budget, but I am in hopes that in the course of a few weeks things will so shape themselves that I can sit down and have a quiet talk with the Foreign Minister, the Prime Minister and Messrs. Herriot and Tardieu, all of whom have promised me that opportunity.

Reports that I get from home continue most cheerful. You have apparently accomplished the seemingly impossible but I hope that your health continues good despite the strain.

Mrs. Straus joins me in kindest regards to you and Mrs. Roosevelt. Very sincerely yours,

Jesse Isidor Straus

[PSF:France:TS]

[1] Not present.
[2] Louis H. Lyautey.
[3] Straus refers to the riots caused by the Stavisky scandal.

662

## Roosevelt to Cordell Hull, Secretary of State

Washington, February 28, 1934

*Private and Confidential*

Memorandum . . . This is for your eyes only.[1] I do not think that any-one else should see it. It is interesting even though there may not be any-thing in it.

[PSF:Italy:CT]

[1] Long to Roosevelt, Feb. 7, 1934, above.

## Press Conference, Executive Offices of the White House
## February 28, 1934, 10:55 A.M.

[*Excerpt*] Q: With regard to the establishment of these three banks to finance the development of foreign trade, can we say what you have in mind with regard to what the Government would be willing to guarantee the railroads?

The President: I do not think we have come anywhere near talking about that, even Peek himself. It would depend on the individual case.

Q: With regard to this bank, it was mentioned twenty million dollars as a possible credit we will extend to the American silver producers to ship silver down there. Is that figure correct?

The President: You had better check with Sumner Welles. My general impression is that it was ten.

Q: The Secretary said a few million and we thought twenty was rather high.

The President: I think it was ten. You had better check on it.[1]

[President's Press Conferences:T]

[1] Following establishment of the First Export-Import Bank, the Second Export-Import Bank of Washington, D.C., was organized under authority of executive order 6638 of March 9, 1934 (*Presidential Executive Orders*, I, 556). Its statement of policy and its officers were the same as the first (Cummings to Roosevelt, March 6, 1934, OF 643). The actual objective was, however, the furnishing of immediate aid to Cuba. This was done by lending Cuba $4,000,000, most of which was used to buy United States silver for conversion into pesos, enabling the new government of President Mendieta to pay long overdue salaries of government employees and to begin certain agricultural reforms and public works (State Department, *Press Releases*, May 5, 1934, p. 244).

It was also suggested in "political circles" that the silver purchase would help remove the opposition of western beet sugar producers to the Cuban sugar quota proposed in the pending Costigan-Jones bill (New York *Times,* Feb. 28, 1934, p. 29). A third bank was proposed to cover world trade not coming within the scope of the first two banks but this was not organized. Instead, the operations of the Second Export-Import Bank were, on July 30, 1934, extended to promote trade in all countries except Russia. This extension of operations was authorized by Roosevelt while at sea on the *Houston* on his vacation (Export-Import Bank trustees to Roosevelt, July 21, 1934; McIntyre to Howe, July 25, 1934; Peek to Howe, July 30, 1934, enclosing a printed "General Policy Statement" of the bank, July 30, 1934, OF 971). The Second Export-Import Bank was dissolved and its business merged with the first bank on May 7, 1936; see note to the executive order establishing the first bank in *Public Papers,* III, 76–81, and press conference of March 9, 1934, below.